Test out of:
B-Ball
F-Ball
Badmitton
Bowling
Tennis
Golf.

Basic skills in sports for men and women

Bryan Fox
Sandison Hall
Room ~~709~~ 405
Box ~~804~~ 505

DAVID A. ARMBRUSTER, Sr., M.A.

Associate Professor of Physical Education and Head Swimming Coach Emeritus, University of Iowa, Iowa City, Iowa; elected to Swimming Hall of Fame, Fort Lauderdale, Fla., 1966

FRANK F. MUSKER, Ed.M., C.A.G.S.

Gymnastics Coordinator and Supervisor of Physical Education, Peabody Public Schools, Peabody, Mass.

DALE MOOD, Ph.D.

Associate Professor of Physical Education, University of Colorado, Boulder, Colo.

Consultants

Robert H. Allen, M.A.

Head Swimming Coach, University of Iowa, Iowa City, Iowa

Helen T. Mackey, Ed.D.

Chairman, Health and Physical Education for Women, and Assistant Dean of Women, Massachusetts State College at Salem, Mass.

Basic skills in sports for men and women

DAVID A. ARMBRUSTER

FRANK F. MUSKER

DALE MOOD

Consultants

Robert H. Allen

Helen T. Mackey

Sixth edition
With 455 illustrations

The C. V. Mosby Company
Saint Louis 1975

Sixth edition

Copyright © 1975 by The C. V. Mosby Company

All rights reserved. No part of this book may be reproduced in any manner without written permission of the publisher.

Previous editions copyrighted 1953, 1958, 1963, 1967, 1971

Printed in the United States of America

Distributed in Great Britain by Henry Kimpton, London

Library of Congress Cataloging in Publication Data

Armbruster, David Alvin, 1890-
    Basic skills in sports for men and women.

    1. Sports. I. Musker, Frank F., joint author.
II. Mood, Dale, joint author. III. Title.
GV701.A75 1973   796   74-14684
ISBN 0-8016-0285-8

CB/CB/CB 9 8 7 6 5 4 3 2 1

PREFACE

A digest of source teaching material for beginning students and instructors in the field of basic skills in sports is amazingly limited. Mindful of this situation, we present the material in this book for a wide variety of sports and physical education skills, which are expertly described and illustrated, to aid those who have little or no knowledge of a sport as well as to aid those who are beyond the beginner's level in improving their performance. A brief history of the skill activity or game, the selection and care of the equipment, a digest of basic rules, fundamentals, techniques, strategy, safety precautions, and terminology, and selected references are included for each activity and sport.

This book will serve not only the student of basic skills but also the professional teacher-training student who is expected to know and perform with competence all of the sports skills during student-training experience.

A considerable number of freshman entering college come from small schools where football and basketball predominate and where few, if any, individual sports skills activities are taught. These men and women are woefully in need of intelligent basic instruction. To this end the teaching and learning techniques are presented in a clear, distinct, and condensed manner for the student, and at the same time they serve as a guide and manual for the instructor.

Mindful of this program, we also hope to stimulate a needed basic skills program of physical education at the elementary and secondary school levels, thus enabling students who are going on to college to attain a level of performance in physical education equal to that required in mathematics, English, reading, and writing. The basic aim is to educate the whole boy and girl in healthful living. Wherever this need has not been fulfilled in the secondary schools, the colleges should be deeply and vitally interested in the boys and girls and set up a basic skills sports program so that their students can engage with proficiency in these recreational experiences for adult living.

In discussing and describing the various skills in this book, we have kept the right-handed person in mind. In the introduction we hope to stimulate the student to attain a more healthful and cultural life, with a knowledgeable guideline of the physical and organic functions that are provided by healthful recreational exercises in everyday living.

Miss Suzanne Chaffee contributed the chapter on Alpine Skiing. She was a member of the United States Olympic Team for four years. In 1966 she placed fourth in downhill skiing in the World Championships in Chile. In 1967 she was the highest ranked woman skier in the United States and competed in the 1968 Olympics in Grenoble, France. She was nominated by the Italian Press as Miss Olympics. She now does ski movies, writes, gives lectures, and models. She has studied at the University of Denver, the University of Washington, the University of Innsbruck, and the University of California at Los Angeles. In 1968 Miss Chaffee was appointed coordinator and publicity director of Vice President Humphrey's Youth Sports and Recreation Program. She received the 1970 New England Council annual award for outstanding contributions to winter sports.

Mr. Charles Hines contributed the chapter on Water Polo. He is Executive Director of the Y.M.C.A. of West Asheville, North Carolina. He is now Vice Chairman and Secretary of the United States Olympic Water Polo Committee and Secretary-Treasurer of the American Swimming Coaches Association, and was coach of the 1969 National Y.M.C.A. Championship Water Polo Team.

Mrs. Dorothy Cleveland contributed the section on Modern Dance. She is Associate Professor of Education at Boston University, Sargent College of Allied Health Professions, Boston, Massachusetts.

We are indeed grateful for the excellent contribution on skin and scuba diving by one of the outstanding West Coast authorities, Dr. George Q. Rich. He is associate professor at San Fernando Valley State College and teaches exercise, physiology, and scuba diving. He also serves as Director of the Human Performance Laboratory at San Fernando Valley State College.

We wish to express our sincere gratitude to the staff in the basic skills program of physical education at the University of Iowa for its untiring efforts in striving to improve teaching procedures of techniques and testing standards and to Dr. Arthur Wendler, formerly of the University of Iowa, for his constant willingness to aid and advise.

Much inspiration and encouragement were received from the late Dr. C. H. McCloy, former Head of Physical Education and Research, University of Iowa.

We are also greatly indebted to past and present varsity coaches at the University of Iowa: Donald Klotz, tennis; Dave McCuskey, wrestling and 1956 Olympic coach; Charles Zwiener, golf; and Richard Holzaepfel, gymnastics.

Grateful acknowledgment is also made to Dr. Helen T. Mackey, Chairman, Health and Physical Education for Women, Massachusetts State College at Salem.

The assistance and valuable suggestions of the University of Iowa's graduate teaching staff, especially Dr. Donald Casady, are gratefully acknowledged.

We greatly appreciate the services of Brian Matchett and Ted Philipps, members of the Boston Young Men's Christian Union, who posed for the photographs of conditioning and isometric exercises.

Self-defense and square dancing have been introduced in this new edition. We are grateful to Dr. Patricia Philips for her contribution on square dancing, and to Sigurd Ogrins for his contribution on self-defense. Dr. Philips is Assistant Professor of Education at Bridgewater State College. For many years she has been well known for her writings and recordings of square dancing. Mr. Ogrins was an instructor of self-defense in the French Foreign Legion during the Second World War. He is presently President of the New England Jiu Jitsu Association, and Director of the Boston Young Men's Christian Union.

We also wish to thank the Rawlings Manufacturing Co., St. Louis, Missouri, manufacturers of athletic equipment, for permission to use their diagram drawings of sports fields and courts.

During the revision of the fifth edition the health and physical education professions lost one of their most creative leaders with the death of Dr. Leslie W. Irwin. Dr. Irwin has written, contributed, and inspired a vast amount of professional literature. A living tribute to this dedicated educator and author will continue far into the future through the lives and programs informed and influenced by Dr. Irwin's extensive professional contributions.

We wish to extend our appreciation to Gregg White for his assistance in the revision of the chapter on skin and scuba diving.

Joining the authors in the overall revision of this edition is Dr. Dale Mood of the University of Colorado. We greatly appreciate Dr. Mood's many hours spent in revising many of this edition's chapters.

David A. Armbruster, Sr.
Frank F. Musker

CONTENTS

1	Introduction	1
2	Operation fitness	16
3	Archery	32
4	Badminton	45
5	Basketball	57
6	Bowling	70
7	Modern dancing and square dancing	80
8	Diving	91
9	Fencing	106
10	Field hockey	114
11	Golf	127
12	Gymnastics	144
13	Handball, paddleball, and racketball	174
14	Paddle tennis	184
15	Alpine skiing	187
16	Self-defense	197
17	Skin and scuba diving	205
18	Soccer	216
19	Softball	228
20	Speedball	240
21	Swimming	250
22	Table tennis	280
23	Tennis	287
24	Touch football	303
25	Track and field	314
26	Trampoline	325
27	Tumbling	335
28	Volleyball	347
29	Water polo	356
30	Weight training, weight lifting, and circuit training	365
31	Wrestling	374
Appendix: Miscellaneous field and court dimensions		387

ix

Basic skills in sports
for men and women

1 Introduction

If you were asked to make a list of the most important things in your life, after some thought, the first item you would record would probably be good health. There is almost unanimous agreement that optimum health is our most prized possession. This thought was expressed by Schopenhauer, the German philosopher, when he wisely remarked, "The greatest of follies is to neglect one's health for any other advantage of life."

A study of the history of nations shows that progress is directly related to the physical, mental, and emotional health of the people. In the process of improving and maintaining optimum health, it is necessary for people of all ages to participate in physical exercise, but there is a wide variation in the types of exercises recommended for different age groups.

A good example of the importance of exercise in maintaining health is the emphasis placed on it in the health regimen of presidents of the United States. In recent years White House physicians have included exercise in the program for maintaining the health of presidents regardless of age or physical defects. One president got his exercise by walking from one to two miles each day, while another preferred to profit by the added psychological and recreational benefits derived from playing golf. Another president included swimming and boating in his conditioning program.

In addition to the value of exercise in maintaining optimum health, there are social and recreational benefits as well.

WHY PHYSICAL EDUCATION?

Although in a majority of colleges and universities students are required to participate in physical education, many institutions have recently eliminated this requirement and instituted a totally elective program. In a large percentage of these cases the number of students taking physical education classes has remained constant or even increased. Why do students continue to elect physical activities even when they are not required to obtain credit toward graduation from these courses? Partially, students have become aware of some of the needs for and values of physical activities discussed in the following paragraphs.

Physical needs and values

There are many things, including physiological, psychological, and sociological factors, which are a part of the process of improving and maintaining physical fitness and health.

Muscular strength

The strength of muscle is increased through use when the "overload" principle is applied—overload meaning to increase the repetitions, the resistance, or both. Muscle increases in size and endurance as it increases in strength. A muscle responds in direct proportion to the extent of demands placed upon it. Short maximal or near maximal exercise develops the kind of strength for efficient, strenuous, short bursts of performance. Repetitive submaximal exercise develops the kind of strength necessary for more prolonged endurance performance. In addition to the increase in size, strength, and endurance of individual muscles, the general muscle tone of the entire body is improved through exercise. Good muscle tone is conducive to an erect bearing and good posture. For example, strong abdominal muscles help in preventing a sagging, protruding abdomen.

A person with adequate strength to satisfy the body's needs will use part of the muscles in relays while others rest. This allows some of the muscles to relax and recover while others carry the load. Trained muscles function more smoothly and more effectively than untrained muscles, enabling them to contract more vigorously with less effort.

Muscular endurance

Muscular endurance and muscular strength are associated with the increase in muscle size brought on through vigorous activity. To accomplish a specific task, only the number of muscle fibers needed are brought into play. When these become fatigued or exhausted, others are called upon. A well-developed muscle has a greater reserve of fibers to call on than a poorly developed muscle and thus has greater endurance.

The gain in endurance from systematic and vigorous physical activity is much greater in proportion than the gain in size. This gain in endurance helps one to continue doing a relatively hard and difficult task over a long period of time without complete fatigue or exhaustion. In a hurried and competitive life with the many varied and continuous demands of daily living, students need an adequate reserve strength and endurance to enjoy and profit most from the college program of activities.

Heart and circulatory system

The effects of proper exercise on the normal heart and circulatory system have been shown through scientific experimentation to be very beneficial. The normal heart and circulatory system increase in strength and efficiency with exercise. Although the heart is a muscular organ and although it differs in type from the muscles of the skeletal system, it responds to exercise in somewhat the same manner as the skeletal muscles as far as strength, endurance, and growth are concerned. As a result of proper conditioning through exercise, the heart is able to fill itself with more blood and therefore have a more efficient volume per stroke. Compared to an untrained heart, a heart conditioned by exercise relaxes more completely, allowing more blood to enter. The larger and stronger conditioned heart is capable of contracting with greater force, thus pumping more blood per contraction. This results in the fact that the trained heart can do more work with fewer beats and it can rest longer between beats than the untrained heart. Another advantage is that a heart kept in good physical condition by exercise not only beats slower during strenuous work, but also returns to normal more quickly than a poorly conditioned heart.

The frequent belief that strenuous exercise may injure the normal heart has no scientific foundation. The term "athlete's heart" as applied to a weakened or injured heart has been found to be erroneous. Scientific evidence indicates that an organically sound heart of children or youth cannot be permanently injured by exercise. The individual will become physiologically and psychologically exhausted before damage is done to the heart muscle. This does not hold true, however, for defective hearts.

When exercise of a vigorous nature is engaged in over a period of time and with regularity, the blood vessels within the muscle tissue itself actually increase in number. Also, the red corpuscles that carry oxygen to the body tissues are increased in number, thus increasing the oxygen-carrying power of the blood.

Another way in which exercise promotes better circulation is through assisting the heart in moving the blood from the extremities of the body back to the heart through muscular contractions.

Improved circulation through regular exercise has a beneficial effect upon the body's heat-regulating mechanism. Exercise warms the body by speeding up circulation and accelerating the blood flow to the legs, arms, and other parts of the body.

Respiratory system

Breathing, or respiration, is the means by which oxygen is taken into the body and the carbon dioxide and waste products are eliminated from the body. Respiration increases during exercise. At rest the trained person will have slower, deeper respirations and can meet the demands placed on the respiratory system with less effort and greater efficiency than the person who is not in good physical condition. Physical conditioning results in more economical and efficient respiratory function. As with heart rate the respiratory rate of a conditioned individual returns to normal faster than that of an untrained person.

There is an increase in the flexibility and a strengthening of the respiratory muscles through exercise. It is possible that the alveoli develop new partitions, increasing the total amount of the area from which the oxygen can be absorbed.

During exercise the spleen contracts, forcing the blood stored there during rest into circulation, thus increasing the number of circulating red corpuscles and consequently, the oxygen-carrying power of the blood.

Vital organs

Physical activity is beneficial to a number of vital organs. The increased metabolism resulting from exercise is met most effectively in the conditioned individual through the coordination of a number of vital organs and functions. There is an increase in size and development of the digestive organs, liver, and pancreas, which may help the individual to care for the increased demand.

The ability of cells to build their nutritive power is heightened by proper exercise. It is recognized in physiology that function and use are closely related. This close relationship starts a power-building cycle that becomes very efficient. As the stored glycogen is burned, releasing heat and energy, there is a demand for more oxygen, more food from blood, and a subsequent elimination of waste from the body. This cycle continually increases the economy and function of all of the internal organs, which adds to the individual's total efficiency and health.

Endocrine glands

Scientific physiological evidence indicates a close relationship between exercise and the function of various endocrine glands, particularly the adrenal glands. As a result of exercise, the adrenal glands seem to have an increased ability to secrete epinephrine (adrenaline) and cortin. The increased production of epinephrine seems to increase the ability of the body to sustain effort by activating more efficient muscular function. The increased cortin seems to give one a generally sustained higher level of energy.

Coordination, skills, flexibility, and agility

The flexibility of the joints of the body can be increased through exercise. Also, there is evidence to indicate that physical activity strengthens bones, thereby increasing their ability to withstand the stress of accidental strains.

Coordination is a term used in describing the proper use of muscles in performing skill activities. Coordination can be developed in the learning of various skills and through frequent practice sessions and the use of correct form. There are no short cuts in the development of coordination. Certain fundamental procedures, however, if properly followed, will help to make the learning and development process more enjoyable and, consequently, increase the satisfactions to be derived from sports participation that requires specific skills.

The best time to develop coordination

and motor skills is at present, due to the fact that your ability to develop neuromuscular coordination passes its peak soon after college age. When you learn new motor skills, it is always best, if possible, to begin under the direction of an expert teacher. Proper advice, particularly in the beginning, can eliminate faulty habits and incorrect techniques. Beginning with incorrect form and developing bad habits in a sport retard the rate of learning and require endless practice to eliminate the bad habits in the process of improvement. Regular practice periods are necessary in developing coordination and skill in most sports. Usually, short and frequent practice periods are superior to long and infrequent periods. Remember, the first thing you should learn is the proper form. You should strive to get the kinesthetic feeling of the correct form and movement at the beginning of the learning process.

Developing coordination and skill is a most satisfying experience resulting from regular participation in physical activities. Constructive recreational activities are some of the best leisure time pursuits. Skills and recreational activities give a great deal of personal satisfaction and pleasure in that they develop poise, confidence, pride, and a feeling of accomplishment.

FATIGUE

The person in good physical condition who is skilled and coordinated uses only the muscles that are needed for the task. This is a great saving in unnecessary fatigue. In the trained person smaller amounts of waste products, such as lactic acid, are formed and generally these waste products are removed more quickly than in the untrained person.

In combating fatigue, exercise is often stimulating not only psychologically, but also physiologically. The contraction of muscles helps in returning the blood to the heart. Consequently, the heart sends additional blood to fatigued areas of the body, resulting in a psychological feeling of recovery and refreshment. This is one of the main reasons why participation in moderate exercise, particularly in the form of a game, often relieves fatigue after a strenuous work day. As a rule, then, people in good physical condition ordinarily tire less easily, and when they do tire, they recover more rapidly than people in poor physical condition.

PHYSICAL FITNESS

It has been mentioned a number of times previously that participation in regular exercise under the proper condition helps to maintain health. This involves not only physical benefits but also certain psychological and sociological benefits.

Exercise does not directly cure disease but may in some instances assist in its prevention or in the recovery process. However, it is known that a person in poor physical condition is more susceptible to illness and that there is a slower recovery from illness as a result of poor physical condition. Proper exercise helps to build up the muscles and vital organs of the body so that they are capable of bearing additional stress and strain due to their greater level of efficiency.

Other needs and values in physical activities

In addition to the physiological needs and values of physical activities, there are other things that are needed and have value in maintaining optimal physical, emotional, and mental health. Some of these are discussed in the following paragraphs.

PSYCHOLOGICAL FACTORS

Many situations in today's world are conducive to producing tension and emotional stress resulting in worry, anxiety, fear, frustration, and the like. Although the evidence is not as definite because the factors involved are more difficult to measure, there is some indication that exercise under the proper conditions can be helpful in improving emotional stability and mental fitness just as it aids in developing physical fitness. Participation in an interesting sport takes the mind from other things and from concentrating on one's self. That is why a healthful sport may be more valuable than walking in maintaining health. Exercise also helps one release emotions through socially approved channels. It is a means of satisfying certain primitive urges that all people have, and it provides for self-expression. Achieving success in developing skills and participating in a physical activity are excellent means of developing confidence and reaping satisfaction that comes from successful accomplishment. There are many individual activities, such as archery, bowling, running, swimming, and golf, in which it is possible to compete against one's own performance.

Knowledge

There is a need for everyone to have a certain amount of knowledge concerning sports, if not as a participant, then as a spectator. One of the dominant factors in the American way of life is the ability of the average citizen both to participate in and to understand sports. To have a knowledge of many sports is a part of the American way of life. Therefore, it is beneficial for the individual to learn the rules of various team and individual sports. Furthermore, in participation as well as in appreciation, it is of value for one to know something about the strategy of games and sports. In addition, knowledge about etiquette, safety, equipment, history, values, rules, techniques, and many other factors can enhance one's enjoyment of watching or participating in team, dual, or individual activities.

Social values

One important aspect of higher education is the attempt of educators to provide a program of activities that helps in the socialization of the individual. Because we are living in an age of great social conflict, it is highly important that colleges everywhere use every means possible to instill positive social habits in their students. A program of physical activities offers unlimited opportunities for developing broad social understandings. One facet of common social interests of people in America is shown by the wide publicity given to sports in American life through radio and television, sports pages of newspapers, magazines, conversations, and discussions of individuals of all ages. There is possibly no better place to learn how to get along with and to live with others than through participation in sports. In sports the individual must show the same qualities that are necessary for successful and happy living in a democratic society. To be most successful, habits and attitudes of courtesy, self-control, initiative, cooperation, and loyalty must be acquired. The experience of being both a follower and a leader can be gained. Successful participation in sports implies that the participant must learn to be a good sportsman and to give credit where it is due, regardless of winning or losing. Participation in team games, particularly, teaches the individual to work with others and to control the emotions to the best advantage of the team.

In college, students are often motivated by the social instinct of belonging. They usually desire to associate with their fellow students. One of the ways that this desire can be satisfied is through participation in sports. Through the congenial atmosphere of sports, opportunity is present to develop friendship that may have lasting value.

Recreation

Recreation has assumed an important place in modern life due to the ever-increasing amount of leisure time available to all. People have been liberated from the drudgery of much work and toil through technological advancements and the development of the machine age. Also, there is every evidence that the leisure time of the average individual will be greatly increased in years to come.

It is readily evident that people can use leisure time either constructively or destructively. One of the aims of a physical activities program is to teach the student to use leisure time wisely. The student should be made aware of the vital place that wholesome recreation can play in the full enjoyment of life, especially the role of sports in this respect.

Recreation, to be helpful, need not be done on an elaborate and expensive scale. To think so is a misconception, for many of the simple forms of recreation available to all of us are the most satisfying and the greatest help to us in maintaining physical, mental, and emotional health.

THINGS YOU SHOULD KNOW RELATED TO THE SPORTS AND PHYSICAL ACTIVITIES PROGRAM

If one is to profit most from participation in sports and physical activities, there are a number of things that should be given consideration at all times. Some of these things are discussed in the following paragraphs.

Training and conditioning

Some physical education and sports directors make a distinction between "conditioning" and "training." Usually, conditioning is considered to be related to such things as proper eating, resting, relaxing, sleeping, and exercising regularly, as well as working toward the improvement of skills in an activity. Training, on the other hand, is considered by some to be the practice of certain movements by constant repetition until a skill is established or mastered. An example of this would be in one's attempting to improve, and master to the greatest possible extent, skills required in such sports as swimming, golf, tennis, or track. There is an overlapping in the meaning of the words "training" and "conditioning," for gains in one generally lead to increases in the other.

It is usually considered necessary to participate in vigorous activity at regular times to develop and maintain maximum body efficiency. To reach maximum body efficiency, it is generally considered best for one to begin with mild exercise with a gradual increase in intensity during subsequent periods. One main reason why this is recommended is to prevent undue stress and strain upon the muscles of the body. The length of exercise periods should be governed by the response of the individual to exercise and past training periods. Other factors such as age and present physical condition will dictate the initial intensity and duration of exercise periods. To develop the greatest muscular efficiency, one should participate in activities which require some use of all muscles of the body. Many sports require repeated use of a limited set of muscles. For this reason it is usually thought best to take part in a wide variety of sports to make proper use of all muscles of the body.

It is very important to follow a regular training routine. It is unwise to engage in any strenuous activity before the body is in condition for it. As mentioned previously, to increase the condition of the body requires the application of a stress or overload. However, it is generally true that to maintain a particular state of physical condition requires less intense activity than it took to get to this level. It is also generally accepted that if participation is discontinued the degree of physical condition will decline at about the same rate required to build it.

Good physical condition is sufficient for participation in most sports. However, it must be kept in mind that certain sports require special kinds of training even though general bodily condition is basic to all sports. There is a difference in conditioning and training on the basis of age. Younger people can train and condition more rapidly than older people.

Conditioning exercises are very valuable in developing flexibility. A well-chosen sequence of exercises such as the one presented below can accomplish this. This sequence involves exercises for the following body areas: (1) shoulders, chest, and back, (2) arms and shoulders, (3) neck, (4) lateral trunk, (5) back and buttocks, (6) legs and buttocks, (7) abdomen, (8) lower back and buttocks, (9) chest and arms, (10) legs, ankles, and feet.

The following exercises can be used with almost all groups and age levels, including businessmen and women as well as college athletes. The number of times each exercise is performed, however, should depend upon the particular group and age level. The exercises can be performed with or without music.

Exercise sequence

The following sample sequence of exercises can be performed by the individual or group.

SHOULDERS, CHEST, AND BACK
Starting position: Standing, feet together, hands at sides.

Movements:
1. Arms forward.
2. Arms sideward.
3. Arms forward.
4. Arms downward.

Repetitions: 32 counts.
Rhythm: Fox-trot.

ARMS AND SHOULDERS

Starting position: Standing, feet spread, arms flexed.
Movements:
1. Extend arms forward.
2. Flex.
3. Extend arms sideward.
4. Flex.

Repetitions: 32 counts.
Rhythm: Fox-trot.

NECK

Starting position: Standing, hands behind neck.
Movements:
1. Pull head forward, resist with neck muscles.
2. Extend head against resistance of hands.

Repetitions: 16 counts.
Rhythm: Waltz.

LATERAL TRUNK

Starting position: Straddle-stand, hips firm.
Movements:
1. Fling left arm sideward-upward and flex body to right.
2. Return left hand to hip and body to starting position.
3. Fling right arm sideward-upward and flex to left. (See Fig. 1-1.)
4. Recover to starting position.

Repetitions: 48 counts.
Rhythm: Waltz.

BACK AND BUTTOCKS

Starting position: Straddle-stand, hips firm.
Movements:
1. Touch toes. (See Fig. 1-2.)
2. Recover.
3. Raise arms over head. (See Fig. 1-3.)
4. Recover.

Repetitions: 32 counts.
Rhythm: Waltz.

LEGS AND BUTTOCKS

Starting position (push-up position): Prone-fall, right leg flexed.
Movements:
1. Jump and change leg position.
2. Return to starting position.

Repetitions: 32 counts.
Rhythm: Fox-trot.

Fig. 1-1. Lateral bend.

Fig. 1-2. Touch toes.

Fig. 1-3. Raise arms over head.

ABDOMEN

Starting position: Supine.
Movements (sit-ups):
1. Touch knees.
2. Touch toes.
3. Touch knees.
4. Return to supine position, arms over head.

Repetitions: 48 counts.
Rhythm: Waltz.

LOWER BACK AND BUTTOCKS

Starting position: Prone, hands behind back.
Movements:
1. Raise chest and head off floor.
2. Lower.

Repetitions: 32 counts.
Rhythm: Waltz.

CHEST AND ARMS

Starting position: Prone, hands on floor.
Movements (push-ups):
1. Extend arms.
2. Lower to floor.

Repetitions: All out (as many as possible).
Rhythm: Waltz.

LEGS, ANKLES, AND FEET

Starting position: Standing, feet together, hands on hips.

Movements:
1. Twelve-inch straddle-jump.
2. Feet together.

Repetitions: 100 counts.
Rhythm: Polka.

Isometric exercises

If muscle strength is desired, isometric exercises may be used with the exercises that have just been described.

TECHNIQUE OF PERFORMING ISOMETRIC EXERCISES

1. Take 4 seconds to reach maximum contraction. Breathe deeply and hold the breath for the next 6 seconds of maximum effort. Exhale and relax on the count of 10. Rest 10 seconds before performing the next exercise.
2. Perform one complete 10-second contraction for each muscle group to be strengthened. This is sufficient for the day's workout.

FULL ISOMETRIC SEQUENCE

The student should perform the full isometric sequence, keeping in mind the necessity of symmetry in proportion.

MUSCLES OF UPPER ARM, FOREARM, AND WRIST

FLEXORS

Exercise position: The feet should be about shoulder width apart and the knees slightly bent.

Rope length and fixation: Use about 5 feet of rope. Pass the rope around the back of the knees and hold each end. The arms should be flexed. (See Fig. 1-4.)

Action: Flex the arms against the resistance of the legs. There should be no visible motion.

EXTENSORS

Exercise position: Stand with the knees slightly flexed, elbows at the sides, and hands forward.

Rope length and fixation: Use about 4 feet of rope. Pass the rope around the back and hold each end. (See Fig. 1-5.)

Action: Pull the rope forward or push it away from the body.

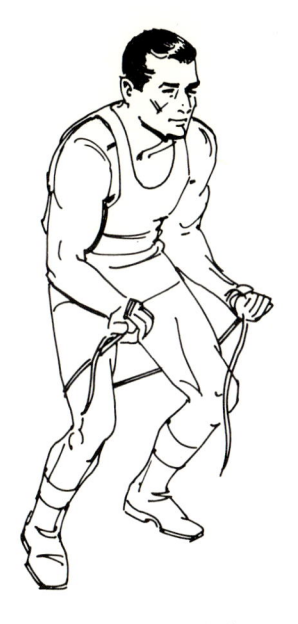

Fig. 1-4. Flexors of the arms.

Fig. 1-6. Lateral deltoids.

Fig. 1-5. Extensors of the arms.

Fig. 1-7. Anterior deltoids.

MUSCLES OF SHOULDER
LATERAL DELTOIDS

Exercise position: Assume a straddle-stand position.

Rope length and fixation: Use about 12 inches of rope. Pass the rope in back of the thighs and hold the ends. (See Fig. 1-6.)

Action: Pull the rope outward away from the body.

ANTERIOR DELTOIDS

Exercise position: Assume a straddle-stand position.

Rope length and fixation: Use about 20 inches of rope. Pass the rope behind the thighs and hold each end. (See Fig. 1-7.)

Action: Pull the rope forward against the resistance of the legs.

Posterior deltoids

Exercise position: Assume a straddle-stand position.

Rope length and fixation: Use about 20 inches of rope. Pass the rope in front of the thighs and hold each end. (See Fig. 1-8.)

Action: Pull the rope backward against the thighs.

MUSCLES OF NECK (WITHOUT ROPE)
Flexors

Exercise position: Assume a straddle-stand position with the arms raised. Grasp the right wrist with the left hand, keeping the elbows high. Place the back of the left wrist on the forehead. (See Fig. 1-9.)

Action: Force the head forward against the resistance of the hands.

Extensors

Exercise position: Assume a straddle-stand position, lace the fingers, and hold the back of the head. (See Fig. 1-10.)

Action: Hold the hands steady and force the head back against the resistance of the hands.

MUSCLES OF UPPER BACK

Exercise position: Assume a straddle-stand position.

Rope length and fixation: Use about 8 inches of rope. Hold the rope across the chest with the arms horizontal, keeping the elbows high. (See Fig. 1-11.)

Fig. 1-8. Posterior deltoids.

Fig. 1-9. Neck flexors.

Fig. 1-10. Neck extensors.

Fig. 1-11. Upper back and shoulders.

Action: Pull apart.

Exercise position: Assume a straddle-stand position.

Rope length and fixation: Hold the ends of the rope (about 30 inches of rope) and extend the arms over the head. (See Fig. 1-12.)

Action: Pull laterally.

MUSCLES OF CHEST, ARMS, AND SHOULDERS

Exercise position: Assume a straddle-stand position with the palms of the hands together in front of the chest, the elbows high, and the forearms horizontal.

Action: Force the hands together.

Exercise position: Assume a straddle-stand position with the feet about shoulder width apart.

Rope length and fixation: Use about 12 feet of rope. Pass the rope under the feet or around the back. Lean back and extend the arms obliquely over the head. (See Fig. 1-13.)

Action: Press or push up as one would do when performing the incline press in weight training.

MUSCLES OF BUTTOCKS AND BACK

Exercise position: Place the feet together, keeping the legs straight and the body flexed.

Rope length and fixation: Use about 36 inches of rope. Loop the rope underneath the feet and hold it with the arms extended. (See Fig. 1-14.)

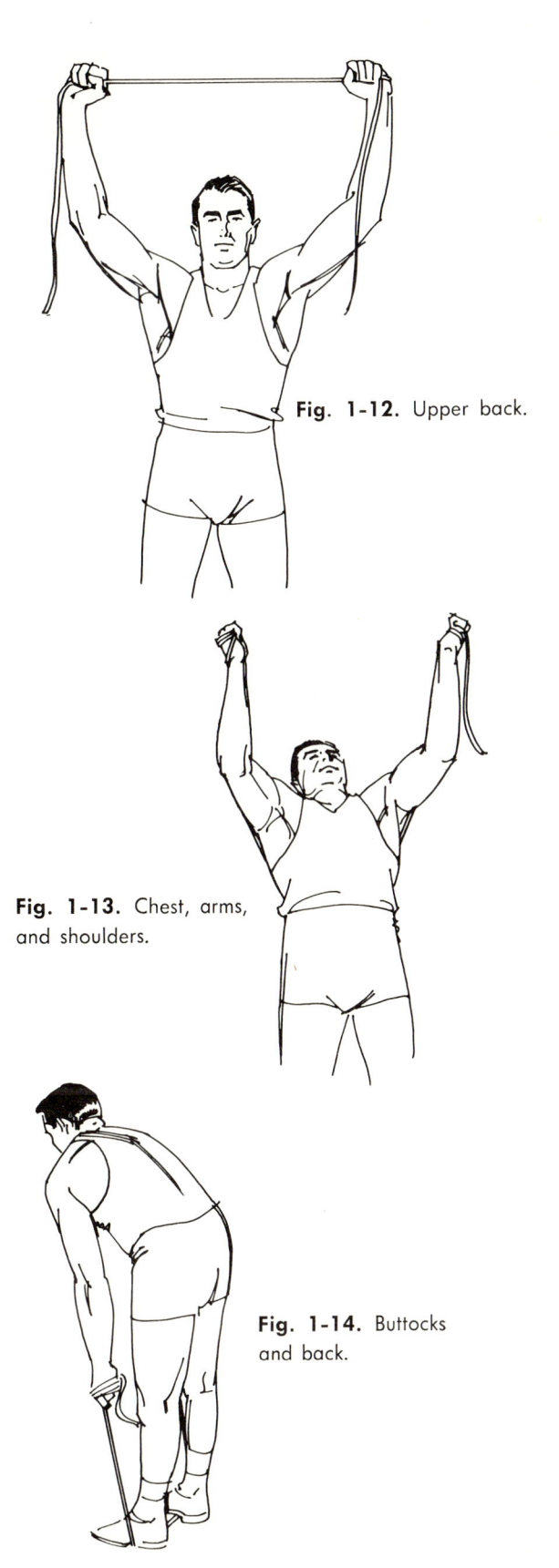

Action: Attempt to straighten the body.

MUSCLES OF ABDOMEN

Exercise position: Stand with the feet together.

Rope length and fixation: Use about 10 feet of rope. Pass the rope under the feet, up the back, and over the shoulders. (See Fig. 1-15.)

Action: Hold the rope tight on the shoulders and attempt to flex the body forward.

MUSCLES OF BUTTOCKS AND LEGS

Exercise position: Do a deep knee bend with the feet together.

Rope length and fixation: Use about 3

Fig. 1-12. Upper back.

Fig. 1-13. Chest, arms, and shoulders.

Fig. 1-14. Buttocks and back.

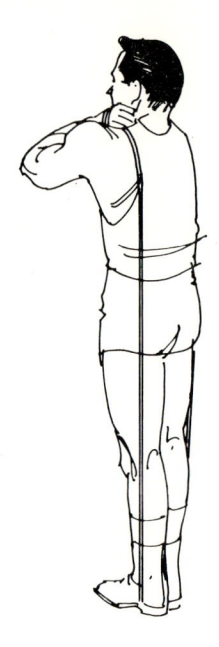

Fig. 1-15. Abdomen.

Fig. 1-16. Legs, buttocks, and back.

feet of rope. Loop the rope under the feet and hold. (See Fig. 1-16.)
Action: Try to extend the legs.
Exercise position (without rope): Do a partial knee bend. Cross the arms and place the hands on the opposite knees.
Action: Hold the knees and try to spread them.
Exercise position: Same as previous exercise.
Action: Hold the knees and try to bring them together.

ADVANTAGES OF ISOMETRIC EXERCISES
1. They may be effectively used for the development of muscular strength.
2. The time required for the activity is quite short—about 10 minutes for a complete workout.
3. Only one piece of rope about 15 feet long is needed.
4. They can be performed anytime anywhere.
5. They are not physically exhausting.

DISADVANTAGES OF ISOMETRIC EXERCISES
1. The performer may experience an increase in blood pressure if the breath is held too long.
2. The performer may become dizzy if the breath is held too long.
3. Isometrics are only part of a good workout. Exercises of flexibility, agility, speed, and endurance should be included.

Physical examination

One should not participate in prolonged and strenuous physical activity without first having had a complete medical examination by a physician. A medical examination is so important that it cannot be overemphasized. The results of medical examinations show that most people do not need to be restricted in physical activity. Regular examinations should be repeated periodically throughout life. There is even greater need for a medical examination before exercise as people grow older. If there are certain defects present, such as a defective heart, participation in unrestricted strenuous exercise can be very damaging to one's health.

Precautions

Before one engages in strenuous physical activity, there should be a period of warming up the muscles. A gradual warming up of muscles eliminates some of the danger of muscle injury. In beginning a warm-up for strenuous activity, the large muscles groups, including the arms, legs, and trunk, should be warmed up first. As a matter of fact, they should receive major attention throughout the warming-up and limbering-up period.

It is usually recommended that one taper

off gradually after participating in vigorous and strenuous physical activity. Sudden and complete relaxation after vigorous exertion without tapering off is more likely to cause dizziness, nausea, and sometimes fainting if the exercise has been particularly strenuous. Giving the bodily processes a chance to slow down gradually is a precautionary measure observed by practically all champion athletes.

There are good reasons for tapering off following vigorous or strenuous exercise. During vigorous exercise the heart rate speeds up to keep the muscles supplied with sufficient oxygen and nutrients. The increased heart rate sends the arterial blood into the veins. Since there is no forceful mechanism like the heart in the venous system to help move blood back to the heart, the action of muscles must be depended on to help the return flow of blood. When the veins fill with blood, the pressure of contracting muscles produces a pumping action on the thin-walled veins to propel the blood back toward the center of the body. If you stop vigorous exercise abruptly, your heart continues for a time to send extra amounts of arterial blood to your muscles. Because your muscles are suddenly quiet, there is not sufficient force for returning the extra blood to the heart. Consequently, the extra blood tends to pool in the muscles. As a result, the imbalance may leave some organs with an inadequate supply of blood. During the tapering-off process following strenuous exercise, the muscles continue to squeeze blood from the extremities of the body back to the main circulation stream.

If you suddenly stop vigorous exercise without tapering off, you may just as suddenly have cramps. Research has not as yet determined the exact reason why cramps sometime follow strenuous exercise. Stiffness as well as cramps may be avoided or reduced by the tapering-off process.

Regardless of the care one may take in beginning training and conditioning for sports, there are times when muscles become sore and stiff. Mild exercise is usually recommended as a speed to recovery when a muscle is only slightly lame. Mild exercise, in cases of this sort, helps the pumping action of the heart that is necessary to bring blood to the sore muscle and thereby speeds up the carrying away of waste products.

Another precaution is to always try to avoid overstraining and overdoing. Excess emotional stress can greatly add to the seriousness of overexertion. The ability to recuperate after strenuous exercise is a good guide at any age to the amount and extent of exercise to participate in at any one time. Recuperation should be reasonably prompt. However, if the breathing and heart rate are still greatly accelerated at the end of approximately ten minutes after exercise, and if there is marked fatigue or weakness after a few hours' rest or a sense of definite fatigue the day following, the exercise likely has been too severe or too prolonged.

A last precaution following strenuous exercise has to do with cooling off. An adequate cooling-off period should follow the tapering-off process. From three to six minutes should elapse between tapering off and entering the shower. Otherwise, the warm water will prevent loss of heat from the body and you will continue to perspire following the bath. Heavy perspiration following a bath and dressing may result in chilling. The results of chilling following heavy perspiration are the same as chilling after being drenched by a cold rain.

Rest and sleep

Sufficient rest and sleep are very necessary to the maintenance of good physical, mental, and emotional health. Although it is thought that the average person needs from eight to nine hours' sleep each night, the amount varies with the individual and with age. Growing children require more sleep than adults. The activities participated in by different people require that some of them get more sleep than others. Regularity in rest and sleep is very important. If one is not getting sufficient rest and sleep, participation in strenuous and vigorous physical activities can be more harmful than helpful. It is recommended that each individual learn to judge the amount of sleep and rest necessary to maintain physical and mental alertness and a feeling of well-being.

Diet and nutrition

A balanced diet is necessary for the maintenance of good nutrition and thus good health. Nutrition is basic to good physical, mental, and emotional health at all times. If the body is poorly nourished, there is little or no chance for a person to be in good health. Those who participate in physical activity usually require more food than those who lead sedentary lives. Participation in physical activities requires energy, and food is the main source of energy within the body.

It is usually not best to eat heavy meals prior to strenuous periods of physical activity due to the fact that so often emotional stress is present if it is a competitive activity. Consequently, it is difficult for the body to digest and assimilate food under such circumstances.

Diet is one of the controlling factors in body weight. Most overweight people consume too much food, which results in an overweight condition. Exercise is sometimes useful in reducing overweight people. However, exercise also stimulates the appetite, and if the overweight person eats more because of the exercise, it is not likely to help in the long run in reducing. If the overweight person uses exercise to reduce and then refrains from overeating, the exercise can be helpful.

Clothing and cleanliness

Proper clothing is important when participating in sports. It is very essential that one change from street clothes to gymnasium clothing when participating in activities of a vigorous nature that will cause perspiration and body odor. Even sports and gymnasium clothing can become so soiled by dirt and perspiration that they become objectionable to others in a class. Therefore, it is important to have sufficient sports and gymnasium clothing and to keep them as clean as possible at all times. It is particularly important to be certain that shoes and hose be properly selected. Gymnasium or other kinds of sports shoes should fit properly in order to safeguard the feet. It is very easy for blisters to form if shoes or hose do not fit properly. All clothing that fits too tightly and that may hinder performance should be avoided.

A shower should always be taken after participation in vigorous physical activity for both hygienic and social reasons. Showers not only cleanse the skin but also reduce chances of infection. For some people it is desirable to take a warm shower followed by a short, cold shower. For others this is a very undesirable practice. It depends on how each person responds to water temperature. For some people a cold shower following a warm shower is very depressing. In such cases, it is not recommended. Rather, the person should taper off the shower from warm to cool only to a point where a favorable reaction occurs.

Injuries and illness

The question is frequently asked as to whether or not one should participate in physical activities during or following periods of mild illness such as colds, influenza, and other infectious diseases. In most cases it is best to refrain from participation in physical activities during any kind of illness caused by infections. The best recommendation is to act only on the advice of a physician.

Care should be given to even slight injuries received while participating in physical activities. Small scratches and cuts should not be neglected but soon be given first aid as soon as possible. Any slight cut or scratch that seems to have become infected should have the attention of a physician immediately. There are other kinds of infections found often in gymnasiums and shower rooms. Students should be careful in taking showers and drying in the dressing rooms to avoid ringworm or "athlete's foot." Sprains and bruises of any seriousness should be given immediate first aid, and then they should be seen by a physician.

Safety

Sports and physical activities should be made as safe as possible. Those who participate in sports should take every precaution to prevent injury to themselves and to others. Equipment, rules, and regulations of games and sports in the modern day are designed to protect players as well as possible. Players should keep in mind that some sports and activities require special protective equipment. To play these games and sports without the protective equipment designed for them is to risk serious injury. For example, special equipment has been designed for the game of football to prevent injury. It would be downright foolhardy for a person to attempt to play football without the usual types of protective equipment. The design of safety equipment for most other sports is not so marked as in football; nevertheless, in many sports, equipment has been designed to prevent injuries.

The beginner in certain sports should recognize that some advanced activities may be dangerous to attempt. An example of this would be in an activity such as tumbling in which some of the advanced tumbling activities require advanced skills. The beginner attempting to do some of the advanced tumbling stunts would likely be in danger of an injury because of a lack of skill. All students should give attention to safety, for it is generally recognized that a high percentage of the deaths and injuries due to accidents could be prevented.

REFERENCES

AAHPER: Youth fitness test manual, 1201 Sixteenth St., N.W., Washington, D. C., 1961, AAHPER Youth Fitness Publications.

Bucher, Charles A.: Foundations of physical education, ed. 7, St. Louis, 1975, The C. V. Mosby Co.

Carlsten, Arne, and Gramby, Gunnar: The circulatory response to muscular exercise in man, Springfield, Ill., 1964, Charles C Thomas, Publisher.

Genasci, J. E., and Klissouras, Vasillis: The Delphic spirit in sports, Journal of Health, Physical Education and Recreation 37:43, Feb., 1966.

Irwin, Leslie W.: The curriculum in health and physical education, Dubuque, 1960, William C. Brown Company, Publishers.

Meredith, Florence L., Irwin, Leslie, W., Staton, Wesley: Health and fitness, Boston, 1970, D. C. Heath & Co.

Morehouse, Laurence E., and Miller, Augustus T.: Physiology of exercise, ed. 6, St. Louis, 1971, The C. V. Mosby Co.

Otto, James, Julian, Cloyd, and Tether, Edward: Modern health, New York, 1967, Holt, Rinehart & Winston, Inc.

Williams, Jesse: The principles of physical education, Philadelphia, 1964, W. B. Saunders Co.

2 Operation fitness*

How about you?

Can you make the team?

Check your scores on the following charts.

*From Youth fitness test manual, Washington, D. C., 1972, American Association for Health, Physical Education, and Recreation.

The AAHPER Youth Fitness Test was announced in September, 1958, and the first edition of the *AAHPER Youth Fitness Test Manual* appeared in October, 1958. There was immediate enthusiasm on the part of AAHPER members and others everywhere. The AAHPER physical fitness test was soon administered to millions of boys and girls throughout the United States. Several states held conferences on fitness, and interest in testing the physical fitness of youth grew at a rapid pace. State units of AAHPER assumed leadership in state fitness activities.

President Eisenhower's Council on Youth Fitness, established in 1956, continued the stimulation of fitness action across the country. The Citizens Advisory Committee of the President's Council on Youth Fitness, chaired by Homer C. Wadsworth, met in September, 1958, at Fort Ritchie, Maryland, and again at the Air Force Academy in September, 1959. Youth fitness was recognized as a major objective.

A National Conference on Fitness of Secondary School Youth was called by the AAHPER in December, 1958, to look at present and future needs of boys and girls in secondary schools and to examine their programs of health education, safety, driver education, physical education, athletics, recreation, and outdoor education. Recommendations provided guidelines for secondary school programs.*

In January, 1959, the AAHPER announced a new program called Operation Fitness—U.S.A., headed by Louis E. Means, AAHPER Director of Special Projects. It was designed to give better leadership to the fitness effort through teamwork among business, industry, and education. It provided organization for action under the auspices of AAHPER and the National Education Association. The AAHPER Youth Fitness Test Project became the first program to be sponsored nationwide, through Operation Fitness —U.S.A.

---

*See *Youth and Fitness, a Program for Secondary Schools.* Report of the National Conference on Fitness of Secondary School Youth, Dec. 1958. American Association for Health, Physical Education, and Recreation (NEA), 1959. 74 pp. $1.50.

Meanwhile, programs of health education, physical education, and recreation were being strengthened. More emphasis was being placed on sports for fitness, on gymnastics for boys and girls, on motivation for fitness. A National Conference on Fitness of Children of Elementary School Age was held November 29 to December 3, 1959. Twenty national organizations cooperated by sending representatives to this AAHPER conference. Leaders in the field of elementary education and AAHPER specialists in health education, physical education, and recreation made recommendations on programs in these areas in the elementary school.

Operation Fitness—U.S.A. added several projects to its national program, among which are the Track and Field Project, the "Lady Be Fit" project, Operation Archery, and projects on sports skills and sports knowledge. Thousands of clinics and demonstrations have been held throughout the country, and over 125,000 kits of materials have been distributed from the AAHPER office.

Results of fitness testing came in from all parts of the United States, involving millions of children and youth. Use of the AAHPER test program soon spread to twenty-nine other countries. A comparison of British and American boys and girls, which showed a very poor picture of physical fitness for the Americans, was widely announced in every newspaper and sounded the alert for action. A Japanese study of 20,000 children revealed that Japanese youth were superior in almost every test element. Results from other nations have given cause for serious concern.

President Kennedy's program

President Kennedy acted vigorously to change the image of the soft American. His concern for the physical fitness of youth was apparent even before his inauguration, when he called attention to the national problem in an article especially written for *Sports Illustrated*. The first presidential conference called by President Kennedy was on the Physical Fitness of Youth (in February 1961). In March 1961, President Kennedy appointed Charles B. Wilkinson special consultant on fitness of youth.

The first document explaining President Kennedy's physical fitness program for youth is now being used in schools throughout the United States.

Concerted action

The AAHPER worked closely with Mr. Wilkinson and his staff in developing the program presented by the President's Council on Youth Fitness. The Council has officially adopted the AAHPER Youth Fitness Test and recommends its use. With this concern on the part of the federal government and the leadership of our professional organization, a national program for health and physical fitness is assured.

IDENTIFICATION OF PHYSICALLY UNDERDEVELOPED PUPILS: ACTIVITIES TO IMPROVE THEIR PERFORMANCE

Screening tests[1]

The screening to identify the underdeveloped pupil consists of the three following simple tests that measure strength, flexibility, and agility:
1. Pull-ups (arm and shoulder strength)
2. Sit-ups (flexibility and abdominal strength)
3. Squat thrusts (agility)

All pupils should be screened at the beginning of the school year. Those who fail any test should be retested on the test or tests failed each six weeks, until they pass.

Instructions for administration of tests

Divide the class into pairs. One pupil acts as scorer for his partner while the other pupil performs the test.

After each test, results are recorded by the teacher on the record form.

The only equipment needed is a chinning bar, a stopwatch (or a watch with a sweep second hand), and record forms.

PULL-UPS—BOYS (see Fig. 2-1, A)

Equipment: A bar, of sufficient height, comfortable to grip.

Starting position: Grasp the bar with palms facing forward; hang with arms and

---
[1]New screening test uses bent knee sit-ups.

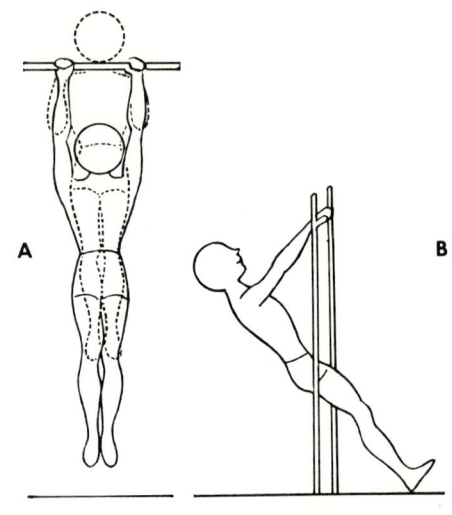

Fig. 2-1

legs fully extended. Feet must be free of floor. The partner stands slightly to one side of the pupil being tested and counts each successful pull-up.

Action:
1. Pull body up with the arms until the chin is placed over the bar.
2. Lower body until the elbows are fully extended.
3. Repeat the exercise the required number of times.

Rules:
1. The pull must not be a snap movement.
2. Knees must not be raised.
3. Kicking the legs is not permitted.
4. The body must not swing. If a pupil starts to swing, the partner stops the motion by holding an extended arm across the front of the pupil's thighs.
5. One complete pull-up is counted each time the pupil places the chin over the bar.

To pass:
Boys, ages 10 to 13 years—1 pull-up.
Boys, ages 14 to 15 years—2 pull-ups.
Boys, ages 16 to 17 years—3 pull-ups.

MODIFIED PULL-UPS—GIRLS
(see Fig. 2-1, B)

Equipment: Any bar adjustable in height and comfortable to grip. A piece of pipe, placed between two stepladders and held securely, may be used.

Starting position: Adjust height of bar to chest level. Grasp bar with palms facing

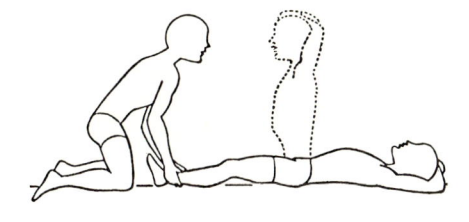

Fig. 2-2

out. Extend the legs under the bar, keeping the body and knees straight. The heels are on the floor. Fully extend the arms so they form an angle of 90 degrees with the body line. The partner braces the pupil's heels to prevent slipping.

Action:
1. Pull the body up with the arms until the *chest* touches the bar.
2. Lower body until elbows are fully extended.
3. Repeat the exercise the required number of times.

Rules:
1. The body must be kept straight.
2. The chest *must* touch the bar and the arms must be *fully extended*.
3. No resting is permitted.
4. One pull-up is counted each time the chest touches the bar.

To pass: Ages 10 to 17 years—eight modified pull-ups.

SIT-UPS—BOYS AND GIRLS (see Fig. 2-2)

Starting position: Pupil lies on the back with legs extended, feet about 1 foot apart. The hands, with fingers interlaced, are grasped behind the neck. Another pupil holds the partner's ankles and keeps the heels in contact with the floor while counting each successful sit-up.

Action:
1. Sit up and turn the trunk to the left. Touch the right elbow to the left knee.
2. Return to starting position.
3. Sit up and turn the trunk to the right. Touch the left elbow to the right knee.
4. Return to the starting position.
5. Repeat the required number of times.
6. One complete sit-up is counted each time the pupil returns to the starting position.

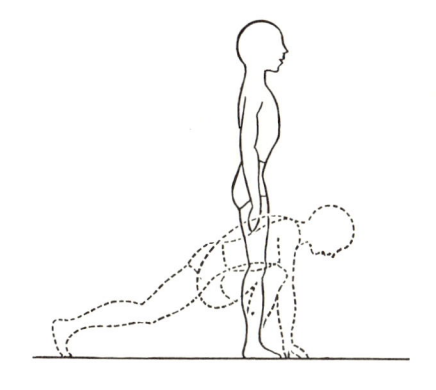

Fig. 2-3

To pass:
Boys, ages 10 to 17 years—14 sit-ups.
Girls, ages 10 to 17 years—10 sit-ups.

SQUAT THRUST—BOYS AND GIRLS (see Fig. 2-3)

Equipment: A stopwatch, or a watch with a sweep-second hand.

Starting position: Pupil stands at attention.

Action:
1. Bend knees and place hands on the floor in front of the feet. Arms may be between, outside, or in front of the bent knees.
2. Thrust the legs back far enough so that the body is perfectly straight from shoulders to feet (the push up position).
3. Return to squat position.
4. Return to erect position.

Scoring: The teacher carefully instructs the pupils how to do *correct* squat thrusts. The teacher tells the pupil to do as many correct squat thrusts as possible within a 10-second time limit. The teacher gives the starting signal, "Ready!—Go!" On "Go" the pupil begins. The partner counts each squat thrust. At the end of 10 seconds, the teacher says, "Stop."

Rule: The pupil must return to the erect position of attention at the completion of each squat thrust.

To pass:
Girls, ages 10 to 17 years—3 squat thrusts in 10 seconds.
Boys, ages 10 to 17 years—4 squat thrusts in 10 seconds.

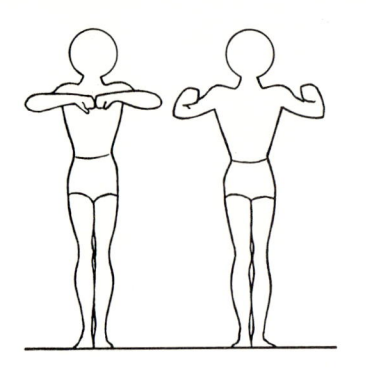

Fig. 2-4

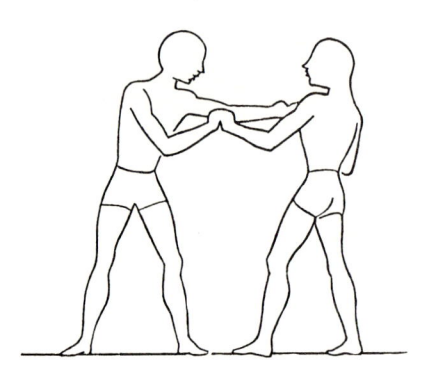

Fig. 2-5

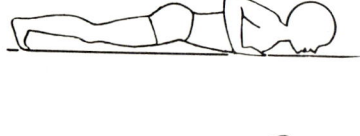

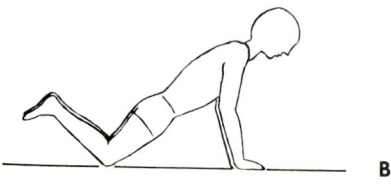

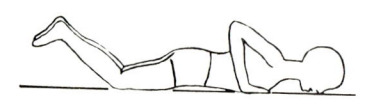

Fig. 2-6

CORRECTIVE EXERCISES
EXERCISE FOR ARM AND SHOULDER STRENGTH
WING STRETCHER (see Fig. 2-4)

Starting position: Stand erect; raise elbows to shoulder height, fists clenched, palms down in front of chest.

Action: Thrust elbows backward vigorously and return. Be sure head remains erect. Keep elbows at shoulder height.

SAWING WOOD (see Fig. 2-5)

Starting position: Pupils pair off, face each other and grasp hands with fingers interlaced.

Action: With a vigorous action, pupils pump the arms alternately as if they were sawing wood.

Note: It is not the purpose of the exercise to make one or the other lose his balance. Resistance should be increased gradually in the forward and backward movement of the arms.

PUSH-UPS

Starting position:

Boys: Extend arms and place hands on the floor, just under and slightly to the outside of the shoulders. Fingers should be pointing forward. Extend body so that it is perfectly straight. The weight is supported on the hands and toes. (See Fig. 2-6, *A*.)

Girls: Extend arms and place hands, fingers pointing forward, on ground just under and slightly outside of the shoulders. Place knees on floor and extend body until it is straight from the head to the knees. Bend knees and raise the feet off the floor. The weight is supported by the hands and knees. (Also for boys who cannot do regular push-ups.) (See Fig. 2-6, *B*.)

Action:

Count 1: Keeping body tense and straight, bend elbows and touch chest to the floor.

Count 2: Return to original position. (The body must be kept perfectly straight. The buttocks must not be raised. The abdomen must not sag.)

RECLINING PULL-UPS (see Fig. 2-7)

Starting position: One pupil lies on back. The partner stands astride the pupil, looking face to face, feet beside reclining

OPERATION FITNESS 21

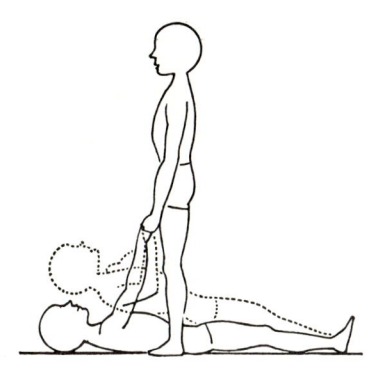

Fig. 2-7

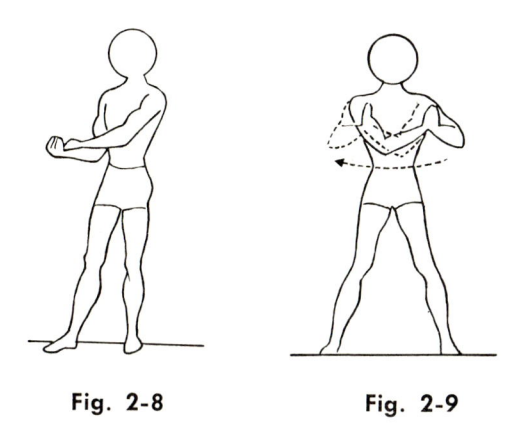

Fig. 2-8   **Fig. 2-9**

Fig. 2-10

pupil's chest. Partners grasp hands, with fingers interlocked. Reclining pupil's arms are fully extended.
Action:
Count 1: Pupil on floor pulls up with arms until chest touches partner's thighs. The body remains straight, with weight resting on heels. The standing partner supports but does not aid action.
Count 2: Return to starting position.

BICEPS BUILDER (see Fig. 2-8)

Starting position: Pupil stands, feet slightly apart. The right elbow flexed, close to body, until forearm is parallel to floor. Right fist clenched, palm up. Place left hand over the right fist.
Action:
Count 1: Inhale, flex right arm slowly and forcefully, while giving strong resistance with the left hand.
Count 2: Return to starting position, pushing forcefully with left and resisting with right.

Relax both arms. Exhale. Repeat exercise several times, then reverse arms.

CHEST BUILDER (see Fig. 2-9)

Starting position: Pupil stands, feet slightly apart, knees slightly bent. Clasp hands, palms together, fingers interlaced, hands close to chest.
Action:
Count 1: Inhale, while pushing the right hand slowly and forcefully, resisting strongly with the left. Keep hands close to chest while they move across the chest.
Count 2: Reverse the action, meanwhile holding breath.
Relax arms and exhale. Do not unclasp the hands. Repeat rhythmically.

EXERCISES FOR DEVELOPING FLEXIBILITY
BEAR HUG (see Fig. 2-10)

Starting position: Pupil stands, feet comfortably spread, with hands on hips.
Action:
Count 1: Take a long step diagonally right, keeping left foot anchored in place; tackle the right leg around the thigh by encircling the thigh with both arms.
Count 2: Return to the starting position.
Counts 3 and 4: Repeat to the opposite side.

SIDE FLEX (see Fig. 2-11)

Starting position: Pupil lies on side, arms extended over head. The head rests on the lower arm. Legs are extended fully, one on top of the other.
Action:
Count 1: With a brisk action, raise the topmost arm and leg vertically. Attempt to make contact with hand and foot, without bending elbow or knee.
Count 2: Return to starting position.

Fig. 2-11

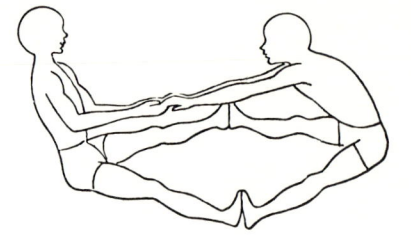

Fig. 2-13

Fig. 2-12

Fig. 2-14

Repeat for several counts, then change to other side.

One-foot balance (see Fig. 2-12)

Starting position: Pupil stands at attention.
Action:
Count 1: Stretch left leg backward, while bending trunk forward and extending arms sideward until this position is reached: The head is up, trunk parallel to floor; the left leg is fully extended with the toes of the left foot pointed. The supporting leg is kept straight.
Hold this position for 5 to 10 seconds.
Count 2: Return to starting position.
Repeat, using the opposite leg for support.

Pull stretcher (see Fig. 2-13)

Starting position: Two pupils sit facing each other, legs apart and extended, so that the soles of their feet are in contact. Pupils grasp hands with fingers interlocked.
Action: One pupil attempts to bring own trunk as close to the floor as possible. The other pupil aids by pulling the partner forward. The exercise is continued as partners reverse actions. The legs must be kept spread and straight throughout the exercise.

Squat thrust (see Fig. 2-14)

Starting position: Pupil stands at attention.
Action:
Count 1: Bend knees and place hands on the floor in front of the feet. Arms may be between, outside, or in front of the bent knees.
Count 2: Thrust the legs back far enough so that the body is perfectly straight from shoulders to feet (the push-up position).
Count 3: Return to squat position.
Count 4: Return to erect position.

EXERCISES TO DEVELOP STRENGTH OF ABDOMINAL AND TRUNK MUSCLES
Knee raise (single and double)
(see Fig. 2-15)

Starting position: Pupil lies on back with knees slightly flexed, feet on floor, arms at side.
Action:
Count 1: Raise one knee up as close as possible to chest.

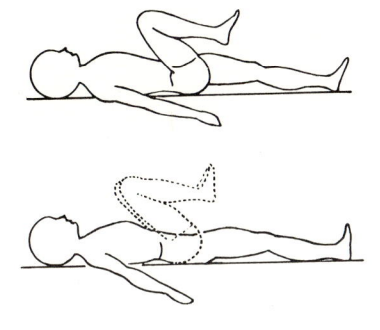

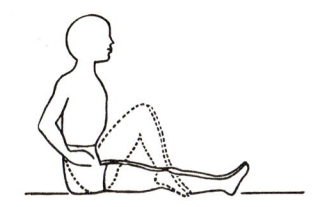

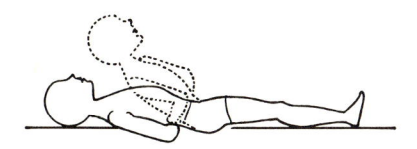

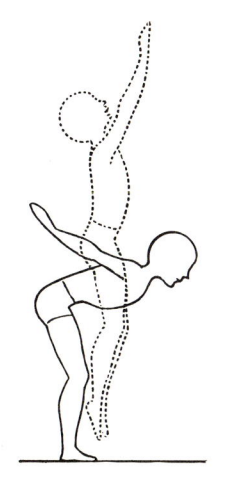

Count 2: Fully extend the knee so the leg is perpendicular to the floor.

Count 3: Bend knee and return to chest.

Count 4: Straighten leg and return to starting position.

Alternate the legs during the exercise. The double knee raise is done in the same manner by moving both legs simultaneously.

Head raiser (see Fig. 2-16)

Starting position: Pupil lies on back, knees flexed, feet pulled close to buttocks, soles of feet on floor, arms at sides.

Action:

Count 1: Raise head and upper back off floor, tensing abdominal muscles.

Count 2: Return to starting position.

As abdominal strength increases, the distance head and upper back are raised from the floor should be gradually increased.

Leg extension (see Fig. 2-17)

Starting position: Pupil sits, legs extended, body erect, and hands on hips.

Action:

Count 1: With a quick, vigorous action, raise and flex the knees by dragging feet backward toward the buttocks with the toes lightly touching the ground.

Count 2: Extend the legs back to the starting position.

The head and shoulders should be held high throughout the exercise.

Head and shoulder curl (see Fig. 2-18)

Starting position: Pupil lies on the back with hands clasped, palms down, behind the small of the back.

Action:

Count 1: Lift the head and pull the shoulders and elbows up off the floor. Hold the tense position for four counts.

Count 2: Return to starting position.

Repeat the exercise.

EXERCISES FOR DEVELOPING AGILITY

Tortoise and hare (running in place)

Starting position: Pupil stands at attention.

Action:

Count 1: Jog slowly in place.

Count 2: On the command, "Hare," the

24 BASIC SKILLS IN SPORTS FOR MEN AND WOMEN

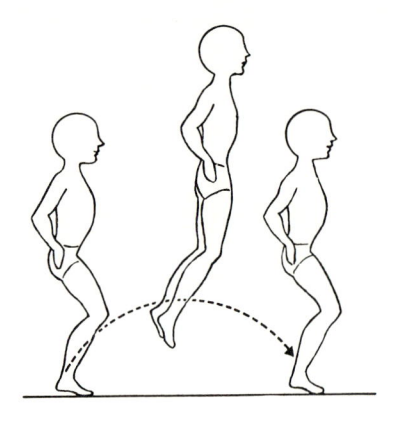

Fig. 2-20

Fig. 2-21

tempo doubles. The knees are lifted high, while arms pump vigorously.

Count 3: On the command, "Tortoise," the tempo is slowed to an easy jog.

Repeat the commands, "Tortoise," "Hare."

JUMP AND REACH (see Fig. 2-19)

Starting position: Pupil stands erect with feet slightly apart, arms extended overhead, palms facing out.

Action:

Count 1: Keeping arms fully extended, swing them downward and back as far as possible, meanwhile bending deeply at the waist and flexing knees slightly.

Count 2: Swing arms upward forcefully, straightening body and leaping as high as possible, landing in starting position.

KANGAROO HOP (see Fig. 2-20)

Starting position: Pupil assumes a semi-squatting position. Knees are flexed with the weight on the balls of the feet and the trunk erect. Place the hands on the hips.

Action: Jump as high and as far forward as possible, keeping hands on hips, landing in the starting position.

BLAST OFF

Starting position: Pupil stands erect, feet slightly apart, hands over head.

Action: While counting downward from 10, the pupil moves slowly to a full squat position. The body is tucked forward, with the head between the knees. The arms encircle the knees tightly. This position is to be reached by the count of zero.

At this point, the class, in unison, shouts, "BLAST OFF," while leaping skyward as high as possible, landing in the starting position.

THE SPRINTER (see Fig. 2-21)

Starting position: Pupil assumes squatting position, hands on the floor, fingers pointed forward, left leg fully extended to the rear.

Action:

Count 1: Reverse position of the feet by bringing left foot to hands and extending right leg backward, all in one motion.

Count 2: Reverse feet again, returning to starting position.

Repeat exercise rhythmically.

THE COORDINATOR (see Fig. 2-22)

Starting position: Pupil stands at attention.

Action:

Count 1: Hop on left foot, swinging right leg forward, touching toe to floor in front of left foot, meanwhile bringing both arms forward to shoulder level, fully extended.

Count 2: Hop again on left foot, swinging right foot to the right side and touching toe to floor, meanwhile flinging arms sideward at shoulder level.

Count 3: Hop again on left foot, returning to position of Count 1.

Count 4: Hop again on left foot, returning to starting position.

Repeat, hopping on right foot. Continue, alternately hopping on each foot. As exercise is mastered, tempo should be increased.

THE PRESIDENT'S PHYSICAL FITNESS TESTS (AAHPER TEST) AND SCORES

PULL-UPS—BOYS (see Fig. 2-23)

Equipment: A bar, of sufficient height, comfortable to grip.

Starting position: Grasp the bar with

palms facing forward; hang with arms and legs fully extended. Feet must be free of floor. The partner stands slightly to one side of the pupil being tested and counts each successful pull-up.

Action:
1. Pull body up with the arms until the chin is placed over the bar.
2. Lower body until the elbows are fully extended.
3. Repeat the exercise as many times as possible.

Rules:
1. The pull must not be a snap movement.
2. Knees must not be raised.
3. Kicking the legs is not permitted.
4. The body must not swing. If pupil starts to swing, the partner stops the

Fig. 2-22

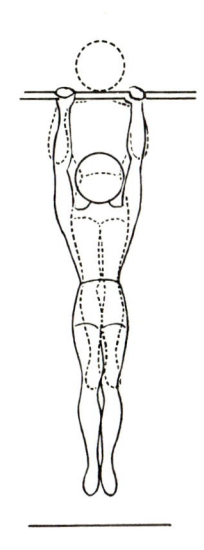

Fig. 2-23

Boys—number of pull-ups

Age	10	11	12	13	14	15	16	17
Excellent	6	6	7	8	10	10	12	13
Good	3	4	4	5	6	7	9	10
Satisfactory	2	2	2	3	4	5	6	7
Poor	1	1	1	2	2	2	3	4

Girls—number of modified pull-ups

Age	10	11	12	13	14	15	16	17
Excellent	45	45	45	45	45	45	45	45
Good	40	40	40	40	40	40	40	40
Satisfactory	30	30	29	30	29	22	25	25
Poor	17	20	20	20	19	12	14	15

Boys—number of sit-ups (see new revised test)

Age	10	11	12	13	14	15	16	17
Excellent	60	67	78	73	99	99	99	99
Good	47	50	51	54	60	60	73	63
Satisfactory	30	31	37	40	44	45	50	50
Poor	22	23	28	30	33	35	40	38

Girls—number of sit-ups (see new revised test)

Excellent	50	50	50	50	49	37	40	42
Good	33	34	30	30	28	26	27	25
Satisfactory	22	25	22	21	20	20	21	20
Poor	15	18	17	17	15	15	16	15

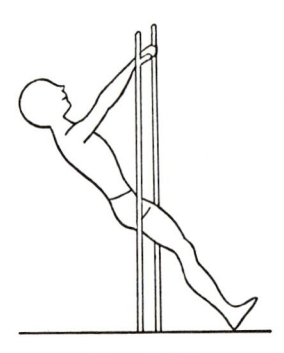

Fig. 2-24

motion by holding an extended arm across the front of the pupil's thighs.
5. One complete pull-up is counted each time the pupil places the chin over the bar.

MODIFIED PULL-UPS—GIRLS
(see Fig. 2-24)

Equipment: Any bar adjustable in height and comfortable to grip. A piece of pipe, placed between two stepladders and held securely, may be used.

Starting position: Adjust height of bar to *chest* level. Grasp bar with palms facing out. Extend the legs under the bar, keeping the body and knees straight. The heels are on the floor. Fully extend the arms so they form an angle of 90 degrees with the body line. The partner braces the pupil's heels to prevent slipping.

Action:
1. Pull body up with the arms until the chest touches the bar.
2. Lower body until elbows are fully extended.
3. Repeat the exercise attempting to achieve the "Excellent" score for your age, but not exceeding that number.

Rules:
1. The body must be kept straight.
2. The chest *must* touch the bar and the arms must then be fully extended.
3. No resting is permitted.
4. One pull-up is counted each time the chest touches the bar.

SIT-UPS (see Fig. 2-25) (see new revised test)

Starting position: Pupil lies on the back with legs extended, feet about 1 foot apart. The hands, with fingers interlaced, are grasped behind the neck. The other pupil holds the partner's ankles and keeps the heels in contact with the floor while counting each successful sit-up.

Action:
1. Sit up and turn the trunk to the left. Touch the right elbow to the left knee.
2. Return to starting position.
3. Sit up and turn the trunk to the right, touching the left elbow to the right knee.
4. Return to the starting position.
5. Pupil should do as many sit-ups as possible, but not exceed the number shown below in the "Excellent" category for the appropriate age and sex.
6. One complete sit-up is counted each time the pupil returns to starting position.

SHUTTLE RUN (see Fig. 2-26)

Equipment: Two blocks of wood, 2 by 2 by 4 inches (blackboard erasers may be

Boys—shuttle run (in seconds to nearest tenth)

Age	10	11	12	13	14	15	16	17
Excellent	10.3	10.4	10.0	9.7	9.4	9.3	9.1	9.0
Good	11.2	11.0	10.5	10.3	10.0	10.0	9.5	9.5
Satisfactory	11.9	11.6	11.1	10.8	10.5	10.4	10.0	10.0
Poor	12.3	12.0	11.7	11.5	11.0	10.9	10.5	10.6

Girls—shuttle run (in seconds to nearest tenth)

Age	10	11	12	13	14	15	16	17
Excellent	11.2	10.9	10.4	10.7	10.5	10.5	10.3	10.4
Good	11.8	11.6	11.3	11.3	11.2	11.0	11.0	10.8
Satisfactory	12.4	12.2	12.0	12.0	11.8	11.8	11.5	11.5
Poor	13.1	12.9	12.6	12.4	12.5	12.3	12.0	12.1

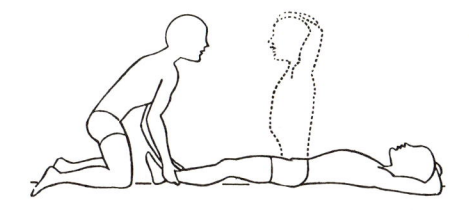

Fig. 2-25

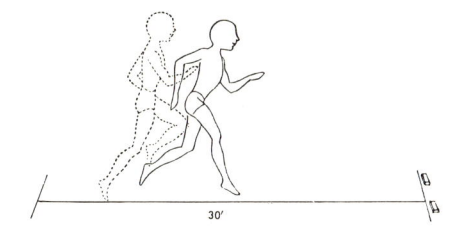

Fig. 2-26

Fig. 2-27

used) and stopwatch. Mark two parallel lines 30 feet apart. Place the blocks of wood behind one of the lines.

Starting position: Pupil stands behind the line opposite the blocks ready to run.

Action: On the signal, "Ready!—Go!" the pupil runs to the blocks, picks up one, returns, and places it behind the starting line. (The block must not be thrown.) The pupil then runs and picks up the second block and carries it back across the starting line.

Rules:
1. Allow two trials.
2. Disqualify any trial in which the block is dropped or thrown.
3. Record the better of the two trials in seconds to the nearest tenth.

STANDING BROAD JUMP (see Fig. 2-27)

Equipment: Any level surface and tape measure.

Starting position: Pupil stands with the feet comfortably apart, with toes just behind the takeoff line. Preparatory to jumping, pupil should have knees flexed and should swing the arms backward and forward in a rhythmical motion.

Action: Jump, swinging arms forcefully forward and upward, taking off from the balls of the feet.

Rules:
1. Allow three trials.
2. Measure from the takeoff line to the heel or any part of the body that touches the surface nearest the takeoff line.
3. Record best of three trials in feet and inches to the nearest inch.

Note: It may be convenient to anchor the tape measure to the surface at a right angle to the takeoff line and have the pupil jump along the tape. The scorer stands to the side with a stick, touches the stick to the point where the pupil lands, and observes the mark to the nearest inch.

Boys—standing broad jump

Age	10		11		12		13		14		15		16		17	
	ft.	in.	ft.	in.	ft.	in.	ft.	in.	ft.	in.	ft.	in.	ft.	in.	ft.	in.
Excellent	5	6	5	10	6	2	6	8	7	2	7	8	8	0	8	4
Good	5	0	5	4	5	8	6	0	6	7	7	0	7	3	7	8
Satisfactory	4	8	5	0	5	4	5	8	6	1	6	5	6	11	7	2
Poor	4	4	4	7	4	11	5	2	5	7	5	11	6	4	6	8

Girls—standing broad jump

Excellent	5	4	5	7	5	8	5	9	6	0	6	2	6	5	6	6
Good	4	10	5	0	5	2	5	4	5	6	5	6	5	8	5	10
Satisfactory	4	5	4	8	4	9	4	11	5	0	5	0	5	2	5	3
Poor	4	1	4	3	4	5	4	6	4	7	4	8	4	10	4	10

Boys—fifty-yard dash (in seconds to nearest tenth)

Age	10	11	12	13	14	15	16	17
Excellent	7.6	7.3	7.0	6.5	6.5	6.2	6.1	6.0
Good	8.1	7.9	7.5	7.2	7.0	6.7	6.4	6.3
Satisfactory	8.6	8.3	8.0	7.6	7.3	7.0	6.8	6.6
Poor	9.0	8.7	8.3	8.0	7.7	7.3	7.0	7.0

Girls—fifty-yard dash (in seconds to nearest tenth)

	10	11	12	13	14	15	16	17
Excellent	8.0	7.5	7.2	7.4	7.3	7.4	7.1	7.3
Good	8.5	8.2	8.0	7.9	8.0	8.0	7.7	8.0
Satisfactory	8.9	8.6	8.4	8.2	8.3	8.3	8.2	8.4
Poor	9.5	9.0	9.0	8.8	8.8	8.9	8.6	8.9

FIFTY-YARD DASH

Equipment: Stopwatch.

Starting position: Pupil stands behind the starting line. The starter takes a position at the finish line with a stopwatch. The starter raises one hand preparatory to giving the starting signal.

Action: When the starter brings the hand down quickly and hits the thigh, the pupil leaves the mark. As the pupil crosses the finish line, the time is noted and recorded.

Rules:
1. The score is the lapsed time between the starter's signal and the instant the pupil crosses the finish line.
2. Record the time in seconds to the nearest tenth.

SOFTBALL THROW FOR DISTANCE
(see Fig. 2-28) (this test has been eliminated)

Equipment: Softball (12 inch), tape measure, small metal or wooden stakes. Within

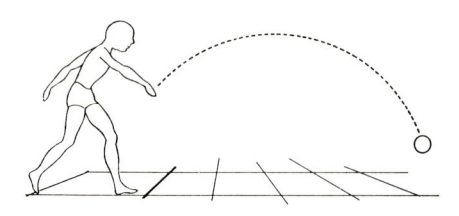

Fig. 2-28

the contestants' limitations, mark lines at 5-yard intervals parallel to a restraining line. A football field marked in conventional fashion makes an ideal area for the test.

Starting position: Pupil stands several feet behind the restraining line, ready to throw.

Action: Moving forward, the pupil throws the ball, overhand, from behind the restraining line, as far as possible.

Rules:
1. Only overhand throws may be used.
2. Mark point where ball lands with one of the stakes.

Boys—softball throw for distance (in feet)

Age	10	11	12	13	14	15	16	17
Excellent	122	130	151	171	190	207	214	231
Good	103	115	132	148	163	182	190	212
Satisfactory	92	103	118	129	147	164	172	185
Poor	82	94	102	115	131	150	156	167

Girls—softball throw for distance (in feet)

Excellent	69	88	94	106	112	117	120	120
Good	56	68	78	88	89	94	99	102
Satisfactory	45	56	65	75	75	80	84	86
Poor	38	48	55	63	64	67	71	72

Boys—600-yard run–walk (in minutes and seconds)

Age	10	11	12	13	14	15	16	17
Excellent	2:15	2:2	2:5	2:0	1:50	1:43	1:40	1:36
Good	2:30	2:24	2:19	2:13	2:5	1:59	1:51	1:51
Satisfactory	2:45	2:37	2:32	2:25	2:18	2:9	2:0	2:0
Poor	2:58	2:50	2:46	2:36	2:30	2:20	2:10	2:9

Girls—600-yard run–walk (in minutes and seconds)

Excellent	2:30	2:25	2:22	2:24	2:20	2:27	2:23	2:30
Good	2:49	2:44	2:41	2:43	2:45	3:5	2:48	2:47
Satisfactory	3:6	3:1	3:3	3:0	3:5	3:6	3:5	3:4
Poor	3:21	3:16	3:21	3:20	3:21	3:24	3:23	3:19

Table 1. Physical fitness test norms—percentile scores for college men

Percentile	Pull-ups	Sit-ups	Shuttle run	Standing broad jump	50-yard dash	Softball throw	600-yard run–walk
100	20	100	8.3	9'6"	5.5	315	1:12
95	12	99	9.0	8'5"	6.1	239	1:35
90	10	97	9.1	8'2"	6.2	226	1:38
85	9	79	9.1	7'11"	6.3	217	1:40
80	8	68	9.2	7'10"	6.4	211	1:42
75	8	61	9.4	7'8"	6.5	206	1:44
70	7	58	9.5	7'7"	6.5	200	1:45
65	7	52	9.5	7'6"	6.6	196	1:47
60	6	51	9.6	7'5"	6.6	192	1:49
55	6	50	9.6	7'4"	6.7	188	1:50
50	5	47	9.7	7'3"	6.8	184	1:52
45	5	44	9.8	7'1"	6.8	180	1:53
40	4	41	9.9	7'0"	6.9	176	1:55
35	4	38	10.0	6'11"	7.0	171	1:57
30	3	36	10.0	6'10"	7.0	166	1:59
25	3	34	10.1	6'9"	7.1	161	2:01
20	2	31	10.2	6'7"	7.1	156	2:05
15	1	29	10.4	6'5"	7.2	150	2:09
10	0	26	10.6	6'2"	7.5	140	2:15
5	0	22	11.1	5'10"	7.7	125	2:25
0		0	13.9	4'2"	9.1	55	3:43

Table 2. Physical fitness test norms—percentile scores for college women

Percentile	Modified pull-ups	Sit-ups	Shuttle run	Standing broad jump	50-yard dash	Softball throw	600-yard run–walk
100	40	50	7.5	7'10"	5.4	184	1:49
95	39	43	10.2	6'6"	7.3	115	2:19
90	38	35	10.5	6'3"	7.6	103	2:27
85	33	31	10.7	6'1"	7.7	96	2:32
80	30	29	10.9	5'11"	7.8	90	2:37
75	28	27	11.0	5'10"	7.9	86	2:41
70	26	25	11.1	5'8"	8.0	82	2:44
65	24	24	11.2	5'7"	8.1	79	2:48
60	22	22	11.3	5'6"	8.2	76	2:51
55	21	21	11.5	5'5"	8.3	73	2:54
50	20	20	11.6	5'4"	8.4	70	2:58
45	18	19	11.7	5'3"	8.6	67	3:01
40	17	18	11.9	5'2"	8.7	65	3:05
35	16	16	12.0	5'0"	8.8	62	3:08
30	15	15	12.1	4'11"	9.0	59	3:13
25	13	14	12.2	4'10"	9.1	57	3:18
20	12	13	12.4	4'8"	9.2	54	3:23
15	11	11	12.6	4'7"	9.4	51	3:29
10	9	9	12.9	4'5"	9.7	47	3:38
5	7	7	13.4	4'1"	10.1	42	3:53
0	0	0	17.3	2'3"	13.7	5	5:29

Table 3. Graded qualifications for the President's physical fitness team

Can you equal or surpass all these marks?

If you can, you are eligible to receive a citation signed by the President and a colorful emblem to prove you earned a spot on the All-America Physical Fitness Team.

Can you make the team?

Boys

Age	Sit-ups	Pull-ups	Broad jump	50-yard dash	600-yard run–walk	Softball throw	Shuttle run
10	100	6	5'8"	7.4 sec.	2 min. 12 sec.	122'	10.4 sec.
11	100	6	5'10"	7.4 sec.	2 min. 8 sec.	136'	10.3 sec.
12	100	6	6'2"	7.0 sec.	2 min. 2 sec.	150'	10.0 sec.
13	100	8	6'9"	6.9 sec.	1 min. 53 sec.	175'	9.9 sec.
14	100	10	7'3"	6.6 sec.	1 min. 46 sec.	187'	9.6 sec.
15	100	10	7'6"	6.4 sec.	1 min. 40 sec.	204'	9.4 sec.
16	100	12	7'11"	6.2 sec.	1 min. 37 sec.	213'	9.2 sec.
17	100	12	8'1"	6.1 sec.	1 min. 36 sec.	226'	9.1 sec.

Table 3. Graded qualifications for the President's physical fitness team—cont'd

Girls

Age	Sit-ups	Flexed arm hang*	Broad jump	50-yard dash	600-yard run–walk	Softball throw	Shuttle run
10	50	21 sec.	5'4"	7.5 sec.	2 min. 20 sec.	71'	10.8 sec.
11	50	20 sec.	5'8"	7.6 sec.	2 min. 24 sec.	81'	10.6 sec.
12	50	19 sec.	5'9"	7.5 sec.	2 min. 24 sec.	90'	10.5 sec.
13	50	18 sec.	5'10"	7.5 sec.	2 min. 25 sec.	94'	10.5 sec.
14	50	19 sec.	6'0"	7.4 sec.	2 min. 22 sec.	100'	10.4 sec.
15	50	18 sec.	6'1"	7.5 sec.	2 min. 23 sec.	105'	10.5 sec.
16	50	19 sec.	6'2"	7.5 sec.	2 min. 23 sec.	104'	10.4 sec.
17	50	19 sec.	6'2"	7.5 sec.	2 min. 27 sec.	102'	10.4 sec.

*The modified pull-ups may be substituted here as found under the President's Physical Fitness Test and Scores. However, if the flexed arm hang test is to be used, the child must be placed on the bar with a 90-degree angle at the elbow.

3. Three throws are allowed.
4. Disqualify throw if pupil steps over restraining line.
5. Measure and record the best of the three throws to the nearest foot.

600-Yard run–walk

Equipment: Stopwatch, and running area with designated starting and finish lines.

Starting position: Pupil stands behind starting line.

Action: On the signal, "Ready!—Go!" the pupil starts running the 600-yard distance (walking only if necessary).

Rules:
1. Walking is permitted, but the object is to cover the distance in the shortest possible time.
2. Record the time in minutes and seconds.

Note: It is possible to test several pupils at the same time. Have the pupils pair off before the start of the test. One of the partners runs, while the other stands near the timer. The timer calls out the time continuously, until the runners have all crossed the finish line. Each pupil near the timer listens for, and remembers, his partner's time as the latter finishes.

3 Archery

HISTORY

The bow and arrow is one of man's oldest mechanical weapons and remains the weapon of many of our still existing aboriginal races and tribes in many parts of the world. The bow and arrow was first used by primitive man for hunting. It was the chief weapon of the American Indians, both for hunting and war. It was used as a weapon of war by the Egyptians in overthrowing Persia and in many other successful wars.

With the discovery of powder and the use of firearms in comparatively recent time, the bow has retired to the realm of sport. In this capacity it has sporadically interested groups in various parts of the civilized world, particularly in England and the United States, but has not flourished to the same extent as many other sports.

The earliest contest in archery, "The Ancient Scorton Arrow," was held in England in 1673, created by the Ancient Scorton Arrow Society. This tournament is still the oldest in existence today.

In the United States the first archery club, known as the United Bowmen of Philadelphia, was organized in 1828. The first tournament was held in Chicago in 1879, and tournaments sponsored by this club are still being continued to the present day.

Within recent years there has been a revival of interest in the sport of archery. Along with the revival of interest in all sports of the individual type, it is being enjoyed by an increasing number of men, women, and children.

Archery has a carry-over fascination for most people from childhood Indian-playing days. Archery is legendary. One need only be reminded of the adventurous glamor and charm of Robin Hood, William Tell, and Hiawatha.

Today, archery as a sport continues to hold interest for several reasons: (1) the evolution of a new method of shooting which is easier to learn and more accurate than the old, (2) the development of more efficient bows and arrows, and (3) the fascination many people find in the activities possible to the archer, ranging from target shooting, clout, roving, field shooting, and novelty shoots to the actual hunting of small and large game.

RULES

Any bow (except a crossbow) and any arrow are permissible in a contest. Tackle may be changed at any time in the competition. Women may shoot in a men's event or in the junior or senior events, but men may not shoot in a women's event. All arrows

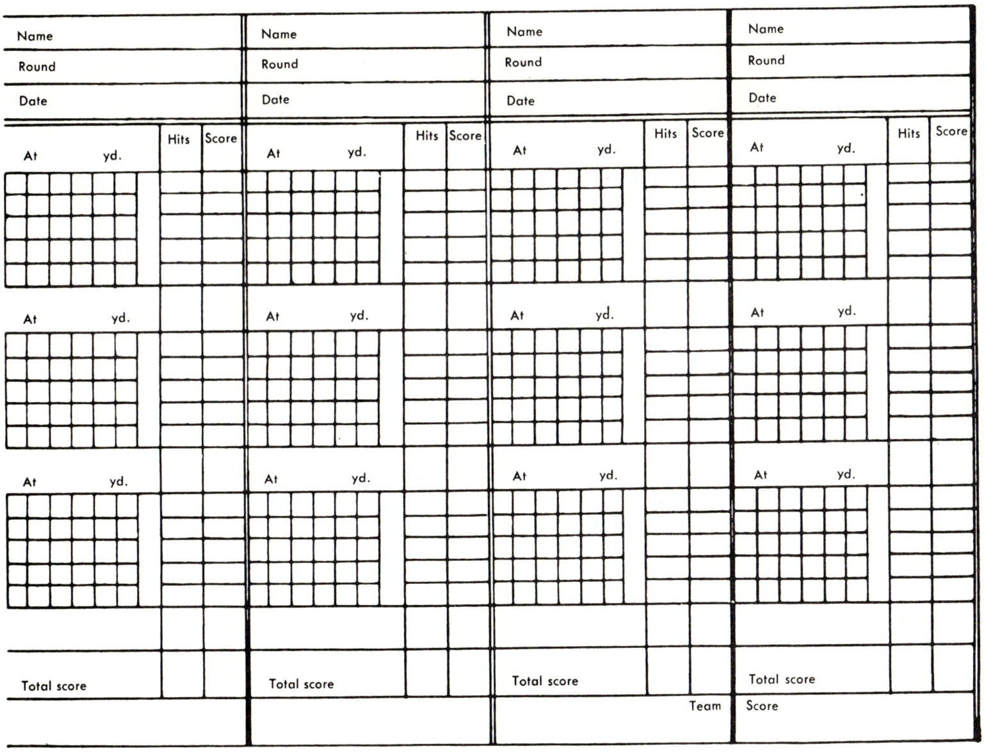

Fig. 3-1. Sample score sheet.

must remain in the target until scored by the range officials.

SCORING (see Fig. 3-1)

Six arrows (an end) are shot at one time. An arrow hitting the wrong target counts as a shot, but its score is forfeited. A loosened arrow may be retrieved if it can be reached from the archer's stance with the aid of the bow. However, it is counted as a shot if it falls beyond the archer's reach without moving the feet.

An arrow which cuts two colors is always given the higher value of the two, even though the greater part of the arrow is in the ring of lower value. An arrow which hits the target at 60 yards or less and bounces off is given a value of 7 points, regardless of what part of the target face has been hit. An arrow which hits the target and passes completely through the scoring face is also given a value of 7 points at 60 yards or less. When an arrow hits the petticoat, it counts for neither score nor hit. Scores are always listed with the highest score first, awarding 9, 7, 5, 3, or 1 point for the gold, the red, the blue, the black, and the white, respectively.

To call back to the archer the location of the arrow, the scorer reads the target like the face of a clock, for example, "6 o'clock red" if the arrow is in that location of the target.

SAFETY PRECAUTION WHILE SHOOTING IN GROUPS

Each archer shoots the end or flight of arrows and waits until the last arrow is shot. All archers then retrieve their arrows and no more shooting takes place until all arrows are retrieved and all archers have returned to the firing line. When this condition exists, a range supervisor will give the commence firing call.

TOURNAMENT SHOOTING
Target competition

Tournaments require the archers to be tested by shooting a prescribed number of arrows from various selected distances. These trial combinations are called "rounds."

1. Miniature round (indoor shooting)—60 arrows from 15 yards on a 2-foot target
2. Range round (indoor shooting)—60 arrows from a single distance, either 50, 40, 30, or 20 yards
3. Junior scholastic round—24 arrows from 30 yards and 20 yards, respectively (new rounds designed for school use)
4. Scholastic round—24 arrows from 40 yards and 30 yards, respectively (newly designed for school use)
5. Junior Columbia round—24 arrows from 40 yards, 30 yards, and 20 yards, respectively
6. Columbia round—24 arrows from 50 yards, 40 yards, and 30 yards, respectively
7. Junior American round—30 arrows from 50 yards, 40 yards, and 30 yards, respectively
8. American round—30 arrows from 60 yards, 50 yards, and 40 yards, respectively (recommended only for advanced coeducational groups)
9. National round—48 arrows from 60 yards and 24 arrows from 50 yards (for women)

Competition in a tournament usually consists of double rounds. Scores are tabulated after each "end" of six arrows is shot.

Clout shooting is a definite round, consisting usually of 36 arrows at 180 yards for men and 120 or 140 yards for women, shot at a 48-foot target laid on the ground. Clout means a marker placed on the ground for long-distance shooting.

Field shooting

Because of the vast increase of bow hunting in this country, The National Field Archers' Association of Redlands, California, now sponsors a new type of tournament and practice range called field shooting, field golf, or archer's golf. Fourteen or twenty-eight targets of different sizes are placed at random over a course which goes over hills and valleys.

Up to four groups of archers shoot a "field round" and advance from target to target, simulating the practice of golf. Targets have a bull's-eye which, if hit, counts 5 points and an outer ring which has a 3-point value. Four arrows are shot at each target. The archer with the highest score is the winner.

EQUIPMENT
The bow

The two types of bows most commonly used by the beginner are the straight and the recurved bow. A bow should be selected that can be pulled back to the pile point of the arrow and held steady momentarily while adjusting for the aim. This is determined by the weight of the bow. In other words, the weight of the bow is the number of pounds pull it takes to pull the arrow to its full length. This, for the beginner, varies with age, sex, and strength.

BOW WEIGHT
1. Women—20 to 30 pounds
2. College women—25 pounds, 28-inch draw
3. High school girls—20 pounds, 26-inch draw
4. Novice archers—15 to 25 pounds
5. Men—35 to 45 pounds
6. Young men—25 to 35 pounds

See Fig. 3-2 for names of the parts of the bow and arrow.

The length of the bow should be determined by the length of the arrow used. If the bow is too long, it will be an inefficient bow in that all of its power will not be used. If the bow is too short, it will tend to be overdrawn and weakened.

Points to look for in selecting a bow:
1. Does the drawn bow bend evenly from the handle to the tips?
2. Do the upper and lower arms bend similarly?
3. When the bow is strung, does the string divide it in half?
4. Does the cut of the bow follow the grain of the wood?
5. Does it feel comfortable in the hand?
6. Does it return to its original shape after it is unstrung?
7. Are pins and knots taken care of by plugging or leaving extra wood around them?
8. Are its weight and strength suitable for your purpose?

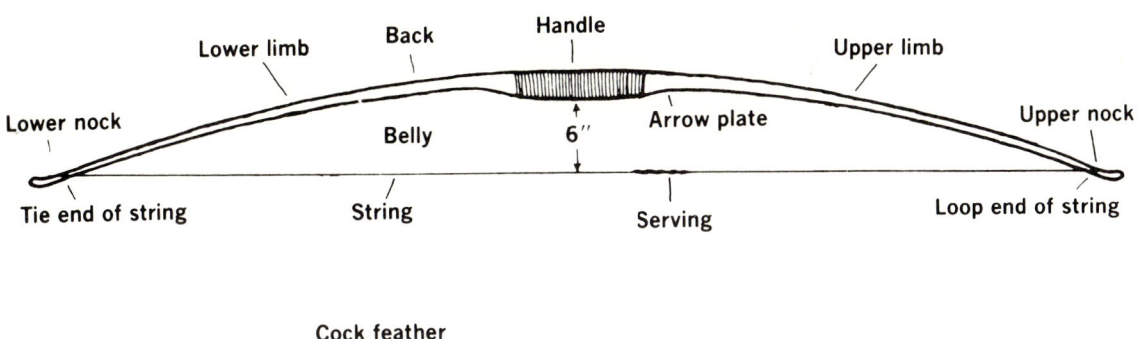

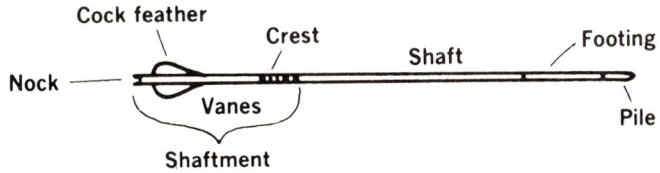

Fig. 3-2. Parts of the bow and arrow.

The arrow

In the selection of arrows the beginning archer should make sure that the arrow is straight and that its length is appropriate for the length of the archer's arm. (See Fig. 3-3.) Port Oxford cedar is the best wood for arrows and should be purchased unless the cost is prohibitive. If so, birchwood is cheap and sufficiently durable. Aluminum and fiberglass have proved to be quite satisfactory.

The string consists of varied numbers of linen threads waxed with beeswax with loops at both ends.

Protective devices (see Fig. 3-4): Finger protection is necessary for all archers. Without it the archer's shots will be inaccurate and painfully executed. There are two types of finger protection: (1) the finger tab, a leather pattern cut to cover index, middle, and ring fingers, and (2) the shooting glove, similar to an ordinary glove with the thumb and little finger of the glove omitted.

The quiver is used for holding the arrows.

The armguard is necessary for the same reasons quoted for the need of finger protection.

Fig. 3-3. Selection of arrow. Measure from fingertip to fingertip.

Target

A target and stand can be homemade and such targets and stands are usually considered best and least expensive.

The tripod stand should consist of three pine boards, 3 × 1 × 6 feet long. It should incline backward about 10 to 15 degrees from the vertical.

Fig. 3-4. Protective devices.

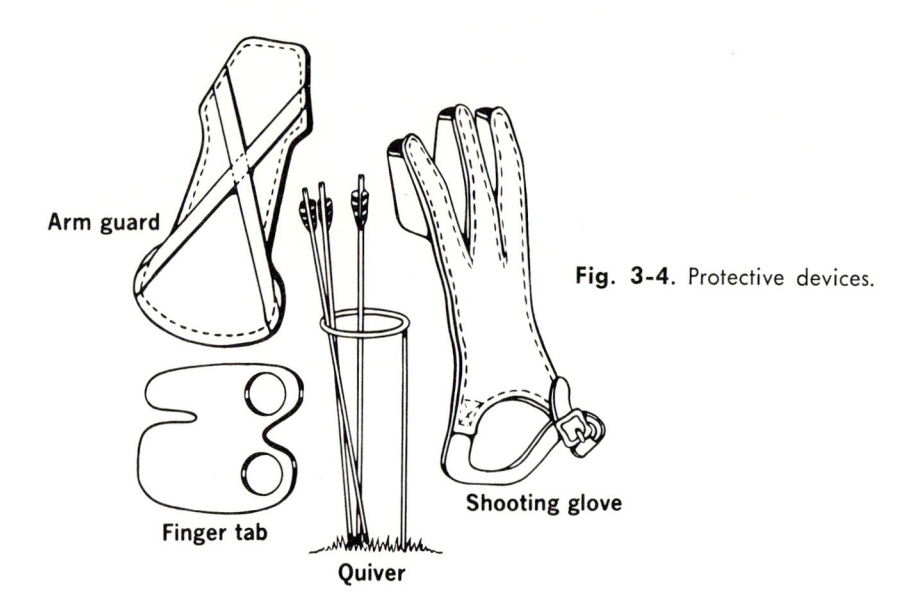

Arm guard
Finger tab
Quiver
Shooting glove

The target is approximately 48 inches in diameter and 4 to 5 inches thick. It is constructed from rye straw or marsh hay wound tightly in a coil and held firmly together with tarred cord.

The target face can be made from canvas, oil cloth, or heavy paper. On the face are painted five colored circles. The "bull's-eye" is painted gold and is 9.6 inches in diameter. The other circles are 4.8 inches in width and are painted, from the center out, red, blue, black, and white, respectively. The target should be hung so that the exact center of the gold circle is 4 feet from the ground.

BASIC SKILL TECHNIQUES
Stringing the bow

Grasp the handle of the bow in the left hand with the back of the bow uppermost. Place the lower end against the inside of the arch of the left foot, making sure that the tip does not touch the ground. Place the heel of the right hand on the back of the bow (see Fig. 3-5) so that the loop of the string may be held between the thumb and first finger. By pulling on the handle with the left hand and pressing with the heel of the right, the bow may be bent and the string pushed up with the thumb and forefinger until it drops into the nock. (See Fig. 3-6, *A*).

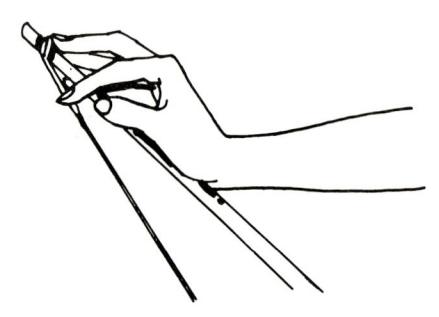

Fig. 3-5. Stringing the bow.

Unstringing the bow

The process is exactly the same as in stringing, except that the string is pulled out of the nock.

Checking the bow after stringing

Make sure the loop is slipped completely into the nock and the bowstring is centered. The distance from string to handle should measure about 6 inches, which may be measured roughly by making a fist and letting the thumb extend perpendicularly from it.

PREPARATION FOR THE DRAW
Stance

The archer should stand astride the shooting line with the target directly out from the left side. (See Fig. 3-7, *A*). The feet should

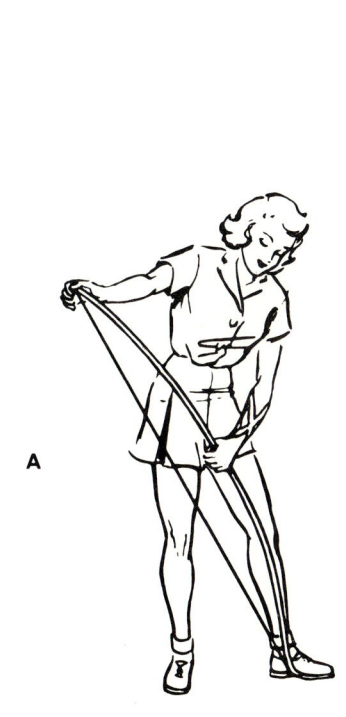

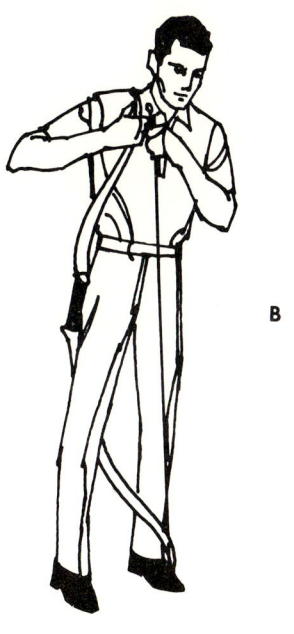

Fig. 3-6. **A**, Stringing the bow. **B**, Stringing a heavier bow.

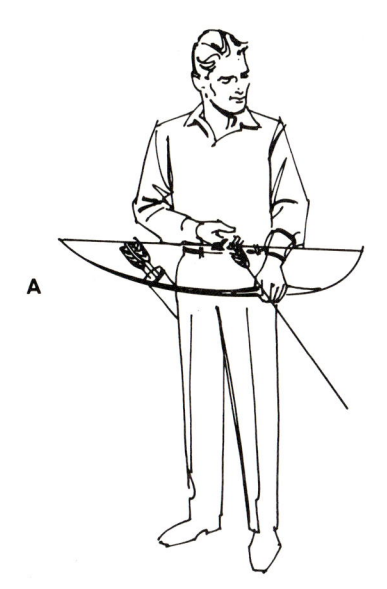

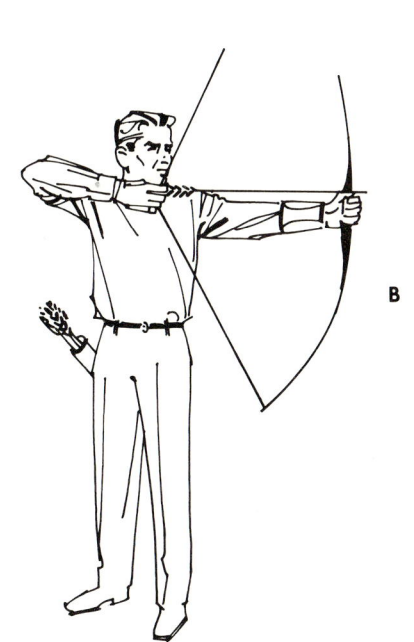

Fig. 3-7. **A**, Stance. **B**, The draw. **C**, The release.

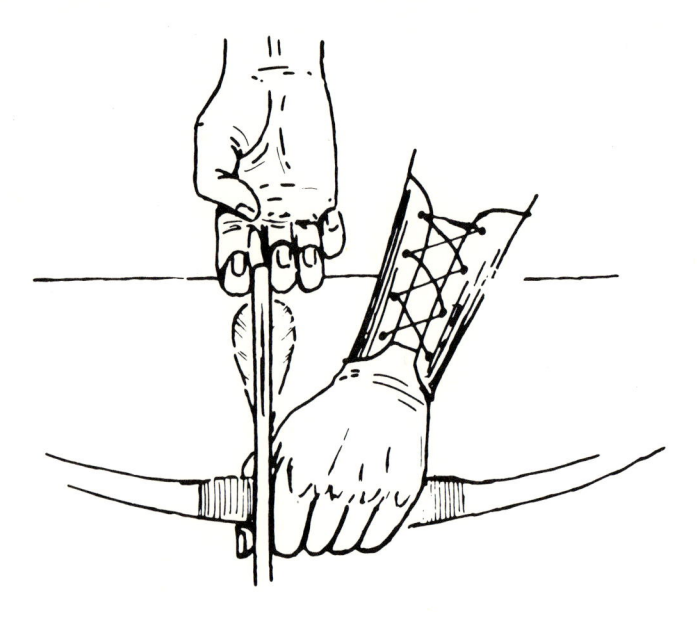

Fig. 3-8. Correct nocking position.

be spread enough to give a firm and comfortable footing. The body and head should be in a normally erect, comfortable position, with a complete absence of tension at any point. (See Fig. 3-7, *B* and *C*.)

Possible errors in stance:
1. Both feet on the same side of the line
2. Feet too close or too far apart
3. Too much weight on one foot

Position of the bow hand

As you take the bow in the left hand, allow the hand to tip up so that the pressure of the bow will come against the part of the palm which is just inside the base of the thumb. The thumb and fingers are allowed to encircle the bow only very lightly—just enough to keep it from falling. Never grip it.

Position of the string hand

Reach under the string and hook the first, second, and third fingers of the right hand onto the string, allowing the whole first joint to hook over the string. Now, as the string is drawn, let it roll down about ¼ inch toward the ends of the fingers. The rolling action will hold the arrow against the bow.

Nocking

Make sure that the cock feather is up and that the arrow is at a right angle to the string, neither too high on the bow nor so low that it slips over the handle. Hold the bow inside down while nocking and have the cock feather toward the bow. (See Fig. 3-8.)

Fig. 3-9. The draw.

THE DRAW

By a simultaneous movement of the arms, pushing with the bow arm and pulling with the string arm (see Fig. 3-9), the bow is brought to the desired position. As the draw is made, the outward pressure with the left arm and the pull with the right arm should be equalized so that both hands come to the position of full draw at about the same time. (See Fig. 3-7, *B*.)

At the full draw, the bow arm is raised to shoulder height, with the elbow slightly bent and pointed downward to a "9 o'clock" position. The string is in such a position that the upper edge of the segment of the forefinger touches just under the corner of the chin. This point is known as the anchor point (Fig. 3-10), and it is of prime importance that the finger touch exactly the same point each time an arrow is drawn and that the elbow and forearm be in line with the arrow.

Possible errors for the arms:
1. Elbow straight or hyperextended
2. Elbow bent too much
3. Left shoulder hunched
4. For the string arm:
    (a) Anchor point too far forward, too high, or below the chin
    (b) Using some part of the hand other than the end segment of the forefinger or the string as the part which touches the anchor point
    (c) Elbow too high or too low

Aiming and releasing

POINT OF AIM

Point of aim method of aiming is the most satisfactory system for the beginner, although sights may be used. With any bow and arrow there is only one distance at which a person may shoot and hit the center of the target by aiming directly at it. This will vary with the weight of the bow and with the length and weight of the arrow. (See Fig. 3-11.) In order that the arrows may be grouped on the target at distances farther or closer than this point-blank range, the archer must use some auxiliary object in the back or foreground. This auxiliary object is known as the point of aim. At the completion of the draw, the point of the arrow should appear to be somewhere near the point of aim. The left hand is then moved slowly and steadily until the point of aim appears to be resting exactly on top of the point of the arrow. (See Fig. 3-12.)

Fig. 3-10. Anchor point.

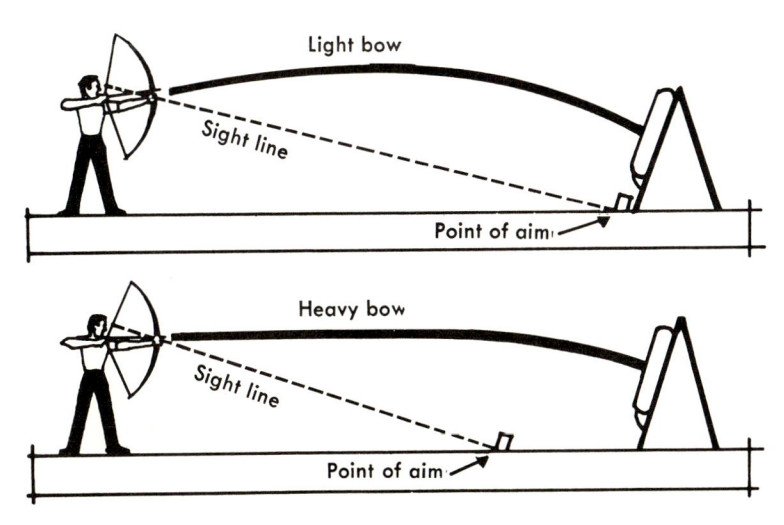

Fig. 3-11. Effect of weight of bow upon point of aim.

Fig. 3-12. Theory of the point of aim.

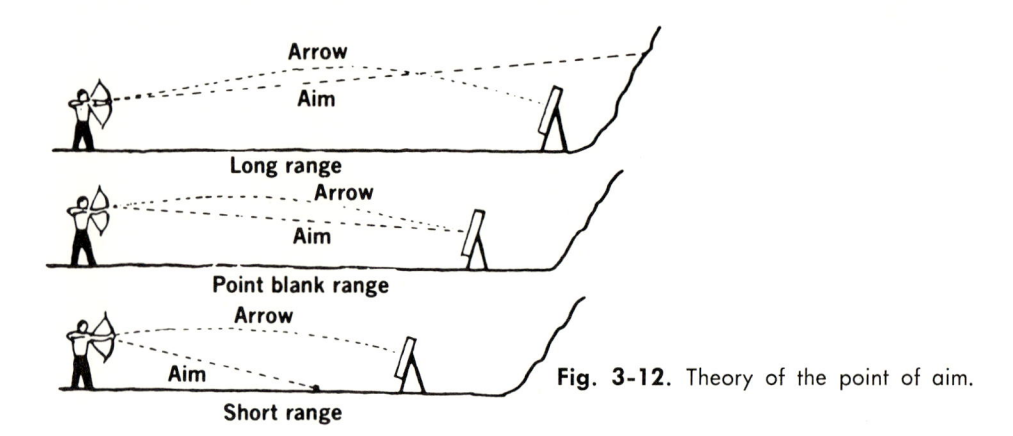

At the instant the aim is adjusted to your satisfaction, the string is released by allowing the fingers to quit holding. But only the fingers are allowed to relax. The muscles of the right shoulder and back must keep pulling, and the muscles of the left arm and shoulder must keep pushing against the bow until the arrow has been released. (See Fig. 3-7, C.)

Note the location of the group formed by the arrows that were properly shot. If they are high on the target, the point of aim must be lowered or brought toward the archer. If they are low on the target, the point of aim must be raised or moved toward the target. If the point of aim is in proper line and they group to the right or left or scatter over the target, check for faults other than the point of aim.

Possible errors in aiming and releasing:
1. Shifting position
2. Relaxing both arms and shoulders at the moment of release
3. Not actually coming to the point of aim before releasing
4. Having the point of aim to the right or left of a line directly between the archer and the center of the target
5. Aiming with the left eye
6. Sighting with both eyes
7. Choosing the "wrong arrow"

RANGE FINDER

A device used for recording the established point of aim is called a range finder. It might be a piece of wood about 6 inches long. For recording the point of aim, the finder is held at arm's length

Fig. 3-13. The range finder.

(Fig. 3-13) from the body toward the target, with the bull's-eye appearing just over the top of it. With the finder in this position, move the thumb up the stick until it is in line with the point of aim already established. At this point place a mark on the stick. In future shooting at this same distance, the point of aim can be reestablished by sighting through the mark recorded on the finder.

BOW SIGHT (FREE STYLE)

A device that is used for sighting and is attached to the back of the bow is termed a "bow sight." It has vertical and horizontal adjustments and is good for short ranges. In use, the line of vision is through the sight to the bull's-eye.

Drawing arrows from the target

The back of the left hand is placed against the target in such a way that the arrow comes between the first and second fingers. (See Fig. 3-14.) Grasp the arrow

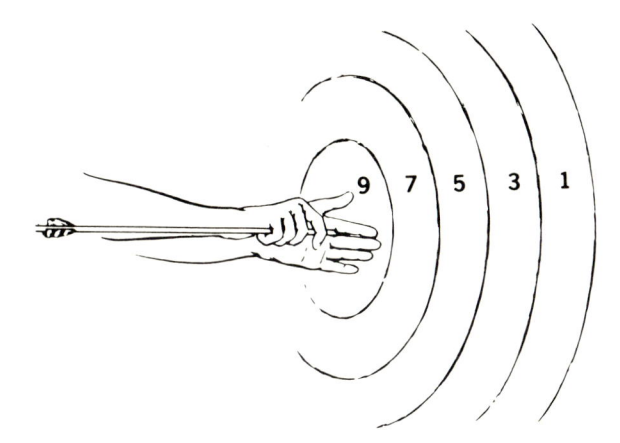

Fig. 3-14. Drawing the arrow from the target.

close to the target with the right hand and exert the same amount of pressure with the left hand required to pull the arrow from the target. Care must be taken to draw the arrow straight out so that it will not be bent or kinked. After being drawn out, the arrows should be held near the point in the left hand with the nock end toward the ground, leaving the right hand free for removing the remaining arrows. If an arrow penetrates until the feathers have entered the target, it must be drawn on through to prevent roughing or stripping off the feathers. If the arrow has penetrated one of the wooden legs or the wooden support of the target, it should be loosened with a pair of pliers before removal. The instructor should be prepared for such an emergency. At times, arrows that miss the target slither along the ground and into the surface grass roots. These must be pulled from the point end, much in the same manner as removing an arrow which has penetrated the target past the feathers. Important also in this connection is the fact that in looking for arrows that have missed the target, one must always keep the eyes on the ground as it is very easy to step on an arrow and break it.

PERFORMANCE TESTS

Probably the best rating of performance in archery is made on the basis of consistently accurate shooting, since accuracy of shots necessarily involves the correct performance of the individual skill fundamentals. In the American round, a rating of 4 is given for the accumulation of 500 points; a rating of 3 for 450 points; a rating of 2 for 400 points; and a rating of 1 for 350 points. No rating is given for a score below 350 points.

SAFETY PRECAUTIONS

Archery contains certain elements of danger if participants become negligent or careless. Proper conduct and behavior while shooting and/or taking care of equipment off range are exceedingly important. Instructors should be very definite in teaching safety rules early in the course. These rules are as follows:

1. Do not go to the target while others are shooting. All participants go at the same time to retrieve arrows.
2. If shooting is finished, step back three paces and wait.
3. Draw an arrow only when directed at the target. (The instructor should also regard this rule unless the arrow can be released without danger to anyone.)
4. Shoot at targets only from the starting line.
5. Participants must remember that bows and arrows are not toys.
6. All participants must faithfully obey the starting and stopping signals.
7. On a field range, "fast" should be shouted before the arrow is released so that persons about will receive adequate warning.
8. While shooting, be certain that there is an adequate backstop behind the

target, or, if there is no backstop, that the area is clear behind target.
9. Bows and arrows should never be left unguarded where children or careless persons might handle them.
10. One should never shoot straight up into the air under any circumstance.
11. One should never shoot with a faulty bow or arrow or permit others to do so.
12. Never take chances or be in the least careless or negligent.
13. Do not pinch the arrow between the thumb and finger to shoot. Always use three fingers for drawing the arrow. This way you cannot accidently release the arrow.

INSTRUCTIONAL AND LEARNING PROCEDURES

1. Discuss the history and values of archery.
2. Discuss the selection and care of equipment.
3. Describe the sport in general.
4. Discuss the safety precautions.
5. Explain and demonstrate the basic skills.
   (a) Stringing and unstringing the bow
   (b) Preparing for the draw
   (c) The draw
   (d) Anchoring
   (e) Aiming and releasing
   (f) Drawing arrows from the target
6. Practice for proficiency.
7. Review the method of scoring.
8. Discuss the rules and mechanics of the skills.
9. Evaluate the course.

GLOSSARY OF ARCHERY TERMS

addressing the target Assuming the proper stance; ready to shoot. Feet should straddle the shooting line.
American round For advanced coeducational groups: 30 arrows shot from 60 yards, 50 yards, and 40 yards.
anchor point A definite point on one's face to which the hand is brought on the draw.
archer's golf An archery game simulating golf; sometimes played on a golf course.
arm guard A protective cover for the lower part of the bow arm.
arrowplate A hard substance inserted on the bow where the arrow crosses it when shooting.
back The side of the bow away from the body and facing the target.
belly The inside of the bow; the side facing the string.
bow-arm The arm that is extended in preparation for release.
bow sight A device used to assist in aiming.
brace To loop the string in the nock when stringing the bow.
broadhead An arrow used for shooting live game.
butt A backscreen to stop free-flying arrows; a backstop.
cast An imperfection in a bow or arrow; the distance an arrow may be shot.
clout shooting Usually 36 arrows shot at a 48-foot target placed or marked on the ground, 120 or 140 yards for women, and 180 yards for men.
cock feather That feather of an arrow set at right angles to the nock; the odd colored feather.
Columbia round A women's round consisting of 24 arrows shot at 50, 40, and 30 yards.
crest The marks identifying the arrow.
drift The motion of the arrow due to wind or weather.
End, American The shooting of six arrows, either six in succession or in two groups of three.
End, English Three arrows shot consecutively.
eye The string loop.
field captain Usually the tournament director.
finger cot An archer's glove.
fistmele The height of the fist with the thumb raised.
fletch The placing of feathers on an arrow.
flight shooting The contest of distance shooting.
flirt An arrow breaking its line of flight.
footed arrow A weighted arrow.
grouping Shooting a group of arrows close together on the target.
head The pile tip of the arrow.
hen feathers The two similar feathers.
hit To hit the target anywhere.

home An arrow that is ready to be released; also called holding.

in game Shooting without error.

instinctive shooting Shooting without the aid of any sighting device.

jerking Jolting caused by too much recoil of the shooting hand on release.

Junior American round For boys and girls: 30 arrows shot at each of 50, 40, and 30 yards.

Junior Columbia round For boys and girls: 24 arrows shot at each of 40, 30, and 20 yards.

Junior Scholastic round For boys and girls: 24 arrows shot at each of 30 and 20 yards.

keeper A piece of binding used to keep the loose end of the string fastened to the unstrung bow.

Lady Paramount Lady directing a women's tournament.

let fly To release an arrow.

limbs Upper and lower parts of the bow.

loose The release of the bow string after the draw.

low strung Less distance than a fistmele between the string and bow.

Minature round Indoor shooting; 60 arrows shot from 15 yards on a 2-foot target.

National round For women; 48 arrows shot at 60 yards, and 24 at 50 yards.

nock The groove at the end of the arrow.

nocking point The point on the string at which the arrow is placed.

over-bowed Using a bow too severe.

perfect end To put six shots in the gold.

petticoat On the target but outside the rings; beyond the white ring.

pile The pointed metal tip of the arrow.

pinsight A device on the bow to help in aiming.

points Units of scoring.

point-blank range The single distance where the true aim is on the bull's-eye.

point of aim The auxiliary object used in hitting the center of the target when the archer is not at point-blank range.

quiver A device to hold the arrows.

range Shooting distance.

range finder A device that the archer uses to determine various distances.

Range round Indoor shooting; 60 arrows shot from a single distance, either 50, 40, 30, or 20 yards.

red The first ring of the target outside the gold center. An arrow hitting in the red counts 7 points.

reflexed bow A bow with limbs that curve out.

release To shoot the arrow.

round To shoot a definite number of arrows at specific distances.

roving Shooting a given number of arrows at targets placed at varied distances over an outside course.

Scholastic round 24 arrows shot at each of 40 and 30 yards.

self arrow An arrow made from one piece of wood.

self bow A bow made from one piece of wood, as opposed to a composite bow.

serving The thread wrapped around the bow string.

shaft The long center part of the arrow.

shaftment That part of the arrow holding the crest and feathers.

shooting tab A protective device for the fingers.

shooting line The line where one stands to shoot. The archer straddles this line.

sight An aiming device which enables the archer to aim directly on the gold.

snake An arrow lost in deep grass.

spine A characteristic of the arrow's strength and flexibility.

stringing To place the string on the bow and made ready to shoot.

tackle Archery equipment.

tassel A bunch of fabric or a piece of cloth to wipe off wet arrows.

timber "Heads up"; a call of warning that an arrow is to be released.

toxophilite One who has studied and mastered the art of shooting.

trajectory The flight of the arrow; the path that the arrow takes.

under-bowed Using a bow that is too light.

vane A feather on an arrow.

wand shoot Shooting at an upright stick.

weight The number of pounds it takes to fully draw a bow.

wide Missing the target to either side.

white The outer ring of the target. Hitting this counts 1 point.

windage The deviation of flight caused by the wind.

wobble The erratic motion of an arrow as it travels in flight.

REFERENCES

Acker, William: Japanese archery, Rutland, Vt., 1965, Charles E. Tuttle Co., Inc.

Bear, Fred: The archer's bible, Garden City, New York, 1968, Doubleday & Co., Inc.

Featherstone, Donald: The bowman of England, London, 1967, Jarrolds Publishing, Ltd.

Gillan, G. Howard: Complete book of the bow and arrow, Harrisburg, Pa., 1971, Stackpole Books.

Jaeger, Eloise: How to improve your archery, Chicago, 1966, The Athletic Institute, Inc.

National Field Archery Association: Official handbook of field archery, Palm Springs, Calif., 1966, The Association.

Niemeyer, Roy K.: Beginning archery, Wadsworth Sports Skill Series, Belmont, Calif., 1967, Wadsworth Publishing Co., Inc.

Official Sports Library for Women: Individual sports—archery, fencing, golf, and riding, National Section on Women's Athletics, Washington, D. C., 1972-1974, American Association for Health, Physical Education, and Recreation.

FILMS

Archery for beginners, 16 mm., 12 min., United World Films, Inc., New York, N. Y.

Archery fundamentals, 16 mm., 11 min., Bailey Films, Inc., Hollywood, Calif.

Archery with Larry Hughes, Bailey Film Service, Hollywood, Calif.

Beginning archery (film strips), The Athletic Institute, Inc., Chicago, Ill.

Bows and arrows, Bailey Film Service, Hollywood, Calif.

Follow the arrow, Teaching Film Custodians, Inc., New York, N. Y.

The world of archery, 16 mm., 30 min., John Lanigan, c/o American Archery Council, Chicago, Ill.

4 Badminton

BRIEF HISTORY

The modern version of badminton is a modification of a game called poona named after a town in India where it was originally played. Poona is believed to be a derivation of the game of battledore, which originated in China. British Army officers are generally credited with bringing the game to England around 1870. The game met with little, if any, enthusiasm until the Duke of Beaufort promoted it at his home, Badminton at Gloucestershire, whence it received its present name. In 1887, the Bath Badminton Club was formed and the rules standardized and arranged for tournament play. The rules were later augmented by the Badminton Association of England, established in 1895 to form the present rules. The game spread from England, where it had its chief development, to Canada, where it is now recognized as the outstanding indoor sport.

The first United States championship tournament was held in Chicago in 1937. Walter Kramer of Detroit and Mrs. Del Barkuff of Seattle were the first American champions.

CARRY-OVER VALUES

Badminton has become increasingly popular throughout the United States since World War II. This growing interest is largely due to the fact that colleges and schools have taught the game in their basic skills program of physical education. There are many more specific reasons for its popularity. It is a game that many people play at home on the grassy lawn. Although the game resembles tennis, it does not require as large a court; neither does it require a hard-surface court, since the shuttlecock must be played before it hits the ground. All that is needed are a net, two posts to support it, and boundary lines. (See court dimensions and layout, Fig. 4-1.) Naturally, it is also an indoor game.

Beginners learn easily and from the start derive pleasure and satisfaction from this game. There is no chasing the ball as in tennis, and action play is more rapid. Action creates interest in any activity, and badminton, because it is a fast game, gives just that. It affords a good workout right at home.

The game demands quick thinking, eye-hand coordination, skill, and mastery of the direction of the shuttle.

Badminton equipment is relatively inexpensive, and for this reason badminton is very popular as a school activity. Plastic shuttlecocks are gaining increasing popularity because of their durability and low cost. Their flight and performance are quite similar to that of the official feathered shuttlecocks.

Because it can be easily mastered, badminton lends itself readily to family recreation and co-ed competition, allowing equal pleasure to children and adults. The game can be played either singles or doubles. The simplicity of the equipment makes badminton an ideal sport for outings.

EQUIPMENT

There are but three items of equipment essential to play the game of badminton: a racket, a shuttlecock, and a net and supports.

The racket

The racket should be selected wisely; it should not be too cheap, but somewhere in the medium-priced range. It should be "whippy." The better grades of badminton racket frames are composed of a wooden head with a wooden or steel shaft. The handle is covered with leather. All-aluminum and fiber glass frames, because of their low cost, light weight, and durability, are finding increased acceptance. Steel rackets, strung with steel strings, are very long-lasting and inexpensive. However, they do not give the "feel" of a hit as well as do wooden rackets.

Badminton rackets may be strung with nylon, gut, or steel string. Gut strings are generally considered best but are expensive. Nylon strings give good service and are relatively inexpensive.

A badminton racket is similar to a tennis racket. The racket head is a pure ellipse. The length is about 10¼ inches and the width is 7⅜ inches. It is much lighter than a tennis racket. Its weight may be 3$7/10$ to 5½ ounces. The length is 26¼ inches, and the handle is octagonal with a circumference of 3¾ inches. A wooden racket should be kept in a press when not in use and be stored in a dry place away from dampness and excessive heat.

The shuttles

The shuttlecock, also called a bird, is made from hard cork with feathers attached.

There are two kinds of birds: outdoor and indoor. The outdoor bird is usually of heavier structure and has a red rubber base to allow for wind resistance and easy identification. The indoor bird is lighter in weight and is a sphere of cork covered with white kid, with feathers bound with silk thread and cemented securely to the cork.

The shuttles have from 14 to 16 feathers fixed in a cork 1 to 1⅛ inches in diameter. The feathers are from 2½ to 2¾ inches in length, have from 2⅛ to 2½ inches in spread at the top, and are firmly fastened to the base with thread or other suitable material.

Plastic shuttlecocks are ideal for use in physical education classes and in intramural sports competition. Plastic birds may be obtained in various weight sizes, the lighter weight bird being used for play indoors.

Care should be exercised in handling the feathered birds. They should be removed from the container base first and be replaced the same way. After each rally take time to straighten out the feathers. The bird should always be put in play with an underhand stroke; otherwise, the racket will hit the feathers and damage them. Pick up the bird from the floor with the fingers, not with the racket; also, avoid striking it along the floor with the racket to the opponents. A good bird is expensive.

A shuttlecock is considered of correct pace if, when a player of average strength strikes it with a full underhand stroke with a reasonably tightly strung racket from a spot immediately above one back boundary line in a line parallel to the sidelines, and at upward angle, it falls not less than 1 foot and not more than 2 feet, 6 inches short of the back boundary line.

The net and standards

The net is made of fine, tan-colored cord of ⅝- to ¾-inch square mesh and may be 17 to 24 feet in length, according to the position of the posts, and 2 feet, 6 inches in depth. The top of the net is 5 feet in height at the center, 5 feet, 1 inch at the posts, and edged with a 3-inch white tape doubled and supported by a cord run

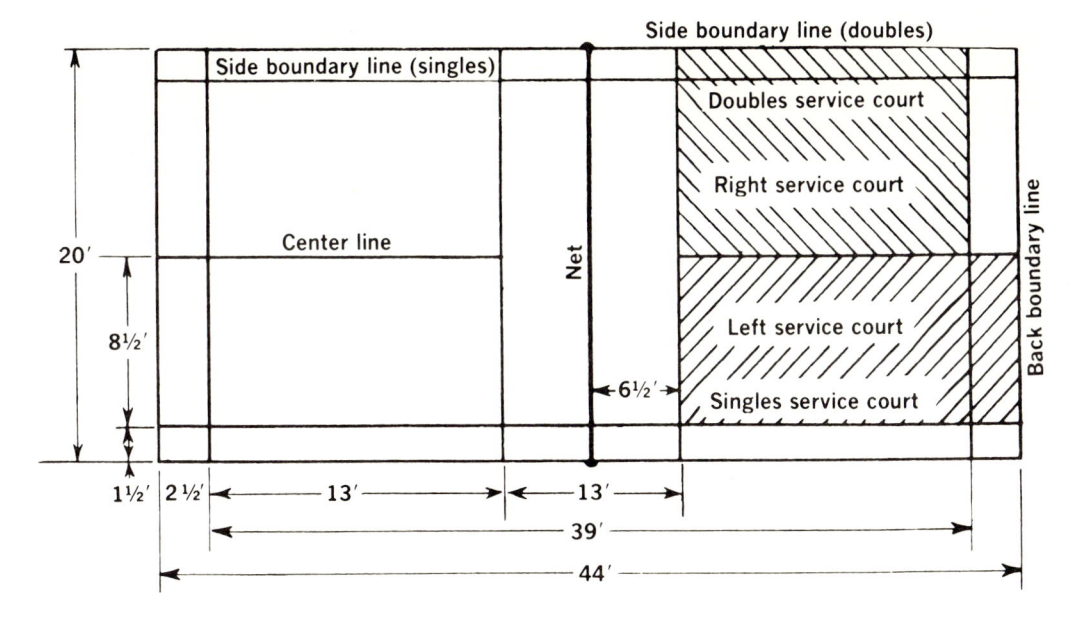

Fig. 4-1. Badminton—double and single courts.

through the tape and strained over, and flush with, the top of the posts.

The posts are 5 feet, 1 inch in height and sufficiently firm to keep the net taut as just described. If possible, the posts should be placed on the side boundary lines of the court; if not possible, a thin post or strip of material not less than 1½ inches in width should be fixed to the side boundary line and rise vertically to the net cord.

HOW TO LAY OUT A COURT

If more than one court is laid out side by side, allow as a minimum at least 3 feet between courts. In laying out a home court in the backyard, use either tape or dry lime for the boundary lines. For the gymnasium, the boundary lines are defined by white or black lines 1½ inches wide. If you are laying out a badminton court at home, it is easier to combine the singles and doubles court into one area. The badminton doubles court is the same length (44 feet) as the singles court but is 3 feet wider.

The court should have a high ceiling. The ideal height is 40 feet at center. A minimum of 15 feet can be used. A room at least 30 × 60 feet is a good size. (See Fig. 4-1.)

ABRIDGED RULES

The object of the game is to hit the shuttlecock back and forth across the net with the racket without permitting it to touch the ground, endeavoring to hit it into the opposing court so that it cannot be returned.

Faults

A fault made by the serving side puts the server out; if it is made by the "out" side (the side receiving the serve), it scores a point for the serving side.

Faults are made under the following conditions:

1. If the serve is made other than underhanded (At the instant it is struck, the bird must be below the server's waist and the head of the racket must be pointing downward to such an extent that the entire head is below the server's hand.)
2. If the server serves the shuttle so that it falls into the wrong court
3. If either the server or the player receiving the service is not standing with the feet in the proper court for the service
4. If the shuttle falls outside the boundary line, fails to pass the net, or goes through the net
5. If before or during the serve any player makes a preliminary feint
6. If a player reaches over the net with the racket and hits the shuttle (The

racket may follow the shuttle over, however.)
7. If a player reaches over the net with the racket or person and touches the net
8. If the shuttle is held on the racket momentarily (carry) or if it is hit twice in succession by players on the same side

It is not a fault if the shuttle is hit by the frame, shaft, or handle of the racket or if the base and the feathers of the shuttle are struck simultaneously.

Let

The word "let" means that the play counts for nothing and is played over. Lets are called under the following conditions:
1. If an unforeseen or accidental hinderance occurs
2. If the server serves from the wrong side of the court or out of turn and scores an ace, provided the let is claimed or allowed before the next serve
3. If a player standing in the wrong half-court takes a service and wins the rally, provided the let is claimed or allowed before the next service
4. If in service or during a rally a shuttle, after passing over the net, is caught in or on the net

It is *not* a let if, on the serve or during a rally, the shuttle touches and passes over the net and lands within the proper boundaries.

Scoring

Points are scored only by the serving side. A point is scored by the serving side whenever the "out" commits a fault. When the fault is committed by the serving side, the server is out.

A service is illegal if the player's serving wrist is above the elbow at the instant of the serve.

Serving

Only an underhand swing of the racket is permitted in serving. The service is considered overhand and illegal if the shuttle, at the instant of being struck, is higher than the server's waist.

The server starting the play stands in the right-hand half of the court and serves to the opposite right-hand half-court. If the server wins the point, the next serve is made from the left-hand half of the court and into the opposite left-hand half-court. Thus the service is always from the right-hand half-court when the server's score is zero or an even number, and in the left half when the score is an odd number. The server continues until an out is scored against him or her. In doubles, the initial serve of one side always starts on the right-hand half of the court regardless of the score.

The badminton court is marked into single and double serving areas. The doubles court service area is reduced in length to compensate for its additional width when compared to the singles court service area.

BASIC SKILLS AND FUNDAMENTAL TECHNIQUES

Grip of the racket

1. Forehand stroke—the handle of the racket is held as if the player were shaking hands with the racket. (See Fig. 4-2.)
2. Backhand grip—similar to the forehand grip except the hand is rotated slightly to the left and the thumb is placed flat against the side bevel for additional power. (See Fig. 4-3.) The changing of grips during play comes somewhat automatically with practice.
3. The racket should be held at the extreme end of the handle with fingers well spread.
4. The standard grip may be secured by placing the racket as you normally would, in front of the body, with the playing surface perpendicular to the floor and then grasping the racket as you would grip the handle of a hatchet.
5. The standrad grip is used for both forehand and backhand strokes. (See Fig. 4-3.)
6. The hand, wrist, and arm should be entirely relaxed, but as soon as the racket hits the shuttle, the fingers tighten automatically on the handle due to the contact.

BADMINTON 49

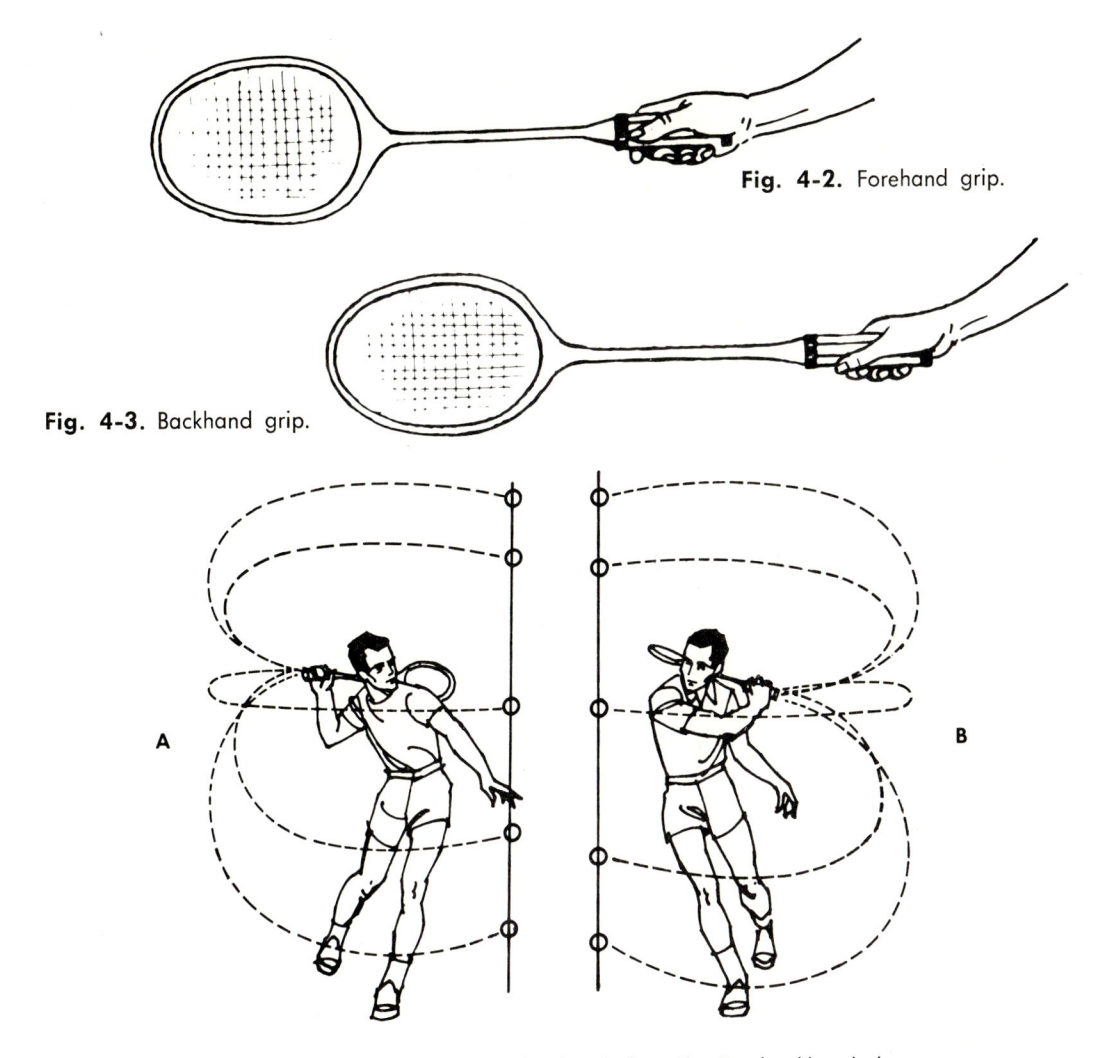

Fig. 4-2. Forehand grip.

Fig. 4-3. Backhand grip.

Fig. 4-4. Footwork. **A,** For forehand shot. **B,** For backhand shot.

Wrist flip

1. A supply wrist and arm should be entirely relaxed but vital.
2. Wrist action is used to disguise intentions. A simple flick of your wrist aids not only in getting direction but also in sending your opponent in the wrong direction, since the flight is concealed until the last fraction of a second.
3. In starting all shots, keep the wrist well back. Do not check the forward swing of the racket; follow through.

Footwork and position

1. Correct footwork is necessary.
2. Never stand flat-footed; be on the balls of your feet all of the time, and have your body weight moving forward with the shot.
3. In receiving any shot, use the ready position; the left foot should be forward and pointing in the direction of the oncoming flight.
4. Agility and body balance are paramount.
5. The cardinal rule in covering the court is to get set first, then hit.
6. When the player changes positions on the court, the knees should be slightly bent and the center of body weight should rest on the forepart of the foot.
7. For forehand shots, the left foot should usually be placed somewhat in front of the other. (See Fig. 4-4, *A*.)
8. On the backhand the right foot must

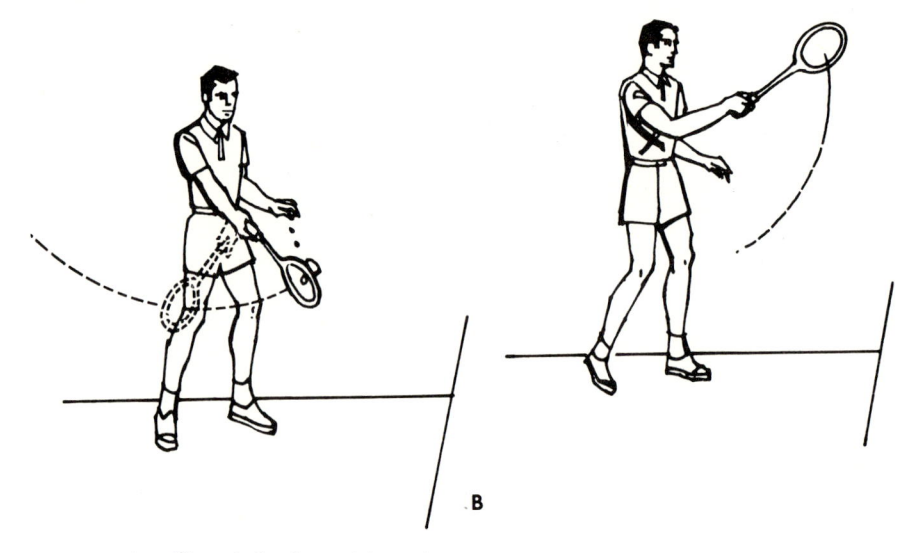

Fig. 4-5. A, Holding the bird for serving. **B,** Service.

be in front of and rather across the left foot to allow free play for arm and racket on the backswing of the stroke. (See Fig. 4-4, *B*.)

STROKES
Service

1. Services are of two kinds: high (clear) and low (drop) serves. High serves generally are used in singles; low serves are generally best in double play. (See Fig. 4-9.)
2. Before you serve, take the ready position.
3. Use "out of the hand" serve, holding the tip of one feather with the tip of the index finger and thumb. (See Fig. 4-5, *A*).
4. The shuttle is dropped in front and away from the body. (See Fig. 4-5, *B*.)
5. After service, the boxer's shift-step is used to get position for service return.
6. Do not use drive serve very often; it gives your intentions away.
7. Both feet must remain in contact with the floor until the service is delivered.
8. The receiver may move across the boundary lines as soon as the bird is hit by the server. (See Fig. 4-6.)

Smash shot

1. The body is held erect, and greater emphasis is placed upon wrist snap.
2. Smash the shuttle well in front of the body while the shuttle is high overhead. (See Fig. 4-7.)
3. Do not smash when off-balance, out of position, or from deep in the rear of the court.
4. The shuttle must be hit at the highest stretch of the arm and racket, not with the elbow bent.
5. Do not hurry a smash stroke.
6. In the backhand smash, the racket is held well in back of the body to get full swing. The side of the body or

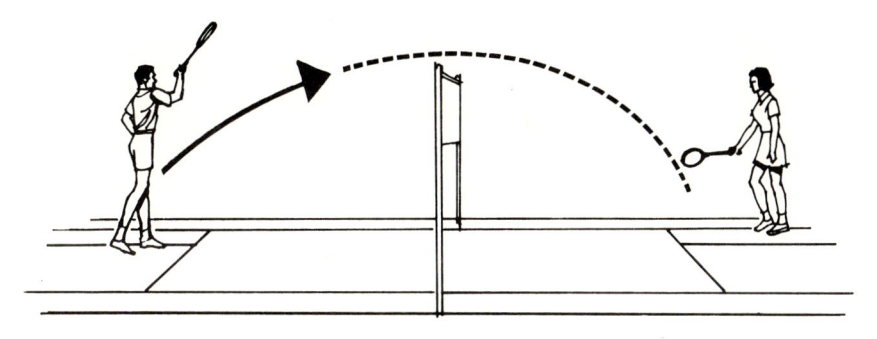

Fig. 4-6. Receiver's position.

Fig. 4-7. Position for smash.

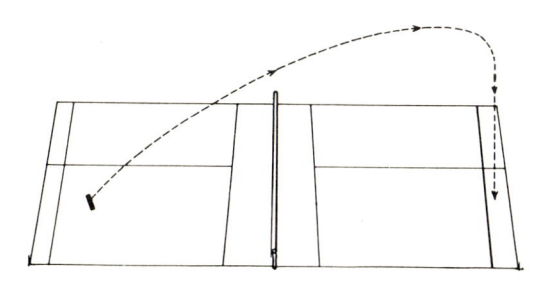

Fig. 4-8. Line of flight of a clear shot.

even the back can be facing the net at the time the bird is hit. This applies only to a backhand smash.

Clear shot (see Figs. 4-8 and 4-9)

1. Primarily defensive strokes, clears should be high and deep.
2. Attempt clear shots when off-balance or out of position.
3. The farther away from the net one stands, the more difficult it is to make an accurate shot of any kind.
4. A clear shot may be hit easily in order that it drop just over the net (as does a drop shot) to take advantage of an opponent who is in the backcourt. This is done by eliminating the wrist action.
5. The racket is held high on forehand clears, left foot in front or across to the the right side.
6. In backhand clears, the racket is held well back of the body so that vigorous swings can be made. Simultaneously with shuttle contact, the weight of the body is transferred to the right foot.

Drive shot (see Fig. 4-9)

1. A flat shot is kept as low as possible.
2. This shot can be sent to any spot desired in the other court without loss of time. Arm and racket are nearly straight at the time of shuttle contact.
3. Firmness and accuracy are needed for the successful production of the stroke.
4. Unlike other forehand strokes, the forehand sideline drive can be best executed off the right foot.

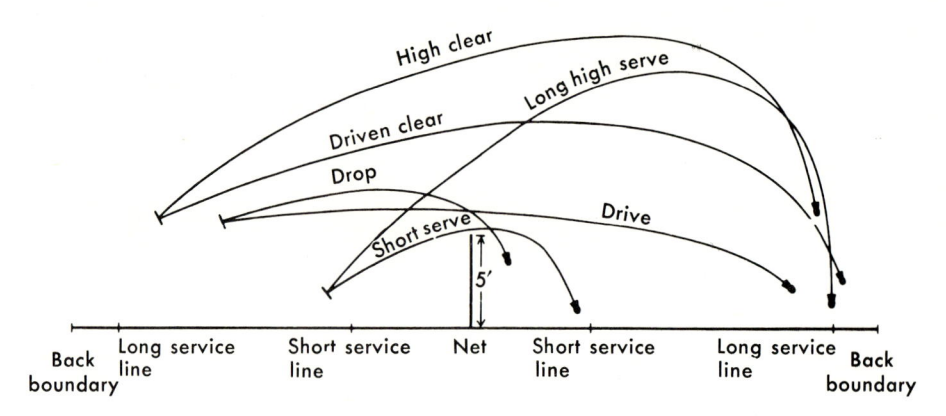

Fig. 4-9. Flight variations.

Drop shot (see Fig. 4-9)

1. In all drops perfect control, as well as sure touch and good wrist action, is necessary to disguise direction.
2. The purpose behind a drop shot is to put your opponent on the defensive, since it forces the opponent to hit the shuttle upward in order to avoid hitting the net.
3. The shuttle must begin to fall immediately after it has crossed the net.
4. On backhand drops, the arm should be perfectly straight and the head high. Stop the racket suddenly, blocking or checking the shuttle. A slow, easy follow-through should complete the shot.

Net shot (see Fig. 4-9)

A cross-court drop shot is particularly effective against most opponents.

Round-the-head shot

The shuttle is struck over the left shoulder by circling the racket over the head. The elbow flexes as the arm circles the head.

POINTS TO REMEMBER
Singles

1. Serve long unless opponent is playing back for just such a serve; in this case, serve short to take advantage of the opponent's poor position.
2. Return a high serve with a drop or clear.
3. The safest return for a low serve is a clear, or if it can be reached before falling too far below the net, use a net shot.
4. Use cross-court smashes or smash at opponent's right hip or shoulder.
5. Return a smash with a drop to the point on the court farthest from the point at which the smash was made.
6. Drive down the sidelines.
7. Play your position; do not try to outguess your opponent.
8. Take advantage of your opponent's weaknesses, but not to the extent that such repeated effort improves the weakness.

Doubles

1. Formations of play
   (a) Side-by-side—Each person is responsible for half the court which runs from front to back. Disadvantages are that it is hard to run from the net to the backcourt and make a good smash or a good attacking stroke, and returns to the center cause confusion as to who will hit them.
   (b) Front and back—One person plays the front court and one the back with the front player taking all net shots and any other shot that could be returned with a better shot than the partner. A disadvantage is the resulting poor defense against smashes and drives down the sidelines.
   (c) Combination formation—This formation combines the best

features of the two previous ones. Here the partners rotate slowly in a counterclockwise circle so that the backcourt player need never return for a backhand shot in the near court.
2. Play shots that will give an opening for your partner on their return. Do not leave your partner open to a heated attack from the opponents.
3. Make most serves low and short, preferably to the corner formed by the center line and short service line.
4. Smash long serves, but occasionally use a drop shot.
5. Rush short serves.
6. Do not play too close to the net. A position around the short service line is best for playing the net.
7. If servers are playing front and back type of play, the best return of a low serve is a half-court shot down the sidelines.
8. Make placements to the least obvious spots.

FOUR-HANDED OR DOUBLE GAME OF BADMINTON

The game is played by two players on a side.

The side winning the toss shall have the choice of serving first or ends. The side winning a game shall always serve first in the next game, but in doubles either of the winners may continue serving and either of the losers may receive the service.

Scoring

The four-handed game consists of 15 or 21 points, as may be arranged by the participants, provided that in a game of 15 points, when the score is 13-all, the side which first reaches 13 has the option of "setting" the game to 5; when the score is 14-all, the side which first reaches 14 has the option of "setting" the game to 3. After a game has been "set" the score is called "love all," and the side which first scores 5 or 3 points, according to whether the game has been "set" at 13- or 14-all, wins the game. In either case the claim to "set" the game must be made before the next service is delivered after the score has reached 13-all or 14-all. In a game of 21 points the same method of scoring may be adopted, substituting 19 and 20 for 13 and 14. (*Note:* "Setting" is not permitted in handicap games.)

A rubber is the best of three games. The players change ends at the beginning of the second game, and also of the third game if a third game is necessary to decide the rubber. In the third game the players also change ends when the leading score reaches 8 in a game of 15 points, 6 in a game of 11 points, or 11 in a game of 21 points, or in handicap games, when either side has scored half the total number of points required to win the game (the next highest number being taken in case of fractions). In matches decided by a single game, the players change ends as provided above for the third game of a rubber.

TWO-HANDED OR SINGLE GAME OF BADMINTON

In games with one player on each side, the rules given for the four-handed or double game hold good, with the following exceptions:
1. The players serve from and receive service in the right-hand half-courts only when the server's score is 0 or when an even number of points has been scored in the game; the service is delivered from and received in the left-hand half-courts when the server has scored an odd number of points.
2. Both players change half-courts after each point has been scored, and consecutive services are received by the same players.
3. In ladies' single matches, the game consists of 11 points, provided that when the score is 9-all, the player who first reaches 9 has the option of "setting" the game to 3 and when the score is 10-all, the player who first reaches 10 may "set" the game to 2.

THE PLAY

It having been decided which side is to have the first service the player in the right-hand half-court at that side begins the game by serving to the player in the opposite right-hand half-court. If the latter player returns the shuttle before it touches the ground, it is to be returned by one of the "in" side and then returned by one of the "out" side, and so on, until a fault is made or the shuttle ceases to be "in play." If a fault is made by the "in" side, the server's hand is out, and since the side beginning a game has only one hand in its first inning, the player in the right-hand court opposite now becomes the server. However, if the service is not returned, or the fault is made by the "out" side, the "in" side scores a point. The "in" side players then change from one half-court to the other, the server now being in the left-hand court and serving to the player in the opposite left-hand court. As long as a side remains "in," service is delivered alternately from each half-court into the one diagonally opposite, the change being made by the "in" side when, and only when, a point is added to its score. Official contests for men are 15 points only. The first service of a side in each inning is made from the right-hand half-court. After the service is delivered, the server and the receiver may take up any positions they choose on their side of the net, irrespective of any boundary lines.

COURTESY OF BADMINTON

Badminton, like tennis, is a gentleman's game. Sportsmanship is foremost in courtesy. One is gracious in playing manners, never "needling" an opponent. If in doubt about a boundary decision, call it in favor of the opponent. The opponent, if a good sport, will disagree. If fouling occurs at the net, one should call it on one's self.

Hand a bird over to an adjoining court player at the end of a rally. Thank a player when your bird is returned.

Be quick to call a foul.

Do not play indifferently against an inferior opponent.

WARMING UP

The older one gets, the more one should warm up before playing. After 40 years of age a person should do considerable free-hand exercises, such as bending, squatting, or free-arm swinging as a safety factor to condition the reflexes and prevent sprains or muscle tears. The play of badminton requires sudden quick movements, which are often a strain on the musculature if one is not properly conditioned.

INSTRUCTIONAL AND LEARNING PROCEDURES

1. To teach the fundamental skills
    (a) Laying out a court, putting up and taking down a net and standards; care of equipment, birds, and rackets
    (b) Proper method in holding or gripping the racket
    (c) Manner of serving, either short or long
    (d) Different types of shots
        (1) Forehand—high, low, and medium
        (2) Backhand—high, low, and medium
        (3) Overhead
        (4) Lift—net tip shot
    (e) Different types of birds in flight
        (1) Smash—a fast straight downward flight, just over the net (kill shot)
        (2) High clear—a long, high flight, with the bird falling in the backcourt
        (3) Drive—a low fast flight with the bird barely clearing the net
        (4) Drop—a rapidly falling flight, just over the net
        (5) Net—low flights, close to and barely clearing the net
    (f) Strategy of the game
2. To teach the rules
    (a) Singles game and scoring
    (b) Doubles game and scoring
3. To be able to play a presentable game of badminton in a class tournament, both singles and doubles
4. Achievement test
    (a) To be able to set up and take down the nets and standards, and to be able to properly care for the equipment
    (b) To be able to demonstrate the

various shots as outlined in 1 (d)
  (c) To be able to demonstrate the various types of birds in flight, as in 1 (e) with grade based upon coordination, ease of swing, path of racket, and accuracy of shot
  (d) To know the rules of the game, both singles and doubles
  (e) To play a presentable game of badminton
  (f) Demonstrate serve:
    (1) Drop—score on five trials
    (2) Clear—score on five trials
  (g) Demonstrate kill or smash: Score on five trials
  (h) Volleying: Average score on two volleys—each volley to be a maximum of five strokes
  (i) Demonstrate in play, tactics of the game:
    (1) When opponent is up close to net right side, left side
    (2) When opponent is in rear of court right side, left side
    (3) When a kill is made by the opponent
    (4) When a drop shot is made
    (5) When serving—singles, doubles
    (6) Meaning of defensive and offensive play

GLOSSARY OF BADMINTON TERMS

ace A point scored by a hard drive into the opponent's court.
alley The area on the sides of the court between the doubles and singles court; the alleys are 1½ feet wide.
back alley The shuttle may not be served into this area. It is 2½ feet wide.
backhand To hit the bird on the left side of the body, if a player is right-handed.
balk To attempt to throw a player off by feinting. The penalty is loss of service or point.
bird The badminton "ball"; the shuttlecock.
carry This is a fault. To hit the bird on the feathers.
clear A lob that falls far back in the court.
cross-court To hit the bird diagonally over the net from one side of the court to the other side.
drive A hard-hit bird just over the net.
driven clear A shot driven high to the backcourt but not high enough to kill.
drop A shot which barely clears the net and then falls into the opponent's front court.
face The hitting surface of the racket.
fault Any violation of the rules.
flight The path of the bird.
forecourt The front of the court.
forehand To hit the bird on the right side of the body, if a player is right-handed.
frame The part of the racket that holds the strings.
hand-out To lose one's serve.
high clear A bird that is hit very high and lands in the back of the opponent's court.
kill A hard hit bird that is impossible to return.
long serve Any serve hit into the back alleys.
match Two out of three games.
miss Failure of the racket to come in contact with the bird; it is not a fault either on the serve or during play.
net flight The bird follows the net when hit.
out-of-hand A bird that is hit just as it leaves the hand.
on-guard stance Ready for the serve or return.
racket The instrument, usually weighing about 5 ounces, used to hit the bird.
rally To hit the bird back and forth.
receiver The player to receive the serve.
round-the-head stroke To circle the racket clockwise around the head and hit it with the overhand motion.
serve To put the bird in play.
server The one who starts the rally.
sling To lift the bird; this is a fault.
setting To decide on the score of the game if it becomes a tie.
short serve Hitting the bird over the net but not into the opponent's court.
shuttlecock The bird.
smash A high shot returned sharply.
throw A carried bird; this is a fault.
toss serve The bird is tossed or dropped out in front of the server.
volley To hit the bird while it is in the air.
wood shot Hitting the bird with the wood of the racket rather than the strings.

REFERENCES

American Badminton Association Rulebook, Lester Hilton, 15 Tanglewood Drive, Cumberland, R. I. 02864.

Davidson, Kenneth R., and Gustavson, Lealand R.: Winning badminton, New York, 1964, A. S. Barnes & Co.

Donnelly, R., Helms, W., and Mitchell, E.: Active games and contests, New York, 1958, A. S. Barnes & Co.

Friedrich, John, and Rutledge, Abbie: Beginning badminton, Belmont, Calif., 1962, Wadsworth Publishing Co., Inc.

Grant, Doug: Badminton, the international textbook of the game, Montreal, 1950, Montreal Graphic Publishing Co.

Official tennis and badminton rules and guide, Washington, D. C., 1972-1974, AAHPER, Division for Girls' and Women's Sports.

Pelton, Barry C.: Badminton, Englewood Cliffs, N. J., 1971, Prentice-Hall.

United States Army Sports Manual, F. M., 21, p. 20.

Vannier, Maryhelen, and Poindexter, Hatty Beth: Individual and team sports for girls and women, Philadelphia, 1968, W. B. Saunders Co.

FILMS

Badminton fundamentals, 16 mm., All American Productions and Publishers, Greeley, Colo.

Let's play badminton, General Sportcraft Limited, New York, N. Y.

Tips on better badminton, Sport Tips and Teaching Aids, Detroit, Mich.

5 Basketball

HISTORY

Basketball was first introduced in 1891 by Dr. James A. Naismith, who at that time was physical education director at the Y.M.C.A. College in Springfield, Massachusetts. The first official game was not played until 1892. Basketball was principally designed as a game to create interest in the gymnasium during the winter months.

The first ball used was a volleyball, and a peach basket was used as the hoop. After each score the ball had to be taken out of the basket before play was resumed.

The game spread rapidly to the nation's playgrounds, community centers, and gymnasiums, until today nearly every boy and girl learns to play basketball.

In 1899 the women formulated their own rules, and in 1901 the first women's *Basketball Guide* was published.

Television has made basketball a great spectator sport.

EQUIPMENT

The playing court is a rectangular surface free from obstructions, having maximum dimensions of 94 × 50 feet and minimum dimensions of 74 × 42 feet. (See Figs. 5-1 and 5-2.) However, many courts are smaller than the dimensions given. For women, the dimensions are the same as for men.

The backboard, with dimensions 6 feet horizontally and 4 feet vertically, is located at the center of each end of the court, 2 feet in from the end line, and 9 feet above the floor. It can be made of hard wood, metal, or glass. Padding is required on the bottom edge of all backboards.

The basket is an open hammock net, suspended from the backboard on a metal ring 18 inches in diameter which must be 6 inches from the rigid surface to which it is fastened, and 10 feet above the floor.

The ball is round, measuring 30 inches in circumference, not less than 29½ inches, and for high schools, not more than 29 inches. It is made of a rubber bladder covered with a leather case, inflated to approximately 13 pounds of air pressure.

Foot comfort and protection should be a primary concern of both coach and player. Basketball sneakers, high with a strong ankle and arch support, should be used. Shoes should fit well. White-soled sneakers will protect the floor from marking.

Head decorations or headwear other than a 2-inch, unadorned headband of specified material are illegal.

BASKETBALL COURT DIAGRAM

Fig. 5-1. Basketball court for men and women.

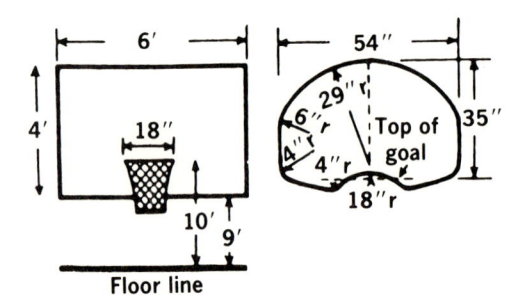

Fig. 5-2. Basketball goal.

GENERAL RULES FOR MEN AND WOMEN

Definite rules govern the entire game and are revised each year by the joint Basketball Rules Committee, representing the A.A.U., D.G.W.S., N.C.A.A., Y.M.C.A., National Federation of State High School Athletic Associations, Canadian Amateur Basketball Association, and chartered Boards of Officials.

1. Common violations of both men's and women's rules include:
   (a) Taking more than one step with the ball without passing, shooting, or dribbling
   (b) Kicking the ball with foot or lower leg
   (c) Stepping out-of-bounds with the ball
   (d) The center's leaving the circle before the ball is tipped in beginning play
   (e) Striking the ball with the fist
   (f) Illegal throwing
   (g) Failure to observe free throw regulations and the three second lane violation
2. Team fouls include:
   (a) Taking time out too often
   (b) Coaching from sidelines by coach or team followers except during a time-out period or intermission
   (c) Failure of substitutes to report to proper officials
3. Individual fouls include:
   (a) Pushing
   (b) Tripping

 (c) Unnecessary roughness
 (d) Holding
 (e) Charging
 (f) Blocking

When a violation is made, the ball is given to the opponents out-of-bounds. When a foul is made, the opponents are given a free throw. A player, fouled in the act of shooting, gets two free throws. If the basket is made, one free throw is awarded and the basket is counted. Only individual fouls disqualify a player. A player cannot have over four personal fouls; a fifth sends the player to the sidelines for the remainder of the game.

Officials

The officials are a referee, an umpire, two timekeepers, and two scorers. One timekeeper and one scorer are assistants.

Scoring

Two points are awarded for each basket from the floor and 1 point for each free throw.

MEN'S GAME
Length of game

The length of the men's game varies in accordance with the age and stamina of the players. College men play for two periods of 20 minutes each, with a 15-minute rest at half time. If the score is tied at the end of the 40 minutes, as many 5-minute periods as needed are played to break the tie.

High school teams play four quarters of 8 minutes each, with a 10-minute half-time rest and 1 minute between quarters. If the score is tied at the end of the fourth quarter, an extra period of 3 minutes is played. Should this fail to break the tie, as many such periods as are necessary to break the tie are played.

Team

There are two forwards, one center, and two guards. Forwards are near the opponent's basket, the center takes his position in the center of the court, and the guards defend their own basket.

Starting the game

The captains toss for the ball and court. A jump ball in the center circle starts the game at each half for college games and at the quarters for high school games.

After each goal, the ball is put into play by the team not scoring from the out-of-bounds area behind the basket at which the score was made.

A jump ball is used if two opposing players have possession of the ball at the same time, or if the officials are uncertain as to which side touched the ball last before it went out-of-bounds. The two opposing players jump where the ball was tied up or where the ball went out-of-bounds.

After a free throw that is not followed by another free throw, the game is started again by the opposing team's putting the ball into play from out-of-bounds behind the opponent's basket if the try is for a personal foul, or by any player of the free thrower's team from out-of-bounds at midcourt if the free throw is for a technical foul.

WOMEN'S GAME
Length of game

The women's official game is for four quarters of 8 minutes each. There is a 2-minute rest between quarters and a 10-minute rest between halves. If the score is tied at the end of the game, an extra period of 3 minutes is played. The game is over when a team is ahead at the end of the extra period. However, if they fail to break the tie, the game continues with periods of 3 minutes until one team leads at the end of an extra period.

Team

Basketball for girls and women is a game played by two teams of five players each. Half of the court is the front court of one team and the back court of the other team. Any three players of a team may be in their front or back court at one time. The ball is passed, thrown, batted, bounced, handed, or rolled from one player to another. The purpose of each team is to get a basket and to prevent the other team from scoring.

There are two forwards, two guards, and one center. The forwards are near the opponent's basket on one half of the court. The guards defend their own basket in their half of the court.

Starting the game

Women allow the visiting team their choice of court. If a neutral court is used, the captains toss a coin or match fingers to determine which team will receive the ball first and which basket each team will play for the first half. The referee puts the ball in play by a jump ball between any two opposing players in the center circle at the beginning of each quarter.

The teams change sides of the court at half time.

After a field goal has been made, the ball is put in play by an opponent out-of-bounds at any point behind the end line.

A jump ball, resulting from a double foul, violation, tie ball, or other situation covered by the official rules, is taken by two opposing players who stand in the restraining circle designated. The ball is tossed between them.

After a free throw, if the goal is scored, the ball is put in play by the opponent from behind the end line. If the free throw is not scored and the ball touches a player, it is in play. If the ball does not touch a player, it is put into play from the sidelines by the opponent's team.

Experimental rules accepted as official 1970-1971

INCEPTION

At the annual meeting of the Joint DGWS-AAU Basketball Rules Committee, held in February 1969, a motion was passed to experiment with a five-player basketball team. The decision was made because of the women's world basketball situation, and the United States basketball players' wish to realign their rules with the rules of other countries.

The Experimental Rules Differential are as follows. All other rules for 1969-1970 apply.
1. There are to be five players on each team instead of six.
2. The 30-second clock shall be used.
3. Two timers, two scorers, and a 30-second clock operator shall assist the officials.
4. Numbers must be worn by players on front and back.
5. Time out shall be taken for all violations.
6. Free throws are not taken following a double foul.
7. For a held ball (5 seconds) a jump ball is given.
8. The hand is considered to be a part of the ball on tie balls, shots, dribbles, interceptions, etc.
9. The penalty for all violations shall be taken on the sideline.
10. The following are not considered dribbles:
    (a) Successive tries for goals
    (b) Fumbles
    (c) Attempts to gain control of the ball by:
        (1) Tapping it from the control of another player
        (2) Tapping it from the reach of another player
        (3) Blocking a pass and recovering the ball
        (4) Blocking a shot and recovering the ball
11. During a free throw the defensive team shall occupy both lane spaces adjacent to the end line.
12. On jump balls, opponents are entitled to alternate positions around the restraining circle if they so indicate before the official is ready to toss the ball.
13. On jump balls, players must hold their established positions around the restraining circle until the ball has been tossed.
14. Either foot or the lower leg may be involved in intentionally kicking.
15. If a player causes the ball to go out-of-bounds by deliberately throwing or hitting the ball against an opponent, the ball is awarded to the player who was struck by the ball.
16. Tagging has been eliminated as a foul, since blocking and holding cover this tactic.
17. Guarding a player from the rear, outside the free throw lane, so closely that contact results when a player

attempts to turn or pivot is a form of blocking, and is a foul.

18. On a neutral court, a toss of a coin shall determine which team is to be designated as the home team.

FUNDAMENTAL SKILL TECHNIQUES
Passing

Passing is the key to successful basketball. A successful team must be able to handle, control, and move the ball downcourt quickly and accurately to create scoring opportunities.

First, learn to catch as well as pass. When the ball is thrown to you, spread the fingers, but keep them relaxed. When the ball hits the fingers, let the arms give slightly toward the body. When the ball is under control, finger it into passing position by placing the hands on each side of the ball so that you can get it away quickly or get set for a shot.

SOME PRACTICAL HELPS

1. The cause of most fumbling is holding arms too stiff while catching.
2. Do not fight the ball; that is, do not pass until full control of the ball is obtained.
3. Try not to rush a throw or pass.
4. Stay relaxed, and carry the head high in order to spot any free teammate.
5. Pay attention to any call by a teammate, but never pass to a player if that player is covered.
6. Move toward a pass rather than away from it.
7. Aim a pass slightly ahead of a receiving player, about chest high.
8. When some mastery in controlling the ball has been gained, learn to pass with deception, for example, looking one way and passing another, or faking high and passing low.
9. Rely upon "split vision," actually looking straight ahead but seeing the receiver out of the corner of the eye.
10. Do not pass blindly.

CHEST OR PUSH PASS

The ball is held with both hands, elbows close to the body, fingers spread with thumbs pointed inward. Step toward the receiver and whip the ball with a strong wrist snap and push of thumbs and fingers, making the arms follow through in the direction of the pass. (See Fig. 5-3.)

CROSS-BODY PASS

Hold and throw the ball with both hands. Assume a crouched position and turn one side of the body to the opponent and bring the ball back to the other side by bending both elbows. Execute the pass across the chest with a strong wrist snap and extension of the arms, letting the hands follow through in the direction of the pass.

OVERHEAD PASS

Hold and throw the ball with both hands. Bring the ball well above and slightly behind the head with both hands and release it

Fig. 5-3. Chest pass.

Fig. 5-4. Two-hand overhead pass.

Fig. 5-5. Baseball pass.

with a strong wrist snap and extension of the arms. Arms and hands follow through in the direction of the pass. The overhead pass is mostly used by tall players. (See Fig. 5-4.)

SHOVEL PASS OR UNDERHAND PASS

Hold and throw the ball with both hands. Spread the legs and crouch, keeping the ball close to the floor, step toward the receiver, and shovel the ball to him or her with both hands with a low underhand sweep.

This pass can also be executed with a semicrouched body and the ball waist high, close to the body, fingers pointing down on the ball, and the ball brought back around to the side of the body. The ball is released with a shoveling motion, a wrist snap, and a step in the direction of the receiver.

BASEBALL PASS OR ONE-HAND
SHOULDER PASS

Shift the ball in front of waist to the throwing hand, turn the opposite side of the body in the direction of the pass, and then whip the ball back as in an infield throw. Step toward the receiver, and throw the ball with a full arm motion and wrist snap. Permit the fingers to follow through without a twist so that the movement will not curve the ball. (See Fig. 5-5.)

HOOK PASS

With the opposite side turned in the direction of the receiver, jump into the air and bring the ball from the hips, up and back.

Fig. 5-6. One-hand hook pass.

Cradle the ball on the wrist with the fingers well spread behind it for control and throw it with a hook motion of the arm and strong wrist action over the head, following through with the hand. (See Fig. 5-6.)

Pivoting

Pivoting is a skill used to elude an opponent when a player has the ball. A forward pivot is executed by keeping one foot in place on the floor and rotating the other forward and across the foot in place. (See Fig. 5-7.) A reverse pivot is executed by keeping one foot in place and rotating the other backward in a semicircle.

Dribbling

Learn to dribble with the body low for protection and the head up, with the ball

Fig. 5-7. Pivot pass.

Fig. 5-8. Fake right.

well out in front where it is easily controlled. Spread the fingers, relax the wrist, and keep the fingers nimble. Control the ball with the fingertips, and push the ball down and forward; do not bat it.

Keep the ball low, below the waist. Avoid a high bounce dribble. A pass can be worked down court faster than a dribble, so never dribble when you can pass.

LIMITED DRIBBLE

For women, one, two, or three bounces are used to elude an opponent or to cover space when a player has the ball.

UP AND UNDER FAKE PASS AND DRIBBLE OR LIMITED DRIBBLE

Stand for the shot in front of the opponent and go through the motion of bringing the ball up for a chest shot. As the guard closes in or leaps to block the shot, duck low and drive past to one side, dribbling with the hand farthest from the opponent.

FAKE PASS AND DRIBBLE
OR LIMITED DRIBBLE

Hold the ball waist high upon receiving it; then fake to the left with the ball and head. As the guard goes in that direction, turn quickly to the right and cross-step with the left foot and dribble down on the right side with the right hand farthest away from the guard. (See Fig. 5-8.) A woman should execute a limited dribble.

Shooting

TWO-HAND SET SHOT

Poise and hold the ball chin high with both hands, the fingers spread along the sides and slightly behind the ball, the thumbs

Fig. 5-9. Two-hand set shot.

Fig. 5-10. One-hand set shot.

directed inward behind the ball and the feet close together with one slightly ahead of the other. Bend the knees slightly, and bring the ball up, extending the knees and arms with a strong wrist snap. The rearmost foot extends enough to lift the feet off the floor in executing the shot. Focus the eyes on the front rim of the hoop. (See Fig. 5-9.)

ONE-HAND SET SHOT

Poise as in a two-hand set shot with the hands in front of the face. Turn the ball so that the shooting hand is behind and under the ball. Bend the knees, bring the ball up, releasing the left hand if shooting with the right, and shoot with a strong wrist action and extension of the arm, letting the feet come off the floor. (See Fig. 5-10.)

FREE THROW OR UNDERHAND
LOOP SHOT

Toe the foul line with spread legs, holding the ball with both hands well extended out front. Carry the ball down between the legs, so that the fingers and thumbs point down. Bring the ball forward and upward, with the arms slightly bent, and release the ball, extending the arms fully. Throw the ball with a backward spin. Spot the eyes on the front rim of the hoop. (See Fig. 5-11.)

LAY-UP SHOT

Hold the ball with both hands waist high, take off with the left foot, leap high into the air, shifting the ball to the shooting hand, and raise the shooting hand as high as possible above and in front of head. Release the ball off the fingertips, laying it softly against the backboard. *Note:* Use both hands to bring the ball up for the shot and do not remove the balancing hand too soon. (See Fig. 5-12.)

HOOK SHOT

Hold the ball with both hands hip high, bring the ball to the right side opposite from the basket, and remove the balance hand (left). Shoot with a full sweep of the right arm, keeping arm perfectly straight. In starting the shot, take a short step with the left foot away from the basket and take off on it. The ball is released farthest from the guard, making the shot difficult to block. (See Fig. 5-13.)

JUMP SHOT

This shot is best executed from a dribble. Come to a stop from the dribble and leap high into the air. At the same time, bring the ball up overhead with the shooting hand behind and underneath the ball and the other hand in front. At the peak of the leap, remove the balance hand and release ball with extension of right forearm and good wrist extension.

Fig. 5-11. Two-hand free throw.

Fig. 5-12. Lay-up shot.

Fig. 5-13. Hook shot.

Defense

TYPES

There are principally two types of defense: man-to-man and zone.

In man-to-man defense, each player is responsible for one opponent. In zone defense, each player is responsible for a certain area or zone. A player must take any player going into it and at the same time watch the ball.

One of the main ideas of zone defense is to form a tightly guarded center so that an opponent cannot drive in for easy lay-up shots. All players must shift with the play of the ball to maintain this tight center. This type of defense is good for small floors. Use zone defense when the opposing team has many set plays, when the opponents have the advantage in height, or when your tall players are in danger of fouling out.

INDIVIDUAL TECHNIQUES

Stance: The feet should be in a forward stride position, knees and hips slightly bent, and the back straight. If the left arm is raised up and the right arm extended to the side, the left foot should be forward. If the right arm is up, the right foot should be forward.

Assumption: From this position one should be able to quickly slide-step in any direction.

ROLE OF DEFENSIVE PLAYER

Position: A defensive player should attempt to position the body between the opposing player and the player's own basket.

Objectives of defensive players:
1. To harrass your opponent by playing in close and moving arms in a distracting manner.
2. To block the shot by staying with the ball as the opponent attempts to throw it. (Don't jump too soon.)
3. If the opponent holds the ball unprotected, to tie up the ball by grabbing it.
4. To knock an unprotected ball out of your opponent's hands.
5. To take a ball that is being dribbled.
6. To deflect a ball, that is being passed by an opponent, to one of your teammates.
7. To intercept a passed ball.

Offensive

Offensive tactics will vary with the defensive play patterns employed by an opposing team throughout a single game of basketball. One type of offensive tactic must be employed to meet a 2-1-2, 2-3, or a 3-2 zone defense and another type to meet a man-to-man defense. Women frequently use a 2-2 or 2-1-1 zone defense.

The most common method of offense against the zone defense is to use a series of short, quick passes around the defense from one side of the court to the other with the object of forcing a defensive player out of an assigned position so that the offensive player can break through for a shot.

Against the man-to-man defense, use dribbling and passing with crisscrossing and blocking and have players follow passes to the basket and try for quick breaks. Plays such as this are spontaneous throughout the game and are never set as a play. The offense is constantly alert for an opportunity for a quick break or shot.

INSTRUCTIONAL AND LEARNING PROCEDURES
Fundamental skill technique practice routines

Passing and catching: One player should stand out in front of a line of five or six players and pass to each player in the line. Rotate the player out front. Passes should be chest high and handled with ease.

Pass and repass for lay-up shot: Two lines are formed on opposite sides of the court and basket along the sidelines. One player on a side stands on the free throw line and receives a pass from a player on the other side; the ball is then repassed back to the player now moving in for a lay-up shot. A player on the free throw line retrieves the ball and play starts over, with players rotating.

Players should be careful not to travel when handling or passing the ball or when driving in for a shot.

When shooting with the right hand, a player should take off on the left foot, and vice-versa with the left hand. The player should lay the ball up and against the backboard, but lay it up softly with underhand, as well as one-hand overhead shots.

Dribbling: Players are arranged in a single line 4 or 5 feet apart. The pivot player dribbles around each of the other players in line to the end of the line and dribbles back. This will develop speed, coordination, and proficiency in dribbling. Have the dribbler change hands.

Pivoting: Form players in a single line and have the front player dribble forward to a spot, stop, pivot, and pass back to the next player in line.

Tipping: Form two lines on each side of the basket, and have one player bank the ball off the board while other players tip it in. Keep this up until the ball goes in. Tip with the fingers, not the palms, Have players jump for height and not stand flat-footed.

Long passes: Have players practice throwing long passes to teammates at midcourt or farther for accuracy. Throw from the ear like a baseball catcher.

Shooting and free throw drill: Show players different ways of shooting from the field and from the free throw line and have them practice their favorite shots. Insist on relaxation and follow-through on shots.

Defensive drills: Have two offensive players try to make a basket while two defensive players try to stop them. Defensive players should not cross the feet when guarding, but

Basketball ability test (Knox)

These tests require no complicated equipment. All that is needed is a basketball, stopwatch, four chairs, and three cups. The tests are based on ability to execute four fundamental movements.

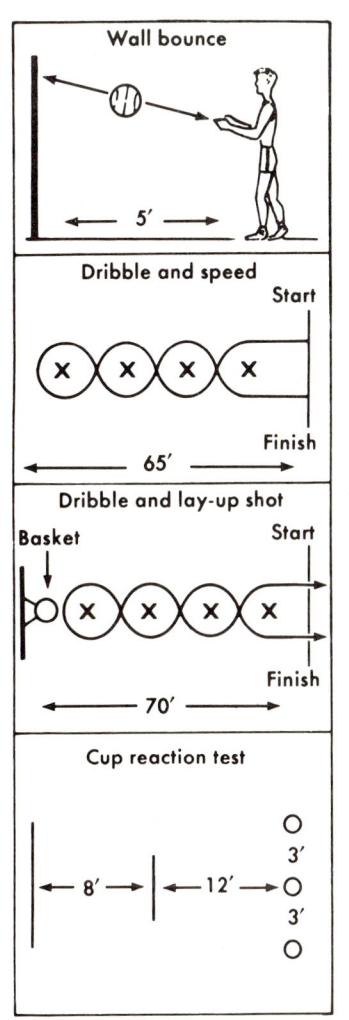

1. Wall bounce—to determine passing and receiving ability. Ball is bounced against a wall fifteen times from a distance of 5'.
   Players with low times are usually the best passers.

2. Obstacle dribble and speed — to determine dribbling ability and speed.
   Course is laid 65' along the sidelines of a court; four objects are placed equidistant apart along the court, and the dribbling player is timed weaving around the object and back to the starting point.

3. Dribble and lay-up shot—to determine ball-handling and shooting ability.
   Course laid out as in the obstacle dribble test but in line with a basket, which represents about an additional 8'. Player is timed dribbling around objects, shoots a lay-up shot, recovers the ball, and returns around objects to starting point.

4. Cup reaction test—tests ability to respond to commands. Three different colored cups 2½" in height, 3" in diameter. Player is given a coin and stands with the back to the cups and the route of travel.
   At a starting signal, player whirls around and starts for the cups 20' away. When the player is 12' from the cups, the examiner barks a command, designating the color cup in which to deposit the coin. Test is completed when a coin plunks in the cup. Multiply time by 4 to obtain equated score.

Take the times made in each test and add them together to obtain player ratings. The scores, in most cases, indicate the potential basketball ability of the candidates.

Names	Wall bounce (15)	Obstacle dribble	Dribble and lay-up shot	Cup reaction × 4	Score

Fig. 5-14

use the boxer's shift, or a sliding movement.

Team offense: Use a five- or six-player team and work the ball into the pivot player for a good shot, cutting around toward the basket for a repass. Teach players to cut after a pass and watch for a repass.

Team defense: Place one team on offense and one team on defense; practice working against a man-to-man defense and against a zone defense. Be sure defensive players have their hands up, waving arms, and batting at all shots and passes. Encourage players to talk to each other to help out the other player who may lose the opponent on a pick-off.

FUNDAMENTALS TO REMEMBER

1. Do not dribble too much when a pass is better.
2. Keep the ball moving.
3. When shooting a free throw, take your time.
4. Practice only those shots you will use in a game.
5. Do not play the other team's game.
6. Play hard around the backboards; control off backboard is very likely to decide the game.
7. Look down the court when in possession of the ball.
8. Do not take wild shots at the basket.
9. Keep at least one player back on offense to pick up any fast breakers in case the ball is lost.
10. A defensive player should never turn the head away from the player who is being guarded. Watch the player from the corner of the eye.
11. Get into shape.
12. Take it easy the first days and do not go at top speed.
13. Keep going when you feel a bit tired; you will soon be able to play longer.
14. Learn to handle the ball well.
15. Use teammate's midsection as a target when passing.
16. Always follow your shots.

GLOSSARY OF BASKETBALL TERMS

air dribble A play in which a player, after giving impetus to the ball once by throwing or tapping it, touches it again before it has touched the floor or has been touched by another player.

closely guarded To guard within three feet.

dead ball A ball which is temporarily out of play. The ball is dead after the whistle is blown.

defaulted game A game is considered defaulted when a team fails (1) to appear for a scheduled game, (2) to be ready to play within 15 minutes after the time the game is scheduled to begin, (3) to be ready to play after one minute at the beginning of the second half or after time out has been called for any reason, (4) to play after being told to do so, (5) to have five players to start play and at least four to continue, (6) to have numbers on front and back, or when a coach or team follower refuses to leave the gym if told to do so by an official.

defensive player A player whose team does not possess the ball.

discontinued game A game that is stopped because of the spectators' conduct.

double violation Violations committed simultaneously by both teams.

dribble To bounce the ball on the floor. The first bounce may be initiated with either one or both hands. The rest of the bounces must be made with one hand only. The dribble ends when the player touches the ball with both hands, permits the ball to come to rest in one hand, or passes it to a teammate. Fumbling is not considered a dribble.

goal A ball legally passed through one's own basket from above.

held ball A ball held more than 5 seconds by a player when closely guarded.

jump ball A ball tossed up between two opposing players.

offensive player A player with the ball.

own basket The basket for which the team is shooting.

pivot To retain one foot on the floor while the other is moved in any direction.

restraining circles The circles on the basketball floor or court.

traveling Illegal progression in any direction with the ball.

REFERENCES

Harkins, Mike: Successful team techniques in basketball, Englewood Cliffs, N. J., 1966, Prentice-Hall, Inc.

Harrell, Bill D.: Championship-tested offensive and defensive basketball strategy, Englewood Cliffs, N. J., 1967, Prentice-Hall, Inc.

Hobson, Howard A.: Basketball illustrated, New York, 1948, A. S. Barnes & Co.

Lowry, Carla: Pictorial basketball, Hollywood, Calif., 1968, Creative Sports Books.

Miller, D. M., and Ley, K. L.: Individual and team sports for women, Englewood Cliffs, N. J., 1955, Prentice-Hall, Inc.

Naismith, James A.: Basketball—Its origin and development, New York, 1941, Association Press.

Neal, Patsy: Basketball techniques for women, New York, 1966, Ronald Press Co.

Official basketball rules and guide, Washington, D. C. (latest edition), 1971-1972, AAHPER, Division for Girls' and Women's Sports.

The NCAA official basketball rules, 1974, College Athletics Publishing Service.

6 Bowling

HISTORY

Through existing records, bowling can be traced back to as far as 7000 years ago. This would easily establish bowling as one of the oldest games known to man. Archeologists trace its origin to the ancient Egyptians, with evidence of crudely shaped implements being used.

The game of modern tenpins had its inception in northern Italy, being derived from variations as played by the ancients. This the Italians called "bowls." Stones were rounded and used as balls without finger holes and were held in the open hand.

Later in the thirteenth century, the game spread to Germany, Holland, and England and was known as ninepins. The playing area on which the game was played was known as the bowling green, because the game was usually played on grass. In 1623, when the Dutch came to this country with the early settlers, they introduced the game to America as ninepins. It was played on grass, clay, and later on a single wide board. This game attracted considerable interest, causing extensive betting to center about it. Laws were passed in several states in the 1840s banning ninepins.

Later, in order to circumvent the existing law and continue the activity, a Dutchman added one more pin and called it tenpins.

In 1895, the American Bowling Congress* was organized, and it formulated rules, alleys, balls, and pins which have become so popular in America that it can safely be said that bowling has more enthusiasts today than any other sports activity. It is now estimated that nearly 40,000,000 people participate in bowling. In recent years high school officials formulated the American High School Bowling Congress (AHSBC).† (The Women's Bowling Congress [WBC] was formed before the AHSBC).

Colleges and universities are building alleys in their student recreation centers, and in many colleges bowling appears on the physical education curriculum as a basic sports skill. Large numbers of students have now enrolled in such bowling courses.

Weekly contests on television have done much to increase the popularity of bowling.

SOCIAL VALUES

In bowling, we have a form of sports skill that appeals to everyone, young and old, men and women, it requires the learning of comparatively few skills. It requires only a single change of shoes and no special uni-

---

*The American Bowling Congress, 2200 North Third St., Milwaukee, Wisc.
†The American High School Bowling Congress, 8142 Indiana Ave., Chicago, Ill.

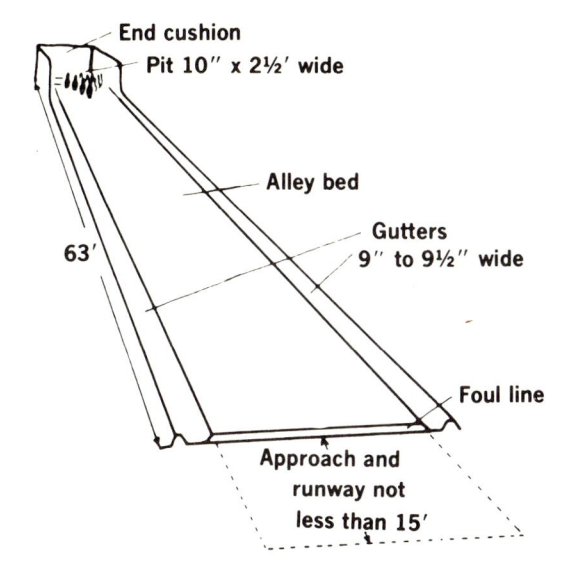

Fig. 6-1. The alley.

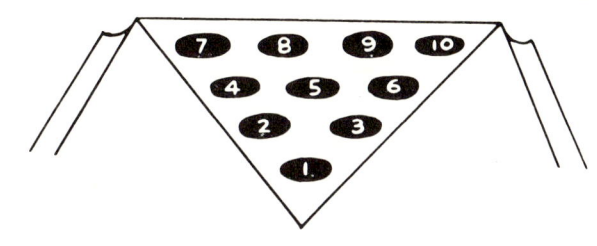

Fig. 6-2. Position of pins and their numbers.

form. One can bowl during lunchtime, after work, or in the evening. This is appealing to the average American. It requires no particularly great strength; rather, rhythm, relaxation, and coordination are the essentials. Once mastered, it is an art. Around the bowling alley, social intercourse is pleasurable and tensions seem to disappear. There is always the challenge, as in golf, to turn in a better score. That one single little pin seems to topple, but sometimes stands up there and wants to fight back. One can play alone to enjoy the game or can easily get on a local team. Bowling, because it brings into play many muscles, is one of our very best modern-day recreational sports skills, and it is relatively inexpensive.

GENERAL DESCRIPTION AND FACILITIES

In bowling, 10 wooden pins are set in triangular position at the far end of a wooden runway called an alley. The alley is 60 feet long from the No. 1 pin to the foul line. It is 42 inches wide. (See Fig. 6-1.)

Behind the foul line is the approach, which must not be less than 15 feet long. The pit is behind the pin spots area and must have a drop of at least 9½ inches from the alley floor. The pins are set 12 inches apart from center to center. (See Fig. 6-2.) The pin is 15 inches in height with a base diameter of 2¼ inches. It is constructed of clear, hard maple.

The balls are constructed of Bakelite or of a hardened rubber substance. The circumference is not more than 27 inches, and the ball weighs from 10 to 16 pounds. The balls have either two or three bored holes for the bowler's fingers for accuracy of delivery down the alley and also for ease in holding and delivering the ball. Special balls with four and five finger holes are now available.

There are other forms of bowling, such as duck pins, barrel pins, and candle pins. They involve the use of small pins and small balls. The fundamentals of all these games are essentially the same. In duck pins 3 balls are rolled per frame.

RULES OF TENPIN BOWLING

1. The bowler is allowed to roll two balls from behind the foul line down the alley at the pins in an attempt to knock down all the pins. In case all the pins are knocked down with the bowler's first ball, the result is called a strike, and it is not necessary to roll the second ball.

2. Two alleys immediately adjoining each other shall be used in all games of league or tournament play, and the bowling of the ten complete frames on the pair of alleys on which the game was started shall constitute an official game.

   The members of the contesting teams shall successively and in regular order bowl one frame on one alley, and for the next frame use the other alley, so alternating each frame until the game is completed. Each player shall bowl two balls in every frame, except where a strike is made.

3. No pins may be conceded, and only those actually knocked down may be counted. Every frame must be completed at the time the player is bowling in regular order.
4. When a strike is made in the tenth frame, the bowler shall then be permitted to bowl two more balls on the same alley. When a spare is made in the tenth frame, the bowler shall be permitted to bowl one more ball on the same alley.
5. In case of a tie game, each team shall bowl one complete frame on the same alley on which its tenth frame was bowled, bowling and scoring said extra frame in exactly the same manner as the tenth frame. If, at the completion of the first extra frame, a tie still exists, teams are to change alleys for additional frames that may be required to determine the winner.
6. A spare is made when a player bowls down all the pins with the second ball in any frame; it is credited and designated with a / in the upper right-hand corner of the frame in which it is made. The count in such frame is left open until such player shall bowl the next ball in the succeeding frame, when the number of pins knocked down thereby shall be added to the 10 represented by the spare, and the total shall be credited therein.
7. Every ball delivered, unless it be declared a dead ball by the umpire, shall be counted against the player.

   If, when rolling at a full frame, it is discovered after the ball has been delivered that one or more pins are misplaced, the ball and resulting pinfall shall be counted. It is the duty of the player to look at the pins before bowling, and if the setup is not satisfactory a request that the pins be respotted should be made.
8. Pins which are knocked down by another pin rebounding in the play from the side partition or rear cushion are counted as pins down, except where pins come in contact with the body, arms, or legs of a pin boy and rebound. Pins which are bowled off the alley bed, rebound, and remain standing on the alley must be counted as pins standing.
9. Should a player by mistake bowl on the wrong alley or out of turn or be interfered with by another bowler or spectator, or should the ball come in contact with any foreign obstacle on the alleys, then the ball so delivered shall immediately be called a dead ball by the umpire, and such ball shall not count and shall be immediately rebowled by the player after the cause for declaring such dead ball has been removed.
10. A foul occurs when the bowler permits any part of the foot, hand, or arm, while in contact with the alleys or runway, to rest upon or extend beyond the foul line, or at any time after the ball leaves the hands and passes over beyond the foul line, the bowler permits any part of the body to come in contact with the alleys, gutters, division boards, wall, or uprights that are on or beyond the foul line.
11. No count shall be made on a foul ball, and any pins that are knocked down or displaced thereby shall at once be respotted. A foul ball shall count as a ball bowled by the player.
12. Pins which are knocked down or displaced by a ball which leaves the alley before reaching the pins, or from a ball rebounding from the rear cushions, do not count, and they shall be immediately respotted, and the removal or interference with pins by a pin boy or girl before they stop rolling shall be cause for the umpire to order the pins respotted.

SCORING

Considerable enjoyment is added to the game if each participant is able to accurately score throughout the game. A perfect score is 300 points. In scoring a game the bowler records the results for each

Frames	1	2	3	4	5	6	7	8	9	10	Total
Name	8 - / 8	7 / / 24	6 3 / 33	G / / 43	F 9 / 52	X / 79	X / 98	7 2 / 107	8 - / 115	9 / 5 / 130	130

Fig. 6-3. Sample method of scoring.

frame, and the accumulative running total for the 10 frames is the final score. In each frame the total of pins knocked down in the respective two tries is recorded except when a strike or spare is made. In case of a strike, the score for the frame is 10 (marked with an X in the small square) plus the count of the next two balls bowled. In case of a spare, the score for the frame is 10 plus the number of pins knocked over with the next ball. If a foul is committed, the score for that ball is not counted. If the foul occurs on the first ball, all pins are reset and the next ball is scored as the second ball of that frame. A sample game (called a line) in which the correct method of scoring is illustrated is shown in Fig. 6-3.

Frame 1: The bowler, on his first ball, knocks down 8 pins. An 8 is placed in the first square of the first frame. On the second ball, the bowler fails to hit either of the 2 remaining pins. The miss is indicated by the mark —, which is called a "blow." The bowler totals the number of pins knocked down with both balls and places the score, 8, in the first frame.

Frame 2: The bowler knocks down 7 pins with the first ball in this frame and places a 7 in the first square to indicate the number of pins scored. The bowler gets the remaining 3 pins with the second ball and thus places the symbol for a spare, /, in the second square. The second frame cannot be scored until the results of the first ball of the third frame are known.

Frame 3: Six pins are knocked down with the first ball in the third frame. The score of 6 is added to the 10 pins gotten in the second frame to give a total of 16 pins. The running score for the second frame is 8 (first frame) plus 16, or a total of 24 pins. Three pins are knocked down with the second ball, giving a total of 9 pins for the third frame. The running score for the third frame is 24 plus 9, or 33.

Frame 4: Unfortunately, the bowler throws the first ball of the fourth frame into the gutter. This is recorded in the first square as a G (gutter ball), which has a zero value. The second ball of this frame knocks down all 10 of the pins. However, as this is the second ball, it is scored as a spare. The running score for the fourth frame cannot be scored until the first ball of the fifth frame has been delivered.

Frame 5: The bowler crosses the foul line while delivering the first ball. Although the bowler knocks down 9 pins, a zero score is received for the first ball since a foul is committed. The fourth frame can now be scored. The score for the fourth frame is 10 plus 0, or 10. The running score in the fourth frame is 43. The foul is indicated by placing an F in the first square. The pins are then reset and the bowler delivers the second ball, which knocks down 9 pins. A 9 is placed in the second square and 9 is added to the score of the previous frame to give a running score of 52 for the fifth frame.

Frame 6: The bowler knocks down all 10 pins with the first ball. This is indicated by placing an X in the first square. The running score cannot be recorded as a strike but is scored by adding 10 to the number of pins knocked down with the next two balls bowled.

Frame 7: The bowler again makes a strike with the first ball. The bowler now has two consecutive strikes, or a "double." The player cannot yet score the sixth or seventh frame.

Frame 8: In this frame the bowler gets 7 pins with the first ball rolled. The bowler records the 7 in the first square. Now the score for the sixth frame can be computed. This score is 10 (strike in frame 6) plus 10 (strike in frame 7) plus 7 (number of pins gotten with the first ball in the eighth frame), or 27. The running score in the sixth frame is 52 plus 27, or 79. The second ball knocks down 2 pins, recorded by a 2 in the second square. Now the seventh frame score can be computed. It is 10 plus 7 plus 2, or 19. The running score is 98 in the seventh frame and 107 in the eighth frame.

Frame 9: In this frame the first ball delivered hits the head pin (No. 1 pin) squarely and a "split" results. The No. 7 and No. 10 pins remain standing. The split is indicated by encircling the 8, shown in the first square of the ninth frame. The second misses both pins and a miss (blow) is indicated by the mark—in the second square. The ninth frame score of 8 is added to the running score of 107 to give a total of 115 pins in the ninth frame.

Frame 10: The bowler gets a spare with the second ball. Since this is the tenth frame, the bowler is entitled to another ball in order that the score may be obtained for the tenth frame. The third ball knocks down 5 pins, giving a score of 15 for the tenth frame. The 15 is added to the ninth frame's running score of 115 to give a total score of 130.

BASIC SKILL TECHNIQUES OF BOWLING

Select a ball, not too heavy or too light, that fits the fingers comfortably for consistent scoring accuracy. Most men should use a 16-pound ball. Women should select a lighter ball weighing from 11¾ to 13¾ pounds. Comfortable fit is essential to good delivery.

Select a ball with finger holes which are neither too narrow nor too wide for finger spread, that is, from thumb to fingers. A good method to determine finger span is to insert the thumb into the thumb hole up to the second joint, or about four-fifths of its length, then lay the hand flat on the surface of the ball with the fingers spread over the holes. The knuckle joints of the fingers should extend about ¼ inch past the inside nearer edge of the finger hole. This allows for proper looseness or slack which is essential for a comfortable grip. This slack or play between the palm and the ball should be about ¼ inch. This is the recommended method of fitting the regular ball; it does not apply to fingertip or semifingertip balls.

The grip

It is a matter of individual preference whether a two- or three-hole finger grip is used. There are champion bowlers who use the two-finger grip, and champions who use the three-finger grip. The two-hole finger grip ball is rarely used today. If a person has an excessively weak grip, a four- or five-hole ball is recommended. The three-finger grip is recommended for beginners or younger bowlers. It is less of a strain on the wrist and arm, and the popular hook ball can be delivered better with the three-finger grip.

When the ball is released, the thumb should come out of the hole first. (See Fig. 6-4.)

The stance

The bowler assumes a stance, prior to throwing, with body facing pins, erect or slightly crouched, about 15 feet back of the foul line. The left foot is slightly in front of the right. The ball is held in the

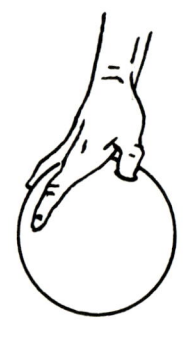

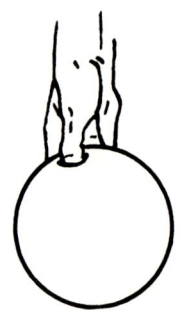

Fig. 6-4. Three-hole grip.

right hand, waist high. Some bowlers hold it higher with the idea of aiming, resting the weight of the ball on the left hand.

Footwork

The most essential and fundamental skills confronting the beginning bowler are footwork, balance, and rhythm. One has the choice of three, four, or five steps before delivering the ball. There are many good bowlers using each style. Today, the three-step approach is rarely recommended or taught unless a person is quite tall or uncoordinated. Probably the most popular among bowlers is the four-step approach. However, each bowler should experiment with the different steps until he finds the number of steps that fit. After this is accomplished, the bowler is ready to synchronize the footstep pattern with the arm movements in delivering the ball. The result of this practice is rhythm and timing. Practice footwork in a straight line, as if walking on a tight wire. This keeps the feet under the weight of the body and prevents shifting the weight of the body laterally with each alternating step. This gives greater accuracy in delivery. Practice a fast walk, a slow run, or a gliding movement, rather than the walk or run.

Delivery and approach to foul line

Once the bowler has mastered the timing of foot and arm movements, a stance is taken, ready for the delivery of the ball. As it was previously mentioned, there are many styles of delivery. Usually the ball is carried anywhere from chest high to waist high and may be centered in the center of the body or in front of the right shoulder. The movements of the approach in general fall into four phases: first, the push-away; second, the swing; third, the forward swing; and fourth, the release of the ball.

The bowler starts the approach toward the foul line by pushing the ball away from the body so that it is extended outward chest high. During this movement a step forward with the right foot is taken if the bowler is using the four-step delivery. If either the three- or five-step delivery is used, start the left foot first. The push-away places the ball forward about shoulder high, and the weight of the ball and gravity give the impetus in making the backward swing arc that is the next phase in the series of movements.

In executing this arc, the bowler should not carry the ball too far backward at the end of the arc, but should end about waist high. The ball is now poised in readiness to gain momentum from this pendulum swing downward and forward smoothly for the release and follow-through.

Release

If the bowler has achieved perfect timing, the ball should be coming forward in its well-executed arc, just as the last step (left foot) is being taken. The body weight should be perfectly balanced over this last step with the left foot.

With continued practice the whole series of arm and step movements blends into a graceful, coordinated, rhythmic pattern.

The approach starts slowly and accelerates toward the end. The last step must stop short of the foul line. (See rules.) The ball should strike the alley floor about 12 to 16 inches beyond the foul line.

Follow-through

At the finish of the forward throw, the bowler's left foot will be in front, the right foot balanced on the floor as a rudder behind, and the bowling arm extended forward and upward in the follow-through so essential in many other sports skills. This finishing movement of the approach is an easy sliding glide that is controlled to stop about 2 or 4 inches short of the foul line.

The bowler's posture at the finish should be smooth, easy, and relaxed, with a bend at the knees and very little at the hips. The opposite arm is used as an aid to balance. For a straight ball, the ball should be laid and rolled smoothly onto the alley beyond the foul line and about 6 or 8 inches from the right gutter. For a hook ball this distance should be doubled.

Style of delivery

The skill techniques just described are common to all delivery styles. The bowler is now confronted with the choice of four styles of delivery: the straight ball, the back-

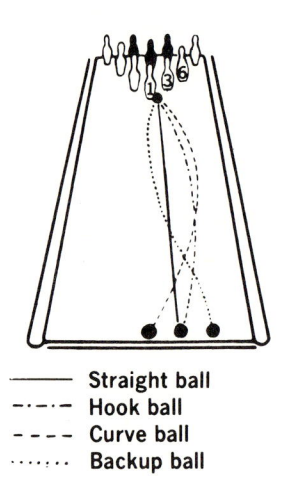

Fig. 6-5. Types of deliveries.

— Straight ball
–·–·– Hook ball
– – – Curve ball
······· Backup ball

up, the hook, and the curve. (See Fig. 6-5.) The beginner should first try the straight ball, as it is easiest, but should also experiment immediately with the hook as it is the most efficient delivery and is the one used by almost all professional bowlers.

STRAIGHT BALL

For this throw, the thumb is placed on top of the ball in a straight forward line directed at the headpin so that it will roll in a straight line. The most universal approach is from the right corner of the alley, so that the aim is directed in a diagonal cross-alley path between the No. 1 and No. 3 pins. During the entire act of bowling, through the stance, approach, and release, the eyes must spot and hold fast that small space between the No. 1 and No. 3 pins if contact of the ball and pins is desired at that point. This is the most popular target for the straight ball roll and the point at which the pins are most vulnerable for a strike possibility. However, many bowlers "spot bowl" by aiming at a spot 16 feet from the foul line.

BACKUP BALL

This style is practically obsolete in strike bowling today and is never recommended. It is a reverse hook with a right-to-left spin. In using it the bowler turns the thumb to the right on the release. The wrist gives an outward or fade-away motion, so that the palm turns upward. It is delivered near the right-hand gutter. The ball fades to the right as it nears the pins, and the aim should be at the 1-2 pocket.

HOOK BALL

The hook ball is the most effective of all bowling styles for producing strikes. This style is universal with leading high-scoring teams. The technique recommended for the beginner's hook ball is as follows: The thumb is placed at a 9 o'clock position, so that the V formed by the thumb and forefinger points down the alley. In a natural hook the wrist or fingers do not turn or rotate. The thumb's coming out first allows the fingers to lift their side of the ball, and a hook results.

The technique for the forced hook ball is as follows: The ball is held with the thumb directed toward the body and the two fingers on the outside of the ball away from the body. The thumb is released first as the wrist and middle and ring fingers apply a turn inward to the ball toward the body counterclockwise, leaving the holes with the back of the hand uppermost. The ball is released near the right alley gutter. The aim is on the No. 3-6 pins. The ball then rolls with a forward motion and breaks sharply toward the left at the No. 1-3 pocket. (See Fig. 6-5.) With the ball coming in on such a sideward angle, the pins are effectively swept off the alley. Unlike other styles, the hook ball, even thinly hitting the head pin, leaves few single pins remaining and few splits.

There is no question of the effectiveness of the hook ball. It will be a question of long practice in mastering it and producing consistency.

CURVE BALL

This ball is usually employed by slow bowlers. It works well on highly polished alleys. This style is not recommended for beginners because of its inconsistency and very difficult control. It requires much practice for its mastery. (See Fig. 6-5.)

The technique is as follows: On the backswing the wrist is rotated to the right, and on the forward swing to the left, which gives the ball a wide, sweeping curve. The release

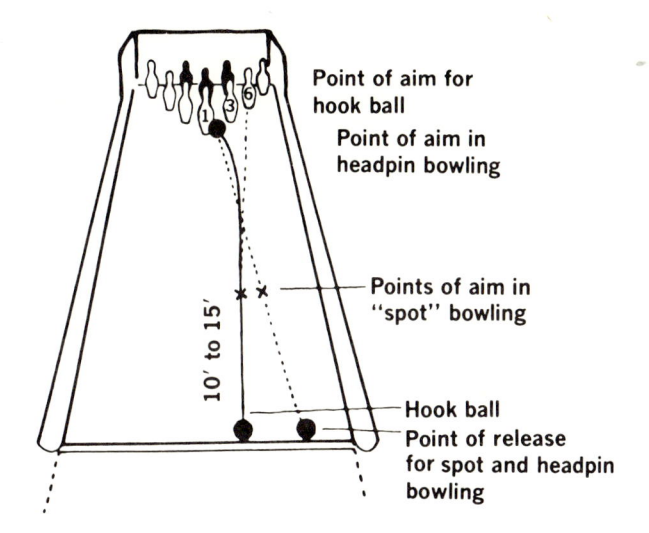

Fig. 6-6. Point of aim for various shots.

is the same as that used in the hook ball. The ball is laid down near the center of the alley. The follow-through is forward.

The aim

There are two methods of aiming: the headpin type and the spot. The most effective balls are rolled to hit the No. 1-3 pocket. For the beginner, the headpin method is best to learn, that is, aiming at the pin or pocket one desires the ball to hit. The eyes should then be focused on that spot throughout the entire delivery and follow-through. (See Fig. 6-6.)

In the spot method the bowler usually aims to roll the ball over a definite spot on the alley floor or over an imaginary line from the foul line down the alley to coincide with the pin or pocket desired to be hit.

THINGS TO REMEMBER IN BOWLING

1. Lay the ball on the alley smoothly.
2. Let the follow-through arm continue in the direction of the pins.
3. Learn the technique of letting the thumb come out of the hole first.
4. Hold the wrist firm when turning and releasing.
5. Develop an even speed roll in all shots and use whichever speed develops the most accuracy and consistency.
6. Do not force a delivery; let the weight of the ball do the work. The arm merely serves as a pendulum.
7. Keep the spin of the ball uniform.
8. Be sure that the run does not become too fast or too slow in the approach.
9. In the straight ball style, be sure the fingers are behind the ball when it is released, to prevent the ball from curving.
10. Relax.
11. To find the correct starting spot in the approach, step off, starting from the foul line, the number of steps desired and add 6 inches to this number.
12. Concentrate on the spot desired to be hit.
13. Experiment in finding the spot that proves most consistent and effective.

TECHNIQUES IN BOWLING FOR SPARES

Spare bowling is quite an art and requires practice to obtain accuracy and confidence. Angle shooting is generally sound. To execute an angle shot, the bowler should assume a stance on the opposite side from that on which the remaining pins are standing. For example, if the No. 10 pin is standing or any number clustered on the right, the bowler rolls from the left diagonally at the cluster in the right corner. The reverse is true if any pins are left standing on the left side of the alley. There are many combinations of pins to be effectively picked off as spares and after a great deal of experience, the bowler will quickly recognize the best ways in which these shots can be made.

TEACHING AND LEARNING PROCEDURES
Equipment and its care
1. Acquainting students with equipment
2. Care of alleys
3. Selecting shoes
4. Rules of etiquette and sportsmanship

Teaching and learning procedures
1. To acquire and develop adequate skill in:
    (a) Selecting a ball
    (b) Various grips in holding the ball
    (c) The stance
    (d) The step approach: three, four, and five steps
    (e) The act of approaching
    (f) The act of delivery
    (g) Aiming the ball
    (h) The styles of bowling: the straight ball, the hook ball, the backup ball, and the curve ball
    (i) Bowling for strikes and spares
    (j) Scoring
    (k) Strategy
    (l) Terminology
    (m) Safety
2. Grade based on performance and true-false knowledge test.

GLOSSARY OF BOWLING TERMS

approach That part of the alley or runway upon which the bowler takes the run or steps to proceed to the delivery point, the foul line.

baby split The No. 3-10 pin split for right-handed bowlers and the No. 2-7 pin for left-handed bowlers.

backup ball A ball delivered in such a manner as to curve toward the arm which delivered the ball. For a right-handed bowler the ball curves to the right.

blow or error A complete failure to knock down any remaining pins after the first ball is rolled.

Brooklyn or crossing over Hitting the headpin and adjacent pin on the opposite side of the alley from which the bowler released the ball on the delivery.

cherry Knocking down one or more of the front pins in a spare and leaving others standing.

double Two consecutive strikes.

foul The act of touching the foul line with the foot. If a foul is made on the first throw, all 10 pins are spotted; on the second throw, only the pins knocked over with the first ball count.

frame The box on the score sheet in which the scores are recorded. Ten frames constitute a game.

headpin The No. 1 pin.

hook A ball that is caused to curve from outside in on its way to the pins.

leave End pins not bowled over on the first shot.

line A complete game recorded in the ten frames across the score sheet.

pocket The gap between any two pins.

rack The trough structure holding the balls beside the runway.

return The ball returned from the pit to the bowler by way of a trough along side of the alley.

runway approach The part of the alley the bowler uses to execute the approach to the foul line.

setup The arranging of 10 pins in regular formation.

spare Bowling over all pins with two balls in any one frame.

strike Bowling over all pins with the first ball rolled.

striking out Rolling strikes for any part of a remainder of a game.

tandem An arrangement of any two pins in a spare formation with one behind the other.

triple or turkey Three consecutive strikes at any time in a game.

zipper A straight fast ball.

zoomer A hook ball that breaks in sharply to the headpin.

REFERENCES

Ainsworth, Dorothy S., and others: Individual sports for women, ed. 2, Philadelphia, 1963, W. B. Saunders Co.

Casady, Donald R., and Liba, Marie: Beginning bowling, Belmont, Calif., 1968, Wadsworth Publishing Co., Inc.

Martin, Joan: Bowling, Dubuque, Iowa, 1971, William C. Brown Company, Publishers.

Official bowling, fencing, and golf rules and guide,

Washington, D. C., 1973-1975, AAHPER, Division for Girls' and Women's Sports.

Women's International Bowling Congress, Inc.: Rules for W.I.B.C., Inc., Sanctioned Leagues, Columbus, Ohio, 1970, The Congress.

FILMS

Better bowling, Ned Day, Films Inc., New York, N. Y.

Bowling aces, Joe Falcaro, Associated Films, Y.M.C.A. Motion Picture Bureau, New York, N. Y.

Bowling fundamentals, Teaching Films, Inc., New York, N. Y.

Bowling skill, Teaching Films Custodians, Inc., New York, N. Y.

Set 'em up, Teaching Films Custodians, Inc., New York, N. Y.

Splits, spares and strikes, Teaching Films Custodians, Inc., New York, N. Y.

7 Modern dancing and square dancing

MODERN DANCING
History

People have always danced. They have used some form of rhythmic movement as a part of their life pattern from the beginning of time. History shows us that dance has been used in worship, as a part of ritualistic ceremonies, for entertainment, and now with modern dance, as a means of expressing thoughts, ideas, and dreams. The beginning of modern dance dates back to the turn of the centutry, when Isadora Duncan rebelled against the formal and unnatural movements of the ballet. She wanted a free and natural form of dance. She felt that anyone could dance and that dance should follow the natural, ordinary but yet beautiful movements of the young child. These movements took the shape of bending, jumping, stretching, running, and turning. She also felt that the dancer should wear very loose and free garments and lightweight sandals on her feet. Many of the goals of modern dance in education today date back to the teachings of Miss Duncan.

In the 1930s great strides were made in this new form of dance. Ruth St. Denis and Ted Shawn started a school for modern dance in California. Martha Graham began to train dancers skilled in this new art and formed a touring company. Doris Humphrey and Charles Weidman did the same. These great artists created some fine dance productions that have stayed a part of the artistic world of dance for many years.

During this same period many teachers of physical education participated in dance classes taught by these outstanding artists and in turn taught this dance to the young people they had in their own classes. Today we find modern dance being taught to all age groups and used as therapy and of course as a performing art in the theater and on television. Many colleges and universities throughout the country presently offer programs of study in which the student may major in dance. Graduates of these programs often turn to teaching as well as to choreography and performance.

Most educators today believe modern dance to be of great importance in the total education of the individual because it deals with the individual's feelings and reactions. The student must be totally involved mentally, physically, and emotionally. Modern dance is concerned with creative development and the desire of the student for self-expression, self-discovery, and self-realization.

The traditional costume for students of modern dance as well as for the professional dancer is the leotard and tights in any color or combination of colors. The tights should come only to the ankles, and the leotard should have long sleeves to protect the arms when moving the body on the floor. This type of outfit is worn because it allows freedom of movement.

Fundamentals of movement

An understanding of the fundamentals of movement is necessary before dance can be used as a means of expression or communication. There are two types of movement—axial and locomotor. Axial movement is movement of the body or any part of the body over a stationary base. This movement may take place on any level and with any part of the body as the base of support. Flexion, extension, rotation, or any combination of these movements plus a variation or forceful release of energy will cause an interesting design pattern. (See Figs. 7-1 and 7-2.)

Locomotor movements are those movements of the body that cause the body to travel from one spot to another spot. There are two categories of locomotor movements. The first group includes moving the body with different parts of the body in contact with the floor. The movements could be rolling, crawling, creeping, or walking on the knees or possibly on the hands. The second group includes all the foot patterns used in moving the body through space. The tempo and rhythm may vary with each pattern. There are only eight possible movements; everything else is a combination or variation of the basic eight.

walk An even transfer of weight from one foot to the other foot.

run An even transfer of weight from one foot to the other foot with a slight spring as the weight leaves the back foot to come down onto the forward foot. The toes touch the floor first, and then the heel comes down. The movement of the legs and feet can cause the body to be carried upward as well as forward.

leap An even transfer of weight from one foot to the other as in a run but a greater spring causes the body to be in the air for a moment with both feet off the floor. The leap may be long and low or short and high. (See Fig. 7-3.)

jump An even movement in which the body may spring into the air from the takeoff from one or both feet but landing must be on both feet. (See Fig. 7-4.)

Fig. 7-2. Extension.

Fig. 7-1. Flexion.

Fig. 7-3. Leap.

Fig. 7-4. Jump.

Fig. 7-5. Hop.

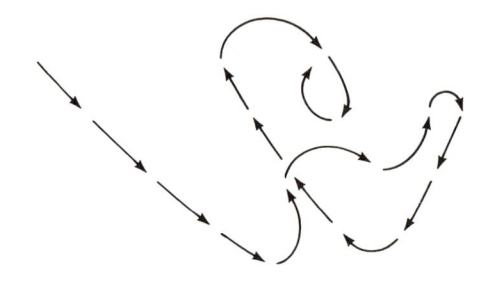

Fig. 7-6. Example of use of direction.

hop An even transfer of weight on the same foot. The body springs into the air from one foot and must land on the same foot. (See Fig. 7-5.)

skip An uneven combination of a walk and a hop. The movement is performed on the same foot. The step, which is the first part of the movement, is rhythmically long, and the hop, the second part of the movement, is short in duration.

slide A uneven combination of two walking steps. The forward step or the first part of the movement is rhythmically long, and the second step, in which the other foot is brought up to the forward foot and the weight placed on it, is rhythmically short in duration.

gallop An uneven combination of a leap and a walk. The leap, the first part of the movement, is rhythmically long, and the walk onto the other foot is rhythmically short.

All dance forms employs these basic eight locomotor movements in some form or style. All eight may be performed in any tempo, meter, or direction in space, such as forward, backward, or sideward. Interesting combinations make challenging and delightful dance patterns. Changes in the space elements, such as level, focus, and size, with the individual's own stylization can be the beginnings of creative endeavors. Examples of this plan could be one of the following:

Three long walks and two jumps, changing level and body direction

Two skips and two gallops, changing size and focus

Any combination of runs and hops, changing position of the arms

Any four movements, stylizing based on a character study

Elements of space

Dance takes place in space. Therefore, a knowledge of the basic space elements is a necessary part of the education of the modern dancer. Space is all around us; we live in it; we move in it constantly; we cannot exist without it. The dance, to be appreciated and to be creative, must concern itself with space, and the dancer must consider how space can be used to full advantage.

First, dance must take direction in space. The individual is capable of moving forward, backward, sideward, and diagonally, and of turning or spinning in one spot. Also, a particular dance pattern should be well placed in the space or area within which the dancer is moving, either on the stage or in a room. This means that the dancer travels toward or away from all sides or corners of the area. (See Fig. 7-6.)

Next, the dancer must be concerned about the level in which the movement occurs.

The dancer may be in a flat position on the floor, seated on the floor, on the knees, on the feet, or in the air, or a combination of all these levels might be experienced during the dance pattern.

The dancer must also be concerned with the dimension or size of the movements being performed. The movements can be very small or they can be extremely large and extensive, or any degree in between the two, depending on the mood or idea being expressed.

Focus of the eyes as well as of the movement must be considered by the dancer. Focus, or the emphasis of the movement pattern, gives the dance more depth and sincere meaning.

All these space elements give the dance a set design pattern in the air as well as on the floor. Again, this makes the dance more interesting and more meaningful.

Rhythm and its relationship to dance

Rhythm is what makes the world go around; it is the pulsation of the universe, the foundation of the world. We would not and could not be alive today if rhythm was not a part of each one of us. The pounding of our hearts in our bodies and the exhalation of the air about us are excellent examples of rhythm. The changing of the seasons, the patterns in the rock formations on the coast, the stars in the heavens, the tides, and the patterns made by the trees and flowers are all rhythmic examples given to us by Mother Nature. We also find a rhythmic pattern in the pattern of our lives. These rhythmic patterns may take shape in the fashion world, in the changes in politics, in economics, and in the many social changes that come upon us during a lifetime. Rhythm, by definition or explanation, is a series of pulsations that can be even or uneven, and these pulsations can be weak and strong. These are grouped together in smaller groups of time. Some of the rhythmic elements a dancer is concerned with are the following:

tempo The rate of speed of the movements, which can vary from very fast to very slow.

accent The stress or force of the movement,

Fig. 7-7. Underlying beat with accent in units of four.

which can vary from very strong and hard to light and weak.

underlying beat The constant pulsation that takes place throughout the dance. This beat is divided into units, thus designating the meter or time in which the dance is performed. (See Fig. 7-7.)

phrase A group of several meters giving a feeling of unity and completion to the rhythmic sentence and movement pattern.

Modern dance may be performed with or without accompaniment, but either way the above rhythmic elements are always present and must be taken into consideration.

Dance technique

Modern dance technique is used to help the dancer develop control of the movements employed and to increase the range of the dancer's movements, or to develop to a greater extent the dancer's vocabulary of movement. In a modern dance class, warm-up techniques are used in the beginning to stimulate and condition the body for the use of more difficult movement patterns. Some of these warm-up movements could consist of stretching in a standing position, on the floor lying down, or while sitting. (See Fig. 7-8.) This can be combined with bouncing movements to increase the individual's flexibility. Various types of strengthening movements are also used to help the dancer gain greater control of the movements, such as exercises for specific parts of the body—the legs, the feet, various joints and segments, as well as the entire torso.

During a modern dance class, different qualities of movement are explored, such as a series of swinging movements, or falling movements as the sit fall, back fall, side fall, and forward fall. Percussive and sustained movements can also be experimented with, as well as vibratory and suspended movements. All these can be patterned, or they can be explored and then created into a set pattern by the members of the class.

Fig. 7-8. Stretching exercises.

Creativity in modern dance

All individuals can be creative in movement to some degree if only because we are creative in movement every day of our lives in the way we go about our daily tasks. Modern dance develops further the individual's creativity in movement. For in a modern dance class the student learns to explore movement and then to solve movement problems. The student learns to improvise or move on the spur of the moment without any previous plan and then to plan a dance pattern or dance study. This study usually is based around some element of the dance the student is studying at the time—qualities of movement, one or several space elements, rhythmic elements, or various forms of axial or locomotor movements. Last, the dancer is prepared to create a composition. This composition has a specific theme or idea and has a definite beginning, a development, a climax, and an ending.

Sources of inspiration for creativity in modern dance come from the world around us. A dance study may be based on an idea, an emotion, an interesting design, or other art forms as music, poetry, literature, art or sculpture, or it may be centered around an experience of an everyday happening or even a sport event. In planning a dance composition or study, the dancer should develop the idea in a personal, perhaps unusual or unexpected manner, but always keeping the main idea present. Also remember that in planning a dance composition, all the elements of time, space, force, and the various types of movement and design, whether symmetrical or asymmetrical, are to be used and to be seen. In a dance composition there must be unity and harmony as well as variety and contrast and yet repetition for emphasis. The ending of one movement should be the beginning of the next. If this is accomplished, a smooth transition of movement and thought will take place, and the composition will relate a well-developed idea and not a series of unrelated and unstructured events.

The following are some suggestions or sources of inspiration in composing a dance:

1. Select an experience such as shopping on a crowded Saturday afternoon at Christmas time. Show accomplishment as well as failure by stylizing the movements with changes in level and dimension.
2. Imagine you are caught in a tunnel that is very small and you cannot find your way out. Express your reactions and fears in a movement pattern.
3. Find a unique way to greet a friend you have not seen for some time. Plan the sequence of movements in relation to various qualities of movement.
4. Draw an interesting design of lines, curves, circles, and wiggly lines that are heavy and light in touch. Then create a dance sequence to interpret the design. (See Fig. 7-9.)
5. Select a game or a sport. Analyze part of the movement patterns used in the sport. Stylize them as to success and failure based on changes in tempo.
6. Choose a simple gesture such as opening and closing a door. Do it as many different ways as you can and relate each to a different character study, such as a fearful, shy individual, a fast-moving, ego-centered individual, a tough tomboy, or a demure, little old lady.

Fig. 7-9. Example of curves and lines.

In composing a dance, the dancer must explore over and over again the various movement patterns possible until one is found that is liked and is comfortable performing. This does take practice. Movements must be clear and set well in space. Rhythmic changes must be exact and well defined. This takes mental, as well as physical and emotional effort, but in the final outcome it is well worth the effort, since it is then that that the complete expression and discovery of the individual is realized.

THE AMERICAN SQUARE DANCE
History

The American square dance had its beginning in England with the English country dance, a dance form that had developed among the people in the rural districts. In the early 1600s the dance did not enjoy tremendous popularity, especially in the larger cities. The impetus that propelled it into prominence came in 1651 when John Playford published the first English country dance book. Most of the dances compiled for this first publication were known as "longways," or what the French later called *contra* dances. In the contra, participants arranged themselves in two lines facing each other. Various sequences of movements were performed that resulted in dancers moving from one position in the line to the next or from one line to the other.

Prior to the introduction of Playford's book, the dances of the Court had been in vogue. These dances sometimes contained intricate dance steps and suggested a romantic or flirtatious attitude on the part of the participants. To understand the significance of Playford's publication in regard to the people's choice of dances, it is necessary to investigate the conditions which prevailed in England during the early part of the seventeenth century.

Segments of England's population had been agitating for change in government. This led to civil war and the eventual beheading of the King. Prior to this event, a group of Puritans, who had been urging separation of Church and State, managed to sail to America in an attempt to set up their own government. As a result of the discontent among the people, as evidence of the desire for a government of their own, and as a sign of their rebellion, the Puritans and other sympathetic groups refused to participate in the dances of the Court, preferring the more simple English country dances. Playford, a Puritan, attempted to meet this need with his publication. Not only was this book accepted with great acclaim among England's discontended, but it also met with favor in America.

It was from this beginning that the American square dance evolved. Instead of the pomp and circumstance attending the dances of the Court and the social etiquette marked by favors given to the most prestigious persons at a dance, participants took their places in lines according to their order of arrival. Gone was the intricate, delicate footwork, and in its place was a steady, even movement of the feet to each beat of the music. The flirtatious attitude among participants of the Court dances was replaced by emphasis on movement patterns and the coordination of all dancers in an attempt to work together to effect these patterns of movement. The dance emphasized the cohesiveness of the people and stressed democracy in action. Today the American square dance is still based on these same principles.

From its beginning, the American square dance has exemplified the very ideals on which the country was founded and which its citizens have attempted to realize in the intervening years. It is the folk dance of North America, not only because it has been a part of the culture since its colonial beginnings, but also because the essence of the dance reflects the philosophy and values of its people.

In the early 1700s the French, who had also found enjoyment in the "longways," introduced the square formation. It was believed that the contra did not allow for sufficient activity or enough excitement. The French realized that they could effect similar figures that were based on the contra in the square formation, thereby assuring more activity for all participants. The new style of dance that emerged as a result of this innovation was called the *cotillion*.

The advent of the French Revolution added further innovations to the cotillion. A faster tempo and more intricate dance steps grew out of the cultural changes taking place in France at this time. People were demanding change and excitement, and they found an outlet for this in their dance.

Eventually, in the mid 1800s the cotillion no longer satisfied the people. By this time the rather short, simple movement patterns were not enough to sustain heightened interest. All facets of the culture were becoming more complicated, and thus it was inevitable that the dance should also articulate this growing complexity. It was the French who combined five to six cotillions into one dance for greater intricacy in dancing. The French *quadrille* became popular in England and America soon after its inception.

The first American innovation to the dance came with the introduction of the caller. It was the caller that set the American square dance apart from all other dances and that has provided the major justification for labelling it the American folk dance. Prior to the advent of the caller in the early 1800s (during or soon after the War of 1812) participants memorized each dance. However, with a "caller" presiding over the dance program, it was possible to perform a new, unfamiliar dance as long as one knew the "basics" or dance patterns (circle, dos-a-dos, promenade, etc.) contained in it. This change heralded a new method of learning how to dance. Sequences of basics no longer needed to be committed to memory. The patter call evolved as an adjunct to this concept. The caller would make-up dances as he or she went along. This introduced the element of anticipation that has drawn many people to the square dance over the years—that which comes from not knowing what will be called next. Participants rely on their knowledge of basics, listening ability, coordination, timing, and rhythm in order to successfully complete a dance.

In the mid to late 1800s the singing call emerged. Currently popular music was used (the practice when choreographing new dances) and a figure was developed by the choreographer in which there was an exchange of partners. This figure was constructed in such a way that if repeated three more times dancers would be back with their original partners in their home positions.

In the late 1800s the waltz, polka, and other couple-dances became overwhelmingly popular in Europe and in the eastern United States. Consequently, ballroom dancing took over as the favorite form of social dancing in the cities and the contra and square dances were eliminated from the dance program. The American square dance receded into the small towns of rural eastern United States.

Meanwhile, the American square dance had been enjoying tremendous popularity in the West. The visiting-couple figure predominated, as did reams of rhyming patter depicting life on the plains. However, by the early 1900s ballroom dancing became popular in the newly formed cities of the West, and here too, square dancing became associated with the small town, the round-ups, and the Granges.

Little change occurred in the American square dance from the early 1900s until the end of World War II. For the most part, those who participated in dancing were content to perform the dances of yesteryear. A study of the evolution of the American square dance shows that change in the dance has occurred during times of social unrest and political upheaval. Thus it was inevitable that World War II would precipitate a new style of the American square dance.

During the war, United Service Organizations, church groups, and other interested organizations presented social activities for service men and women. The square dance seemed a logical activity to inspire congenial social cohesiveness among strangers. After the war many of the young men, who had enjoyed this experience, turned to calling in order to provide home-town neighbors with a similar experience. Overnight, it seemed, the American square dance gained tremendous popularity, and with this popularity came many changes in the dance.

The wave of popularity grew in the West and quickly spread eastward. In Southern California in 1941 there were approximately ten clubs and five callers. By November 1948 there were some thirty callers and seventy-five square dance clubs. Six months later in May 1949, the number had risen to some 400 active groups in the same area.[1] By the end of 1950 there were an estimated 50,000 square dancers in Los Angeles alone and five million in the nation.

By the time the wave of popularity hit the east coast in the late 1940s and the early 1950s, a new dance style—the modern American square dance—had developed. There were few differences in dancing from one section of the country to the other. For this reason, dance historians believe it was at this point that the square dance finally emerged as the national dance—the American folk dance.

The square dance as it developed from the 1940s to the 1970s is vastly different from the square dance of the early twentieth century. From some ten or twelve basics prior to 1940, there are now over 800 basics or movements. Twenty or more new singing calls are released each month from the fifteen-odd commercial square dance record companies now in existence. A year to two years of instruction is required of participants in order to prepare for community dancing. The simple visiting-couple figure of the Western square dance is no longer performed. Instead, the line, posting, and star-thru figures are used along with the traditional circle formation. Participants learn to perform basics, not dances. They rely on their ability to listen to the calls; to coordinate their movements with each other; to time each basic correctly while dancing; to move to the beat, tempo, and phrasing of the music; and to space their steps appropriately for the various formations and basics used in the dancing.

It is estimated that some six to ten million people belong to square dance clubs in the United States. To many, square dancing takes up at least two to four evenings a month, while for others dancing two or three evenings a week is not unusual. The American folk dance knows more participants than any other national folk dance. It continually changes as the culture changes. It is a vibrant, living folk dance articulating the values of its people.

Objectives

1. To provide satisfaction and self-pride by giving to the participant a new "ability."
2. To promote gracefulness.
3. To provide an opportunity to develop coordination.
4. To help develop self-discipline.
5. To help the participant develop good timing and rhythm.
6. To provide an opportunity to learn to relax with the opposite sex.
7. To provide an opportunity to develop emotional and social values.
8. To provide an activity that will promote "togetherness and fun" for everyone.

The square dance formation

The square dance is performed by sets of four couples. The lady is always situated to the right of the man. The couple in front of the caller is One. Couple Three faces One. These two couples are the *head* couples unless otherwise designated. Couple Two is to the right of One. Couple Four is opposite Two. These two couples, Two and Four, are the *side* couples. Home position is the starting position. If a mistake is made by a couples while performing, a figure, "Square the Set," is called and all couples return to starting position.

---

[1] Robert Osgood, ed., "How Many Squares Are Dancing?", *Sets in Order,* I, No. 8, p. 7, 1949.

Relative position of partners

The lady on the man's right is always his *partner*. The lady on his left is his *corner*. The man on the lady's left is her *partner*; the man on her right is her *corner*. During the dance the man may be separated from his starting partner. If he is separated and if the word *partner* is called, he must take the lady who at that time is to his right. Partners hold hands whenever possible.

Shuffle-step

The dance should be performed in a light-footed, lively shuffle-step, with the dancers changing from one basic to another. One step is taken on each beat or count. The feet slide forward on the floor. When moving to the right as in "Circle Right," step right foot to the side, then step left foot in front of the right. Continue this sequence with toes pointed toward the center of the circle.

Composition of the square dance

basics Individual movements, for example, "Go forward and back."

phrase A number of basics making eight or sixteen counts.

figure A group of phrases, usually sixty-four counts in which the couples start at home position and return to home.

dance Enough figures to take a couple through a song.

name of square dance Usually the main figure, for example, "Ducking for the Oyster" or "Taking a Peek." The dance could be identified by the name of the music to which it is danced.

"Honor your partner" or starting the dance

The call, "Honor your partner," starts the dance: participants first bow to their corners and then to their partners.

Basics or fundamental skills of the square dance

circle 8 beats halfway, 16 beats all the way. Designated dancers join hands, turn slightly in the direction designated, and shuffle-step around. This may be to the left or to the right. The call may be for ladies, for men, or for everybody.

forward and back 8 beats or counts. Designated couples take four steps toward the center of the circle and then back out four steps.

dos-a-dos 8 counts. Partners, corners, or opposites shuffle forward, go to the right of each other past each other's right arm, go back to back, and then back out to starting position.

promenade 8 counts halfway, 16 counts all the way. Pairs take right hands as though shaking hands and position themselves side by side, facing counterclockwise with the man on the inside of the circle and the lady on the outside. The man reaches under his right arm with his left hand and grasps the lady's left hand. They then shuffle-step together around the circle.

ladies chain 8 counts. Ladies, heads or sides, shuffle across the set touching right hands as they pass each other in the center of the circle. They then extend their left hands to the men. The men take the ladies' left hands with their left hands, place their right hands on the ladies' waists and all turn counterclockwise to home and starting position.

allemande left 8 counts. The man joins his left hand or arm with whomever allemande is to be made. Both then shuffle counterclockwise around each other, back to starting position.

star 8 counts. Designated partners extend designated hands into the center of the circle and shuffle around in an inner circle one full circle, returning to starting position. Dancers may be called to do a right or left star.

right hand round the partner 8 counts. Partners face each other holding right hands and go around each other moving in a clockwise direction. Return to starting position. This basic is opposite allemande left.

grand right and left 8 counts halfway, 16 counts all the way. Partners face each other and hold right hands. They walk by each other and take opposite hand of the dancer they are facing. They advance around the circle alternating from side to side until they meet. Men go counterclockwise while ladies advance clockwise.

sashay round your corner 8 counts. Using sideward sliding steps and always facing the center, the man goes to the left, outside and around his corner, returning to his original position.

seasaw round your own 8 counts. The man uses sideward sliding steps to the right, outside and around his corner, returning to his original position.

around that couple take a peek 16 counts forward and back. Couple One faces couple Two. Couple One goes forward, splits, goes past Two, peek at each other, and then backs up to starting position. The call may be for heads or for sides to take a peek.

dive for the oyster 16 counts. First and second couples face by shuffling together. All hold hands and circle half-way to the left. Second couple joins hands and raises arms while the first couple goes four steps under and four steps back. Again all join hands and circle half-way around and back to starting position.

to balance Take two steps back from partner and curtsy.

to balance and swing Balance as above. Now take two steps forward, join hands or arms, and rotate twice around each other.

The construction of the figure

First "Bow to your corner," "Bow to your partner," and all join hands.

1. Circle to the left half-way.	8 counts
2. All go forward and back.	8 counts
3. Circle right half-way.	8 counts
4. Circle to the left all the way.	16 counts
5. Circle to the right all the way.	16 counts
6. All go forward and back.	8 counts
	64 counts

"Bow to your corner," "Bow to your partner."

1. Dos-a-dos your corner.	8 counts
2. Dos-a-dos your partner.	8 counts
3. All join hands and circle left.	16 counts
4. Heads go forward and back.	8 counts
5. Sides go forward and back.	8 counts
6. All join hands and circle right.	16 counts
	64 counts

Take a Peek

1. Circle left all the way.	16 counts
2. Heads Take a Peek round the couple on the right.	16 counts
3. Sides Take a Peek round the couple on the right.	16 counts
4. Circle right all the way.	16 counts
	64 counts

Music to square dance to

PATTER OR HOEDOWN MUSIC

The patter call is used for timing and rhythm. It usually does not have a familiar melody, and, as a rule, it is used to teach the basic skills.

SINGING CALL

The singing call music has a definite melody and there is a specific set of figures written for it. Examples of singing calls are:
Oh Johnny!
Hot Time in the Old Town Tonight
Hello, Dolly!
Cabaret
Buffalo Girls
Pop Goes the Weasel

Teaching and learning procedures

1. Explain the activity and let participants hear a recording of the fundamentals.
2. Use a blackboard, draw a "set," explain positions: home, head, sides, partner, corner.
3. Explain what is meant by "Honor Your Partner," and have students practice: bow to the corner, bow to your partner.
4. Teach the class the shuffle step. Have them perform and repeat. Stay with this until all students do this well. Have them hold hands, go forward and backward, and to the right and left in a circle.
5. Explain and demonstrate the beat or count of the square dance, and explain how square dances are phrased. Play a recording and let the class hear the beats and phrases as you count.
6. Teach each basic until all participants are familiar with the mechanics and the call, and until they react quickly.

This can best be accomplished by using one figure. A figure is a group of basics put together to make 64 beats.

REFERENCES

Modern dancing

Brown, Margaret C., and Sommer, Betty K.: Movement education: its evolution and a modern approach, Reading, Mass., 1969, Addison-Wesley Publishing Co., Inc.

Ellfeldt, Lois: A primer for choreographers, Palo Alto, Calif., 1967, National Press Books.

Hawkins, Alma M.: Creating through dance, Englewood Cliffs, N. J., 1964, Prentice-Hall, Inc.

Gates, Alice A.: A new look at movement: a dancer's view, Minneapolis, Minn., 1968, Burgess Publishing Co.

Lockhart, Aileene, and Pease, Esther, E.: Modern dance: building and teaching lessons, Dubuque, Iowa, 1966, William C. Brown Company, Publishers.

Norris, Dorothy, Koch, E., and Shiner, Reva P.: Keynotes to modern dance, Minneapolis, Minn., ed. 3, 1964, Burgess Publishing Co.

Pease, Esther E.: Modern dance. Physical education activities series, Dubuque, Iowa, 1966, William C. Brown Company, Publishers.

Sherbon, Elizabeth: On the count of one: a guide to movement and progression in dance, Palo Alto, Calif., 1968, National Press Books.

Square dancing

Hall, J. Tillman: Dance: a complete guide to social, folk and square dancing, California, 1963, Wadsworth Publishing Company.

Kraus, Richard: Square dancing of today, New York, 1954, S. S. Barnes and Company, Inc.

Piper, Ralph: Developing the creative square dance caller, Minneapolis, Minnesota, 1956.

Phillips, Patricia: Contemporary square dance, Dubuque, Iowa, 1968, William C. Brown Company, Publishers.

RECORD COMPANIES

Burns Record Company
755 Chickadee Lane
Stratford, Connecticut

Columbia Records
1413 Barnum Avenue
Bridgeport, Connecticut

Education Record Albums, David McKay Company, Inc.
119 West 40th Street
New York, New York

Folkraft Records
1159 Broad Street
Newark, New Jersey

Kimbo Educational Records
Box 55
Deal, New Jersey 07233

MacGregor
729 South Western Avenue
Hollywood, California

8 Diving

HISTORY

Diving is a form of aerial acrobatics. It is an outgrowth of tumbling. Instead of landing on a mat, the diver dives into water, either headfirst or feetfirst, and descends under the surface.

Diving into water at its beginning was more or less a form of feats, such as high dives from bridges, from flying rings suspended over a pool, or from a rope suspended from a tree branch to swing the performer far out over the water.

In 1905, diving was performed from a springboard, and it then became a competitive sport in England. At that time only a few simple dives were perfected. The dives were named after their originators, such as the Mollberg, later changed to the full gainer, and now known as the full reverse. The half reverse was first called the flying dutchman, later, the half gainer, and now is known as the reverse dive. However, competition was the needed impetus to challenge youth. During the past forty years of competition, diving has developed and has become one of the most beautiful, thrilling, and spectacular of all aerial acrobatics. It is fun and great sport.

Rules were formulated which were few and simple and are now quite generally standardized internationally. Briefly, some of these rules are as follows:

1. A dive is executed either from a standing or running position.
2. It can be performed from either a rigid platform or a springboard.
3. It must be executed in one of four body positions:
   (a) Tuck, in which the body is flexed at both hips and knees
   (b) Pike or jackknife, in which the body is flexed at the hips
   (c) Lay-out or straight dive, in which the body is held straight throughout the dive
   (d) Free, which is some combination of the other positions (usually pike and layout), used only in certain twisting dives
4. The legs must be held together at all times, with toes pointed.
5. Entry can be made either headfirst or feetfirst.
6. Competitive springboard diving must be performed from either a 1- or 3-meter height from the water.
7. Platform diving must be performed from a height of 10 meters.
8. A springboard must be either 14 feet or 16 feet in length by 20 inches in width.

ELEMENTARY DIVING TECHNIQUES (PROGRESSIVE LEARNING FOR BEGINNERS)

The beginner

Before attempting springboard diving, the beginner should first start in the shallow end of the pool, pushing off from the sidewall and gliding as far as possible on the surface, with the entire body stretched out straight, arms and legs held together, head down between the arms, and toes pointed. Note the distance of the glide.

Undersurface dive

Push off as described in the preceding paragraph, but direct the arms and head at a shallow angle toward the bottom. When nearing the bottom, turn the hands and head upward and the body will again glide to the surface.

Shallow water surface dive on handstand

Stand away from the wall in waist-deep water. Execute a light spring upward, then quickly bend at the hips (pike) and thrust and direct the arms to the bottom about 8 to 10 inches in front of where the feet were standing. Then lift the legs up over the head out of the water and balance on handstand. Give a slight push backward with the hands, and raise the head up sharply with the arms trailing at sides to regain the surface.

Deep water surface dive—pike

This dive requires considerable skill in the use of the hands and arms, since one cannot push with the feet from the bottom or sides of the pool as in the shallow water dive. But it is not too difficult for the beginner. It teaches the diver to pike with the legs straight at the knees and with the ankles stretched and held together. This is a swimming and lifesaving skill. It is performed from the surface of the water in a breaststroke swimming position.

Take a deep breath, duck the head sharply, pull the arms laterally to the hips as in the breaststroke, face the palms down and press the water downward and sweep the arms forward. When the trunk is vertical or upside-down, the body is in a jackknife position with the legs lying on the surface. Now lift the legs vertically above the hips, using the hands and arms for support. The weight of the legs above the water will weight and glide the body down toward the bottom. Tuck, place the feet on the bottom, and push up to the surface, arms trailing at the sides. Repeat several dives continuously, getting a breath above the surface between each dive.

Deep water surface dive—tuck

The deep water surface dive is performed exactly as the pike, except that the knees, as well as the hips, are bent. This teaches a closely bunched tuck for somersault dives. Note that the body turns down more easily than in the pike position.

The student should now be prepared with pool deck diving before attempting the springboard. For each of the three elementary dives from pool deck described in the next section, start at the shallow end of the pool but be sure there is sufficient depth to avoid hitting the bottom of the pool. Also, be sure that in each dive the legs are higher than the head at the instant of entry to avoid a "belly flop."

ELEMENTARY DIVING FROM POOL DECK

Sitting dive

Sit on the edge of the pool, feet on the handrail. Join thumbs, arms straight, and sight the hands at a point one body length out from the takeoff wall. Lean forward to lose sitting balance, take a deep breath through the mouth, guide the arms and hands to the desired spot, lower the head between the arms, close the eyes, and push gently with the legs until the knees are straight. Continue to hold the knees and ankles straight and the legs together. As soon as the body has entered the water, direct the hands upward toward the surface, thumbs still locked, and permit the body to glide until the momentum is spent.

At the entry, the water should hit the top of the head, not the forehead. When the head hits the water, do not let reflex bend the knees.

Standing squat dive

Stand on the edge of the deck, toes of both feet gripped over the edge of the pool deck. Assume a full squat position with the buttocks close to the heels. Extend the arms and direct them at a spot one body length out from the pool wall of takeoff, plus one head length. The eyes are only a few inches higher from the water level than from that of sitting on deck. Take a deep breath, lean forward, and push with the feet until the knees are straight, and continue as in sitting dive entry.

Standing semicrouch

Stand on the edge of the deck, toes hooked over, knees slightly bent, trunk bent over at the hips to a horizontal position. The arms are held back at hip level. Spot water at a point one body length plus one arm's length away from the takeoff wall in order to determine where you are to hit water. Raise the trunk and arms slightly by straightening the knees, take a deep breath, drop the knees, and swing the arms forward in a "pump-handle" swing. As the arms pass the knees, push with the legs. As the feet leave the takeoff, lower the head between the arms. Close the eyes for entry. Glide as far as possible. A one-knee dive from the deck is omitted because there is a danger of scraping kneeling legs on the takeoff ledge.

When diving from the pool deck is mastered in the shallow end, try the deep end of the pool. Execute the same dive as described except dive higher into the air, duck the head sharply as in a surface dive, and dive straight down to bottom. The pupil is now properly conditioned for springboard diving.

SPRINGBOARD JUMP DIVES— TECHNIQUES

Progressively the student should now advance to the next category of elementary dives, the jump dives.* All of these dives are foot-entry dives. They are first executed from a standing position at the takeoff end of the board. The student has the sensation of a springing takeoff from a slightly higher takeoff than from the side of the pool.

Front jump—straight

As the body leaves the board, the arms reach upward, shoulder width, fingers and thumbs squeezed together. The head and shoulders are pressed backward to keep the body from falling forward and to keep it aligned erect for entry. Just before the entry the arms swing down along the sides of the body. Spot water straight ahead. At takeoff lean slightly, not more than 2 or 3 degrees from the vertical. The toes stretch toward the bottom, legs straight and tightly squeezed together. When the body has entered the water, flex the feet at the ankles toward the knees to prevent an injury on the bottom of the pool. Repeat dive often for balance. (See Fig. 8-1.)

Front jump—pike

Arms reach for the ceiling as in the straight front jump. Just before the body reaches maximum height, the legs are held

---
*See Springboard diving fundamentals in Armbruster, D. A., Allen, R. H., and Billingsley, H. S.: Swimming and diving, ed. 6, St. Louis, 1973, The C. V. Mosby Co.

Fig. 8-1. Standing or running front jump dive—straight position.

Fig. 8-2. Standing or running front jump dive—pike position.

Fig. 8-3. Standing or running front jump dive—tuck position.

together straight at knees, toes pointed, but the body is flexed at the hips. The head is erect and the eyes spot straight ahead, level with the eyes. The arms are lowered to the legs, hands touching the toes. Unpike immediately and slide the hands along the legs to the side of the body for the entry. Entry is the same as in the straight front jump. This dive requires considerably more skill of balance and control to effect a vertical entry. (See Fig. 8-2.)

Front jump—tuck

This dive is easier to perform than the pike, but it teaches, nevertheless, the fundamentals of tucking and untucking. Reach high at the takeoff and, instead of piking, tuck the body. To execute this dive, the knees are brought up to the chest, and the knees and ankles are held together and the ankles extended. The arms are lowered, the hands grasping the lower legs and pulling them in so that the heels are brought toward the buttocks in a tight tuck. The hip and knee joints must be relaxed. The head is maintained erect throughout the dive, with eyes directed forward. Tuck is held until after the diver has passed the peak of height.

As legs are untucked, they shoot downward and are pressed backward in line with the trunk. The hands slide down to the sides of the body. On all foot-entry dives, the arms are to be held at the sides of the body, not overhead. (See Fig. 8-3.)

Front jump—half twist

At takeoff, the arms are reached upward and a slight twist is started with the feet as they lose contact with the board by pushing the left foot forward and the right foot backward for a twist to the right. Once airborne, the right arm remains elevated as the turning mechanics are executed with the left arm. The left arm is swung downward across and close to the chest and is pushed upward past the opposite shoulder and slightly beyond head level. As the left arm passes in front of the right shoulder, the right arm is lowered with the elbow bent and is pushed backward to square the shoulders. As the right arm is brought down across the chest, the head and eyes, which were originally spotting forward, turn with the body to the right, and the eyes focus to the rear behind the board. The entry is effected like all foot-entry dives. (See Fig. 8-4.)

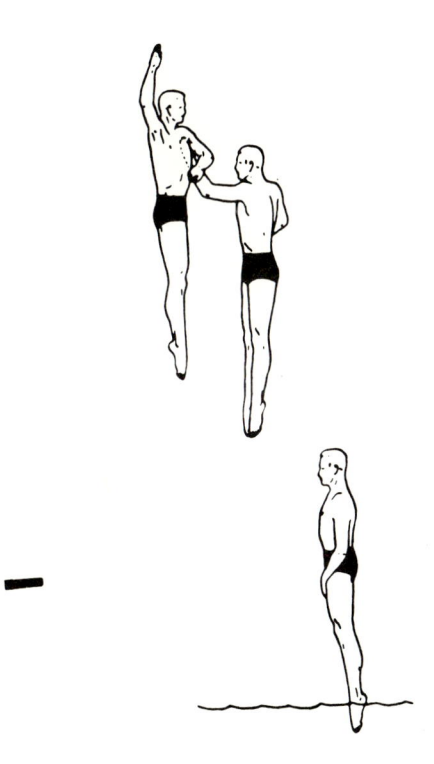

Fig. 8-4. Standing or running front jump dive with half twist to right.

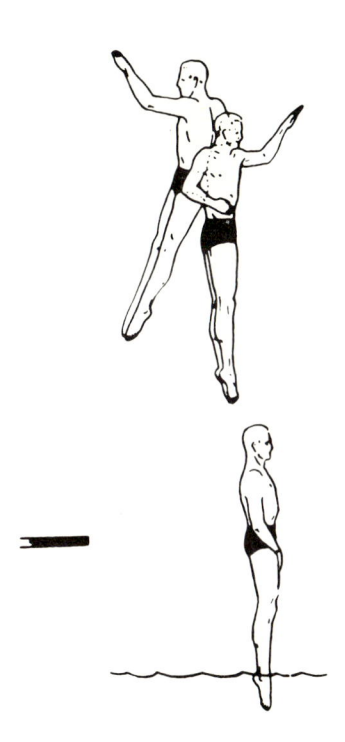

Fig. 8-5. Standing or running front jump dive with full twist to right.

Front jump—full twist

From the half twist we try the full twist. It is merely an exaggerated movement of the half twist. The success of execution depends upon an exaggerated movement of the arms as in the half twist. Also, slightly more twist is initiated from the board with the feet than in the half twist. However, in the arm action, as one half twist has been executed, the right arm is bent and brought down forcibly with the elbow pushing back behind the body. Another fundamental principle in a twist dive is to control the body balance in an erect position, that is, on the longitudinal axis, upon which it twists easily. If the body is bent or arched too much, it is difficult to execute twisting dives. (See Fig. 8-5.)

Back jump—straight

As the body leaves the board, the arms lift with the hands passing closely in front of the face. The arms are stretched upward. (See Figs. 8-6 to 8-10.) As the body jumps upward and backward from the board, the head and body must be held erect.

Fig. 8-6. Standing backward jump dive—straight position.

Fig. 8-7. Standing backward jump dive—pike position.

Fig. 8-8. Standing backward jump dive—tuck position.

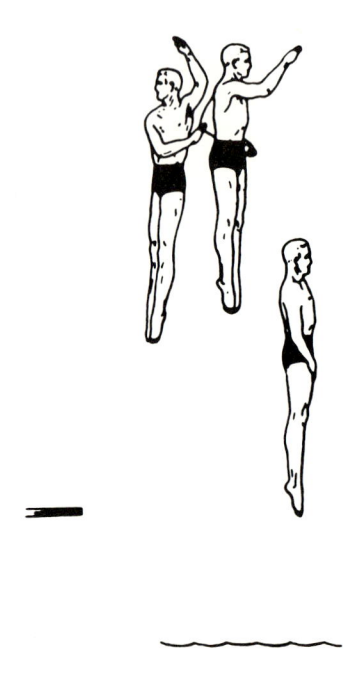

Fig. 8-9. Standing backward jump dive with half twist to left.

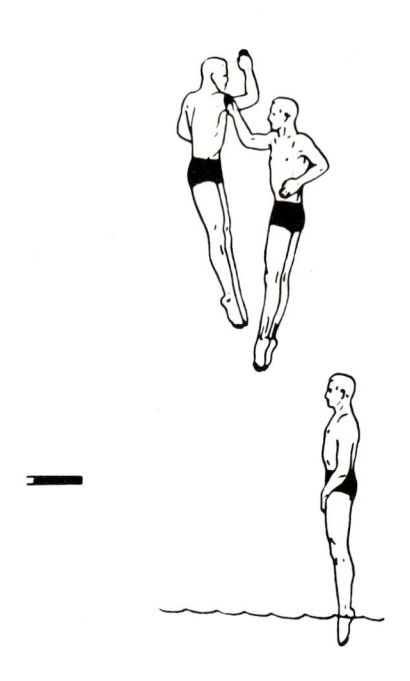

Fig. 8-10. Standing backward jump dive with full twist to left.

Avoid a falling takeoff. As the diver descends from the peak, the hands are lowered to the thighs and a vertical entry is made. The eyes should remain focused on a spot on the wall at eye level at the rear wall. The eyes then aid the body to control itself during the dive.

FUNDAMENTAL TECHNIQUES OF RUNNING SPRINGBOARD DIVING
Approach—running dive

There are many different skills to be learned in the art of diving. Two of the most essential are good body control and coordination. This means proper movement of arms in the hurdle and proper handling and straightening of knees and ankles in dropping and springing on and from the board. Obtaining adequate height above the water is one of the most essential prerequisites for becoming a good diver. The trampoline is an excellent piece of training apparatus for developing height in dives, for losing the fear of height by bounding up and down, and for maintaining balance. This same exercise can be practiced on the end of the springboard and is often called "working" the board.

The approach is a skill consisting of the stance, walk, hurdle, and takeoff.

STANCE

Assume an erect position, with the chest and chin up, stomach drawn in, and arms along the sides of the body, feet together. In this stance concentrate and measure with the eyes from the tip of the board to an imaginary point of desired height. (See Figs. 8-11 to 8-13 for the progressive stages of the approach.)

RUN OR WALK

All running dives must have at least three steps. The hurdle is not a step. Most divers prefer a four-step run with a hurdle from the third step to the end of the board. The steps should be rather quick and strong, yet natural. During the run, focus the eyes on the tip of the board until the feet are in contact with the board; then raise the eyes to a desired focal point, usually straight ahead. This is called spotting and is an im-

Fig. 8-11. Series of ideal forms for executing three-step run, hurdle, and takeoff in springboard diving.

Fig. 8-12. Series of ideal forms for executing standing takeoff—facing water.

Fig. 8-13. Series of ideal forms for executing standing takeoff—facing springboard.

portant fundamental in good diving. It aids in balance, control, and correct angle of lift or flight from the board.

The steps in the run should be natural rather than long.

HURDLE

The hurdle steps should be about 2 feet long. If one uses the four-step run, assuming, that the left foot is one's best takeoff foot, then start the run with the right foot. As one steps onto the hurdle foot, the shoulder girdle and head should pull up erect from the forward lean of the run, eyes focused on the end of the board. The hands are slightly behind the hips, fingers and thumbs straight and squeezed together. From this position the arms are lifted up above the head. The knee opposite from the takeoff leg is sharply raised to aid the takeoff leg and arm to reach maximum height in the hurdle for a longer drop onto the end of the board. Depress both ankles during the hurdle. During the drop, stretch the body straight with both legs together. Just as the feet are about to contact the board, raise the toes slightly to drop onto the balls of the feet and bend the knees. The arms are now moving downward toward the hips to aid the weight of the body in bending down the board. As the board rebounds, the diver resists it by straightening the knees and ankles. The arms are now lifting, not swinging, upward in a reaching position, aiding the legs in the takeoff for desired maximum height. Do not stomp the feet onto the board from the hurdle. Stay with the board until it is through bending down and until it rebounds. Do not hurry the leap-off. Weeks and weeks of practice are required to acquire an accurate hurdle and line of flight from the takeoff.

Height and line of flight

Height in diving is the vertical distance of the highest peak reached by the body's center of motion in the line of flight. The line of flight is the path described by the center of body weight from the takeoff to the entry. Height and correct line of flight are a natural result when the run, hurdle, and takeoff are well controlled and timed. Too much effort or muscular power in the run and takeoff will result only in jerky and unbalanced motions.

Some persons have a natural gift of springing legs and, therefore, not all divers can obtain the same height.

Entry

The point of entry of a dive should be at a spot on the surface directly under the center of body weight, on a line with the descending flight of the body, and projected downward to the bottom of the pool. The diver should go all the way to the bottom and follow this projected line of flight. Arching the body upward too soon under the surface can result in a bad back sprain.

For headfirst entries, the arms should be sharply closed several feet above the surface and held in line with the spine. The head is held between the arms so that the water hits the head on the top forehead. The legs must be stretched and closed tightly, the ankles and toes stretched and pointed in line with the legs. The feet should pass into the same hole in the surface that the head entered. The body should not be too arched at the entry.

On foot-entry dives, the body is held erect and the arms are closed snugly along the sides of the body, and the head is held erect.

GROUPS OF DIVES

In competitive diving there are five groups into which all dives are categorized.*

    Group   I—Forward dives
    Group II—Backward dives
    Group III—Reverse dives
    Group IV—Inward dives
    Group V—Twisting dives

All dives are combinations of the forward or backward dive with either a somersault or a twist in one of the straight, pike, tuck, or free positions.

*See Rules for springboard diving. Intercollegiate swimming guide and A.A.U. swimming handbook.

In learning to dive, one should begin with the most elementary of the dives in each of the groups. As these are mastered, the successively more difficult dives are attempted. The following order may be used in learning all of the required dives and a few of the most elementary of the optional dives.

Group I: Forward dive—layout

This dive is commonly known as the swan or plain front dive. It is, in reality, a half somersault. The difficulty of this dive lies in the large amount of body control required to maintain the body in good alignment throughout the flight through the air. As the feet come in contact with the board at the end of the hurdle, the eyes are lifted from the board and are focused on the front wall. The face is held directly forward until after the peak of the dive has been reached. When the diver leaves the board, the body should be stretched. The hands are lifted from the hips and are spread out to a position straight from the shoulders with a slight angle forward. A line across the upper back should follow along the top of the arms when the body is in the layout position.

The chest is pushed forward and a slight arch is formed in the lumbar or the small-of-back region. From the hips downward the body should be straight and the legs held close together with the toes pointed backward.

As the peak of the dive is reached, the body rotates forward around its center of weight, which is just above the hip joint. This rotation lifts the legs upward and levels the trunk, so that the heels are just above the head level when the body is at its peak.

The rotation continues as the body falls from the peak, and the head is slowly dropped between the arms as the eyes are shifted from the wall to the point of entry. The hands are brought close together as the vertical entry is made.

The diver should reach for the bottom as the entry into the water is made.

If the rotation at the peak has been too great, overcast of the legs can be prevented at the entry by bringing the arms together sooner for the entry. (See Fig. 8-14.)

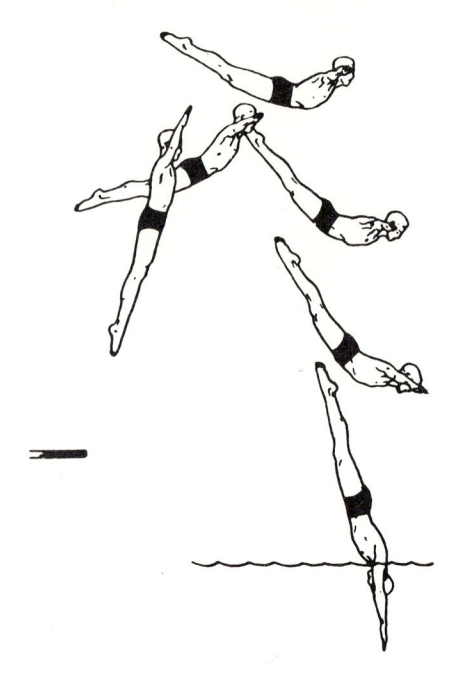

Fig. 8-14. Forward dive—layout position.

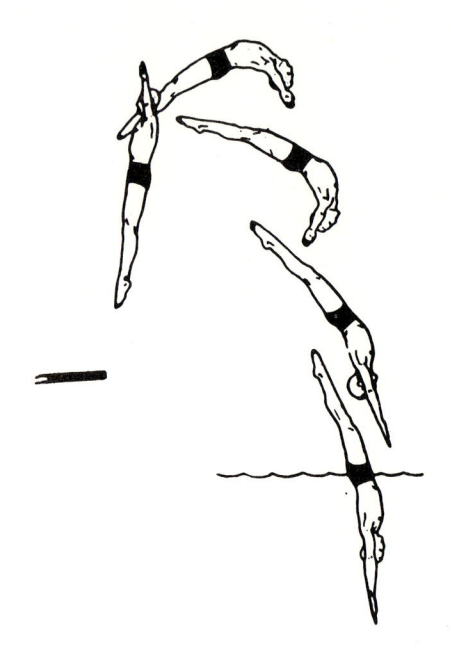

Fig. 8-15. Backward dive—layout position.

Group I: Forward dive—pike

This take off is made with the hands held close together in a modified reach. The pike is started at the end of the reach. The feet are pressed forward, the arms are depressed, and the hips are lifted above the head as the body rises into the peak of the dive. The eyes are spotted well down the course of the pool. As the peak of the dive is reached, the hands are brought into contact with the feet. The legs at this point are in a vertical position, with the toes pointing downward.

As the body drops below the peak of the dive, it has slightly rotated forward, so that its position resembles an inverted V. The legs are then lifted slowly as the body starts to open up, and the continued rotation of the body places it in a vertical position for the entry. As the legs lift upward, the arms reach forward to a position along the sides of the head, and the hands are held close together at the entry.

Common errors in executing this dive include the following:

1. The pike is not sharply formed in the hip joint but takes place in the spine.
2. The legs are not pressed forward as the hips lift toward the peak of the dive.
3. In unpiking, the hands follow the legs back too far, giving the body too much rotation forward with loss of entry control.

Group II: Backward dive—layout

Although the backward takeoff dives are blind dives, they are easy to perform since the body is simply levered backward and additional movements are then made.

As the body lifts from the board in the backward dive, layout, the eyes are first focused overhead. The arms reach upward and slightly backward and are spread in line with the back of the spine. At the height of the lift, when the head is about at the peak of the dive, the head is stretched backward and the eyes begin to look for the entry spot in the water behind the diver.

During this head and arm action, the hips and legs should be lifted and the knees and ankles must be stretched. The arms are brought together when the body has dropped to a point opposite the board and the entry is made with the hands close together and the head between the arms. (See Fig. 8-15.)

Group III: Reverse dive—layout

As the body drops onto the board preliminary to the takeoff for this dive, the weight should remain over the toes and the diver should not shift the weight backward as the heels contact the board. As the board lifts the diver, the center of the body weight (in the hips) should be shifted to a position just in front of the base of support (balls of feet), so that the body is easily projected forward and upward.

The reverse dive is one of the most graceful of all dives. It is, essentially, a backward dive from a forward takeoff. The diver actually gains distance in a forward direction; thus, the name "gainer" or "reverse" is given to it.

At the takeoff, the arms lift to a spread position and the eyes focus overhead. At the end of the lift from the takeoff, the head, arms, and shoulders are levered backward and the chest, hips, and legs are lifted, as well as stretched. When the body reaches the horizontal position at the peak, the legs remain lifted as if anchored since the backward rotation causes the head and shoulders to drop. The arms are closed, the head is brought between the arms at board level, and the body is straightened as it drops in a vertical entry. (See Fig. 8-16.)

Group IV: Inward dive—pike

While the body is poised over the end of the board, the center of weight is over the balls of the feet. During the preliminary arm movements of the takeoff, the center of weight moves vertically, but should not move forward or backward.

At the lift from the board, the arms are raised to a moderate reach above the head and in front of the face. Palms are facing forward and are slightly depressed.

At the end of the reach, the hips are flexed and raised, the arms are brought forward and downward, and the hands touch the front of the feet at the peak. The hips have lifted above the head to the peak of the dive. The legs are vertical when the pike is effected. The eyes focus on the touch at the peak of the dive, and then shift to the water for the entry.

The body is held piked for a small rotation as it falls a short distance from the peak, and it is then unpiked quickly.

As the body drops to the vertical entry,

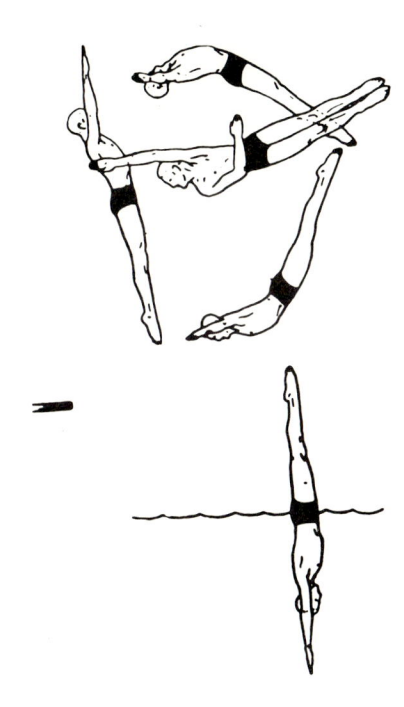

Fig. 8-16. Reverse dive—layout position shown with one-half twist.

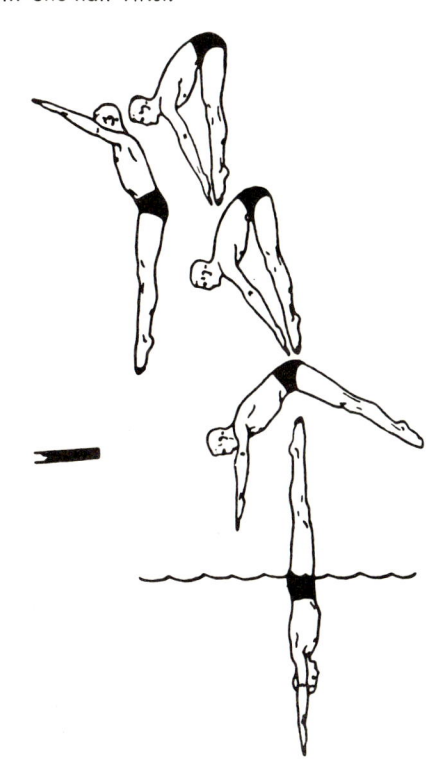

Fig. 8-17. Inward dive, backward spring (back jackknife)—pike position.

the arms reach forward and stretch toward the bottom of the pool while the hips and legs are straightened in a well-controlled movement. (See Fig. 8-17.)

Group V: Forward dive, half twist—layout

The takeoff is somewhat similar to the front jump, half twist in that the twist is initiated from the board by the feet. The arms are spread to a Y position as the body lifts into the reach. To twist to the right, as the diver is ascending, the left arm and shoulder are rotated forward while the head remains stationary with the eyes focused forward. As the diver rotates in a somersaulting direction the water should come into view directly below the left hand. (See second position in Fig. 8-18.) The right shoulder is raised and the arm is pressed backward firmly. The arms move as though the hands were grasping and turning a large steering wheel counterclockwise. The legs constantly bear upward during the twist and the drop of the trunk.

The head should not resist the downward movement of the dive by pulling backward, but should be allowed to follow the downward rotation movement. Once the eyes spot the point of entry, they should not lose sight of it. Following this rule aids in obtaining the necessary arch to rotate the body.

The hands are closed slowly above the head, and the arms are pressed to the ears as the body is straightened for the headfirst vertical entry. (See Fig. 8-18.)

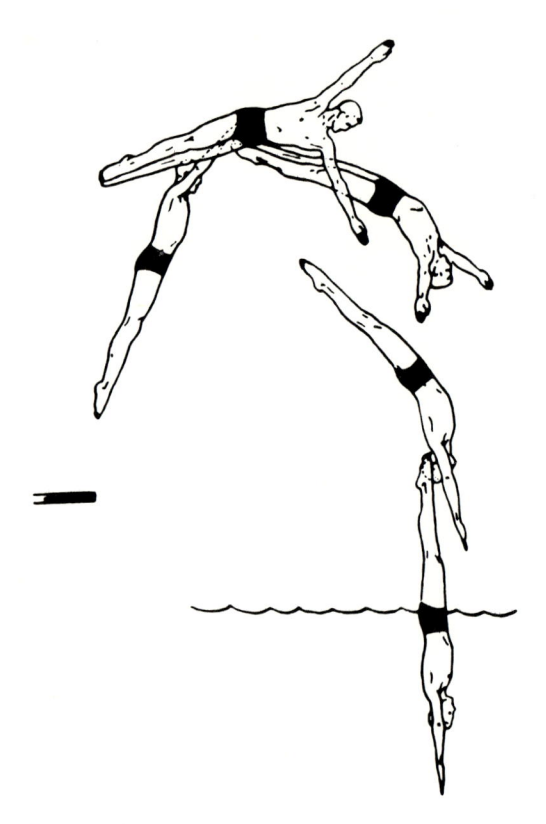

Fig. 8-18. Forward dive, half twist—layout position.

Group I: Forward somersault— tuck or pike

The body leaves the board in the same manner for both the forward somersault tuck and pike. The somersaulting rotation of the diver is produced from a shortening of the radius by tucking or piking.

In the tuck, the heels are brought toward the buttocks while the diver bends at the knees and waist, and grabs the legs with the hands. This position is not held too long as the tucking action causes a rapid acceleration in the rotation of the body. As the body reaches a position in which the diver's back is approximately parallel with the water, the legs are extended. This produces a "sitting

Fig. 8-19. Forward somersault—tuck position.

Fig. 8-20. Forward somersault—pike position.

in air" appearance as shown in diagram 4 of Fig. 8-19. Complete extension follows with the entry being the same as for all feet-first dives.

In pike, the actions are the same except that the body is bent at the waist only and the pike should be held slightly longer than the tuck since the velocity of the rotation is slightly less.

The angle of entry can be adjusted in both dives by remaining either tucked or piked or by opening, and this adjustment is learned quickly with practice. (See Figs. 8-19 and 8-20.)

Group II: Backward somersault—tuck

The tuck is made soon after the upward and backward reach so that the body is tucked at the peak of the dive. The tuck is made by lifting the knees to the chest, and the hips follow behind this action to get the desired continuous rotation.

During the turn the diver should concentrate on the center of rotation. Again, as in the forward somersault group of dives, in

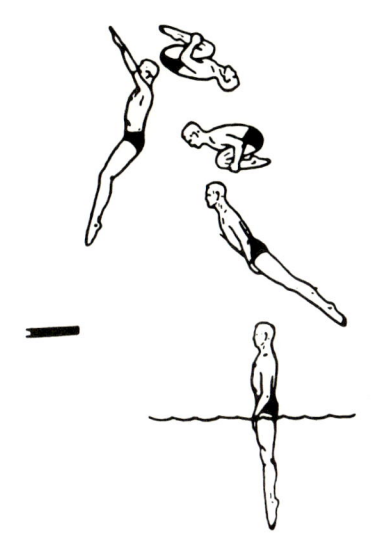

Fig. 8-21. Backward somersault—tuck position.

order to effect speed and balance during the rotation, the diver must be constantly aware of the dominating angular movement of the hips.

When the chest is horizontal to the surface and well above the board, the legs are thrust to full extension and the toes are kept pointed. The head and shoulders are made erect so that the body is perfectly aligned at the entry.

As the body is opened, the eyes can focus on the board until the entry is made. The hands simply slide from the shins to the front of the thighs. (See Fig. 8-21.)

Group III: Reverse somersault—tuck

At the takeoff, the eyes are focused upward and the reach is made slightly in back of vertical. The arms will move forward slightly in reaction to the legs coming toward the chest when going into tuck position (See diagram 1 of Fig. 8-22). The tuck is held until the chest is parallel to the water, at which time the legs are thrust out, the hands ride up the legs to the thighs, and the body is readied for a feet-first entry. (See Fig. 8-22.)

Group V: Forward dive, full twist—layout

The diver leaves the board as in the forward dive, half twist layout. If the twist is toward the right, the left arm cuts in across the hip and bears downward. This movement

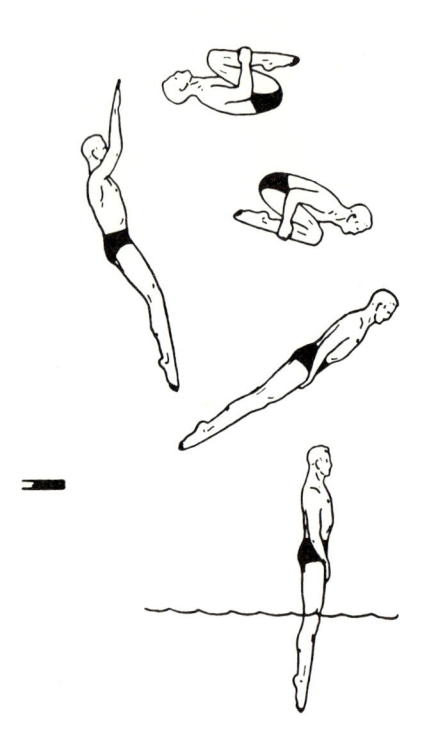

Fig. 8-22. Full reverse somersault—tuck position.

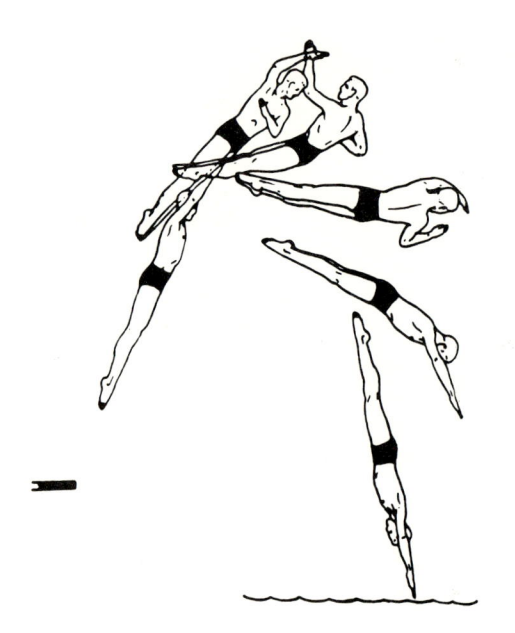

Fig. 8-23. Full twist forward dive—layout position.

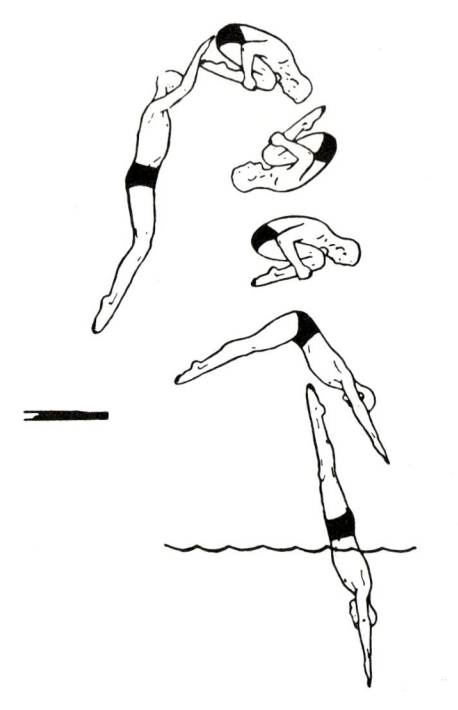

Fig. 8-24. Forward one and one-half somersault—tuck position.

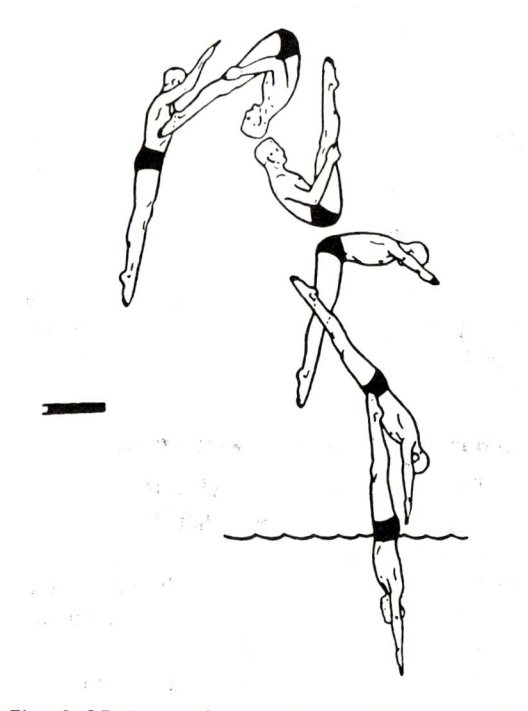

Fig. 8-25. Forward one and one-half somersault—pike position.

lowers the left shoulder. The right arm is bent at the elbow and is moved behind the head. The legs bear upward during the whole movement. A quarter twist is started and the eyes hold a spot on the point of entry until the twist is far enough to pull the head away. The half twist has been made during the ascent to the peak, and the diver is now in a horizontal position. The twist is fairly rapid and is continuous.

The head is now turned sharply to the right as the right elbow drives backward and the eyes spot the water at the point of entry. The left arm is then extended toward the point of entry and the right arm joins the left in stretching toward the vertical entry. This stretching action should be emphasized in this dive since it squares the body so that the hips and shoulders are straightened at the entry.

All movements in this dive should center around the longitudinal axis of the diver. Movements of the shoulders must be loose in order to avoid any lateral action caused by strained movements of the arms.

A common error in performing this dive is a failure to bear the legs upward during the twisting movements. (See Fig. 8-23.)

Group I: Forward one and one-half somersault—tuck

This dive is very similar to the forward somersault, tuck, with the exception that an additional half forward somersault rotation is made while the body is in the tuck position.

The tuck is entered at the end of the reach, the hips are lifted, and the head and shoulders are depressed. The heels are brought sharply to the buttocks. The chin is tucked in as the head is brought toward the knees and the back is rounded. The tuck starts to open when the body is horizontal on the one and one-fourth turn. The legs are extended and press backward as the hips are moved forward to straighten the body. This elongation of the longitudinal axis decreases the speed of rotation.

The arms reach for the point of entry and the body slides down the parabolic line of trajectory and into the water. (See Figs. 8-24 and 8-25.)

REFERENCES

Armbruster, D. A., Allen, R., and Billingsley, H. S.: Swimming and diving, ed. 6, St. Louis, 1973, The C. V. Mosby Co.

Billingsley, Hobie: Illustrated diving, New York, 1966, The Ronald Press Co.

Official N.C.A.A. swimming guide (issued annually), New York, The National Collegiate Athletic Association.

Official N.S.W.A. aquatic guide, Washington, D. C. (latest edition), American Association for Health, Physical Education, and Recreation.

FILMS

Elementary to advanced swimming, American Red Cross, Washington, D. C.

Aquatics artistry, Teaching Films Custodians, Inc., New York, N. Y.

Fundamentals of diving, Norman Sper, Hollywood, Calif.

Springboard champions, Teaching Films Custodians, Inc., New York, N. Y.

Springboard diving, Bell and Howell Co., Lincolnwood, Ill.

9 Fencing

HISTORY

Fencing is defined as the "art of fence," both offensively and defensively. It was originated as a form of deadly combat before the Christian Era and has continued as such for more than 2000 years.

Fencing has a fascinating and exciting history. It had its beginning with a crudely shaped spear in the hands of men as a deadly weapon in war, similar to that of the bow and arrow. The invention of gun powder ended its use as a weapon of war, which was also true of the bow and arrow. Later, gentlemen and nobility dueled to the death to avenge an insult or to restore honor that had been smudged in one way or another.

In the fourteenth century the Germans first attempted to make dueling a sport as well as a fight to the death. It made little headway, but it did point the way to developing fencing as a sport during the fifteenth and sixteenth centuries.

Different swords and sabers were devised by the Italians, French, and Germans down through the years to the modern-day foil, épée, and saber. Schools of instruction in fencing flourished in all European countries. The early, heavier sword was replaced by a lighter weapon to obtain greater speed, dexterity, and precision. Surprisingly enough, this formerly deadly combat was converted into an excellent and popular modern sporting event of skill and precision.

Fencing is an excellent event in the combative category of sports skills which is important in the modern program of physical education. It is also well adapted for the physically handicapped (even amputees). Age is no barrier. It is an excellent coeducational activity and therefore ranks very high socially.

Women are limited to one weapon, the foil, while men have a choice of three weapons: the foil, épée, and saber.

The purpose of the sport of fencing is to hit, or score a clean touch, on an opponent without being hit oneself.

In America, fencing other than intercollegiate is controlled by the A.F.L.A. (Amateur Fencers' League of America).

EQUIPMENT

1. Competition uniforms (light canvas jacket for foil fencing, heavy jacket for the dueling sword, very heavy jacket for the saber)
2. Mask to protect the face and neck
3. Pigskin gloves
4. Foil
5. Épée

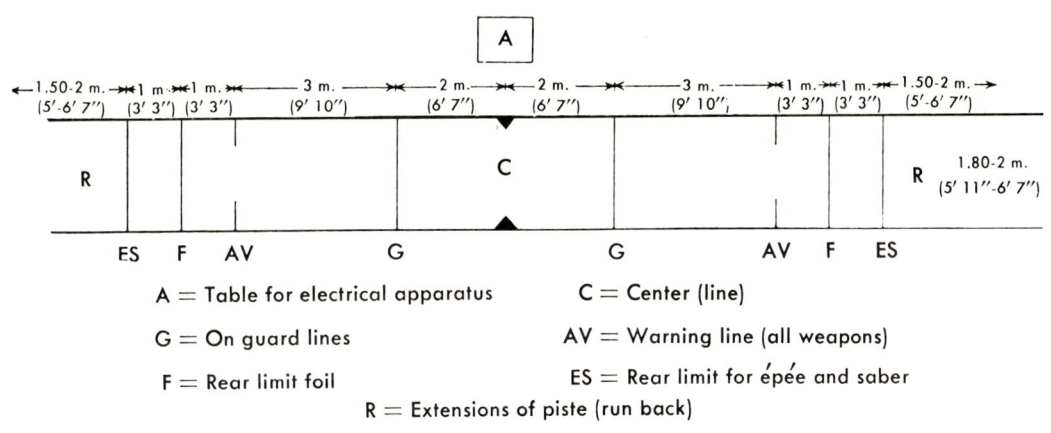

FENCING 107

Fig. 9-1. Regulation piste for all three weapons. (Excerpted from AFLA Fencing Rules and Manual.)

A = Table for electrical apparatus
G = On guard lines
F = Rear limit foil
C = Center (line)
AV = Warning line (all weapons)
ES = Rear limit for épée and saber
R = Extensions of piste (run back)

For electric foil and épée the metallic piste must cover the whole of the length and breadth of the piste, including its extensions (run back)
Note: Measurements given to nearest inch, the distance from ES to AV is 6' 7"

6. Saber
7. Mats: The strip or piste on which the bouts take place, between 5 feet, 10⅞ inches and 6 feet, 6¾ inches wide and 40 feet in length; three parallel lines to be drawn across the strip—one in exact center, the other two warning lines at a point 3 feet, 3⅜ inches from the ends. (See Fig. 9-1.)
8. Tennis shoes and gymnasium costume satisfactory for class use

For schools, about 20 to 25 foils and an equal number of masks are sufficient to conduct class instruction.

MODERN FENCING WEAPONS
The foil

The foil is the basic weapon of fencing. It is a thrusting weapon. Its maximum weight is 17.637 ounces and its maximum length is 43.307 inches. It is rectangular and tapers out from the guard to a very thin, flexible upper section toward the buttonlike tip, which must be covered with a single layer of adhesive tape. The guard is circular and concave for protection to the hand. The grip handle may be wooden, cordwrapped, or molded metal. (See Fig. 9-2, *1*.)

The target in foil fencing includes any portion of the trunk from the collar to the

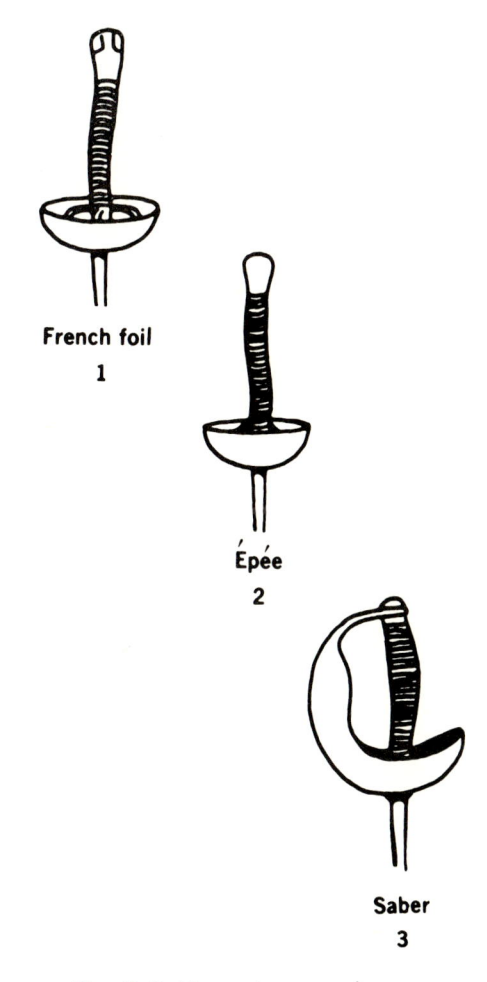

French foil
1

Épée
2

Saber
3

Fig. 9-2. The various swords.

groin lines in front or to a horizontal line passing across the tops of the hip bones in the back. For women, the lower limit of the target, both front and back, is the hip bone line. Touches, to be valid, must arrive on the target clearly and cleanly with the point and in accordance with certain convictions, or rules of order, frequently called "right-of-way," or privilege of attack. The attacker is said to have the right-of-way. A successful parry gains for the defendant the right-of-way. When both fencers are hit simultaneously, the touch is awarded to the one who has the right-of-way. Touches scored on the head, arms, or legs are called "foul" but carry no penalty other than halting the bout. The contestant who first scores 5 touches against his opponent within 10 minutes wins the bout in men's competition. For women, 4 touches constitute the bout. A women's bout lasts 5 minutes.

The first person scoring the winning number of points, 4 for the women and 5 for the men, wins the bout. If the time runs out and the score is tied, the tie score is carried over into the second bout, and the one completing the necessary number of points is the winner. If the time runs out and neither contestant scores the winning point, the one with most points wins by the number of points with which the lead is held at the end of the bout.

The épée

The épée, or dueling sword, is also a thrusting weapon. It is more pointed, heavier, and more rigid than the foil. It weighs 27.16 ounces and has a maximum length of 43.307 inches.

The target for épée dueling includes every portion of the body. A bout is won by the first contestant scoring 3 touches. (See Fig. 9-2, *2*.)

The saber

The saber is a pointed weapon with cutting edges along the entire front and one-third of the back of the blade. Cuts and countercuts as well as thrusts are valid.

The saber has a maximum weight of 17.637 ounces and a maximum length of 41.338 inches. (See Fig. 9-2, *3*.)

The saber target includes all portions of the body, including the head, arms, and hands, above a horizontal line drawn through the greater trochanter (hip bone).

ABRIDGED RULES OF FENCING
Scoring

Individual competition: The individuals usually compete on a round-robin basis.

Team competition: In intercollegiate team competion, a team consists of nine men, three using each of the three weapons. Each contestant fences a bout with each of the three opponents in the same weapon, making a total of twenty-seven bouts.

Officiating contests

1. The contests are ruled by a jury of five officials, of which one is the director and four are judges. In addtion there is a scorer.
2. The director is in charge of the bouts and stands an equal distance from each contestant, usually about 4 meters back from the strip on which the bouts are staged.
3. The director advises the fencers when to be ready with a call "on guard," starts action with a call "play," and ends it with "halt."

Contestant rules

1. In all types of fencing bouts the idea is to wound or touch an opponent with the sword without being touched.
    (a) The attack may be directed toward any one of four quadrants and the defender is therefore called upon to make different parries (decisive blocks or guards). The attacks are aimed above or below the level of the elbow of the weapon arm and inside or outside the arm.
    (b) General: Because of the rapid action and exchange of sword play in competition, certain rules of orderly sequence have been established in order to control them.
2. An offensive action should be executed with an extension of the sword and

sword arm toward the opponent's target. If such an extension is executed ahead of any such action by the defense, it takes the right-of-way and must be parried before any counteraction may be taken.

3. A slow extension out of line or withdrawal of the point or arm will result in loss of the right-of-way, provided that the defender responds by an immediate and timely counterextension of the sword and arm. Any improper extension against a properly executed attack has no rights in the event the attack scores. Whenever an attack is parried successfully, the defender takes the right to execute a counteraction. Following the successful parry of a riposte (return), the original attacker then retakes the right-of-way for counterripostes.

4. In order to minimize what may seem to be confusing rule technicalities, the student should carefully study the basic techniques of fencing and apply them to the rules of technical sequence and right-of-way regulations for competitive fencing.

FUNDAMENTAL SKILL TECHNIQUES OF FENCING

In fencing, as in many other skill sports, the student must acquire not only eye-hand coordination, but also the technique of the use of the body, legs, feet, arms, and hands, and must coordinate them skillfully into the use of the weapon in hand. In addition, the student must also acquire a keen sense of distance, speed, force, and precision in all movements.

The grip

The convex side of the curve of the handle should be placed in the palm at the heel of the thumb. The thumb is placed on the top of the broad surface of the handle close to the circular guard. The tip of the index finger is placed on the opposite side of the handle, so that the foil is controlled between the thumb and forefinger. The other three fingers curl around the three sides of the handle so that the tips rest on the concave surface and press the handle firmly against the base of the thumb. The wrist is held slightly flexed so that the flat of the pommel rests flat against the wrist in such a manner that the sword will form a direct straight line of extension with the forearm. (See Fig. 9-3.)

Fig. 9-3. The grip.

Fig. 9-4. Front and side views of on guard position.

On guard

On guard position in fencing is similar to that in boxing. The on guard position is designed to give the greatest balance and efficiency in performing either offensive or defensive movements in advancing, retreating, or directly attacking. The body in this position also offers the smallest possible target.

Using the proper grip, the sword arm is extended toward the opponent, the elbow flexed in an obtuse angle and held closely in line with the body. The hand is about level with the lower sternum, the sword pointing slightly upward, directly toward the opponent. (See Fig. 9-4.)

To assume this position the feet are apart and at right angles to each other, heels in line. The feet are approximately 1 foot apart. The body weight is distributed evenly over both feet. The knees are bent so that they extend over the instep of the foot. The torso is held erect with the right side and right toe facing the opponent. The head is erect and turned to face the opponent. The left arm is raised behind so that the upper arm is horizontal, the forearm vertical, and the hand completely relaxed behind the head.

Advance and retreat

Advancing and retreating in fencing are the fundamental and basic movements from the guard position. They are identical to the advance and retreat in boxing. To advance, the (right) forward foot is first moved forward and the rearmost (left) foot follows. To retreat, the rear (left) foot is moved back and then the forward (right) is moved back. The steps are short, varying from a few inches to about 1 foot. The on guard position of the legs is always to be maintained. The purpose of the advance movement is to get within attacking distance of an opponent, and the purpose of the retreat is to get out of reach of an opponent.

Another advancing step used is a jump, called the balestra. In this jump, both feet leave the floor at the same time, with the right foot slightly ahead, and come in contact with the floor at the same time. In the retreat jump the right foot lands slightly before the left and in the correct on guard position.

The lunge

The lunge is one of the most important actions in fencing. It is a method used to reach an opponent with the tip of the foil to make a touch. It is executed from the guard position and is preceded by an extension of the sword arm, followed by lunging with the foremost leg while the rear foot holds in place. If well executed with speed and precision, at the right moment in a bout, it is very likely to make possible a score on an opponent.

Execute the extension of the weapon arm as quickly as possible without locking the elbow. Do not rotate the wrist or hunch the shoulders. The body should be held erect, not leaning. Simultaneously with the lunge, the left arm is extended fully to the rear for balance. (See Fig. 9-5.)

Fig. 9-5. The lunge.

Recovery from lunge

To recover to the guard position, bend the left leg and simultaneously push back with the right. Bring the right foot back quickly to the guard position. Try not to raise the body during recovery, but remain low.

It is sometimes necessary to recover forward to take up ground given by the opponent when retreating from a lunge. This action simply involves bringing up the rear foot to the on guard position. This enables the attacker to defend if the attack has failed, to attack again, or to retreat if the opponent counterattacks.

SIMPLE ATTACKS

A simple attack is a single movement without feint or previous threat to the opponent's target. There are three main types: the straight thrust, the disengage, and the cutover or coupe.

The straight thrust

The straight thrust is simply the lunge as already described.

The disengage

The disengage is a simple method of engaging the foil in the opposite line from that in which it is originally engaged. It is accomplished by passing the point under the opponent's blade to the opposite line of engagement, after extending the arm. The movement is semicircular and is executed by the wrist and fingers. The foil is kept close to the opponent's blade at all times. This attack is usually followed by a lunge to score. During a bout, fencers are continuously trying to keep their opponents in a closed line while trying for an opportunity in an open line.

The disengage is used as an attack in an effort to hit the target in an open line.

The cutover or coupe

This simple method of attack is exactly the opposite of the disengage, since the point is passed over the top of the opponent's blade. It is another method of changing the line of engagement. It is principally used when an opponent has lowered the weapon or uses pressure with the weaker leverage of the blade nearer the tip of the foil against the strong part of the attacker's blade. It is easier then to cutover and to disengage to pass under. The action is executed by sharply lifting the top of the foil over the opponent's foil, using the fingers, wrist, and forearm. The arm is extended as the foil goes downward and forward to the target to score, followed immediately by a recovery.

COMPOUND ATTACKS

Compound attacks are known as attacks on the blade. The purpose is to knock the defending blade aside and control it. These attacks are accomplished by several methods.

The beat

The beat is a quick, sharp blow of the middle of the blade on the weak part of the opponent's blade for the purpose of making an opening or feint before an attack.

The press

The press is made when an opponent's grip is weak or tiring, and it has the same purpose as the beat. It is executed by simply bringing pressure to bear on the opponent's blade with the arm in the normal guard position.

The pressure glide

The pressure glide is a quick, sudden pressing down on the opponent's blade and gliding the foil into the target for a score.

Combinations

Combinations are made using the attacks described with one or more disengages.

DEFENSE

Parries are movements of defense executed by the blade and guard to either block or divert the blade of the opponent's offensive action at the target so that a touch is avoided. All parries are executed by the fingers and wrist with just enough movement to catch the opponent's blade and prevent a thrust to the target. Always parry with the strong base of the blade, not with the weak tip of the blade. A successful parry takes the right-of-way from the offensive and permits an immediate counterattack.

There are two simple parries for each position: (1) the opposition parry, which maintains pressure against the opponent's blade until the return, and (2) the beat parry, which is a sharp, light tap against the opponent's blade with a return to the on guard position.

The target is divided in half, at breast level, into high and low lines of defense. In the high line the point of the foil points at or above eye level. In the low line the point is at the level of the knee. These positions of the sword will give sufficient leverage to deviate the attacking blade to one side or the other.

The sword hand must protect four areas: the inside-high, inside-low, outside-high, and outside-low. (See Fig. 9-6.) This gives eight parries in their terminal position, where the hand is either pronated or supinated:

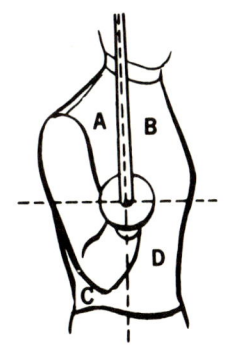

Fig. 9-6. Four areas to be protected by sword.

1. First defends the inside-high line, *B*, hand pronated.
2. Second defends the outside-low line, *C*, hand pronated.
3. Third defends the outside-high line, *A*, hand pronated.
4. Fourth defends the inside-high line, *B*, hand supinated.
5. Fifth defends the inside-low line, *D*, hand pronated.
6. Sixth defends the outside-high line, *A*, hand supinated.
7. Seventh defends the inside-low line, *D*, hand supinated.
8. Eighth defends the outside-low line, *C*, hand supinated.

THINGS TO REMEMBER

Fencing weapons are used quite differently from weapons in other sports. In fencing, the weapon is used for thrusting rather than for hitting or swinging. Thus, it is very essential for the beginner to learn the fundamental skills because they will not be skills that beginners ordinarily are accustomed to or carry-overs from other sports. Fencing is a game of leverage. The defender uses the strong part of the weapon against the weak part of the attacker's blade.

Practice positions, movements, and footwork.

Study the rules carefully.

TEACHING AND LEARNING PROCEDURES

1. History
2. Description of equipment
3. Grip
4. On guard position
5. Call (appel)
6. Advance and retreat
7. Lunge
8. Combination of Advance and retreat with the lunge
9. Explanation of the target:
    (a) Its divisions
    (b) The lines of engagement
    (c) The position of engagement
10. Lunging for a touch in each of the four divisions:
    (a) On wall target
    (b) On opponent without defense
11. Direct attack in high 4 and the parry of 4
12. Direct attack in high 6 and the parry of 6
13. Direct attack in low 6 and the parry of 2
14. Direct attack in low 4 and the parry of 7
15. All four direct attacks and parries
16. Disengage in the high line and parries of 4 and 6
17. Disengage from 4 to low 6 and parry of 2
18. Disengage from 6 to low 4 and parry of 7
19. All four disengages and parries
20. Short bouts of direct and single disengage attacks with one fencer defending, the other attacking, and vice versa
21. Beat
22. Beat combined with disengage
23. Cutover
24. Cutover combined with disengage
25. Riposte
26. Short bouting periods employing all skills learned
27. Counter
28. Press
29. Glide
30. Stop thrust

GLOSSARY OF FENCING TERMS

advance Moving forward on an opponent to gain ground and attack.

attack Moving forward on an opponent, attempting to score a hit.

attack of second intention An attack that is intended to be parried, so that the attacker may parry the return and score on the counterattack.

attack on the blade The beat, pressure, and glide attacks used to deviate the defensive weapon point.

balestra or jump lunge A forward movement employing a jump before the lunge.

benefit of the doubt When two side judges disagree and the director has no opinion, no score is awarded.

blade parts:
  strong Near the guard, parrying surface.
  middle Midsection of the blade.
  weak Near tip end, weakest leverage for force to be exerted.

bout A contest between two individuals.

call Signal given by director of the bout to call fencers on guard.

pass A hit that does not touch validly (would not inflict a puncture or penetrating wound).

retreat To move backward, to open the distance from an opponent.

right-of-way Established by a fencer who first extends the weapon arm with point in line of attack.

remise Following an attack, the defender delays the riposte. The attacker, without recovering from the lunge, may merely move the sword so that the point is replaced in the target area.

riposte or return An offensive action after a successful defense; it may be a simple or compound return.

touch A hit on the target which would puncture or wound if weapons were pointed.

REFERENCES

Amateur Fencers' League of America: Fencing rules, New York, 1971, The League.

Castello, Hugo, and Castello, James: Fencing, New York, 1962, The Ronald Press Co.

De Beaumont, Charles: Fencing: ancient art and modern sport, New York, 1966, A. S. Barnes & Co., Inc.

Garret, Maxwell, Fencing, New York, 1961, Sterling Publishing Co., Inc.

Official bowling, fencing, and golf rules and guide, Washington, D. C., 1973-1975, AAHPER, Division for Girls' and Women's Sports.

Sports illustrated book of fencing. New York, 1971, J. B. Lippincott Co.

Vince, Joseph: Fencing, New York, 1962, A. S. Barnes & Co.

FILMS

Basic training of foil fencing, 22 min., University of California Extension Film Center, Berkeley, Calif.

Instruction film on fencing, 400 ft., Castello Fencing Equipment Co., New York, N. Y.

Instructional films on fencing, 400 ft., Castello Fencing Equipment Co., New York, N. Y.

Techniques of foil fencing, United World Films, New York, N. Y.

Techniques of foil fencing, 10 min., University of California Extension Film Center, Berkeley, Calif.

Theory of foil fencing, Castello Fencing Equipment Co., New York, N. Y.

10 Field hockey

HISTORY

Field hockey is undoubtedly the oldest sports game played with a stick and ball. About 2500 years ago, the early Greeks and other ancient nations played a game very similar to our present-day hockey. Some centuries later it was found that the game was being played in France and was called "hoquet." Then the English liked the game and began to play it under the name of "hokay." The French pronounced "hoquet" as we would pronounce hockey. The game became generally known as hockey by its English spelling and pronunciation. However, later when ice hockey, a similar game played on ice, became popular, the game of hockey was called field hockey, and so it remains today.

Between 1880 and 1890 field hockey was played exclusively by men in England, France, and other European countries and is still very popular with them. In the United States, men tried the game but it met with little favor.

A group of women, who formerly lived in England, formed the Livingston Association on Staten Island about this time, but it was short-lived.

Then in 1901, Constance M. K. Applebee, of the British College of Physical Education, demonstrated the game of field hockey during a visit to the Harvard summer school. She recommended it as a health-building form of combative recreation for college women.

Miss Applebee was then invited to several eastern women's colleges (Smith, Vassar, Wellesley, Bryn Mawr, and Mount Holyoke), and on each campus field hockey was accepted with high favor. Women's teams were formed and the first interclass contest was held in 1902.

The women enjoyed the game so much and became so vitally interested in it that they adopted it and revised the rules to make them uniform and suitable for women's play. In 1920, an American women's team traveled to England, and later, an English team visited the United States to play games in Philadelphia, New York, Boston, and Baltimore, thereby establishing field hockey as an international game.

In 1922, the United States Field Hockey Association was formed in Philadelphia to govern the sport for women, its purpose being to stimulate more enthusiasm for and advance the best interests of hockey for women and girls. The game's popularity spread rapidly among schools, colleges, and clubs.

In 1927, this widespread interest throughout the world brought about an International Federation of Women's Hockey Associations, and tournaments were held in Philadelphia and Denmark. In July of 1950, another such tournament was held in South Africa with representative teams from England, Australia, New Zealand, Wales, Ireland, Scotland, South Africa, and the United States.

In 1963, the United States Field Hockey Association (USFHA) played hostess to eighteen of the twenty-five nations which are members of the International Federation of Women's Hockey Associations (IFWHA). Plans have been made for this Federation to meet on a four-year basis for conference games and discussion of international rules and hockey problems.

The Field Hockey Association of America is the rules governing body for men's play.

GENERAL DESCRIPTION

Field hockey is played by two teams of eleven players each. Only the goalkeeper is permitted certain kicking privileges. All other players may use only the stick to play the ball.

The game is started at the center of the field with the "center." The ball is then moved toward the goal only by the use of

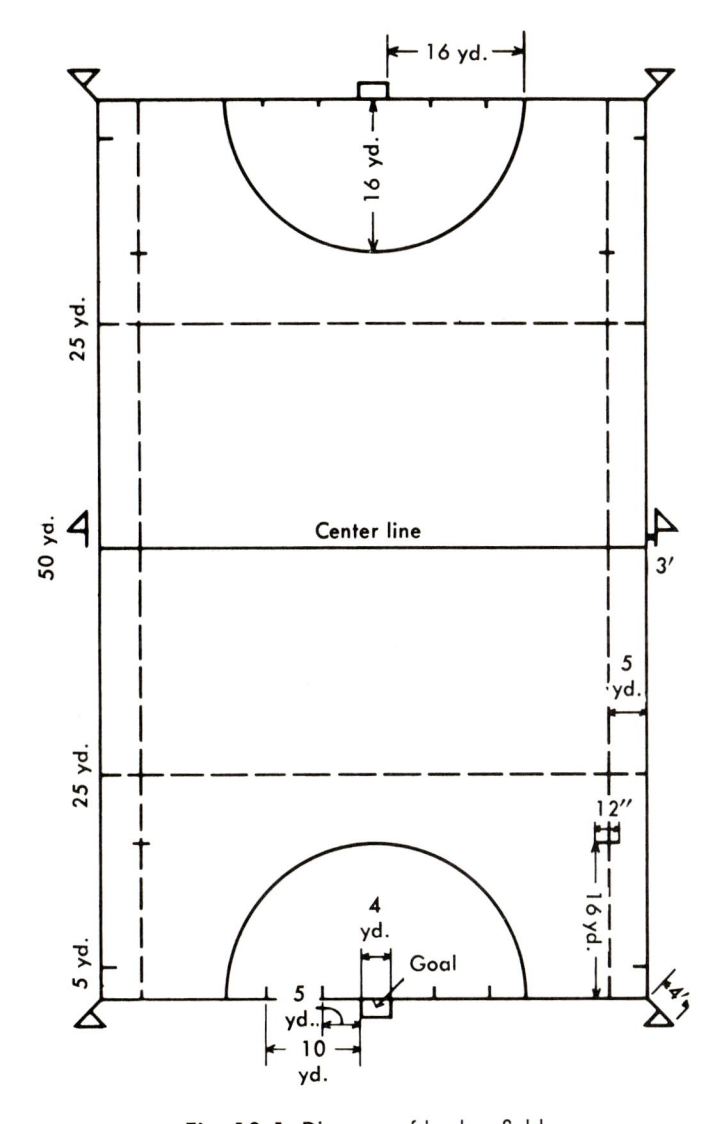

Fig. 10-1. Diagram of hockey field.

the hockey stick. A goal scores 1 point and can be scored only if an attacker's stick touches the ball inside the striking circle.

The official game is played in halves of two 35-minute periods with 5 minutes between halves. School and college games are usually 20- to 25-minute halves. There is no time out allowed except for injury or a broken stick. There is no overtime played if the game is tied.

DIMENSION OF FIELD

The hockey field is about the size of a football field (100 yards by 60 yards) with a goal at opposite ends. Goalposts are 4 yards apart and 7 feet high joined by a crossbar. The goal is enclosed by a net or wire screen, supported by two additional posts 4 to 6 feet behind the goal. (See Fig. 10-1.) A smaller field can be used for junior play.

EQUIPMENT
The ball

The ball is made of cork and string, covered with white leather. It is slightly larger than a baseball and is quite hard. Its weight must not be less than 5½ ounces, nor more than 5¾ ounces; its circumference not less than 8 13/16 inches, nor more than 9¼ inches.

The stick

The usual stick weighs about 18 or 19 ounces. It varies between 35 and 38 inches in length. Select a stick by standing erect, grasping it as for a drive, and swinging it in front of the body past the feet. It should just clear the ground.

The stick is constructed with a handle made of cane with rubber or cork inserts and a blade of ash or mulberry wood. The left side of the blade is flat and is used in hitting the ball. The right side of the blade is rounded and may not be used for hitting the ball at any time. The crook of the stick is composed of the heel and toe.

After using the stick, store it in a cool, dry room, not in a heated room. If the stick has splinters, use sandpaper or tape. Wax may be applied at intervals to keep moisture from penetrating the wood.

Costume

The usual gymnasium costume is worn. However, many players prefer to wear a tunic. In chilly weather, a sweater or jacket is recommended. Shoes are of great importance. They should have soles with leather or rubber cleats—*not* metal. Cleats are recommended to prevent slipping in quick maneuvers on grassy playing surfaces.

The goalkeeper has specially built shoes which are well padded along the sides and have hard toes. They should be fitted large enough so that the player can wear two pairs of heavy socks. The goalkeeper should wear guards or pads from the thigh down to the ankle. Other players should wear lightweight shin guards.

FUNDAMENTAL SKILL TECHNIQUES

Footwork with the stick in hockey is just as important as foot and racket handling in tennis, perhaps even more so. There are so many varying and changing situations constantly arising on the field of play that one must react quickly and coordinate with stick and footwork. The feet must maneuver the player into the proper relationship to the ball, not the ball to the feet. Players must at all times keep their eyes on the ball.

The grip

Set the heel of the stick on the ground in front of the left foot and then drop the handle of the stick into the left hand near the top of the handle. Place the right hand directly below the left. Lift the club to a horizontal position with the toe of the stick pointing directly upward. The V formed by each thumb and index finger of each hand is directly in alignment with the toe of the club. The grip is firm but not tense. The left forearm is also in alignment with the stick. The heel of the stick is placed to the right front of the right foot. This is the basic fundamental position for all strokes. The left hand seldom changes its grip for any strokes. The right will adjust and readjust itself down or up on the stick to the situation of each stroke. (See Fig. 10-2.)

Dribbling

One dribbles the ball with the hands in basketball or with the feet in soccer, but in

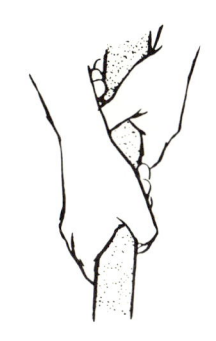

Fig. 10-2. The grip.

Fig. 10-4. The back lift.

Fig. 10-3. Dribbling.

Fig. 10-5. The drive.

hockey a stick is used to dribble or maneuver the ball downfield. The ball should be kept close enough to the dribbler to control it. As running speed increases, strokes should be played stronger.

In dribbling the ball, the arms should be relaxed, the left arm held away from the body with the left shoulder slightly in front, and the right-hand grip several inches below the left hand. The stick is held perpendicular, and the impetus given to the strokes in the dribble is principally a wrist action.

In dribbling on the run, the player should maintain the ball slightly to the right front of the right foot to prevent running into or kicking it. (See Fig. 10-3.)

The drive

The drive in hockey is somewhat similar to that of a shortened golf drive. The hands are gripped close together; a backswing and forward drive are executed with the body weight following through. However, the stick should not be lifted higher than the shoulders on the back lift nor higher than the shoulders on the follow-through. The wrists bend very little at either end of the stroke, thus controlling the height of the stick during the drive. (See Figs. 10-4 and 10-5.)

Drive to left

The ball is played from in front of the feet. The stick swing is similar to the drive. The direction of movement is from right to left.

Drive to right

The ball is played to the right and behind the feet well back from the fundamental drive position. The left foot steps forward after the drive is made. A pivot of the shoulders and hips to the right is made on the backswing and then a follow-through to the right on the drive stroke.

Straight-ahead or goal drive

The ball should be to the right front of the right foot. If a hard drive is to be executed, it is well to have the left side of

Fig. 10-6. The push pass.

the body aligned in the direction the shot is to be made with either the left or right foot forward. Players should practice this interchangeable foot skill with the drive since it is often done at a full run during a game.

The push pass

The push pass is used when there is not sufficient time to execute a drive. It is usually employed for short and more accurate passing. There is no backswing. The right hand should be well down the stick to execute a quick pass. The stick is facing the direction of the pass and in contact with the ball. The body weight should be transferred to the right leg. The ball is pushed with the stick. The left leg follows through at the end of stroke. (See Fig. 10-6.)

When this pass is smoothly and skillfully executed, it is accurate and powerful and can be easily received by a teammate.

The flick

The flick is a shot made with the face of the stick in contact with the ball and without a backswing. It is performed by the wrist and arm action of pushing the club head behind the ball and flicking the ball into the air to a teammate. The follow-through movement of the stick, in the direction of the flick, is important to the successful execution of this stroke.

The job

The job is used only in spoiling a drive or shot by an opponent. It is merely jabbing the heel or toe of the club against the ball. It is used when no other stroke can be used. The stick is held in one hand, and the ball is pushed aside just before an opponent can complete a dribble or drive.

RECEIVING, FIELDING, AND PASSING

Fielding or receiving a ball may be done while the player is either stationary or moving. Because hockey is a running game, most stops are made while the player is on the move except during a corner play. The feet should be in line with the oncoming ball. The right hand drops slightly down the handle of the stick for better ball control. There are several important fundamentals to remember as a ball is approaching the receiver:

1. Keep the eyes on the opponent's stick and ball and go to meet the ball.
2. Point the fact of the stick at the ball as it approaches and lower the stick to graze the ground.
3. Keep the stick close to the ground until the tackle is completed.
4. As the ball comes in contact with the stick, let the blade give with the ball so that the hands on the handle are ahead of the ball.
5. Stop the ball and possess it.
6. Maintain an easy grip.
7. In stopping a hard-driven ball, let the handle of the club give with the blade of the club so that the ball does not rebound.
8. Get the ball in a position diagonally opposite the front foot before playing it.

After successfully performing the skills just described, a player is ready to pass, drive, or dribble.

TACKLING

Tackling is usually an attempt made to take the ball away from another player. The approach for the tackle can be made from the front, right side, or left side. The players should always practice these techniques in pairs, one dribbling, the other attacking. The instant the opponent's stick is away from the ball is the moment to tackle. Try always to move and not stand still while tackling.

Approach from the front— head-on tackle

1. Keep the eyes on the opponent's stick and ball.
2. Place the stick in the path of the ball.

3. Keep the stick on the ground until the tackle is completed.
4. Time the tackle.
5. Play the ball not the person.

Approach from the right—left-hand lunge

This approach is used when the would-be tackler was unsuccessful in tackling an opponent. The tackler must turn around and make another attempt to stop or deflect the ball from the opponent. The stick is carried with both hands and finally one hand as a lunge step is being made to deflect the ball from the opponent's possession. Make the attack as the opponent taps the ball.

1. Do not get too close to an opponent.
2. Allow sufficient room to complete the lunge stroke and body movement.
3. Carry the stick low during the attack.
4. Judge the lunge accurately and time your stroke to hit the ball while your opponent's stick is in the backswing of the dribbling stroke.
5. Be alert to pivot when capturing the ball.

Approach from the left—circular tackle

The attack from the left side is a weak play because the dribbler will control the ball on the side front. The attacker then must outrun the opponent by at least a stride or two, circle around in front, and then with quick short taps take the ball or pass to a teammate. The movement is called the circular tackle.

WAYS TO EVADE AN OPPONENT

One method of evading an opponent is by the use of the scoop. This is executed by facing the flat side of the stick upward. The toe of stick is flicked under the ball, lifting the ball a few inches above the ground and over the opponent's stick. The most effective scoop is forward and to the dribbler's left, which is the attacker's stick side. This play seldom slows down the dribbler's speed downfield, and almost certain repossession of the ball is assured.

Dodging

RIGHT DODGE

Dodging is another effective method of being skillful in avoiding a would-be opponent. The ball is passed to the non-stick side close to the opponent's left foot, but the passer runs around the opponent's stick side and meets the ball behind the opponent.

LEFT DODGE

To perform the left dodge, the dribbler should keep the ball on the stick (right) side. Just before the ball reaches the opponent, the dribbler steps to the left, quickly pulls the ball directly to the left only a few inches, and then quickly taps the ball forward. This maneuver requires skill and accurate timing.

ZIG-ZAG DODGE AND PASS (TRIANGULAR PASS)

In this situation, as the dribbler approaches the attacker, the ball is passed diagonally forward either to the right or left to a teammate. The teammate, in turn, passes back to the dribbler, who already has run around and to the rear of the attacker to again meet the ball. This is one of the most fundamental and most used plays on the hockey field.

ABRIDGED RULES OF FIELD HOCKEY
The bully

The bully is the play used to start or restart a game of hockey. One player from each team will make the bully. They face each other in the center of the field if starting a game. Each player must stand squarely with feet astride the center line. The ball is placed on the line between them. They cannot move the feet until the bully is completed. The bully is then started with each player alternately striking the ground with the face of the stick on his or her own side of the ball and then striking the opponent's stick above the ball for three consecutive times. With the third meeting of sticks above the ball, the bully is completed and players are free to move into playing or attacking areas. After the players hit the sticks for the third time, the ball is hooked back out of the opponent's reach by inverting the toe of the stick, and from this position of the ball a pass left or right is executed to a teammate. Offensive plays are initiated from the bully. (See diagram of field for position of players, Fig. 10-7.)

120 BASIC SKILLS IN SPORTS FOR MEN AND WOMEN

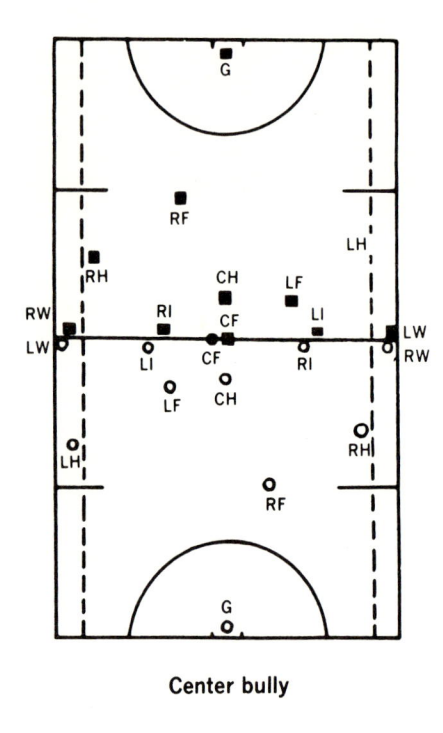

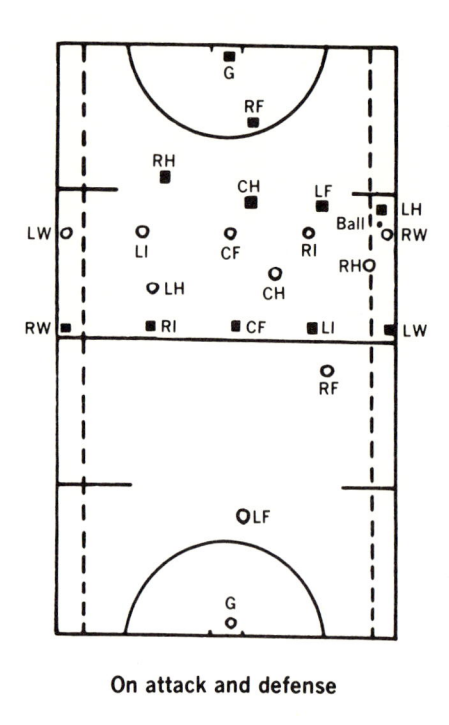

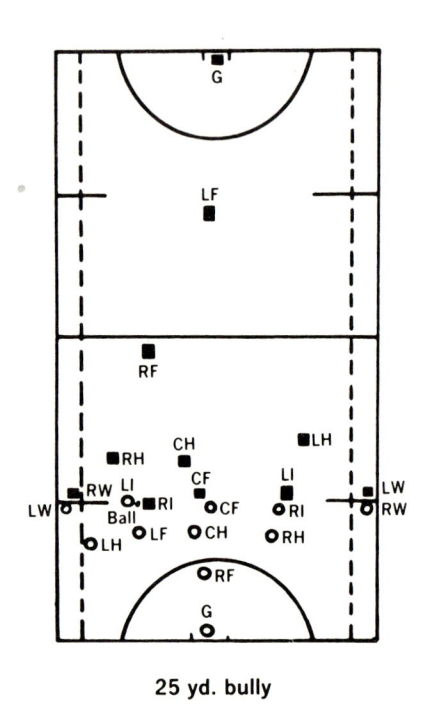

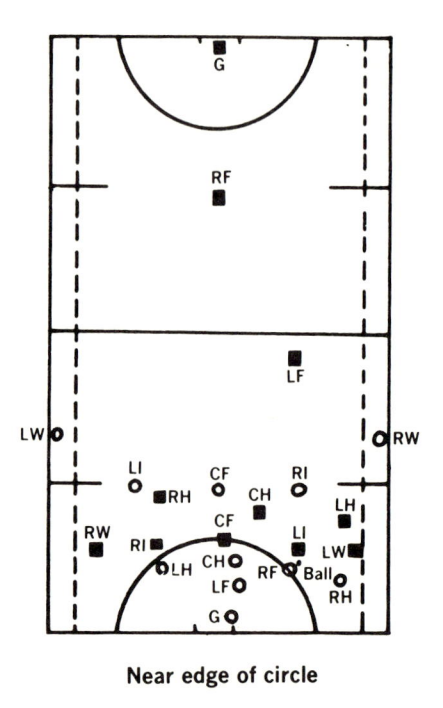

Center bully

On attack and defense

25 yd. bully

Near edge of circle

Fig. 10-7. Diagram of hockey field showing positions of players.

The bully is used to:
1. Start the game at the beginning, after half time, and after a goal has been scored.
2. Restart the game on the 25-yard line after the ball has gone over the end line off the attacker's stick.
3. Restart the game on the 25-yard line when the ball has gone over the end line off the sticks of two opponents simultaneously.
4. Restart the game after a penalty bully.
5. Restart the game after a simultaneous foul by two opponents.

Penalty bully

A penalty bully is given for a foul by the defensive team.
1. A foul preventing a certain goal from being scored
2. A foul that is a willful breach of the rules
3. For deliberate or repeated fouling

A penalty bully is taken 5 yards out from the center of the goal line by the player who fouled and any player chosen by the attacking team.

All other players, including the goalkeeper if he or she is not the defense member participating, are beyond the 25-yard line and may not take part in the game until the penalty bully is completed. One of the following situations will result:
1. A goal is awarded to the attacking team and the penalty bully is completed when:
    (a) The ball goes over the goal line between the goalposts off the stick of the attacker or the stick or person of the defense.
    (b) The defender commits a foul.
2. There is no score, the penalty bully is completed, and the game is restarted with a bully in the center of the 25-yard line when:
    (a) The ball goes outside of the circle.
    (b) The attacker hits the ball over the goal line but not between the goalposts.
    (c) The attacker fouls.
3. The penalty bully is repeated when:
    (a) The defense hits the ball over the goal line, not between the goalposts.
    (b) The ball goes out of the circle or over the goal line off the sticks of the two opponents simultaneously.
    (c) There is a double foul.
    (d) There is an improper bully.
    (e) The ball unavoidably touches the person of the defense.

Corner

This formation is awarded as an advantage to the attacking team and has two variations: long corner and short corner.

Long corner: This formation, sometimes called a corner, is awarded when the ball is *unintentionally* sent over the goal line, not between the goalposts, off the stick of a defender. The ball is placed 5 yards from the corner on either the goal line or sideline, preferably on the goal line, on that side of the goal where the ball went out.

Short corner: Sometimes called a penalty corner, this formation is awarded when:
1. The ball is sent over the goal line intentionally played by the defense.
2. The defense fouls in the striking circle.

The ball is placed not less than 10 yards from the nearer goalpost on either side of the goal on the end line. The attacking team may choose the side on which the penalty corner will be taken.

Corner play

Usually the wing of the attacking team takes the hit for the corner. The other forwards stand at the edge of the striking circle, sticks and feet just outside the circle line. The halfback backs up the forwards.

Six players of the defending team are stationed with their feet and sticks behind the goal line. Each player is opposite the stick of the person he or she is to cover. The five forwards of the defending team remain at the 25-yard line.

No player is to be nearer than 5 yards to the player taking the hits. As soon as the ball is hit, these players may move. Other defending players may not be nearer than the 25-yard line and cannot cross this line until the ball has been touched by a player other than the hitter or has come out of the circle.

The wing usually passes to one of the other forwards. No player may shoot for the goal unless the ball has been stopped on the ground or has touched the stick or person of a defender.

To execute a good corner play, the wing hits hard but the ball stays on the ground and does not bounce. The forward executes a good stop and a quick shot at the goal.

Free hit

When a foul is committed, unless it is a foul by the defense in the circle, a free hit is given to the opposite team.

For a free hit outside the circle, the ball is placed on the spot where the foul occurred and is put into play by the defensive player in whose area the foul occurred. All other players must be 5 yards away. The ball must be motionless. The player taking the free hit can use any legal stroke, but after taking the free hit cannot play the ball again until it has been touched by another player. The free hit shall not rise above knee height. A free hit play should be made quickly before the opposing team can get set to meet it.

For a free hit inside the circle, the ball is usually played from the edge of the striking circle by a back.

When the ball is sent behind the goal line by one of the attacking team and no goal is scored, or if it is in the opinion of the umpire unintentionally sent behind the goal line by one of the defending team who is beyond the 25-yard line, the game shall be restarted by a free hit to be taken by one of the defending team exactly opposite the place where it crossed the goal line and 15 yards from the inner edge of that line.

Roll-in

When a ball goes out-of-bounds it is put in play again at the point at which it went out-of-bounds by a member of the team opposite to the player who last touched the ball before it crossed the line.

Usually the halfback takes the roll-in; the stick is held in one hand and the ball in the other. The ball is rolled onto the field of play, as in bowling. It must not be thrown or bounced. The player rolling the ball in may not play it again until it has been touched by another player. The other players may enter the alley as soon as the ball crosses the outside line. Excellent plays can be formulated from a roll-in play if a formation can be executed quickly.

Goalkeeper rules

The goalkeeper has many more different skills to learn and acquire than do any of the other players. He or she must not only be able to do well-executed stick work, but must be clever in stopping the ball with the feet, legs, hands, or stick. The goalie has the privilege of even kicking the ball. The goalie may stop the ball with the flat hand but cannot bat it. Above all, the goalie must have a courageous and competitive spirit of play.

The goalie takes the position in front of the goal line, never on it. The goal line to the goalie is an imaginary line extending from goalpost to goalpost but extending in a semicircle about 1 yard out onto the field. The goalie faces the attacking field with feet together and knees bent in readiness to shift to left or right. The feet or legs should be used to stop and clear a ball. The stick is used to clear only in an emergency. To clear is to get the ball out of danger of the goal. It should be cleared with the inside of the foot and passed out accurately to a back or parallel to the end line. At times the goalie has little time to clear. High-kicked balls in the path of onrushing forwards should be discouraged.

If a forward is dribbling toward the goal alone, the goalie can rush out to meet the attack as the forward enters the striker's circle. If a shot is going to miss the goal, the goalie should not touch it, but permit it to go over the end boundary.

A goalie should never permit his or her vision to be blocked. The goalie should follow the game closely at all times.

Rules on fouls

1. When playing the ball, a player shall not:
   (a) Raise the stick above the shoulder at either the beginning or end of a hit.

(b) Hit the ball dangerously into a player at close range, hit a hard ball that rises, or hit a ball on the fly.
(c) Undercut, or execute a drive stroke with the blade of the stick laid back.
(d) Use the rounded side of the stick.
(e) Allow the ball to rebound or be moved by any part of the body. However, the goalkeeper is privileged to stop the ball with the body, provided he or she is in the striking circle.
(f) Hit the ball between his or her own feet.
(g) Take part in the game without a stick in his or her hand.

2. With regard to an opponent, a player shall not:
(a) Push, charge, shove, trip, strike at, or in any way personally handle an opponent.
(b) Strike, hook, hold, lift, or in any way interfere with an opponent's stick.
(c) Place the body between the opponent and the ball.
(d) Allow the feet, shoulders, or any part of the body to interfere with an opponent's playing the ball.
(e) Break an opponent's stride by running in front of the opponent.

3. Off side play: A player of the same team as the striker or the roller-in is off side if he or she is nearer the opponent's goal line than the striker or roller-in at the moment when the ball is hit or rolled in, unless the player is in his or her own half of the field or there are at least three opponents nearer to their own goal line than he or she is. A player who is in an off side position shall not be put on side by reason of the ball having touched, or glanced off the stick or person of an opponent. The player should not be penalized unless an advantage is being gained from having been in an off side position. An attacking player may run forward to meet a pass after the ball has been hit.

Rules on penalties for fouls

Outside circle: A free hit is awarded to the team not committing the foul.
Inside circle:
1. By the attacker: A free hit is awarded from anywhere in the striking circle. This hit is usually taken on the circle by a back of the opposing team.
2. By the defense:
   (a) A short corner (penalty corner) is awarded to the attacking team.
   (b) A long corner is awarded to the attacking team.
   (c) A penalty bully is given.

Out-of-bounds play

ACROSS SIDELINE

1. The ball is put in play by a roll-in by a member of the team opposite the player last touching the ball as it crossed the sideline.
2. When the ball goes out-of-bounds off the sticks of two opponents, the ball is put in play by a bully within the 1-yard line opposite the spot at which it went out-of-bounds.

OVER END LINE—NOT BETWEEN GOALPOSTS

1. Off the attacking team: A 25-yard bully is taken opposite the spot where the ball crossed the goal line.
2. Off the defensive team:
   (a) A corner when the ball is *unintentionally* hit over the goal line.
   (b) A short or penalty corner when the ball is intentionally hit over the goal line.
3. Off the sticks of two opponents: A 25-yard bully opposite the spot where the ball left the field.

OVER GOAL LINE BETWEEN GOALPOSTS

1. A legal goal is scored when the ball is touched by the stick of an attacker inside the striking circle. The goal counts even though the ball was last touched by the stick or person of the defending team. Play is again resumed by a center bully on the center line at midfield.
2. If the ball was not touched by a stick

of the attacking team inside the striking circle and (a) was touched by a stick of the defensive team, a long corner, or (b) was not touched by a stick of the defensive team inside the circle, a goal is scored and a bully on the 25-yard line resumes play.

MEN'S FIELD HOCKEY

Men's rules vary slightly from women's.
1. The striking circle is 16 yards in, and the alleys are seven yards wide.
2. A penalty flick replaces the penalty bully. This is played eight yards from the center of the goal.

OFFENSIVE PLAYING

When an offensive player has the ball, the other four forwards should keep on the line with the player with the ball. In this formation the ball can easily be seen and each forward is in a good position to receive a pass. The ball should be passed from one forward to another to prevent the defense from becoming set for a defensive maneuver. This is a shifting attack and is hard to stop if the ball is strategically played, controlled, and passed as it progresses downfield to the striking circle where a hard shot should be attempted at the goal. This shot should be followed in hard and rushed by the inner players and center. In the scoring area the attack should be sustained and relentless. The center goes to the center of the circle with an inner player rushing on either side of the center to prevent the goalie from executing a successful clear. Wings can often pass back to the center or center halfback who would shoot from the edge of the circle.

DEFENSIVE PLAYING

If the ball has been taken away from the forwards, they should immediately tackle back to regain possession. If the ball is regained, the other players should be in readiness and in a receptive position to receive a pass and again form an attack upon the goal.

Ordinarily each defensive player should be responsible for the area and the player he or she marks.

The halfback must mark his or her opponent in such a way that he or she is close enough to intercept a pass or make a tackle. The halfbacks must always be alert to shift from offense to defense and vice versa as possession of the ball changes from one team to another.

The fullbacks may play or come up as far in the field as the halfbacks. But they must be alert and in readiness to meet any break-away opponent dribbling downfield.

The backs, in marking an opponent, should be close to the opponent on the stick side and nearer the goal than the opponent, with stick down in readiness.

One back should cover another back if the play is on his or her side of play.

When the ball approaches the striking circle, all the defensive players should be marking very closely with no covering player.

HELPFUL AIDS IN PLAYING

1. Control a ball before hitting it.
2. Run straight up and down the field and move only in your own territory.
3. A player should move away from a teammate with the ball, but be close enough to receive a pass.
4. In receiving a ball from a teammate, face the direction of the goal you are attacking and look back over your shoulder to see the oncoming ball.
5. Hold the stick so that it does not touch another player.
6. Try not to pull the ball around you, but rather move yourself around the ball.
7. Pass to a free teammate when free, on his or her open side.
8. If a teammate is running to open space, pass ahead into this space.
9. Forwards must not crowd.
10. Be courteous, play fair, and know and observe the rules of the game.

INSTRUCTIONAL AND LEARNING PROCEDURES

Costume and equipment
1. Explanation and description of suitable costume and necessary equipment

Reading assignments
1. Suggested readings from references listed at end of chapter

Objectives

1. To know the rules
2. To know the fundamental strokes
3. To have a fair knowledge of offensive and defensive play and team tactics
4. To be able to play the game and enjoy it

Progressive techniques

1. Drive in all directions
2. Field with stick and hand
3. Dribble
4. Push pass
5. Flick
6. Scoop
7. Left-hand lunge
8. Job

Note: Practice these techniques individually, in two's, in relays, and in technique games.

9. Tactics and techniques of play
    (a) Passing and fielding
    (b) Shooting
    (c) Dodging
10. Fundamentals of the game, offensive play
    (a) Position on field
    (b) Open out after bully
    (c) Tackle back, from offense to defense
11. Fundamentals of the game, defensive play
    (a) Back up forward line
    (b) Tackle
    (c) Clear
12. Strategy of play

Tests

1. Performance and achievement test
2. Knowledge test

GLOSSARY OF FIELD HOCKEY TERMS

advancing Rebounding of the ball from a player's body; a foul.
alley That area of the field between the sideline and the five-yard line.
backing up Play of defense directly in back of a bully.
bully The name of the play to start or restart the game. Each player alternately strikes the ground with the face of the stick on his or her own side of ball and then strikes the opponent's stick above the ball for three consecutive times.
circular tackle Circling around in front of the opponent from left to right and taking the ball or passing it to a teammate.
corner Formation where the ball is placed 5 yards from the corner on the goal line on that side of the goal where the ball went out.
dribble Using the stick to maneuver the ball downfield.
drive A swing somewhat similar to that of a shortened golf stroke or drive.
fielding Receiving a ball while a player is either stopped or in motion.
flick A shot made with the face of the stick in contact with the ball and without a backswing.
free hit A hit with which the opponent may not interfere; awarded when a foul is committed.
goal A legal goal is scored when the whole ball has passed entirely over the goal line under the bar after it has been touched by the stick of an attacker inside the striking circle; 1 point.
lunge A play to take the ball away from an opponent on his left side.
marking Guarding an opponent by a defensive player.
offside Receiving the ball in an illegal position.
own goal The goal one's own team defends.
penalty bully A bully taken 5 yards out from the center of the goal line by the player who fouled and any player chosen by the attacking team; given for a foul by the defensive team.
penalty corner A play awarded when the ball is sent over the goal line intentionally played by the defense, or when the defense fouls in the striking circle. The ball is placed not less than 10 yards from the nearest goalpost on either side of the goal on the end line.
push pass A maneuver in which the ball is pushed with the stick; used when there is not sufficient time to execute a drive.
reverse stick To play the ball on the left by turning the stick over; or to tackle an opponent on the right.
roll-in A play in which the ball is rolled onto

the field of play at the point at which it went out-of-bounds.

scoop A play executed by facing the flat side of the stick upward. The toe of the stick is flicked under the ball, lifting the ball a few inches above the ground and over the opponent's stick.

sticks Raising the stick above the shoulder either fore or back; a foul.

REFERENCES

American Association for Health, Physical Education and Recreation: physical education for high school students, Washington, D. C., 1970, AAHPER.

Delano, Anne Lee: Field hockey, Dubuque, Iowa, 1967, William C. Brown Company, Publishers.

Hickey, Melvyn: Hockey for women, London, 1962, Nicholas Kay Ltd.

Lees, Josephine T., and Shellenberger, Betty: Field hockey, New York, 1969, The Ronald Press Co.

Mackey, Helen T.: Field hockey, Englewood Cliffs, N. J., 1968, Prentice-Hall, Inc.

Mackey, Helen T.: Field hockey: an international team sport, Englewood Cliffs, N. J., 1963, Prentice-Hall, Inc.

Official field hockey and lacrosse rules and guide, Washington, D. C., 1972-1974, AAHPER, Division for Girls' and Women's Sports.

FILMS*

Hockey—improve your game, All England Women's Hockey Association, 60 min., AAHPER.

Hockey strokes—fundamentals of the game, Scottish Women's Association, 40 min., AAHPER.

Goalkeeping techniques, 15 min., AAHPER.

---

*Information on the purchase of these films or on the latest films taken may be obtained from the USFHA Film Distribution Chairman, Gladys Thomas, 3935 N. Palmer Ave., Milwaukee, Wis. 53212.

11 Golf

HISTORY

The royal game of golf as we know it today is one of the most ancient of our modern sports. Historians are not agreed on its origin, but as early as 1457 the Scottish Parliament ordained that golf should not be played by the people because it was distracting from the practice of archery, which was deemed necessary for defensive purposes. It appears certain, therefore, that golf was played in Scotland more than 500 years ago. Old paintings and drawings show that similar games were also played about that time in Holland, Belgium, and France. The Dutch term "kolf," meaning a club, is considered by some to have given rise to the name of the present-day game. Regardless of how much Scotland invented on her own and how much she borrowed from others, it appears quite certain that that country was the source from which the game of golf as it is known today spread to all parts of the world.

Courses or links of those days differed greatly from those of the present time. Golf was then distinctly a seaside game. It was played over stretches of land that linked the waterline of the seashore with tillable lands farther inland. It was this condition which led to calling the scene of play "links," which in fact means a seaside golf course.

Location of holes followed no definite plan. The landscape was partially covered by bushes, trees, and the like. Open areas were chosen as finishing points or putting greens. No official number of holes was adopted as standard for a round of play until 1858, when eighteen holes were designated as a round.

Historic documents tell of the organization of golf clubs in the United States in the closing years of the eighteenth century. However, the game as we know it today had its start in the United States approximately fifty years ago. A few clubs were started in the eastern United States, and the rapid increase in popularity since then has greatly enlarged the number of private and municipal courses. Colleges and universities own and operate their own golf courses, whereas high schools use private and municipal courses.

Physical education classes have done much in recent years to stimulate and create this interest by giving class instruction to the general student body. It has been estimated that more than 7,000,000 Americans play golf sometime during the year.

There are at least 16,000 driving ranges in America. Many persons who have never been on a golf course become enthusiasts and start playing golf as a result of experience on a driving range.

Golf today is no longer a game for those with a high income. It is played by the poor as well as the rich, by women as well as men, by the very young and the very old, and by the duffers as well as the masters.

Truly, golf is a sport which offers a lifelong source of pleasure. One or two perfectly timed and directed shots are often sufficient cause for the player to return for many more rounds.

The social values and aspects of golf include the following: (1) it encourages excellent compatibility of mixed groups; (2) it clears and freshens the mind by diversion of interest; (3) it brings urban dwellers into sunshine and nature; (4) it provides restful activity for the working individual; (5) one is pitted against one's self as well as opponents; (6) each hole is a separate contest and challenge; and (7) the game is played by people of all ages, sizes, and builds. As recreation, golf is one of the most desirable of all sports.

THE COURSE

A golf course is usually built and constructed to conform best to the locale of the plot of land. A complete golf course consists of eighteen holes, which would require not less than 100 acres of land. Many small communities construct a nine-hole course.

A well-constructed golf course is architecturally planned so that each hole differs from the rest, yet has elements common to all.

Each hole is composed of a tee, fairway, rough, boundary, green, sand traps, bunker, cup, flag, tee markers, trees, and sometimes water hazards. The shape and size of greens, as well as the placing of traps, bunkers, and water hazards, are usually left to the golf course architects.

Par for the course is usually determined by the distance of the holes from the middle of the tee down the middle of the fairway to the middle of the green. Holes up to 250 yards are usually designated as par 3; holes from 251 to 470 yards are designated as par 4; holes from 471 to 600 yards are designated as par 5. Par 3 is a score usually obtained by reaching the green in 1 shot and rolling the ball into the cup with 2 putts. On a par 4, the golfer must reach the green in 2, and on a par 5, reach it in 3. A championship course usually has a par of 72, or an average of 4 strokes per hole. A course usually has a certain number of par 3, par 4, and par 5 holes.

Par for women differs somewhat from that for men, depending upon the difficulty of each hole as to distance, hazards, etc.

Refer to the sample of the University of Iowa Finkbine Field scorecard (Fig. 11-1) in regard to par for men and women, distances of each hole, and how to score self, partners, and opponents.

GENERAL DESCRIPTION

Eighteen holes make up the average course. The 1st, 9th, 10th, and 18th holes are generally near the clubhouse. One can play any multiple of nine holes, and each hole varies in length and general layout. Hazards are generally placed to penalize a poor shot. One endeavors to score as few strokes as possible for each hole. Play starts at the tee behind two markers, continues along the fairway, which is generally bounded by rough, and finishes at the green, which is generally surrounded by traps. The ball is rolled into the hole marked by the pin.

Note: For definition of all terms, see glossary.

FACILITIES FOR PRACTICE

1. Any large room in school, preferably the gymnasium
2. Two or three large pieces of canvas hung in front of a wall with fish netting along sides to form a cage-type setup
3. Several mats from which to hit
4. Several clubs and balls, which most professionals at the city club would be glad to help furnish to a school (most students will bring their own clubs)
5. One large rug with rather long nap for putting

Hole	Yards	Men's par	Ladies' par	Self	Partner	We + 0	Handicap strokes	They + 0	Opposing team	Opposing team
1	356	4	4				10			
2	472	5	5				4			
3	533	5	6				2			
4	162	3	3				7			
5	183	3	4				5			
6	280	4	4				14			
7	360	4	4				12			
8	160	3	3				15			
9	380	4	4				11			
Out	2886	35	37							
10	211	3	4				16			
11	403	4	5				6			
12	398	4	5				8			
13	297	4	4				13			
14	539	5	5				3			
15	570	5	6				1			
16	150	3	3				18			
17	388	4	4				9			
18	160	3	3				17			
In	3116	35	39							
Total	6002	70	76							
Handicap										
Net score										

S. U. I. FINKBINE FIELD — SCORES — Side matches

Scorer / Date

Fig. 11-1. Scorecard.

6. One or two rubber cups for individual putting (water glasses can be used)

CLOTHING

Dress according to local custom on the course you play.

Spiked shoes are an important part of golfing equipment. However, if they are not available, a pair of tennis shoes will suffice. It is necessary to keep the feet from slipping, for if they move during the swing it is difficult to make a good shot.

EQUIPMENT

This country has contributed a large share to the improvement of the game of golf, for Americans are responsible for the type of ball in use today, the steel shaft clubs, the graduated set of irons, and the peg tee.

It is not necessary to have the best set of clubs on the market to enjoy playing golf and to play it satisfactorily. On the other hand, it is a poor policy to handicap your game with poor equipment. Buy a medium-priced club made by a popular and dependable manufacturer. In so doing you have assurance of satisfaction and long wear.

Clubs

As you may well know, golf clubs come in a variety of lengths, weights, and flexibilities of the shaft. If you live in a community in which there is no professional golf instructor and you must make your own choice, select clubs that feel best to you, that is, that are neither too heavy nor too light, and neither too "whippy" nor too stiff in the shaft. Usually, the faster the swing, the less whip you should have in your club shafts. To determine the proper length of the clubs, assume a proper stance with a club. If the sole of the club head rests flatly on the ground without your having to move closer or farther away, chances are that the length is satisfactory.

Beginner's set of clubs

In the event you wish to buy only a bare minimum of clubs with which to start, get a brassie (#2 wood), putter, #2, #3, #5, and #7 or #8 iron. The key clubs are the #3, #5, and #7 irons, and if you learn to use these well you will have little trouble with the other irons. It might be well to add that it is to the player's advantage to fill out the set of clubs as soon as possible in order to learn the proper use of each one. In buying, remember to buy all the same brand.

Woods

For four common types of woods, see Fig. 11-2.

Driver: Hits 220 to 300 yards (women, 150 to 180) and is used only on the tee.

Brassie: Hits 210 to 250 yards (women, 150 to 170) and is used from a good lie for long shots.

Spoon: Hits 200 to 230 yards (women, 145 to 160) and is used from a good lie where distance and height are needed.

Wood: Takes the place of the #1 iron in newer sets.

Irons

For the various irons and distances made with each, see Figs. 11-3 and 11-4.

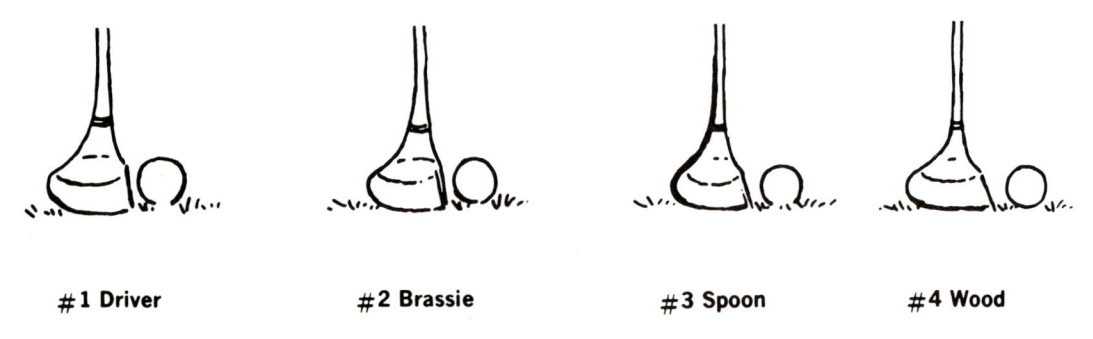

#1 Driver   #2 Brassie   #3 Spoon   #4 Wood

Fig. 11-2. The four woods.

GOLF 131

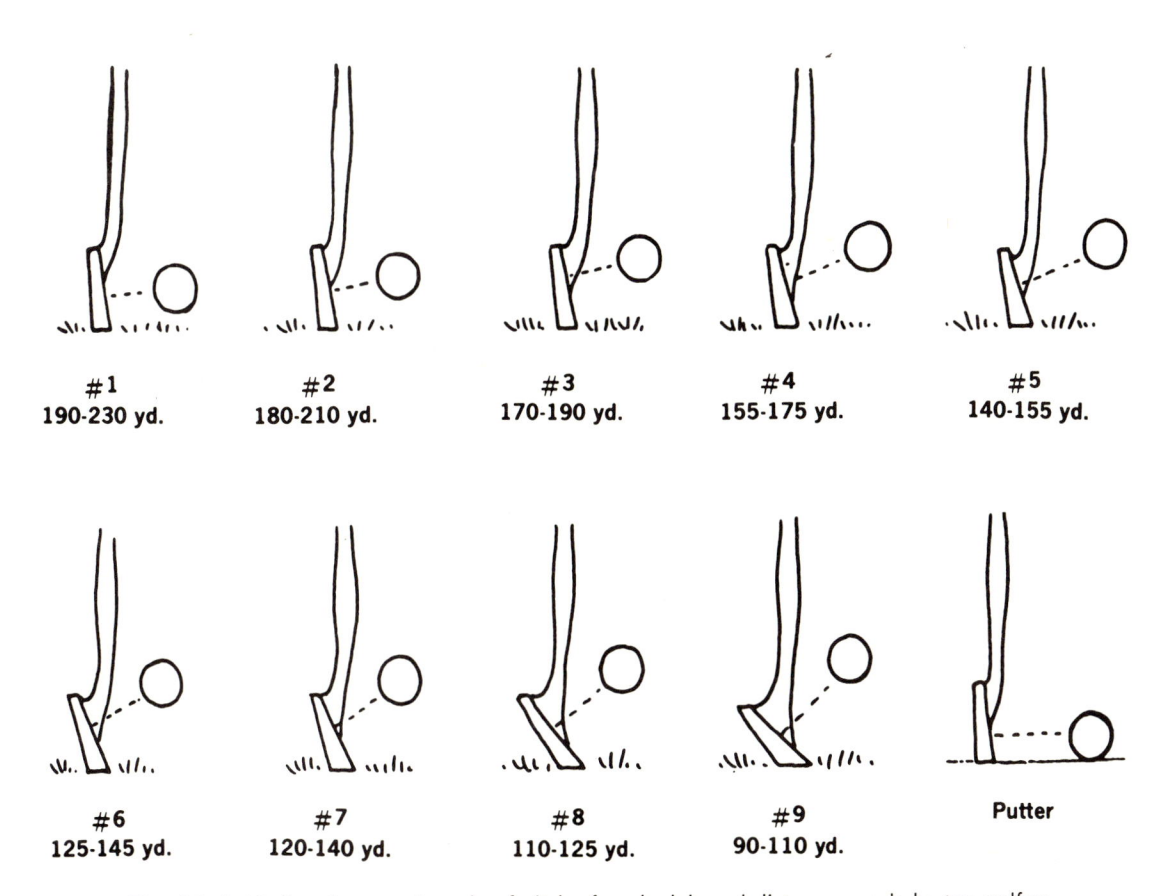

#1
190-230 yd.

#2
180-210 yd.

#3
170-190 yd.

#4
155-175 yd.

#5
140-155 yd.

#6
125-145 yd.

#7
120-140 yd.

#8
110-125 yd.

#9
90-110 yd.

Putter

Fig. 11-3. Various irons and angle of pitch of each club and distances made by top golfers.

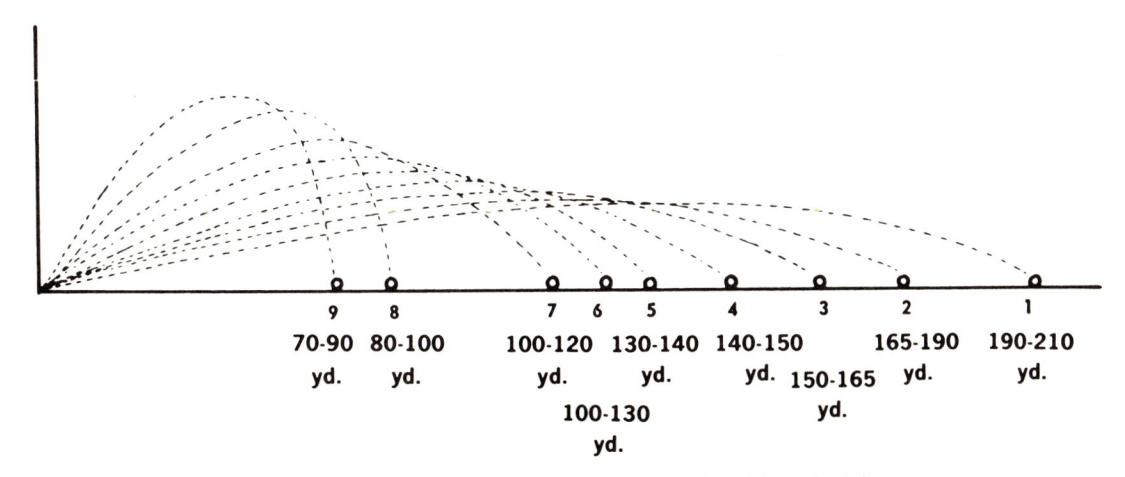

9
70-90
yd.

8
80-100
yd.

7
100-120
yd.

6
130-140
yd.

5
140-150
yd.

4
150-165
yd.

3
165-190
yd.

2

1
190-210
yd.

100-130
yd.

Fig. 11-4. Distances made by average golfer with each club.

#1 iron: Hits 190 to 230 yards (women, 140 to 155) and is used from the tee or a good lie.

#2 iron: Hits 180 to 210 yards (women, 150 to 165) and is used on the fairway or short rough.

#3 iron: Hits 170 to 190 yards (women, 135 to 150). It is similar to the #2 iron.

#4 iron: Hits 155 to 175 yards (women, 125 to 140). It is used on the tee for short holes and from the fairway and rough for long approaches.

#5 iron: Hits 140 to 155 yards (women, 115 to 130). It is the most popular club and is used for approaches from the fairway and rough, for chips, and for run-up shots.

#6 iron: Hits 125 to 145 yards (women, 110 to 120). It is used for approaches from the fairway and rough and for chips or run-up shots near the green.

#7 iron: Hits 120 to 140 yards (women, 100 to 110). It is used for approaches from the fairway and rough and may be used for pitch-and-run shots.

#8 iron: Hits 100 to 125 yards (women, 90 to 100). The #8 iron is used for approaches from the fairway and rough and may be used for pitch-and-run shots.

#9 iron: Hits 90 to 110 yards or less (women, 70 to 80). It is used for approaches from the fairway and rough, pitch shots, and pitch-and-run shots. It may be used from sand traps.

Putter: This club is used for putting on the green or just off the green and may be used to roll the ball out of sand traps onto the green.

Pitching or sand wedge: This club is used for short approaches from the rough and fairways and as a trouble club for tall rough or sand traps. It is very versatile when properly used.

FUNDAMENTAL SKILLS AND TECHNIQUES

Because certain clubs and types of shots fall into natural groupings, the following material has been arranged to take advantage of these categories. For the left-handed player, it will be necessary to reverse the outlook presented here since consideration has been given only to the right-handed player.

The woods

There are three common woods: the driver, the brassie, and the spoon. They have longer shafts than any of the iron clubs and can consequently give more distance than an iron club having a similar loft or tilt to the club face.

GRIP OR POSITION OF THE HANDS

1. Natural, no overlap, or 10-finger grip; used by players with small weak hands or extremely short fingers. Ladies generally use the 10-finger grip.
2. Interlocking grip; used by players with small hands or short stubby fingers.
3. Overlapping, 9-finger, or Vardon grip (Fig. 11-5); the most popular grip, used by most topflight players (described below).

Open the left hand, and with the thumb and fingers together, place the club diagonally across the hand from the middle joint of the index finger across the heel of the hand. Close the hand over the club so that it is held by the fingers (Fig. 11-5, *1*). The V formed by the thumb and index finger should point approximately to the right shoulder. When the club is held in the position of address, you should see the first three knuckles of the fingers. The thumb is above, one-quarter turn over the club with the pad of the thumb on the grip of the club, formed by the first and second fingers of the left hand (Fig. 11-5, *2*). The right rotation of the left hand allows the cocking of the wrist at the peak of the backswing. It also allows the left arm to deal a backhand blow to the ball. Try swinging the club head with only the left arm. Watch that the arm remains comfortably straight and that the wrist cocks at the top of the backswing.

Place the right hand in position (Fig. 11-5, *3*). The handle should first contact the middle joint of the right forefinger. When the hand is closed, this forefinger knuckle must be on the right side of the shaft—never under it. Close the hand, placing the thumb to the left, diagonally across the shaft

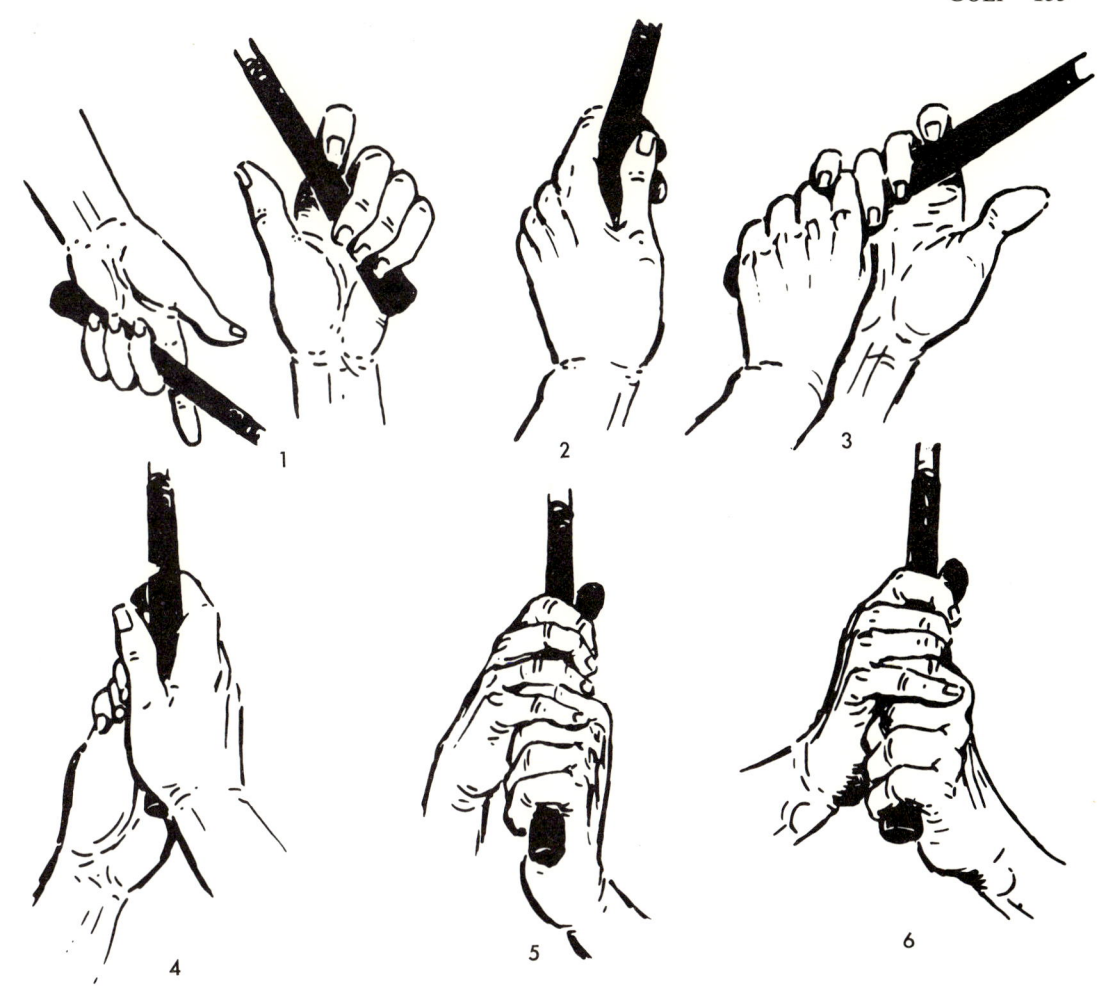

Fig. 11-5. Overlapping grip.

so that it helps the forefinger to grip (Fig. 11-5, 4). The feel of the club head is controlled mainly by the forefinger and thumb of the right hand, giving more power and control. The left thumb should fit snugly into the palm of the right hand (Fig. 11-5, 5). The little finger of the right hand should be wrapped around the crevice formed by the first two fingers of the left hand (overlapping grip) (Fig. 11-5, 6).

POSITION OF THE BODY (IN RELATION TO LINE OF PLAY)

For various foot stance positions, see Fig. 11-6.

Square stance: The feet, knees, hips, and shoulders are parallel to the line of play. This stance is used for almost all long shots of both woods and irons since it allows free movement of either side of the body. The toes turn slightly outward with the weight evenly distributed. The arms hang away from the body but do not reach. The body curves naturally, but not sharply, forward. The eyes are on the ball, resting there easily. The knees are *very* slightly bent.

Open stance: The left foot is withdrawn slightly from the line of flight, but the knees, hips, and shoulders remain square. This stance is used rarely for woods, but more often for the shorter iron shots. It tends to restrict the turning and pivoting of the left side but allows a better follow-through.

Closed stance: This is directly opposite to the open stance. It is used when playing a pull shot (later) and to correct a flat swing for chunky builds.

The leg action during the swing should be

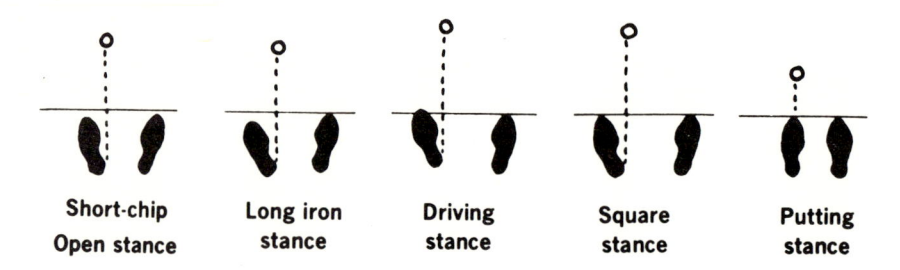

Fig. 11-6. Various foot stance positions.

Fig. 11-7. Progressive steps of swing.

natural, without overemphasis of the movements. On the backswing the right foot is flat and the leg straight, carrying most of the body weight. The left foot is pulled up on the toe and the knee is bent. It is a rather common fault to raise the left foot high and bend the knee more than is needed, which throws too much weight on the right leg. On the downswing, the leg positions go from this to the swinging position at the base of the swing and then to a reversed position in the follow-through.

Shoes are important in that the feet must not slip. Rubber-soled shoes are acceptable in dry weather, although they are warm. Short golf spikes in leather soles are best since they will grip in all kinds of weather.

Full swing

For the progressive steps in the swing, see Fig. 11-7.

Pivot: The full left arm swings back from the shoulder to the hand with the elbow straight. As the club head comes back to a wide upward arc, the complete left side (foot, knee, hip, and shoulder) turns fully to the right until the golfer is looking down at the ball over the left shoulder. Pivot while holding the head stable.

Backswing: The backswing is not rushed but rhythmic. At the peak the hands should be in a position just above the level of the right shoulder. The hands are under the club with the wrists cocked. The club face is open or the toe is pointing down. The left arm should be comfortably straight and the right elbow should be away from the body but pointing down. The following are possible errors in the backswing:
1. Swaying or bending to the right instead of pivoting the body over the ball
2. A backswing which is too fast and throws the golfer off balance
3. Bending the left arm
4. Raising the left shoulder
5. A backswing which is too flat or horizontal
6. Moving the head from its original position
7. Pausing too long at the peak or not pausing long enough

Downswing:
1. As both arms come down, the right elbow is kept fairly close to the body with the left arm leading until the hands are about waist high.
2. At the waist-high position the wrists uncocked strongly and reinforce the speed of the club head as it hits into the ball. The face of the club must meet the ball squarely without the right wrist turning in.
3. The hands must neither precede nor follow the club since this will cause a slice or a hook.
4. The follow-through should be natural, finishing up in a position just above reverse of the backswing.
5. The position of the head is of the utmost importance. From the time you step up to the ball until the follow-through, the eyes should focus on the ball. The head should not move in any direction during the swing since the movement takes place beneath it. The follow-through should pull the head up.

Other common faults in the full swing:
1. Uncocking the wrists too soon, which throws the golfer off-balance
2. Pushing with the right arm, which drops the right shoulder
3. Bringing in the right hip, which causes the hands to go in too early and results in a severe slice
4. Relaxing the wrists at the moment of impact
5. Failing to complete the follow-through

Addressing the ball

Grip the club and let the head rest on the ground in a natural way. The feet should be placed in their relative position for the club used. For the woods, the ball is generally in line with the left heel. As the length of the club and the required distance decrease, the ball is addressed farther to the right.

Long irons and short irons (half swing)

Take a few swings with only the right hand on the club. Feel the guide of the forefinger and thumb.

Stance:
1. The stance is slightly open.
2. Arms are comfortably close, with the left arm hanging.
3. The ball is at the center.
4. Feet are about 1 foot apart.

Grip:
1. The club is held a little shorter.

Backswing:
1. The club comes back in the intended line of flight.
2. This is a shot of direction, not distance.
3. The swing stops at a point where the club is about vertical.
4. The length of the swing is controlled by the left arm.
5. Hold the left arm fairly close.
6. Keep the right elbow close.
7. Keep the left arm straight, breaking sharply at the wrists.

Downswing:
1. The speed of the club head is controlled by the partially cocked wrist.
2. The follow-through is not so strong as the downswing, but the club head must continue in the direction of flight.
3. Both arms are straight when the club head meets the ball.
4. Hit very easily at first.
5. Let the club head do the work.
6. Keep body movement at a minimum.

Long irons

Stance:
1. The feet are placed in a square stance.
2. The ball is at center.
3. The feet are spread about the same as for the woods.

Backswing:
1. The swing is almost full or full.
2. The mechanics of the backswing are similar to those for the woods, although the head travels more of an up and down course.

Downswing:
1. Contact the ball just before the base of the swing.
2. The pivot is taken out after the ball is contacted. The swing should be long and narrow in the direction of the intended flight of the ball. This will show that the follow-through is complete. The base of the iron swing is a little flat because of the follow-through.
3. The follow-through is more complete than that of the woods. The woods tend to contact the ball at the point where the upswing begins.

Short approaches (quarter swing)

PITCH-AND-RUN APPROACH

Stance:
1. The feet are only 8 to 12 inches apart.
2. The ball is about dead center.
3. The bend of the hips and knees is increased.
4. The stance is well open.

Grip:
1. The club is held a little shorter.

Backswing:
1. Body movement is at a minimum with no hip sway.
2. The wrists, partially cocked, do most of the work.
3. The club head stops just above the hips.
4. The left arm is straight throughout.
5. Both feet remain flat on the ground.
6. The swing is flat and in the line of flight.
7. The left arm is straight and close.
8. The right elbow is close.
9. Swing easily but deliberately, without tightening the shoulders or stiffening the arms.

Downswing:
1. The wrists dominate the shot.
2. Feel the swing with the right forefinger and thumb.
3. Follow through in the line of the shot.
4. At the end of the swing, the club head should point at the hole, emphasizing the follow-through.

HIGH BACKSPIN APPROACH

Stance:
1. The stance is generally quite square.
2. The feet are quite close and the knees bent.
3. The ball is at center.

Backswing:
1. The backswing is longer than that for the pitch-and-run approach.
2. The arms are brought back higher,

with the wrists cocked not quite so sharply.

Downswing:
1. The left arm pulls the club down strongly and dominates the action.
2. When the ball is contacted, the club is hitting down, so that the base of the swing comes just past the ball.
3. The swing is not quite so flat as that of the pitch-and-run approach.

The high backspin approach is used where terrain is irregular and over obstacles.

CHIP SHOT

1. The chip shot is used as a variation of either of the other two approaches.
2. The club head is not brought much higher than the hips.
3. The stance is the same as for the high approach.
4. The wrists control almost all of the action since the arms move back very little.
5. The action is a chop down at about a 45-degree angle.
6. There is no follow-through since the club head sinks into the ground where the ball previously rested.
7. The club head brushes the ball sharply down and forward at the same time, giving a low shot with much backspin.

PUTTING

Stance (see Fig. 11-8):
1. The stance is fairly upright with a sharp bend at the neck and shoulders.
2. The feet are 8 to 12 inches apart.

Fig. 11-8. Putting stance.

3. The stance is slightly open.
4. Most of the weight is on the left foot.
5. The left arm is close.
6. The right forearm is close to the right thigh.
7. The ball is at center.

Grip:
1. The back of the left hand and the palm of the right hand are square to the line.
2. Both thumbs are directly on top of the grip.

Swing:
1. The swing is very short and is flat and close to the ground.
2. It is totally in line with the intended roll of the ball.
3. It is completely relaxed, slow, and steady.
4. There is no body movement.
5. Follow through with the club head.
6. Play to pass the hole slightly.
7. Feel with the forefinger and thumb of the right hand.

Testing:
1. Check the grass for texture to determine the speed of roll.
2. Sight the hole from behind the ball to determine any hazards or tilts.
3. Play up any hill and let the ball roll down.

Practice: Practice is of the utmost necessity in this shot since it can be the cause of losing ten or fifteen strokes in eighteen holes.

Sand traps

GENERAL PRINCIPLES:

1. Sand traps vary from deep, soft sand to shallow, hard clay and sand, so that each situation will be different.
2. When you enter the trap, do so from the point nearest your ball so that you do not unduly disturb the surface.
3. Find your foot positions and then move them back and forth in position so that you will have a firm stance.
4. When you address the ball, do not touch the sand with the club head until the ball is hit.
5. When you leave the trap, cover the irregularities you have made by smoothing them out with the club head.

TRAPS IN WHICH THE SAND IS HARD OR
SHALLOW—BALL ON SURFACE

1. Use chip shots if the edge of the trap is not too high and the ground underneath is either hard or has a very shallow soft surface.
2. Use a short, high approach if the surface is soft but the ball is found set up high. If the edge of the trap is high and the hole close, lift the club head sharply as the ball is contacted.

TRAPS OF SOFT, DEEP SAND—
BALL EMBEDDED

1. Explosion shot:
    (a) The grip, stance, and swing are about the same as for the short, high approach.
    (b) The right forefinger and thumb control the club and carry it through the sand.
    (c) The stance is open with the feet fairly close together and well set in the sand.
    (d) The grip must not be tense, but firm.
    (e) The swing must be fairly long, upright, and U-shaped.
    (f) The club head must not stop in the sand since sand pushed ahead of the club causes the ball to rise. Follow through very definitely with power.
    (g) The amount of sand taken, or how far back of the ball the club head enters, controls the distance the ball will travel. Thus, the closer you are to the green, the more sand you must take.

Uneven ground shots

PRINCIPLES

1. Disregard distance to a great extent.
2. Play for accuracy.
3. Allow the club head to follow the contour of the ground.

UPHILL

1. There is a tendency to pull or hook, so aim to the right.
2. Stand close with the feet in slightly closed position.
3. Weight will be more on the right foot, which will make the backswing flat and awkward.
4. The club will come into the ball with a flat downswing, followed by a quick rise.
5. Play the ball forward of the normal position in stance.

DOWNHILL

1. There is a tendency to slice, so aim to the left.
2. With a steep slope, avoid wood clubs since it is difficult to achieve a rise.
3. Play the ball back of normal position in stance.
4. Weight will be more on the left foot, which will restrict the action of the pivot to the left. Shift the weight to the right foot.
5. The backswing will be more vertical with a flat follow-through.

BALL BELOW FEET

1. There is a very strong tendency to slice, so play to the left.
2. The weight is on the toes, so open the stance somewhat.
3. Avoid topping by holding the club long and concentrating on staying down until the ball is contacted.
4. Do not pivot as much as on level ground since more of a U-shaped swing is natural.

BALL ABOVE FEET

1. The tendency is to pull or hook, so play to the right.
2. Use a short club and hold it short.
3. Swing slowly since a fast swing will throw you back, causing you to top the ball.
4. There is a tendency to toe the ball with the club, so play it close.

ROUGH

1. General principles:
    (a) Do not press in trying for too much distance.
    (b) Use the U-shaped swing.
    (c) Play the shot safely rather than gamble on a "lucky one."

(d) Open the face of the club slightly to cut the grass better and to give a quicker rise in long grass.

(e) Each position will differ from the last, so judge each one as the occasion arises.

SOME OF THE MORE ESSENTIAL GOLF RULES

1. The ball must be played as it lies except as outlined by the rules. Local rules may permit preference lies, or "winter rules," in which case the ball may be moved with the club head provided that it is not moved nearer the hole.
2. The ball must be fairly struck with the head of the club and must not be pushed, scraped, or spooned.
3. The player whose ball is farthest from the hole shall play first.
4. If a ball goes out-of-bounds, the player must play the next stroke at the spot from which the ball was last struck. If the stroke was played from the tee, the ball may be teed; in all other cases it must be dropped. The penalty is loss of stroke and distance. (Add two strokes to score for the hole.) If any part of the ball lies in bounds, the ball remains in play. If a ball is thought to be out-of-bounds, a provisional ball may be played.
5. In match play, if a player's ball is moved by the opponent's ball, the opponent has the option of allowing the ball to remain in the new position or replacing it as near as possible to the original position. In stroke play, the ball must be moved back to its original position.
6. Irregularities of surface which might in any way affect the player's stroke shall not be removed or pressed down by the player, any partner, or caddies.
7. A ball lying on or touching an obstruction such as clothing, lumber, vehicles, ground under repair, etc. may be lifted and dropped away from such an object without penalty but may not be moved closer to the hole.
8. If a player's stroke is interfered with by any object such as just mentioned, the ball may be moved two club lengths, no nearer the hole, without penalty.
9. If a ball interferes with the play of another player, or lies in his line on the green, the player may ask the partner or opponent to move and lift the ball while the stroke is played. It must then be returned to its original position.
10. A ball to be played from a sand trap must be played without grounding the club prior to the actual shot.
11. There should be no more than four persons in one party, and each person should have at least four clubs in the bag.

A DIGEST OF IMPORTANT RULES

1. **Ball played as it lies:** A ball must be played wherever it lies or the hole must be given up except as otherwise provided for in local rules and for unplayable lies. Winter rules mean that the lie on the *fairway* may be improved.
2. **Moving or bending fixed or growing objects:** A player shall not move, bend, or break anything fixed or growing before striking at a ball in play. This applies to holding branches out of the way and to trampling weeds in order to improve the line of the ball.
3. **Lost or unplayable ball:** If a ball is lost or is deemed by the player to be unplayable, the player shall play the next stroke as near as possible to the spot from which the lost or unplayable ball was played, adding a penalty stroke to the score for the hole. *Note:* If a ball is believed lost or unplayable, a provisional ball may be played before the golfer leaves the point from which the first ball was played.
4. **Out-of-bounds:** If you drive out-of-bounds from the tee, you may tee another ball at once and play again. Where not remitted by local rules, the penalty is stroke and distance; that is, you count the next ball as your third

stroke. Otherwise the next drive will count as your second stroke.

5. **Play in a bunker:** When a ball lies in a hazard, nothing shall be done which can in any way improve its lie; the club shall not touch the ground in addressing the ball or during the backswing; nor shall anything be touched or moved by the player before the ball is struck.

6. **Ball in water hazard or in casual water:** If a ball lies or is lost in a recognized water hazard (whether the ball lie in water or not, or in casual water in a hazard) the player may drop a ball, under penalty of one stroke, either (1) behind the hazard, keeping the spot at which the ball crossed the margin of the hazard between himself or herself and the hole, or (2) in the hazard, keeping the spot at which the ball entered the water between himself or herself and the hole. If the ball was played from the teeing ground, a ball may be teed under the penalty of one stroke, as near as possible to the spot from which the original ball was played.

   If a ball lies or is lost in casual water (unintentional hazard), the player may drop a ball without penalty on dry ground as near as possible to the spot where the ball lay but not nearer to the hole.

7. **Putting (condensed):** In match play, if a player's ball knocks the opponent's ball into the hole, the opponent shall be considered to have holed out on the last shot. A ball which has been moved by an opponent's ball may be left at that point or replaced in its original spot. In stroke play, the ball moved must be replaced as near as possible to its original spot. The golfer playing the putt has the right to ask the opponent to mark the ball.

   In holding the flagstick, the player has the option of having it left unattended, removed, or attended. If the ball strikes the flagstick unattended, there is no penalty. If the ball strikes an attended flagstick or a person attending the flagstick in stroke play, there is a two-stroke penalty. In match play, if the flagstick is held by an opponent or an opponent's caddy, the opponent loses the hole. If it is held by the player's caddy, the player loses the hole.

ETIQUETTE

Students should study golf etiquette carefully and govern their conduct accordingly. Golf developed as a gentleman's game and it still remains so. Play the game by the rules without exception.

1. No one should move or talk or stand close to or directly behind the ball or the hole when a player is making a stroke.
2. On the putting green, the player whose ball lies nearest the hole should hold the pin while other players putt.
3. No player should play until the golfers in front are out of range.
4. Players looking for a lost ball should allow other players coming up to pass them. They should signal to the players following them to pass, and, having given such a signal, they should not continue their play until these players have passed and are out of range.
5. A player should see that any turf cut or displaced by him or her is at once replaced and *pressed* down.
6. No practice shots should be attempted on any part of the course when other golfers are following.
7. Slow players should allow a faster group to pass through.
8. Observe local course rules.
9. Play all shots according to the rules of the game.
10. The player farthest away from the hole shoots or putts first.
11. Avoid walking ahead of your partners or opponents.
12. The tee shot should be played from behind the markers.
13. If any player or person on the course is in danger of being hit by your shot, call "fore" as a warning.

14. Always lay your golf bag off the green.
15. Smooth out footprints in a sand trap after a shot.
16. When holding the flag on the putting green, stand so that your shadow does not fall across the cup.
17. When all players have holed out, leave the putting green immediately for oncoming players.
18. When one member of a twosome, threesome, or foursome has lost a ball, all members of the group should help look for it.
19. Above all, be courteous.

The game of golf teaches the highest principles of sportsmanship and consideration for others.

The game is no longer enjoyable when rules are broken at random. The code of golf etiquette is easily understood and, when correctly observed, affords pleasure and enjoyment of the game.

THE BALL

Golf balls are made by many manufacturers. Their construction is essentially the same. One should have at least three or more balls in the golf bag when going out to play.

Plastic balls are used for the gymnasium, small field, or backyard practice.

LEARNING PROCEDURES
Equipment

1. Balls (supplied by students)
2. Wood driver and several irons (supplied by the school)

Object

The object in required physical education is as follows:
1. To become acquainted with a fundamental knowledge of the various clubs
2. To help develop a sound fundamental swing
3. To learn to use the wood and iron clubs:
   (a) Grip
   (b) Stance
   (c) Address
   (d) Swing
4. To learn different types of shots:
   (a) Drive
   (b) Pitch-and-run
   (c) Chip
   (d) Putting
5. To stress rules of the game and play
6. To stress rules of conduct and etiquette on the course
7. To learn to play the game with confidence and the knowledge that strokes are fundamentally sound
8. To learn the psychology of golf

Achievement tests

1. Demonstrate use of the various clubs.
2. Analyze own swing.
3. Understand rules of play such as:
   (a) Handicap play
   (b) Medal play
   (c) Match play
4. Play eighteen holes of medal play, keeping own score and that of opponent.
5. Pass written examination on rules of play and etiquette of golf. Practice is confined to driving, approaching, and putting.

Grade

The grade is based upon the tests just listed. There should also be a written examination on rules, tournament play, and etiquette on the golf course.

GLOSSARY OF GOLF TERMS

ace Making the hole in one stroke.
addressing the ball Placing the body and club in position.
approach shot A shot played to the green: (1) played with run-up club, #3 or #4 iron; (2) played with #5 or #6; (3) played with #7 or #8; (4) shots played to land at the edge of the green and roll to pin.
away Ball farthest from the hole—to be played first.
birdie Making a hole in one less than par.
bisque Strokes of handicap—may be taken on any hole.
bogey Any phantom score played against, generally one over par.

brassie Wooden club #2, generally has a brass or metal base. (See Fig. 11-2.)
bunker Hazard, usually artificial, of exposed ground or sand.
caddie Assistant to the player—watches the ball, carries the clubs, etc.
carry The distance the ball travels through the air; sometimes used in estimating the height of clearance of a shot. (*Note:* the higher the number of the club, the more altitude and the less distance and roll.)
clubs Implements used to propel the ball.
course Ground within the limits.
cup Hole into which the ball is played.
dead Ball does not roll after flight.
divot Slice of turf cut out with club.
dodo Double eagle; three under par for any hole.
dormie As many holes up as are left in match place, unbeatable.
down Number of strokes or holes by which the opponent leads.
driver Wooden club #1 (see clubs).
eagle Two under par for any hole.
face Contact surface of the club head.
fairway The mowed or well-kept part of the area between the tee and green.
flag On pin, indicates number and position of hole.
flagstick On pin, indicates number and position of hole. The flagstick in the hole.
fore Warning signal.
foursome Two players on a side or four people.
green Short-cropped grass around a hole.
grip Handle of the club or method of grasping.
gross score Actual score shot by a player in stroke play.
halved Tied score on a hole or a complete game.
handicap Strokes given to a player to enable him to shoot a score of par, computed on the basis of 80% of the difference between the player's average score and par.
hazard Natural or unnatural obstacle on a course.
head The weight at the end of the shaft; part used for hitting.
heel Back part of the club head.
hole The cup into which one rolls the ball.
hole out Final stroke for a hole.

honor Right to play first from a tee by low score on the last hole.
hook A shot which curves to the left.
iron A club with an iron head (see clubs).
lie Position of the ball on the course.
links The entire course.
loft The elevation of a shot or angle of the club face.
match A game.
match play Competition based on a hole-by-hole basis.
medal play Competition based on total strokes per round.
par Perfect score for a hole; a set number of strokes.
pin The flagstick in the hole marking it.
press Too much tensing of muscles.
pull A slight hook with a long roll, generally intentional.
rim the cup The ball rolls around the edge of the cup without falling in.
rough Intentional rough ground and long grass off the fairway.
round Any series of holes, generally eighteen.
shaft The stick which holds the club head.
slice The ball curves to the right.
stance Position of the feet.
stroke Act of swinging at the ball even though it may be missed.
tee An elevation, generally a wooden peg, upon which the ball is placed and from which it is to be driven.
tee-ground Starting point for each hole; a designated area behind markers.
toe Front portion of the club head.
trap Usually a sand pit in the fairway and around the green.
up The number of holes or strokes by which one leads an opponent.
waggle Preliminary movements with the club as the ball is addressed.
wood A club with wooden head.

REFERENCES

Ainsworth, Dorothy, and others: Individual sports for women, ed. 3, Philadelphia, 1963, W. B. Saunders Co.

Barnes, J. L.: Picture analysis of golf strokes, Philadelphia, 1963, J. B. Lippincott Co.

Boros, Julius: How to play golf with an effortless swing, Inglewood Cliffs, N. J., 1964, Prentice-Hall, Inc.

Casper, Bill: Chipping and putting: golf around the green, New York, 1961, The Ronald Press Co.

Gaskill, Bud: Golf at a glance, New York, 1960, Arco Publishing Co., Inc.

Hogan, Ben: Power golf, New York, 1957, Pocket Books, Inc.

Hogan, Ben: Five lessons of modern fundamentals of golf, New York, 1957, A. S. Barnes & Co.

Snead, Sam: Natural golf, New York, 1953, A. S. Barnes & Co.

The rules of golf, New York, 1973, United States Golf Association.

FILMS

Beginning golf (film strip), The Athletic Institute, Inc., Chicago, Ill.

Golf doctor, Wilson Sporting Goods Co., Chicago, Ill.

Golf mistakes, Teaching Films Custodians, Inc., New York, N. Y.

Play better golf (Part I, fundamentals; Part II, advanced), Official Films, Inc., New York, N. Y.

Saving strokes with Sam Snead, Teaching Films Custodians, Inc., New York, N. Y.

12 Gymnastics

BRIEF HISTORY

The word gymnastics means "naked art" and comes from the early Greeks. It is believed that the Chinese were the first people to develop activities that resembled gymnastics. The Greeks worked with an apparatus rather than upon it, whereas the Romans used an apparatus in the form of a wooden horse upon which to practice. The word gymnasium is also a Greek word and means "the ground, or place for gymnastic performances."

When the Roman civilization weakened, the common people were discouraged from participating in strenuous activities, and through the middle ages, only the knights engaged in much physical activity. Using people as apparatus, human towers were formed during sieges and at public performances.

Johann Basedow (1723-1790) was the first European to teach organized gymnastic exercises. Then Johann Guts Muths (1759-1839) published the first book on gymnastics. Guts Muths is also referred to as the "great-grandfather of gymnastics."

After the Napoleonic victories over the Germans, a plan for building up the national strength of Germany was formulated by Frederick Jahn during the period from 1810 to 1852.

Jahn is credited with introducing the parallel bars, the horizontal bar, the side horse with pommels, and the vaulting buck. He believed that the Germans should be united to protect themselves, so he took the boys of Berlin to nearby woods on hikes and there they invented these different types of apparatus. In 1842, ten years before Jahn's death, gymnastics was introduced into the German public schools but in a formal nature.

Mats were first used in Copenhagen, Denmark when the Military Gymnastic Institute was opened to train teachers in gymnastics.

About 1850, a wave of German immigration brought these clubs to America, where they were called Turner Societies.

In 1865, the American Turners established a Normal College of the American Gymnastic Union for the purpose of training gymnastic teachers.

Gymnastics took a thorough hold through these Turner Clubs and through Y.M.C.A.s, schools, and colleges. In an elementary form for modern recreational use in our parks and community centers are the jungle gyms, teeter-totters, slides, rings, swings, etc. Heavy apparatus such as parallel bars, horizontal bar, side horse, buck, and flying rings are the equipment used in most schools, colleges, clubs, and Y.M.C.A. gymnasiums.

Gymnastics in modern usage and competition generally refers to bodily movements on apparatus, tumbling on mats, trampoline, and calisthenics.

The use of apparatus in American public schools and colleges was impeded by three main factors:

1. About 1800 Dio Lewis introduced exercises that did not require apparatus and the schools accepted them enthusiastically.
2. The Swedish influence about 1900 emphasized calisthenics.
3. Between World War I and World War II gymnastics did not occupy its rightful place in the total program of high schools and colleges in this country. The trend was toward mild recreational activities for the majority whereas strenuous competition was encouraged for the small minority.

Following World War II, the pendulum swung once again back to resistive forms of exercise, including gymnastics. Today there is considerable emphasis on competitive gymnastics in the secondary schools, Y.M.C.A.'s, Turner Clubs, and many of the colleges throughout the United States. The foundation of our whole physical education program seems to be moving toward heavy apparatus work.

Noteworthy developments after World War II were the organization of the National Association of American Gymnastic Coaches in 1946 and of the National Gymnastic Clinic in 1951.

SAFETY RULES

1. There should be a regular inspection of apparatus for detecting faults, making proper adjustment, and removing obstruction hazards.
2. Remember that accidents on apparatus never "just happen." They are caused, usually through carelessness.
3. Provide an adequate number of mats around the apparatus, and keep them clean. Carry mats; do not drag them over the floor. Do not overlap the mats when placing them around the apparatus.
4. Build strength and skill progressively; the need of progression from the simple to the more complex must be recognized.
5. Master the art of spotting by alternately acting as performer and spotter, respectively.
6. Use magnesium chalk and resin wisely. Sand the bars to prevent hand tear.
7. Strict discipline should be maintained; fooling and horseplay are absolutely forbidden.
8. Warming-up exercises are essential before practicing stunts.

DUAL MEET COMPETITION

Competition rules for high schools and colleges are written by the N.C.A.A. The A.A.U. writes rules for competitions other than those in schools. In a number of states rules for high school competition are being formulated by state high school coaches associations.

Order of competition

MEN

The events in order of competition for a dual meet shall be as follows: floor exercises, pommel horse, rings, vaulting bars, parallel bars, and high bar. There will be no warm-up allowed after the meet starts.

Gymnasts from both teams shall be alternated in the events. The visiting team shall compete last in floor exercises, rings, and parallel bars.

Number of entries: Each team shall be limited to a maximum of five entries per event. Three of the men must be designated as all-around contestants. A gymnastics team shall be limited to fifteen men.

WOMEN

For women the order of events in competition are as follows: floor exercises, vaulting, balance beam, and uneven parallel bars. Gymnasts alternate the same as men.

Number of entries: The number of gymnasts from each team to compete in each event should exceed the number of scores that will count for the final team totals (for example, five entries using three scores per team; or four entries using three scores per team).

SCORE

The best three scores for each team in each event are added to determine the team's score for that event. This includes the all-around score. The event scores are added to determine the final team score.

JUDGES

Four judges plus one superior judge conduct the competition. Each of the four judges flashes a score based on 10 points, four points for composition and six points for execution. (See DGWS Gymnastic Guide, June 1973-June 1975, p. 66.) Then the low and high scores are dropped and the other two averaged. If the middle scores are out of range, the superior judge's score is added to the average of these two scores and then this score is divided by two to get the final score.

EQUIPMENT
Personal

1. Gymnastic shoes, except on trampoline where the contestant may go barefooted
2. Gym shorts or pants
3. Athletic supporter
4. Athletic shirt

Gymnastic

1. Side horse
2. Long horse
3. Parallel bars
4. Uneven parallel bars
5. Horizontal bars
6. Rings
7. Balance beam
8. Mats
9. Carbonate of magnesium
10. Emery paper to clean bars
11. Trampoline
12. Free exercise—40 × 40 foot area

FUNDAMENTAL SKILL TECHNIQUES

The gymnastic exercises in this chapter are basic movements primarily for developmental purposes. Advanced stunts and routines may be found in other sources. However, these are advanced enough to qualify a beginner for the gym team. We have included the flying rings as a fun piece of apparatus to be used by the physical education class. Many of these flying exercises can also be accomplished on the still rings.

Safety and assistance procedures on the apparatus

Each of the illustrations accompanying the discussion of the movements on the horse, parallel bars, horizontal bar, and flying rings has a figure with a spot ♂ and a circle O. Both the spot and the circle may be on the same figure, or a spot may appear on one and a circle on another. The spot indicates the area of the body that should be controlled by the spotter throughout the exercise or movement, whereas the circle indicates the crucial part of the movement or stunt. For example, as shown in Fig. 12-13, a beginner may have weak arms and may fall forward as the body swings back when starting to hand walk forward on the parallel bars. For protection against falling through the bars, a spotter should help support the performer's body as the weight is transferred from one arm to the other while moving forward. *The spotter should follow the movement from beginning to end.* The crucial part in this movement is the point at which the weight is transferred to a single arm. This is the point of difficulty. Spotting should continue as the performer dismounts.

Side horse,* buck, Swedish box, and elephant

FLANK VAULT

This is also termed the "side vault." Use a two-foot takeoff and vault so that the side of the body passes over the horse. Keep the legs extended and the toes pointed. Land in a partial knee bend with the arms extended to the side. (See Fig. 12-1.)

SQUAT TO REAR SUPPORT

Use a two-foot takeoff and pass over the horse by lifting the hips high, keeping the head up and bringing the knees between the arms. After the feet pass over the horse, come to rest in a rear support. (See Fig. 12-2.)

---

*Many of these vaults can be performed on the side horse with or without pommels.

Face vault

Use a two-foot takeoff and pass the body over the horse by doing a quarter turn so that the body faces the horse as it passes over it. Land with the side to the horse, with one hand on the pommel and the other extended to the side. (See Fig. 12-3.)

Feint left or right

Do this from the front support. Swing the leg up and over the end of the horse, either the right side, which is called the croup, or the left side, which is called the neck. If the right leg passes over the horse, turn the face to the left. If the left leg passes over the horse, turn to the right. Keep the arms fully extended, legs stiff, and toes pointed. Pass the leg over the horse and then bring it back. (See Fig. 12-4.)

Courage vault

This is also termed "knee vault." Jump to the knee stand. Now throw the arms into the air and push with the shins. Land in the partial knee bend with the arms extended to the side. Be sure that a spotter is present. (See Fig. 12-5.)

Wolf vault

Approach the horse as you would in performing the flank vault. This is a combination of the flank and squat vault. If the vault is to the right, keep the right leg extended and bend the left leg under. Land with good form. (See Fig. 12-6.)

Cut left or right

From the front-leaning support, pass the leg over the end of the horse and under one hand. To accomplish this, the weight of the body must be transferred to the opposite hand. Attempt to keep both arms and legs extended. (See Fig. 12-7.)

Flank vault from feint left or right

As the flank vault is thrown from the feint, keep the weight back on the arm opposite the side over which the flank is performed. Land in the partial knee bend with the arms extended to the side. (See Fig. 12-8.)

Straddle vault

Instead of stopping on top of the horse, pass the body completely over. Keep the

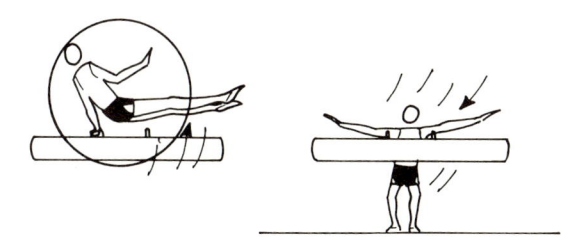

Fig. 12-1. Flank vault.

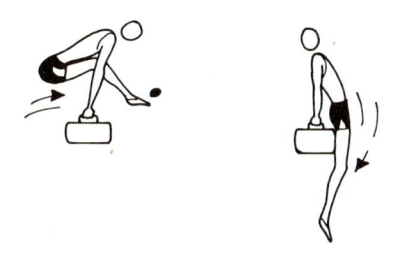

Fig. 12-2. Squat to rear support.

Fig. 12-3. Face vault.

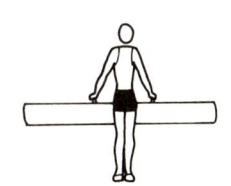

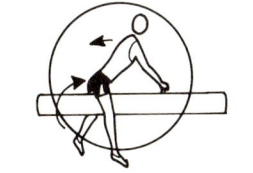

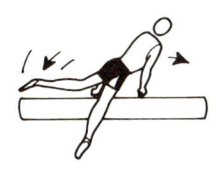

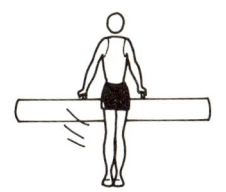

Fig. 12-4. Feint left or right.

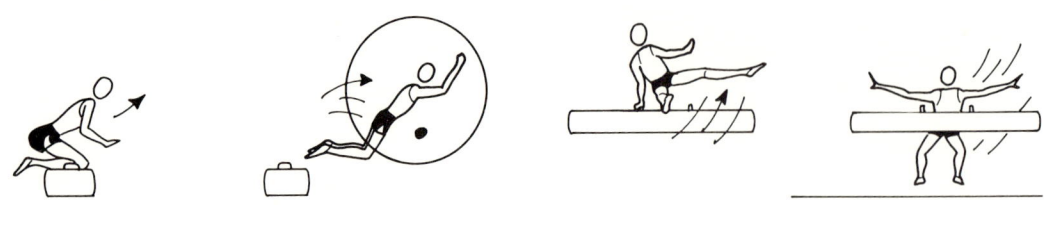

Fig. 12-5. Courage vault.

Fig. 12-6. Wolf vault.

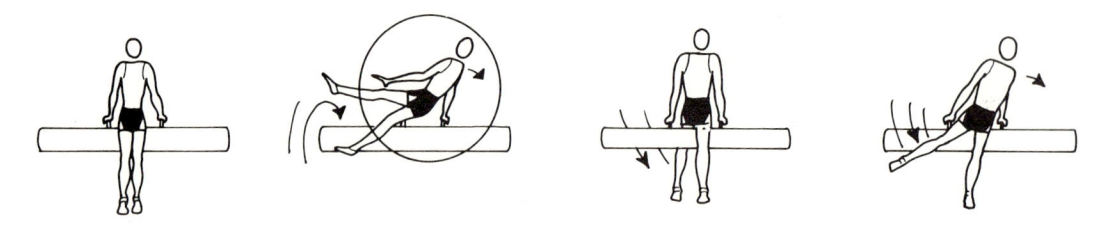

Fig. 12-7. Cut left or right.

Fig. 12-8. Flank vault from feint left or right.

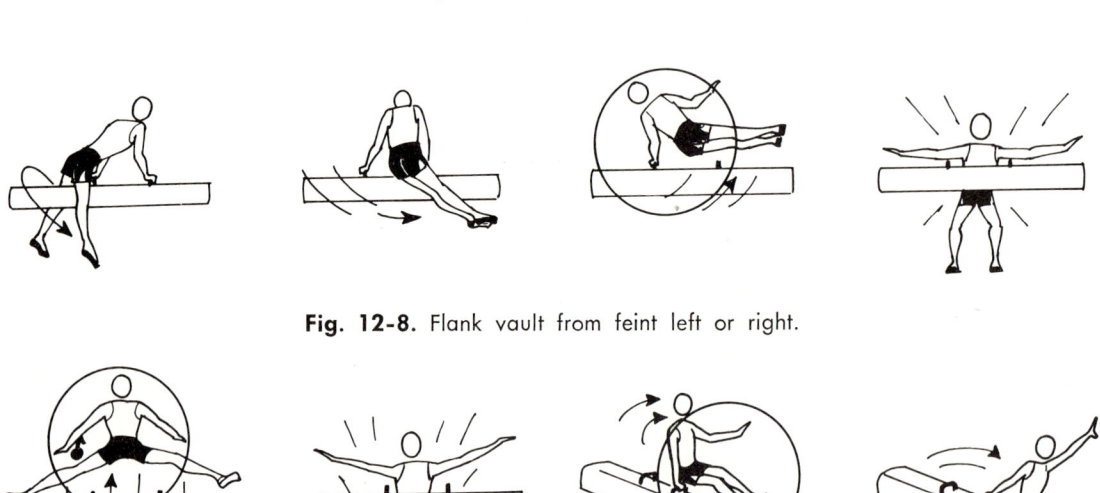

Fig. 12-9. Straddle vault.

Fig. 12-10. Rear vault.

head up. This vault should be spotted very closely. (See Fig. 12-9.)

REAR VAULT

This is termed a "rear vault" because the rear or back of the body passes over the end of the horse. If the vault is a rear vault to the right, the body makes a quarter turn to the right and passes over the horse in this position. After the body passes over the horse, regrasp the right pommel with the right hand and extend the left to the side. (See Fig. 12-10.)

THIEF VAULT

This is something like a hurdle and done from a one-foot takeoff. Before placing the hands on the pommels, kick one leg up and over the saddle and then bring the other foot to it. Drop onto the hand support as shown in the second maneuver in Fig. 12-11. Push off to a good landing.

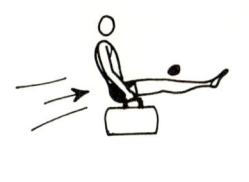

Fig. 12-11. Thief vault.

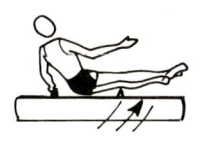

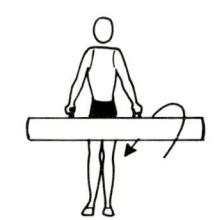

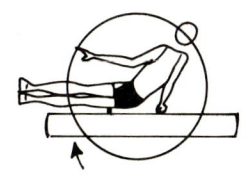

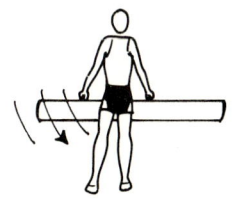

Fig. 12-12. Right flank to rear support, reverse flank left to front support.

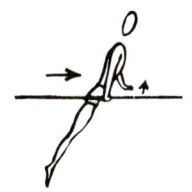

Fig. 12-13. Hand traveling.

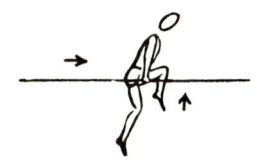

Fig. 12-14. Bicycle riding.

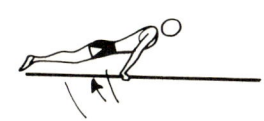

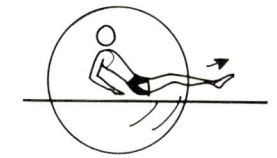

Fig. 12-15. Intermediate swing with hop.

RIGHT FLANK TO REAR SUPPORT,
REVERSE FLANK LEFT TO FRONT SUPPORT

If the weight is kept over the horse as the flank is performed, the catch to the rear support is not difficult. To perform the reverse flank, throw all the weight on the right arm. The secret of the vaults and catch is proper weight distribution. (See Fig. 12-12.)

Parallel bars

HAND TRAVELING

1. Hand over hand, walk forward the length of the bars. Keep the chest out, head up, back arched, and toes pointed. (See Fig. 12-13.)
2. Hop the length of the bars in a straight-arm support position. In this hop forward the hands are moved simultaneously.
3. Riding a bicycle with the legs increases the difficulty. (See Fig. 12-14.)

INTERMEDIATE SWING WITH HOP

In doing the intermediate swing, keep the arms extended, flex the body on the front swing, and extend it to the back swing. The hop is executed on the front swing. *Spot this for a possible collapse right after the catch.* (See Fig. 12-15.)

FORWARD SWINGING DIPS

1. Swing from the shoulders.
2. At the end of the rear swing, flex the arms, keeping the back arched and head up. (See Fig. 12-16.)

Fig. 12-16. Forward swinging dips.

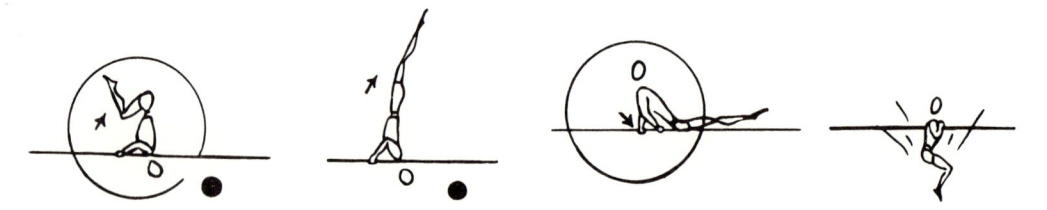

Fig. 12-17. Shoulder balance.

Fig. 12-18. Rear vault dismount.

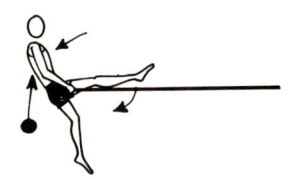

Fig. 12-19. Single-leg cut-off.

3. Swing forward in a bent-arm position so that the chin is even with the bars in the middle of the swing.
4. At the front end of swing, straighten the arms and shoot the feet forward. This must be done four times for credit.

STRADDLES

1. Execute a series of straddle seats going across the bars.
2. Execute a straddle seat to the center of the bar with a front dismount.

INTERMEDIATE SWING

From a cross support position in the center of the bars, start to swing the body from the shoulders forward and backward. Learn to balance the center of body weight over the hand supports by leaning backward when the legs are swinging forward and by leaning forward when the legs are moving backward.

SKIN THE CAT

From the end of the bars, bring the feet forward and up through the bars and back, trying to touch the floor with the toes. Return to the original position. The hands must keep their grip on the bars.

SHOULDER BALANCE

Be in the center of the bar and extend elbows to be level with the shoulders. The forearms should be flexed at the elbow with the hands on the bar. Flex the knees and place the feet on the bars. Roll the hips up first, then the legs, and arch the back to maintain balance. If you start to fall backward, keep the elbows well spread and swing downward, using the upper arms as rockers. Have a spotter on each side always when practicing this. (See Fig. 12-17.)

DISMOUNTS

From a cross support at the center of the bars, execute one of the following dismounts over either bar:

1. Rear vault dismount, in front of hands. (See Fig. 12-18.)
2. Front vault dismount, behind hands.
3. Side vault dismount, facing outward. This vault is made in front of the hands.

From the outside cross seat on one bar, execute a rear vault over the other bar.

SINGLE- AND DOUBLE-LEG CUT-OFFS

Single-leg cut-off: At the end of the forward swing, push back and cut off. *Watch*

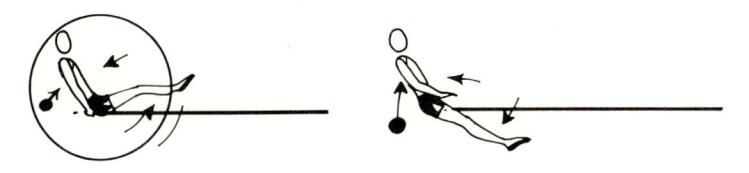

Fig. 12-20. Double-leg cut-off.

Fig. 12-21. Run and jump to cross support.

Fig. 12-22. Hip rise.

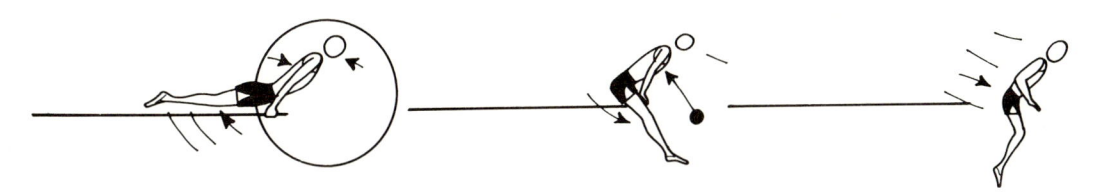

Fig. 12-23. Split-off.

out for the face. Keep the head back so that the face will not hit the bar. *Spot this on both shoulders from the back.* The backward lean before the cut-off is very important. (See Fig. 12-19.)

Double-leg cut-off: Apply the same principle to this as you did in the single-leg cut-off. Cut off with both legs. Use the same spotting technique as you did before. (See Fig. 12-20.)

RUN AND JUMP TO CROSS SUPPORT

Take the jump as in the dive and roll. Land in the forward-leaning position and then swing forward. *Spot for a collapse on the backswing.* Spot under the bar on the chest if a collapse takes place. (See Fig. 12-21.)

HIP RISE

Swing forward vigorously in the upper arm hang. Approaching the front end of the swing, pull forward with the arms, and then push up to a cross support. (See Fig. 12-22.)

BACK ROLL FROM SITTING POSITION

From a straddle seat position in the center of the bar, grip the bar behind the back with the thumbs in. Spread the flexed elbows to make rockers. Slowly roll backward to a straddle seat position.

SPLIT-OFF

This is nothing but a straddle vault. Be sure to keep the head up. Do not raise the hips too high. *Spot this forward on the chest and shoulders.* (See Fig. 12-23.)

KIDNEY ROLL

While in a straddle seat position, reach forward with the left hand. Place the right hand palm up on the left bar between the left hand and thigh. Twist onto the small of the back with the head under the left bar and the legs toward the ceiling. Keep twisting in the same direction until the body is back in the sitting position but in the opposite direction. *Spot the legs.* (See Fig. 12-24.)

High horizontal bar

GRASPS

Show the correct grasps and significance of each one, including the wide grasp, mixed grasp, ordinary grasp, cross grasp, and the reverse grasp.

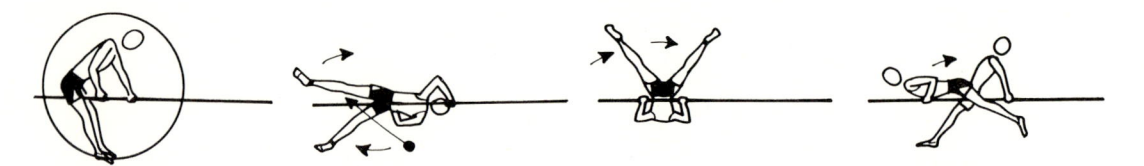

Fig. 12-24. Kidney roll.

Fig. 12-25. Seat swing up from swing.

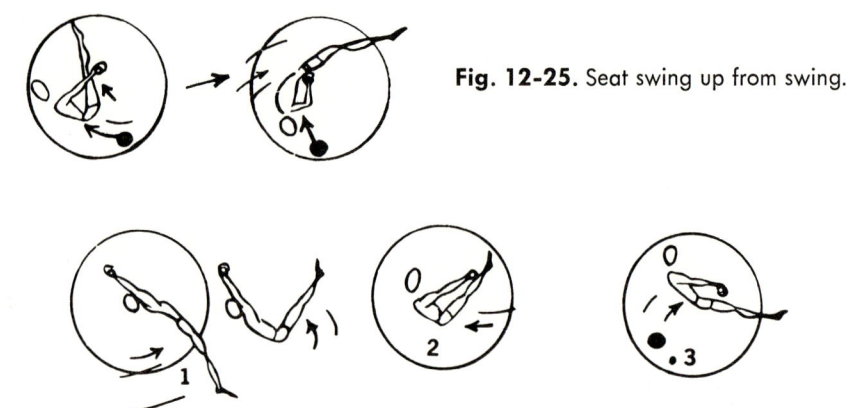

Fig. 12-26. Kip or upstart.

SWING

Execute a short underswing from the hang and dismount.

CHINS

1. Use the ordinary grasp and pull up to the chest six times.
2. Use the wide grasp and pull up to back of the neck four times.
3. One hand grasps the bar and the other hand grasps the wrist of the chinning arm. Chin two times.
4. One hand grasps the bar and the other hand grasps the bicep of the chinning arm.

SKIN THE CAT OVER THE BAR

From a hanging position, pull the legs up through the hands and then over the bar; do not allow the body to swing.

SKIN THE CAT

From a hanging position, bring the legs up through the arms and over the head until the feet point toward the floor. Return to original position.

MONKEY HANG

From a hanging position, bring the legs up through the arms and over the head until the feet point toward the floor. Release one arm and swing a complete turn on one arm and then regrasp the bar.

SEAT SWING-UP FROM SWING

Pull the legs up through the hands and then over the bar. Arch the back and slowly pull the body up over the bar into a sitting position on top of the bar. (See Fig. 12-25.)

KIP OR UPSTART

Stress arching the back at the front of the swing and wait for the hips to start the return swing before bringing the instep to the bar. Bring the instep to the bar and shoot the legs up, out, and down. Press down and in with the shoulder muscles. Get a little wrist motion when going above the bar. Do not push away from the bar. Force the shoulders well forward. (See Fig. 12-26.)

SINGLE-KNEE MOUNT

From a hang position with an ordinary grasp, swing one knee over and hook it on the bar, outside or inside the arms, using either leg. Swing the other leg hard downward and backward, and pull in with the arms, mounting to a cross seat on the top of the bar.

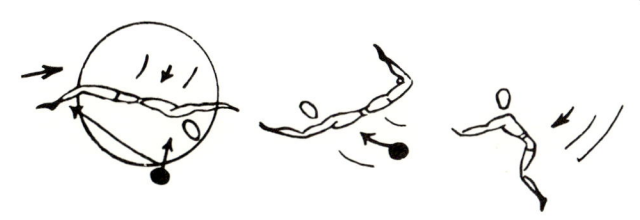

Fig. 12-27. Hock swing dismount.

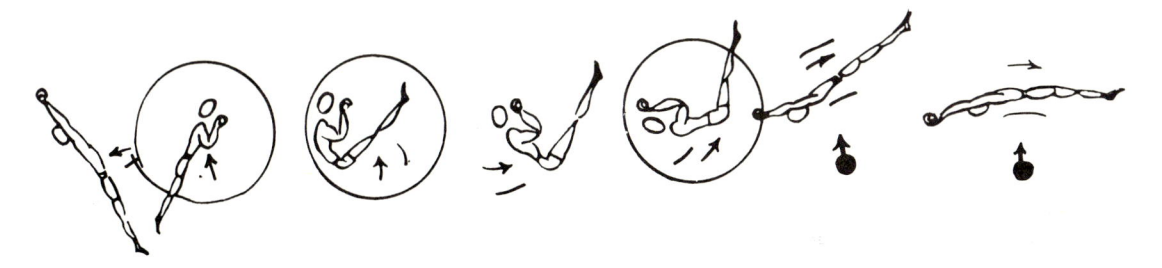

Fig. 12-28. Cast.

Hand and knee circles

From a cross-riding seat on the bar (one leg on each side of the bar), and with an ordinary grasp (thumbs in direction circle is made), reach back with the rear leg and swing it downward hard and forward. The other leg is hooked at the knee over the bar and a complete circle backward around the bar is made. The instructor stands by to assist.

Hock swing dismount

Sit on the bar, then let the body back slowly with both knees hooked on the bar between the hands. Release the hand grip and make an underbar swing. At the end of the forward swing, snap the knees straight, and swing the legs down to a stand on the mat. (See Fig. 12-27.) The instructor stands by for protection. (Students should wear long pants for knee hooks.)

Short underswing dismount

Stand under the bar; jump up and grasp the bar. From a hang position, pull the body up over the bar to a front rest, drop the trunk backward, and at the same time pike at the hips and raise the legs (straight at knees) forward until the ankles are at the bar. As the body swings downward under the bar, shoot the feet forward and pull backward and upward with the arms, shooting out forward to a stand on the mat.

Crotch circles

From a side-riding seat and an ordinary grasp, fall backward to start the circle. When the body is under the bar, flex and pull on the arms somewhat to complete the circle. This circle can also be executed forward with the reverse grasp, with the thumbs in the direction of the circle. This can also be performed sideways from a cross-riding seat, the hands grasping in front. Dismount with a short underswing.

Cast

From a hang position with a regular grasp, pull up to a half chin, lean the shoulders and head back, and at the same time raise the legs, holding the knees and ankles stretched and together. Shoot the legs forward and upward, at the same time extending the elbows. *Note:* As the legs swing upward and shoot outward, also shoot the body forward by pushing on the elbows for a big swing. (See Fig. 12-28.) Practice this swing several times.

Heel circle forward with reverse grip

Sit on top of and grasp the bar with a reverse or undergrip. Keep the legs extended, extend the arms, and raise the hips backward until the heels rest on the bar. Keep this position and let the body drop. Slightly alter the hand and leg relationship. Start the hip extension. Drive the legs over the bar.

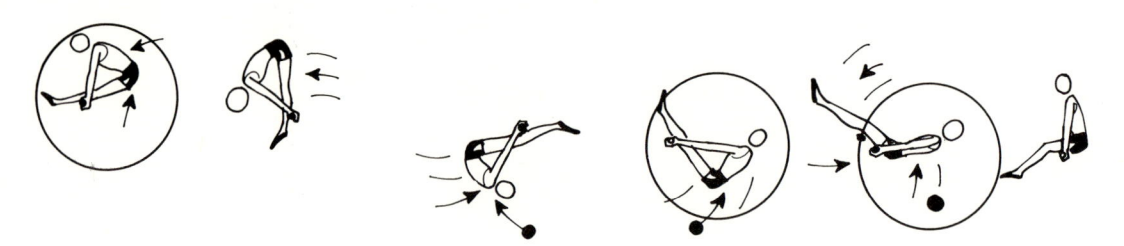

Fig. 12-29. Heel circle forward with reverse grip.

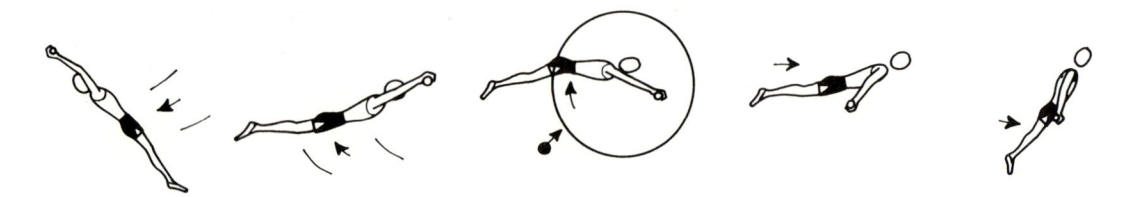

Fig. 12-30. Stem rise.

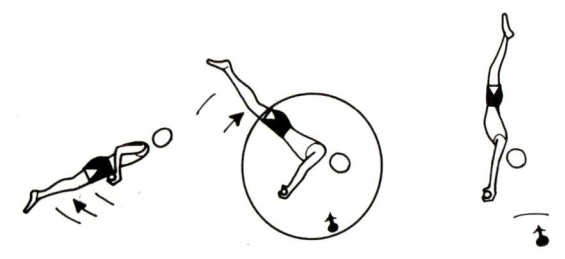

Fig. 12-31. Cast to handstand.

Return to a sitting position. (See Fig. 12-29.)

STEM RISE

A requisite for this skill is a good cast. After the cast, swing down and back in an extended posture. At the end of the back swing, pike, raise the back and shoulders, and lift the body above the bar by pushing down with the hands. Place the body weight over the bar by leaning over the bar and arching. Come to the front-leaning support. (See Fig. 12-30.)

HIP CIRCLE FORWARD

Pull over to a front-leaning support. Push down with the arms and raise the body so that the thighs will rest on the bar. With the head held up, fall forward, keeping the thighs in contact with the bar. Hold this position. Shorten the radius on the upswing by forcing the head forward and bending the arms. Come to a rest over the bar.

CAST TO HANDSTAND

Practice this first on the low bar. Practice with both grips. Assume a front-leaning support position. Slightly flex the arms so that the bar contacts the lower abdomen and swing the legs under the bar as the body leans forward. Forcefully hyperextend the body and push with the arms as the body weight remains over the bar. (See Fig. 12-31.)

HALF GIANT SWING

Use the overgrip (palms down). Start cast as in going for a handstand but push back. Swing down fully extended. At the 5 o'clock position, break at the waist and come to a rest on the bar. (See Fig. 12-32.)

BACK GIANT SWING

Use the overgrip (palms down). Cast to a full handstand. Keep the arms extended and drop the chest first. Retain this extended position down and under the bar.

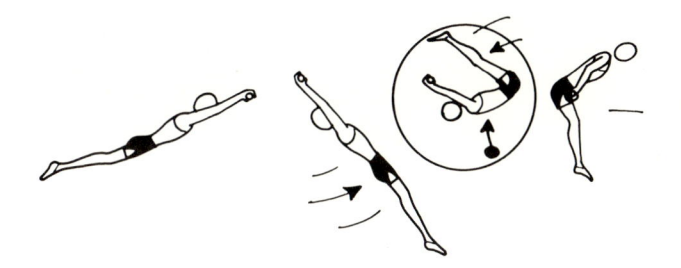

Fig. 12-32. Half giant swing (overgrip).

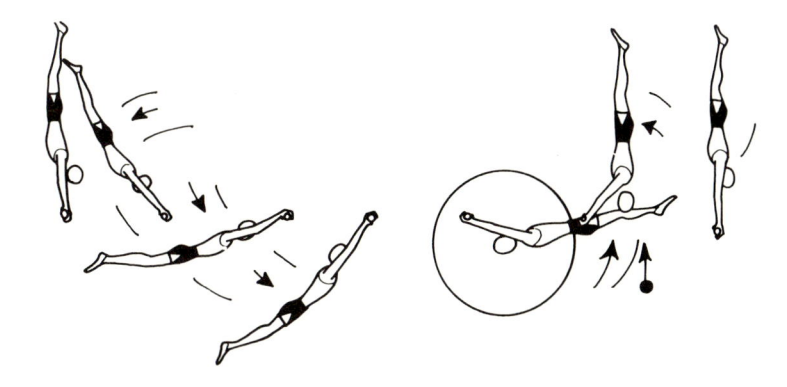

Fig. 12-33. Back giant swing (overgrip).

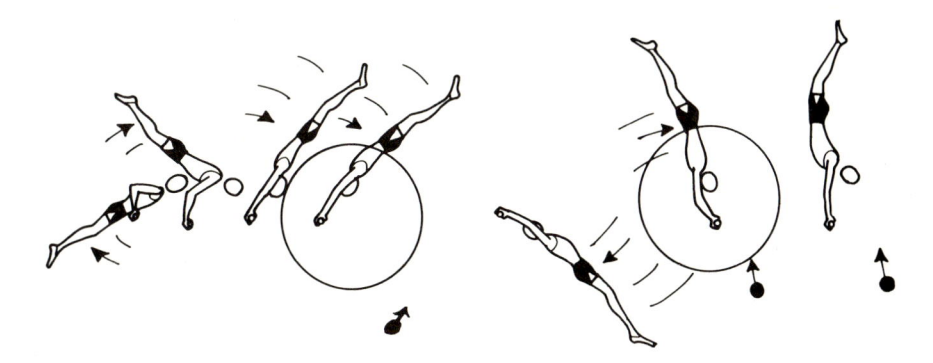

Fig. 12-34. Front giant swing (undergrip).

Flex at the shoulders and hips to shorten the radius on the upswing. Direct the legs over the bar and extent the shoulders. (See Fig. 12-33.)

FRONT GIANT SWING

Use the undergrip (palms up). Cast to a handstand. Extend the arms fully and duck the head. Fall forward. Continue to revolve in this position until about three-quarters of the way around and then flex the hips slightly and pull in slightly toward the bar. Look at the bar. (See Fig. 12-34.)

Fig. 12-35. Double front cut-off.

FLYING RINGS
DOUBLE FRONT CUT-OFF

From a pike hang position, rotate the body forward vigorously, bending the elbows, and at the same time bring the separated legs, with the knees bent, down

156 BASIC SKILLS IN SPORTS FOR MEN AND WOMEN

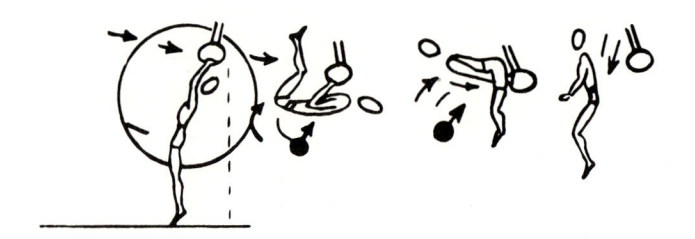

Fig. 12-36. Double back cut-off.

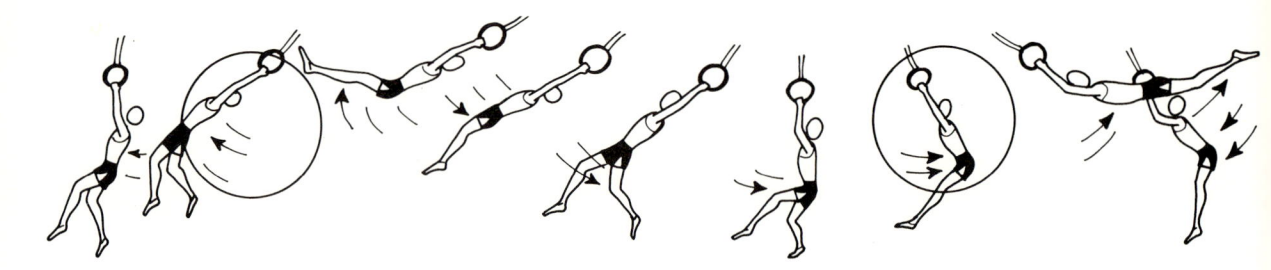

Fig. 12-37. Fundamental swing. (Observe from right to left.)

across the elbows. Immediately after this, and while still rotating forward, release the rings and land standing on the mat. (See Fig. 12-35.)

DOUBLE BACK CUT-OFF

From a bent-arm hang, swing the legs and hips upward vigorously, spreading the legs held straight until the crotch is astride the wrists. While the body still has momentum, release the rings and land in a standing position. (See Fig. 12-36.) *Spot the back and shoulders.*

FUNDAMENTAL SWING

As the body leaves the mat on the forward swing, it is in an arched position. To acquire maximum height on the forward swing, flex at the waist. On the return from the forward swing, let the legs swing back and reach for the mat with one foot, as shown in Fig. 12-38. Take one step (a large step) and then push back into a sitting position. Lastly, swing the legs back into a hyperextended position as shown in Fig. 12-37. Flex when coming out of this hyperextended position, reach forward, take two steps, and push the chest forward again for the forward swing. Repeat. *The two most important movements are spotted.* Observe Fig. 12-37 from right to left.

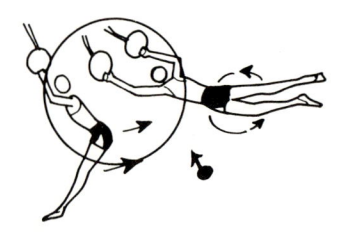

Fig. 12-38. Fundamental swing with turn on backswing.

FUNDAMENTAL SWING WITH TURN ON BACKSWING

The turn is performed while extending on the backswing. The twist is made with the shoulders. If twisting to the right, drop the right shoulder and raise the left. This is really a *twist* and not a turn. (See Fig. 12-38.)

DISLOCATION AT BACK END OF SWING OR ON STILL RINGS

From a pike hang position in the swing, wait until the end of the backward swing is reached, then extend the legs upward and about 20 degrees backward. At the same time turn the thumbs out. (See Fig. 12-39.) The body will swing around through the shoulders and the performer will come to an ordinary hang. *Spot this movement on the downswing.*

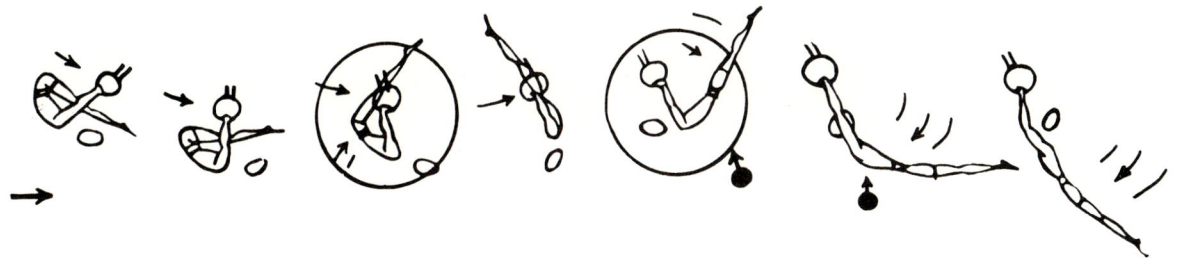

Fig. 12-39. Dislocation at back end of swing or on still rings.

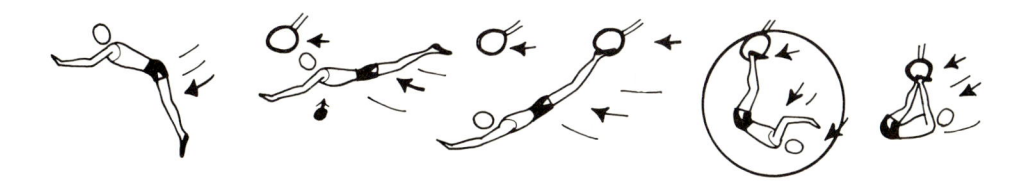

Fig. 12-40. Toe snap on front swing. (Observe from right to left.)

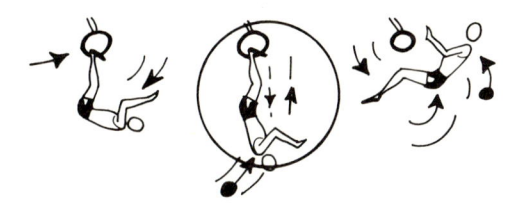

Fig. 12-41. Toe snap on backswing.

TOE SNAP ON FRONT SWING

First work on the toe hang. Assume the hand and toe hang. Turn the toes up and hold tight. Let go with the hands and let the body down very slowly until a toe-supported handstand is performed. Now walk forward on the hands and drop off. *Spotter should hold performer as he lets his body down.* Next, do the same thing on a little swing, then a little longer swing, and on the forward swing do not drop off but hyperextend the body forward and up. As the body gets enough height, drop off to the feet. *Spot the head and shoulders.* Observe Fig. 12-40 from right to left.

TOE SNAP ON BACKSWING

Before attempting to do this toe snap, go through the learning procedure for the toe snap on the front swing. The difference between these is the recovery from the extension or hang. This has to be executed faster than the previous exercise. Just before the end of the backswing (with the body in a toe and hand hang), release the hands and drop the body down to near vertical. Keep the chin on the chest at all times. Do not extend the head. Immediately flex at the waist forcibly and drop to the mat on the feet. *Spot this under the shoulder of the performer.* (See Fig. 12-41.)

CUT AND CATCH ON BACKSWING

Learn the split-off on the backswing first. This is very easy with a good spotter. Use very low rings about chest high. The performer is given just a little lift by the spotter while executing the cut-off. If the performer does not throw the rings away, they should be able to be regrasped after the legs pass forward. The high ride up is the important thing to work on. *Spot this under the armpits.* (See Fig. 12-42.)

FRONT ROLL WITH ARMS FLEXED

This is a good stunt for the weight lifter, the body builder, or the student who has been working apparatus for quite a while. It takes strength. Use a low ring to spot. Jump to the cross support position as seen in Fig. 12-43. Lower the shoulders and raise the

Fig. 12-42. Cut and catch on backswing.

Fig. 12-43. Front roll with arms flexed.

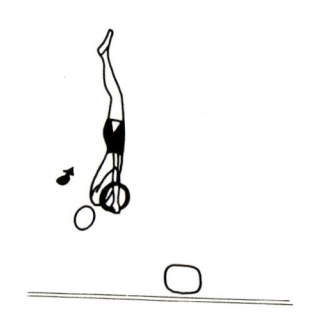

Fig. 12-44. Shoulder stand.

Fig. 12-45. Muscle-up or pull- and push-up.

hips. Do not turn the hands as you perform this first move. As the body falls over, supinate the hands. Do not let the shoulders drop. As the body turns forward, pull up as high as possible and pronate the hands. This move should bring the weight above the rings and on the arms. Now perform a push-up. *Spot by lifting the performer above the rings.* (See Fig. 12-43.)

SHOULDER STAND

Lower the rings to about 3 feet from the floor. Now stand up on a chair or stool. Grasp the rings from the inside. Raise the hips slowly as the shoulders are lowered. On the first couple of tries steady the body by locking the legs around the ropes. Keep the eyes at all times on the mats. If the head is flexed, the body will somersault. Eventually arch the back and bring the feet together. Keep the rings close to the shoulders at all times. *Spot this by keeping the performer from turning over too quickly.* (See Fig. 12-44.)

MUSCLE-UP

Grasp the rings with the false or high grip. The body should be suspended on the wrists. Execute a pull-up as high as the chest. As the height of the pull-up is completed, the feet should be raised to about a 30-degree angle. Now drop the legs down and pronate the hands as the arms are inwardly rotated. This action should place you above the rings. Now push up, arch the back, and hold the head up. *Spot this by helping to lift the performer above the difficult level.* (See Fig. 12-45.)

KIP

Put the rings down to chest high. Grasp them from the outside. Now take a half step backward. Lift one leg and then the other into the pike position. Swing forward, and on the backward swing, extend rapidly at the waist as you push down with the hands. Force the head and shoulders forward and up. This action should place the body in a cross support position. *Spot this in the middle of the back through the waist extension.* (See Fig. 12-46.)

SWINGING KIP

Keep the rings low so that the performer can easily be spotted. This kip is the same

Fig. 12-46. Kip.

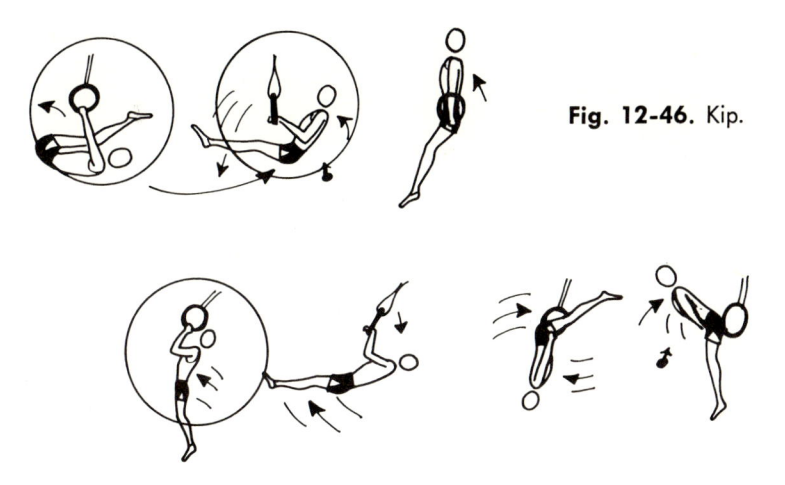

Fig. 12-47. Standing back or reverse cut-off.

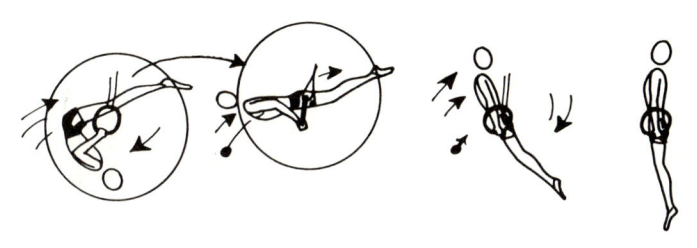

Fig. 12-48. Reverse uprise or back kip.

as the previous one, but it is executed on the end of the swing. *Spot an overthrow. The danger here is not being able to control the cross support.*

Standing back or reverse cut-off

This is not a difficult stunt to master. The important thing is the timing. The level of the rings should be just above the head. Grasp the rings from the outside. While holding the rings, fall off balance. Just as the body falls off balance, pull up to a half bend, throw the head back, and flex rapidly at the waist. Hold on as the body rotates until you can see the mat and then release the hands. *This is spotted with the spotter's right hand over the performer's left arm and on the chest, the left hand turning the performer in the small of the back.* (See Fig. 12-47.)

Reverse uprise or back kip

Study the figures very closely. On the forward swing, go into the pike. Immediately, without a swing in the pike position, lift the hips above the rings by quickly pulling up. Now, without losing a moment, extend the head and shoulders into the hyperextended position. Push down forcefully with the hands. End up in a cross support position. This is accomplished most easily with the false grip. *Spot this under the shoulders.* (See Fig. 12-48.)

Stem rise

The important move in this stunt is from the pike to the hyperextension. The hips should drop out of the pike first, as shown in Fig. 12-49. After the hips drop, whip the legs back and then up. Push down hard with the hands and bring the body to rest in the cross position. *Spot a possible overthrow.*

Dislocate on front swing

Begin this the same way as you would the backswing. However, keep the arms bent all the way through. Shoot for the extension just before the peak of the front swing. *Spot this closely on the first forward swing after the dislocate. This is the point where the hands might slip off.* Observe Fig. 12-50 from right to left.

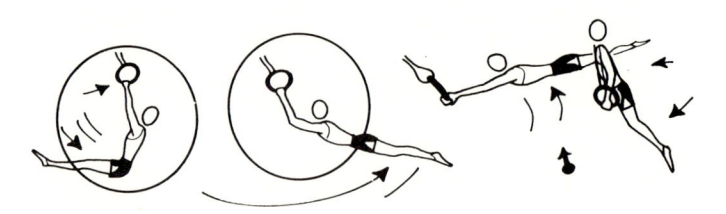

Fig. 12-49. Stem rise.

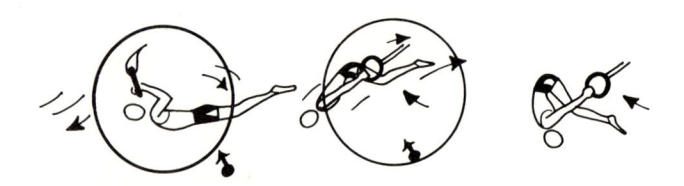

Fig. 12-50. Dislocate on front swing. (Observe from right to left.)

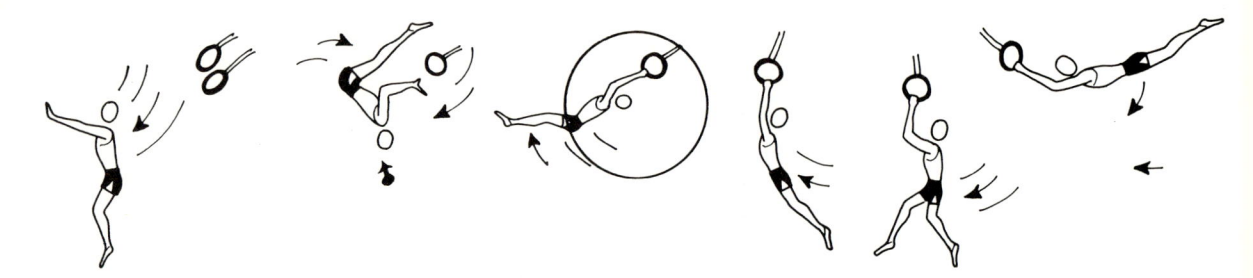

Fig. 12-51. High cut-off on front swing. (Observe from right to left.)

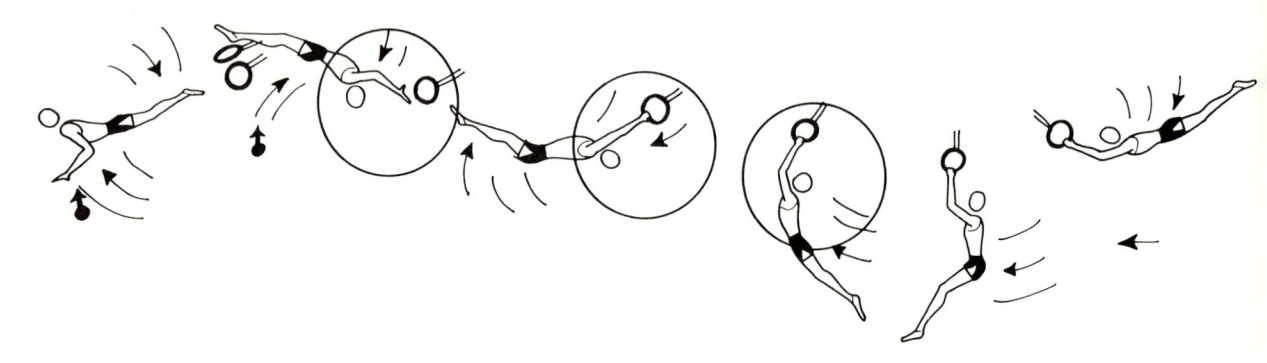

Fig. 12-52. Fly away on front swing (back airo). (Observe from right to left.)

HIGH CUT-OFF ON FRONT SWING

The level of the rings should be reach high (to learn). Take a walk beat, as seen in Fig. 12-51, from the high backswing. Then arch forward. Whip forward with the legs, extend the head, and pull. Let go after the body passes the horizontal. Do not hold on until the body rides up, as shown in Fig. 12-51. *Spot this for an overthrow.* Observe Fig. 12-51 from right to left.

FLY AWAY ON FRONT SWING

Follow the mechanics of the preceding exercise to the flexion on the forward swing. Then arch back with the head and shoulders. When you can see the mat, pike down to the landing. *Spot this in the safety belt.* Observe Fig. 12-52 from right to left.

FREE EXERCISE

Free exercise is performed on the floor or on a thin, resilient pad or mat, within a square area 40 × 40 feet.

Free exercise contains ballet movements, leaps and poses, elements of dance combinations, acrobatics, and tumbling grouped in rhythmical and harmonious patterns. Through these and other movements, the gymnast explores tempo, height, distance, mood, direction, and precision or form. The basic elements of form are balance, composure, pointed toes, straight knees (except for dismounts), full extension, and good body alignment.

The routines, which are performed to music (piano, organ, or taped) for women and without music for men, generally begin and end with an opening and closing sequence of tumbling. The main part or body of the routine consists of ballet movements, balancing, agility, and flexibility stunts.

The gymnast tries to create an artistic image. The composition is not only a physical exercise but is developed into a coherent pattern showing a change of pace, vitality, expression, individuality, and originality.

A great part of an individual's success is to adhere to an established and well-defined routine which includes elements that are not too difficult for the performer.

The gymnast must decide which stunts are to be performed and practice the routine at least three or four times during daily workout periods throughout the season. He or she should not wait until meet time to decide on a routine.

An optional routine is not created in its entirety at one time. It is a synthesis of a long period of developing individual elements, passages, and their combinations. This reserve grows as training progresses and is constantly drawn upon by the gymnast for the enrichment of the optional exercise.

PURPOSES

1. To express understanding of beauty through effective use of the body
2. To reflect perfection through form
3. To improve poise and grace

VALUES

1. Development of coordination and balance
2. Development of rhythm, timing, agility, and flexibility
3. Development of muscle tone, power, strength, and endurance
4. Development of a sense of creativity
5. Development of a sense of aesthetic value

LEARNING METHODS

The elementary movements, as well as combinations, must be adapted not only to the age and sex of the students but also to their mental and physical abilities.

1. Learn skills first—simple, fundamental, elementary movements.
2. Combine various exercises; combine dance steps and tumbling and make them into a simple routine.
3. Set combinations to music if the gymnasts are women.
4. Allow each person to make up his or her own routine.

Note: Acrobatics should be well-dispersed throughout each routine, and fast-moving sequences followed by an abrupt stop or pose should be included to give the variety that is needed.

A few movements that may be used in a free exercise routine will be described.

TOE RISE OR STAND

Take a standing position. Rise up on your toes and extend your arms sideward with the palms of your hands facing downward. Lower your heels to the floor as you drop your arms at your sides to get back to a full standing position. (See Fig. 12-53.)

BODY SWEEP

Kneel on one knee and place your hand at a comfortable distance and on line with the knee to acquire equal distribution of weight. Swing the other arm forward and extend the other leg backward. (See Fig. 12-54.)

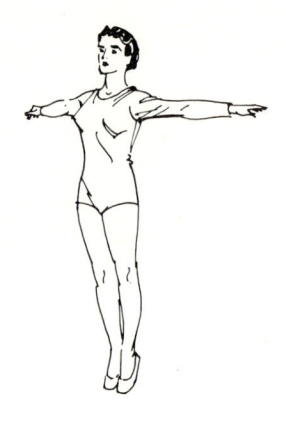

Fig. 12-53. Toe stand.  **Fig. 12-54.** Body sweep.  **Fig. 12-55.** Stag leap.

Fig. 12-56. Split.  **Fig. 12-57.** One-leg balance.  **Fig. 12-58.** Front walkover.

STAG LEAP

Take three running steps forward—left, right, left—and leap into the air, touching the right knee with the left foot as you lift your arms upward overhead. (See Fig. 12-55.)

SPLIT

Stand with one leg ahead of the other and slowly lower the body downward into a splits position. (See Fig. 12-56.)

ONE-LEG BALANCE

Take a standing position. Raise one leg to the side and upward as high as possible. Grasp the instep of your raised leg with one hand and extend the other arm to a horizontal or upward position. (See Fig. 12-57.)

FRONT WALKOVER

Take a standing position. Go into a handstand position and let your feet continue on over to the floor. Land on one foot. Lift your hands off the floor, bringing your body to an upright position, and then bring your other foot to the floor. (See Fig. 12-58.)

HANDSTAND

Place your hands on the mat, shoulder width apart with your fingers pointing forward. Keep your arms straight, head up, and eyes looking forward. Kick upward, arch your back, and grip the floor. (See Fig. 12-59.)

BALANCE SEAT

Sit on the floor with your back straight, legs together, and your hands on the floor

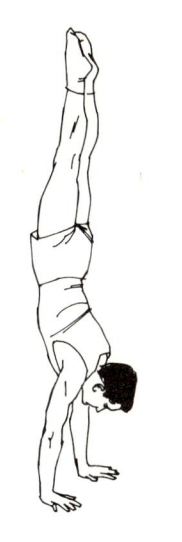

Fig. 12-59. Handstand.

Fig. 12-60. Balance seat.

Fig. 12-61. Front scale.

Fig. 12-62. Arabesque.

in back of your hips. (You may raise your arms outward from the shoulders.) Raise your legs to make a V with your trunk. (See Fig. 12-60.)

FRONT SCALE

Take a standing position. Raise one leg backward and upward so that your leg is fairly straight and your toes are pointed. Balance on one foot and extend your arms horizontally in front of you for a more perfect balance. Allow your body to lean forward to a position parallel to the floor. Keep your head up and arch your back. (See Fig. 12-61.)

ARABESQUE

Take a standing position. Raise one leg horizontally backward. Balance on one foot and hold your arms out to the side and slightly back for better balance. (You may have one arm upward and one sideward, as in Fig. 12-62.) Allow your body to lean slightly forward and at the same time keep your head and chest almost vertical. Hold this position with ease and grace.

VALDEZ TO HANDSTAND

Sit on the floor. Place one hand on the floor in back of your hip and to the side. (See Fig. 12-63.) The hand needs to simulate a wide grip. Raise your other arm shoulder high and turn the palm of that hand upward. Bend one leg so that the sole of your foot is on the floor near your seat and your knee is near your chest. Extend the other leg. (A Valdez can be done on the same arm with either leg bent. For some it is easier to have the bent leg on the same side as the supporting arm.)

From this position, throw your head straight back and your raised arm overhead

Fig. 12-63. Valdez to handstand.

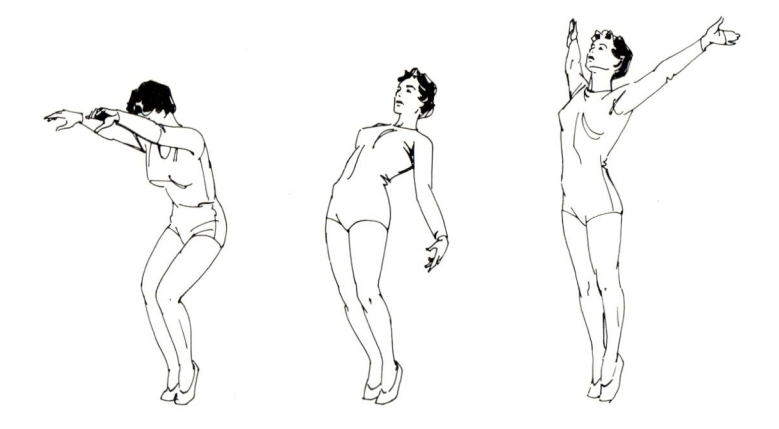

Fig. 12-64. Body weave.

and directly to the rear. (The hand is twisted, but the throw is directly back.) Lift the extended leg upward. (The move will be on one plane with one dimension—a straight line back like a flip-flop.) Speed is picked up with a vigorous leg push and a strong head and arm throw.

A handstand is assured with an extended head throw.

BODY WEAVE

Start with the body partially flexed—knees, hips, back, and head. The body is balanced on the toes, the arms reaching forward but relaxed, then hyperextend the body and drop the arms down and back and the head forward. Lastly, extend the head, raise tall the body, and elevate the arms. (See Fig. 12-64.)

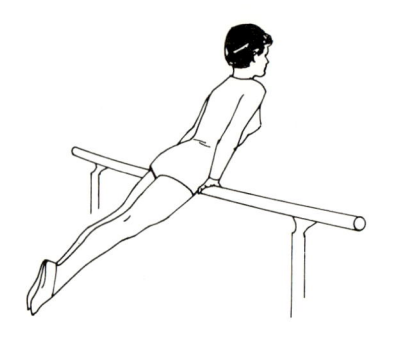

Fig. 12-65. Jump to front-leaning support.

Fig. 12-66. Crotch seat.

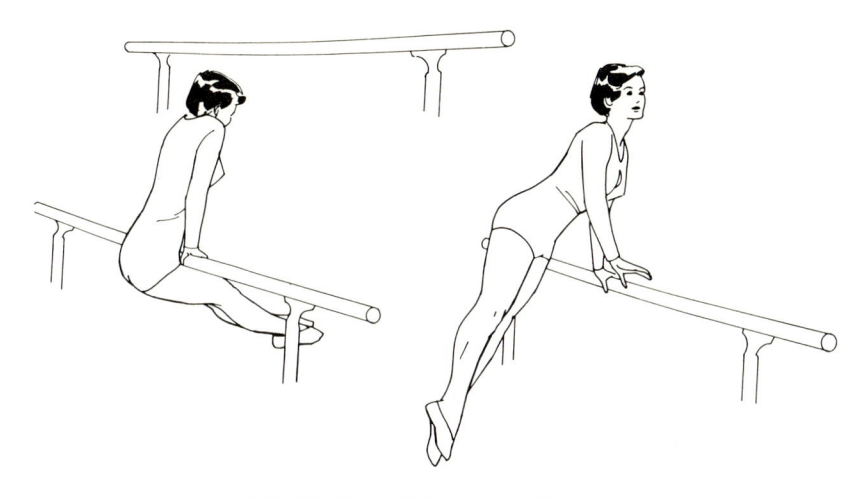

Fig. 12-67. Cast off low bar with quarter turn.

UNEVEN PARALLEL BARS

One of the last pieces of apparatus to be added to the sport of gymnastics is the uneven parallel bars. These are used in women's competition. However, as a developmental tool the uneven bars are challenging to the junior and senior high school boy. Many of the stunts illustrated in this book on the parallel bars can also be utilized by the girls for developmental purposes. Following is a list of stunts with their explanations that can be performed by the average gymnast.

JUMP TO FRONT-LEANING SUPPORT

Stand facing the low bar. With the hands on the bar and with the over-, under-, or mixed-grip, jump so that the body comes to rest on a straight-arm support. (See Fig. 12-65.)

CROTCH SEAT

Do this from the front-leaning support. Raise the right leg up and over the bar while making a quarter turn counterclockwise. Now reach up and grasp the high bar with the left hand. (See Fig. 12-66.)

CAST OFF LOW BAR WITH QUARTER TURN

Do this also from the front-leaning support. Swing the legs under the bar with a forward lean of the body. Swing the legs back, push with the right hand, and execute a quarter turn clockwise. Land in a side stand, knees partially bent and arm (right) extended obliquely upward. (See Fig. 12-67.)

166 BASIC SKILLS IN SPORTS FOR MEN AND WOMEN

Fig. 12-68. Single-leg flank vault dismount.

Fig. 12-69. Cross seat mount.

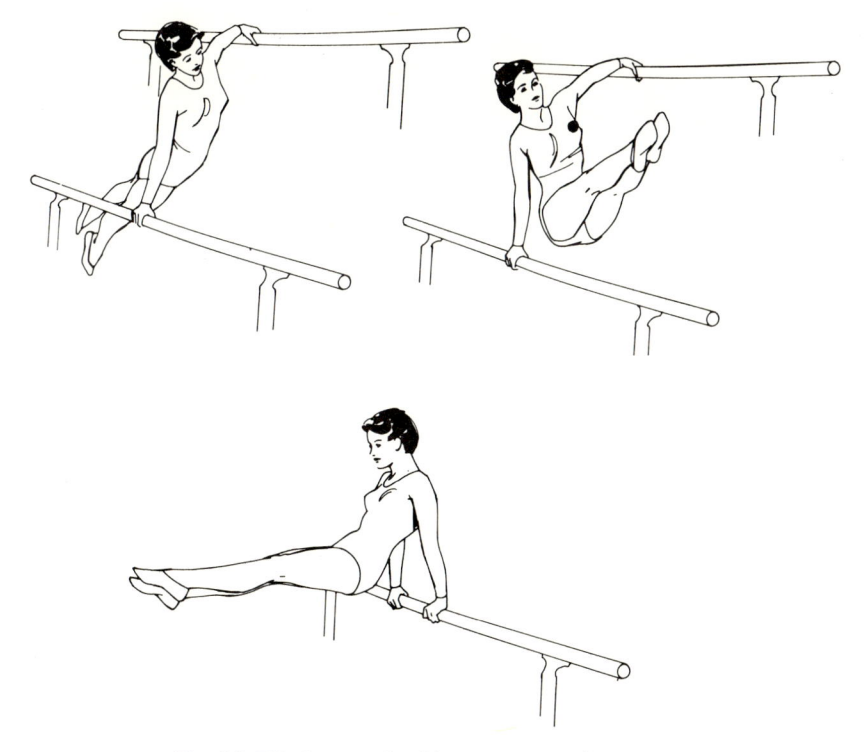

Fig. 12-70. Rear vault with quarter turn dismount.

SINGLE-LEG FLANK VAULT DISMOUNT

From a single-leg cross seat, using a left-hand supinated grasp and a right-hand pronated grasp, raise the right leg up and over the low bar. Pivot on the left arm as the body is supported and turned by the right arm. Land in a partial knee bend with the right hand and arm extended obliquely upward. (See Fig. 12-68.)

CROSS SEAT MOUNT

Swing to a back-leaning support or a rear seat. Notice the hand position in the illustration. Now swing the feet and hips up and over the bar clockwise. Come to rest with the left hand still on the high bar. (See Fig. 12-69.)

REAR VAULT WITH QUARTER TURN DISMOUNT

From an elbow and arm cross support, swing the legs up and over the low bar with a half turn clockwise, push away from the bar, and land in a partial knee bend with the arms extended obliquely upward. (See Fig. 12-70.)

Fig. 12-71. Back hip circle mount.

BACK HIP CIRCLE MOUNT

From a supine arm-hanging and heel-resting support (hands on the bars, body under and forward of the bars with heels on the mats), kick the right leg up and over the bar, bring the left leg to it, and pull up so that the weight of the body passes over the bar. Come to a front-leaning support. (See Fig. 12-71.)

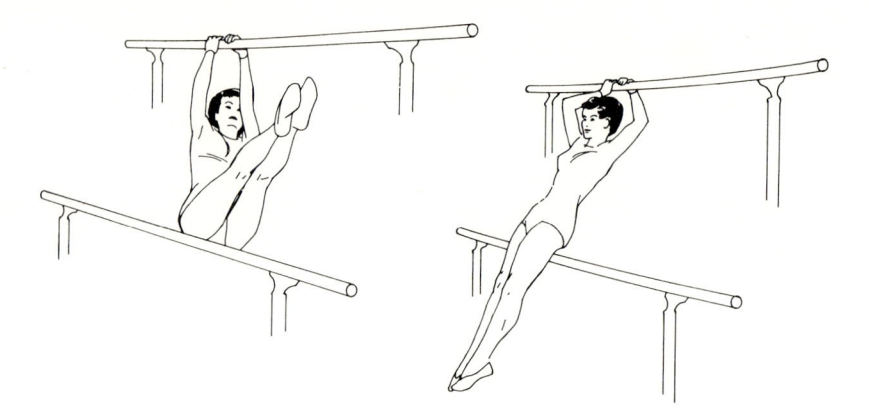

Fig. 12-72. Double-leg circle over low bar from cross hang.

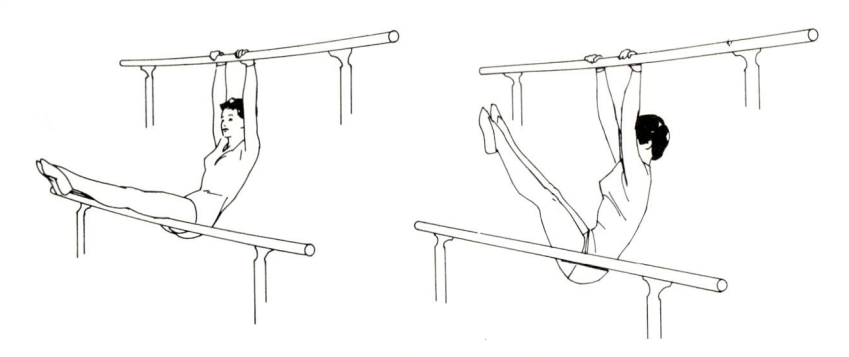

Fig. 12-73. Double-leg circle over low bar from rear seat.

Double-leg circle over low bar from cross hang

Use a mixed grip. Start the exercise by hanging on the high bar facing the low bar. With the legs extended and the toes pointed, raise both legs to the left up and over the low bar. The exercise may be completed by coming to a rest on the low bar in a rear seat position or by continuing the leg motion over the right side of the low bar back to the hang position. This may be executed with both hands in the overgrip position. (See Fig. 12-72.)

Double-leg circle over low bar from rear seat

Hang from the high bar with an overgrasp, thighs resting on the low bar. Take all of the weight on the arms. Now swing the legs over the low bar to the right or left, lower the legs to the hyperextended position of the body, and then continue to circle the legs to the left and up over the bar. (See Fig. 12-73.)

Half-turn swing

From a front seat on the low bar, with the right hand under and the left hand over the high bar, slide off the bar, swing forward, and execute a half turn counterclockwise. (See Fig. 12-74.)

Thigh rest

From the cross hip support, reach forward and grasp the low bar with the overgrip. Now hyperextend the body. (See Fig. 12-75.)

Back hip circle

Execute this from the front-leaning support position. Lean forward and swing the legs up. Swing the legs forward and under the bar, slightly bending the arms and letting the bar contact the body just above the

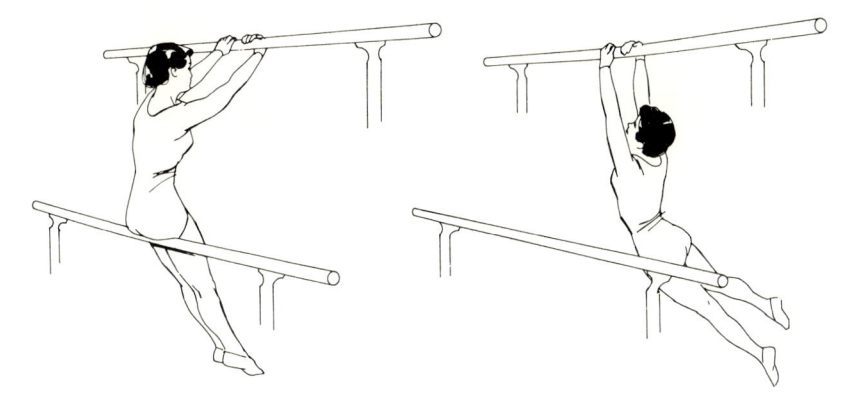

Fig. 12-74. Half-turn swing.

Fig. 12-75. Thigh rest.

Fig. 12-76. Back hip circle.

170 BASIC SKILLS IN SPORTS FOR MEN AND WOMEN

Fig. 12-77. Arch back.

Fig. 12-78. Balance beam; pass through positions.

GYMNASTICS 171

thighs. Hold tight with the slightly bent arms, and the body will rotate around bar and back to front-leaning support. (See Fig. 12-76.)

ARCH BACK

From a knee hang on the high bar, facing the low bar, grasp the low bar with the overgrip. Pull in to the low bar and then push up. (See Fig. 12-77.)

BALANCE BEAM

The movements on the balance beam must be continuous and smooth. All fundamental movements may be used, including steps, runs, jumps, and turns, some of which may be dance types. Positions from lying to sitting to kneeling should be used to make up the routine. Balancing and tumbling skills are to be included in the sequence.

The judges look for slow beautifully blended combinations of movements.

The sequence of exercises should take from 1:20 to 1:45 minutes to complete. A fall, or a stop for 10 seconds or more terminates the routine.

Chart of positions and movements

Any number of sequences may be set up from the many positions illustrated in Fig. 12-78. Examples: 6-9-13-2-11-15-19-4-19-10-8-17-16-20-5 or 18-2-3-5. Short two- or three-movement sequences may be good for class work. The long sequence may be used for individual developmental purposes. Compose your own sequence.

INSTRUCTIONAL AND LEARNING PROCEDURES
Objectives

1. To develop habits of regular exercise
2. To develop habits of practicing proper mental attitudes
   (a) To enjoy doing a thing well
   (b) To encourage others to do well
   (c) To help others with their stunts
   (d) To learn the nomenclature of skill exercises on apparatus
3. To develop and build up physical efficiency and endurance through the use of activities that will develop:
   (a) Balance
   (b) Strength
   (c) Courage
   (d) Rhythm and timing
   (e) Coordination
   (f) Good body mechanics

Plan for course

Four pieces of apparatus should be used: side horse, parallel bars, horizontal bars, and rings.

The first day of a class is known as the explanation period. This period is used to acquaint the students with the apparatus and with the class rotation plan of instruction and its safety methods for each piece of apparatus. All the various stunts for each class period are demonstrated. The students then become acquainted with the apparatus, moving from one piece to another, never staying on one longer than 15 minutes.

A list of six stunts of moderate difficulty on each piece of apparatus should be provided. Students may select any three from each of the lists of six stunts on each piece of apparatus for the final performance skill test near the end of the term. Successful performance of the stunts selected by the student will ensure passing the tumbling and apparatus skill requirements. These standards are within the ability of almost any student who is willing to exert reasonable effort in practice.

As soon as a student has mastered the required stunts, specialization may be attempted on any piece of selected apparatus or stunts on different pieces of apparatus may be learned. Individual instruction will be given in the learning of new stunts.

Consistent practice on the apparatus will not only give a great deal of pleasure in graceful performance, but will also contribute to the development of strength in the arms, shoulders, and abdominal area, and improve agility and control of the body in motion.

A written knowledge test will also be conducted at the end of the term.

REFERENCES

Babbitt, Diane H., and Hass, Werner: Gymnastics apparatus exercises for girls, New York, 1964, The Ronald Press Co.

Carter, Ernestine Russell: Gymnastics for girls and

women, Englewood Cliffs, N. J., 1969, Prentice-Hall.
Cochrane, Tuovi S.: Gymnastics for women, Reading, Mass., 1969, Addison-Wesley.
DGWS: Gymnastic guide, 1973-1975, AAHPER.
Johnson, Charles: Procedures for teaching gymnastics in physical education, Englewood, Ohio, 1970, Gym Master Co.
Loken, N., and Gagnier, E. N. (eds.): Sequence gymnastics, Ann Arbor, 1959, University of Michigan.
Musker, F., Casady, D., and Irwin, Leslie: A guide to gymnastics, New York, 1968, The Macmillan Co.
Official gymnastic rules, 1973, The National Collegiate Athletic Association.
Price, Hartley D., Hewlett, Joseph M., and Loken, Newt: Gymnastics and tumbling, New York, 1950, The Ronald Press Co.
Thulin, Josef G.: Gymnastic handbook, London, 1954, Bailey Bros. and Swinfen, Ltd.
West, W. D.: Gymnast's manual, New York, 1955, Prentice-Hall, Inc.

13 Handball, paddleball, and racketball

HISTORY
Handball

There is some evidence that handball was originated about the "thermaeor" baths of Rome and that it is one of the oldest of all sports. Ireland is credited with first developing the game and holding the first championship tournament. John Kavanagh of York was the leading player and champion in 1840. In this same year handball was introduced into the United States.

The first international match was played in 1887 for a purse of $1,000. The match was between Phil Casey of Brooklyn and John Lawler, the Irish Champion. Casey emerged the winner. The match consisted of twenty-one games. Of the ten games played in Ireland, Lawler won six, and of the eleven played in the United States, Casey won seven straight games and the championship. The matches were played on a four-wall court. Casey retained the championship for many years and was called the father of the game in America.

In 1897, the Amateur Athletic Union sponsored the first American tournament, won by Michael Egan.

In the early years of the game, four-wall courts were used. Later, in about 1913, a one-wall court game on the beaches of New York became very popular. This was a modification of the four-wall game. The use of one wall brought the game outdoors. This court is used today in gymnasiums where building space is limited.

The A.A.U., the Y.M.C.A., and the United States Handball Association, formed in 1951, conduct national championships in this sport at the present time.

The first four-wall championship was held in Los Angeles in 1919 and the first one-wall A.A.U. Championship was held in New York in 1924. The first Y.M.C.A. National Championship was held in Cleveland in 1925.

One of the great players of modern times was Joe Platak, who won the national championships from 1935 to 1945.

Paddleball and racketball

The game of paddleball is generally believed to have been formulated at the University of Michigan in the early 1920s. The rules are identical to handball except that a wooden paddle is used instead of the hand in striking the ball and a different type of ball

174

is used. Racketball is identical to paddleball except that a strung racket is used. For both paddleball and racketball various types of balls are manufactured. The balls differ in color and in the amount of rebound.

Novice paddleball or racketball players should be very careful to avoid swinging wildly at the ball because the paddles and rackets can injure a partner or opponent. In fact, the paddles and rackets have attached to the handle a thong that must be secured to the player's wrist to prevent a paddle or racket from slipping from the hand. For this reason, it is illegal to switch the paddle or racket from hand to hand during play.

Paddleball and racketball are often more enjoyable than handball for beginners because success in contacting and placing the ball is more immediate with the paddle or racket than with the hand.

NATURE OF THE GAMES

A rubber ball is batted alternately by the players against the front wall of the one- or four-wall court, the object being to cause the ball to rebound to such a position and in such a manner that the opponent cannot return it before the second bounce. The ball may be played either on the rebound fly from the front wall or after one bounce. It is put in play by a serve which must first hit the front wall. A point is scored only by the side serving. A game consists of 21 points. A tennis ball can be used for paddle ball.

VALUES OF THE GAMES

One of the best of the many features of these great recreational sports is that they combine a good hard workout in a short time with a great deal of fun. A pair of gloves, the proper ball, a paddle or racket, and a suitable gym outfit and tennis shoes are the only equipment needed. Most Y.M.C.A.s, recreation centers, and athletic clubs have courts. A one-wall court can be marked off in any gym or be erected outdoors on a tennis court or other playing field. The rules are very simple and can easily be learned in a very short time. These games require only two, three, or four persons to play, so it is easy to play a game almost any time without getting a lot of people together.

Any of these games can be played at any age. However, due to the requirements of fast reactions, quick reflexes, and good eye-hand coordination, it is important to play with partners and opponents of comparable ability. Generally, paddleball and racketball are played more frequently by older participants than is handball.

EQUIPMENT AND FACILITIES FOR THE GAMES

The official ball for handball is a black ball $1\frac{7}{8}$ inches in diameter and $2\frac{3}{10}$ ounces in weight. It is often suggested that beginners use a softer, larger ball, such as a tennis ball, until some of the basic footwork and shot fundamentals are mastered. The ball used for paddleball and racketball is about the size of a tennis ball. They are manufactured by several companies and come in different colors and degrees of "liveliness."

In handball, gloves must be worn. The gloves may be made of leather or a soft material and must be light in color. The fingers of the gloves cannot be webbed, and no foreign substance (tape, rubber bands, etc.) can be worn on the gloves. Padded gloves are available and are recommended for beginners. After the hands become toughened and the player's skill increases so that batting the ball does not result in sore hands, tight-fitting, unpadded gloves are recommended to allow increased control of the ball.

The only difference between paddleball and racketball, as the names imply, is the implement used to strike the ball. In paddleball, a flat wooden paddle is used. Sometimes holes are drilled through the paddle surface to reduce air resistance. In racketball, a strung racket, resembling a tennis racket with a short handle, is used. For safety in both activities, a thong must be attached to the paddle or racket and is wound around the player's wrist.

THE COURTS
One-wall court

The one-wall court is 20 feet wide, 34 feet long, and 16 feet high with at least 6 feet of clear space beyond the side and long lines. The 34-foot line is called the long line.

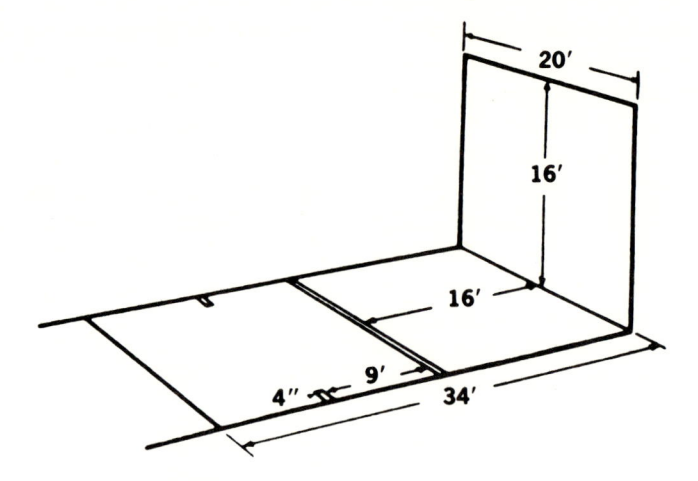

Fig. 13-1. One-wall handball court.

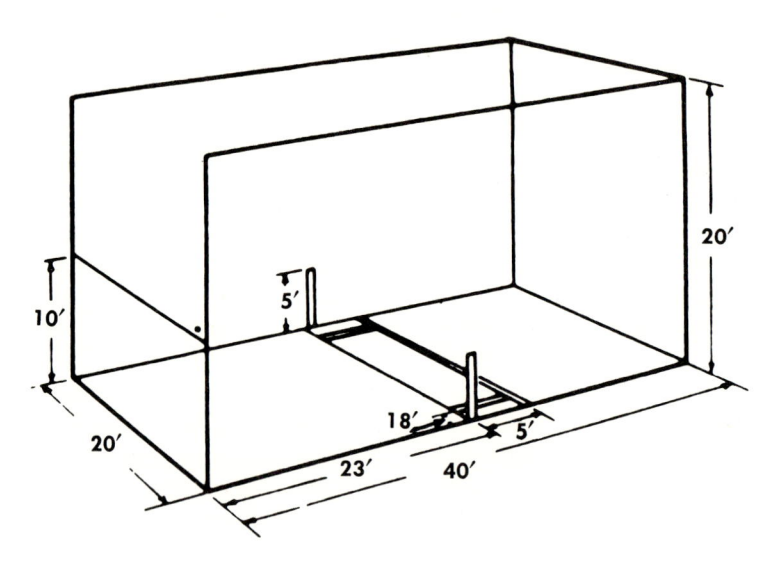

Fig. 13-2. Four-wall handball court.

There are no official specifications for playing surfaces. The surface is usually wood, cement, or clay. (See Fig. 13-1 for dimensions.)

The short line is drawn across the court 16 feet out from the front wall and parallel to it. The service line is drawn across the court 5 feet behind the short line and parallel to it. The space between the service line and short line is the service zone.

Four-wall court

The four-wall court should have a hardwood floor, and sidewalls should be constructed of smooth plaster, tile, concrete, glass, or even brick. (See Fig. 13-2 for dimensions of court.) The court should not measure less than 20 × 20 × 40 feet or more than 23 × 23 × 46 feet.

RULES
One-wall court

The rules for the four-wall court also apply to the one-wall court with the exception of those rules pertaining to sidewalls, back wall, and ceiling plays where there is no ceiling adjoining the front wall, and with the following other considerations.

Serving: The server drops the ball to the floor within the service zone, and on the first bounce he strikes it in such a manner that it hits the wall and returns to the floor beyond the short line and in front of the long line. The opposing side must make a legal return by striking the ball after the first bounce or on the fly.

Following are terms that pertain to serving:

long ball A long ball is one that passes over the long line on the serve.

short ball A short ball is one that does not pass over the short line on the serve.

outs An out results from serving two short ball, two long balls, one short ball and one long ball, serving the ball out-of-bounds, or hitting the floor before the wall.

Special rules for paddleball:
1. Loss of 3 points for throwing the paddle
2. Loss of 2 points for dropping the paddle
3. Loss of 3 points and serve for throwing the paddle while serving
4. Loss of 5 points and serve for hitting any player with the paddle

Four-wall court
1. The game may be played by two (singles), three (cutthroat), of four players (doubles).
2. A game shall consist of 21 points. (There are no deuce points in handball as in tennis. The player or team who first reaches 21 points is the winner.)
3. A match shall consist of the best two out of three games.
4. Only one hand may be used in striking the ball. The use of the foot, or any portion of the body other than one hand, to return the ball is barred.
5. In attempting to return the ball, a player cannot strike it more than once.
6. Serving:
   (a) To make a legal service, the server drops the ball to the floor within the service zone and strikes it on the bounce, so that it hits the front wall first and on the rebound lands upon the floor back of the short line, either before or after striking one of the side-walls.
   (b) Three types of serve are possible: a legal serve, an out serve, or a fault serve. If the serve is legal play continues; if the serve is an out serve the server is retired; if the serve is a fault serve another serve is permitted. What constitutes each of these types of serve is explained under playing regulations.
   (c) After the ball has been legally served, the opposing side makes a legal return by striking the ball on the fly or first bounce, causing it to hit the front wall before hitting the floor. The ball may hit the ceiling, back wall, and either one or both sidewalls on its way to the front wall.
   (d) The serving and receiving sides alternate in attempting to make legal returns until one side fails. If the serving side fails, it scores an out; if the receiving side fails, a point is scored for the server.

PLAYING REGULATIONS

Service:
1. The choice for the right to serve shall be decided by the toss of a coin, and the player winning the toss starts the first and third games.
2. The server may start serving from any place in the serving zone.
3. In singles, when the server loses his service, he shall become the receiver; the receiver then becomes the server, and so on alternately in all subsequent services of the game.
4. In serving, the server must start and stay within the service zone; if while serving the server steps outside the service zone, a fault shall be charged. Stepping outside the service zone twice in succession shall retire the server and count as an out.

   The words "stepping over" shall be defined as the act of putting any part of the foot past the short or service lines.
5. In serving, the ball must be bounced on the floor and struck on the re-

bound from the floor. The server is out if the attempt to hit the ball on this rebound fails. Not more than three bounces may be used in making a service. Bouncing of the ball by a server in any part of the court prior to serving shall be counted as a bounce within the meaning of this rule. Violation of this rule retires the server.

6. The server shall not serve until the opponent has had fair opportunity to get placed or the referee calls play.

7. A ball coming from the front wall on a fly or bounce that goes into the gallery or an opening in a sidewall shall be a hinder, but if it goes into the gallery or opening after a player has touched it, it shall be a point or an out against the player attempting the return.

8. In doubles, the server's partner must stand within the service zone with the back against the wall until the ball passes the service line on each serve. Two consecutive violations of this rule retire the server.

9. If a player's partner is hit by a served ball while standing in the service box, the serve counts as a "dead ball" without penalty, but any short or fault preceding the service is not eliminated. Two consecutive faults retire the server.

10. In the doubles game only one player is allowed to serve in the first inning. When this player is put out, each of the opponents is allowed to serve until put out. Upon resuming service, the player who served first again serves until put out, and then the partner serves.

11. In doubles, each partner must serve in the regular order of service. Failure to do so shall count as hand out, and the points scored on the illegal serve shall not count.

12. Every effort shall be made to keep the ball dry, particularly on the service. Deliberate violation of the spirit of this rule shall result in forfeiture of serve. The ball may be inspected at any time during a game, and the referee shall put a new ball in play if deemed advisable.

Receiving service:

1. The receiver must stand back of the short line while the ball is being served.
2. A receiver may play the service either on the volley or the first bounce.
3. Only a legal serve may be played by the receiver.

Faults:

1. A serve is considered short when the served ball hits the front wall and fails to strike back of the short line on the fly.
2. A short also occurs when a served ball hits the front wall and two sidewalls before striking the floor back of the short line.
3. A serve is considered long when the served ball rebounds from the front wall and touches the back wall before touching the floor.
4. A serve is also considered a fault if the ball rebounds from the front wall and touches the ceiling.
5. Stepping over the outer edges of the service or short line with any part of the foot in the act of service is considered a fault.
6. Serving the ball in doubles when the server's partner is not in the service box with his back against the wall is considered a fault.

Hinders:

1. A returned ball which strikes an opponent on its way to the front wall is considered dead even if it continues to the front wall before striking the floor.
2. A player's unintentional interference in such a way as to prevent the opponent from having a fair chance to return the ball is considered a hinder.
3. In doubles, both players on a side are entitled to a fair and unobstructed chance at the ball.

The referee should be alert in rendering decisions under this rule in order to discourage any practice of playing the ball where an adversary

cannot see it until too late to get into position. It is no excuse that the ball is "killed" or that the adversary "could not get it." A player is entitled to a fair chance to recover any ball.
4. The principle just cited holds true also in singles. It is the duty of the side that has played the ball to get out of the way of the opponent.
5. It is the duty of the referee to decide all hinders and covered balls.
6. When a player is interfered with by his or her partner, a hinder cannot be claimed.
7. When, in the opinion of the referee, a player is hindered intentionally, the referee shall decide the point against the offending player.
8. A ball coming from the front wall on a fly or bounce that goes into the gallery or an opening in the sidewall shall be a hinder, but if it goes into the gallery or opening after a player has touched it (a ball caroming off of a hand or glove), it shall count as a point or an out against the player attempting the return.

Outs:
1. Intentional interference with an opponent
2. A partner serving out of turn
3. A served ball touching the server in singles or doubles
4. A served ball striking the server's partner when the latter is outside the service box
5. A legally returned ball striking the partner of the one returning the ball
6. Failure to play a ball properly returned from a service
7. A served ball hitting the ceiling, floor, or sidewalls before striking the front wall
8. A served ball hitting the front wall and sidewall, front wall and floor, or front wall and ceiling at the same time (crotch ball)
9. Two successive infractions by the server (two shorts, two faults, or a short and a fault)
10. More than three bounces on the serve

BASIC SKILL TECHNIQUES AND FUNDAMENTALS OF THE GAMES

The beginner playing with an experienced player soon learns that there are certain fundamentals common to most sports. The beginner is often out of position, off-balance, and unable to get a good, accurate shot, while the more experienced opponent seems to always be in the correct position. The beginning student should therefore work on these fundamentals.

Position on floor

Study the possible angles that a ball can travel and rebound within the four rectangular walls of the court as you would in studying angles while playing billiards. Throw the ball at the walls at different angles and heights and observe the rebounds. Try to move to that spot where the ball is expected to be best played. (See Fig. 13-3.)

Footwork

The fundamental skill of footwork is essential for proficiency and accuracy in playing the ball. If the ball is played with the right hand, the left foot is forward; if the ball is played with the left hand, the right foot is forward. The body should be slightly crouched and the knees bent for faster reacting movements in any direction. (See Fig. 13-4.)

Accuracy of playing shots

Accuracy depends upon good footwork, good balance, and keeping the eye on the ball with good arm action and follow-through. The player, by experience, should gain split vision, or the ability to choose the angle and spot it is desirable to hit without looking at the spot. This not only gives one accuracy but avoids telegraphing one's play to the opponent.

Practice using split vision often. Practice low corner shots that have little or no rebound. These shots are called kill shots. The sidearm stroke is most accurate for this shot.

The hand

Snug-fitting gloves should be worn. The tips of the fingers should be slightly squeezed together, and the entire hand slightly cupped

180 BASIC SKILLS IN SPORTS FOR MEN AND WOMEN

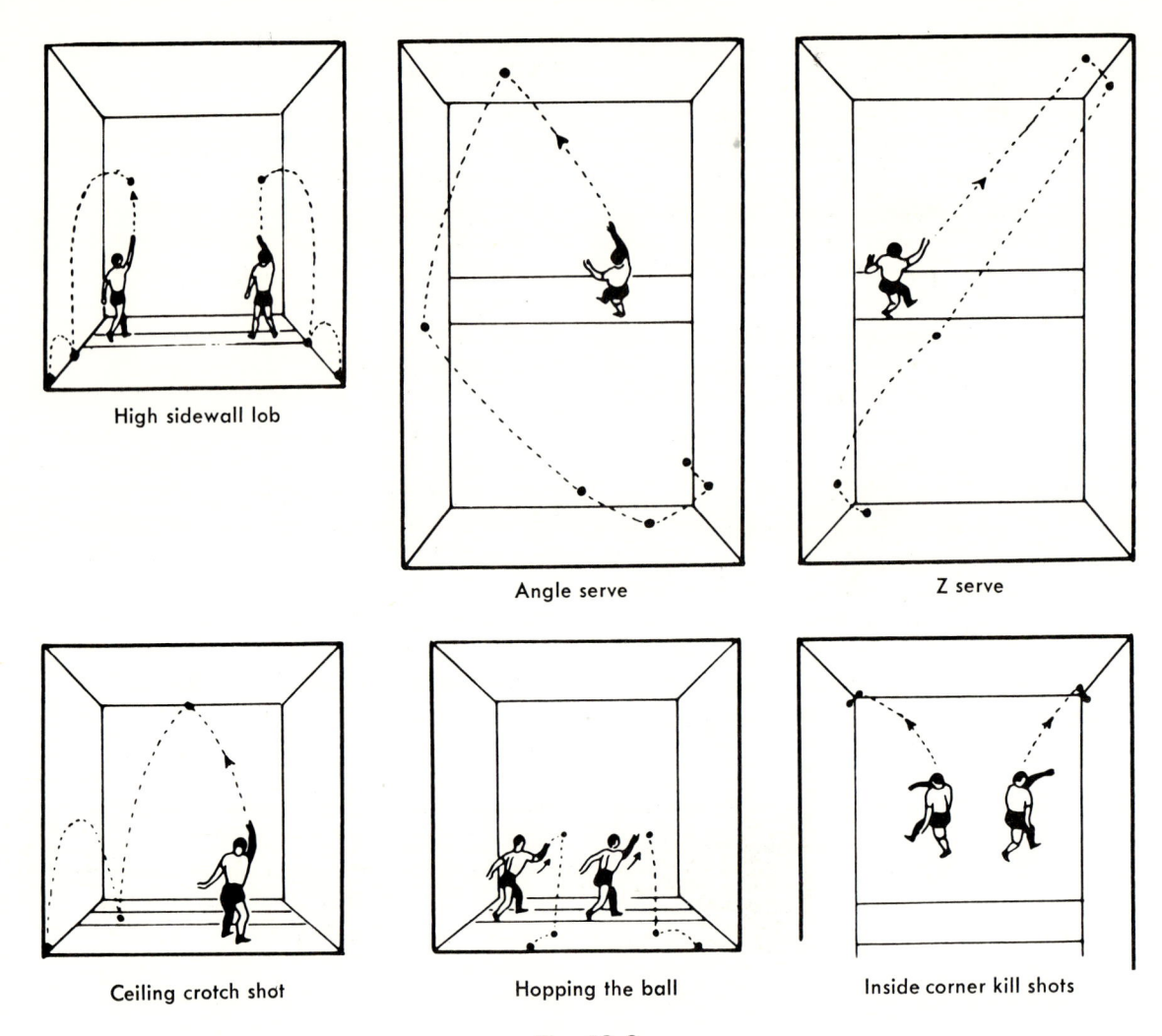

High sidewall lob

Angle serve

Z serve

Ceiling crotch shot

Hopping the ball

Inside corner kill shots

Fig. 13-3

Fig. 13-4. Stance for an open-hand forehand shot in handball.

like a swimmer's hand. The wrist and elbow should be flexible to accommodate a wrist snap shot or an overarm stroke similar to that of throwing a quick fast ball. In stroking the ball, the hand should follow through toward the spot that the ball is directed before the arm swings across the body in completing the follow-through. The hand can also be tightly closed. (See Fig. 13-5.)

Arm strokes

Arm strokes are fundamentally the same as in throwing a ball. These are the overarm, underarm, and sidearm.

The overarm: The overarm stroke is very similar to that of throwing a ball fast, for example, from catcher to second base. The arm swings back as in throwing so that the

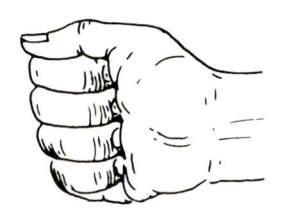

Fig. 13-5. Punch fist handball position.

hand begins the stroking action from behind the ear. If a ball is hit from a high reach, the arm is usually held almost straight while stroking.

The sidearm: The sidearm stroke is similar to a sidearm throw delivery. If the player hits with the right arm, the left foot should be in front of the right, and vice versa. Often the stroke is made without changing feet and with a quick, flexible wrist snap. However, the feet should always be ready to react if a more accurate stroke can be delivered by shifting the feet.

The underarm: Several variations of the arm action in this stroke are universally common to other sports skills such as bowling and softball.

In the more or less straight underarm stroke where power is desired, the hand contacts the ball on the heel of the hand. This part of the hand is strong and muscular and can withstand constant and repeated contacts of the ball.

For wrist action in a stroke requiring speed, the ball contacts the hand toward the tips of the fingers. This permits a longer leverage to the hand, and a wrist whip gives the ball terrific speed and accuracy. To master this stroke requires a great deal of practice.

The ball can be hit with the palm of the hand, but this shot is not so accurate, nor can speed or power be obtained from it.

Kill shots

There are many varieties of kill shots. A kill shot is one which hits the front so close to the floor that there is practically no bounce or several bounces before an opponent can reach the ball and play it.

Straight kill shot: The straight kill is a shot to the front wall which does not touch either sidewall but hits the wall low.

Right outside corner kill shot: In the right outside corner kill shot, the ball is played with the right hand, the ball first hitting the right sidewall, bouncing to the front wall, and then bouncing to the floor.

Right inside corner kill shot: In the right inside corner kill shot, the ball first hits the front wall, bounces to the sidewall, and then bounces to the floor. Again, this shot is most easily executed with the right hand. The left side of the body faces the front wall with the left foot well in front. When executed from the left hand, the reverse is true. (See Fig. 13-3.)

Fly kill shot: In the fly kill shot the ball is hit on the fly from a front wall rebound so fast that the opponent has no opportunity to play the ball.

A player should constantly strive to direct a ball into an area, or at such an angle into the sidewalls, so that the opponent has no opportunity to play the ball. This is a skill that can be mastered only by practice and experience.

The serve

There are many types of, and variations in, serving a ball. There are, however, several common types used by famous handball players. A serve is first put in play by dropping the ball on the floor behind the service line before it is batted with the hand. The ball must first hit the front wall. It can then either rebound directly back behind the server or rebound from the front wall onto the sidewalls, as long as it rebounds to the floor behind the short line to make it a legal serve. The server gets another serve if a fault is committed. Two faults retire the server.

Power serve: In the power serve, the player hits the ball close to the floor so that it hits the front wall close to the floor and rebounds just behind the short line, but it is directed at an angle so that it drops dead against the sidewall.

Sharp-angle serve: In the sharp-angle serve, the player serves from the side so that the ball rebounds from the front wall to the sidewall opposite the server at such an angle that the ball lands behind the short line. This type of serve can also be hit high so that the ball rebounds to the back wall and corner behind the server.

Clenched-hand serve: In a clenched-hand serve, the ball is hit with the clenched hand. This serve gives speed and power, but lacks accuracy.

Direct high lob: The server stands close to the right or left sidewall and serves the ball high up on the front wall and close to the sidewall, so that the ball rebounds far back in the court but is very close to the sidewall on its entire flight. This type of serve often drops dead in the back corner and is difficult to return. Some of these serves may just touch the sidewall on their rebound flight, causing the ball to drop dead.

Two-wall serve to back corner: The server takes a position close to the right wall and serves the ball about head high and about 4 or 5 feet from the left sidewall. The ball rebounds to the left sidewall just back of midcourt, rebounds to the floor and on back to the right corner, and hits the back wall and then the right wall before hitting the floor.

The flight of this serve causes the receiver to run around following the ball, looking for an opportunity to play it, which is difficult.

In doubles play, the server's partner must stand within the service box with the back against the wall until the ball passes the service line on each serve. Violation of this rule is a fault.

HINTS ON PLAY AND STRATEGY

1. Throughout a game it is well to keep in mind that in the various serves, situations identical to those described may arise, and the ball can be directed and played like a serve. Handball is similar to tennis; in both there is a need for quickly sizing up an opponent's weaknesses and strong points. Play to an opponent's weakness and disadvantage.
2. Pace changes constantly from fast play to lob shots and runaround plays to keep an opponent off-balance. One should strive to place shots accurately.
3. Be constantly on the alert for low hit balls or corner kill shots.
4. Constantly work for a desirable position on the court. A good spot is usually the "hole" or "well" near the center of the court and service area. This is also known as the offensive spot and backcourt defensive spot.
5. By skillful playing, the opponent can be kept out of the "well."
6. Strive to think ahead and set up a series of play situations that will keep the opponent off-balance and therefore at a disadvantage.
7. Continue to use and practice with the weaker arm. On either a serve or rebound, concentrate on hitting a spot on the front wall but keep the eyes on the ball until it is hit. After a serve, come up quickly to midcourt. Continue to maneuver for the offensive position throughout the game.

SKILLS TO PRACTICE ALONE

1. Practice by throwing the ball to the wall at various angles and receiving the rebounds.
2. Practice hitting lob rebounds and receiving them accurately.
3. Throw the ball to the back wall and take it with an underhand snap of the hand to return it to the front wall. In practicing this skill, do not rush. Take it easy, keep the eye on the ball, and wait for the ball to reach you.
4. Practice serving and study angles and an imaginary opponent's position.
5. Practice and master the skills mentioned and develop the skill of directing the ball to the areas impossible for an opponent to cover.
6. A ball hit low on the wall is difficult to return. Practice this type of return regularly by using the underarm stroke.

COURT COURTESY

If there is any doubt about any play, it should be played over. It is not good sportsmanship to deliberately hit an opponent with the ball in order to get a hinder on the play. One's opponent is entitled to a fair, unobstructed opportunity to play the ball.

INSTRUCTIONAL AND LEARNING PROCEDURES

1. History of the game
2. Assigned reading from the references at the end of this chapter
3. Equipment and facilities
4. Discussion of the nature of the game
5. Discussion of the rules
6. Fundamental basic skills
   (a) Correct position on floor
   (b) Footwork
   (c) Correct position of the hands and how to hit the ball
   (d) Types of strokes and serves
      (1) Overarm
      (2) Sidearm
      (3) Underarm
   (e) The kill shots
      (1) Straight kill shot
      (2) Right outside corner kill shot
      (3) Right inside corner kill shot
      (4) Fly kill shot
   (f) The serve
      (1) Power serve
      (2) Sharp-angle serve
      (3) Direct high lob serve
      (4) Two-wall serve to back corner
   (g) Playing strategy and hints
   (h) Practicing playing skills
      (1) Throwing the ball at the wall at different angles and taking rebounds correctly
      (2) Practicing serving
      (3) Practice in taking rebounds from back wall with both the right and left hands
      (4) Practicing lob shots
      (5) Practicing contacting the ball with the open hand, on the fingertips, on the heel of the hand, and on the closed hand

GLOSSARY OF HANDBALL, PADDLEBALL, AND RACKETBALL TERMS

ace A service which completely eludes the receiver.

crotch ball A ball hitting at the juncture of the front wall and the floor, or the ceiling, sidewall, and corner.

dead ball A ball out of play, following a fault not played, a penalty, or a hinder.

fault An infraction of the rules that involves a penalty other than shorts.

hinder An accidental interference or obstruction of the flight of the ball not involving a penalty.

kill A ball returned to the front wall in such a manner that it rebounds from the front wall or sidewall so close to the floor that it is impossible to get.

out Sometimes called hand out. It is scored against the serving side when the server fails to serve legally. In a doubles game when each of the two partners has been put out, it is a side out. In a singles game, retiring the server retires the side.

point Scored only by the serving side and made when an opponent fails to play a legal serve or a legally returned ball.

receiver The player or players to whom the ball is served; also called the receiving side.

server The person serving the ball.

service line The line running parallel with and 5 feet in front of the short line.

service zone The space between the outer edges of the short and service lines in which the server must remain while serving the ball.

short line The line running parallel with the front wall and dividing the court into two equal parts.

REFERENCES

Menke, Frank: Encyclopedia of sports, ed. 2, New York, 1960, A. S. Barnes & Co.

Mitchell, E. D. (ed.): Sports for recreation, New York, 1952, A. S. Barnes & Co.

Official handball rules, New York (latest edition), The Amateur Athletic Union of the United States.

Unified Handball Rules Committee: Official unified handball rules, 1968, courtesy of Champion Glove Mfg. Co., Des Moines, and Seamless Rubber Co., New Haven.

Yukic, Thomas: Handball, Philadelphia, 1972, W. B. Saunders Company.

14 Paddle tennis

HISTORY

The game of paddle tennis was originated in America in 1898 by a 14-year-old boy, Frank Peer Beal, at Albion, Michigan. He observed a game of tennis but could not afford a racket, nor was his backyard large enough for a full court. He fitted a court to his own backyard about a fourth as large as the full-sized tennis court. As a substitute for rackets, he shaped paddles out of a 1-inch maple plank.

The game grew slowly at first, but it eventually took hold and spread country-wide to churches, Y.M.C.A.s, schools, and similar places where adequate space for tennis was limited. Tournaments were held.

By adding a covered playing surface, F. S. Blanchard and J. K. Cogswell created a variation of the game, platform paddle tennis, which can be enjoyed in all seasons.

The game became very popular indoors as well as outdoors through the efforts of Mr. Beal.

The National Recreation Association is more or less responsible for the promotion and development of paddle tennis, which has become a widely accepted form of recreation and a must on the playground, in the gymnasium, on blocked-off pavement, or in the backyard.

Paddle tennis is like tennis on a smaller scale or like table tennis on a larger scale. There is a junior court and a senior court, and only in the height of nets and size of paddles does paddle tennis differ from regular tennis.

EQUIPMENT

The junior court

See Fig. 14-1 for a diagram and dimensions of a junior court.

The senior court

See Fig. 14-2 for a diagram and dimensions of a senior court.

The paddle

There are several types of paddles, and all are made of plywood. However, for school use the standard paddle (Fig. 14-3) is recommended since it is the least expensive. For the junior court it must not be more than 15 inches in length, and for the senior court it must not be more than 17 inches in length. It is resin-bonded birch, with handles glued, doweled, and fitted with leather handguards. It is rectangular in shape, with rounded corners, and its weight is between 8 and 9 ounces. It is about 7¾ inches wide.

PADDLE TENNIS 185

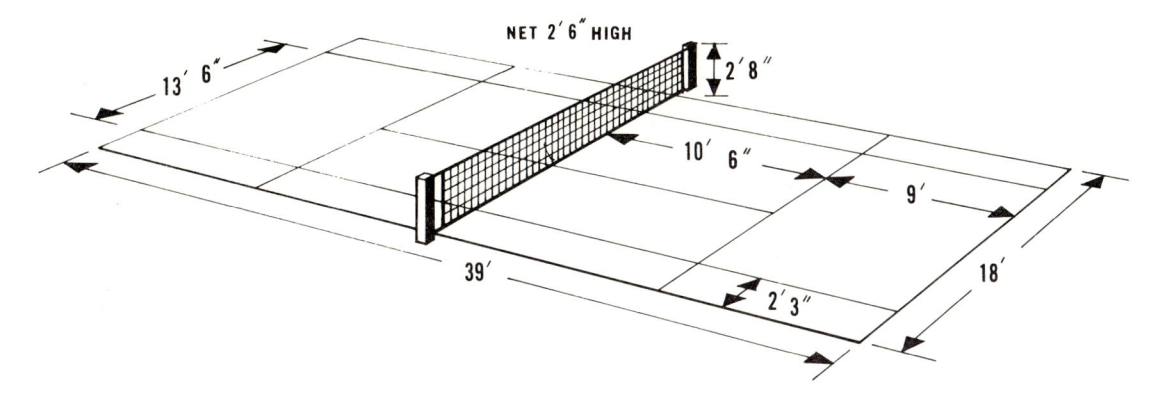

Fig. 14-1. Junior court.

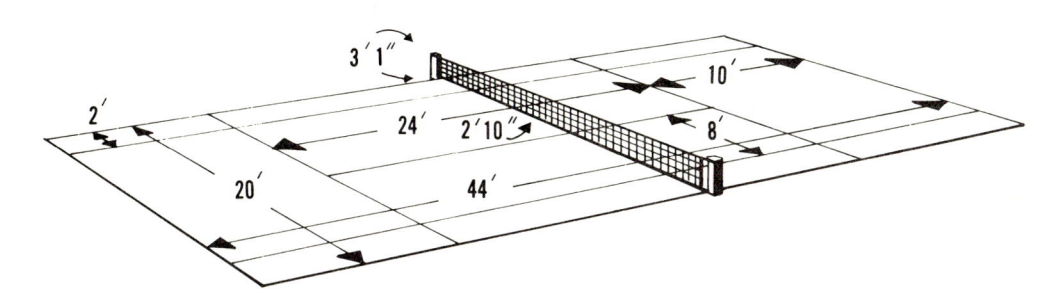

Fig. 14-2. Senior court.

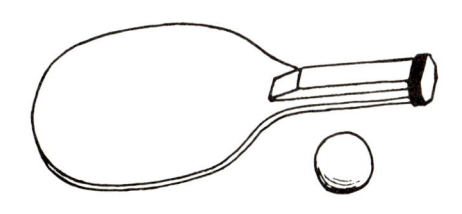

Fig. 14-3. Standard paddle and ball.

The ball

The ball is of a light, sponge rubber, approximately 2⅝ inches in diameter, and almost the same size as a tennis ball. New tennis balls are too lively, but old tennis balls can be used. The official ball is not so lively as a tennis ball and can be best controlled in this small-sized court.

The nets

The junior net is made of white twine, and is 18 feet long and 2 feet deep, with 1½-inch mesh.

The senior standard net is heavier and is constructed of white twine, with a heavy canvas-banded top. It is taped at the bottom and bound by green tape at the ends. The net is 22 feet long and 2½ feet deep, with ½-inch mesh. All-weather tarred nets can also be secured.

RULES

The rules are the same as in tennis with a few exceptions. For junior courts the height of the net is 2 feet, 6 inches at the center and 2 feet, 8 inches at the sides. For senior courts the height of the net is 2 feet, 10 inches at the center and 3 feet, 1 inch at the sides. Two serves are allowed as in regular tennis in the junior game but only one in the senior game. Also in senior games, if the serve is a fault, the server loses the point; after the service the entire doubles court is used for singles play.

Playground and paddle tennis are sponsored by the United States Paddle Tennis Association, and the rules are included in the *Official Tennis Guide*. Platform paddle tennis interests are sponsored by the American Paddle Tennis Association.

TECHNIQUES AND STRATEGY

The techniques and strategy of paddle tennis are not different from those of tennis. For rules, techniques, grips, and learning procedures, the reader's attention is directed to the chapter on tennis. The procedures are no different from those followed for tennis, even to the use of the generally popular eastern grip for the forehand. For the backhand shots, there is more of a shift of the hand behind the handle so the face of the paddle is open at an angle, and the power of the wrist can produce full strength behind the stroke.

If there is a difference in strategy, it would be that in paddle tennis it is best to play the net as often as possible since the court is not so wide as in tennis.

REFERENCES

Lawn tennis annual (published annually), New York, American Lawn Tennis, Inc.

Official paddle tennis equipment and rules, New York (latest edition), The Paddle Tennis Co.

Spalding tennis annual (published annually), New York, Spalding Sporting Goods Co.

15 Alpine skiing

HISTORY

Skiing started as a form of travel in hunting and war during the Stone and Bronze Ages. Snowshoelike skis have been found in the bogs and marshes of Finland, Norway, Sweden, and Russia, as well as on rock-wall carvings in Norway and Russia. The primitive toe-strap bindings were too loose for any real control, but a single solid pole acted as a downhill brake and "pusher" on the flats. The short ski, 6 to 7 feet, for pushing off and the long ski, 9 to 12 feet, for gliding were the first skis commonly used in Scandinavia. As the sport spread to the Alps, skis of equal length evolved.

Skiing as a modern recreational and competitive sport owes much to Sondre Norheim, Mathias Zdarsky, and Sir Arnold Lunn. Norheim, a Norwegian, invented the "stiff" binding in the early 1800s. Zdarsky, in Austria, developed the first dynamic ski technique and started the first ski school. It took a British scholar, Sir Arnold Lunn, to devise slalom and downhill racing. Later he devised the Arlberg-Kandahar races and was knighted for his contribution to skiing and mountaineering and for the improvement of Anglo-Swiss relations.

Although the Americans did not have great ski techniques during the 1850s, they are probably credited with the first professional races. The gold rush in the snow-covered California Sierras attracted many Scandinavians, who could get around on "snowshoes" easily. Skiing became instantly popular and was even used in delivering mail in winter. Records verify that in 1855 a ski competition was held in Onion Valley, California, for a prize of $25,000 in gold nuggets.

The first ski club in the United States was formed in 1872 in New Hampshire and was called the Nansen Ski Club. In 1904 seventeen ski clubs met in Michigan to form the National Ski Association. Again, skiing was supported mainly by Scandinavians. Since then, skiing has become a major American sport and industry. The United States Ski Team is considered one of the best in the world. And now modern technology makes it feasible to ski and to learn to ski without snow, utilizing artificial snow, portable revolving ski decks, or dry-land turf skis. This is a real boon to diehards and those living outside of snow country.

PRESEASON CONDITIONING

To really enjoy the winter ski season, speed up the learning process, and prevent overtiring and injuries during the first few

Fig. 15-1. Author Suzy Chaffee, Olympic ski star, executing royal christie. (Courtesy Hart Ski Manufacturing Co. and the Student Ski Association.)

weeks of skiing, fall conditioning is important. The most fun and effective way to stay in shape is participation in sports, especially tennis, waterskiing, football, soccer, gymnastics, bicycling, lacrosse, basketball, sprints, and jogging. If facilities for these sports are not available, or if you want to supplement your conditioning, by October start a 15-minute daily program concentrating on the three groups of muscles used most in skiing—stomach, thighs, and calves.

1. Stomach—sit-ups
2. Thighs—phantom chair (sitting with your back against a wall)
3. Calves—squat jumps and walking on your toes

All forms of yoga and dance are good for concentration and agility.

One should remember always to loosen up before doing conditioning exercises and all sports, especially the first ski run of the day. Stretch the muscles by rotating the neck, arms, waist, hips, knees, and ankles.

EQUIPMENT
Boots

Boots are a priority item in equipment, demanding a combination of stiffness and proper fit to ensure good control of your skis and happy feet. Generally speaking, the better the skier, the stiffer the boot.

Because the price of boots is relatively high, the beginner should first rent a pair of buckle boots carefully fitted at the ski shop. The boots should feel snug with one thin pair of nylon or silk socks plus one pair of thermal socks. If you can lift your heel inside the boot, or your buckles are not tight enough, or your boots are too soft, your turns will lack precision, regardless of how good a skier you are. If your boots are too small, you will cut off your circulation, causing numbness and possible frostbite. For maximum comfort, it is well to loosely fasten buckles while riding the lifts, then tighten them before the descent. If purchasing, the student should buy a comfortable pair of plastic, buckle boots because they retain their stiffness, comfort, and appearance longer than do leather boots. A boot press is often used to hold and carry the bulky boots about.

Skis

Skis are available in wood, metal, and fiberglass. Wood is outdated because of its lack of durability and performance. Metal is more durable than fiberglass and is a good bet for the soft snow found mainly in western America. Stiff fiberglass skis are great for hardpack and icy conditions. Metal skis tend to *chatter* on ice. Generally, the shorter and more flexible the skis, the easier they are to handle. Shorty skis are rapidly gaining popularity, not only for trick skiing but also as a safe, easy way of learning. Skis with the new three-dimensional or fish scale bottoms facilitate climbing and give additional security for turning.

The proper length of skis is determined by your height, weight, and ability. In general, the ski tip should stand 4 to 6 inches above your head. If you are lightweight and a beginner, 4 inches are appropriate; if you are solid and advanced, 6 inches should do. Fill in the shades of gray. Borrow or rent skis the first few times you try the sport. If you become addicted, invest in new skis costing over $70 or buy good secondhand ones. Have the shop attendant "flat-file" new skis before your first run. All skis should be sharpened at least twice a year for best ski performance as well as safety.

Waxing

The plastic running surface on the latest skis has minimized the need for waxing to reduce friction. However, under certain conditions, especially racing, wax is a must. New skis have a dry, slow surface and should be ironed with paraffin and scraped. Wax can be applied by hand, cork, or brush. For best results, skis should be dry and warm before waxing. Variety packs of waxes are available at ski shops.

Green—very cold snow
Blue—new fallen snow
Red—old, corn snow
Silver—moist, sticky snow

To repair gashes in running surface, melt a P-tex or Kofix stick into holes and scrape level.

Bindings

Release bindings disengage the boots from the skis in a hard fall. They do not guarantee against a broken leg, but they do reduce risks. Step-in bindings with the direct release at the toe and heel are the most up-to-date. Be absolutely sure to have your bindings adjusted and tested by a ski shop mechanic. Do not swap skis with friends until the skis have been checked. Bindings that are too loose or too tight are dangerous. They should not release unless you lunge forward, and hopefully then there will be someone to catch you. Bindings should be mounted ½ inch in front of the median point of the ski, between the tip and the tail. Safety straps should be worn to prevent runaway skis when bindings release.

Poles

Ski poles are built with handles, wrist loops, and metal alloy or bamboo shafts. The rings or baskets attached near the pointed tips of poles prevent the shafts from sinking into the snow too deeply. Poles range in quality, weight and flexibility, according to price. The expensive thin-walled steel poles with adjustable grips are light and easy to manipulate but could break at the end of their flexibility. The cheaper poles, made of aluminum alloys are heavier and nonadjustable but usually bend instead of break.

For length, poles should hit a few inches below the arm pit when standing on hard ground with boots on. Poles that are too long get in the way and cause bad habits in technique. Ski shops can easily cut down ski poles to a length suitable for you.

Ski pole grips

To get the most out of your pole action and to prevent dropping it, the loop of the pole must be in the correct position. With

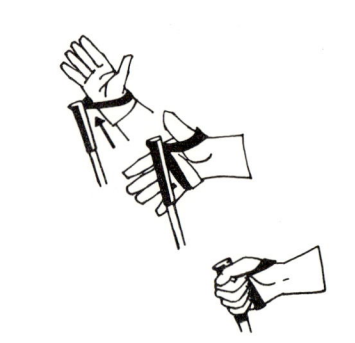

Fig. 15-2. Ski pole grips.

Fig. 15-3. Walking and gliding.

Fig. 15-4. The side step.

loop facing you, slip palm of hand underneath and entirely through the strap (see Fig. 15-2), close fist around handle and strap and slide hand down so that the loop is snug around the wrist. When skiing, hold pole firmly in this position.

Ski poles are used by the skier to help maintain balance, walk or glide, climb, assist in making turns, get up from falls, and to go faster.

BEGINNING TECHNIQUES
Walking and gliding

Walking on skis is the same motion as walking without skis, except for the sliding tendency. Here poles are used for stability and pushing. The change of weight from one ski to another "sets" the ski, making it easy to push off for the next step. Following the natural inclination of the arms, the skier extends the arm and pole opposite the extended leg and pulls against it. As he brings the other leg forward he braces against the opposite pole. Keep the weight on the balls of the feet so the knees can bend properly. (See Fig. 15-3.)

The exaggerated form of walking is *gliding*. The skier lunges forward and upward from a slight crouch and pulls against the poles to create the momentum for a gliding movement.

The side step

When a hill becomes too steep to walk up, the side step is recommended. (See Fig. 15-4.) With skis pointing across the hill, the skier places the uphill ski a foot above the next, then draws up the lower one. For very steep slopes put pressure on your edges and poles.

Falling and getting up

The best way to fall is backward and to one side. Remember even the best skiers fall. If you start to lose your balance try to stay on your feet as long as possible. But if gravity gets the best of you, try to relax.

The best way to get up is to place your skis on the downhill side of the slope. Next tuck your legs up under your hips on the

Fig. 15-5. Downhill schussing.

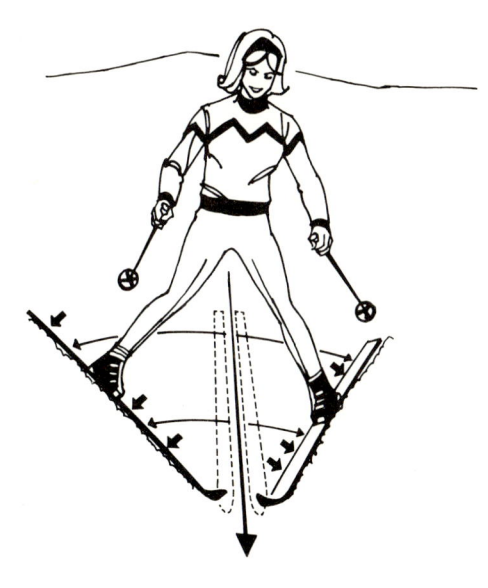

Fig. 15-6. Snowplow braking technique.

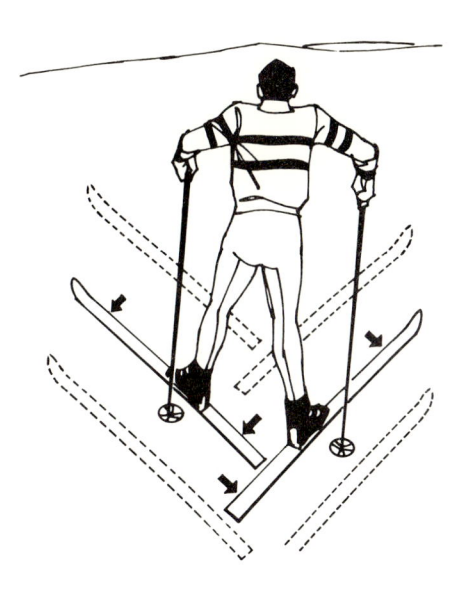

Fig. 15-7. The herringbone.

uphill side and push your body up with your hands or poles.

Downhill schussing

The key to the downhill schuss is correct body position and relaxation. (See Fig. 15-5.) Build your confidence by starting with a ski teacher on a gentle slope. The run-out should be sufficient to stop safely. Find a fairly flat area and point your skis straight down the *fall line*. Skis should be parallel and about a foot apart, with weight evenly distributed. The body should lean slightly forward, bending at the ankles, knees, and hips. Do not bend forward at the waist. Let your legs absorb the bumps by leaning forward and tucking up the legs as you go over them.

Remember, when schussing from deep snow to a hard surface or from packed snow to ice, a skier should lean farther forward so that the ski cannot run away with him. In contrast, to schuss from hard snow to powder, lean slightly back.

The snowplow

The snowplow (see Fig. 15-6) is the basic braking technique used by beginners and experts alike. Facing down the fall line in the downhill schuss position, push off with a brushing motion into a V-shaped ski position, with the ski tips together and the tails wide apart. The wider the V, the slower the speed.

The herringbone

The herringbone is a faster means of climbing up a hill than is the side step, provided the hill is not too steep. (See Fig. 15-7.) Face directly up the hill with skis in a V-shaped position, this time with the tips wide apart and the tails close together. Weight is on the inside edges, and the poles are used to propel upward and prevent backslip as the weight is shifted from one ski to the other.

Fig. 15-8. The kick turn.

The kick turn

The kick turn is used not only as a fine balance exercise on flat ground but also for changing direction when a skier ends up facing dangerous terrain. (See Fig. 15-8.) The turn is actually a stationary 180-degree change of direction. Starting with the skis parallel, poles halfway between boots and ski tips, and weight on left ski, kick up right ski high enough so that the ski stands on its tail. Next, rotate the raised ski to face in the opposite direction, as the pole comes around as a brace. Weight transfers to the right ski as the left ski and pole shift around next to the right ski. On a steep slope with skis facing across the fall line the lower leg is always the kick-up leg.

SAFETY PRECAUTIONS

1. The best assurance against first-day injury is a ski school instructor lesson.
2. Have ski shop man or instructor adjust and check bindings with skis and boots on. Do not swap skis with friends without the same adjustment.
3. Do not ski on unmarked trails or where avalanche warnings have been placed even though the snow looks sensational.
4. On hazardous days do not ski alone, and when ski touring, at least three people are necessary.
5. On subzero days, wear thermal underwear and/or warm-up pants, insulated parka, goggles, and mask or scarf to avoid frostbite. If a white spot appears on the face, place bare hand on the spot for a minute, but do not rub, then head for shelter.
6. Do some loosening-up exercises before the first run. Warming up from the neck down prevents strained muscles and eliminates that first stiff run.
7. Be a patient learner. Ski in control and build up confidence. In *schuss booming*

Fig. 15-9. Traversing.

Fig. 15-10. Stem turn.

not only could you ruin yourself but you might also ruin a nice relationship.

INTERMEDIATE TECHNIQUES
Traversing

If you are skiing in a straight line other than the fall line you are traversing. (See Fig. 15-9.) Skis are parallel and slightly apart, weight is over the balls of the feet, with two thirds of the weight on the lower ski and one third on the upper ski. Ankles and knees are rolled into the hill, causing the inside edges of the skis to bite into the snow without slipping. To compensate, the upper body leans slightly downhill, but essentially square over the skis. The amount of bending motion, called *angulation,* depends on the steepness of the slope and the radius of the turn. During the traverse, the arms should be slightly forward about waist level.

Stem turn

The stem turn, which combines the snowplow turn and the traverse, is useful for a slow speed turn. (See Fig. 15-10.) The

Fig. 15-11. Parallel.

skier enters the turn from a regular traverse position, then stems the uphill ski into a half-V position. As the weight transfers, the body *angulates* over the ski causing both skis to come around in the turn. As the new direction is established, the skis can run back into the parallel position. Problems in turning are usually due to insufficient weight shift to the uphill ski.

ADVANCED TECHNIQUES
The parallel turn

The parallel turn is a progressive form of the stem christie but is more complex because of its dependence on *up-unweighting* and precise edge control. (See Fig. 15-11.) The turn starts from the *traverse* position standing square over the skis. The skier sinks slightly as he plants his pole lightly in the snow on the downhill side between boot and ski tip in anticipation of the turn. As he exposively up-unweights, the pressure on the *inside edges* transfers to the *outside edges* and the ankles and knees power the skis around in the turn, ending in a traverse position. The upper torso should be kept as still as possible throughout the turn.

The hop turn

The hop turn is an exercise for coordinating the parallel turn. To execute, thrust the heels of the skis in the direction of the turn, either in quick rhythmic thrustings or subtle hops in between long traverses.

Wedeln

The wedeln is an advanced form of parallel skiing where the ankles and knees manipulate a series of rhythmical half-completed turns.

RULES OF ALPINE COMPETITION
Slalom

The racer with the fastest time without missing any gates is the winner. A gate is two flagged poles of the same color 10½ feet apart. Course setters use about fifty-five of these gates in a blue, yellow, red sequence in various combinations, like the open gate, close gate, hairpin flush, and elbow. Quickness and agility are prerequisites for a good salom skier. Slalom skis are shorter than giant slalom or downhill skis.

Giant slalom

Giant slalom uses half as many gates as the slalom, and the gates are twice as far apart. The red and blue sequential double-pole gates are often spread out over a mile of undulating terrain. Strength, agility, and explosiveness when diving into the turns are important for this event. The skating turn is often used.

Downhill

Downhill is the fastest, most exciting event where speeds up to 80 miles per hour are reached. Courses are of up to 3 miles long, utilizing the natural terrain. Red or blue control gates are used as guidelines and to check speed. The aerodynamic egg position is used on smooth terrain and flats. Protective helmets are required.

Nordic competition

The nordic competition includes cross-country and jumping.

SKI ORGANIZATIONS GOVERNING COMPETITIONS

F.I.S.

All races are run according to the rules of the Fédération Internationale de Ski (F.I.S.). This representative body supervises the Olympic Games and World Championships, which are held every four years; the World Championships follow two years after the Olympics.

U.S.S.A.

The United States Ski Association is the governing body for the sport of skiing in the United States. There are eight geographical divisions, each with its own membership, classification of racers, and schedule of competitions, ranging from juniors through veterans. National, Olympic, and World Championship teams are selected on the basis of qualifying races.

N.C.A.A

The National Collegiate Athletic Association is the governing body of intercollegiate ski racing. The top teams and individuals compete at the N.C.A.A. Championships. The individual winners of the various events, including Alpine and Nordic, are named to the All-American Ski Team at the end of each season.

NASTAR

National standard race operates on a handicap system as in golf, utilizing a simple giant slalom course especially designed for recreational skiers of all ages. With the aid of computers and professional pacesetters, skiers can compare their skiing with that of other skiers throughout the country.

TEACHING AND LEARNING PROCEDURES

Beginners

1. Ski pole grip
2. Positioning
    (a) Stretching exercises
    (b) Ski tip lift
    (c) Ski tail lift
    (d) Ankle and knee bending
3. Walking and gliding on skis
    (a) Walking—skier's choice
    (b) With poles
    (c) Without poles
    (d) Gliding with poles
4. Falling and getting up
5. Climbing techniques
    (a) Side step
    (b) Diagonal side step
    (c) Herringbone
6. Kick turn
7. Downhill schussing
    (a) Skiing down, bending ankles and knees
    (b) Skiing down, moving body position up and down
    (c) Skiing down, alternating picking up skis
    (d) Skiing down, leaning back and forward

Intermediates

1. Exercises
    (a) Stretching exercises
    (b) Gliding and skating on flat ground and the hill

2. The traverse
   (a) Traverse in prepared track
   (b) Traverse moving up and down
   (c) Traverse leaning forward and back
   (d) Changing degrees of angulation
   (e) Turning up the hill
3. Stem turn
   (a) Assume snowplow position on slope
   (b) Slide into snowplow from downhill schuss and back
   (c) Snowplow straight down the hill leaning from side to side.

Advanced

1. Exercises
   (a) Stretching exercises
   (b) Review stem turn, side stepping, forward, back, up, and down movements, and turning up the hill
2. Parallel turn
   (a) Hopping turns
   (b) Smooth turns
   (c) Alternate making big smooth turns and quick little turns

GLOSSARY OF ALPINE SKIING TERMS

angulation Body position where edges bite into the snow from pressure exerted by the ankles and the knees being rolled into the hill; to compensate, the upper body leans slightly downhill.
chatter Undesirable vibrations of edges while skiing on ice or hardpacked snow.
fall line The imaginary line of gravity straight down a slope.
inside edges Those gripping the snow on the inside of the arc of the turn.
outside edges Those on the downhill side of the slope not gripping the snow.
traverse Skiing on inside edges at an angle to the fall line.
schuss booming Skiing dangerously out of control.
up-unweighting A down-up movement of the ankles and knees for reducing weight on the skis prior to turning, to facilitate changing of edges.

REFERENCES

America's ski book, editors of *Ski Magazine* and John Henry Auran, New York, 1965, Charles Scribner's Sons.
Casewit, Curtis: Ski racing, advice by the experts, New York, 1969, Arco Publishing Co., Inc.
Joubert, Georges, and Vuarnet, Jean: How to ski the new French way, New York, 1967, Dial Press, Inc.
Lunn, Sir Arnold: The story of ski-ing, London, 1952, Eyre & Spottiswoode (Publishers), Ltd.

PERIODICALS

Snow Magazine, published eight times a year by Snow Publishing Co., Bloomfield Hills, Mich.
Ski Magazine, published eight times a year by Universal Publishing Corp., New York, N. Y.
Skiing, published six times a year by Ziff Davis Publishing Co., New York, N. Y.
The Student Skier, published six times a year by the Student Ski Association, West Dover, Vt. *Note:* This newspaper is perfect for college students and is free.

FILMS

The moebius flip, Summit Films Productions, Denver, Colo.
Ski the outer limits, Summit Films Productions, Denver, Colo.
Incredible skis, Summit Films Productions, Denver, Colo.
Ski country USA, Summit Films Productions, Denver, Colo.
The great ski chase, Summit Films Productions, Denver, Colo.
NASTAR, Joseph Schlitz Brewing Co., Milwaukee, Wisc.

16 Self-defense

HISTORY

The art of self-defense was developed by the Chinese Monks in the twelfth century. The monks were forbidden to use weapons in combat by the monastic rules. Because they were constantly being attacked by nomads and roving bandits, they were forced to devise a defense without the use of weapons of any kind. Through trial and error, often with the loss of life, the monks eventually developed a method of defense that has remained basically unchanged throughout the centuries. During the last half of the twelfth century the Japanese discovered this art, copied it, claimed it as their own, and called it "jiu jitsu." Jiu means *gentle* while jitsu means *art* or *practice*. Not one but many systems of jiu jitsu were developed by the Japanese. In 1882, Professor Jigora Kano, a Japanese instructor who had spent many years practicing many of the systems of jiu jitsu, established the Kodokan, *a school for studying the way* and labeled his system "judo," which means *the way or principle*.

One branch of the Kodokan was established in 1921 in New York City. However, because this system was mainly competitive, young Americans were not interested. In 1925 a group of these young Americans developed their own system of self-defense, and called their organization The American Judo Club. They produced a system of self-defense that during World War II proved to be superior to any other in the world. After the war, judo, as a competitive sport, started to grow and today is a recognized sport throughout the world.

Because of the recent upsurge in violence "all around us," we feel that basic instruction in self-defense is beneficial for the student, both man and woman. The basics of self-defense that are to follow were taught during World War II in the U. S. Air Corps School of Physical Training and were presented to the Air Corps Training Units, Air Cadets, and Guards.

THE BASIC PRINCIPLES
Balance

An individual is off balance in some direction no matter what position is assumed. It takes only a small amount of effort to move a person off balance if you know in what position that person is weak.

Strength

Intensive development and use of the internal and external oblique muscles of the abdomen is the second principle. Much of the strength needed in the execution of most of the defensive maneuvers must come from these muscles.

Opponent's momentum

Utilization of an opponent's momentum and strength to bring about the downfall is the third principle.

Power against weakness

The object of the attack is to apply one's maximum amount of power at the opponent's minimum amount of leverage.

Knowledge of the basic defenses

Understanding the techniques of getting the hold and applying the pressure in many different situations is another basic principle. It is suggested that in practice, caution must be used during the application of pressure, to guard against broken bones.

METHOD OF INSTRUCTION

Students should be paired off so that two students of approximately the same height and weight are standing facing each other. They are then designated as One and Two. On the command "Attack," One attacks Two, for example, by executing the "overhand thrust," in which One raises the hand as though intending to strike. On the command "Break," Two executes the defense. This procedure is repeated many times, until all participants are thoroughly familiar with the mechanics of each basic. Next the command "Attack" is given and the defender responds immediately. After a variety of attacks have been practiced, each of the participants should act as both attacker and defender. The attacker should attack using any one of the basics, and the defender should try to respond quickly with the correct break.

BASICS OF SELF-DEFENSE

There are many basics of self-defense. It would take volumes to cover them all. We have attempted to describe a few of them.

The chest push

One puts a hand on Two's chest. Two immediately places both hands on top of One's hand. Holding the hand tightly against the chest, Two then flexes sharply at the waist and knees, sending One to the floor. (See Fig. 16-1.)

The collar grab

One grabs Two's collar in front. Two takes One's right thumb in the left hand and places the left thumb on the back of One's hand. Two then, with the help of the right hand, twists One's hand counterclockwise putting pressure on One's wrist. This will force One to the floor. This break is the same as that shown for the front choke. (See Fig. 16-4.)

Single-hand grasp

One grasps Two's wrist: right on left, left on right, or opposites. Two makes the break by twisting the hand toward the opponent's thumb. (See Fig. 16-2.)

Double-hand grasp

One, facing Two, reaches forward and grasps Two's wrists from above. Two makes the break by stepping in quickly, dropping the elbows and lifting the hands up and toward One's thumbs. Two may use the left hand to assist in the break. (See Fig. 16-3.)

The front two-hand choke

One places the hands around Two's throat. On the command "Break," Two clasps the hands together, spreads the elbows and then drives the arms up against One's arms, forcing them free. A knee to the groin at this point can easily be executed. (See Fig. 16-4.)

This same defense may be used while lying on the floor.

The second break, which may be used against the front choke, is the two-hand thumb grab and twist. Two reaches up with the right hand and grasps One's thumb, then with the other hand Two rotates One's hand clockwise. (See Fig. 16-5.)

Choke from the rear

One assumes a choke hold from the rear. Two grasps One's wrist and pulls One's arms forward over the shoulder. Then quickly bends forward, and tosses One over the head. (See Fig. 16-6.)

SELF-DEFENSE 199

Fig. 16-1. The chest push.

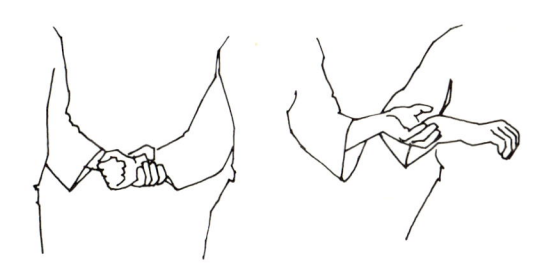

Fig. 16-2. Single-hand grasp.

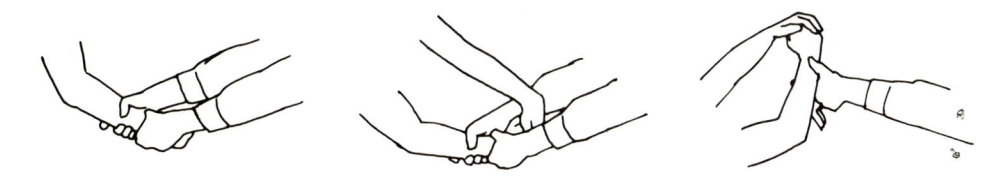

Fig. 16-3. Double-hand grasp.

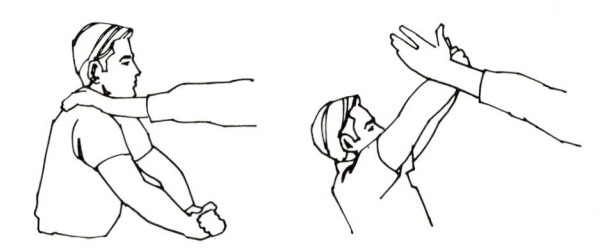

Fig. 16-4. Front two-hand choke.

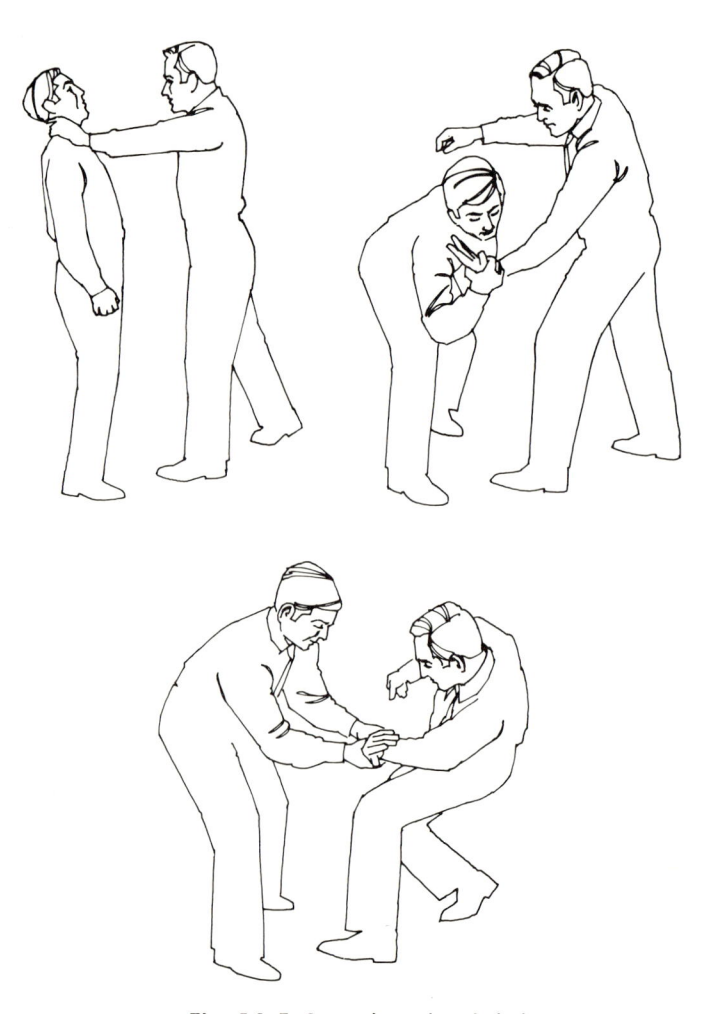

Fig. 16-5. Second two-hand choke.

SELF-DEFENSE 201

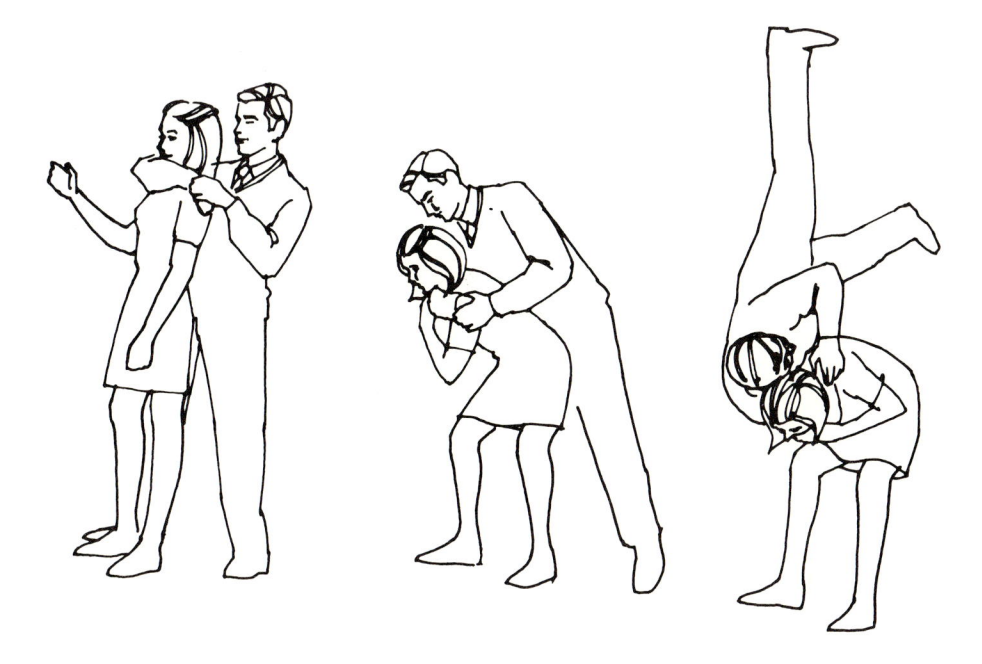

Fig. 16-6. Choke from the rear.

Fig. 16-7. One-hand overhead thrust.

Fig. 16-8. Underhand thrust.

Overhead smash

One raises the hand to attack. Two steps in with the left foot and at the same time, reaches high over the head with crossed arms, right over left. When One smashes the arm down, Two stops it between the wrists. Two then grabs One's wrist with the right hand and applies pressure with the left hand just above One's elbow.

One-hand overhead thrust

On the command "Attack," One raises the right hand high over the head. As One starts to bring it down, Two grabs it with the right hand, and then reaches in back of Two's right arm and up between the biceps and forearm and grasps his or her own right wrist. Pressure is then applied on the arm. (See Fig. 16-7.)

Underhand thrust

One attacks by thrusting the right hand upward and forward from the hip. Two breaks the attack by bringing the little finger edge of the left hand against Two's lower forearm and at the same time dodging to the left. Next, Two grabs One's right hand with the thumb of the right hand on the knuckles of One and the fingers around the palm side of One's hand. With a twist of the hands counterclockwise, Two easily forces One down. (See Fig. 16-8.)

Hip throw

As the attacker approaches, Two grabs the attacker by the right arm or sleeve with the left hand. The defender then pivots clockwise extending right leg in front of One, so that the hip is directly in front of the

Fig. 16-9. Hip throw.

Fig. 16-10. The front hug.

attacker. At the same time, Two places the right arm around One. By flexing forward at the waist and pulling with both the left hand and the right arm, Two easily throws the attacker to the back. (See Fig. 16-9.)

Leg trip while lying down

The defender lies on the floor on the back with the legs extended and apart. The attacker stands straddling the defender's right leg.

To take the attacker down, the defender rolls to the left side, hooks the right shin on the attacker's right knee, and applies pressure.

The defender may also execute this by diving feet first into the starting position.

Foot pry take down

The attack position is the same as that of the leg trip while lying down. The defender places the instep of the left foot behind the attacker's right heel and pulls it forward while placing the right foot on the attacker's knee and forcing it backward.

The front hug

The attacker approaches the victim and wraps the arms around the victim's waist. The defender manages to keep arms free. The defender closes the fist and places the thumb underneath the base of the attacker's nose and presses. By pressing forward and pulling the attacker forward with the other arm, the attacker can be forced over backwards. (See Fig. 16-10.)

Fig. 16-11. Front hug—thumbs press in jaw line.

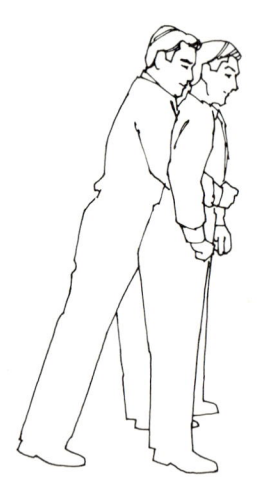

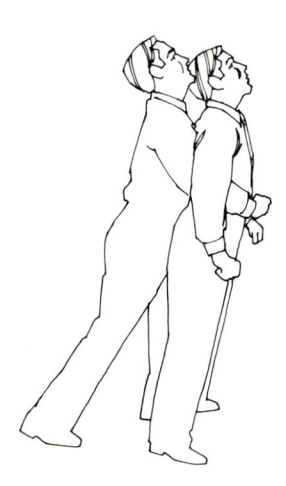

Fig. 16-12. The back underarm hold.

A second defense for the same hold is to place the thumbs in the jaw line of the opponent's face. Pressure should be applied along this line and up underneath the ear lobes. The pain from this technique is terrific. The attacker must release the hold. (See Fig. 16-11.)

The back underarm hold

The attacker wraps the arms around the victim's waist leaving the arms free. The victim slams the head back into the face of the attacker. Then the victim raises the arms high and twists rapidly, hitting the attacker in the face with the elbows. (See Fig. 16-12.)

REFERENCES

Basic field manual: Unarmed defense for the American soldier, Washington, D. C., 1942, U.S. Government Printing Office.

Callum, Miles: Body-building and self-defense, New York, 1962, Barnes and Noble, Inc.

Yerkow, Charles: Official judo: sport judo and self-defense, New York, 1953, A. A. Wyn, Inc.

17 Skin and scuba diving

INTRODUCTION

The underwater world is relatively unexplored and filled with beauty beyond description. It is a world of greater depths than the highest mountain peaks and covers nearly seven-tenths of the surface of the earth. It is inhabited by uncountable varieties of animal and plant life. It is a restless, dynamic, changing world possessing rhythm, design, movement, and power. Man is inexplicably drawn to this underwater world. He must, however, proceed with care and skill. This new world can be hostile and sometimes cruel. For these reasons the following information, though brief, is explicit, definite, and important for those who venture below the surface. Learn these lessons well, then enjoy the underwater world with confidence and skill.

HISTORY

The exploration of the land surface dates from the very beginning of man, and the wanderings of man over the surfaces of the world's water masses date from the beginning of recorded history; but the exploration of the underwater world is a relatively recent adventure. Though Aristotle wrote about diving devices as early as 360 B.C., and the great historian Pliny in A.D. 77 described the use of breathing tubes for underwater activity, man's real opportunity for extended underwater movement and investigation did not occur until the introduction of the scuba* regulator in 1943 by Jacques-Yves Cousteau and Emile Gagnan of France.

The forerunners to modern methods of underwater exploration and sport are many. Early Greek and Roman strategists, in an effort to perfect the art of warfare, trained and equipped soldiers of strong swimming ability to approach enemy craft from below the water surface. They were supplied with air through a short length of hollow reed. Soldiers of the fifteenth and sixteenth centuries were fitted with surface-breathing bags connected to the diver by means of a hose and leather hood arrangement, and wore weighted shoes. These divers were restricted to the shallow depths because of their crude equipment. Benjamin Franklin, in his autobiography, described his making of hand and foot fins to facilitate faster swimming. William Forder, in the early 1800s, developed a metal helmet covering one-half of the diver's body and supplied with air from the surface by means of a hand-operated bellows. In 1837, Augustus Siebe developed a full, dry diving suit with a rigid

---

*Self-contained underwater breathing apparatus.

helmet. In the latter part of the 1800s the French developed a rubber diving suit and mask, supplied with air from a metal canister carried by the diver. A mechanical regulator was employed to control the flow of air. The American C. J. Lambertsen patented a successful closed circuit–rebreathing unit in 1942. This unit was adopted by the Navy for underwater demolition teams, because with this equipment the diver's expired air did not bubble to the surface to reveal his position as he worked underwater.

In the past two or three years the design of the scuba has been refined and sophisticated, but the basic principle remains the same as the Cousteau-Gagnan design.

DIVING PHYSICS

As the diver goes beneath the water surface, there is an awareness of an increase in the surrounding pressure. This pressure has an important effect on parts of the diver's body and the air the diver breathes.

The air mixture compressed in a scuba tank is atmospheric air, never pure oxygen, and contains the same gas percentages (79% nitrogen, 20.93% oxygen, and 0.03% carbon dioxide) as atmospheric air. When these gases are breathed under pressure as in scuba diving, there are several basic laws of physics that must be carefully considered.

Boyle's law states that if temperature is constant the volume of a gas will vary inversely with the absolute pressure, while the density varies directly with the pressure. If the pressure of a gas is doubled, the volume is decreased by one-half, but the density is doubled. This simply means that when a skin diver is descending, the air in the lungs is compressed and as the diver surfaces it expands. This phenomenon is only important to the skin diver diving to exceptional depths. If the scuba diver, breathing air at the ambient pressure (pressure equal to the surrounding water), does not exhale and breathe normally when ascending, the volume of air taken into the lungs at depth is going to expand as the pressure of the surrounding water is lessened during the ascent. This gas expansion can cause serious medical problems and might result in a fatal injury.

Henry's law states that the quantity of gas that goes into solution in any liquid is directly proportional to the partial pressure of the gas. This means that if a certain quantity of liquid is capable of absorbing one quart of gas at one atmosphere of partial pressure, the same quantity of liquid would absorb two quarts of gas at two atmospheres. An understanding of gas absorption by the blood while diving is important to the diver in appreciating the need for computing a decompression dive.

We live under a constant pressure of 14.7 pounds per square inch, or one atmosphere; but when we dive beneath the surface of the ocean, we add about 0.445 pound per square inch for every foot depth. When we reach the 33-foot depth, we have added another 14.7 pounds per square inch and are at two atmospheres of absolute pressure. For each additional 33 feet we add another atmosphere of pressure. It is the effects of this pressure of water and atmospheric pressure above the water that the diver must understand and appreciate. It is this pressure that causes pain in the diver's ear during the descent, drives gas into solution, and presses the face mask against the face.

Sight and hearing are dramatically affected by the water. Due to the water's refraction and absorption of light, underwater objects appear to be about one-third closer than their actual distance and about one-fourth larger than their actual size. Sound travels much more rapidly in water than in air. When a tank is struck with a hard object such as a knife, the noise can be easily heard for quite a distance; however, it is more difficult to determine the direction from which the sound came in water than it is in the atmosphere. Communicating by voice underwater is very unsatisfactory, so divers must develop a system of hand signals that all divers in the party understand and are able to use.

SKIN DIVING

The term "skin diving" is used to describe diving activity when the diver uses mask, snorkel, and fins and holds the breath while swimming underwater. "Scuba diving" refers to underwater swimming when the diver adds to the basic skin diving items, equipment designed to take an air supply beneath the surface. "Sport diving" is commonly used to include both skin and scuba diving activities.

Prerequisites

The skin and scuba diving student should first possess an advanced swimming ability and be the holder of a lifesaving certificate issued by the American Red Cross, Y.M.C.A., or other recognized agency. A standard first aid card is also desirable.

SWIMMING TEST

The following test must not only be the minimum level of swimming competency but should be executed with a high level of skill and with relative ease.
1. Swim 300 yards using overarm, side- and breaststrokes.
2. Swim 50 feet underwater without swim aids.
3. Tread water for 5 minutes.
4. Rest on back for 10 minutes with little or no movement.
5. Execute surface dives to 10 feet.

MEDICAL EXAMINATION

In addition to being a strong swimmer, the student must be in sound medical health. The physician should carefully examine for functional or structural deficiencies in the following organs:
1. Ears—average hearing with the drum intact
2. Nose and throat—normal breathing
3. Sinuses—unobstructed
4. Heart and circulatory system—capable of strenuous work loads
5. Respiratory system—clear, normal, and capable of supporting heavy work
6. Eyes—20/30 or better

Chronic symptoms of nervousness, ear infections, sinus irritation, lung disease, and heart aliment should eliminate a person from this sport. No diver can be subject to fainting spells, blackouts, epilepsy, or other neurological disorders. In addition, anyone prone to phobias, fears, and panic should be advised to find interests in other sports.

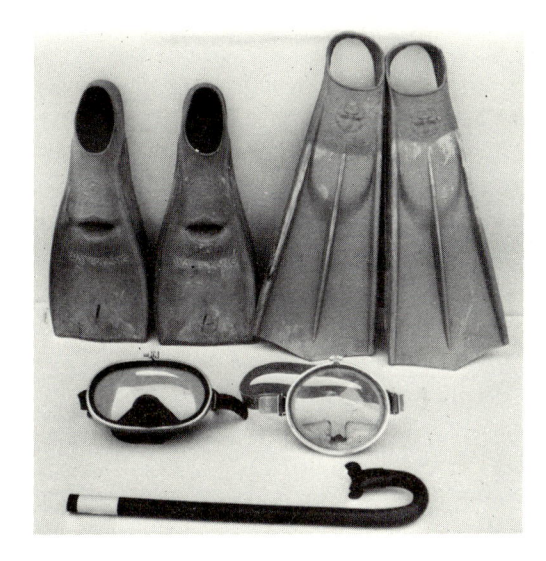

Fig. 17-1. Full-footed fins; open-heeled fins; purge-valve mask; equalizing mask; and snorkel.

Equipment

Items essential for skin diving are the mask, snorkel, and fins. (See Fig. 17-1.) When diving in cold water, the diver should wear a neoprene-rubber wet suit. When a wet suit is worn, a weight belt must also be used to overcome the buoyancy of the suit. Most diving authorities insist that a personal float, such as an inflatable vest or belt, is absolutely essential for safe diving.

Supplementary items of equipment are the surface float, such as a tire tube or paddle board, knife, spear gun, game and collecting bags, diver's flag, compass, depth gauge, watch, and photographic equipment. Some of these items are required by law in some states.

MASK

The mask, sometimes called a face-plate, keeps the water from coming in contact with the surface of the eye and eliminates distortion, thereby enabling the diver's vision to be limited only by the light and clarity of the water. It also prevents water from being inhaled through the nose. The mask should fit the face with comfort and provide a water-tight seal when the diver is submerged. The lens should be made of safety glass, not plastic, and secured in the mask by a metal retaining ring with a tension screw. The adjustable strap should attach on or near the front of the mask to assure a snug watertight fit. Some models have a one-way purge valve which enables the diver to clear water from the mask without changing the swimming position. Also there are masks with molded depressions that permit the diver to close off the nostrils by pressing with the fingers which facilitates easy clearing of the ears.

Snorkel

The snorkel is a tube that is held in the diver's mouth and extends above the surface of the water. It enables the diver to swim and breathe without lifting the head from the water. Although several types are available, a semirigid rubber or plastic tube in the form of the letter J is the most advisable and popular among experienced divers. Those with ping-pong valves and rubber flutter valves are very dangerous and are not recommended for sport diving. A rubber mouthpiece allows the diver to maintain control of the tube and breathe with the head submerged for easy underwater viewing. The snorkel should have a soft rubber mouthpiece that is comfortable to the diver's mouth, permitting extended use without undue mouth fatigue.

Fins

Fins are mainly of two types: open heeled and full footed. Either is satisfactory, depending on the diver's preference, but an adjustable strap model is usually preferred. The purpose of the fins is to give extra power in swimming, not to increase speed. The fin should fit comfortably to allow circulation and prevent the feet from cramping, but be snug enough to be secure when going through the surf. Fins of extra large design can cause undue fatigue, particularly when used by an untrained diver. Beginning divers should use a medium-sized fin of medium flexibility.

Exposure dress

Wet suits made of cellular foam neoprene rubber and designed to fit snugly over the whole body are superior and preferred to the old dry suit model. A small amount of water enters the wet suit, is quickly warmed by the diver's body, and then serves as insulation between the body and the surrounding water. These suits increase the diver's buoyancy significantly, so weights must be worn to enable the diver to submerge and swim with ease underwater.

Weight belt

This item deserves special attention. Lead weights attached to a web belt are used in varying amounts to overcome buoyancy. Most important is the quick-release buckle, which must be designed to operate effectively with one hand. When the diver is in any questionable situation that could possibly lead to an emergency, the diver must be able to quickly and surely release the weight belt and allow it to fall away free and clear.

Accessory equipment

Descriptions of, and information concerning, other equipment for skin diving may be found by consulting the references at the end of the chapter. However, let it be understood that no one should dive without some type of personal float, such as an inflatable vest, in addition to a surface float. A good automobile inner tube with attached line makes a very effective and practical surface float for resting. A canvas or burlap bag tied to it serves to carry the diver's equipment.

Skin diving skills

All basic strokes can and will be used while diving; however, the open, enlarged flutter kick with very loose knee action is the most common source of propelling force. Many divers alternate the dolphin kick with the flutter kick to help prevent undue fatigue. A strong kick allows the diver freedom for the hands and arms to carry equipment, shoot fish, take pictures, and pick up interesting objects. Usually when the diver is swimming, the arms are trailed in a comfortable position at the sides and are not specifically in use. (See Fig. 17-2.) This position allows for maximum balance and relaxation. However, when swimming in turbid, murky water with poor visibility, the diver should extend both arms forward at full length to ward off undetected obstructions. When underwater, the diver should

Fig. 17-2. Skin divers in proper underwater swimming position.

always swim as effortlessly as possible, conserving oxygen and thereby extending the length of "down time."

Diving Down

When in open water, the diver should use either the tuck or pike surface dive to submerge. If the dive must be made through kelp or other plant life or into unfamiliar water, a feet-first dive should be executed.

Hyperventilation

Some divers extend their down time by means of rapid and deep breathing with exceptionally full exhalations just before submerging. No other practice in diving is more hazardous. Hyperventilation, combined with the exertion of swimming under water and a change in the normal regulatory responses of carbon dioxide and oxygen caused by the pressure changes, can cause anoxia (lack of oxygen) and could result in drowning. Instead, the diver should take two or three deep breaths and then hold a third at about two-thirds capacity just as the dive is started.

Clearing

When the diver submerges, the snorkel will be filled with water, but the air pressure in the diver's mouth prevents the water from entering the mouth and throat. Upon surfacing, the diver can blow out the water in the tube by a short forceful exhalation while keeping the face submerged.

Sometimes a small amount of water seeps into the face mask during the dive. This water should be evacuated to prevent its being inhaled through the nose. To clear the mask, the diver should roll to one side, press the upper edge of the faceplate inward, and exhale through the nose into the mask. The water pooled in the bottom side of the mask is forced out by the air pressure. Care should be taken to release hand pressure on the mask while still blowing; otherwise water will flood into the mask through the released seal. Another method is for the diver to tilt the head back, press on the top of the mask, and exhale. (See Fig. 17-3.)

Equalizing

To provide for comfort and prevent injury, it is essential that pressure inside and outside the eardrum always be equal. When the diver descends, the pressure on the eustachian tube side of the drum and that developed by the increasing pressure of water on the outside must be equalized. Swallowing and sliding the jaw from side to side sometimes will accomplish this. Pinching the nose while blowing gently against the closed nostrils can also be used to equalize the

Fig. 17-3. Clearing mask—head tilted to side; head tilted back.

pressure. However, other methods should be tried first because mucus can be forced into the middle ear with this technique. The diver must never use ear plugs or place anything in the ears while diving.

ENTRIES

Always enter the water from as close to the surface as possible. When hunting, slip, drop, or slide feet first into the water as quietly as possible so as not to frighten game from the diving area. When the entry is from a point well above the surface, such as the side of a boat which is not equipped with a diving platform, the entry should be made with a giant stride, feet-first jump. When executing this entry, cover the face mask with one hand to prevent its being dislodged by the impact of the water. Keep other gear, such as cameras or spear gun, well away from the body. Take a giant stride well away from the takeoff point, keeping the body erect and eyes looking forward. After settling in the water, level off and make an approach swim to the diving area.

ASCENDING

When ascending, always extend one hand and arm overhead, looking up and turning 360 degrees around. This method should always be used to ensure the diver from coming up headfirst under another diver's tank, boat, floating object, or obstruction that could cause serious injury.

PERFORMANCE TECHNIQUES

When beginning a dive, snorkel on the surface, pushing a tube in front with the face submerged until reaching the diving location. Swim easily and relaxed, conserving energy and strength for the dive. The dive should be planned so that both buddies know the intentions of the other. A well-planned dive is the first step toward a safe dive. Surface dives should be made steep to the bottom; then, when underwater, swim slowly. Over-all bottom time and total dive time can be increased by limiting the time of each single dive and by making more rather than fewer extended dives.

Buddy diving

Never dive alone. This is the first and most important rule of safe diving. Diving and staying together takes practice between partners, but it must be done to ensure enjoyable and safe diving. You enter the water together, you dive together, and you leave the water together.

SCUBA DIVING

Several types and arrangements of self-contained underwater breathing apparatus enable the diver to take a supply of air below the surface. Scuba has been the greatest advancement in man's effort to explore the underwater world. Such equipment extends diving time to over one hour and at depths of well over 100 feet. Scuba also frees the diver to swim with relatively complete freedom and to roam the depths at will. Though time and depths can be extended dramatically over skin diving limits, the novice scuba diver is cautioned to limit the dive time to 90 percent of tank capacity and to restrict depth for the first 25 or 30 dives to 33 feet. After this, the diver can move to depths of 60 or 70 feet and use up two or three tanks on a given day. However, this should not be done without consulting U.S. Navy standard decompression tables. (One standard tank provides approximately one hour of diving time depending on dive depth, water temperature, and breathing pattern.) Not until well after a year of regular sport diving at the depths and times just listed should the diver move into depths approaching 100 feet. These may seem to be unduly restrictive diving limits, but it is interesting to note that many amateur and recreational divers find their most interesting and enjoyable diving in around 35 feet of water. Remaining within this depth limit enables the diver to avoid a decompression dive even though several dives may be made during a 12-hour period.

Equipment

Two general classifications are recognized: the closed circuit or rebreather and the open-circuit scuba. Although other equipment is sometimes used, only the open-circuit scuba is recommended for sport divers. Open-circuit scuba means that all exhaled air is exhausted into the water and none is reused. In closed-circuit scuba the breathing gas is recirculated, the carbon dioxide being absorbed by granulated chemicals and the oxygen being added to a breathing bag as needed from a high pressure supply tank. Open-circuit scuba uses compressed atmospheric air and never pure oxygen as in closed circuit, because 100% oxygen becomes toxic when breathed under pressure greater than 29 pounds per square inch. This pressure is reached when diving

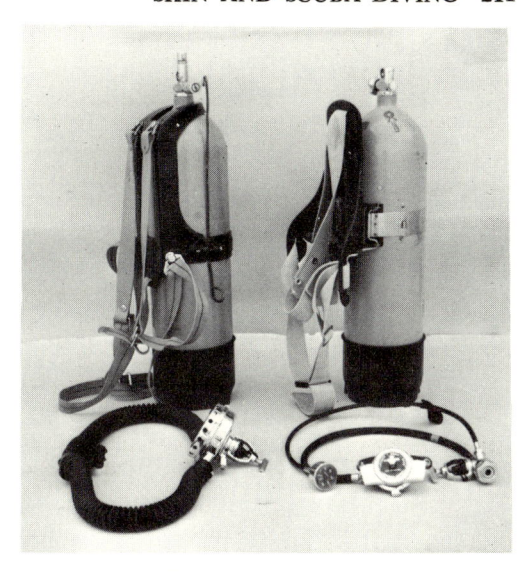

Fig. 17-4. Tank with reserve valve (J type) and harness; tank with no reserve (K type) and backpack harness; two-hose regulator; and single-hose regulator with pressure gauge.

deeper than 33 feet. There are three main components of open-circuit scuba: the regulator, the tank, and the valve. (See Fig. 17-4.)

Regulator

The regulator is the heart of the scuba as it is responsible for the delivery of the diver's air at exactly the correct pressure and whenever the diver inhales. For this reason the regulator is often referred to as a *demand* regulator because it permits air to flow into the diver's mouth each time the diver demands by the slightest inhalation. This inhalation causes a drop in the pressure on one side (dry side) of a rubber diaphragm. The water pressure on the other side (wet side) of the diaphragm is then able to push the diaphragm inward, which in turn activates a lever that opens a valve and allows air to flow through the diver's air hose. When the pressure on both sides of the diaphragm again becomes equal, the valve closes and the air flow is shut off. This pressure balance is regained when the diver discontinues inhaling.

Regulators are designed either with a single or double hose. Both types are popular and have their strong points. The student should consult a detailed reference for specifications of each design.

Valves

The valve is located between the tank and the regulator. Basically, there are two types of tank valves: the constant reserve (J type) and the nonreserve (K type). The J valve mechanism is preset to provide air as long as tank pressure remains above 300 pounds per square inch, but below this pressure a spring-actuated piston restricts the diver's air and breathing becomes difficult. This is a signal to the diver that the air supply is low and the reserve lever should be pulled to open the reserve valve and allow the last 300 pounds of air to flow freely. The diver should end the dive at this time by returning to the surface station for another tank or rest period. Never continue diving when on reserve air and always check to make sure the reserve lever is in the up or loaded position before entering the water.

The nonreserve or K type valve has no reserve feature and is simply an on-off valve control. Divers using this valve usually attach an air pressure gauge to their regulators to keep themselves constantly informed as to the air remaining in the tank. Both arrangements are popular among good divers.

Tanks

Air cylinders for diving are available in many sizes and in single, double, and triple units. The size and air pressure of the tank will generally determine the time a diver can remain submerged. However, breathing rate, water temperature, depth, and working rate are also important determinants of underwater time. The tank size usually recommended is the "standard 70." This means the tank contains 70.2 cubic feet of air when filled to 2250 pounds per square inch and will provide air for single dives within the limits of "no decompression" dives.

Harness

A harness, often arranged in combination with a plastic form-fitting backpack and made of canvas webbing, must be fitted with quick-release buckles or safety hitches and must never be put on over the weight belt. The harness must secure the scuba to the diver with comfort and allow freedom of movement in all positions, but it must also be designed to be "ditched" without hesitation or fumbling.

Scuba diving skills

Fundamentally the swimming skills employed in scuba diving are the same as those used in skin diving; however, one point of caution should be noted at this time. No one should attempt scuba diving until well skilled and experienced in skin diving.

Entries

When entering and exiting through the surf while wearing a scuba, the diver must remember that though carrying a supply of unrestricted air he or she is also more vulnerable to wave action in the surf and can be easily tumbled and thrown about when attempting to come to a standing position. When exiting through the surf, the diver should remain in an extended swimming position until well up on the beach before attempting to stand, then quickly turn about and shuffle backward until clear of all surge and water action.

When entering from an elevated point, boat dock, or land, the diver should use a feet-first entry but never into unknown water. The diver should grasp and protect the mask with one hand as in the skin diving entry, and with the other hand hold the tank down to prevent its being forced up and striking the head.

When entering unknown water, the diver should make a feet-first drop or slide-in entry. This method also reduces the chances of frightening game from the diving area. Other methods, such as forward and backward rolls, are interesting stunts but really have no place in safe sport diving.

Scuba drills

These drills should only be practiced with a partner and with a trained instructor observing.

1. *Submerging and swimming without a mask.* Replace and clear the mask without surfacing. (See skin diving skills for clearing.)
2. *Mouthpiece clearing.* Remove the mouthpiece underwater. Return it to the mouth, give a short sharp exhale

Diving disorders

Disorder	Cause	Symptoms	Treatment
Drowning	Physical exhaustion; running out of air; loss of mask or mouthpiece; flooding of apparatus; entanglement	No respiration; blueness of skin	Immediate artificial respiration, preferably by mouth-to-mouth method; start at once
Air embolism	Failure to breathe normally or holding breath while ascending results in blockage of circulatory system by excessive pressure rupturing lung tissues and allowing air to enter bloodstream	Weakness; dizziness; loss of speech; paralysis of extremities; visual disturbance; staggering; bloody frothy sputum; unconsciousness; death could occur within seconds after reaching surface, if not before	Recompress immediately to 74 pounds per square inch (165 feet); medical care; lower head to allow bubbles to go to feet rather than head
Decompression illness (bends or caisson disease)	Bubbles of nitrogen expand in bloodstream and tissues of body from inadequate decompression following exposure to pressure; nitrogen absorption depends on depth, time, and working rate; nitrogen more soluble in fatty tissues	Skin rash; itching; pain deep in joints, muscles, and bones; choking; visual disturbances; dizziness; convulsions; weakness in arms and legs; loss of hearing or speech; paralysis; unconsciousness; death	Recompress by Navy treatment tables; if caught in time, there are usually no serious aftereffects
Nitrogen narcosis	Intoxicating effect of nitrogen when breathed under pressure; no prevention; occurs usually at about 130 feet, though reported at 30 feet	Loss of judgment and skill; feeling of greatness; slowed mental activity; fixation of ideas; similar to alcohol intoxication	Stop work; reduce pressure; effects disappear when ascending; no aftereffects
Oxygen poisoning	Using pure oxygen below 33 feet for longer than 30 minutes; depends on CO_2 tension and work rate; not probable on compressed air until about 132 feet	Nausea; dizziness; headache; twitching of muscles around mouth and eyes; disturbance of vision (tunnel vision); numbness; unconsciousness	Surface; rest; medical care; never dive below 30 feet on pure oxygen; use only compressed air in tanks
Carbon monoxide poisoning (CO)	Contaminated air supply from internal combustion engines; improperly lubricated compressors; CO combines with blood, causing internal asphyxiation; improper exhalation	Same as symptoms for CO_2 poisoning except lips and mouth are bright cherry red; 10% in blood causes headache and nausea; 30% causes shortness of breath; 50% causes helplessness	Surface; artificial respiration if not breathing; oxygen; medical care; may seem to be all right on bottom but lose consciousness on ascent
Apnea	Hyperventilation and extended dives in skin diving	No warning symptoms to speak of (perhaps moment of blackness before total unconsciousness)	Fresh air; artificial respiration; do not hyperventilate excessively
Squeeze	Pressure differential over concerned area; middle ear and sinuses usually first place where pain felt; also teeth, face mask, suit, lung (thoracic) squeezes	Usually sharp pain due to stretched or damaged tissues; damage can occur without pain, however	Equalize pressure on affected areas

to clear it of water, and resume breathing. Use surge valve if available. Always take the first breath slowly after clearing the snorkel or mouthpiece of the regulator.

3. *Buddy breathing.* Two divers share one air supply. The diver with air passes the regulator mouthpiece to the buddy, who receives and clears the mouthpiece and takes two breaths before returning it. The diver with the air supply always retains control of the mouthpiece. The second diver uses the hands to help swim and keep the two divers close together.

4. *Free ascent.* Practice this emergency skill to be able to function calmly in an emergency situation resulting in the complete loss of an available air supply while submerged. In this situation the diver looks up, starts the ascent with one arm extended over the head, and exhales continuously for the entire ascent. The student in the class drill of free ascent should remove the mask and then the mouthpiece before starting the free ascent. The diver's buddy and instructor, with air functioning and mask in place, must always accompany the free-ascending diver to the surface.

5. *Buoyancy testing.* This is essential because the addition of a scuba adds several pounds of negative buoyancy to the diver. A slight positive buoyancy is recommended for the start of a scuba dive, as most surface buoyancy is lost at 33 feet of depth. Weights should be added or subtracted to allow the diver to gradually sink after a full exhalation on the surface.

6. *Ditching and recovering.* Do this exercise involving complete mastery of equipment underwater to gain familiarization and proficiency underwater. For details of the drill, consult one of the texts in the reference list.

DIVING MEDICINE

Most diving disorders or medical problems in diving are classified as barotrauma, or a change in normal conditions due to changing pressure. Usually it is an injury resulting from unequal pressure between a space inside the body and the outside water pressure. The cavities of the middle ear and the sinuses are most susceptible to changing pressure, but serious problems can also develop from pressure on the breathing gas. Nitrogen narcosis, oxygen toxicity, and carbon monoxide poisoning are examples of these disorders. A chart of some of these problems and their causes, symptoms, and treatment appears on p. 213.

TEN BASIC RULES OF SKIN AND SCUBA DIVING

1. Be in top physical condition and have an annual medical examination.
2. Be a good swimmer.
3. Secure certified training from recognized agency.
4. Never dive alone.
5. Use safe, time-proved equipment.
6. Join a reputable diving club.
7. Be familiar with your diving area *before* diving.
8. Always use a float with surface identification, usually a diver's flag.
9. Heed all pains and strains as warning symptoms.
10. Know basic first aid.

FIVE SUPPLEMENTARY RULES OF SKIN AND SCUBA DIVING

1. Know the basic laws of diving physics and physiology.
2. Practice skin diving frequently *before* scuba diving.
3. Use only time-proved regulators of reputable manufacturer.
4. Secure certified training in the use of scuba from recognized agency.
5. Never hold your breath while scuba diving.

REFERENCES

Ciampi, Elgin: The skin diver, a complete guide to the underwater world, New York, 1960, The Ronald Press Co.

Cousteau, J. Y., and Dugan, James: The living sea, New York, 1963, Harper & Row, Publishers.

Empleton, Bernard E. (ed.): The new science of skin and scuba diving, a project of the Conference for National Cooperation in Aquatics, New York, 1962, Association Press.

Lee, Owen S.: Complete illustrated guide to snorkel and deep diving, Garden City, N. Y., 1963, Doubleday Co., Inc.

Navy Department: United States Navy diving manual, Washington, D. C., 1963, U. S. Government Printing Office.

Parker, Eugene K.: Complete handbook of skin diving, New York, 1965, The Hearst Corp.

The new science of skin and scuba diving, ed. 3, Association Press, 1968, New York.

Tillman, Albert A.: Underwater education, Dubuque, 1962, William C. Brown Company, Publishers.

Tassos, John: The underwater world, Englewood Cliffs, N. J., 1957, Prentice-Hall, Inc.

Underwater Unit: Underwater recreation, Los Angeles, 1965, Department of Parks and Recreation, County of Los Angeles.

18 Soccer

HISTORY

The true origin of soccer is difficult to determine. One historian reports that soccer originated in Greece where it was called "harpaston." The Romans obtained the game from the Greeks and, in turn, passed it on to England.

The early games were rugged and irregular. Two towns, three to five miles apart, sometimes engaged in a game with no rules being enforced. Occasionally a river had to be crossed. The market place of the town was the goal.

Rugby was devised accidentally at Rugby College, England, in 1823 when one of the players on Rugby's team tucked the ball under his arm and ran across the goal line. This act was recognized as unsportsmanlike conduct. The game gained tremendously in popularity through the next forty years, and when the word football was used, some people asked, "Which kind?"

In 1848, the advocates of football met in Cambridge to draw up a list of rules which became known as the Cambridge Rules. This meeting was unsatisfactory since some schools favored carrying the ball as permitted in rugby. The result was a meeting in 1863 of the group that favored the kicking type of game. This group voted to confine play entirely to kicking and later became known as the London Football Association. To distinguish between the two types of football, they called one "rugby" and the other "association." Later this was shortened to "assoc" and finally to its present designation, soccer.

Soccer has been played in American colleges since 1830.

In 1868, Princeton challenged Rutgers, and the first intercollegiate soccer game was played in New Brunswick, New Jersey. Rutgers won, but Princeton asked for a return game and won.

Soccer became a national sport in 1913 with the organization of the United States Football (Soccer) Association.

In 1919, soccer was introduced at Bryn Mawr, a women's college. It was not until 1927, however, that the National Section on Girls' and Women's Sports published the first soccer rules for women.

Outside the United States soccer is the most widely played and watched game in the world.

OBJECTIVE VALUES

Soccer should be taught in every basic physical education program from the elementary grades up through high school and college if for no other reason than to teach boys and girls the skillful use of their legs. Today, about all the average American boys and girls do with their legs in everyday living is walk, run, jump, and dance. However, if these four basic fundamentals can be skillfully synchronized by means of a game like soccer, perhaps we may have pedestrians better prepared for crossing streets and drivers with better-trained reflexes behind the wheel on our highways. One should be better able to develop stronger knee, ankle, and arch (foot) supports. More and more the American youths are taking exercise off and away from the feet through the use of the automobile.

The automobile has taken the lives of more Americans than has any weapon. The game of soccer trains one to avoid body contacts. It requires a split-second vision of impending dangers and teaches how to maneuver out of, or into, openings. Such abilities should aid one to use good judgment in driving a car.

It is thus reasonable to assume that in their early years the average boy and girl will not get sufficient and proper strengthening exercises for their underpinnings to carry them through many healthful years of living unless physical educators do something to correct this situation. As one gets older, body weight increases, placing greater stress and strain on the small base of support, the feet and leg joints. Soccer is an excellent game and form of exercise to develop sturdy and more skillful legs and feet.

Soccer is well adapted to both sexes because it can be played fairly well the first time it is attempted. It develops such qualities as coordination, speed, endurance, strength, good spirit, self-control, sportsmanship, and sociability.

GENERAL DESCRIPTION OF THE GAME

In soccer a team of 11 men or women seeks to advance a round, inflated ball toward and between an opponent's goalposts and under its crossbar by dribbling, kicking, striking, or pushing the ball with any part of the body except the arms and hands. The goalkeeper, however, is less limited.

THE FIELD

In men's soccer the game is played on a rectangular field not more than 360 feet nor less than 300 feet in length and not more than 225 feet nor less than 165 feet in width. (See Fig. 18-1.)

For women's play, the field length ranges from 240 to 300 feet and the width from 120 to 180 feet. (See Fig. 18-2.) The side field boundary lines are called touchlines in men's rules and sidelines in women's rules.

Penalty areas are designated at each end of the field, and a penalty kick mark is indicated at each goal.

EQUIPMENT

Shoes are the most important part of a player's equipment. Regulation shoes are high-laced and have leather or rubber cleats to protect the player against slipping. Shin guards are worn inside knee-length socks. A gym suit completes the necessary equipment.

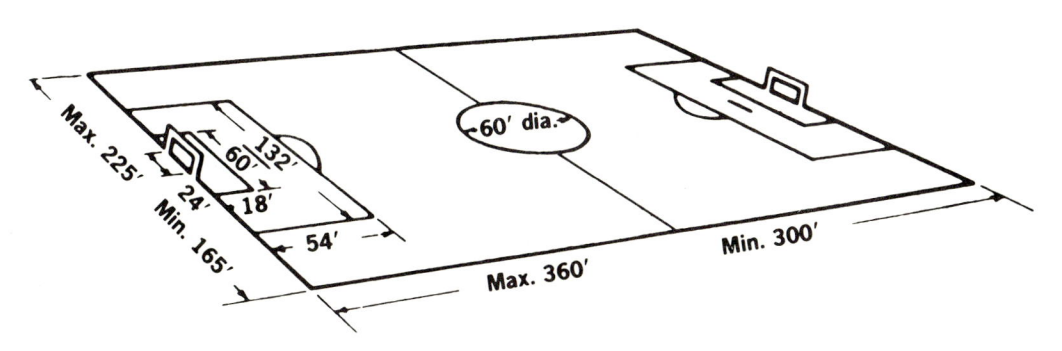

Fig. 18-1. Soccer field for men.

218 BASIC SKILLS IN SPORTS FOR MEN AND WOMEN

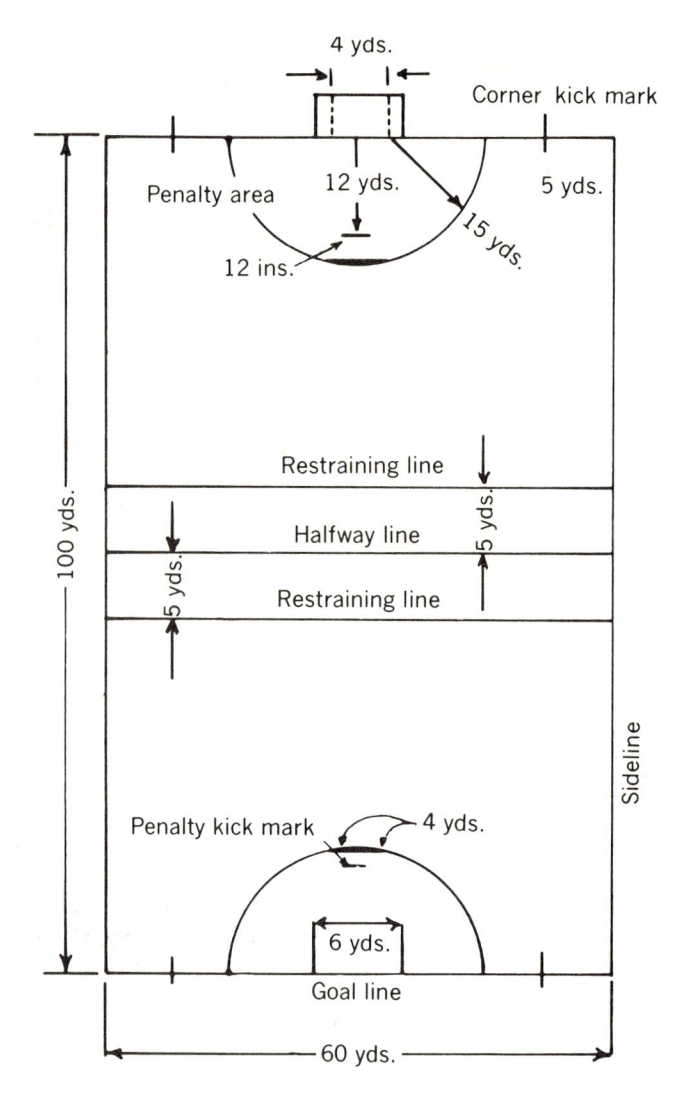

Fig. 18-2. Soccer field for women.

RULES FOR MEN
Officials

Two referees have control of the game and enforce all penalties and decide all disputed points.

Two linesmen shall be provided by the home team; their duties shall be to carry an extra ball and to act as ball retrievers, to avoid delay of the game. All linesmen shall be instructed by, and under the direct supervision of, the game referee. The linesmen also indicate when the ball is out-of-bounds or play and which side is entitled to the corner kick, goal kick, or throw-in, and assist the referees in controlling the game.

One scorekeeper and one timekeeper are required.

Duration of game

A regulation game consists of two equal periods of 45 minutes, with 10 minutes between halves. The score stands as official with the following exception: time shall be extended beyond the examination of the normal period of either half only to permit a penalty kick to be taken. The clock is stopped when a goal is scored. It is started on the kickoff.

Number of players

The game is played by two teams of eleven men each:
 1 goalkeeper
 2 fullbacks—right and left
 3 halfbacks—right, left, and center

5 forwards—outside right, inside right, center, inside left, and outside left

Playing privileges to goalkeeper

A goalie within the penalty area may have the following playing privileges:
1. The goalie may throw, drop-kick, punt, pick up the ball, or bounce it once.
2. The goalkeeper when in possession of the ball may not carry it more than four steps without bouncing it on the ground.
3. The referee will remove without caution any player who intentionally charges the goalkeeper.
4. The goalkeeper must not be interfered with.
5. The goalkeeper outside the penalty area has no more privileges than any other player.

Playing privileges to other players

1. A player may dribble, shoulder, or head the ball.
2. A player in possession of the ball may place himself between his opponent and the ball.
3. A player may stop the ball by trapping it under his feet, between his feet, or between the front of his legs and the ground.
4. A player may kick the ball while it is trapped by an opponent, providing he does not commit a foul.
5. A player may stop the ball by blocking it with any part of his body except the hands or arms.

Start of play

At the beginning of the game a coin is tossed to decide the kickoff and which goal each team is to defend. The ball is put in play by a place-kick (a kick at the ball while it is stationary on the ground) taken from the center of the field by the center forward at the start of the game, at the start of the second half, and after each goal. After a goal is scored, the team scored against shall kick the ball. Opposing players must stand at least 10 yards away at the time of the kick. The ball is in play after it has rolled at least 27 inches. A goal cannot be scored direct from a kickoff. The kicker cannot play the ball again until it has been played by another player.

Ends must be changed after each period and the team that did not score kicks off.

When resuming the game after a temporary suspension of play, except on a free kick, the referee shall drop the ball at the place where it was when play was suspended, except in the penalty area. If suspended in the penalty area, the ball is dropped in the nearest point outside of the penalty area. A goal may be scored direct from the dropped ball.

Ball out-of-bounds

1. A ball that goes out-of-bounds over the touchline (side boundries) is thrown in by a player on the team opposite to that which last touched the ball. The throw-in is made with both hands, the throw coming from behind and over the head.
2. When a ball goes out-of-bounds over the goal line, excluding that portion between the goalposts, either in the air or on the ground, and has been last touched by a member of the attacking team, it is put into play by a kick (ball is put on the line where it went over) in any direction beyond the penalty area by one of the defending players. If the ball does not go beyond the penalty area, kicker kicks again.
3. When a ball goes out-of-bounds over the goal line and has been last touched by a member of the defending team, it is put into play at the nearest corner by an attacking player. From the corner kick, a goal may be scored directly or indirectly.

Off side

A player is off side if he is nearer his opponent's goal line than the ball at the moment the ball is played unless:
1. He is in his own half of the field.
2. There are two of his opponents nearer to their own goal line than he is.
3. The ball last touched an opponent or was last played by him.
4. He receives the ball direct from a goal

kick, corner kick, a throw-in, or when it is dropped by the referee.

Note: A player not ahead of the ball when it is last played cannot be off side.

On side

A player once off side cannot put himself on side, except in the following ways:
1. If an opponent next plays the ball
2. If he is behind the ball when it is next played by one of his own team
3. If he has two of his opponents between him and their goal line when the ball is next played by one of his own team farther from the opponent's goal than himself
4. A player cannot be off side in the following cases:
   (a) When an opponent last plays the ball
   (b) On a corner kick
   (c) On a goal kick
   (d) On a drop ball
   (e) On a throw-in

An indirect free kick is given to the opponents if the off side player has interfered with the play or with the opponent. Otherwise, an off side player is not punished.

Direct free kick

Offenses for which a direct free kick is given:
1. Handling the ball
2. Kicking, tripping, striking, charging, holding, or pushing an opponent
3. Goalkeeper handling the ball outside the penalty area

Note: All direct free kicks awarded in the penalty area are penalty kicks.

Indirect free kick

The following are the offenses of which an indirect free kick is awarded:
1. Charging at improper time
2. Attempting to play the ball when it is in possession of the goalie
3. Touching the ball a second time before another player touches it after a free kick, throw-in, corner kick, or penalty kick
4. A goalkeeper carrying the ball more than four steps within the penalty area without bouncing it
5. If goalkeeper delays getting rid of the ball
6. Illegal coaching after warning by referee
7. Ungentlemanly conduct
8. Dangerous play
9. Off side

Position of players on taking free kick

Opposing players must not be within 10 yards of the ball.

Penalty kick

Any infringement of rules that ordinarily requires the awarding of a direct free kick shall be punished by a penalty kick if the foul is committed by a defending player within the penalty area.

A penalty kick shall be taken any place on the penalty mark line. All players must be 10 yards away, with the exception of the goalie. The goalie must be standing on his own goal line without moving his feet until the ball is kicked. The ball is in play if it hits the goalposts and bounces back.

Throw-in

When a ball passes out-of-bounds over the touchline it must be brought back into play by an opposing player by a two-hand over-head throw-in. If the throw-in is improper, it shall be taken over by a player on the opposing team.

Goal kick

When the ball is sent over the goal line, except that part between the posts, by the attacking team, it shall be kicked back into play by the defenders.

Corner kick

When the defending team moves the ball in back of its own goal line outside of the goalpost area, the opposing team takes a corner kick. Opposing players must not be within 10 yards of the kicker. A goal may be scored direct from the corner kick.

Method of scoring

A goal counts 1 point. The ball must have been kicked legally between the goalposts and under the crossbar.

RULES FOR WOMEN*

The team members and positions played are the same as in men's rules. They are 5 forwards, 3 halfbacks, 2 fullbacks, and 1 goalkeeper. Substitutes may enter the game when time is taken out, and a player who has been taken out for any reason other than disqualification may reenter the game any number of times.

Duration of game

The length of the game shall be four quarters of 8 minutes each, with a 10-minute interval between halves and 2 minutes between quarters. A penalty kick may be taken after the whistle blows. Two 2-minute time outs may be taken by each team during a game. A roll-in is used if the referee calls time out during play on the field.

The game

A toss decides the kickoff and the goal each team will defend. Teams alternate kick-offs at quarters. Ends are changed at the half.

The game shall be started by a kickoff (place-kick) from the center of the field by the center forward. The ball must go 27 inches. The kicker cannot touch the ball again until another player has touched it. Opponents must be at least 5 yards away from the kickoff. A goal cannot be made from the kickoff.

After a goal is scored, the team scored against shall make the kickoff.

Penalty: If a foul occurs, an indirect free kick is made at the place of the foul.

Equipment

High cloth shoes with a rubber or leather disk over the inner ankle and extra tips for protection of toes are worn along with shin guards.

Officials

Two umpires, two scorekeepers, and two timekeepers are required.

---

*Official soccer and speedball rules and guide, Washington, D. C., 1974, AAHPER, Division for Girls' and Women's Sports.

Playing privileges to goalkeeper

A goalie within her own penalty area may have the following playing privileges:
1. The goalie may throw, drop-kick, punt, pick up the ball, or bounce it once.
2. The goalie may combine a bounce with a punt, dropkick, or throw.
3. The goalie may take two steps with the ball in the hands preceding a punt, dropkick, or throw but will incur a penalty if the punt, dropkick, or throw is combined with a bounce.

Privileges to other players

1. A player may dribble, shoulder, or head the ball.
2. A player in possession of the ball may place herself between her opponent and the ball.
3. A player may stop the ball by trapping it under her foot, between her feet, or between the front of her legs and the ground.
4. A player may kick the ball while it is trapped by an opponent, provided she does not commit a foul.
5. A player may stop the ball by blocking it with any part of the body except the hands or arms.

Fouls

A foul is an infringement of the rules of soccer for which a free kick or a penalty kick is awarded the opponents. The following violations are fouls: charging, playing the ball with the hands or arms, holding, off side, kicking, punishing, tripping, and carrying (except by the goalie who may not take more than two steps).

PENALTIES

Inside the penalty area:
1. For any breach by the attacking team, a free kick is awarded the defending team at the spot where the violation occurred.
2. For any breach by the defending team, a penalty kick is awarded the attacking team from the penalty kick mark.
3. For any breach committed simultaneously by both teams, a roll-in shall be awarded at the spot where the double foul occurred.

Outside the penalty area:
1. For any breach by either team, the penalty shall be a free kick awarded at the spot where the foul occurred.

Note: A goal may be scored directly from a free kick awarded for kicking, tripping, striking, jumping at, pushing, holding, charging an opponent, or handling the ball. A goal may not be scored directly on a free kick following a penalty against the goalkeeper for carrying the ball.

Off side

A player is in an off side position if she is nearer her opponent's goal line than the ball at the moment the ball is played by one of her own team unless:
1. She is in her own half of the field.
2. Three of her opponents are nearer their goal line than she is.
   (a) The player is not to be penalized for being off side unless she is playing the ball, interfering with another player, or gaining some advantage from standing in an off side position.
   (b) Once off side, a player can be put on side only in the following ways:
      (1) If she is behind the ball when it is next played by one of her own team.
      (2) If there are three opponents between her and their goal line when the ball is played by one of her own team farther from her opponent's goal than she is. An indirect free kick is awarded as a penalty for being off side, if the offender interferes with the opponent's play. A goal cannot be scored on this kick.

Out-of-bounds

THROW-IN

If a ball during play passes over the sidelines a throw-in is taken by the opposing team. Any type of one- or two-hand throw is permissible. Players must be at least 5 yards away. The ball must be touched by another player before thrower can again handle the ball. A goal cannot be scored from a throw-in.

Penalty: The other side gets the ball to throw-in if the thrower handles the ball before it is touched by another player or if a teammate of the thrower stands within the 5-yard limit.

DEFENSE KICK

When the ball is sent over the crossbar or over the goal line outside the legal goal area, a place kick is taken by the defending team at a point anywhere on the quarter circles marking the penalty area. All players must be at least 5 yards away.

Penalty: If a foul occurs, an indirect free kick is given to the opponent.

CORNER KICK

A corner kick is taken by the attacking team if the defending team kicks the ball over their own goal line outside their goalposts. Corner kicks are made five yards from the nearer corner. The halfbacks, fullbacks, and goalkeeper must stand on or behind the defender goal line. The forwards can be anywhere on the field. All players must be at least 5 yards from the kicker. A goal may be kicked directly from the corner kick.

Penalty: For a foul by the kicking team, an indirect free kick is given opponents.

ROLL-IN

If a double foul sends the ball off field, the umpire shall put the ball in play by a roll-in 5 yards inside the field from where the ball went out.

Free kick

A *direct free kick* is awarded for the following fouls:
1. Those committed by either team outside the penalty area
2. Those committed by the attacking team inside the penalty area
3. Those resulting in disqualification of a player or players

An *indirect free kick* is awarded for the following:
1. A free kick, corner kick, kickoff, penalty kick, defense kick, or roll-in that is not taken correctly

Fig. 18-3. Kicking.

2. Fouls on the goalkeeper
3. Off side

Penalty: An indirect free kick is given to the opponents if the direct free kick is fouled.

Scoring

A field goal scores 2 points, and a penalty kick scores 1 point. In a tie game the score stands. A team winning by default is awarded 2 points.

FUNDAMENTAL TECHNIQUES

Essentially and primarily the game of soccer is a kicking game. The players should therefore master first the techniques of controlling the ball with the feet. These skill techniques are dribbling, trapping, blocking, and passing. Other skills to be mastered are heading and blocking. When these skills are learned, attention is given to field positions, team play, and strategy conforming to the rules of the game.

Kicking

The kick may be performed with the top of the foot as in regulation football, or with the inside or outside of the foot or heel. (See Fig. 18-3.)
1. Volleying is meeting the ball before it touches the ground with either the foot or knee. The foot volley is used to gain distance or direction and is generally used when the ball comes at the player in a low line of flight. The knee or thigh volley is used to take a ball from an opponent if it is coming from a high line of flight.

Fig. 18-4. Dribbling.

2. Dribbling is a series of short, zig-zagging, controlled kicks made by a player with either one or both feet in advancing the ball or eluding an opponent. It is accomplished with either the inside or outside of the foot and at times with the toe. (See Fig. 18-4.)
3. In a placement kick the ball is stationary, the kicker taking a few steps before kicking and striking the ball with the toe of the shoe, except in the case of the penalty kick, for which the top of the instep is used.

Trapping

Trapping is the stopping of a rolling or bounding ball or a ball in flight with the body or feet and taking possession of it. Trapping a ball in flight is accomplished by keeping the heel of the shoe on the ground and bringing the sole of the shoe down on the ball the instant it strikes the ground. A ball may be stopped by stepping on it lightly if it is rolling slowly, getting it between the foot and leg and the ground if it is moving fast, or clamping it between the legs and the ground if it is a high bounder or fly ball. It may be trapped between the knees or in the midsection of body by jackknifing over it. (See Fig. 18-5.)

Intercepting or blocking

Interrupting the progress of the ball by the use of any part of the body except the hands and arms is interception. Heading is

Fig. 18-5. Trapping.

Fig. 18-7. Blocking.

Fig. 18-6. Heading.

Fig. 18-8. Blocking.

one form of interception. (See Fig. 18-6.) This is accomplished with the head by meeting the ball wtih the front top of the head and jumping at the same time, holding the neck stiff and the spine rigid with the shoulder girdle hunched, against the impact of the ball. Another form of interception is made with the chest, or for women, with the arms folded across the chest. (See Fig. 18-7.) Still another form utilizes the hips, thighs, or knees to intercept a kick. (See Fig. 18-8.)

Passing

Passing the ball from one teammate to another is accomplished with the toe, the inside or outside of the foot, or the head. This is a team skill and can be practiced by dribbling down the field with two or three players using the feet to control the ball.

Tackling

Tackling may be accomplished by means of several generally recognized methods. The idea in tackling is to get possession of the ball from an opponent. This method is accomplished by the use of the legs alone. A side tackle is made with the inside of the foot and inside of the leg. This method involves playing the ball instead of the player. The split tackle is made by dropping to one knee and kicking the ball forward with the toe of the other foot.

Playing the player instead of the ball involves contact with the opponent passing the ball, which is accomplished by charging the offensive player in possession of the ball and hitting the opponent with the shoulder below the shoulder. The idea is to force the opponent from the ball.

Body contact tackling under women's rules is not permitted. Women confine tackling to a front approach, and possession of the ball is obtained by the use of the feet in intercepting the ball as it leaves the opponent's foot. This is accomplished by a straight, hook, or split, depending on the method of approach in intercepting the ball.

Playing positions

The five forwards are the offensive line. The center forward is usually the shooter of goals and the pivot of the forward line. The inner forwards play slightly behind the center and the wings, roving back and forth to cooperate with the latter players, and the outside forwards and wings usually attempt to kick the ball across the field for the center or inner forwards to shoot. The forwards must be good feeders to the forward scoring zone and must therefore be good passers. The three halfbacks back up the forward line, feed passes to the forwards, and cover the opposing outside forwards and center forward. The two wing halfbacks make the throw-ins and take the free kicks.

The center halfback is usually the team captain. The halfbacks are the backbone of the soccer team play. They must learn to dribble, tackle, and pass accurately and cleverly.

The two fullbacks assist the goalkeeper in defending the goal and seldom advance very far in front of the penalty zone. They take the goal kicks and cover the wing forwards. The fullback must learn to kick well and accurately. The goalkeeper rarely leaves the zone immediately in front of the goalposts. The goalie is permitted to use the hands or arms and to catch, throw, hit, or kick the ball, or use the body to prevent goals from being scored. When the goalie catches the ball, it is usually kicked out of the wings.

PRACTICE TECHNIQUES

Practice dribbling around the field, in and out of obstacles. Practice with two or more players dribbling down the field. Form a small circle or have partners facing each other to practice heading the ball. Learn to tackle with the feet only. Study and learn to play your position properly. In passing, time the pass, make it accurate, and look for openings and uncovered teammates to whom to pass. Develop team work. Be alert.

In dribbling, keep as close to the ball as possible. Strike the ball below its center with the foot. Do not dribble too much or come too close to an opponent. Keep your eyes on the ball. Be deceptive. Learn the technique of trapping the ball.

Offense and attack

Vary the attack and go after the goals. Do not give the defense a chance to organize. Rush the opposing goalkeeper on every shot. Do not pass too much in front of the opponent's goal. Keep one eye on the ball and the other on the opponent, taking advantage of every opening.

Defensive tactics

In tackling from the front, always play the ball. Rush the opponent, jam the foot down on the ball, and use a body block in making the recovery. In using a hook, tackle from the side and use the inside of the feet with a body block.

Use the split tackle from the side; extend the leg nearest the opponent across in front of the ball and drop on the other knee.

In charging, hurry your opponent but do not be violent or dangerous. Make use of standing tall and nudge.

In blocking an opponent, use a wide stance; get in the way and keep your feet on the ground.

Soccer is a rugged game requiring endurance, speed, and skill. On the field of play, complex situations may arise that require quick thinking, speed, and maneuvering, which are not always covered by rules or techniques. This makes the game interesting and challenging to youth.

TEACHING AND LEARNING PROCEDURES
Fundamental skill techniques

1. Kicking (both right and left foot)
   (a) Power kick
      (1) Instep to the inside of foot

(2) Straightway instep
  (3) Outside of foot
 (b) Passes (stress accuracy)
  (1) Power kicks for long passes
  (2) Inside-of-foot "shove"
  (3) Outside-of-foot short pass
  (4) Straightway short pass
  (5) Back heel pass
 (c) Volley and half-volley kicks
  (1) Ball kicked on the fly
  (2) Ball kicked as it bounces
2. Trapping (both feet)
 (a) Sole of foot
 (b) Side of foot and lower leg (either side or outside of foot)
 (c) Double knee trap (between knees and ground)
 (d) Stomach trap
3. Dribbling (both feet, stressing control)
 (a) Inside or outside of instep
  (1) Around post and return as a drill
  (2) Weaving in and out around markers and return
  (3) Shuttle relay dribbling, combined dribble and pass
4. Heading
 (a) Straight forehead; head meets ball at hairline
 (b) Side of head; head snap to send ball in different direction
 (c) Heading underball; ball continues in same direction
 (d) Jumping and heading; used to beat an opponent to the ball
5. Ball control (both feet)
 (a) One, two, or three players working with one ball, keeping it off the ground or bouncing under control
6. Shooting
 (a) Using power kicks
 (b) At goal, with goalie on defense
 (c) Against backboard
 (d) Shooting a stationary ball
 (e) Shooting a moving ball
 (f) Against opposition; two or three forwards against a back and goalie
7. Tackling and charging
 (a) Straight-on tackle, using either foot
 (b) Hook tackle from side
 (c) Race for ball; proper charging of players off the ball
8. Practice of combinations (preferably through drills)
 (a) Dribbling and passing
 (b) Heading and dribbling, following the ball quickly after heading
 (c) Heading, dribbling, and shooting
 (d) Trap, dribble, pass, and shoot
9. Special skills
 (a) Free kick; accuracy plus power
 (b) Corner kick; accuracy, 6 feet high and 10 feet out from far goalpost
 (c) Goal kick; accuracy plus power
 (d) Penalty kick; emphasis on accuracy
 (e) Kickoff; plays from kickoff
 (f) Throw-in; proper method, accuracy, plays
10. Game drills
 (a) Keep-away, forming a circle with one player in the center who attempts to intercept passes, with the player who last touched the ball before interception becoming the next center player
 (b) Take-away, having a given number of players attempt to keep the ball away from an equal number of players
 (c) Line against backs with a line of three halfbacks attempting to score through a backfield of fullback and goalie

Play starts at center of field. For variation, add halfback line to defense.

Tests

1. Achievement and proficiency performance test
2. Knowledge test of rules, scoring, strategy, etc.

GLOSSARY OF SOCCER TERMS

attacking team Team that has possession of the ball.
blocking Stopping the motion of the ball with some part of the body.
carrying An infringement of the rules when

the goalkeeper takes more than two steps while holding the ball.

defending team The team that is trying to get possession of the ball.

direct free kick A free kick from which a goal may be scored directly.

double foul An infringement of the rules committed by two opposing players at the same time for which a roll-in is awarded.

dribbling A succession of forward kicks in which the player keeps the ball under control.

dropkick A ball that is dropped on the ground and kicked just as it bounces. Only the goalkeeper in women's games within the penalty area can take this kick.

holding Impeding the progress of a player by placing the hand or extended arm in contact with the player.

indirect free kick A free kick from which a goal cannot be scored.

own goal The goal the team is defending.

passing Moving the ball from one player to another.

place-kick A kick made while the ball is stationary on the ground.

punt A ball kicked by the goalkeeper within the team's own penalty area.

throw-in To put the ball in play from outside the side line by a two-hand over-head method.

trapping To stop the progress of the ball. This is done with the foot, between both feet, or between the leg or legs and the ground.

unnecessary roughness Any act that might cause injury to an opponent.

volley Meeting the ball in the air with some part of the body and directing it to a teammate. It is legal to use the upper part of the arm if it is held next to the body.

REFERENCES

Bailey, Ian C., and Teller, Francis: Soccer, Philadelphia, 1970, W. B. Saunders Co.

DiClemente, Frank F.: Soccer illustrated for coach and player, New York, 1968, Ronald Press.

Ensing, Walter: Fundamentals of soccer, Cleveland, 1968, Charles Merrill Publishing Co.

Menke, Frank: Encyclopedia of sports, ed. 2, New York, 1960, A. S. Barnes & Co.

Meyer, M. H., and Schwarz, M. M.: Techniques of team sports for women, Philadelphia, 1947, W. B. Saunders Co.

Miller, Donna Mae, and Ley, Katherine L.: Individual and team sports for women, Englewood Cliffs, N. J., 1955, Prentice-Hall, Inc.

Official N.C.A.A. soccer guide, New York, 1970, The National Collegiate Athletic Association.

Official soccer and speeedball rules and guide, Washington, D. C., 1972-1974 AAHPER, Division for Girls' and Women's Sports.

Vogelsinger, H.: Winning soccer skills and techniques, Nyack, 1970, Parking Publishing Co.

19 Softball

HISTORY AND GENERAL DESCRIPTION OF THE GAME

The Y.M.C.A. perhaps did more than any other organization to inaugurate softball by transferring the game of baseball from the outdoors to the indoors. This took place about 1900. Naturally softball is an adaptation of baseball. Because of the lack of indoor space and the hardness of the ball, the Y.M.C.A. directors made the ball softer, the bat smaller, and the base lines and pitching distances shorter. The pitcher delivers the ball with an underhand throwing motion. Base stealing is not permitted until the ball has left the pitcher's hand. Briefly, this is a description of the increasingly popular game of softball.

Several years later the Playground Association of America, now known as the National Recreation Association, needed such a game that could be adapted to small outdoor spaces and could be played by all ages, especially by both young boys and girls. It took on different names at different times, such as playground ball, kitten ball, recreation ball, and ladies' ball, but in 1933 the name softball was adopted as the official name by the Amateur Softball Association. That year a National Tournament was held at the World's Fair in Chicago. At the same time this organization set up and standardized rules which are the official rules today. Following the year 1929, when thousands were unemployed, the game was a great source of recreation at community centers.

Prior to World War II, public interest in softball grew so much that teams were organized into leagues all over the country, and it was estimated that well over 5,000,000 people engaged in this genuinely popular American game. Because of its great appeal to Americans of all ages, and because only a small amount of equipment is needed and any ordinary playground is adequate, this game has become the first choice of all recreational playgrounds.

There exists only one set of official rules, but different communities adopt varying rules to fit local conditions.

EQUIPMENT

The bat should be round and made of hardwood, no more than 34 inches long, and not more than 2⅛ inches in diameter at its largest part.

The ball should be a smooth-seamed, leather-covered sphere containing yarn and kapok, measuring no less than 11⅞ inches and no more than 12⅛ inches in circumference and weighing from 6¼ to 7 ounces.

SOFTBALL

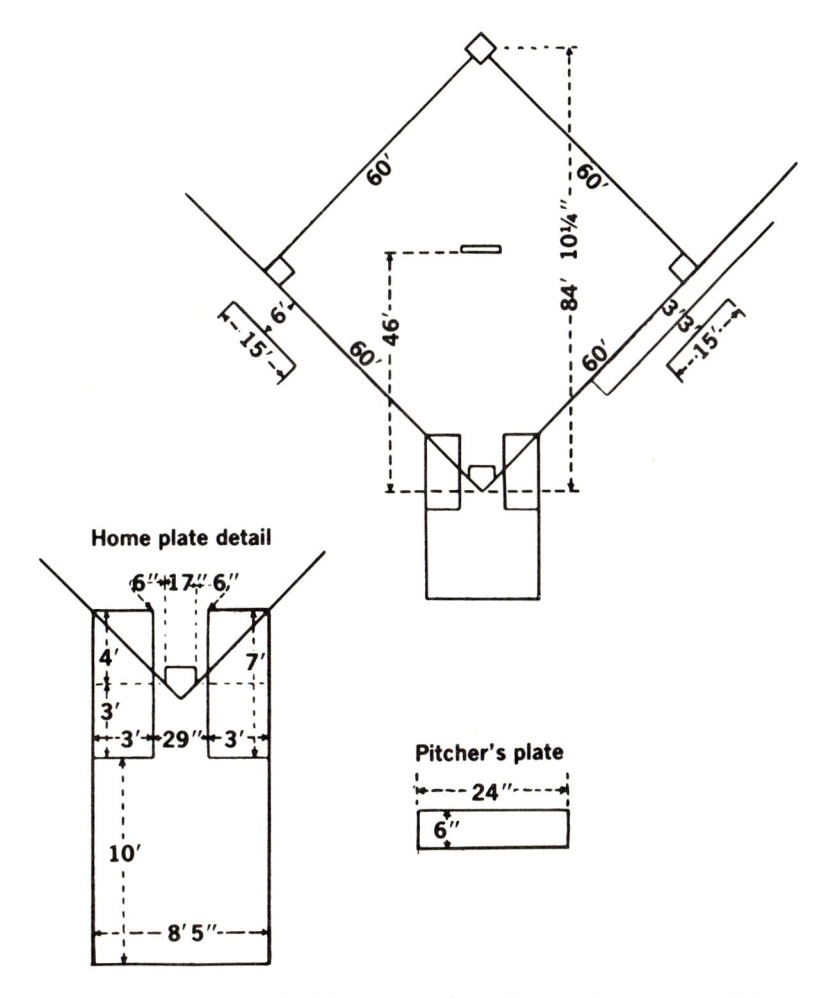

Fig. 19-1. Softball playing field for men. Pitching distance for women is 40 feet.

The home plate should be made of solid rubber or other suitable material. (See Fig. 19-1 for design and measurements.) The distance to the pitcher's box is 38 feet for women and 46 feet for men.

Gloves may be worn by any player, but mitts are limited to first basemen and catchers.

Masks must be worn by catchers.

Spikes or any other type of sharp projections on the shoes are prohibited.

Playing field dimensions are given in Fig. 19-1.

ABRIDGED RULES

Teams, players, and substitutes

A team shall consist of nine players whose positions shall be designated as follows: catcher, pitcher, first baseman, second baseman, third baseman, shortstop, left fielder, center fielder, and right fielder. With the exception of the pitcher, who must take position as defined in the pitching rules, and the catcher, who must be within the lines of the catcher's position, players in the field may be stationed at any points on fair ground.

A substitute may take the place of a player whose name is in the team's batting order, but the removed player may not thereafter re-enter the game, except as coach.

The game

1. A regulation game shall consist of seven innings, unless the team second at bat scores more runs in the six innings than the team first at bat has scored in seven innings.
2. It is a regulation game if the team last at bat in the seventh inning scores

the winning run before the third player is out.

3. It is a regulation game if it is called by the umpire because of darkness, rain, fire, panic, or other cause which puts the patrons or players in peril, provided five or more innings have been played by each side or that the team second at bat has scored more runs at the end of its fourth inning or in any part of its fifth than the team first at bat has scored in five complete innings.

4. When a game is called in any inning after the fifth, the score is what it was at the time the game was called if the team second at bat has more runs than the first team at bat. Or, if the team second at bat has fewer runs than the team first at bat when the game is called, the score is that of the last inning completed by both sides.

Pitching rules

1. Preliminary to pitching, the pitcher shall come to a full stop, facing the batter with the ball held in both hands in front of the body and with both feet squarely on the ground and in contact with the pitcher's plate. A pitch should be made not less than 1 second nor more than 20 seconds before taking one hand off the ball at the start of the windup or backswing.
2. The pitcher shall not be considered in pitching position unless the catcher is in position to receive the pitch.
3. In the act of delivering the ball to the batter, the pitcher may not take more than one step, which must be forward and toward the batter. The step must be taken simultaneously with the delivery of the ball to the batter.
4. A legal delivery shall be a ball which is delivered to the batter underhand and with a follow-through of the hand and wrist past the straight line of the body before the ball is released. The pitcher may use any windup desired, provided that in the final delivery of the ball to the batter, the hand shall be below the hip and the wrist not farther from the body than the elbow.
5. At no time during the progress of the game shall the pitcher be allowed to use tape or other substance upon the pitching hand or fingers or on the ball. Powdered resin may be used to dry the hands.

"No pitch" shall be declared whenever the pitcher pitches during a suspension of play or when a quick return of the ball is attempted before the batter has taken position or when the batter is off-balance as the result of a previous pitch.

Illegal pitches

An illegal pitch, entitling the base runners to advance one base, shall be called by the umpire as follows, and in each of the cases cited a ball also shall be called in favor of the batter:

1. Any delivery of the ball to the batter without previously taking position as defined in points 1 and 2 of the pitching rules
2. Taking more than one step before releasing the ball
3. Final delivery of the ball to the batter with the hand above the hip and the wrist of the pitching arm farther from the body than the elbow as described in point 4 of the pitching rules
4. Failure to follow through with the hand and wrist past the straight line of the body as described in point 4 of the pitching rules
5. Rolling the ball along the ground or dropping the ball while the pitcher is in pitching position
6. Holding the ball more than 20 seconds
7. Making any motion to pitch without immediately delivering the ball to the batter
8. Delivery of the ball to the batter when the catcher is outside the lines of the catcher's position
9. Continuing the windup after taking the step described in point 3 of the pitching rules
10. Taking a pitching position on or near

the pitcher's plate without possessing the ball

In each of these cases the ball shall be dead and not in play until again put in play at the pitcher's box. If, however, the batter strikes at, and hits into fair territory, any of the illegal pitches just mentioned, there shall be no penalty for such illegal pitch; the ball shall remain in play, and the base runners may run bases or be put out as though the ball had been legally pitched.

Foul tip

A foul tip is a ball that is batted by the batter while standing in the lines of the batter's position and that goes sharply and directly to the hands of the catcher and is legally caught. A foul tip caught is a strike and the ball remains in play. A foul hit ball which rises higher than the batter's head shall not be a foul under this rule.

When batter is out

1. If the batter makes a foul hit other than a foul tip as just defined and the ball is caught by a fielder before touching the ground, provided that it is not caught in the fielder's hat, cap, protector, pocket, or other part of the uniform or does not strike some other object before being caught
2. If the ball is batted illegally
3. If a bunt is fouled after the second strike
4. If an attempt is made by the batter to hinder the catcher from fielding or throwing the ball by stepping outside the lines of the batter's position, or if in any way the batter obstructs or interferes with that player; the exception to this rule is that if a base runner attempting to steal is put out, the batter shall not be out
5. Immediately after three strikes, whether there are no outs, one out, a runner on first base, runners on first and second bases, runners on first, second, and third bases, or runners on first and third bases
6. If the third strike is swung at and the ball does not touch any part of the batter's person
7. If, before two players are out, while first and second, or first, second, and third bases are occupied, the batter hits a fair fly ball that is handled or, in the opinion of the umpire, would have landed within or near the base lines
8. If the batter steps from one batter's box to the other while the pitcher is in position ready to pitch

FUNDAMENTAL SKILL TECHNIQUES

Softball, like any other sports activity, has basic skills which must be learned and practiced often if they are to be performed with any degree of skill. The techniques necessary for good performance are given below.

Throwing

Although throwing is a natural activity for both boys and girls, there are some skills in throwing the ball in softball that differ from the natural way of throwing.

OVERHAND FULL ARM SWING

In the overhand full arm swing (see Fig. 19-2), the ball is grasped with two fingers on the top, the thumb on the left side, and the third and fourth fingers on the right side for support. The hand is brought back with a swing, well behind the shoulder at shoulder height. The left side of the body is turned in the direction of the throw. The left arm is raised and carried around to the front of

Fig. 19-2. Overhand full arm swing.

Fig. 19-3. Stance for overhand full arm swing. Practice swing.

Fig. 19-4. Short arm swing.

Fig. 19-5. Underhand pitch.

the body. The left foot is in front, the toe touching the ground. The weight of the body is on the right foot. The ball is thrown with a downward snap of the wrist. The snap of the wrist increases the speed the ball already has received by the arm motion. The weight of the body is brought forward into the throw. (See Fig. 19-3.)

SHORT ARM SWING

In the short arm swing (see Fig. 19-4) the hand is brought into position above the right shoulder, elbow pointed backward and down. Snap the throw forward by an elbow extension and sharp wrist flexion. The right shoulder, arm, and wrist do most of the work, since it is impossible to get very much body weight into the throw. This is the type of throw the catcher uses.

UNDERHAND PITCH

The throw starts below the shoulder with the arm fully extended. The hand is turned with the palm down at the start and then is brought forward with a pendulum swing of the arm to the front. The elbow is slightly flexed throughout. The follow-through brings the hand, with the palm up, about chest high. (See Fig. 19-5.)

From this underhand throw, two kinds of balls can be thrown: (1) a fast-breaking inshoot and drop and (2) an upward and outward curve. Speed, balance, and relaxation are necessary in order to throw expertly.

Catching

FIELDING FLIES

There are two methods for fielding flies: (1) holding the thumbs together and the fingertips up (see Fig. 19-6) and (2) placing the little fingers together and letting the ball drop into the nested hands.

The advantage of the first method is that the throw can be made faster; the advantage of the second is that the catch is more sure. The ball is visible and if it spins it is more likely to remain in the hands. One should be at the spot at which the ball is descending in order to get set for it.

Fig. 19-6. Fielding flies.

Fig. 19-7. Fielding ground balls.

If a ball goes over the head, one should turn and run (never run backward) to the spot where the ball is expected to drop, glancing over the shoulder while running.

When the ball drops into the hands, let them give back slightly with the impact. Shield the eyes from the sun with the gloved hand. Do not hold the ball after catching it. Be careful that revolving balls do not spin out of the glove.

Back up other fielders when making a play.

FIELDING GROUND BALLS

A bouncing ground ball should be fielded in either of two ways: (1) as it hits the ground (trap) (see Fig. 19-7) or (2) as it is at the height of its bounce. For the sake of a quick play, advance to meet the ball. Time the speed of advance with the speed and bounce of the ball. The success of this play lies in exact timing and judgment of movements with the moving ball.

If the ball is coming above the waist, catch it with the fingertips turned up.

Fig. 19-8. Batting grip and stance.

The waist-high ball can be caught either way, depending on whether the ball is dropping or coming up.

In order to maintain balance when running in for a ball, run with the legs and feet apart. Meet the ball out in front of the body with the left foot slightly advanced. Keep the eyes on the ball until it is in the hands. Throw the ball directly to the bag.

A ground ball may take unexpected hops to the right or left, and these should be fielded with the feet apart, the knees slightly bent, and the body crouched. In fielding fast and hard hit balls, it is well to close the feet or block balls by dropping on one knee.

Batting

Good batting ability and clever base-running are the key to successful offensive softball. It is therefore essential that beginners practice and observe the following skill fundamentals:

1. Assume a natural and comfortable position at the plate with the feet well apart and with the left side of the body toward the pitcher. The elbows should be well away from the body to allow for freedom in swinging the bat. (See Fig. 19-8.)
2. Start the swing of the bat with a hip roll. Take a step forward and swing the bat parallel to the ground with a follow-through.
3. If the ball is coming into the strike area, keep the bat poised at shoulder height, ready to swing. Never rest the bat on the shoulder while waiting for the pitch.

4. Keep the eyes on the ball from the moment the pitcher starts the windup until the ball reaches the plate.
5. Look the pitches over carefully and swing only at the good strike area pitches.
6. Try not to swing too hard.
7. Select a bat that feels comfortable in weight, grip, and balance.
8. Use a grip that best controls the bat.
9. Run quickly to first base as soon as the ball is hit.

FREE-SWING AND CHOKE HITTER

A free-swing hitter stands farther back of the plate with the feet well apart and parallel to the side of the box.

A choke hitter will stand closer to the plate and in stride position to the box when first learning. Later a position can be taken with the feet together, and a stride taken forward when the hitter swings. The trunk should be slightly inclined forward.

The free-swing hitter should grip the bat down near the small end, the right hand above the left.

The choke hitter grips the bat several inches from the small end of the bat.

USE OF ELBOWS IN HITTING

The elbows are held well out from the body. The left elbow is on a level with the hand and slightly below the left shoulder.
1. Swing forward on a horizontal plane.
2. Have a quick eye and accurate muscle control in batting at a curve ball.

BUNTING

Bunting is just as effective an offensive weapon in softball as it is in baseball.

A bunt can be made from a choke stance, or the batter can change from a feint bunt to a swing.

The arms and elbows are held well out from the body and the right hand holds the bat while the left hand acts as a steering hand. A slight recoil of the bat is made when it meets the ball.

There are two kinds of bunts: (1) the swing bunt, sending a roller down third, and, (2) the drag bunt, pushing the ball toward first. Hold the bat as if to choke or hit a free swing. As the pitcher lets go of the ball, run the right hand about halfway down the bat. Hold the bat loosely to deaden the bunted ball and at an angle to lay the ball down either the first or third base line.

Fig. 19-9. Catching.

Catching

The catcher should be in a half-squat position in order to move quickly and reach out to the right or left or to jump up and move forward for a throw. Practice a quick snap throw. (See Fig. 19-4.) Work as close under the bat as possible. Keep the eyes on the ball. Get the ball before attempting to tag a player. Hold the thumb of the bare hand close to the fingers to prevent injury. (See Fig. 19-9.)

Pitching

The pitching position is assumed with both feet on the rubber plate. The pitch is an underhand throw to the batter. (See Fig. 19-5.) Preliminary movements may be taken by the pitcher in any motion as long as the final delivery to the batter is underhand and parallel to the body.

The pitcher should develop a wrist snap and a finger flip with a complete follow-through. A pitcher should have a slow ball for a change of pace.

Practice spinning the ball to create a curve which will cause the batter to hit a pop-up ball. (See Figs. 19-10 to 19-13 for various types of pitches.)

To prevent a bunt, pitch high.

Practice getting the arm to act as a whip which snaps the ball away and yet controls its direction.

SOFTBALL 235

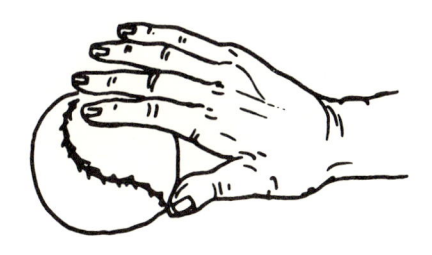

Fig. 19-10. In-curve and out-curve releases.

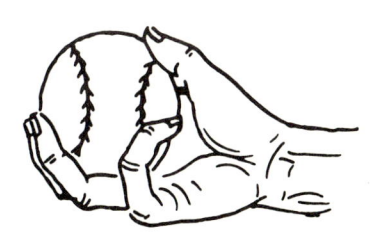

Fig. 19-11. Drop grip and drop release.

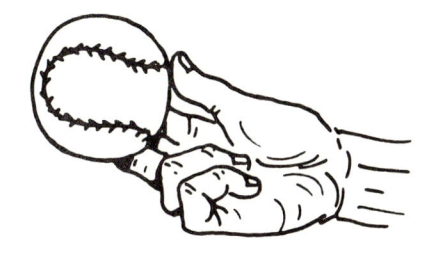

Fig. 19-12. Grip and release for fast ball in-curve and out-curve.

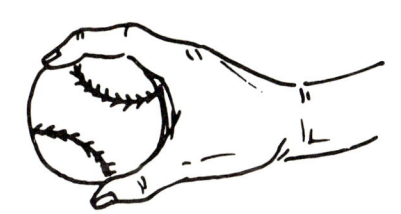

Fig. 19-13. Grip and release for upshoot.

Baserunning

In softball the runner must hold the base until the ball leaves the pitcher's hand. Readiness to start for the next base requires assuming a runner's stance with the left foot on the base ready to sprint for the next base the instant the pitcher releases the ball. A runner leaving first base should watch the third base coach to determine whether to stop at second base or try for third base. The base coach has a better view of the entire field of play and can make a better judgment. The run should be made on a straight line between the bases and not a circle; it is farther to circle.

A runner on occasion must be able to slide into second base, third base, or home plate correctly. One should first learn a hook slide. (See Fig. 19-14.) This is performed by sliding on the thigh and hip and hooking the bag with the toe of the foot. The runner slides to the right of the bag, making

Fig. 19-14. Hook slide.

Fig. 19-15. First base position.

it difficult to be tagged. The slide should be started soon enough in front of the bag so that the runner can slide to the bag and not plunge on it.

Playing bases

FIRST BASEMAN

The first baseman (see Fig. 19-15) should cover the bag in such a way that does not cause interference with the runner, but balls from all sides of the plate can still be played. The first baseman (see Fig. 19-16) should have good footwork in order to handle high and low throws. It is correct to push the hands toward the ball in receiving pickups and come up in the same movement. The first baseman should play the bag on the inside when receiving throws from the infield. If no runner is on the base, the first baseman stands about 8 feet off the bag and about 10 to 12 feet behind the base line toward right field. With a runner on base, the first baseman stands inside the diamond with the heel of the left foot on the bag and the right foot extended toward second base.

SECOND BASEMAN

The second baseman must have ability and agility to go either way for ground balls. The best position is a little nearer second base than first and back of the base line. It is important to tag runners quickly, while maintaining a good grip on the ball. The second baseman should back up other infielders.

Fig. 19-16. First baseman techniques.

THIRD BASEMAN

The third baseman should play about 5 to 7 feet inside the diamond from the base and in front of the base line. When receiving the ball behind the bag, an overhand throw should be used because an underhand throw is not fast enough.

In tagging a runner, the infielder must be alert at all times for a slide since the runner will attempt to get around the baseman with a hook slide. Worry the runner but do not leave an opening in your position. The third baseman should not compete with outfielders on flies and should not run in until the batter is seen to go into a bunting motion by sliding the hand down the bat.

The outfielders

The outfielders must have speed, must be able to judge accurately the flight of a fly ball, and must be able to throw accurately and hard. A throw must be long with smooth execution of a full arm swing rather than a wrist snap. Outfielders should study hitters to know where they hit. In playing a ground ball, the outfielder should place the body in front of the ball in order to block it. An outfielder should watch every pitch and be ready to move in any direction at each pitch.

Team offensive strategy

Players should sacrifice individual record performances for team success. A batter should sacrifice a runner on first for a runner on second so that a possible hit can score the runner on second.

A hit and run is good offensive team strategy. The squeeze play is another offensive weapon that may be used with a runner on third. When the game is in the late stages and there are fewer than two outs, it is good strategy to bunt in an attempt to score the runner. The runner starts for home on the pitch and the batter bunts.

The double steal is another excellent offensive play used to catch the defensive team off balance. This play is usually attempted with runners on first and second or first and third. It is most often attempted in the latter case, the idea being to score the runner on third if the catcher throws the ball to second base in an effort to retire the runner coming from first base.

Any offensive or defensive strategy that is effective in baseball is also good softball strategy.

Defensive strategy

Good defense playing includes breaking up and meeting any crucial situation that may arise. For example, to break up a double steal, the shortstop or second baseman runs over behind the pitcher and in front of second base takes the throw from the catcher to second and throws it back to the catcher.

The infield can draw in for a play at the plate. A double play is always perfect defense if it can be executed.

Always get the runner nearest the plate if possible. Good team defense requires that infielders help and cooperate with the other infielders.

An intentional pass is good defense, as well as a pitch out to make a play at second or first.

SLOW-PITCH SOFTBALL

Slow-pitch softball is becoming very popular in high school and college recreation programs. The rules are as follows.

Playing field

The playing field is the same as that for fast-pitch softball. (See Fig. 19-1.)

Equipment

The bat shall be no more than 34 inches long and not more than 2½ inches in diameter at its largest part. "Official softball" should be marked on the bat. The ball shall be a regular, smooth-seam, concealed stitch or flat-surfaced ball not less than 11⅞ inches nor more than 12⅛ inches in circumference, and shall weigh not less than 6½ ounces nor more than 7¼ ounces. The ball shall be marked "official slow-pitch softball."

Players

A team shall consist of ten players: pitcher, catcher, first baseman, second baseman, third baseman, shortstop, left fielder, center fielder, right fielder, and short fielder.

A player removed from the game can re-enter the game only as a coach.

The game

A regulation game shall consist of seven innings. In case of a tie game more innings shall be played. A forfeited game goes to the team that is ready to play.

Pitching regulations

The pitching arm must come to rest holding the ball in front of the body, with a pivot foot in contact with the pitcher's plate. This position cannot be held longer than 20 seconds. The ball is to be thrown on the first forward swing past the hip. The pivot foot must remain in contact with the plate until the ball leaves the hand.

Batting

The batter shall take position within the lines of the batter's box. The batter has 1 minute to take the place after the umpire calls "play," or the batter is out. All batters must bat in their batting order or an out is called on the person at bat. However, if this error is discovered in time, an adjustment can be made.

A *strike* is called (1) for each legally pitched ball, (2) for each pitched ball missed by the batter, (3) for each foul tip—the batter is out if the tip is on the third strike, (4) for each pitched ball struck at and missed that touches any part of the batter, and (5) for hitting a batter positioned in the strike zone.

A *ball* is called for a pitched ball that does not enter the strike zone.

A *fair ball* is one that (1) lands in fair territory—between first and third bases, (2) lands on any one of the bases with the exception of home base, or (3) falls on fair ground beyond first or third base.

The batter is out immediately when an *infield fly* is hit with base runners on first and third, or first, second, and third with less than two outs. This is called the infield-fly rule.

A *foul ball* is a legally batted ball that (1) settles on foul ground outside the first or third base line or behind home plate or (2) bounds past first or third base on foul ground or outside of bases. *If a foul fly is caught the batter is out*. The batter is out if there are two strikes and the next batted ball is a foul tip. A foul tip is a batted ball that goes from the bat, not higher than the batter's head, to the catcher's hands and is legally caught.

The batter is out under the following circumstances:

1. On three strikes
2. When the ball is bunted or chopped downward
3. When a fly ball is legally caught
4. On an infield fly
5. When the batter interferes with the catcher
6. Intentional interference puts a runner out plus the batter who hit the ball

Baserunning

1. All bases must be touched in order.
2. If two base runners are on the same base, the last runner on can be tagged out.
3. The batter becomes a base runner when four balls are called.
4. An over-thrown ball to first or third allows the base runners two bases.
5. When a fair ball bounds or rolls into a stand, over, under, or through a fence or other obstruction marking the boundaries of the playing field, the ball is dead, and all base runners are awarded two bases from the time of the pitch.
6. There is no base stealing. Only after the ball has passed home plate can the base runner run.
7. The base runner is out if running outside the 3-foot line. The base runner is not out, however, if it is necessary to run around a fielder taking the ball.
8. The base runner is out if another base runner is passed.
9. The base runner is out if struck by a fair ball before it passes a fielder. The base runner must be off base.

OBJECTIVES

1. To help the student develop individual skill for playing the game as well as for participating in intramural events
2. To teach techniques, rules, and strategy of baseball

TESTS
Achievement test

1. Throwing and catching (5 trials in each)
2. Batting (hit 5 straight-pitched balls)
3. Base playing
   (a) Run bases for time
   (b) How to cover the bag
   (c) For a right- or left-handed hitter
   (d) With one man on base, two men on base, three men on base

Written examinations

1. Examination on rules
2. Examination on tactics

GLOSSARY OF SOFTBALL TERMS

appeal play A play upon which an umpire cannot make a decision until requested by a player. The request must be made before the next play.

assist Throwing or deflecting, by a player, of a thrown or batted ball by which a possible out could be made.

base on balls Reaching first base after four balls are called.

base path An imaginary line three feet to either side of a direct line between bases.

battery The pitcher and catcher.

batting average Number of hits made by a batter divided by the times at bat.

batting order The official listing of the sequence of the players to bat.

bean ball A ball thrown at the batter's head.

bunt A ball softly touched by the bat and landing within the infield.

double play A play in which two players are legally put out.

fair territory The part of the playing field within, or including, the first and third base foul lines from home base to the bottom of the extreme playing field fence and perpendicularly upwards.

error A play that fails to account for the out of a runner or allows the advancement of a runner.

foul tip A ball that goes directly from the bat to the catcher's glove.

infield That portion of the field within the base lines.

inning That portion of a game in which a team plays both offense and defense, starting with the first team at bat.

passed ball Failure of the catcher to hold a pitched ball; the runner is allowed to advance. An error is charged against the catcher if the third strike is dropped; the runner is allowed to go to first.

pivot foot The foot that the pitcher must keep in constant contact with the pitcher's plate until the delivery of the ball.

play "Play ball" means to resume the play or to begin the game.

sacrifice bunt A bunt play for the purpose of advancing a runner.

sacrifice fly A fly ball hit to the outfield allowing a runner, after tagging up after the ball is caught, to advance.

stolen base A man on base advances to the next base without the ball being hit.

strike zone The area between the batter's knees and armpits.

switch hitter A batter capable of batting either right-handed or left-handed.

Texas leaguer A ball that lands between the infield and outfield.

wild pitch A ball thrown in such a way that the catcher cannot catch it.

REFERENCES

Blake, O. William, and Volp, Anne M.: Lead up games to team sports, Engelwood Cliffs, 1964, Prentice-Hall.

Dobson, Margaret J., and Sisley, Becky L.: Softball for girls, New York, 1971, The Ronald Press Co.

How we do it game book, Washington, D. C., 1968, American Association for Health, Physical Education, and Recreation.

Jacobs, J., and McCrory, J. R.: Softball rules in pictures, Newark, N. J., 1968, Amateur Softball Ass.

Meyer, M. H., and Schwartz, M. M.: Technique of team sports for women, Philadelphia, 1959, W. B. Saunders Co.

Mitchell, E. D. (ed.): Sports for recreation (revised ed.), New York, 1952, A. S. Barnes & Co.

Noren, Arthur T.: Softball, New York, 1959, A. S. Barnes & Co.

Official softball guide, Washington, D. C., 1972-1974 American Association for Health, Physical Education, and Recreation.

Official softball rules, Albany, N. Y., 1969, J. deBeer & Son, Inc.

Softball rule guide, Oklahoma City, 1971, Amateur Softball Association.

20 Speedball

HISTORY

Prior to 1920 the main sports used for fall outdoor participation in physical education classes and intramural programs were touch football and soccer. Because of the restrictions on the use of the hands, the game of soccer was not very popular with many students. Although touch football was perhaps more popular than soccer, it nevertheless had certain limitations in that all players did not regularly get an opportunity to throw, catch, and kick the ball.

By 1920, many physical education teachers and coaches felt the need for a vigorous outdoor game that would provide for the development of many basic skills on the part of participants. After much experimentation, Elmer D. Mitchell of the University of Michigan developed and formulated the rules for speedball, combining many of the fundamental elements and skills found in basketball, touch football, and soccer. Because speedball is designed to permit all players on a team to participate in all phases of the game, including catching, throwing, and kicking, it developed rapidly and is now widely used in physical education classes and intramural programs throughout the entire country.

Speedball gradually became popular with both men and women. However, the original rules of speedball needed to be adapted to girls' and women's sports since basketball and soccer rules for women differed from those for men. Consequently, in 1933 the National Section of Women's Athletics of the American Association for Health, Physical Education, and Recreation revised and adapted the speedball rules to meet the needs and abilities of girls and women. Rules for girls' and women's speedball are published periodically.

PLAYING AREA AND EQUIPMENT

Although fields of varying sizes can be used for speedball, the area most commonly used by men is a field the size of a football field. Figs. 20-1 and 20-2 show the dimensions of speedball fields for men and women. A middle line divides the playing area in half. There are two restraining lines that run parallel to the middle or halfway line. There is a penalty area at each end of the field that extends the width of the field. The end zone penalty area for men is 10 yards and the penalty area for women is 5 yards. The ball used for the game of speedball is slightly larger than a soccer ball. Although the regulation ball is recommended for use, many schools throughout the country prefer to use

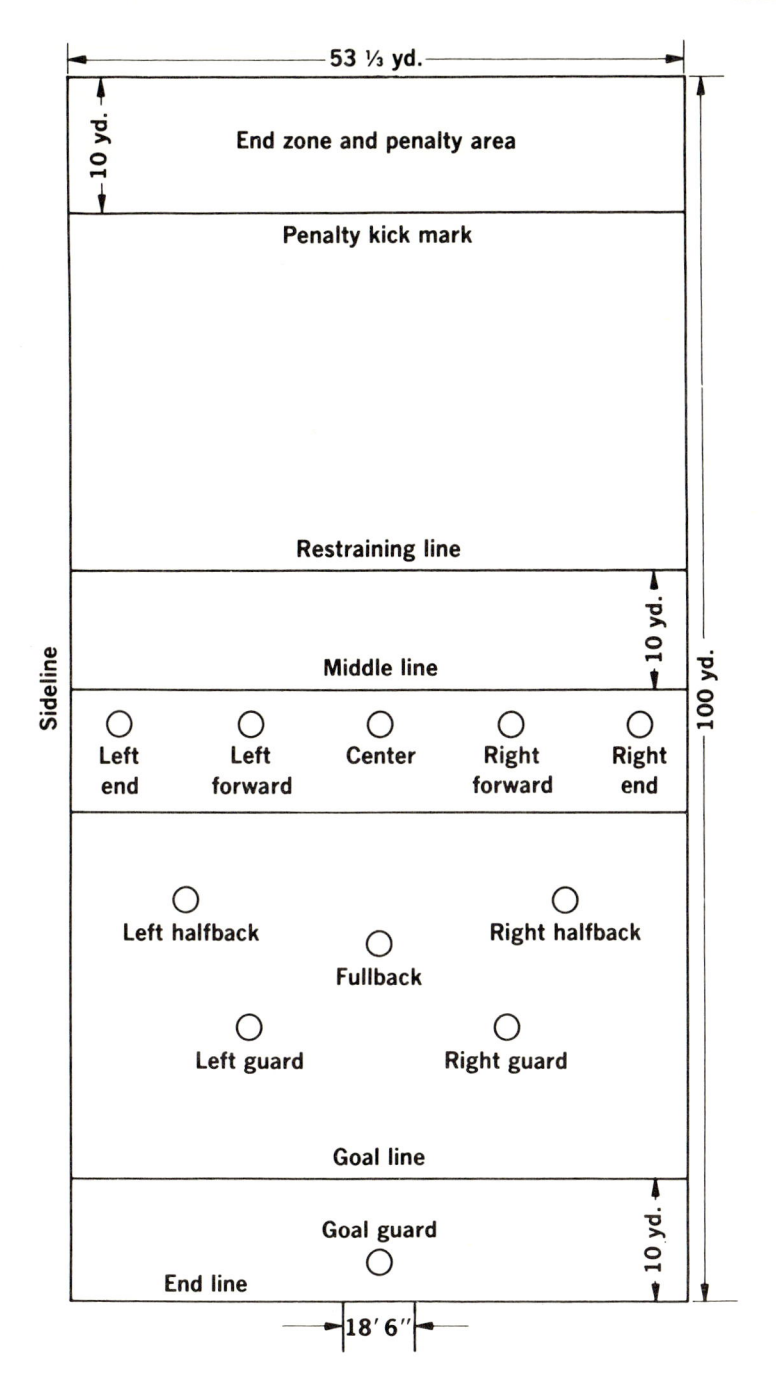

Fig. 20-1. Speedball field and lineup for men.

a soccer ball. No special equipment other than the ball and the playing field is required for speedball.

GENERAL DESCRIPTION

The game of speedball is played by two teams of eleven players each. Although eleven players constitute a regulation team, the game can be played with fewer members making up each team. A wide variety of techniques is employed in speedball, including kicking and dribbling the ball with the feet as in soccer, catching and throwing the ball as in basketball, and punting and passing the ball as in football. Since speedball combines the elements of basketball, soccer,

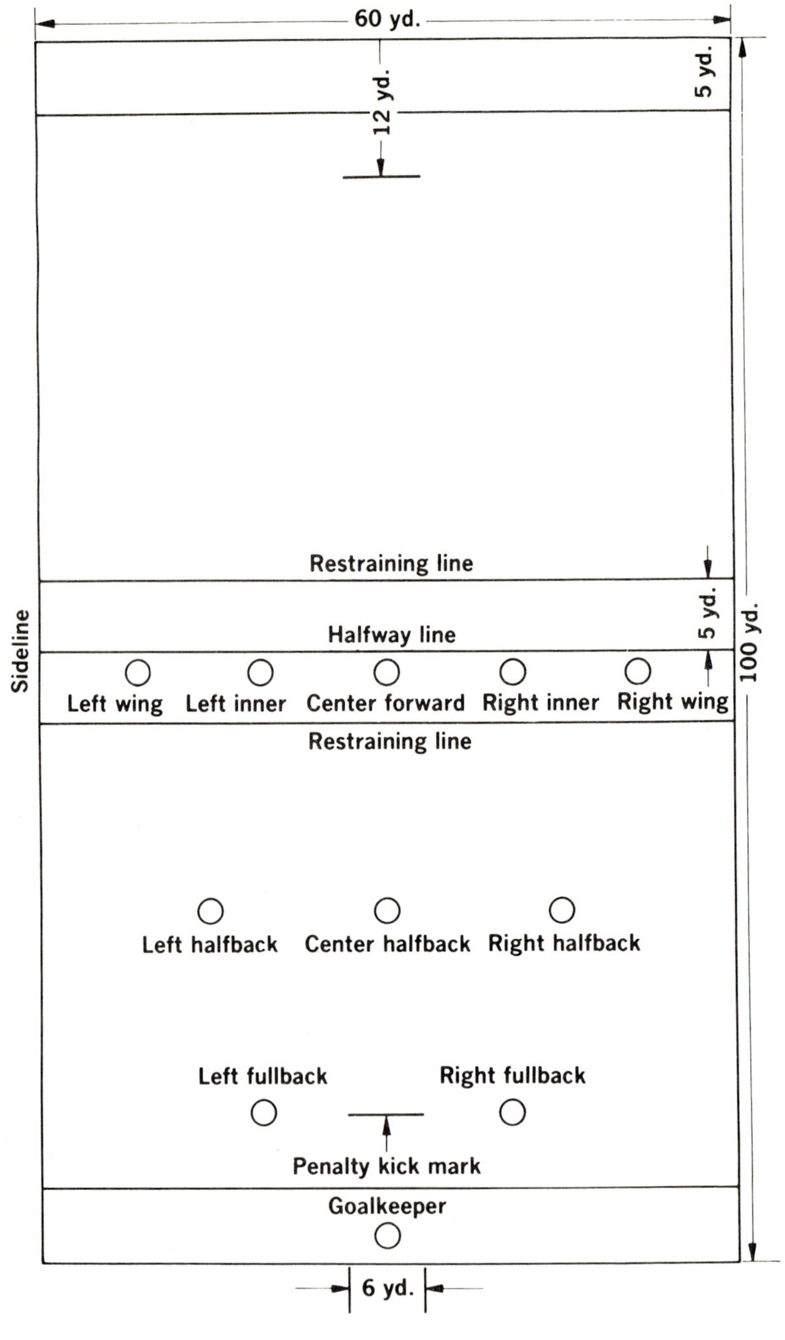

242 BASIC SKILLS IN SPORTS FOR MEN AND WOMEN

Fig. 20-2. Speedball field and lineup for women.

and touch football, in general, the soccer rules apply when the ball is on the ground; basketball rules apply to aerial or fly balls; and football rules usually apply in the forward passing of the ball and scoring. The names of the playing positions for men and women are listed in Table 4, as well as in Figs. 20-1 and 20-2.

The object of the game is for the team in possession of the ball to advance the ball down the field toward the opponent's goal line and attempt to score. The opponents of the team in possession of the ball try to intercept and obtain possession of the ball in order to move it toward the opposite goal line in an attempt to score.

Table 4. Playing positions of men and women

Women	Men
Left wing	Left end
Left inner	Left forward
Center	Center
Right inner	Right forward
Right wing	Right end
Left halfback	Left halfback
Center halfback	Fullback
Right halfback	Right halfback
Left fullback	Left guard
Right fullback	Right guard
Goalkeeper	Goalkeeper

Table 5. Values of different types of scoring

	Points	
	Men's rules	Women's rules
Field goal	3	2
Dropkick	2	3
Touchdown	1	2
Penalty kick	1	1
End goal	1	

SCORING

Points may be scored in four different ways by women and in five different ways by men as follows:

1. Field goal: A field goal is scored when a ball that has been kicked or legally played with any part of the body passes between the goalposts and under the crossbar. A field goal counts 3 points in men's rules and 2 points in women's rules.
2. Dropkick: A dropkick is made when the ball passes over the crossbar after having been drop-kicked from the field of play outside the penalty area. A dropkick counts 2 points for men and 3 points for women.
3. Touchdown: A touchdown is scored when an offensive player passes the ball to a teammate who catches it behind the opponent's goal line. A touchdown counts 1 point for men and 2 points for women.
4. Penalty kick: A penalty kick is scored when the player awarded the try kicks the ball between the goalposts and under the crossbar. A penalty kick counts 1 point for men and 1 point for women.
5. End goal: The end goal applies to men's rules only. An end goal is scored when an offensive player who is in the end zone legally causes the ball to pass over the end line but not between the goalposts. An end goal counts 1 point.

The values of different types of scoring are given in Table 5.

FUNDAMENTAL PLAYING REGULATIONS
Officials

The officials for a game of speedball consist of two umpires, two timekeepers, and two scorers. The umpires have final authority in all decisions pertaining to the conduct of the game.

Length of game
MEN

A regulation speedball game consists of four 12-minute quarters with a 10-minute rest period between halves and a 2-minute interval between quarters. Each team is allowed three time-out periods during a game. Each additional time out taken by a team constitutes a technical foul.

WOMEN

The women's game is made up of 4 quarters of 8 minutes each with a 10-minute interval between halves and 2-minute intervals after the first and third quarters. Each team is allowed three time-out periods during a game. Each additional time out taken by a team constitutes a team foul.

Beginning the game

The game and each quarter are started by having one team kick off (place kick) into its opponent's territory from the center of the field. The members of the kicking team line up on the middle or halfway line. They remain behind the ball until it is kicked. The opponents of the kicking team must remain behind their restraining line until the ball is kicked. In men's rules the kickoff must travel 10 yards or be touched by a member of the receiving team before the kicking team can touch it. In women's rules the kickoff must travel the length of the circumference of the ball, and may be lifted by the foot to a teammate. It may not be touched by the kicker until another player has touched it. Goals are changed at half time.

Playing the game

When the ball is in play, it is referred to as an aerial or fly ball or a ground ball.

AERIAL OR FLY BALL

A ball which has been kicked into the air is referred to as a fly ball in the men's rules and an aerial ball in the women's rules. A fly ball that has been caught may be passed from one player to another as in basketball or moved by a forward pass as in football. It can continue to be played in this manner until it again touches the ground, becoming a ground ball. A player catching an aerial or fly ball is allowed to take one step in making a pass if the ball is caught while the player is standing still, or two steps if the player caught the ball while running.

GROUND BALL

A ball that is in contact with the ground is called a ground ball, whether it is stationary, rolling, or bouncing. The ball remains a ground ball, even though it may bounce into the air, until it is lifted into the air from a direct kick. A ground ball can be kicked, headed, or played with any part of the body except the hands and arms.

Dribbling the ball

A player may dribble a ground ball with the feet with a succession of short kicks. A player may use one overhead dribble; that is, after catching the ball, the player may toss it into the air and catch it again. The player may toss it in any direction and run and catch it before it strikes the ground. Any number of steps may be taken before catching the ball after tossing it. Only one overhead dribble is permitted before passing to another player. A touchdown cannot be scored by an overhead dribble.

Goalkeeper

The main work of the goalkeeper is to keep the ball from going through the goal. The goalkeeper has no special privileges or restrictions but is governed by the same rules as other players.

Illegal play

Although defensive play is allowed in speedball, blocking and tackling as in football are illegal. A player must attempt to secure the ball legally and without undue body contact or roughness.

In women's rules, striking the ball from the hands of a player is considered a foul, but in men's rules a player may legally take the ball from an opponent.

Tie ball

A tie ball is called when two opposing players catch the ball simultaneously, hold the ball without gaining possession, or commit a double foul, or when the officials are in doubt as to which side last touched the ball before it went out-of-bounds. In case of a tie ball, the official puts the ball into play by a jump ball as in basketball. All players must remain at least 5 yards from the spot where the ball is being put into play as a jump ball until it is touched by one of the jumpers. Following a jump ball, the ball may be played as a fly or aerial ball. A score may not result from a jump ball that is caught in the end zone, even though the ball is still in play. A jump ball at the center of the field is used to begin play after a double foul or at the beginning of an overtime period in men's rules. In women's rules the jump ball is used at the spot of the foul in the case of a double foul. If the ball drops to the ground after the jump, either jumper can kick it.

Out-of-bounds

When a player causes the ball to go out-of-bounds over the sidelines, it is put into play with a pass by a player of the opposing team. In returning the ball to the field of play, the player can use either an underhand or overhand pass, and can use one or both hands. In the case of a double foul over the sideline, a jump ball is used 5 yards in from where the foul was committed. When a player causes the ball to go over the end line without scoring, the opponents put the ball into play by a pass or kick.

Penalty kick

A place-kick is used in making a penalty kick in the men's game, while a dropkick is used in the women's game. A penalty kick is awarded as the result of a foul. In men's play the kick is made from the 10-yard line; in women's play the kick is made from the 12-yard line. In the men's game the defensive players must line up on the end line until the kick is made. In women's play the defensive players may be behind the goal or on the field so long as no one is within 5 yards of the kicker.

Free kick

The free kick is part of the women's game. The free kick is awarded in the cases which follow:
1. For an individual or personal foul committed on the field outside the penalty area
2. For a personal foul behind the goal line committed by the attacking team

When a free kick is awarded, the ball is placed at the spot where the foul was committed. The ball may be kicked in any direction and must travel at least the full circumference of the ball. No opposing player may approach within 5 yards of the kicker. The ball must be kicked, but it may be turned into an aerial ball.

MEN'S RULES FOR VIOLATIONS, TECHNICAL FOULS, PERSONAL FOULS, AND PENALTIES
Violations

The following infractions of rules are considered violations:
1. Traveling with the ball
2. Touching a ground ball with the hands or arms
3. Dribbling overhead more than once
4. Kicking or kneeing a fly ball before catching it
5. Causing the ball to go out-of-bounds
6. Interfering with a kickoff or jump ball
7. Illegally interfering with a penalty kick
8. Illegally interfering with a player returning the ball from out-of-bounds

Violation penalties

The penalty for a violation committed on the field of play outside of the end zone is that the opponents are awarded the ball out-of-bounds for a throw-in. If a violation is committed within the penalty area, one penalty kick is given the opponents. If the penalty kick is missed, the ball continues in play.

Technical fouls

The following infractions are considered technical fouls:
1. Illegal substitutions
2. Unsportsmanlike conduct
3. Unnecessary delay of the game
4. Taking more than three time outs
5. Having more than eleven men on the playing field at one time

Technical foul penalty

A penalty kick is awarded for a technical foul committed outside the penalty area. Any member of the team may make the penalty kick. If the penalty kick is not successful, the ball is dead and a touchback is awarded the opponents.

Personal fouls

Personal fouls include the following infractions:
1. Pushing, holding, kicking, tripping, charging, or blocking an opponent
2. Unnecessary roughness

Personal foul penalties

If a personal foul is committed by a player within his own penalty area, the offended team is given two penalty kicks. If the second kick is missed, the ball remains in play. If a player commits a personal foul outside his own penalty area, the opponents are given one penalty kick. If the penalty kick is not successful, a touchback is declared.

WOMEN'S RULES FOR INDIVIDUAL FOULS, TEAM FOULS, AND PENALTIES
Individual fouls

The following infractions are regarded as individual fouls:
1. Kicking, tripping, holding, or blocking an opponent
2. Charging, pushing, or obstructing an opponent
3. Boxing up an opponent

4. Entering the game illegally
5. Delaying the game
6. Traveling with the ball
7. Touching a ground ball with the hands or arms
8. Juggling the ball more than once
9. Holding the ball more than 3 seconds
10. Attempting a dropkick within the penalty area
11. Forward passing for a touchdown within the penalty area
12. Unnecessary roughness, including knocking the ball out of an opponent's hands after it had been legally caught, kicking the ball in the hands of a player who is in the act of converting a ground ball into an aerial ball, or using any other form of rough or dangerous play

Penalties for individual fouls

Penalties for individual fouls are as follows:
1. For an individual four occurring outside the penalty area, a free kick is awarded where the foul occurred.
2. If a player commits an individual foul within her own penalty area or behind her team's own goal line, a penalty kick is awarded.
3. If an individual foul is committed by the attacking team inside the penalty area or behind the goal line, a free kick is awarded.
4. In case of a double foul, a jump ball is declared between the two offenders; in the case of a double foul behind the goal lines, the toss-up between the two offenders occurs on the 5-yard line opposite the place where the fouls occurred.

Team fouls

Team fouls include the following infractions:
1. Taking more than three time-out periods
2. Having more than eleven players on the field of play at one time
3. Failing to report to the officials before going into the game

Penalties for team fouls

One penalty kick is awarded for each team foul.

FUNDAMENTAL TECHNIQUES AND SKILLS

Dribbling with the feet

Dribbling with the feet is used in moving the ball toward an opponent's goal line. It is most often used in situations where it is not advisable to kick up or kick to a teammate. In dribbling the ball it is extremely important that the player keep control of the ball at all times, which means that it must not be kicked with force. In most cases, the inside surface of the foot should be used for best control although experienced players may use the outside of the foot along the area of the little toe. Ordinarily, for best control the ball should be kicked from an even run about every third step.

Passing

Many types of basketball passes may be used. Any kind of one- or two-hand throw is acceptable depending upon the particular situation. The baseball-type pass is used extensively in speedball because of the wide playing field available. A player with the ball may pivot as in basketball if one foot is stabilized. This sometimes helps in finding a teammate open to receive a pass.

Overhead dribble

Only one overhead dribble is allowed. The overhead dribble is made by tossing the ball into the air and running to catch it before it strikes the ground. There is no restriction on the number of steps that may be taken after tossing the ball and before catching it again. The overhead dribble is particularly useful when a closely guarded player tosses the ball over the head of the opponent in order to get free.

Place-kicking

The place-kick is used in an attempt to score following a foul. The ball is placed on the penalty kick line or 10-yard line for men and on the 12-yard line for women. The object is to kick the ball past the goalkeeper between the goalposts and under the crossbar. The goalkeeper is the only player on the opposing team who is permitted to defend against the place-kick.

Drop-kicking

For the best control of the ball in drop-kicking, hold the ball at a level just above the knees, flex at the waist, drop the ball to the ground, and kick it just as it bounces; take one step with the left foot and kick the ball with the right foot. If the player kicks with the left foot, the reverse technique should be used.

Punting

Punting in speedball is used to advance the ball toward the opponent's goal line as quickly as possible. Techniques of punting in speedball are similar to those in football. The ball should be kicked with the upper surface of the instep of the foot. The kicker should take one step forward with the left foot, drop the ball from extended arms, and kick the ball with the right foot. The ball should be dropped as the foot starts its upward swing. If the player kicks with the left foot, the reverse technique should be used.

Catching

The ball should be caught with the entire hand since many of the passes are vigorously thrown After the catch, the ball should be held with the fingers. Since catching the speedball is similar to catching a basketball, the same technique should be practiced in perfecting this skill.

Blocking

Any part of the body, with the exception of the hands and arms, may be used to stop or slow the speed of the ball. Women should cross their arms in front of the chest in trying to stop the ball at shoulder level. To prevent the ball from rebounding too vigorously off the body as it strikes, the player should move back slightly at the instant of the impact.

Trapping with the feet

In trapping the ball with the foot, the player extends the leg forward toward the ball with the heel 4 or 5 inches above the ground and the toe pointing upward. The sole of the foot is presented to the ball as it approaches. When the ball comes within reach of the foot, press down and trap the ball between the sole of the foot and the ground.

Trapping with the legs

In trapping the ball with the right leg, the player slightly advances the left leg diagonally forward and outward and flexes the right leg as though intending to kneel. The flexion should be inward over the right toe. The ball should be trapped between the lower leg and the ground. In double-leg trapping the feet are close together as the rolling ball approaches from the front. The ball is trapped by kneeling on it. However, the weight of the body should remain over the feet.

Kickup

There are many situations in the game of speedball in which a ground ball may be played more advantageously by converting it into an aerial or fly ball. A player may convert a ground ball into an aerial or fly ball by kicking it into the air.

KICKUP WITH TWO FEET

With the ball held firmly between the insides of the feet and ankles, the player jumps into the air, lifting the ball upward. (See Fig. 20-3.) When the ball is released by the ankles and feet, the player catches it before it touches the ground. Since the kickup is one of the easiest ways to pick up a ground ball, players should practice and develop considerable skill in its use.

KICKUP WITH ONE FOOT

The play can be made on a rolling ball by flipping the ball into the air with the foot and catching it after it leaves the foot and before it touches the ground. As the rolling ball approaches, the player should extend the leg forward with the pointed toe touching the ground. As the ball rolls onto the instep of the foot, the player flips the ball into the air and catches it.

The one-foot kickup can be made on

Fig. 20-3. Kickup with two feet.

Fig. 20-4. Kickup with one foot.

a stationary ball by placing the foot on top of the ball and drawing it backward to start the ball rolling toward the player. Then the toe is quickly placed under the ball so that it will roll onto the instep. When it rolls onto the instep, the player quickly flips the ball into the air and catches it before it touches the ground. (See Fig. 20-4.) The kickup technique on both a rolling ball and a stationary ball can also be used to lift the ball to a teammate.

OFFENSIVE PLAY

In moving the ball down the field, the forward line should be spread and the players should attempt to keep in front of the ball. As the ball approaches the goal line, the wings should go across the end line to receive a forward pass. The halfbacks should remain in a position to back up the forwards or try to score if an opportunity presents itself. Also, the halfbacks should be ready to guard against the opposing team if the ball is intercepted and lost. In the men's game a long kickoff deep into the opponent's territory usually is best. The kicking team should move rapidly down the field following the kickoff to prevent the opponents from returning the ball toward their goal line. In the women's game a long kickoff downfield is not always the best strategy, depending somewhat on the ability of the players. Since the kickoff in the women's game need not travel more than the circumference of the ball, the best strategy often is to keep control of the ball by dribbling it along the ground or converting it into an aerial ball or to gain possession of the ball by a kickup or by using a short control pass.

DEFENSIVE PLAY

Player-to-player defense is most often used in the game of speedball. Fullbacks, guards, and halfbacks guard the opposing forwards. The goalkeeper may leave position to assist in stopping a touchdown play when necessary.

GLOSSARY OF SPEEDBALL TERMS

aerial ball A ball that has been raised into the air by either a one- or two-foot kick; a punt, dropkick, kickup, or thrown ball that has not touched the ground.

air dribble A ball that is tossed or tapped into the air and caught by the same player.

attackers The team in possession of the ball.

blocking the ball Intercepting the ball with any part of the body. A player cannot block a ground ball with the arms or hands unless they are in contact with the body.

closely guarded Being guarded within three feet.

dead ball A ball no longer in play; out-of-bounds, after a score, after a foul, during time out, or a tie ball.

defenders The team not in possession of the ball.

double foul Fouls committed at the same time by both teams; a toss-up is awarded.

dribble Advancing the ball by a series of kicks.

dropkick Dropping the ball to the ground and kicking it just as it bounces from the ground.

end goal Passing the ball over the end line but not between the goalposts; counts 1 point for men but does not apply to women's rules.

field goal Passing the ball between the goalposts and under the crossbar; 3 points for men, 2 for women.

foul An infringement of the rules for which a free kick, free throw, or a penalty kick is awarded the opponents.

free kick A place-kick from which a goal can be scored directly.

free throw A throw taken by any player on the team that has been fouled during the play of an aerial ball.

goalkeeper A player whose duty it is to defend the goal.

ground ball A ball that is in contact with the ground whether it is stationary, rolling, or bouncing.

handling the ball Putting the hands or arms on a ground ball.

indirect free kick A free kick from which a goal can not be scored directly.

kickup The play converting a ground ball into an aerial ball.

own goal The goal one's team is defending.

own half The half of the field in which own goal is located.

passing Means of moving the ball by passes or batting with the hands to another player.

penalty kick A free kick awarded as the result of a foul; men use a place-kick from the 10-yard line and the ball must go under the crossbar; women use a dropkick to pass the ball over the crossbar.

place-kick A stationary ball kicked by a player.

punt A play in which a player drops a caught ball and kicks it before it touches the ground.

trapping Stopping the motion of the ball by placing the sole of the foot on it, by kneeling on it, or by catching it between the front of the legs and the ground.

volley A play in which a player fields a fly or aerial ball with some part of the body such as the head, hip, or shoulder.

REFERENCES

DeWitt, R. T.: Teaching individual and team sports, Englewood Cliffs, N. J., 1953, Prentice-Hall, Inc.

Fait, Hollis F.: Speedball for men, Washington, D. C., 1967, AAHPER.

Meyer, M. H., and Schwarz, M. M.: Sports for girls and women, ed. 3, Philadelphia, 1965, W. B. Saunders Co.

Official soccer and speedball rules and guide, Washington, D. C., 1972-1974, AAHPER, Division for Girls' and Women's Sports.

Scott, M. Gladys, and French, Esther: Sports skill tests—speedball in measurement and evaluation in physical education, Dubuque, Iowa, 1959, William C. Brown Co.

Vannier, Maryhelen, and Poindexter, Hatty Beth: Individual and team sports for girls and women, Philadelphia, 1968, W. B. Saunders Co.

FILM

Soccer for girls, 16 mm., 11 min., Coronet Instructional Films, Chicago, Ill.

21 Swimming

HISTORY AND EVOLUTION

No one knows when, where, or how the first human being discovered how to swim. It was undoubtedly learned by observing animals that usually set up a running motion to move about on or in the water. Water is an unnatural medium for humans because it interferes with their breathing mechanism. The animal is better equipped anatomically for swimming simply because it holds its nose higher. The human being cannot easily do this successfully and remain in the horizontal position. The human being must therefore learn to breathe in water in order to swim.

Carvings showing swimming have been found dating as early as 9000 B.C. In the middle ages, accounts in the Greek, Roman, Anglo-Saxon, and Scandinavian classics dealt only with great feats of swimming prowess of the heroes of their day and left the type of swimming stroke used to the reader's imagination.

In 1538, Nicolaus Wynman, a German professor of languages, wrote the first book on swimming. In 1696, M. Thevenot, a Frenchman, wrote a more scientific treatise.

The breaststroke was the first basic stroke to be taught just for the joy and pleasure of swimming. Competition soon changed this in England, and the English sought ways and means of speeding up the breaststroke, just as competition has always been an accelerating factor in any sport.

England had a great merchant fleet sailing the seven seas. Its captains observed natives swimming in all parts of the world. Their style and manner of swimming were brought back to England, and hence the development of strokes for speed swimming began to materialize. The strokes listed below are still fundamental and seaworthy for all utility purposes, but have been considerably refined for competitive swimming.

The evolution of these strokes occurred in the following order:

1. The "doggy" or human paddling strokes.
2. The breaststroke (sailor stroke), the first scientific stroke taught.
3. The underarm sidestroke. This stroke was still too slow for speed because both arms recovered under the water as they did in the breaststroke. The kick was a scissor-like kick.
4. The side overarm or the English overarm stroke. This stroke was faster than either the breaststroke or the side underarm stroke because the uppermost arm recovered above the surface and thereby reduced resistance.

5. The trudgeon stroke, discovered in South America in 1860 by an Englishman, John Trudgen. This stroke employed the method of recovering both arms above the water hand-over-hand and still further reduced resistance to water and created greater speed. It was similar to the side overarm stroke except that the body turned over to the uppermost side to also permit the under arm to lift out of the water for recovery. In this stroke the scissors kick was used just as it was in the sidestrokes.
6. The Australian crawl, introduced to England by Richard Cavell of Australia in the 1902 championships. This was the first true hand-over-hand stroke with vertical thrash of the legs. Cavell, as well as Trudgen, took a trip to the South Seas and there observed the natives thrash their legs up and down. Trudgen did not observe the kick and therefore used the scissors kick. Cavell explained the stroke as "crawling through the water." This style eliminated the scissors kick for speed swimming, since recovering the legs caused great resistance.
7. The American six-beat leg kick crawl. The Australian stroke then became scientifically refined by American coaches. This style broke all existing freestyle records in speed swimming and became known as the fastest human stroke in water.
8. The inverted breaststroke. This is the breaststroke executed upside down while one is swimming on the back.
9. The back crawl. About 1910, the crawl was turned upside down and was much faster in competition than the inverted breaststroke. Here again there was no recovery of arms or legs underwater as in the inverted breaststroke. It, too, minimized resistance and created faster speed on the back.
10. The butterfly breaststroke.* This stroke was beginning to make its appearance in competition about 1934. The kick in this stroke remained the same as the breaststroke kick, but the arms recovered above the water simultaneously. They lifted out of the water at the hips and were swung laterally forward to the entry, resembling a butterfly in flight; thus the stroke received its name.
11. The dolphin fishtail breaststroke.* The newest of all the swimming strokes was created by one of us (Armbruster) through the specific ability and skill of Jack Sieg. The purpose of this stroke is to obtain greater speed with the breaststroke by eliminating the recovery underwater of the legs in the kick. This is accomplished by beating the legs up and down in unison. This kick actually creates greater speed when used without arms than does the alternating crawl flutter kick. It synchronized beautifully with the butterfly arm stroke and created greater speed.

This discussion is presented to show briefly the origin and evolution of each style of stroke and kick as it has been used in water to obtain speed. Keen competition in swimming and the search for new techniques to obtain greater speed in water are the constant goals of coaches, teachers, and competitors. These strokes have been originated in less than 100 years. This is certainly a creative accomplishment by coaches, research technicians, and teachers. Undoubtedly greater advances will be made.

Not only have all of these strokes been developed and refined, but they also have been put to practical and utilitarian usage for the average swimmer and are expressed in many different categories of swimming, usually called aquatics. Some of these categories of aquatics are listed below:
1. Recreational
2. Lifesaving
3. Competition
4. Synchronized or ballet

---

*See Armbruster, D. A., Allen, R. H., and Billingsley, H. S.: Swimming and diving, ed. 6, St. Louis, 1973, The C. V. Mosby Co.

*Also see Armbruster, D. A.: The dolphin breast stroke, Journal of Health and Physical Education 6:23, April, 1935.

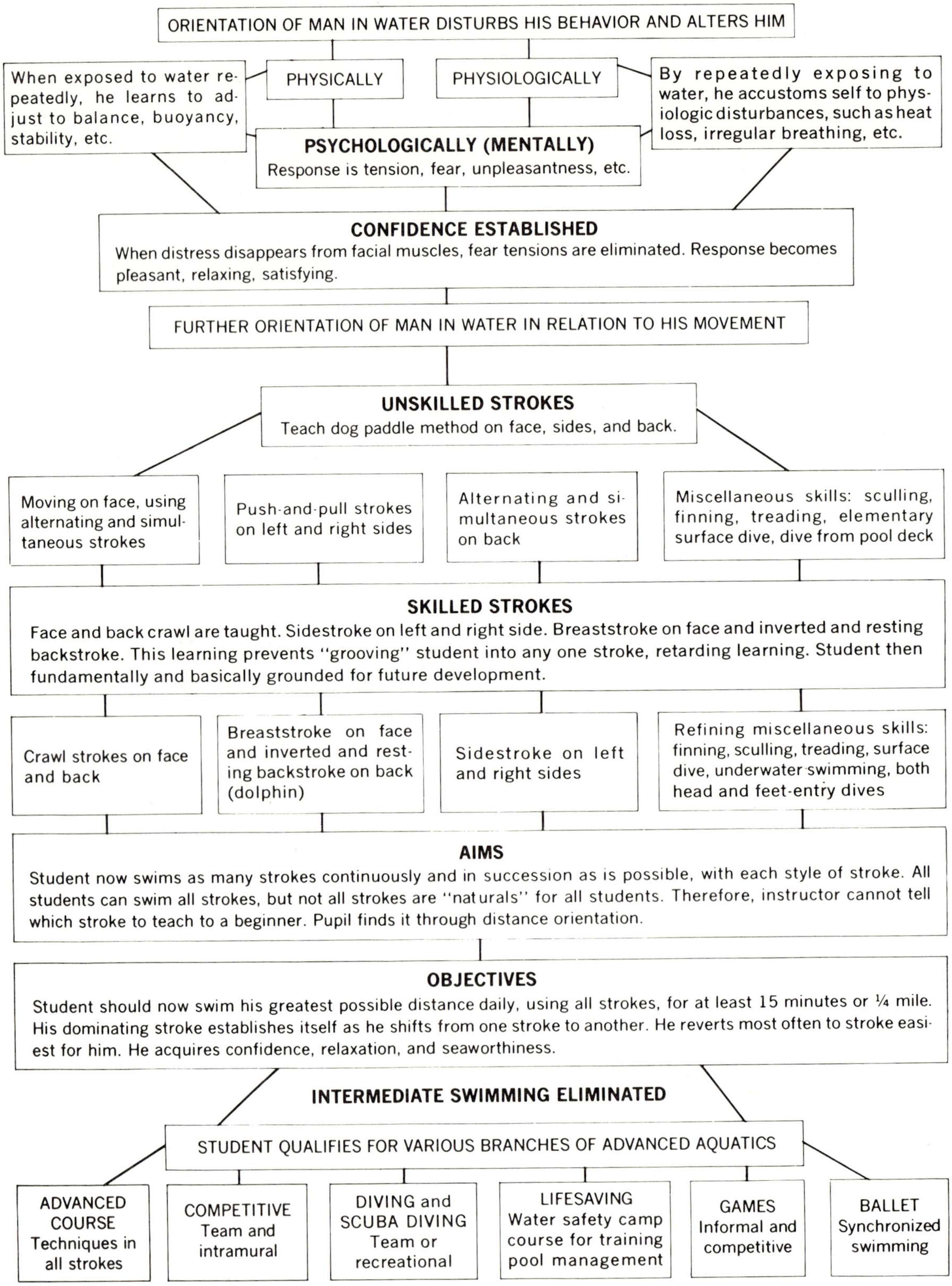

```
┌─────────────────────────────────────────────────────────────────────┐
│ ORIENTATION OF MAN IN WATER DISTURBS HIS BEHAVIOR AND ALTERS HIM    │
└─────────────────────────────────────────────────────────────────────┘
```

| When exposed to water repeatedly, he learns to adjust to balance, buoyancy, stability, etc. | PHYSICALLY | PHYSIOLOGICALLY | By repeatedly exposing to water, he accustoms self to physiologic disturbances, such as heat loss, irregular breathing, etc. |

PSYCHOLOGICALLY (MENTALLY)
Response is tension, fear, unpleasantness, etc.

CONFIDENCE ESTABLISHED
When distress disappears from facial muscles, fear tensions are eliminated. Response becomes pleasant, relaxing, satisfying.

FURTHER ORIENTATION OF MAN IN WATER IN RELATION TO HIS MOVEMENT

UNSKILLED STROKES
Teach dog paddle method on face, sides, and back.

| Moving on face, using alternating and simultaneous strokes | Push-and-pull strokes on left and right sides | Alternating and simultaneous strokes on back | Miscellaneous skills: sculling, finning, treading, elementary surface dive, dive from pool deck |

SKILLED STROKES
Face and back crawl are taught. Sidestroke on left and right side. Breaststroke on face and inverted and resting backstroke. This learning prevents "grooving" student into any one stroke, retarding learning. Student then fundamentally and basically grounded for future development.

| Crawl strokes on face and back | Breaststroke on face and inverted and resting backstroke on back (dolphin) | Sidestroke on left and right sides | Refining miscellaneous skills: finning, sculling, treading, surface dive, underwater swimming, both head and feet-entry dives |

AIMS
Student now swims as many strokes continuously and in succession as is possible, with each style of stroke. All students can swim all strokes, but not all strokes are "naturals" for all students. Therefore, instructor cannot tell which stroke to teach to a beginner. Pupil finds it through distance orientation.

OBJECTIVES
Student should now swim his greatest possible distance daily, using all strokes, for at least 15 minutes or ¼ mile. His dominating stroke establishes itself as he shifts from one stroke to another. He reverts most often to stroke easiest for him. He acquires confidence, relaxation, and seaworthiness.

INTERMEDIATE SWIMMING ELIMINATED

STUDENT QUALIFIES FOR VARIOUS BRANCHES OF ADVANCED AQUATICS

| ADVANCED COURSE Techniques in all strokes | COMPETITIVE Team and intramural | DIVING and SCUBA DIVING Team or recreational | LIFESAVING Water safety camp course for training pool management | GAMES Informal and competitive | BALLET Synchronized swimming |

Fig. 21-1. The Armbruster all-stroke method—a progressive learning procedure chart for school swimming.

5. Springboard diving
6. Water games—polo, basketball, baseball, etc.
7. Water safety
8. Survival
9. Skin and scuba diving

All of these skill activities in water have as a basic background the fundamental skill strokes.

Not all of the strokes mentioned will be taught to the beginners. However, it is strongly recommended that the beginner be taught all of the basic strokes, which have as their purpose not only combining seaworthiness and practical utility, but giving the learner an assurance of self-preservation, an at-home feeling, and a joy of relaxation for pleasurable and recreational swimming. To accomplish this, the beginner must be versed in all the fundamental skill strokes This method of learning will be called the "Armbruster all-stroke method for beginners."* (See the all-stroke progressive learn-chart, Fig. 21-1.)

THE ARMBRUSTER ALL-STROKE METHOD FOR TEACHING BEGINNERS

The all-stroke method has been used successfully at the University of Iowa for the past twenty years. It has been taught with equal success to persons of all ages, from 5 years to 60 years, both sexes. All the time that is necessary to teach this method is 2 to 3 hours per week for an entire semester or 3 to 4 hours for one-quarter semester.

This method utilizes the word picture-modified Brink method for adjusting students to water, but adds several skilled and some low-skilled techniques. When the student has been comfortably adjusted to water and basically "stanced" so to speak, all of the basic skill strokes can be learned quite rapidly.

At the beginning all persons can learn all of the strokes and make reasonable progress; however, not all persons can swim all strokes equally well. Therefore, we teach the student all of the strokes and the student will find naturally the stroke most comfortable and suitable through a distance orientation program after the stroke skills are learned. There is no instructor capable of meeting a class for the first time and saying, "In this course we will learn the following two 'pet' strokes," because not all students can swim those strokes easily and naturally. People differ anatomically, as well as aesthetically. If the student is taught all strokes, in the distance orientation program the stroke that takes the least effort will naturally most often be selected. The student is now beginning to find the stroke that gives the student the most self-satisfaction and pleasure, although the student is basically "grounded" in any stroke. The student is not first "grooved" in one or two strokes but is basically grounded for advanced swimming, lifesaving, or any other form of aquatic interest. The idea, too, is to do away with the in-between intermediate level of swimming.

The secret of this method is really to punish the legs by drilling them in the different kick skills. Ordinarily legs are clumsy and awkward, being composed of big muscles that in everyday living are trained only to walk, run, jump, and perhaps dance. To get legs to relax in water and become skilled, to get the feel of a semisolid medium, water, one must train and overlearn.

Swimming instructors must move ahead and keep abreast of the rapid developments in swimming that have taken place in the past decade. The instructor should not limit a student in the learning experience but should give a foundation upon which the student's greatest capabilities and talents can be developed if they lie in the aquatic field.

Correct breathing habits are the next important essential skill to teach. One must breathe in order to swim. Water interferes with the breathing mechanism of the human being. Even the quadruped holds its nose at the highest point of its body in relation to the surface level in order to swim. It, too, must breathe to swim. The human being has learned to exhale under the surface and inhale above the surface.

---
*Armbruster, D. A.: Teaching beginners to swim, a physical, physiological and psychological method, Journal of Health and Physical Education 7:233, April, 1936.

Instructors of swimming should eliminate too many testing programs during the learning class time. Testing wastes good teaching time. Emphasize skill-learning repetitions by constant drill and action. Action creates interest and results in interested students, which in turn results in good class discipline. Students like to work hard if they feel and know they are learning. Swimming taught progressively and quite intensively accomplishes just that. If students become fatigued (not exhausted) from constant exercise, they will naturally take it easy, and when they take it easy, the response is relaxation. Relaxation is learned through constant repetitions.

OBJECTIVES

1. To orient the student to water, a medium which disturbs a person physically, physiologically, and mentally, and brings about the following body changes:
   (a) Unstableness
   (b) Apparent loss of body weight
   (c) Loss of sense of balance
   (d) Change in body position for locomotion
   (e) Change in heat-regulatory mechanism
   (f) Change in respiration
   (g) Change in normal muscle tonus
2. To give confidence, drill to adjust the student to the above responses and reactions from water, using drills that have the following objectives:
   (a) To eliminate mental hazards
   (b) To teach inspiration and expiration properly
   (c) To bring about relaxation in the water
   (d) To encourage enjoyment of swimming
3. To teach self-reliance for self-preservation
4. To teach an appreciation of distance over water no matter how short or long the distance
5. To teach respect for water generally while swimming
6. To impart confidence in one's own skill and ability of accomplishment
7. To achieve personal health and body cleanliness before swimming
8. To teach strokes in such a way as to motivate the student to persistent practice
9. To encourage swimming as a source of life-long pleasure
10. To teach distribution of effort and the conservation of strength
11. To teach how to delay fatigue
12. To teach the student how to dive into water

PERSONAL EQUIPMENT

1. Swimming trunks for men and full suits for women
2. Bathing caps if needed for hair protection
3. Ear plugs only if swimmer has a perforated eardrum
4. Nose clip recommended only in severe case of chronic sinusitis
5. Clogs for going to and from pool to protect feet from fungus infection between toes

HYGIENIC RULES FOR USE OF SWIMMING POOLS

1. Solo swimming is prohibited; you must swim with a partner or under the supervision of an attendant.
2. Running in shower rooms or around pool is prohibited.
3. Spitting, spouting, or blowing the nose in the pool is prohibited.
4. Street clothes and shoes are not to be worn in pool area.
5. Chewing gum is prohibited.
6. Persons with skin diseases, sore or inflamed eyes, nasal or ear discharges, bandaged cuts or scratches, severe athlete's foot, or any communicable disease must consult the instructor.
7. Before and after using the pool, all students must shower thoroughly without their suits, using lukewarm water and soap for 3 minutes.
8. Never call for help in fun.
9. Flinging or throwing objects except in a water game is prohibited.

10. Know the depth of the water before jumping or diving into it.
11. Swimmers should run the shower water over the head to wash out all falling hair.
12. Women should remove all pins from the hair.

INSTRUCTION BEFORE ENTERING WATER

Water is a very strange medium to the beginning nonswimmer and very often to those who can swim. As a person enters the water slowly and the water level comes up to the naval area, the respiratory center is affected, and breath is gasped inward irregularly. Difficulty in exhaling is experienced momentarily. While standing in water waist deep or deeper, the swimmer has difficulty maintaining balance. The person stands on tiptoes because the body is buoyant and loses body weight. The loss of body heat in cool water is almost four times as great as on land causing the body to become chilly and shivery, and the muscles to become tense.

When the face is placed in water, the person becomes disturbed not only because it becomes difficult to breathe, but also because the sensory organs, such as the eyes, nose, mouth, and ears, are irritated by water. This is not pleasant and also disturbs the beginner. All of these physical and physiological disturbances cause the person to be disturbed mentally. However, the experience does become pleasant when the beginner is properly adjusted. It is essential therefore that the beginner swimmer be:

1. Oriented with regard to being at home in this new element
2. Taught the basic principles of body-buoyancy behavior in water
3. Taught to open the eyes and ship water with the open mouth, under and above the water
4. Given instruction in proper breathing habits
5. Given instruction regarding the action of specific gravity pressing upward upon the body, buoying it to the surface, called floating

BASIC SKILL TECHNIQUES IN ADJUSTING BEGINNER TO WATER

Adjustment to water

1. Wade waist deep into the pool and submerge repeatedly to chin level, rinsing up and down and washing the face.
2. By holding on to the overflow trough, allow water to lift the legs and body to the surface. Keep relaxed.

Breath control

1. Standing in waist-deep water with the body inclined forward, practice breath holding; inhale through the mouth, close the mouth, shut the eyes, and submerge the face flat beneath the water. Hold for 3 counts and recover. Repeat several times, lengthening the time of holding the breath underwater.
2. Inhale through the mouth, submerge the face with the eyes closed, exhale through the nose and recover. Repeat several times.
3. Inhale through the mouth, submerge the face with the eyes closed, and exhale through the nose, mouth, or both, steadily but as slowly as possible. Recover and repeat several times.

Use of eyes underwater

Inhale, close the eyes, submerge, open the eyes, count the number of fingers visible on a partner's hand, and recover. Repeat.

Ship water with mouth

Submerge, open the mouth, recover, and ship out water by squeezing the mouth from the rear. Repeat several times.

Balance and control of the body

The following floating and gliding activities are designed to aid the student in developing confidence in the water. To ensure that confidence is generated and fear is not enhanced, it is important to discuss and practice (with partners) the procedures of returning to a stable position before assuming the various floating and gliding positions.

Jellyfish float: This float may be performed in either the jackknife or tuck position. Take a deep breath, submerge the face,

Fig. 21-2. A, Jellyfish float, jacknife and tuck positions. **B,** Recovery from jellyfish float.

raise the knees to the chest or extend the legs, and hold with the arms for 3 seconds. Release the hold, extending the legs until the feet touch the bottom of the pool, and recover. (See Fig. 21-2.) Repeat.

Prone floating position: The prone floating position is taken by lifting and extending the arms forward beyond the head beneath the surface with the head held low in the water and extending the legs (this is the only difference between the prone float and the jellyfish float). (See Fig. 21-3.) On recovery to the standing position, pull the knees to the chest, round the back, then simultaneously press firmly downward with the extended arms, and extend the legs to the bottom of the pool and lift the face from the water. With the legs extended downward, the feet will settle on the pool floor. (Water must be at least waist deep.) Keep the eyes open. After recovery, exhale through the nose, open the mouth, inhale, and flutter the eyes open.

Prone glide and stand: In the prone glide, the student bends forward at the waist; the arms are extended forward. Lay the upper body and arms in the water. A deep breath is taken at the side, the knees bend, and the face is rolled under the surface. The knees are straightened, the feet push off the bottom, and the student slides into a prone position and the glide. At the end of the glide, draw the knees into the chest and recover as in the prone float.

Back floating position: In floating on the back, have your partner stand directly behind you, submerge to the chin, and with your partner supporting the back of your neck with one hand and the small of the back with the other, lift the hips and extend the arms sideward. Keep your ears underwater. The partner gradually removes support, first from the small of the back, and then from the neck. The partner should aid the student to recover the first few times. To gain own recovery from the back float, move

SWIMMING 257

Fig. 21-3. Prone float and recover.

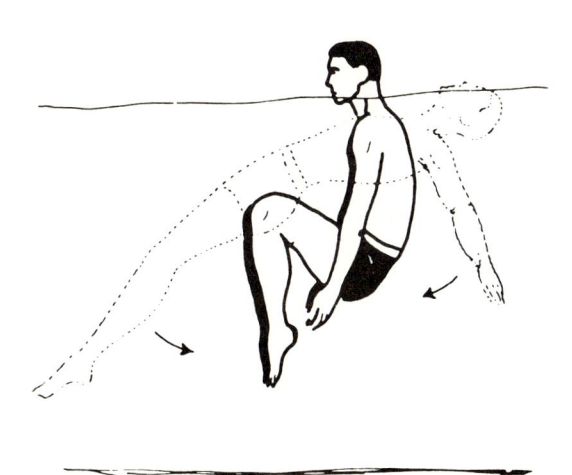

Fig. 21-4. Back float and recover.

the arms downward and forward in the water, round the back, bring the knees to the chin, and lift the head slowly forward. When the body settles to a vertical position, the legs are extended to the bottom and the student stands. (See Fig. 21-4.)

Back glide and stand: In the back glide, the student sits back, pushes off with the feet, glides until forward motion stops, and then recovers as in the back float. In the glide, keep the arms at the side and the legs straight and together.

Simple leg movements to keep body horizontal and to aid propulsion

Kick glide, prone position: In the kick glide, prone position, the student starts in the same manner as in the prone glide, but as the body straightens out on the surface, the legs pick up an alternate up-and-down thrash, delivered with a fairly loose knee, and continue to the limit of breath-holding ability. (For additional practice, hold on to the overflow trough and kick the legs in the above manner or hold on to a kickboard.)

Kick glide, back position: In the kick glide, back position, assume a back floating position, but with the back flat and chin tucked well into the throat. The legs are used in a slack-kneed flutter kick of slightly greater depth than that used in the front position. (For additional practice, hold on to the overflow trough and execute the flutter kick.)

Simple arm movements for support, propulsion, and balancing of body

Arm stroke on the front: In the arm stroke on the front (dog paddle), the prone position in the water is assumed and arms are extended alternately forward and downward, followed by a press backward under the body. Cup the hands slightly on the pull backward. In the recovery forward of each arm, straighten the hand, draw it up under the chin, and extend it to a forward position; cup the hand and repeat the stroke.

Arm stroke on the back: The arm stroke on the back (finning) is a paired movement of the hands and arms in a back position. The arms are first extended by the sides and then drawn up about 1 foot, at which point the demands are thrust outward and then downward toward the feet in a sort of pushing movement, supplemented by a sort of fishtail flip of the hands and wrists.

Coordination of breathing, leg, and arm movements

Combined stroke on the front: The combined stroke on the front is composed of the up-and-down alternating thrash of the legs and the dog paddle of the arms with breathing done entirely above the surface or alternately inhaling above and exhaling below the water. Two or more beats of the legs should be delivered in the cycle of a stroke of the arms. (The right arm pulls as the left leg delivers the downward drive; the left arm pulls as the right leg beats downward.)

In breathing, inhalation should be taken to the side. If you turn the head to the left to get air, inhale when the right arm is extended forward. Rotate the head into the water on this cycle and when the left arm is extended, exhale underwater through the nose. If you inhale to the right side, the left arm should be extended and on this cycle, as the right arm is extended, rotate the face into the water and exhale.

Combined stroke on the back: The combined stroke on the back consists of finning with the hands and flutter kicking with the legs. Take the back floating position with the back flat and the chin tucked well into the throat. First, the leg thrash is started using greater speed and more flexibility than is used in the front kick. The thrust of the hands (finning) is let into the stroke at regular intervals. Breathe naturally.

Turning, right and left: Begin the front stroke (dog paddle), maintaining a nearly horizontal position of the body, and execute a right turn and then a left turn. Try executing a complete turn. (Extend the hands and pull in the opposite direction of the turn.)

Change positions: In changing position or turning over from the front position to the back position, start swimming, keep the body nearly horizontal, and at the point of changing positions, roll the body either right or left to a back floating position. Keep the shoulders and head low in the water. The arms will aid in rolling the body. In changing from a back float to the front, roll in a similar manner to a front position and resume the stroke.

Jumping into water

From the side of the pool, practice jumping into waist-deep water feet-first. At first, the student may desire to hold the nose if the body is being completely submerged.

Elementary diving skill

Diving from sitting position: In diving from a sitting position, sit on the side of the pool, raise the arms forward, hold the arms tightly against the ears, and push off across the pool, keeping the feet in contact with the overflow trough as long as possible.

Standing front dive in deep water: In the standing front dive, extend the arms overhead, push off with a jump from the side of the pool simultaneously driving the head and arms downward and the legs upward, and dive to the bottom of the pool. On reaching the bottom, turn the body upward by tucking the knees under the body and push off from the bottom of the pool to reach the surface of the water.

• • •

The method just described is recommended if only limited class time per week is allotted. This is principally the universal method of teaching beginners sponsored by the American Red Cross. However, it is inadequate for school instruction. In the schools, two, three, or more periods per week per semester are allotted to swimming. For this reason, the all-stroke method has been devised as described previously in this chapter.

The success of this method lies in drilling the legs intensively daily if performing all of the kicks, spending from 2 to 5 minutes on each kick. The legs are composed of big muscles and ordinarily are awkward in learning new skills. Therefore they must be thoroughly trained. This is the overlearning principle. The arms differ since they have smaller and more highly coordinated muscles. Almost every action in everyday living involves the hands and arms; therefore, they are more skilled than the legs and do not require as much training. If the legs are then well trained and the kick patterns established, the arms will easily fit into the stroke pattern.

SKILLED STROKE TECHNIQUES
Resting backstroke

The resting backstroke (see Fig. 21-5) should be the first stroke to be taught to beginners. It requires little coordination and gives the student a sense of motivation without throwing water all over the face or sinking the head during recovery of the arms, as in the elementary backstroke. This is principally a resting stroke for an emergency or for easy swimming while resting, and it lays a sound foundation for the breaststroke and elementary backstroke, as well as for towing or treading water. It was greatly stressed by the service forces in World War II as recommended by one of us (Armbruster).* By holding the arms straight during the recovery, the swimmer eliminates the interference of a service uniform with shoulder action. Underwater breathing is eliminated and breathing is not a disturbing factor.

WHIP KICK (INVERTED FROG OR BREASTSTROKE KICK)

The kick is first thoroughly drilled at the side of the pool before the stroke is attempted.

The body is in the back floating position. The ears are submerged at all times, the chin held high, the eyes open and looking over the forehead, the chest high, and the hips level with the rest of the body.

The recovery is executed by spreading the knees but holding the heels together. Press the heels down as they recover toward the buttocks so that the knees do not lift out of the water, and at the same time lift the hips to prevent the drop. Separate the heels and cock the feet outward toward the knees. Start the drive by sweeping the legs out and together, and engage the water with the soles of the feet, extend-

*See FM-21-20 Physical training, Department of the Army Field Manual.

ing the feet as they kick. During this kick, when the knees are not quite straightened, squeeze the thighs together forcefully with the knees relaxed to give a whiplike motion to the foreleg and feet, resulting in greater propulsion.

ARM STROKE

The arm recovery starts from the sides of the thighs by turning the palms downward and slightly at an angle in the direction of recovery, the little finger side of the hand leading and knifing through the water. The arms are held perfectly straight. The arms move outward away from the thighs to a point just above the shoulders.

The pull is executed by turning the palms to the rear and slightly downward and moving the straight arms forcefully to the sides of the thighs.

At no time during either the recovery or the pull of the hands or arms should they be in or above the surface water.

WHOLE STROKE

The reason this stroke is easy to execute is that the arms and legs work in unison. The arms and legs recover at the exact moment and kick and pull at the same moment. When the stroke is closed, stretch out straight and pause until momentum from the previous stroke is spent. Repeat.

Points to remember
1. Hold the chin and chest high at all times.
2. Recover the arms and legs slowly, but kick and pull forcefully.
3. Do not drive. It is not a speed stroke.
4. To prevent water from splashing in the face, press the hands under the surface all the way on the recovery; keep the palms down and facing against the movement.
5. Do not bend the elbows on the recovery. (See Fig. 21-5.)

Elementary backstroke (or inverted breaststroke)

This stroke (see Fig. 21-6) should be taught after the resting backstroke has been mastered. This is true especially for men, since they are not as buoyant floaters as

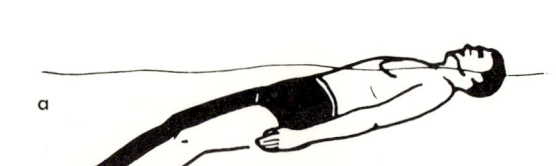

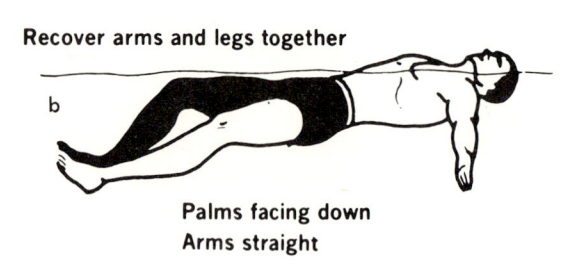

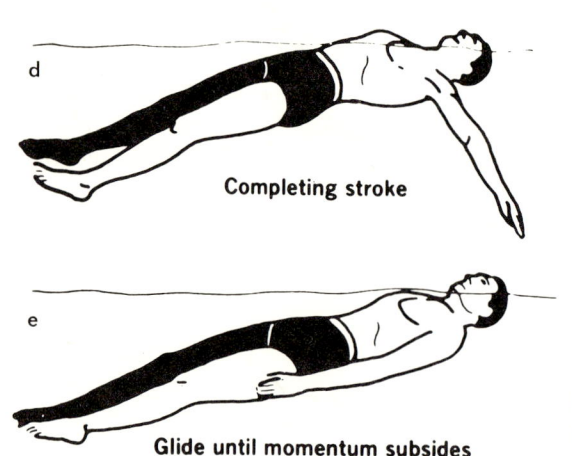

Fig. 21-5. Progressive steps in swimming the resting backstroke—the first skilled stroke to learn.

a. Starting position
b. Recover arms and legs together — Palms facing down, Arms straight
c. Kick and pull together
d. Completing stroke
e. Glide until momentum subsides

women. However, it is equally successful for women.

This style affords a little more speed than does the resting backstroke and is still restful and easy to learn. However, more coordination skill is required to execute it because the arms are partly recovered before the legs recover; that is, the arm recovery is partially staggered against the leg recovery.

Whip kick

The kick is executed exactly the same as in the resting backstroke kick.

Arm stroke

The arm recovery in the elementary backstroke differs from that in the resting backstroke. The arm recovery is executed by bending the elbows downward and sliding the hands from the sides of the thighs up along the sides of the body toward the shoulders. Then the hands, palms facing up, reach out diagonally from the armpit under the water until the arms are straight. Turn the palm facing backward and pull, straight-armed, to the sides of the thighs. Pause until the momentum from the pull subsides.

Whole stroke

In the recovery phase, hold the legs straight while the arms recover to about armpit level; then start the leg recovery at the same slow speed as the arms recover. When the arms have reached the pulling position, the legs have recovered to the kick position; that is, the knees and heels apart, feet pointed outward. Then kick and pull must start at the same instant. Stretch the body and legs straight, though relaxed, and pause in this position for the momentum to spend itself. Breathe regularly. (See Fig. 21-6.)

Points to remember
1. Recover the arms and legs slowly.
2. Recovering the hands above the water splashes and submerges the face.
3. Flexing the legs too much at the hips causes the knees to lift out of the water, submerging the body.
4. Keep the hands and arms close to the body in the recovery movement.

a — First learn to float on back

b — Starting position

c — Recover arms and legs together

d — Start of arm and leg drives

e — Completing the driving stroke

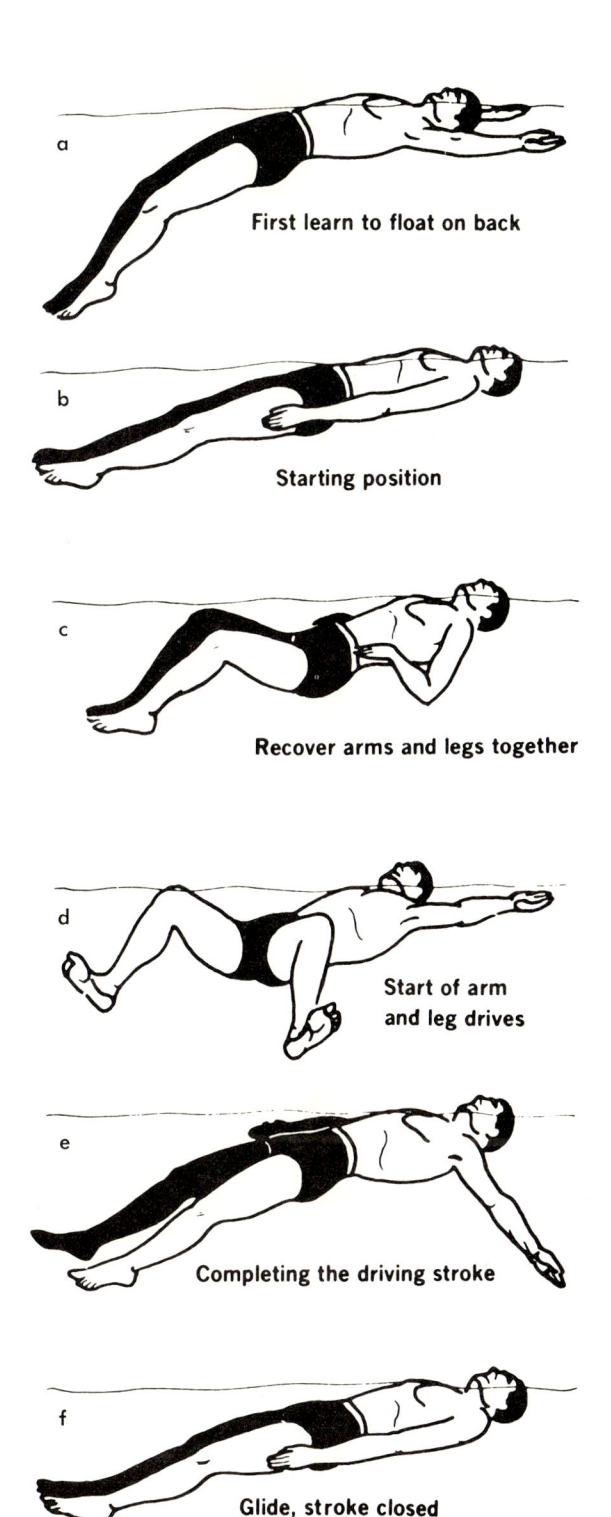

f — Glide, stroke closed

Fig. 21-6. Progressive steps in swimming the elementary backstroke.

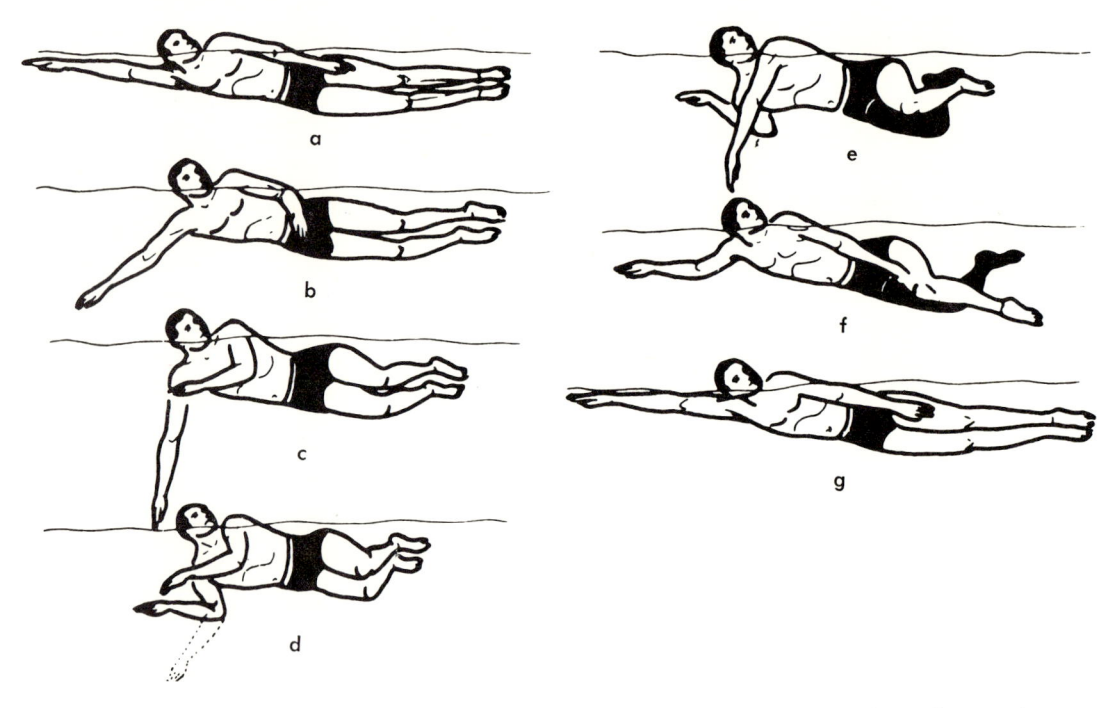

Fig. 21-7. Progressive steps in swimming the underarm sidestroke. This stroke is illustrated on the right side, which most instructors prefer. However, we prefer the left side for starting beginners.

Underarm sidestroke

The underarm sidestroke (see Fig. 21-7) is without doubt the most seaworthy and utilitarian of all swimming strokes. It is easy to learn, is easy to swim, and is preferred by most women. It is the foundation stroke for lifesaving. With this stroke, by means of towing, one can swim for two. The scissors kick can be used in treading water. Breathing is not a hazard since the nose and mouth are turned to the rear and the water passes by the side of the face. It is not one of the modern competitive strokes. The stroke is swum on the side. If one side is dominated, it should be on the left side, because the upper arm, not under arm, is the driving stroke. Also, in lifesaving the right arm is usually used for reaching and this permits the swimmer to tow easiest on the left or dominant side, holding the subject with the right hand.

The side overarm recovery and the trudgeon strokes are outgrowths of the underarm side stroke. This development came about in the early years of competition for speed.

Scissors kick

The scissors kick is so called because it resembles the blades of a house shears. The scissors kick is perhaps the most powerful of all kicks in the water. That is why it is used so much in lifesaving.

First the kick is learned on both sides by holding onto the sides of the pool. Start on the left side; then practice on the right side. The body is held straight on its side, legs straight, feet extended, and the right or upper leg on top of the left or under leg. To start the recovery movement, flex at the knees and slowly draw the heels backward. Both legs are held together and move simultaneously. This drawing of the heels backward gives just the proper amount of flexion at the hip joint. In this position, if an imaginary line were passed through the midpoint of the shoulder and hip joints, it would project out over the legs at a midpoint between the knees and ankles when the legs are in a full recovery position. The scissors now open by moving the under leg back and the top leg forward, still maintaining the fully flexed knees. The foot of the top leg cocks itself, or flexes toward the knee. The under foot remains extended. From this position the legs start the drive, sweeping outward and together by extension of the knees and the foot of the top leg. The under leg hooks the water and acts in the same manner as kicking a ball, whereas the top leg has a whip motion similar to a horse's pawing. The legs come together stretched straight and relaxed and pause long enough for momentum to be spent in the glide.

Practice 50 kicks on both sides daily for six to eight class periods to establish the neuromuscular pattern.

Points to remember
1. Hold the shoulder girdle and pelvic girdle in a vertical plane.
2. Prevent the under knee from dropping down during recovery; hold it up against the upper leg.
3. Stretch the entire body as the legs close.
4. Close the legs at the completion of the stroke and hold there momentarily during the glide; do not let them pass each other.
5. Emphasize the under leg by reaching back as the kick is started.

ARM STROKE

While the body is on its left side, with the shoulder girdle in a true vertical plane, the under left arm is extended forward directly under the head, with the palm facing down and the hand just under the surface. The upper right arm is pulling back, hugging closely along the upper front part of the body with the palm of the hand resting on the front side of the upper leg, never on the top of the leg. If held on top, the palm will sink the body easily and also waste pulling motion at the completion of its stroke.

The learner should first get a clear mental picture of the arm stroke from this starting position, that is, both arms moving simultaneously along the longitudinal plane of the body. They meet just under the head, change direction, and simultaneously extend again to their starting position. The under arm moves forward; the upper arm moves backward. The student can "singsong" to himself "everything drawn in, everything thrust out." Actually, what should take place is that as the upper arm slides forward to recover to meet the under arm, the under arm pulls diagonally downward and backward to a line under the head. Here it changes direction and starts the recovery movement with the hand and fingers pointing forward to its starting position. Even though the hands move in and out together, the under arm is always pulling on the "in" movement, while on the "out" movement the upper arm is pulling, or vice versa.

UNDERARM TECHNIQUE

The underarm must never pull beyond a line directly under the head; otherwise, its support for the head is gone. The elbow flexes back, however, and is hugged close to the under and back side of the chest as the hand starts the beginning of the recovery.

The underarm will guide the swimmer's direction and is a support to the head. When extended ahead, the under arm must be in a direct line with the body and near, but not above, the surface.

UPPER ARM TECHNIQUE

The upper arm is held closely to the front, upper part of the body with the palm of the hand resting on the front of the thigh and the arm straight. As the hand recovers, it slides away from the thigh, palm facing downward and slightly forward toward the face. The elbow bends but hugs close to the lower chest until the hand is well on its way forward to meet the under hand. There is a special skill technique for the beginner to learn at the start by facing the palm downward and forward. If a slight pressure downward is brought to bear on the hand sliding forward, well under the surface, close in front of the chest, and moving on a horizontal plane, it will support the learner's face above the surface. The elbow and upper shoulder must be submerged as much as possible to prevent the upper arm from pushing a wave toward the face, causing choking and difficulty in breathing. The hand recovers about a hand's length beyond the face and passes above and beyond the under hand, which is just releasing the water and starting on its recovery. The

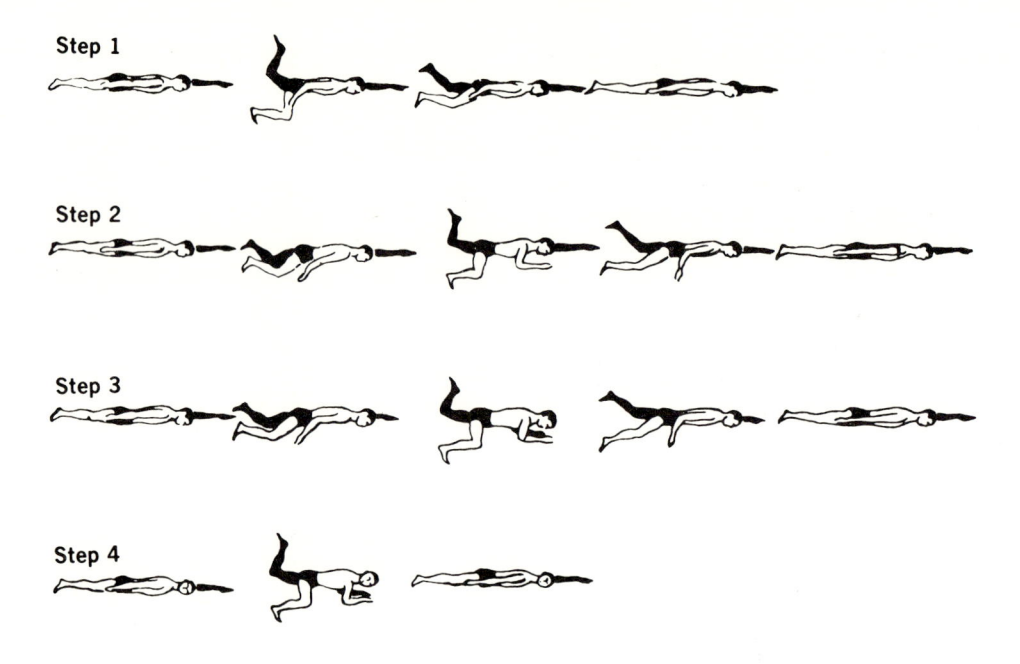

Step 1
The kick only

Step 2
The kick and upper arm; must be timed to work together

Step 3
The kick, upper arm and under arm; timed to start the stroke simultaneously and to kick simultaneously

Step 4
In steps 1, 2, and 3 the face is held underwater. Now the face is turned out and looks over top shoulder to rear.
Whole stroke

Fig. 21-8. The four steps of learning the sidestroke.

upper hand now starts its pull by pressing downward and backward to its starting position in front of the thigh. (See Figs. 21-7 and 21-8.)

The planing effect of the upper hand and the submerging of the elbow are very definitely factors in quick learning, even though they may be resisting movements to forward progress.

WHOLE STROKE—COORDINATED IN FOUR STEPS

It is recommended that each of the four steps be learned thoroughly before advancing to the next step. (See Fig. 21-8.)

Step 1—scissors kick only: Take a deep breath and lie on the left side floating position with the body straight and the left under arm extended in a line with the body. The face is turned down into the water on top of the under arm, holding the breath. The upper right arm is in front of the upper thigh. Take at least four kicks in succession and pause between each stroke for the glide. The upper hand is in front of the upper thigh and remains on it during these kick exercises. This trains the upper arm to work in unison with the kick as it must do in the whole stroke.

Step 2—the kick and upper arm: The body is still on its extended left side, with the face under as in step 1. To execute step 2, the upper hand and arm recover at the same time that the legs recover. The hand planes forward beyond the face, with the elbow and hand submerged to a point beyond the face. The arm pull starts at the same time as the kick. Here again, as in the resting backstroke, the upper arm and legs recover at the same time and the kick and pull at the same time.

Step 3—the kick, upper arm, and underarm: The body with the face under is still in the same position as in step 1. To execute step 3, press, do not pull, the underarm diagonally down and in a backward direction to a point under the face. At the same instant that the underarm starts its press, the legs and upper arm are recovered. The hands meet, cross over, and repass as the hand of the underarm recovers, and thrusts forward to guide the glide. At the same time the underarm recovers, the upper arm and legs start the kick and pull. Pause and glide. Repeat the same singsong, "everything in, everything out," as in the underarm sidestroke. Glide. This makes the arms and legs simple to coordinate into the whole stroke. Take at least four stroke repetitions before stopping for air.

Step 4—breathing: Take one or two strokes in step 3 position and then turn the face out of the water and face to the rear with the chin in line with the upper shoulder. Breathe in at the same time that the arms and legs come in; breathe out at the same time that the arms and legs go out. Remember, "everything in, everything out." Once four or five strokes are correctly timed and coordinated, the student has learned the skill of coordinating the whole stroke. Now repeat the same four-step procedure on the right side. The water level should remain constant at the face, leveling at the corner of the lower eye and lower corner of the mouth.

Note: These four-step procedures can also be performed with flotation devices, such as kickboards.

Points to remember
1. Depress the upper elbow and shoulder during the recovery movement.
2. Time the stroke so that the upper arm pulls the instant that the under hand releases press for the recovery.
3. Emphasize the reaching and stretching back of the under leg as it starts the positive kick phase.
4. Fully stretch the legs as the kick is closed.

Breaststroke (orthodox)*

The orthodox breaststroke was the first competitive stroke. In modern competitive swimming the dolphin butterfly stroke has surpassed in speed the orthodox breaststroke. This is due to the fact that the arms are simultaneously recovered above the surface. The dolphin butterfly is principally a speed stroke and is primarily used in competition. It is of little value in the beginner's program. However, the orthodox breaststroke will remain in the school aquatic program as an excellent utility stroke as well as an excellent seaworthy stroke.

KICK

There have been many modifications of the breaststroke kick in recent times. These modifications have resulted primarily from an interest in increasing the speed of the entire stroke. In competitive swimming the type of kick used is often selected to suit the body build and musculature of a particular swimmer. In general, the main characteristic of these recent modifications has been to reduce resistance by narrowing the knee spread and adding a slightly downward thrust in the propulsive phase of the kick. However, for the beginner the traditional kick is probably easiest to learn initially.

The breaststroke kick (frog) is the same as used in the inverted or the resting backstroke. The body is in the prone position, arms extended, face under. The legs are recovered by spreading the knees and are drawn down slightly. The heels remain close together and are drawn toward the buttocks just under the surface. As the knees are brought forward, however, the angle of the thighs to the upper body should be something greater than 90 degrees. In other words, the knees should not be drawn up so far as to be directly below the pelvis. (See

---

*For the breaststroke and the dolphin butterfly stroke, see Armbruster, D. A., Allen, R. H., and Billingsley, H. S.: Swimming and diving, ed. 6, St. Louis, 1973, The C. V. Mosby Co.

Fig. 21-9, *E*.) When the heels are fully drawn up to the buttocks, the feet separate outward and the ankles are cocked, or the feet flexed outward at the ankles and toward the knees. The legs are now in position to drive. The drive is made with an outward and together sweep, extending the ankles until the legs are again closed to the starting position, with the legs straight and the toes pointed. Pause with the legs fully extended until momentum from the kick is spent. During the propulsive phase of the kick the swimmer should feel as though water is being pushed backward by the soles of the feet. Also attempt to get a whiplash to the legs during the kick phase. This is accomplished by driving the thighs in toward each other before the knees have fully extended. This movement gives the powerful whiplash kick. Practice 50 kicks at the side of the pool and then use a kickboard until the movement is natural and propulsive.

Arm stroke

In the starting position, the arms are extended forward, hands close together, palms facing down. The arms spread out and pull simultaneously in a lateral downward and backward movement. First, execute a slight stretch forward and at the same time press down on the hands. During this stretching and hand press preliminary to the pull, the face is lifted to clear the mouth and to inhale. This elevating movement makes breathing easier for the learner. The hands are pulled to a point under the chin. Pulling them farther removes the support from under the shoulders and head, causing them to drop and sink, which disturbs the body balance. Here the hands join each other and are thrust forward to the starting position. At this point, pause to allow for a glide. The entire arm stroke is a continuous, uninterrupted movement. Practice walking across the pool and executing the breathing with arm action technique.

Whole breaststroke

Push off from the side of the pool with the body prone on the surface, fully extended, the face underwater. The arms go into the stretch, press, and pull while the face lifts out to clear the mouth for inhaling. The arms pull as just described to a point lateral to the shoulders, at which time the legs are recovered with the feet spread and cocked for the drive. By this time the arms are already thrusting forward. When the arms are almost fully extended, the legs start the drive. The arms pause for the glide when they have reached full extension. The legs also pause for the glide when they have closed at the end of the drive. The body is now fully extended. Exhale slowly during the glide. Repeat several strokes to time the movements smoothly and continuously from the start of the stroke to the end of the leg drive. (See Fig. 21-9.)

The breaststroke can easily be executed with the face out of the water. The glide is shorter and requires more effort.

Points to remember

1. In first attempts at coordinating the arms and legs, start recovering the arms and legs simultaneously, emphasizing a long glide before attempting the next stroke. As in learning the other strokes, singsong "everything in, everything out." When this skill is mastered, then attempt the correct timing movements as described.
2. In learning, do not pull the arms but merely press the hands and plane the palms for support by holding the forearms horizontal during the stroking.
3. Make the kick, not the arms, do the propelling.
4. Try to feel the hold of water with the sole of the feet.
5. In breathing, lift and drop the head easily. Keep the shoulders underwater while breathing.
6. Take it easy; relax and give over to the water. Easy will do it.

Crawl stroke

The crawl stroke (see Fig. 21-10) is the speed king of all strokes. It has an alternating overhand arm stroke and a constant flutter kick of the legs. Breathing occurs under and out of the water during an arm stroke cycle. Neither arms nor legs recover underwater, which accounts for its greater

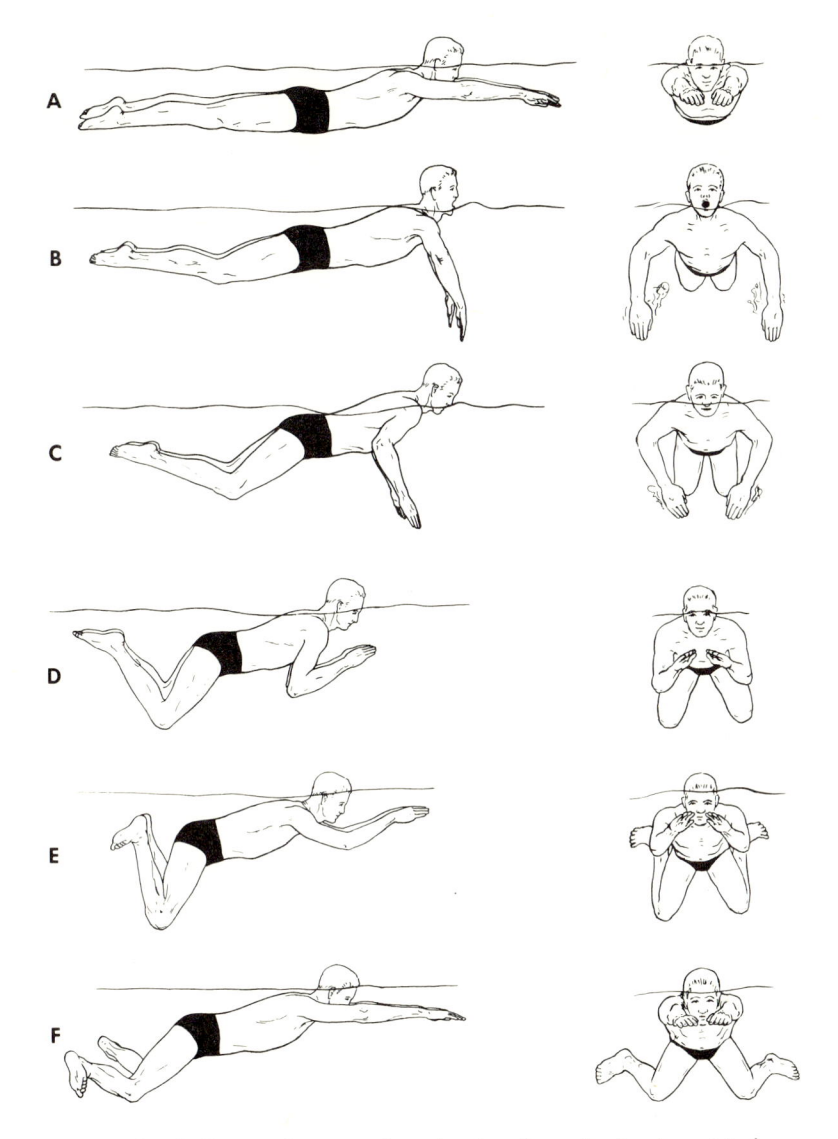

Fig. 21-9. Progressive steps in swimming the orthodox breaststroke.

speed. The modern speed crawl is truly one of the most refined and specialized skills of all sports skills. The crawl stroke was developed through the evolution of the side and trudgeon strokes.

Flutter kick

The body is lying prone, with arms and legs fully extended, face under, and ankles stretched and close together. From this position the flutter kick is executed by alternately oscillating the legs vertically from the hips, forcefully and regularly. On each downward beat the foot turns inward (pigeon-toed). This occurs naturally if the ankles and feet are held loosely. This increases the surface area of the foot. In the upward beat the foot is extended, not pigeon-toed. Beginners should first attempt this kick while learning to hold the legs straight, yet not rigid. This originates the movements from the hips. When this is learned and the thighs move up and down, the knee action can be learned. For example, let us look at the action of one leg only. It is very similar to the pedaling of a bicycle. As the leg drives up, the sole of the foot pushes upward and remains there until the knee is almost straight on the downward beat. (See action of right leg in *A* thru *D* of Fig. 21-10.) This

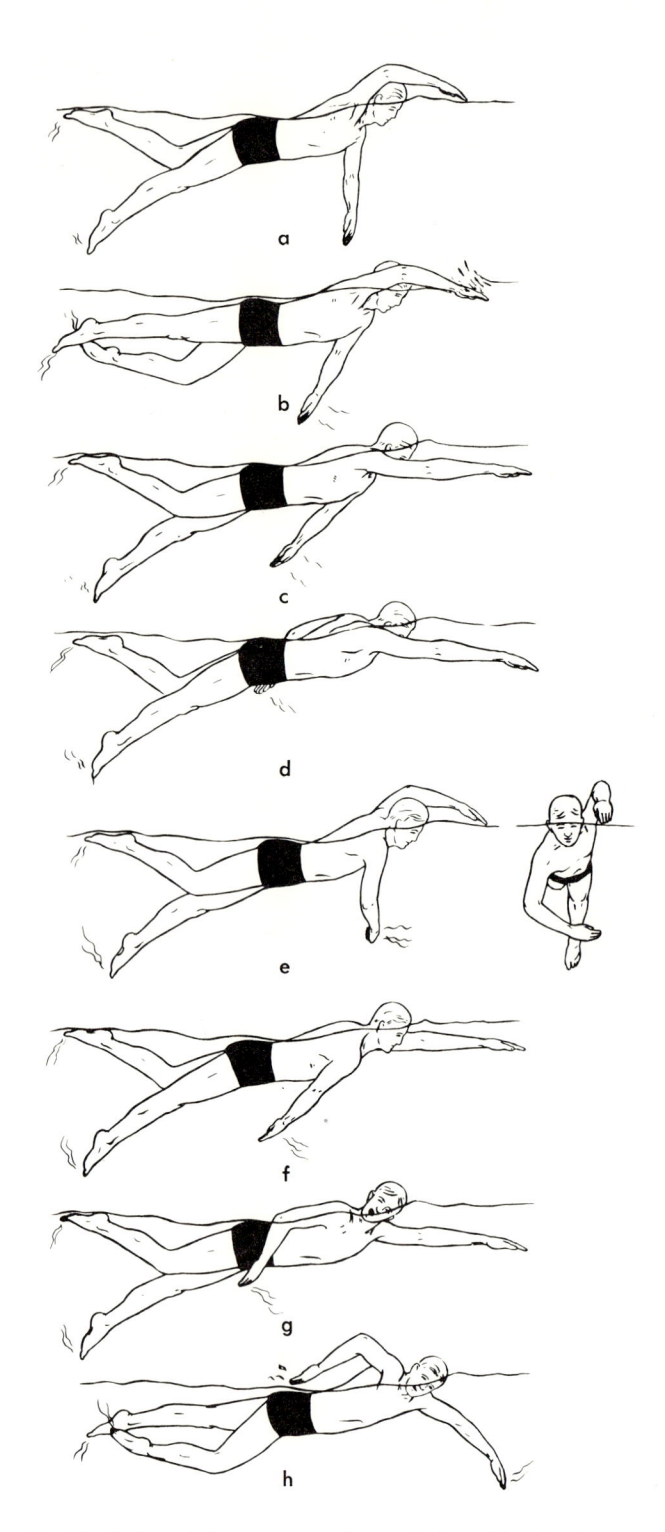

Fig. 21-10. Timing of the arms and legs with breathing in the crawl stroke.

movement results in a quick down-up whiplash of the foreleg and foot at the end of the downbeat, the same principle used in the breaststroke kick. This skill can be accomplished by daily drills with the aid of the kickboard.

ARM STROKE (ALTERNATING)

This stroke is executed by alternately reaching hand-over-hand forward into the water and pulling the body forward over the surface. The arm stroke has seven components: (1) entry, (2) support, (3) catch, (4) pull, (5) push, (6) release, and (7) recovery.

For the entry, place the hand in the water at a natural arm's length reach, directly in front of the face. The hand should enter before the elbow or shoulder. A comfortable reach should be made; never overreach. (See Fig. 21-10, examples *A* and *B*.)

In the early years of teaching the crawl stroke, one arm was staggered against the other in performing the stroke; that is, while one arm entered the water, it paused there as a supporting aid to prevent the body from sinking, while the opposite arm recovered above the surface. In modern speed swimming, as well as in teaching the crawl stroke to beginners, this method is no longer followed. Instead, an opposition rhythm type of stroke is prevalent among the topflight swimmers. The term "opposition type stroke" means that the arms are more nearly opposite to each other at all times. The "Dutch windmill," which was used in the early learning procedures of the arm crawl action, is a good example. However, if speed is wanted, the fundamental mechanics of the stroke become quite complex, and are highly technical in obtaining the ease and balance necessary for good performance as well as speed. These technical essentials can be overcome once the fundamentals of the stroke have been mastered.

The beginner should not be concerned with speed in learning but should merely be able to execute the arm stroke with reasonably good opposition timing. The learning procedure for this phase of the stroke can be practiced by walking across the swimming pool.

The catch and pull should start, first in the hand and then bending the elbow slightly for good leverage. The pull shifts into a push motion just as the arm is passing under the chest toward the opposite hip. Then the push continues the drive to the release with the forearm and hand. At this point the shoulder begins to lift in preparation to recover the arm until the hand clears the surface at the hip.

The arm is then recovered to the entry by lifting the shoulder, bending at the elbow, and turning the hand so that the palm faces to the rear and gradually faces the water at entry. The arm recovery movement is up and outward, away from the hip, and forward to the water. The shoulder is held high while the hand and forearm enter the water. (See Fig. 21-10.)

WHOLE STROKE*

While the arms execute a complete revolution, the legs complete six evenly measured beats. In walking, the arms and legs move in a 1:1 ratio, an opposite arm and leg counterbalancing movement. In swimming the crawl, the leg-to-arm ratio is 3:1. The legs perform three beats to each arm stroke, or six beats to each complete cycle of both arms. This ratio gives the stroke a true counterbalancing movement, like that in walking or running. (See Fig. 21-10.)

BREATHING

Breathing in the crawl stroke is executed in the following manner: just as the arm opposite the breathing side is set into the water for support, the head is turned to inhale and then immediately recovered. When turning the mouth for air, keep the chin in close to the throat and spot with open eyes near the surface where the mouth is opening to determine if the mouth is inside the trough of the bow wave formed by the head. Take a quick breath as the mouth is opening; do not pause after opening the mouth. Curl the lips out away from the teeth when

---

*For a critical analysis of the crawl stroke, see Armbruster, D. A., Allen, R. H., and Billingsley, H. S.: Swimming and diving, ed. 6, St. Louis, 1973, The C. V. Mosby Co.

opening the mouth. (See Fig. 21-10, examples *G* and *H*.)

Back crawl stroke

The back crawl stroke (see Fig. 21-11) is the crawl stroke inverted. However, it is much easier to learn than the crawl for two main reasons: (1) the face is not under the water during the stroke, so that breathing is simplified, and (2) the arms are always opposite each other; that is, one arm is not staggered against the other. When the arms enter, there is only a slight supporting phase other than the natural press of the hand and arm.

INVERTED FLUTTER KICK

Essentially the kick is the same as the flutter kick in the crawl stroke. The body is extended on its back, legs held closely together, ankles and toes pointed, chin low on the throat, water level at the lower ear lobes. The legs move alternately up and down with action originating from the hips. On the upward beat the toes turn in, and on the downward beat they are extended. At the end of the upward beat the kneecap should not break through the surface and the foot should throw some water above the surface without projecting out of the water. To accomplish this skill, the thigh, as in other styles of kicks, forcefully drives down just before the knee has straightened. This action gives the foreleg and foot an effective propulsive up-down whip. The ratio of leg kicks to one complete stroke revolution is 6:1, the same as in the crawl stroke.

ARM STROKE

The arms move in opposition to one another as if the swimmer has a broomstick across the back of the neck and shoulders with the arms extending out along the broomstick.

The moment the arm has finished its pull along the side of the thigh, the hand gives a final downward press as the shoulder is lifted out of the water and the hand is turned to face outward. The arm is bent slightly at the elbow at the beginning of the recovery phase, but it is straightened for the entry. The arm recovers to the entry with an outward swing away from the body and continues to the entry at a point not more than 6 inches outside the shoulder line. The hand and forearm should not be slowed as they near the point of entry, but should accelerate so that they are in the water before the shoulder can sink under.

The power or pull phase of the stroke can be done with either a bent arm or a straight arm. The bent arm stroke is used by almost all high level competitive swimmers but is more difficult to learn than the straight arm pull, which is generally recommended when learning the backstroke. In the initial part of the straight arm pull, the arm is shallow, about 2 to 6 inches underwater. As the arm reaches a point directly out from the shoulder the depth should be about 6 to 10 inches. From here, the arm continues until it reaches the leg and begins the recovery phase. (See Fig. 21-11.) The bent arm pull is initiated slightly deeper than the straight arm pull. As the pull progresses, the arm is drawn in toward the body by bending at the elbow. Just prior to when the hand reaches a point directly out from the shoulder the pulling action turns into a pushing action. The arm and hand continue and finish near the leg as in the straight arm pull to begin the recovery phase. In both types of pulls the arm stroke should be smooth and relaxed throughout.

BREATHING

Breathing should be continuous; inhale through the nose and exhale through the mouth. Hold the head with the chin always lined up on dead center, never moving from side to side. Try to retain a stretched body. This prevents sagging down at the hips. (See Fig. 21-11.)

Dolphin butterfly stroke

The dolphin butterfly stroke was created by Armbruster at the University of Iowa in 1935 with the aid of one of his swimmers, Jack Sieg. The author immediately named it the dolphin butterfly stroke.* The legs in

---

*Armbruster, D. A., and Sieg, J.: The dolphin breast stroke, Journal of Health and Physical Education **6:**23, April, 1935.

Fig. 21-11. Progressive steps in swimming the back crawl stroke showing the six leg beats and one revolution of the arm stroke cycle.

this stroke move in unison in an up-and-down wavelike action that resembles the tail of a dolphin in swimming. The arms also move in unison in both the propulsive and recovery phases. The arms recover low above the surface, are held straight, and resemble the wings of a butterfly in flight.

The new stroke is definitely dominated by the kick. This dolphin wavelike kick by the legs only has become the fastest means of human movement through water. It is even faster than the alternating flutter kick used in the crawl and back crawl strokes; yet, the basic characteristics of the dolphin kick are the same as those of the alternating flutter crawl kicks.

This new kick has now replaced the old double overarm butterfly stroke with the orthodox breaststroke kick. In the dolphin kick there is no underwater recovery phase as there was in the previous butterfly breaststroke. With the elimination of the resistance factor of the recovery phase, this kick has gained tremendous and amazing speed. In speed, the dolphin butterfly stroke is now ranked second only to the crawl stroke.

The dolphin butterfly stroke is very exhausting to the untrained individual. It has little, if any, value to the human being in water. It is exclusively a speed stroke and is used as such in competitive racing. However, the stroke is included in this edition because many students have a great desire to learn it, if for no other reasons than for its rugged, challenging action and for a self-satisfied feeling of being able to perform it. When the stroke is mastered and used correctly, it gives the swimmer a feeling of well-being, because of its rhythmic ease of performance.

KICK

It is essential that before learning the dolphin kick, the beginner thoroughly master the flutter kick of the crawl stroke since the basic characteristics of the two are the same. When the flutter kick is learned and performed with ease, the student is well conditioned to attempt the dolphin kick. In daily training class drills the practice of this kick works in well with the other stroke kicks in the all-stroke practice method.

As practice sessions progress, the student should be trained to lie facedown on the surface of the water, kicking only, with the hands finning at the sides of the hips. As a final step of conditioning and training, and before the whole stroke is attempted, the student should submerge and practice the kick underwater during breath-holding intervals. The hands should be finning at the sides of the hips, rather than extending in front of the head. By practicing the kick underwater, the student is able to determine if the progress is true forward and not down or up. If either occurs, adjustment should be made to equalize the up-and-down beat in relation to the forward plane of progress. It is also essential while performing underwater to stress relaxing the entire spine from the shoulders down through all the joints to the end of the toes. When the true shortened up-and-down beat of the kick, as well as the up-and-down action of the hips, has been mastered, the student has been properly trained and conditioned for learning the arm action.

ARM STROKE

The student should first practice the arm stroke by walking across the swimming pool, bent over at the hips, water level at the chin, stroking with the arms. The stroke can also be practiced while in a bent-over, stationary position.

The arms start the stroke from the point of entry, just outside the shoulders, pressing downward into a short lateral spread. The hands and forearms continue the pull backward with a quick inward action, elbows bending, until they reach a point just under and ahead of the shoulders. From this point the power drive is completed backward to the sides of the hips until the arms and hands have cleared the surface of the water. This final kick is delivered by straightening the elbows until shoulders, arms, and hands have cleared the surface of the water. From this final kick action the arms also derive the impetus to swing laterally forward through the recovery phase to again reach the correct point of entry. During the recovery the arms are held straight, palms facing the surface. The recovery should be executed

SWIMMING 273

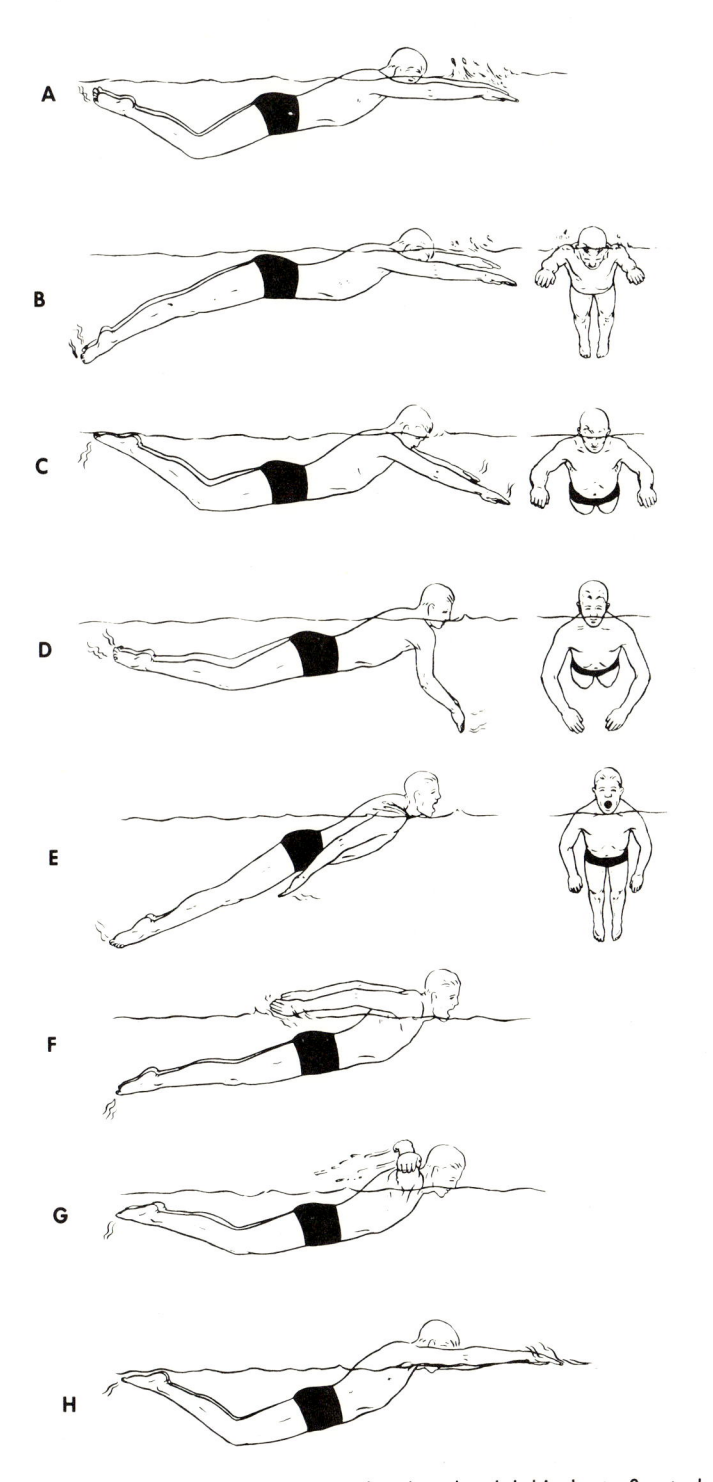

Fig. 21-12. Progressive steps in swimming the dolphin butterfly stroke.

without hesitation at the end of the power drive. The arms should enter the water with a soft plunge, the wrists slightly flexed down toward the surface as they enter. Actually, the hands and forearms should enter the water slightly ahead of the upper arms and shoulders. At this point, without hesitation, the catch of the next stroke is started.

When walking or swimming across the pool practicing the arm stroke, the student should imagine the body moving toward the face of a large clock; the left arm should enter the water pointing to 11 o'clock, while the right arm should point to 1 o'clock.

There is no pause in the entire stroke turnover. It is what is known in swimming terms as a fast turnover type of stroke; that is, the moment the arms complete the power drive, they go into the recovery to start the next stroke. Not only must the arms recover quickly, but the power drive of the arms must also be rapidly executed. It is this fast turnover cadence that makes the stroke so strenuous for the beginner, especially if the beginner is poorly conditioned. However, most students who already swim other skilled strokes well have an inherent urge to learn the challenging complex skills involved in performing this rugged stroke.

Whole stroke

The stroke is started by throwing the arms forward laterally to the point of entry. The hands enter the water just outside the shoulders simultaneously, pointing to the 11 and 1 o'clock positions, respectively. As the hands execute the catch, with a slight spread and downward press, the first downward beat of the kick takes place. (See Fig. 21-12, examples *A* and *B*.) This downbeat of the kick is a natural counteraction caused from the powerful downward catch and pull of the forearms, similar to the counterswing of the arms and legs in walking or running. While the hands and arms execute the inward drive or pull to a point just ahead of and under the shoulders the first upbeat of the kick has taken place. (See Fig. 21-12, examples *C* and *D*.) From this point the arms continue to complete the final power drive as the second downbeat of the kick takes place. (See Fig. 21-12, examples *D* and *E*.) This action is again a natural counter-balancing movement of legs and arms. As the arms drive out of the water at the hips and move into the recovery phase, the legs execute the second upbeat. (See Fig. 21-12, examples *F* to *H*.) Note that during the entire arm recovery phase there is but one beat of the legs, which is up, and none supporting the body. For this reason it is essential for the swimmer to move the arms quickly from the end of the drive to the entry. This quickened movement will prevent the body from sinking below swimming level. The most troublesome part of learning the whole stroke occurs during this latter phase. If the arms move too slowly or hesitate at any point between the final drive and the entry, rhythm and timing are lost.

In executing the entry, the arms plunge lightly into the water and immediately go into the catch to start the next stroke. The stroke should first be practiced without breathing until reasonably satisfactory timing is attained. Then too, in learning, beginners often make the mistake of starting the recovery of the arms prematurely before the arms and hands have cleared the surface of the water well back of the hips, and straightened elbows. (See Fig. 21-12, examples *E* and *F*.)

Breathing

Correct breathing in the dolphin butterfly stroke is not too difficult, providing the beginner does not develop a tendency to climb too high to get a breath. In learning this skill, the student should again walk the arm stroke across the swimming pool with the face submerged while executing the breathing and correct timing action of the head in the arm stroke cadence. Taking a breath every stroke should be practiced. Correct breathing habits in this stroke are essential in order to obtain ease of performance of the entire stroke.

In taking air, the beginner should lift the head just far enough for the mouth to clear the surface of the water. This action takes place just as the arms have passed backward from under the shoulders and are completing their drive. Air is actually taken just as the arms are clearing the water and are moving into the recovery phase. (See Fig. 21-12, examples *D* to *F.*) Note how the finishing "kick" of the arm stroke gives the head the necessary lift to inhale. Emphasis is placed on dropping the head quickly into the water (but not too deeply) after air has been taken and before the arm recovery has reached the point of entry. (See Fig. 21-12, examples *G* and *H.*) It should now be easy for the beginner to visualize why it is essential to recover quickly both the head and arms to again give support to the body during this phase of the stroke. Both the head and arms are well above the surface of the water with the kick also executes its second upward beat. If this phase of the stroke is not well timed and executed, the beginner will have a tendency to sink too deep in the water and then have to climb too high to get air. With continued practice, proficiency is acquired, and error is minimized and smoothed to a high degree of greater efficiency.

Points to remember
1. Minimize the up-and-down action of the hips by reducing the range of the legs.
2. Relax the neck and entire spine. Be firm but not tense.
3. Do not stress lifting of the hips in the kick.
4. Avoid lowering the head too deep in the water after air is taken.
5. Use the entire leg to execute the kick, and avoid excessive knee bending.

The teaching and learning procedures have already been stressed throughout this discussion of the stroke. The instructor and student should have no difficulty from the previous discussion in following a teaching and learning progression plan. The dolphin butterfly stroke lends itself well to the category of the other skilled swimming strokes and should be included in the all-stroke method of teaching.*

TESTS

At the end of a semester or quarter, a test can be given over all the strokes and skill items taught. Four students can swim across the pool and be tested by the instructor at the same time regarding form, timing of stroke, and ease of performance. Speed is not essential. The instructor can rate them rapidly as they swim across the pool with each style of stroke. The students stop at the end of each length while the instructor scores and then start again at the signal. The instructor scores in the following manner:

4 = excellent
3 = good
2 = fair
1 = poor, such as doggy paddling or struggling
0 = student knows nothing about stroke

---

*For further advanced techniques of the dolphin butterfly stroke, see Armbruster, D. A., Allen, R. H., and Billingsley, H. S.: Swimming and diving, ed. 6, St. Louis, 1973, The C. V. Mosby Co.

Rating chart for beginning swimmers' performance test

Name	Dive from pool deck	Crawl stroke	Back crawl	Breast-stroke	Resting backstroke	Right side-stroke	Left side-stroke	Treading	Surface dive	Sculling	Finning	Total score	% improvement
John Doe	2	2	3	1	4	3	4	2	2	1	2	26	
Bill Rowe	1	2	1	0	2	1	3	1	2	2	0	15	
Robert Smith	1	2	1	1	3	0	2	0	1	1	0	12	
Charles Brown	2	3	2	3	4	3	3	3	2	3	4	32	
Henry Jones	4	4	3	1	3	1	4	4	4	3	3	34	
Peter Black	3	3	4	3	4	4	0	3	3	2	3	32	

Testing should be held to a minimum. Too much testing is a waste of teaching time and is not good pedagogy.

In addition to the stroke technique test just mentioned, distance with any or all strokes can be added, such as 50 or 100 yards, and/or remaining afloat for 5, 10, 15, or 20 minutes. Other testing items can be added, such as treading water for 30 seconds, diving from a springboard, and using a surface dive to retrieve an object in deep water. Another possibility is to test the efficiency of some strokes such as the resting backstroke, the elementary backstroke, and the breaststroke by counting the number of strokes required to go to a specified distance.

In a class of thirty or forty students, this test gives a very good scattergram as to what the students individually have accomplished. This can be posted for them to study. With a class of forty, this test can be conducted in a half-hour period at the end of the term.

This test is also given at the beginning of an advanced course and again at the end of the course. The instructor, as well as the students, can determine at the beginning of the course where the greatest weakness of the class lies; that is, in what stroke area instruction is most needed. The instructor can then plan the course and work on the weaknesses of the class. Students can study their own weaknesses and good points.

TEACHING AND LEARNING PROCEDURES FOR BEGINNERS

Lecture

The instructor should lecture on pool sanitation, personal health, and hygiene.

Objectives

1. Orientation and adjustment to water in order to overcome loss of body weight, loss of balance, and loss of body heat, all of which disturb the beginner psychologically, physiologically, and physically.
   (a) Submerging the face, opening the eyes, and holding the breath
   (b) Shipping water with the mouth
   (c) Breathing with bobbing exercises
   (d) Floating, tucked and body straight on both the face and back
   (e) Safety methods
2. Adjustment of the hands and feet to paddling in shallow water
   (a) Sculling with and without the feet
   (b) Finning with and without the feet
   (c) Treading water with and without the feet
3. Unskilled strokes on the face, sides, and back
   (a) Human stroke, windmill fashion, breaststroke fashion
4. Skilled strokes (basic strokes)
   (a) Kicks
      (1) Flutter
      (2) Scissors (both sides)
      (3) Frog
   (b) Arm strokes (basic strokes)
      (1) Alternating stroke with breathing
      (2) Sidestroke with breathing
      (3) Breaststroke
      (4) Resting inverted breaststroke
5. Synchronizing or timing of arms and legs in all strokes
   (a) Part-whole method; that is, breaking down each stroke from the whole into its component parts and by progressive stages building it again into the whole stroke
6. Orientation in distance swimming
   (a) This is neuromuscular memory learning.
   (b) The student should now take as many strokes in succession with breathing as is comfortably possible.
   (c) At this stage of learning one must breathe to swim.
   (d) Daily improve prolonged swimming time and distance without stopping.
   (e) At this stage the instructor assists the student to refine timing movements and relaxation.
   (f) The objective is to have the student swim all strokes 20 yards and then swim ¼ mile, changing strokes as often as desired.

Distance orientation is now the most important, interesting, and exciting phase of

learning for the student. In this stage, the longest remembered lessons in watermanship are learned.
1. A sensory feel of distance over water, which is too often misjudged by the inexperienced, is gained.
2. Once the student swims continuously from 100 to 150 yards, he or she can go on almost indefinitely.
3. The most natural stroke is learned by the swimmer, and is the one most often reverted to.
4. Relaxation is learned as distance is increased.
5. Breathing becomes natural and rhythmic.
6. The student also breathes more easily and more naturally.
7. Water strength and a confident feeling of seaworthiness are developed as the student becomes adequate and safe in water.
8. The student is now prepared, ready, and basically grounded for any branch of advanced aquatics.

INTERMEDIATE SWIMMING
Prerequisite

Instruction in intermediate swimming is given to those who have taken and passed the beginner's course; those who have never had instruction but can pass the beginner's test, although they have no knowledge of stroke technique; or those who can swim in deep water.

Reading assignments

The instructor may choose reading assignments from the references at the end of the chapter.

Aims
1. To teach the fundamental techniques of the following strokes so that the students may be able to determine which stroke is easiest and most practical for their own use and enjoyment:
   (a) Modern crawl
   (b) Modern back crawl
   (c) Breaststroke
   (d) Sidestroke, both left and right sides
   (e) Resting backstroke (safety)
2. To serve as a prerequisite course to advanced swimming and lifesaving
3. To give the student practical demonstrations and knowledge of skills as to safety and utility uses and their application for each of the strokes learned

Objectives
1. To teach skill techniques in all the strokes
2. To develop some skill in diving
3. To develop for each student the ability to perform one stroke and one dive in good form, as well as the ability to perform all other strokes in passable form
4. To teach relaxation
5. To teach self-safety in the water
6. To enable the student to keep afloat for 15 to 30 minutes
7. To teach the miscellaneous skills such as surface diving, sculling, finning, and treading

Teaching progression
First week
1. Lecture on pool sanitation and personal health and hygiene.

Second week

2. Test students' knowledge of skills of all strokes in water, review strokes, and review techniques of proper breathing.

Third to eighth weeks

3. Explain, demonstrate, and drill on the techniques and timing of the leg action in all the stroke kicks.

Ninth and tenth weeks

4. Coordinate and time the technique of the arm action with the leg action and breathing action. Review the technique of diving.

Eleventh to sixteenth weeks

5. Provide orientation in distance swimming, emphasizing relaxation and natural breathing.
6. Practice fundamental dives from the springboard.
7. Teach safety factors for self and others, such as tired swimmer's stroke, a sim-

ple rescue, simple carries in towing, and performing resuscitation.
8. Have students swim distances stressing ease in breathing, relaxation, and the distribution of effort over distance comfortably.

Achievement test and proficiency tests

1. Swim each stroke 20 yards in good form and with proper timing.
2. Execute one dive in good form from the springboard.
3. Tread water for 3 minutes.
4. Retrieve an object in 10 feet of water.
5. Be able to swim any stroke or alternating strokes ¼ mile in 10 minutes or less.

Grades

Grades are based upon the achievement test, as well as the ability to keep afloat in water for 15 minutes or to swim ¼ mile. The written examination is based upon knowledge and use of skills and safety factors in water.

ADVANCED SWIMMING
Prerequisite

Instruction in advanced swimming is given to those who have passed the intermediate course or have achieved the ability to swim ¼ mile and have demonstrated all of the standard strokes.

Reading assignments

The instructor may choose reading assignments from the references at the end of the chapter.

Aims

1. To teach proficiency in all-around watermanship
2. To teach safety factors pertaining to watermanship

Objectives

1. To time the strokes perfectly so that ease of performance with added power and speed is developed thereby gaining confidence
2. To swim each stroke 100 yards with correct timing
3. To be able to swim 60 feet on each side, holding the upper arm out of the water fully extended
4. To be able to swim 60 feet on the back, holding both hands out of the water
5. To swim ¼ mile in 8 minutes or less
6. To accomplish a good racing start and good technique in turning at the end of the pool
7. To accomplish at least three dives from the springboard in good form
8. To learn safety factors in boat craft
9. To swim safely for 20 minutes
10. To learn how to wade properly in water of unknown depth
11. To learn how to swim out of a swift current
12. To learn how to assist another person temporarily in distress in deep water
13. To learn how to swim for two people
14. To swim under water for a distance of 60 feet
15. To learn how to conserve strength
16. To learn how to rest while tired in deep water
17. To learn boatmanship
    (a) Paddling and rowing
    (b) What to do when capsized
    (c) How to land safely when capsized
18. To be able to teach others how to swim
19. To learn how and when to make a safe rescue
20. To be able to demonstrate proper resuscitation

Achievement test

1. A performance test in strokes and different skill items is given at the beginning of the course, emphasizing good form and timing of all the moving parts.
2. The performance test is repeated after a review of stroke techniques and skills.
3. Tests are given over items listed in the aims of the course.
4. The students are tested for time in the ¼-mile swim and graded on a graduated sliding scale, from 8 to 12 minutes

for men and from 10 to 15 minutes for women. For children, eliminate the time element but substitute remaining afloat from 15 to 20 minutes.

Proficiency test

1. Be able to swim ¼ mile in 8 minutes or less.
2. Be able to score a grade of 90 or better in the American Red Cross lifesaving test.

Grades

Grades are based upon achievement tests and the various items that include both oral and written tests.

REFERENCES

Armbruster, D. A., Allen, R. H., and Billingsley, H. S.: Swimming and diving, ed. 6, St. Louis, 1973, The C. V. Mosby Co.

Beach and Pool (a monthly swimming magazine), Baltimore, Hoffman-Harris, Inc.

Cureton, T. K.: How to teach swimming and diving, New York, 1934, Association Press.

Intercollegiate and interscholastic swimming guide, official rules of swimming and diving (published annually), New York, The National Intercollegiate Athletic Bureau.

Keifer, Adolph, Gabrielsen, M. A., and Gabrielsen, B. W.: Learning to swim (twelve easy lessons), New York, 1951, Prentice-Hall, Inc.

Official N.C.A.A. swimming guide (issued annually), New York, The National Collegiate Athletic Association.

Official N.S.W.A. aquatic guide, Washington, D. C. (latest edition), American Association for Health, Physical Education, and Recreation.

FILMS

Oars and paddles, American Red Cross.

Heads up, American Red Cross.

Swimming—elementary, advanced and fundamentals of diving (directed by Fred Cady), Division of Audiovisual Education, Los Angeles County Schools, Los Angeles, Calif.

Learn to swim (Olympic champions at Silver Springs), Castle Films, New York, N. Y.

Swimming: the front crawl, Bell & Howell, Chicago, Ill.

Swim and live, photographed by Army Air Forces at Miami Beach, Fla.

The dolphin butterfly stroke, underwater, D. A. Armbruster, University of Iowa Extension Division, Iowa City, Iowa.

22 Table tennis

HISTORY

Table tennis is a relatively new sport. The exact date of its origin is not definitely known; however, it is generally agreed that table tennis started in about 1890 as a game called ping-pong. It had a brief popular following throughout America and then subsided as a sport.

In 1921 it was revived to the extent that a place was provided for a table in the recreation area of almost every home.

In 1926 the International Table Tennis Federation was established in Berlin, and in 1933 the United States Table Tennis Association* was established.

The game is popular the world over and is a major sport in England, Hungary, and Czechoslovakia. It is becoming more and more popular in America and is being more scientifically studied and played. It has been estimated that about one in every six Americans plays the game.

SOCIAL VALUES

Table tennis is one of the best of the home recreation room games for the entire family. One of the reasons for its popularity is that persons of any age and any sex can play the game the year round. It can be played both indoors and outdoors. It is popular at the "rec" and community center. Table tennis causes no destructive damage in the home because a small paddle and "light as a feather" type of ball are used.

There is no difficulty in finding a partner to play a game. It provides fun and exhilarating exercise for everyone. This game is a natural for rehabilitation physical education programs.

EQUIPMENT

Any type of clothing and shoes allowing freedom of movement and comfort is acceptable.

The paddle

A wooden, rubber-faced paddle is most satisfactory. If paddles are homemade, they can be faced with sandpaper.

The size, weight, and shape of the paddle are immaterial, but it must be nonreflecting or of a light color. The handle can be covered with leather.

The ball

The ball is small, celluloid, spherical, white in color, and restricted by rule as to

---

*Table tennis for you, Philadelphia, 1946, United States Table Tennis Association.

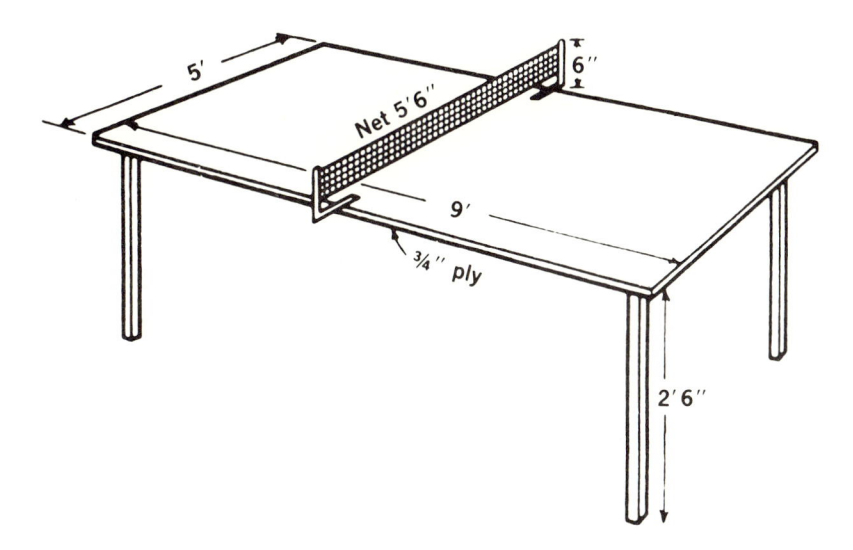

Fig. 22-1. Table and net for table tennis.

size and weight. It is fragile but very hard to break unless stepped upon when left on the floor. When purchasing a ball, be sure to rely upon the U.S.T.T.A. approved standardization ball that has a uniform bounce. If it is dropped from a height of 12 inches upon a ¾-inch plywood table, it should bounce 8 to 9 inches.

The table

If the table is homemade, it should be constructed of ¾ inch-thick, fine plywood. The playing surface should be dark (usually green) and nonreflecting. The sidelines and end lines are white and should be ½ to ¾ inch wide. The center line is also white, but only ⅛ to ¼ inch wide. (See Fig. 22-1.)

The net

The net is light in texture. It is stretched across the center of the table and attached to the outside by vertical standards. The net should be from 6 to 6¾ inches above the table.

RULES* (ABRIDGED)
Singles

A game is won by the player who first scores 21 points, unless both players have scored 20 points, in which case the one who

---
*The laws of table tennis, New York (latest edition), United States Table Tennis Association.

first scores 2 points more than the opponent is the winner.

The choice of playing position at the table and order of service are determined by the toss of a coin. If the winner of the toss prefers to have first choice of playing positions, the opponent then has the choice of whether to serve first or receive service, and vice versa.

The change of ends (position) and service shall take place after 5 points have been scored. The receiver then becomes the server and the server becomes receiver and so on after each 5 points until the end of the game or the score 20-all. At the score 20-all, the receiver becomes the server and the server the receiver and so on after each point until the end of the game.

In the start of a new game, the player who served first in the previous game becomes receiver and the receiver becomes server and so on, alternating after each game.

The players also exchange ends after each game, and, if play consists of more than one game, in the deciding game of the match the players change ends at the score of 10.

Service

A good service is delivered by releasing the ball by hand only without imparting a spin. The ball is then struck so that it touches the server's court first and then, passing directly over or around the net, touches the receiver's court. At the moment of impact of the paddle on the ball in service, both handle and ball must be behind the end line of the server's court and between an imaginary continuation of the sidelines.

A good return of a served ball must be struck by the receiver on first bounce so that it passes directly over the net or around the net and touches directly on the opponent's court. However, if a ball that has been served or returned in play returns with its own impetus over the net or around the net, it may be struck, while still in play, by the player so that it directly touches the opponent's court.

Law 11—points

Either player may lose a point due to the following circumstances:
1. If failing to make a good service except as provided for in Law 12
2. If failing to make a good return of a good service or a good return made by the opponent, except as provided for the Law 12
3. If the player, the racket, or anything that the player wears or carries touches the net or its supports while the ball is in play
4. If the player, the racket, or any wearing apparel moves the playing surface while the ball is in play

Law 12—let

A let ball is called in the following cases:
1. If the served ball, in passing over the net, touches it or its supports, provided that the service would otherwise have been good or volleyed by the receiver
2. If a service is delivered when the receiver is not ready, provided always that the receiver may not be deemed unready if an attempt to strike at the ball is made
3. If either player is prevented by an accident not under his or her control from serving a good service or making a good return
4. If either player loses the point, as provided in Law 11 (3, 4, 5) or Law 13, owing to an accident not within his or her control

Law 13—points

Either player loses the point in the following cases:
1. If, before the ball in play has passed over the end lines or sidelines, not yet having touched the playing surface or the player's side of the table after being struck by the opponent, it comes in contact with the player or anything the player wears or carries
2. If at any time the player volleys the ball, except as provided in Law 12 (1)

Scoring

A point is scored by the side that makes the last successful return prior to the end of a rally. In an unsuccessful return the ball is missed, hit off the table, sent into the net, or hit onto the player's own half of the court on the return. Failure to make a good serve also scores a point against the server unless it is a let as in Law 12.

In play

The ball is in play from the moment it is projected or dropped from the hand in service until one of the following has occurred:
1. It has touched one court twice consecutively.
2. It has, except in service, touched each court alternately without having been struck by the racket intermediately.
3. It has been struck by either player more than once consecutively.
4. It has touched either player or anything that the player wears or carries, except the racket or the racket hand below the wrist.
5. It has touched any object other than the net and supports.

Doubles

Law 19—good service

The service should be delivered as previously described and should touch first the right half of the server's court or the center line on the server's side of the net, and then, passing directly over or around the net, touch the right half of the receiver's court or the center line on the receiver's side of the net.

LAW 20—CHOICE OF ORDER OF PLAY

The pair who have the right to serve the first five services in any game decide which partner shall serve, and the opposing pair decide similarly which will first be the receiver.

LAW 21—ORDER OF SERVICE

The first five services must be delivered by the selected partner of the pair who have the right to do so and must be received by the selected partner of the opposing pair. The second five services must be delivered by the receiver of the first five services and received by the partner of the server of the first five services. The third five services must be delivered by the partner of the server of the first five services and received by the partner of the receiver of the first five services. The fourth five services must be delivered by the partner of the receiver of the first five services and received by the server of the first five services. The fifth five services must be delivered as the first five services, and so on, in sequence until the end of the game or the score 20-all, at which point each player serves only one service in turn until the end of the game.

In a one-game match or in the deciding game of a match of more than one game, the pair that served the first five services have the right to alter their order of receiving or that of their opponents at the score of 10.

BASIC SKILL TECHNIQUES

Table tennis is a game similar to lawn tennis. However, it is played on a wooden table with a light celluloid ball that is struck with a wooden paddle or racket over a net attached to the table.

The grips

FOREHAND GRIP

In the forehand grip the short handle of the racket is gripped very close to the blade, with the blade itself partially held in the hand and the forefinger and thumb bracing opposite sides of the blade. The index finger is used behind the blade for support. (See Fig. 22-2.)

BACKHAND GRIP

The backhand grip is the same as for the forehand, except that the thumb is used on the left side or in back of the blade.

The forehand and backhand grips are very similar to the tennis grips. It is recommended that the beginner learn these grips.

The penholder is a holdover from ping-pong and is no longer recommended for good sound table tennis play. (See Fig. 22-2.)

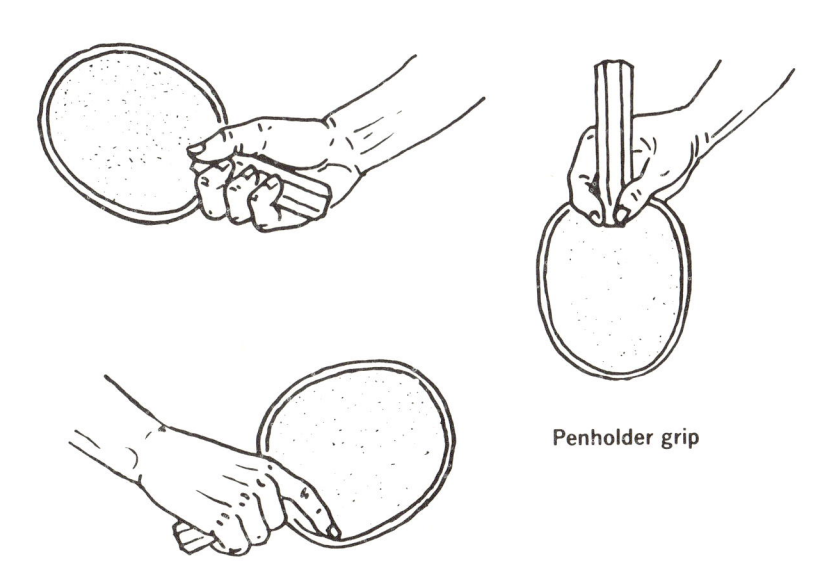

Fig. 22-2. Forehand and backhand grips for table tennis.

Points to remember

1. Do not grip the racket too tightly; relax.
2. Hold the wrist firm.
3. Face somewhat to the side in forehand and backhand shots as in tennis.
4. Constantly check the racket head, making sure that it is not dropped.
5. Regularly check the thumb and index finger in order to keep them in the proper place.

Serving

For an ordinary forehand serve, the ball is put in play either by a toss into the air or by dropping the hand away from under the ball. As soon as the ball is released, it is met by the racket, which is swung in the same manner as in a forehand drive.

For a forehand side-spin serve, the racket is brought across the ball from right to left just as the racket strikes the ball, with the racket head moving to a nearly vertical position and the ball being struck directly in front of the server.

For a backhand side-spin serve, the racket is swung across the ball from left to right and the ball is released from the left hand just as the racket passes in front of the server. The essential part of all effective serves is giving the ball the proper spin.

In putting the ball in play by either a toss or a drop, the server must keep the fingers straight and together and the thumb free. No cupping or pinching of the ball is permitted. If this rule is violated, a let is called and the server warned. If the violation is repeated, a point is awarded to the opponent.

Footwork and stance

Proper stance and footwork in serving or receiving are just as important in learning table tennis skills as they are in tennis, badminton, or any sport skill that requires a constantly alert player.

A good beginner's stance in serving the ball is a position from about 1½ to 2 feet directly behind the center line of the court. Face slightly to the right side with the feet well apart and the left foot forward (for a right-handed player). Remember the service rule stating that at the moment of impact, both racket and ball must be behind the end line and within hypothetical extension of the sidelines.

A good stance position in receiving is from about 2 to 2½ feet directly in back of the center line of the court. The feet are spaced well apart, the knees are slightly bent, and the body is inclined forward in an alert position. From this position one can quickly step forward, backward, or to the side to effect either a backhand or forehand shot. After the shot is made again, recover to this position for the next return.

For a forehand or backhand return, the feet should be placed, at the moment of contact of the racket with the ball, so that they are perpendicular to the line of flight of the ball. The feet are well spread in order to shift weight forward and backward in delivering a shot. This is effective body weight follow-through. In going after a ball for an effective shot, remember to face the ball as you play it. Also remember to return to midcourt quickly after the shot is made. Keep your eye on the ball.

Stroke techniques

HALF VOLLEY OR PUSH SHOT

The half volley or push shot is the basic defensive shot. This shot is accomplished by meeting the ball as it touches the table and gently pushing it back over the net with the racket, which lifts and carries it forward at the same time. To add deception, the racket can be turned to either side and the shot angled. It can be played either forehand or backhand.

FOREHAND TOP-SPIN SHOT

The forehand top-spin shot is the basic offensive drive and is similar to the tennis drive. This drive is accomplished by striking the ball with a vigorous motion on either the dropping part of the bounce or at the dead height of the bounce with an upward forward motion to give it top spin. The racket is tilted or angled forward at the point of contact with the ball. The upward motion imparts the over spin. This shot is best played on deep or high-bouncing returns. As skill and accuracy are acquired, learn to shift body weight forward to add power to the shot.

Backhand drive

The backhand drive is similar to the forehand drive, except that the drive is shorter because the arm crosses the body and the ball is hit preferably on the rising part of the bounce. The racket is held with the thumb supporting the blade, and a snap of the wrist is used at the end of the drive.

Forehand chop

The forehand chop is primarily a defensive stroke. It is executed with a hatchet-chopping motion. The stroke starts from shoulder height, hitting forward and downward, and the top of the racket blade is tilted back away from the ball. Finish the stroke with the arm almost fully extended in front of you. Cutting with the blade down behind and under the ball gives the ball a back spin as it leaves the face of the racket. This stroke should be executed with considerable speed, making it very difficult to return.

Backhand chop

The backhand chop also requires that the racket be tilted and is the reverse of the forehand chop, except that it is a shorter stroke and employs the stronger use of the forearm and wrist. The stroke is started at about chin height and ends at about waist height. This shot requires a great deal of practice to acquire a worthwhile degree of control and accuracy.

Drop shot

The drop shot is executed by swinging the racket as if beginning a drive but stopping the forward motion of the racket just before hitting the ball and letting the ball hit the racket, causing the ball to return short over the net and drop dead. This shot should be used only occasionally as a change of pace or to catch an opponent off guard.

Smash shot

The smash shot is actually what its name implies. It is used on a higher-than-net bounce—the higher, the better. It is hit straight forward and down without spin upon the opponent's court. Use it only as a setup shot when an advantageous situation presents itself. Play it accurately and put weight behind the smash. It is a kill, or point, shot. Make it good when used.

Points to remember

1. Rely upon the pebble surface of the rubber-faced racket to execute cuts and spins.
2. Practice spins for control and accuracy.
3. Do not smash when a drive is more desirable and safer.
4. Concentrate on the ball.
5. Do not smash too soon or be overanxious.
6. Do not telegraph your intentions or your shot.
7. Do not try to return a chop with a chop.
8. If shots are hitting the net too often, try an upward lifting motion instead of a straightforward swing.
9. In a drive be sure to follow through.
10. Do not hit harder than your form justifies.
11. Always strive to perfect form.
12. Adhere to form and do not sacrifice it for speed or power; speed and power will naturally follow well-executed form and good technique.

Strategy

For singles play

Probably the best strategy for the defensive, as well as offensive, game is similar to that of tennis—relying upon the opponent to commit an error. Concentrate on returning the ball safely to the opponent's court. Mix the speed of the returns. Try different shots and study the opponent's weaknesses or strong points. Size them up quickly and play to an opponent's weaknesses. Keep the opponent guessing and avoid setting up easy shots. Keep the ball in play.

For doubles play

Essentially, strategy in doubles play is the same as that for singles play. Alternating each shot makes the doubles type of play actually a singles game. Offensive strategy therefore consists of keeping the opponents running and off balance as in lawn tennis. Do not drift into a slow, deliberate game but mix the type of shots and tempo.

If one wins the toss at the start of the game, it is good strategy to take the choice of first receiving. This causes the opponents to determine who is to serve first, and the receivers can then choose wisely as to who is to receive, since the same player must receive from the same opponent throughout the game. Receiving first puts one in a strategic position in the crucial closing moments of a game. Keep the eye on the ball. Learn to react with lightning speed in choosing which type of shot to make in each situation of the game. Use cross-court angling shots and keep opponents off-balance. Constantly strive for a versatile, deceptive attack and defense so that opponents cannot guess your shots in advance.

TEACHING AND LEARNING PROCEDURES
Teaching objectives
1. To explain the history of the game
2. To explain the type of equipment and facilities needed
3. To explain the rules
4. To teach the method of scoring
5. To suggest effective strategy
6. To organize tournament play

Basic skills techniques
1. The grips
2. Serving
3. Returning
4. Stance and footwork
5. Spins
   (a) Top spin—stroke forward and upward
   (b) Under spin—stroke forward and under
   (c) Side spin, left—stroke across the ball from right to left
   (d) Side spin, right—stroke across the ball from left to right
6. Strokes
   (a) The half volley
   (b) The drives, forehand and backhand
   (c) The chops, forehand and backhand
   (d) Drop shot
   (e) The smash

GLOSSARY OF TABLE TENNIS TERMS
ace A point scored on a shot that is impossible for the receiver to return.
ad Advantage.
angle shot Moving a shot diagnoally across the table.
backhand Hitting the ball with the back of the hand turned in the direction of movement.
backspin Revolving the ball the opposite way of its flight.
blade The face of the racket.
chop To hit the ball downward on the back of the ball giving the ball a backspin.
deuce A tie game at 20-all; two points scored consecutively are needed to win.
drive Giving a stroke top spin by turning the racket or paddle slightly forward as the ball is hit.
drop shot A shot barely crossing the net.
end lines White stripes on the ends of the table.
fingerspin Spinning the ball with the fingers on the serve; illegal.
flick A short return.
follow-through Completing the swing after hitting the ball.
forehand Hitting the ball with the back of the hand turned toward the body.
half-court Either half of the net.
let To play the ball over; occurs when the ball hits the top of the net and passes over it on the serve, when the receiver is not ready, or when an accident prevents a good service or return.
smash Executing a "kill shot" usually after receiving a high bounce.
top spin A forward rotating ball.

REFERENCES
Cartland, Douglas: Table tennis illustrated, New York, 1953, A. S. Barnes & Co.
Menke, Frank G.: Encyclopedia of sports, ed. 3, New York, 1966, A. S. Barnes & Co.
Official Sports Library for Women: Official recreational games and sports, 1968, National Section on Women's Athletics, Washington, D. C. (published biennially), American Association for Health, Physical Education and Recreation.
United States Tennis Association: Table tennis for you, Philadelphia, 1952, The Association.

23 Tennis

HISTORY AND ORIGIN

There are some historians who trace the game of tennis to the ancient Greeks. Others consider it an outgrowth of the game of handball, which was first played in Ireland and Scotland as early as the tenth century. However, most authorities trace its origin to "le paume" (game of the hand), which was first played in France as early as A.D. 1300. The game at this early time was played either indoors or outdoors. A cork ball or a ball of hair covered with leather was batted with the hand back and forth over a mound of earth on blocks of wood about 3 feet high. Gloves were used to protect the hands. Soon, however, a paddle was used, which later was replaced by a racket with tightly drawn strings. The cork ball was replaced by an inflated ball, and a net replaced the mound of earth. Undoubtedly, the original game of batting the ball with the hand has continued to the present day and is known as handball.

The game received its present-day name when English visitors heard French officials call "tenez," which meant to resume play, an expression similar to "play ball" used by baseball umpires. The English thought "tenez" was the correct name for "le paume." In time the English word tennis was substituted.

It is peculiar that, while the game was widely played during the middle ages, there appears to be no record of any rules governing it.

In 1874, Major Walter Wingfield, a British army officer, patented a game called "sparistike." This was the first known attempt to develop a tennis-type game with standardized rules and regulations. This peculiar name was not well liked and was soon replaced by lawn tennis because the game was being played on a lawn. As the game became increasingly popular, hard-surfaced courts became popular. Today the game is usually played on clay, concrete, or asphalt courts, although some matches are still being played on lawn courts.

A British officer introduced the game into Bermuda where it gained popularity. Miss Mary Outerbridge of New York was vacationing in Bermuda at the time and was very much attracted to the game. She immediately set about learning the game and its rules and bought equipment. In the same year, 1874, at the Staten Island Cricket Club, she introduced tennis in the United States. By 1879 the game had spread over the entire nation to the West coast.

In 1881, E. H. Outerbridge, the brother of Miss Outerbridge, called together the leading players of the day and formed the

United States Lawn Tennis Association. In this same year Championships were played. In 1900, Dwight Davis, a former doubles champion, donated a cup for a match between leading players of England and America. From this famous dual competition has developed an annual series of worldwide elimination tournaments for the coveted Davis Cup.

Mrs. Hazel Hotchkiss Wightman, a national singles titleholder, donated the Wightman Cup for a similar tournament; however, it is limited to competition between women's teams from England and the United States.

SOCIAL VALUES

Tennis is, without a doubt, the most popular of universally accepted games. There are many reasons for its great appeal:
1. It can be played by every member of the household, very young or very old.
2. It is a co-ed recreational game, and is well suited for mixed competition.
3. It requires only two or four people to play.
4. It can be played both indoors and outdoors.
5. Only a short duration of time is needed to play either a mild form of game or a very strenuous game that taxes one's ability, endurance, speed, and agility.
6. It is an excellent game of eye-hand coordination.

For these and many other reasons it is one of the best of all the carry-over basic skill sports. Every boy and girl should learn to play this game sometime within his or her school experiences, for its social values have a far-reaching influence on the achievement of a full and rich life.

EQUIPMENT

Students should be able to buy, care for, and discuss equipment as well as use it.

The racket

The racket should be selected with considerable care as to weight, balance, grip, and feel as it is wielded. It should balance evenly over the index finger at its throat. It consists of a handle and an oval head frame across which strings are woven. No exact specifications exist. The rackets are made of wood, steel (not recommended), aluminum, and plastic, and strings are made of nylon, silk, steel wire, or sheep gut. Nylon is considered best for class situations; it is moisture proof, inexpensive, and has better elasticity. Silk loses life quickly and is not recommended although it is the cheapest of all strings.

The grip on the handle should be selected by the size of the player's hand. The grip is from $4\frac{1}{3}$ to $4\frac{3}{4}$ inches in circumference, and the weight of the racket will vary for children, women, and men: for the younger beginner, $12\frac{1}{2}$ to 13 ounces; for women, $12\frac{1}{2}$ to $13\frac{1}{2}$ ounces; and for men, $13\frac{1}{2}$ to 15 ounces. The most popular weight for men is $14\frac{1}{2}$ ounces.

The ball

The ball is an inflated, hermetically sealed rubber sphere covered with stitchless felt cloth, about $2\frac{1}{2}$ inches in diameter, and weighs 2 ounces.

Clothing

The player should be guided by the conventional custom of selecting whites. They should feel comfortable. Women may use either a dress or shorts that allow for freedom of movement. Men may wear either a light jersey or T-shirt with shorts or slacks. Only low white tennis shoes with smooth soles should be worn on clay courts, so no indentations are left in the clay surface. Two pairs of socks should be worn to prevent blisters. Usually a light pair of socks underneath a heavier cotton or wool pair is best. A visored tennis cap is useful on bright days.

The net

The net should be 3 feet high at the center and $3\frac{1}{2}$ feet high at the posts, with the bottom touching the ground or held down at the center by a net band. The posts should be located 3 feet outside the sidelines and be equipped with a winch to raise or lower the net to desired height.

Cotton nets are best for indoor courts. The tarred hemp-type nets are best for outdoor courts because they are waterproofed.

Courts

The surface of the court should be smooth, firm, and level. It may vary from grass to hard-surfaced cement. The hard-surfaced courts, which afford playing soon after rains, are best for schools. Asphalt is probably best for school purposes because asphalt courts can be used for additional parking space during football and basketball games or be used for band marching practice. Clay courts are best suited for team competition. Although hard-surfaced courts cost more to build, they cost less in upkeep. In some communities they are used in winter for skating rinks. For various types of construction, see references at the end of this chapter.

DIMENSIONS

1. Singles court—78 × 27 feet
2. Doubles court—78 × 36 feet (4½-foot alley added to each side)
3. Height of the net at center—3 feet, commonly measured by taking the length of the racket plus the width of the racket head
4. Height of the net at the posts—3½ feet
5. Height of the posts—3½ feet
6. Distance of the posts away from the sidelines—3 feet
7. Distance between the baseline and the service line—18 feet
8. Distance between the service line and the net—21 feet

The end lines are called base lines, and the sidelines are called sidelines. The forecourt is near the net, and the backcourt is near the base lines. (See Fig. 23-1.)

START OF GAME

Tennis is played by either two players (singles) or four players (doubles) on a rectangular court using rackets and an inflated ball, which is hit over a waisthigh net until one side fails to return the ball.

The choice of serve or court is commonly made by flipping a coin. The winner receives the choice of service or court.

The server serves a complete game before the opponent starts to serve. The server always starts serving from the right side of the center line behind the base line. The server serves diagonally into the right service court, receiving two serves or chances to place the ball in this designated area. Having first served from the right and the point decided, the player then serves from the left side of the center line behind the base line. This time the serve is made diagonally into the left service court, and the server receives the same number of chances to place the ball in the designated area.

HOW TO KEEP SCORE
Game

The sequence of scores in tennis for each successive point won by each player is 15, 30, 40, and game. For example, if both the server and the receiver win a point, the score will be 15-all. If the receiver wins the next point, the score becomes 15-30 (remembering the server's score is always first).

Deuce refers to the score of 40-all, not 30-all. When the score is tied after the point of 40-all, it is also referred to as deuce. In order for a player to win a game after the score becomes 40-all, two successive points must be won.

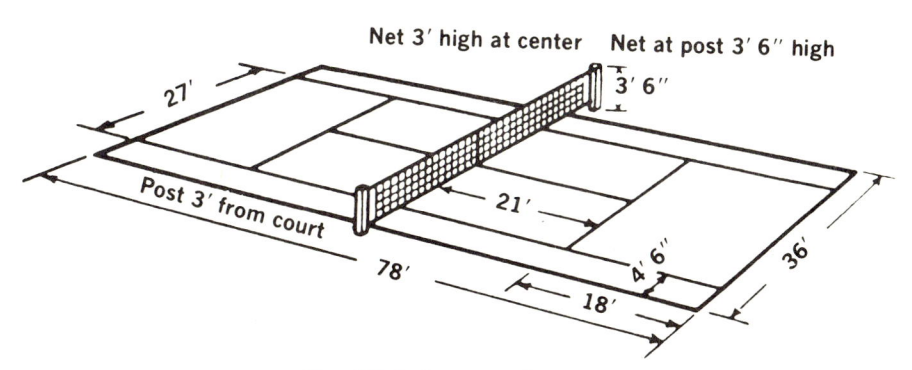

Fig. 23-1. Lawn tennis court.

Love, in tennis, means that a player has a score of nothing. For example, if the score is 30-love, the server has won two points and the receiver has won none.

Ad in or advantage in means that the server has won one point after the 40-all mark. To win the game, the server must win the next point.

Ad out or advantage out means that the receiver has won one point after the 40-all or deuce mark. If the receiver wins the next point, the game is over. However, if the server wins the next point, then the score is deuce again, meaning that a player must win two successive points to win the game.

Set

A set consists of six games, provided that the player or team wins by two or more games (6-0, 6-1, 6-2, 6-3, or 6-4). In the case of a 5-all set, the winner is the player or team winning the next two consecutive games (7-5, 8-6, 9-7, 10-8, etc.).

Match

A match consists of the best three out of five sets for men's national rules, both in singles and doubles.* For collegiate rules, a match consists usually of the best out of three sets. A match consists of the best two out of three sets for women's and mixed (woman and man) tournament rules.

Men may rest 10 minutes after the third set, while women may rest 10 minutes after two sets.

Let

The player serving receives two chances; if one of the serves (either the first or second) hits the net and lands in the proper service area, the serve is considered a let. The player is only permitted the let service over. For example, if the let occurs on the first ball served, the server still is entitled to two serves. However, if the let occurs on the second service, the player is entitled to one service. Outside interference, either by another player or ball from a nearby court, results in a let and the point is played over. If the receiver is not ready (in ready position), a let may be called. If the receiver makes an attempt to hit the ball, a let cannot be claimed.

The term "let" in tennis is an abbreviation of the early use of the phrase "let's play it over," used when there was a questionable decision on any point of play.

RULES

1. Players change courts on an odd number of games (1, 3, 5, 7) of the total number of games.
2. A player loses a point in the following cases:
   (a) If the player allows the ball to bounce twice on the player's own side of the net. The ball must be returned after the first bounce or on a volley (volley meaning the ball is hit while in flight before striking the ground for the first time).
   (b) If the server or receiver returns a ball to any point outside the designated area.
   (c) If a player stops a ball before it goes out-of-bounds, regardless of whether or not it was going out-of-bounds. The player must let the ball bounce. A player may play a ball that is going out-of-bounds; however, if the return is not good, the point is lost.
   (d) If a player strikes at the ball twice with the racket, for example, a slice stroke in which the ball strikes the frame plus the gut before going over the net.
   (e) If a player reaches over the net to play a ball. The ball must be contacted on the player's own side of the net. After contacting the ball on the player's own side of the net, it is legal to follow through with the stroke, provided that the net is not touched in the execution.
   (f) If the ball in play hits any part of a player or racket, regardless of whether it is the player's own partner or not, or whether it is going out-of-bounds.
   (g) If a player throws a racket at the ball.

---

*See N.C.A.A. rules.

3. A player cannot at any time invade the opponent's court with any part of the body or with the racket.
4. There are occasions when a player can reach over the net to play a ball. If a player puts a cut on the ball and the wind returns it over the net to the player's own side, the receiver, in order to win the point, must reach over the net and hit the ball, but must not touch the net in so doing.
5. A net ball is any ball hit into the net. In all cases the player committing this fault loses the point.
6. If the server fails to get the first serve into the serving court, it is called a single fault; if failing on both serves, it is a double fault, and the server loses the point.
7. Any ball striking a permanent fixture other than the net is considered out-of-bounds and a point is lost. Balls hitting the top of a net post and falling in the court are good.
8. A player wins a point in the following instances:
   (a) By delivering an ace. An ace is a serve or return that the receiver does not touch and is unable to return.
   (b) During play when an opponent fails to return a shot.
   (c) When a receiver fails to return a serve upon contacting the ball (called a fault).
   (d) After the service, when a ball touches the net and goes over into the opponent's court without being returned.
   (e) If a ball strikes a line, making it good, and is not returned.
9. If a player must go out beyond the net posts to play a ball, the player may do so legally, even though returning the ball outside the posts, below or above net height, provided the ball is played back into the opponent's court before it touches the ground.

Foot faults

Foot faults pertain only to the server. During any serve, if the server commits a foot fault, that serve only is lost, not the point. In order to lose a point, the server must commit two foot faults in succession or a combination of a foot fault on one serve and another type of fault on the other. The following are considered foot faults:
1. Touching the base line while serving.
2. Stepping on the base line while serving.
3. Having both feet off the ground while executing the serve. One foot must remain in contact with the ground from the start of the execution to the finish.
4. Moving both feet along the ground in a walking or running fashion. One foot must remain stationary.

Additional rules
1. An underhand service is legal.
2. Receivers may stand anywhere on their own side of the net. After the serve is hit, servers play anywhere on their side.
3. The server's partner may stand anywhere on his own side of the net during service, but usually plays within 8 feet of the net on the side opposite that in which the serving partner stands.

FUNDAMENTAL SKILLS AND TECHNIQUES
The grips
CONTINENTAL

For the forehand grip, use the right hand only if right-handed, and place the palm near the end of the handle with fingers spread and wrapped diagonally forward around the handle with the thumb around the opposite side. The V formed by the thumb and index finger should bisect the left ridge on top of the handle. This grip does not shift for the backhand; it remains the same for both.

EASTERN

For the forehand drive or volley, have the palm of the hand behind the handle. "Shake hands with the racket," placing the first finger slightly up the handle. (See Fig. 23-2.)

For the backhand drive or volley, place the palm of the hand above the handle so that the thumb can be put diagonally up the handle behind. The back of the hand is parallel to the direction of the stroke. The

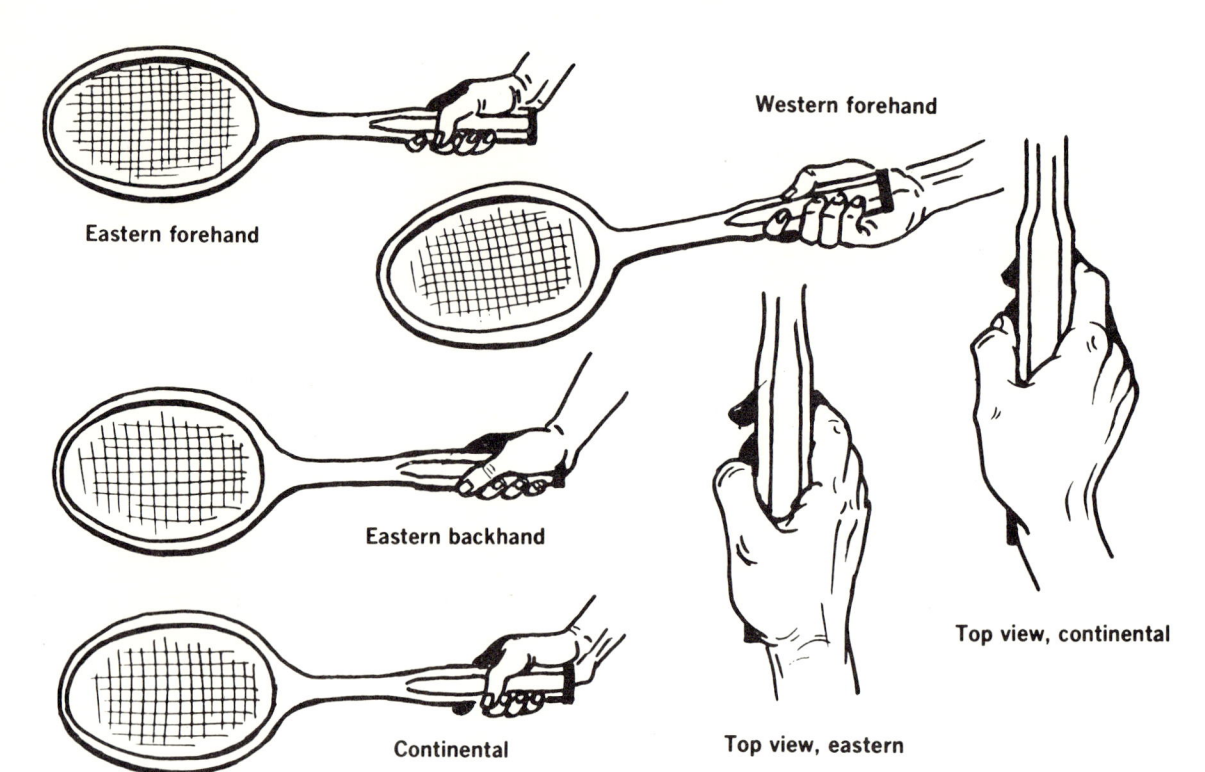

Fig. 23-2. Various grips for tennis.

hand shifts slightly to the left of the handle for the backhand.

Hold the racket at the end of the handle as indicated in Fig. 23-2 or perhaps up a couple of inches for volleying. A higher grip makes for accuracy, but a lower one makes for power. The western grip is no longer generally used.

To cut services to the right, grip the racket as in a backhand stroke. For a straight service without cut, use a grip that is either halfway between these two grips or like a forehand grip.

Some good players use slightly different grips from those described. Try these out first, then experiment a little, but do not change too much.

Between strokes, hold the racket at the throat (the place where the handle joins the head) with the left hand, keeping the feet apart and the knees bent. Stand facing the net, racket head up and away from the body, held chest high. This makes it easy to change from one grip to the other.

Stance

Stand with the weight forward over the toes and with the feet spread moderately. Bend forward a little.

Crouch down a bit for all low shots so that the eyes will be nearer the level of the ball.

Footwork

In all ground strokes, try to have the side of the body, not the front, toward the net. The body should face the sideline. Right-handed players should have the left foot toward the net on the forehand strokes and the right foot toward the net in backhand strokes. Never play a ball with the feet parallel to the net if you can help it.

On volleys, the turning of the body is not so marked, but there should be some turn. The footwork should be used in the same way, but with not so long a step.

In all smashes, except when the ball is on the left of the body, and in all services, have the left foot forward.

Fig. 23-3. Service.

The main factor in hard hitting is getting the weight of the body to assist the arm stroke. Transfer the weight from the rear foot to the forward foot *before contact*.

If you wish to smash a lob that is over your head and is going to come down behind you, *run backward*. If you have to turn around, let the ball bounce, especially if it is a sliced or chopped ball. If you let it bounce, run to one side of the ball, not under it. Adjust position so that you are able to hit the ball with your best shot.

The service

Hit the ball at as high a point as you can *efficiently* reach.

Put your body weight into the shot.

Have your left foot forward. As you serve, transfer your weight from the rear foot to the left foot, and, at the moment of impact, you should be on the left foot only. Bend the knee of the right leg so the foot will not cross the line before the ball is struck. (See Fig. 23-3.)

Swing the racket with a kind of "Indian club swing"; that is, do not just swing it with your strength but use the *momentum* of the racket head.

Watch the ball until you have struck it.

Get settled before each service. *Do not hurry your second service.*

For a flat service, throw the ball up in front of the face and hit it straight and hard. Reach high. For a slice service, cut over top to right, throw the ball up in front of the face and hit it as hard as you can with a glancing blow.

For the American twist serve, cut upward and to the right with the racket and throw the ball up opposite the left shoulder, so that it would alight back of that shoulder when it came down. The body should be facing the right sideline and should bend backward before the ball is hit. When the ball is hit, the body should straighten *upward* and the racket should cross the ball upward and to the right.

If it is desired to rush to the net after the the service, it is best to serve not too fast but with a good cut. *The American twist is the best serve to use.*

In doubles, serve as many down the center line as can be done without having the opposing team play for them all the time.

Serving down the center line narrows the angle to be defended and prevents wide-angle cross-court returns and passes down the alley.

Strokes

GENERAL HINTS

Watch your foot position carefully. More bad playing results from this fault than from bad swinging.

Keep your eyes on the ball. Violation of this rule is responsible for over half the errors made.

Swing smoothly and easily. Do not press the shots. Prepare in time to hit easily. Use force at the moment of hitting, not before or after.

Follow through after the shots. Sweep the ball across; do not just pat it over.

Do not get too close to the ball. It is

Fig. 23-4. Forehand drive.

better to have to lean forward to hit it and reach for it than to be cramped and have to bend the elbow and hold it close to the body.

Watch the timing of the stroke. Watch the ball from the time it leaves the racket of your opponent and get ready for it in your mind. If you do this, you will not be hurried, and you will time the swing accurately.

Try to hit the ball to a place in the court, not just over the net. Remember that the net is 6 inches higher at the sides than at the middle, and you must hit it higher to get it over on down-the-line shots.

Forehand drive

Learn to hit with the left side to the net so that the impact will come about opposite the belt buckle. Learn to transfer the weight before the time of hitting. The weight should be over the right foot at the start of the swing, then, as ball is hit, transferred to the forward foot.

There are two kinds of backswing: circular and straight. The straight is the easiest to master. The arm is brought straight back. Learn first to hit the ball without a cut (Fig. 23-4, *A*); then learn to hit with an upward cut or top spin (Fig. 23-4, *B*). After this is learned well, and not before, learn to slide or hit with a slight downward cut to the stroke. In both of these cuts the major part of the movement should be forward, not up or down.

Things to remember in making a forehand swing:

1. Try always to keep the eye on the ball.
2. Stand left side to the net.
3. Move the body into the stroke.
4. Start the backswing early. Give yourself plenty of time to hit the ball accurately.
5. Do not play on top of the ball. It is better to reach for it.
6. Keep a good distance from where the ball strikes the ground as it is hit to you. Give yourself plenty of room to swing.
7. Try to get behind and under a low bouncing ball.
8. When you hit the ball follow through with the racket. Use the whole arm.

Backhand drive

Hit in front of the body and more to the right side; that is, with the right side toward the net, the ball is hit out in front of the right side, not just in front of the belt buckle. (See Fig. 23-5.) As the racket hits the ball, the weight is transferred from the left to the right foot. On the backswing of the backhand drive the weight moves back over the left foot. The racket should be held firmly, but the arm should not be rigid. As the arm moves back there should be a slight twist of the body to the left to get ready for the swing. This movement is made to add power to the swing. The arm should be brought back so that the forward swing can be well timed.

The ball should be met about one foot in front of the right foot. The arm on meeting the ball should be extended. After the contact, the arm should follow through in the direction of the flight of the ball.

Things to keep in mind in relation to the backswing:

1. Keep your eye on the ball.
2. Try to meet the ball with the right side toward the net.
3. Try always to play ahead of the ball.
4. Give yourself plenty of room—don't let the ball get too close to you.
5. Use your arm not the wrist. Follow through after the stroke.
6. Watch out for rigidity. Don't tense up. Try to stay loose.

Learn first to hit straight, then to hit with a "top," and finally to hit with a slice. The slice is used more with the backhand than with the forehand shot.

Volleys

Grips for the volley should be the same as for ground strokes.

Slice all volleys except the ones above the level of the net. The ball is hit with the head of the racket above the wrist.

Hit the ball hard with a sort of forward lunge with the shoulder that is similar to striking in boxing. It is a punch without much backswing or follow-through.

Use the elbow motion, not the motion from the shoulder, and keep the wrist stiff. The weight should be well forward and

Fig. 23-5. Backhand drive.

on the toes. The footwork of the volley is not so marked as in other shots.

Hit the ball well ahead of the body and crouch for all low balls.

If you are playing near the net, volley the ball to the feet of the opponent or hit the ball at a sharp angle away from the opponent. If you cannot volley to kill the ball, volley deep.

Given the option of going forward or sideward to volley, the volleyer should always go forward, for the angle is smaller and the return is faster, giving the opponent less time to recover. Also, the angle of the return can be sharper, and it is easier to make a stop volley.

Lobs

A cut lob is defensive and gives the lobber more time to get back into position. A topped lob is harder to execute but is an offensive stroke, since it bounces high and deep and is harder to reach.

A lob must be hit high enough to get it over the heads of the opponents. It should hit between the service line and the base line, the nearer to the base line the better. Also, the lower it can be hit and still be too high to hit back, the more effective it will be. Lobs are usually hit to the backhand corner.

Lobs have the following uses:
1. A high lob drives the net player back to the base line.
2. A high lob enables the receiver to get back into position.
3. A low lob tires the net player by requiring a lot of running.
4. A low lob can be used to win the point.

Smashing

Hit the ball in front of the head like a serve. Let it fall as if to hit the face, and hit it at as high a point as is possible. Hit for depth; most failures go into the net.

If you can get to the ball easily, learn to hit it for a kill. This is not difficult.

In singles, smash to the sidelines. In doubles, hit to the center unless close to the net.

Do not hurry or press the shot. *Follow through*.

In hitting when close to the net, it is almost always safe to hit to the opponent's feet.

Learn the backhand smash, but use it only on balls you cannot get on the forehand.

Run *backward* using a sidestep to get all overhead balls that are to be *smashed*.

Watch the opponent to anticipate lobs. You can often detect a lob from the nature of your opponent's preparatory swing.

HALF VOLLEY

Watch the ball all the way to the racket.

Use no preliminary swing, but execute a full follow-through, hitting with a great deal of lift to make the stroke drop in court.

Use a firm, rigid twist and get the proper angle to the racket. This angle is somewhat over the ball.

DROP VOLLEY

On the drop volley shot the racket face is open, extra underswing is imparted by downward movement of the racket, and the touch is soft.

DROP SHOT

The drop shot calls for a much lighter touch than the chop and has a shorter follow-through. It is aimed to just clear the net and almost drop dead.

It is all *wrist* chop, unlike a hard volley, which is made with the elbow.

Crouch on the low drop shots.

LENGTH

Hit the ball to the base line or within 6 feet of it in singles or in doubles when the opponent or opponents are back. Short balls are easy to advance on and easy to hit for a pass.

Hit the ball to the feet of the player rushing up to the net.

When playing to a player at the net, hit low balls, just over the net, with a great deal of top spin to give them drop.

Spin

A *top spin* (forward spin) causes the ball to drop rapidly and hence may be hit hard and fairly high above the net and still fall in court.

A *cut* or *slice* (backward spin) causes the ball to float or sail; it has a short, low bounce and bounces slowly. It may cause the net player to hit the ball into the net or out-of-bounds.

On service, an out cut bounces to the left and curves to the left. An out-and-out cut (American service) curves to the left and down but bounces to the right and high.

Stroke combinations

Against a driving, top-spin game, slice the ball or chop it.

Against a slice or chop game, volley from the net.

Against a net game, drive with a great deal of top spin.

Do not chop to net players, especially in doubles. *Drive*.

Chop to a good driver, especially to the backhand, unless the player is close enough in that a drive can be made to the feet.

Return of service

Never play to return a falling ball. Always play to take it at the top of the bounce or, best of all, hit the rising ball from close in—about 4 to 6 feet inside the base line. This hurries the server more than a shot from any other place.

In singles, hit either cross court or straight down the sideline.

In doubles, usually hit cross-court shots. However, if the server is rushing up after a *soft* ball, hit a semilob down the sideline over the net player's head. It will go for an ace.

Play the cross-court shots at the feet of the oncoming net player.

When going to the net, play deep to the corners on either side in about 5 feet.

Do not hit the ball at sharp angles until you can ace the shot. Play rather to get the opponent out of position.

Fast shots with a lot of spin must be hit back hard, or they will go out of the court or into the net.

Always play the court angles on the server, and stand in the middle of the probable hitting angle.

If the serve pulls you out of position, hit a lob or a slow, deep shot to allow you to get back in position.

Singles court position

Keep out of the zone between the service line and the base line for receiving balls because they can be too easily hit at your feet.

When a difficult shot comes to you, try to play your return to the middle of the opponent's court and as deep as possible.

When in doubt as to whether to advance or retreat, *always* go forward and volley rather than retreat and take a ground stroke.

After each stroke, get back in position.

Step toward the ball, not away from it, when you can. Have the weight going forward.

If you are caught out of position on an easy shot, *guess* where your opponent will return it and jump for that place just as the ball is hit. If you guess right, you make a save. If wrong, you would have probably lost the shot anyway.

Watch the opponent's favorite strokes and the places they are usually put, *but* do not make use of this knowledge all the time. Save it for times when a point may be needed.

In singles, play close to the net three-fourths of the time if it is possible to do so.

Doubles court position

Both players should be parallel to the net, not one up and one back.

Run up on *every* service. (This presupposes good and hard service.)

Players should smash their players own lobs.

Hit many shots down the middle between the other players.

Take the net on *every* opportunity as follows: (1) on long drives to the other team at the base line, (2) on *deep* lobs, (3) whenever else you get a chance on a hard-hit ball, not a soft one.

The receiver's partner should generally play just in front of the service line and in about the middle of the service court.

If you can always control the other player's service and return it where you wish, the partner of the striker can play up just inside the service line, but the return *must* be kept away from the net player.

On service, the partner should stand from 8 to 10 feet from the net. If the service goes to the center line, the net player can stand slightly closer to the middle line.

In doubles, it is well to serve as many balls to the middle line as can be done without having the opponent always in position for it.

Always keep on the offensive in doubles. Do not go on the defensive if it can be helped.

GENERAL POINTS TO REMEMBER

The most important thing to remember in tennis is to keep your eye on the ball.

Do not be hurried. Watch the opponent's stroke from the moment the ball is hit, *mentally* and *physically* prepare to hit it, and *time* it accurately. This will improve your game at least 50 percent.

Give adequate attention to every stroke. Concentrate on it as though it were the deciding stroke of the match—it may be.

Try to anticipate shots, especially when you are at the net.

Play to win.

Be a good sport and give your opponent the benefit of the doubt.

Play with *confidence*—do not be afraid. If you lose, it will be because your opponent was the better player that day. Timid playing usually is unsuccessful.

Never lose your temper over poor shots. They are usually balanced by your lucky shots.

Never dispute the referee's decision.

Play with spirit and joy, just as though you felt so good you *had* to play hard to feel right.

Play every stroke you can get your racket on. Strokes that you *nearly* make worry your opponent, and if you do make a stroke, it is one less for your opponent.

Save some reserve strength and energy for

the pinches. Do not get played out too early. If you are out of condition, use lobs and sideline shots and run your opponent around.

Do not worry, but play your own game. Do not change the plan of your game without a reason. Your opponent may be lucky for a few minutes. Keep at it. Your opponent may have bad luck, or tire, or take his or her eye off the ball. However, a player should always change a *losing* game and never change a *winning* game.

Be sure that the technique you use in a losing game is the cause of your losing before you change it. To change your game, change the style of strokes, for example, from drive to slice; change the style of the game, as base line to net or vice versa; or change the pace, for example, from fast to pat-ball, or slow to fast.

Always play to increase the score. Do not take chances. Take chances *only* when there is no other hope.

When an opponent is running from the sideline to the center of the court, hit a ball to the place you opponent has just left. It is nearly always a winner.

HELPFUL HINTS

It is not generally good tennis to play the ball close to the top of the net. Clear it by 2 feet or more.

A good drive generally has depth, that is, lands within 2 feet of the base lines.

In singles, go to the center of the base line or close to the net after each shot has been executed.

The tougher the shot, the easier the swing.

One should hit strokes only as hard as they can be controlled.

Tennis is a game of great skill, speed, agility, and endurance, both mental and physical. It is also a game of courtesy, sportsmanship, and gentlemanly behavior. Coarse behavior or language is inappropriate.

There are no home runs in tennis—easy does it. Develop steadiness, then accuracy, and finally speed.

The most necessary fundamental is to *watch the ball* until it hits the strings.

The next most important fundamental is *position,* that is, standing somewhat sidewise, feet apart, and racket back as soon as possible.

Remember to swing level and follow through.

EFFECTIVE PRACTICE

A little guidance as to the best methods of practice will be of invaluable aid in developing in students the proper attitude toward practice.

No amount of study will take the place of practice.

It is ideal to have a teacher or critic. Discovering your own faults and weaknesses is difficult.

A certain amount of drill (for example, shadow practice and ball tossing) is helpful in establishing neuromuscular patterns. This form of practice requires neither court nor partner.

Backboard practice is another aid. (Backboard games add interest to this type of practice.)

Concentrate on weaknesses.

A beginner should hit to a practice partner. This takes as much precision as does hitting away from the partner, and it facilitates keeping the ball in play.

Never practice aimlessly. Try for each ball.

Do not practice indifferently against an inferior player.

Have a definite objective for each shot.

Do not be discouraged easily.

Vary your opponents.

Do not be satisfied with incorrect strokes. Changing form may upset your game for a time, but it will make the game more effective in the end.

Usually it is better not to play games when trying to develop strokes. If you do, concentrate on form rather than on score.

Work with accuracy rather than speed.

Avoid underplaying, pressing, patball and slugging.

There are no substitutes for persistence and concentration.

Practice against a wall when you have time, and try to hit hard and to a definite place. Practice keeping your eyes on the ball.

Know the rules and follow them. Expect your opponent to do the same.

When you practice, have a stroke-practice schedule with your partner in the practice. The practice schedule might resemble the following drill:

1. Practice ground strokes, both drive and slice.
2. With one player at the net and the other back (reverse later), try these shots:
   (a) Volleying
   (b) Stop volleys
   (c) Drop shots
   (d) Lob volleys
   (e) Half volleys
3. With both players on the service line, try volleys and half volleys.
4. Have one player lob while the other smashes. Hit some behind and run back for them.
5. Serve a dozen balls in succession—hard.
6. Serve a dozen balls and run in on them.

After each has practiced these, then play some. The practice is worth more than the play.

Progress in tennis is made by constantly trying to eradicate one's faults and by trying to learn something new. It may take five years to learn to do all the strokes even passably well, but it will be worth it. Study your game; always play with a purpose to develop something definite in your game. Above all, learn early in your career to play with skill and not by brute force. Tension is fatal. Learn to hit hard with the skill and timing of the stroke, not by tensing the muscles. Learn to move like a cat, not like a cow. Study all the pictures of good players that you can, and learn from them.

FACTORS RESPONSIBLE FOR POPULARITY OF TENNIS

The main factors to which tennis owes its increasing popularity are the following:

1. Availability of courts
2. Availability of teachers
3. Relatively low cost of equipment
4. Stimulus of tennis associations and tournaments
5. Trend toward individual sports
6. Suitability of the game to both sexes and to a wide range of ages

ETIQUETTE

Growing out of the game's aristocratic background is an appreciation by tennis enthusiasts of the spirit of clean competition that characterizes the game, as well as a respect for its fineness and precision. This appreciation and respect are reflected in many of its rules of etiquette.

1. Keep your temper.
2. Obey the following rules of lawn tennis:
   (a) Do not foot fault.
   (b) Do not stop a ball that is going out until after it has bounced.
   (c) Do not touch the net, and do not volley a ball until it has crossed the net.
   (d) Do not serve either service until your opponent is ready.
   (e) Opportunity should be given your opponent to clear a ball off the court.
3. You may speed up or slow down the play by your shots as you please and as you are able to do so, but do not unduly hurry or delay the game otherwise.
4. Accept decisions of officials graciously.
5. Respect your opponent's decisions.
6. Always shake hands after a tournament match.
7. Win or lose pleasantly and without excuses.
8. After a point has been played, return balls directly to the server; do not hit them back carelessly.
9. If your ball goes into the adjoining court, wait until the players on that court finish their point before calling for the ball.
10. If a ball from an adjoining court comes into your court, return it to the owners as soon as possible. If it interferes with your point, play a let.
11. In tournament play, speak when changing courts, even if you do not know your opponent. This is espe-

cially important if your opponent is a novice.
12. Keep score. Establish the habit of calling the score after each point.
13. If the ball touches the ground twice before you hit it, call "not up" immediately.
14. If possible, do not return a first service which is a fault. If the ball is too fast and too close for you to call before returning it, say that you are sorry.
15. In doubles, the receiver's partner should call service faults.
16. If it is impossible for you or your opponent to decide whether or not the ball was good, the point should be played over, but this is disturbing to both players and should be resorted to only when unavoidable.
17. Try for every point. Tossing points and playing to the audience are insulting to your opponent.
18. In nontournament play, insist on furnishing the balls half of the time, and perhaps more often if you are much the inferior player.
19. Be on time.
20. Do not tear up the court unnecessarily.

STRATEGY
1. Learn to outthink rather than outrun your opponent.
2. Study your opponent, yourself, and the situation.
3. Look for your opponent's weaknesses.
4. Be aware of your own weaknesses and learn to protect them.
5. Vary your game with the court surface and weather conditions.
6. Understand and learn to use, at the correct time, the following strategy:
    (a) Change of pace
    (b) Lob game and chop game, etc.
    (c) The dash to the net (center theory)
    (d) Parallel play in doubles
    (e) Deception

TOURNAMENT AND PLAYERS
Handicaps may be applied to any of the following types of tournaments:

1. Elimination (consolation and double elimination)
2. Round robin
3. Ladder

The following procedures may be included in making an elimination tournament draw:
1. The seed
2. Byes and preliminary rounds
3. Recording scores, schedules, etc.

CONTRIBUTIONS
It is well for teacher and students to formulate objectives at the beginning of the course. These may be posted so that students may keep them in mind.
1. Neuromuscular coordination
2. Health and vigor
3. Recreation
4. Transferable fundamentals
5. Social development
6. Broadened scope of appreciation

WARM-UP
One should thoroughly warm up before the start of play, using such exercises as free arm-swinging movements, bending and rotating trunk, and knee-bending exercises. It is a safety factor in preventing muscular strains and also improves the neuromuscular responses and reflexes.

TEACHING AND LEARNING PROCEDURES
Objectives
1. To teach fundamental tennis strokes
2. To teach knowledge of the game and its etiquette
3. To encourage a desirable attitude toward a healthful, recreational sport

Teaching procedures
1. Rules
2. Etiquette
3. Grips
4. Stance
5. Forehand
6. Backhand
7. Service (elementary)
8. Receiving, footwork
9. Playing positions
10. Class play with coaching

Achievement tests

Achievement tests are given over the items just mentioned. The following strokes should be practiced and used with supervision from a coach:

1. Forehand drives
2. Backhand drives
3. Forehand returns of service
4. Backhand returns of service
5. Service from right and left courts

Final grade

The final grade is based on an achievement performance test over the skills mentioned previously with all balls landing within a playing area, written test over rules, etiquette, and court positions, and written reports and assignments.

GLOSSARY OF TENNIS TERMS

ace A point scored on a shot that is impossible to return.
ace on service A hard hit ball impossible to return.
advantage in One point won by the server after the 40-all mark.
alley The lane between the singles and doubles sidelines.
backhand Hitting the ball with the back of the hand turned in direction of movement.
backspin Spinning of the ball in the opposite direction of its flight.
blocked ball A ball stopped and returned without swinging the racket.
base line The boundary at the end of the court.
choke To shorten the grip on the racket.
chop stroke A forward downward motion giving the ball a backspin.
cross court Driving the ball diagonally across the court.
deuce The score of 40-all; also a tied score after the point of 40-all.
game Reaching a score beyond 40 and being two or more points ahead of the opponent.
ground strokes Strokes used after the ball has bounced.
let To play the ball over; occurs when the ball hits the net and passes over it, when outside interference occurs, or when the receiver is not ready.
lob To hit the ball high into the rear of the opponent's side of the court.
love No score.
match Contest play; may be two out of three sets, or three out of five.
rally To hit the ball a number of times.
set Six games, provided that a player or team wins by two or more games.
short ball A ball dropped just over the net.
smash A hard hit ball from a position over the head.
spin A side, front, or back rotation of the ball caused by cutting the ball as it is hit.
stop volley A short ball play; to let the ball hit a held racket so that it will rebound over the net.
stroke The action of hitting the ball with the racket.
underhand To hit the ball by bringing the hand forward and up from below the shoulders.
volley To hit the ball before it bounces.

REFERENCES

Barnaby, John M.: Racket work: the key to tennis, Boston, 1969, Allyn and Bacon.
Driver, Helen I.: Tennis for teachers, ed. 2, Philadelphia, 1959, W. B. Saunders Co.
Jaeger, Eloise, and Leighton, Harry: Teaching of tennis for school and recreational programs, Minneapolis, 1963, Burgess Publishing Co.
Johnson, Joan, and Xanthos, Paul: Tennis, Dubuque, Iowa, 1967, William C. Brown Co., Publishers.
Kenfield, John: Teaching and coaching tennis, Dubuque, Iowa, 1964, William C. Brown Co., Publishers.
King, Billie Jean: Tennis to win, Evanston, Ill., 1970, Harper and Row.
Menke, Frank G.: Encyclopedia of sports, ed. 3, New York, 1966, A. S. Barnes & Co.
Official tennis and badminton rules and guide, Washington, D. C., 1968-1970, AAHPER, Division for Girls' and Women's Sports.
Talbert, William, and Olds, Bruce S.: Stroke production in the game of tennis, Philadelphia, 1971, J. B. Lippincott Co.
United States Lawn Tennis Association: Official tennis guide and yearbook with official rules, New York, 1970, A. S. Barnes & Co.

FILMS

Beginning tennis, The Athletic Institute, Chicago, Ill.
Technique of tennis, Lloyd Budge, Bell and Howell Co., Chicago, Ill.
Tennis rhythm, Bobby Riggs, Teaching Films Custodians, Inc., New York, N. Y.
Tennis tactics, Fred Perry, Teaching Films Custodians, Inc., New York, N. Y.

24 Touch football

HISTORY OF THE GAME

Football as we see it today came to us through soccer and rugby. Harvard, Yale, Princeton, and Rutgers were the schools that made early attempts at playing this game. The early attempts at football were not much more than gang fights over a round ball.

However, through the years since 1869, rules have been formulated, equipment has been adopted and qualified, and coaches and members of the medical profession have worked toward making football a relatively safe game.

From tackle football the game has been modified in such a way that it can be played without pads and still be played safely. Playing the game without the costly equipment has enabled children and young adults to participate. Touch football as it is played today is an interesting and beneficial game for all who desire fun and competition.

In 1932, the Intramural Sports Section of the College Physical Education Association drafted and adopted an acceptable set of rules for school and college play. These rules are not as yet standardized as official rules. Variations are found in many colleges and universities in different parts of the United States.

BRIEF DESCRIPTION

Touch football is similar to regulation rugby football and to a modified form of American football except that the ball carrier is stopped by being touched rather than by being tackled, and blocking as in regulation football is eliminated. These modified rules lessen the danger of injury and encourage a more open style of game. Forward passing is the principal offensive weapon, with all players eligible to receive the pass.

EQUIPMENT

Playing field: The dimensions of the field are the same as those of a regulation football field—160 × 360 feet. (See Fig. 24-1.) The dimensions can be made shorter for class play if space is limited.

Ball: The ball used is a regulation American football.

Uniforms: No special uniform is necessary; however, a regulation gym uniform consisting of T-shirt or sweat shirt, trunks, athletic socks, supporter, and basketball shoes can be used. Cleats are not necessary. Teams should be equipped with distinctively colored jerseys.

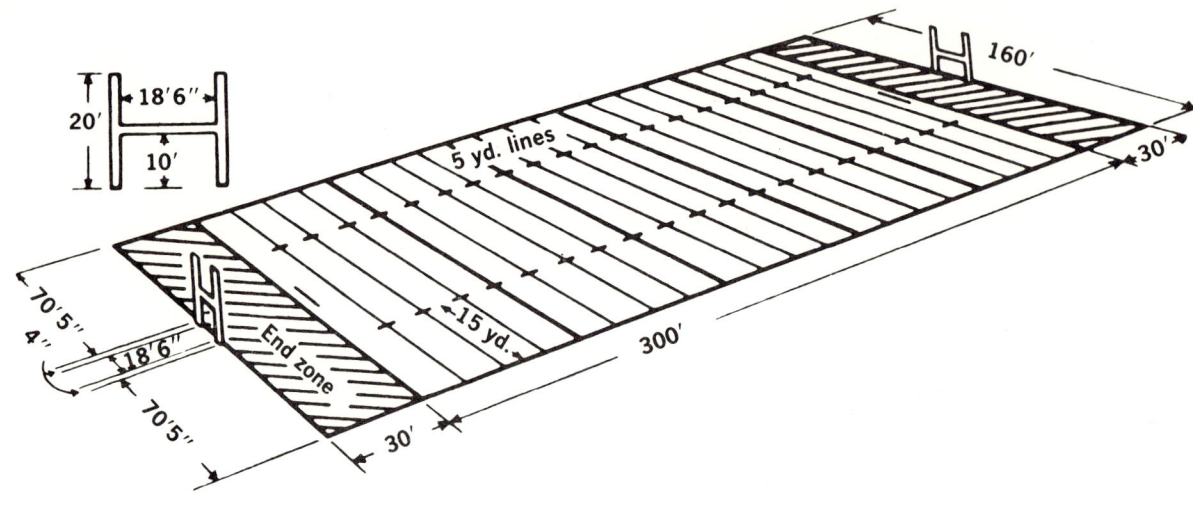

Fig. 24-1. Football field.

MODIFIED RULES
Length of game

1. The game consists of four 10-minute periods with 3 minutes between quarters and 5 minutes between halves.
2. An overtime period is added in case of a tie. Each team is given four downs from the same 20-yard line; the team advancing the ball the farthest in the four downs is declared the winner.
3. A team failing to appear within 15 minutes after the appointed time forfeits the game.
4. Time out may be called two times in each half of the game by each captain. Additional time outs result in a yard penalty. Time out will be taken in the following instances:
   (a) When the ball goes out-of-bounds
   (b) When the referee calls time out for a captain
   (c) After a score is made
   (d) At the discretion of the referee

Scoring

1. Touchdown—6 points
2. Field goal—3 points
3. Safety—2 points
4. After touchdown—1 point

Players and substitutions

1. A team shall consist of six to nine players. The offensive team must have at least three players on the line of scrimmage.
2. Any number of substitutions may be made during the game. Substitutions must report to the referee before entering the game.

Playing regulations

1. The game is started by the following procedure:
   (a) Choice of goals and kickoff. A coin is tossed and the winner gets the choice of goals, of kickoff, or of receiving. The loser of the toss has choice of option. These privileges of choice are reversed at the beginning of the second half.
   (b) Putting the ball in play. The ball is put in play at the beginning of the game, at the beginning of the second half, and after a score by a place-kick from the kicker's 40-yard line. The kickoff must go 10 yards or the ball shall be kicked over. Kickoffs are free balls and may be recovered by either side.
2. Ball kicked over opponent's goal line on kickoff. If the ball is kicked over the opponent's goal line on the kickoff, it goes to the opponents for scrimmage on their own 20-yard line.

3. Ball going out-of-bounds on kickoff. If the ball is kicked out-of-bounds on the kickoff and it had gone 10 yards before going out-of-bounds, the receiving team shall have its choice of taking the ball where it went out-of-bounds or on its own 20-yard line.
4. Fumbled ball. At any time the ball is fumbled, during scrimmage, after lateral passing, or after a kick or a run, the ball is dead and belongs to the team that fumbled the ball at that spot, the down and the point to be gained remaining the same.
5. Necessary gain in downs. If in four consecutive downs a team fails to advance the ball to the second white stripe, it shall go to the opponents at that point.
6. Downed ball. The player is downed and the ball is dead when an opposing player touches the first player with both hands simultaneously.
7. The following regulations apply to passing:
   (a) All players of the offensive team are eligible to receive passes. Any member of the defensive team may intercept passes.
   (b) Passes may be thrown anywhere back of the line of scrimmage.

Note: To increase passing and receiving proficiency, passes could be thrown anywhere on the field in any direction.

Fouls and penalties

1. It is considered a foul to tackle, trip, push, or rough another player.
2. It is a foul to use the hands or to leave the feet in an attempt to block an opponent. The penalty for blocking is loss of 15 yards from the spot of the foul.
3. It is a foul for a player to be off side before the ball is put in play. The penalty is loss of 5 yards from where the ball was put in play.

Officials

1. The referee has absolute charge of the game and decisions made by the referee are final.
2. The umpire pays particular attention to holding and interference on forward pass plays.
3. The linesman measures distance and reports off side and fouls of personal type such as holding and roughness. The linesman may also be the timekeeper if no special individual is assigned this duty. (See Figs. 24-2 and 24-3 for official football signals.)

Unsportsman-like conduct   Roughing kicker   Clipping

Personal foul   Delay of game   Holding by defense

Fig. 24-2. Football signals.

Fig. 24-3. Football signals.

BASIC SKILL TECHNIQUES
The stance

The rules state that both hands or both feet or one hand and opposite foot must be within 1 foot of the scrimmage line.

Offensive line stance: The stance used by linemen must be one that will enable them to move forward, backward, and laterally; therefore, it must be a position with feet well apart, knees bent, and the feeling of explosive effort.

Three-point stance (staggered)
1. The feet are about 2 feet apart, with the toe of one foot on a line with the heel of the other and both feet pointing straight ahead.
2. Execute a full knee bend, dropping the right hand to the ground and resting the left forearm on the left knee. Balance on the balls of the feet.
3. The body is relaxed and balanced, the right arm is straight, the hips lower than the shoulders, and the head up with the eyes ahead.

Defensive line stance: This stance is similar to the offensive stance except that the body is closer to the ground and more weight is on hands or hand. Weight must be forward for a lineman in charging forward.

Offensive backfield stance (two-point stance)
1. The feet are 18 inches apart, with the toes straight ahead.
2. Weight is equally distributed on the balls of both feet.
3. The hands are on the knees, arms are straight, thumbs are on the inside of the knees, the head is up, with the eyes straight ahead.

Defensive backfield stance: Stand with natural ease in a comfortable position with feet apart and staggered.

Blocking

Offense depends upon blocking by obstructing the opponents. that is, by body contact with the opponent to prevent the opponent from tagging the ball carrier.

Shoulder block
1. Shoulder contact should be made to the opponent's shoulder. (See Fig. 24-4.)
2. Feet should be well spread and under the player's body.
3. The follow-up should consist of short steps used to drive the opponent to the rear.

Tagging

Tagging is used as a substitute for tackling. The location of the ball carrier when tagged will determine the start of the following play.
1. Approach the ball carrier with maximum speed and body control.
2. Tag the opponent with both hands simultaneously.

Kicking

The punt is the most important play in football. It generally determines the outcome of the game. The punt is used to gain yardage or to better a team's position on the field. Punting is highly specialized, and constant practice is necessary to develop a player into a good kicker.

Punting
1. Be physically relaxed but mentally alert.
2. Hold the ball with both hands, laces up, and pointed up the field.
3. Hold the ball on the kicking foot side just below the chest.
4. Stand with the feet slightly apart and staggered, legs flexed at the knees,

Fig. 24-4. Shoulder block.

and weight equally distributed on the balls of both feet.
5. Incline the body forward from the waist, arms and hands extended in front of the right leg, fingers spread, and palms up.
6. Keep the toe of the kicking foot pointed in.
7. Take only three steps before contacting the ball.
8. Have the kicking foot ahead at the start of the kick.
9. Follow the ball with the eyes from the center and after the ball is caught, keep the eyes on it until it has been kicked.
10. Release the ball so that it remains in its long axis until after being kicked.
11. Catch the ball between the toe and upper part of the kicking foot.
12. Swing the leg from the hip through a perpendicular arc, the center of the long axis of the ball meeting the outside part of the instep approximately 2 feet above the ground.
13. As the foot meets the ball, straighten out the lower leg and lock the knee joint.
14. Make a good follow-through.
15. Do not necessarily put a lot of power into the kick.
16. Take your time in kicking.
17. Kick the ball as high as possible.
18. If possible, kick out-of-bounds.

Catching punts
1. Keep the eyes on the ball.
2. Form a basket when catching and give with it to a certain extent.
3. Always run up to the ball so that after you catch the ball you can continue on and complete the play.
4. Run straight ahead and when players are bearing down on you, change direction.
5. Keep relaxed.
6. Always keep the body in motion.

Place-kick
1. A spot should be picked in advance and the eyes kept on this spot.
2. The kicker should place himself so that the path of the kicking leg will be in line through the point of the kick

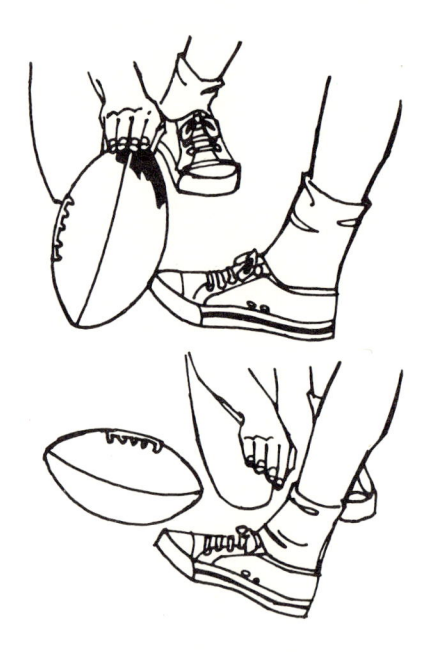

Fig. 24-5. Place kick.

and over the center of the crossbar. (See Fig. 24-5.)
3. The feet should be comfortably spread, knees slightly bent, and body slightly inclined forward from the hips.

Passing or throwing

Forward pass or overhand pass: The forward pass is an offensive weapon used to advance the ball and to hold secondary defense in deep enough position to make the running game function.

Grip for pass
1. The passer should grip the ball slightly behind the middle with the fingers on and across the lace.
2. The fingers and thumb should be relaxed and well spread.
3. In the event that the front part of the ball fails to drop in flight, the index finger should be extended toward the rear point of the ball.
4. The right foot should be firmly planted upon the ground and the left foot pointed in the direction of the pass.
5. The ball should be raised toward the right shoulder with both hands, and as the delivery starts, the right hand should come back with the ball to a position behind the ear. The upper

Fig. 24-6. Foreward pass.

Fig. 24-7. Center pass.

arm should then be parallel to the ground. (See Fig. 24-6.)
6. The ball should be delivered directly over the right shoulder with the index finger pointing the direction of flight.
7. The passer should plan to lead the runner just a little and should throw at medium speed, not too hard.
8. Body weight should be put into the throw.

Lateral pass: The lateral pass is very valuable and is one of the most successful methods of producing touchdowns provided a few general rules are followed.
1. Do not pass over 5 yards.
2. Do not lateral when you have a chance to break away and run.
3. Do not float for a lateral when you are in a position to block for the ball carrier.
4. Do not lateral too soon.
5. Do not throw laterals indiscriminately.
    (a) Basketball pass
        (1) Hold and deliver by both hands with an arm and wrist action, the ball turning end over end.
        (2) There is very little arch and the ball should travel slowly enough to be easily handled.
    (b) One-hand underhand pass
        (1) The ball rests in the right hand and is held there by the left hand until the actual toss is made, the ball rolling off the fingertips with a slight spiral action.

Center pass
1. The center pass is just like a forward pass, but is upside down.
2. Hold the ball on the ground with the right hand.
3. Have either the fingers or thumb on the lace.
4. Use the left hand to guide the ball.
5. Place the feet at opposite corners of a rectangle.
6. Spread the feet as far apart as is comfortable. (See Fig. 24-7.)
7. Advance the left foot with the right foot a little behind.
8. Lead your runner a little with the ball on an end run.
9. With the quarterback right behind center, pass the ball with only the right hand.

Pass receiving or catching the ball

1. The receiver should keep the eyes on the ball and catch it with the hands rather than trap it against the body.
2. The arms and hands should be loose and relaxed prior to actual reception of a pass.
3. As the ball touches the hands, a slight giving movement should occur, doing away with resisting or fighting the ball.
4. The ball should then be brought against the body and put in a carrying position.
5. Try to catch the ball over the left or right shoulder.

310 BASIC SKILLS IN SPORTS FOR MEN AND WOMEN

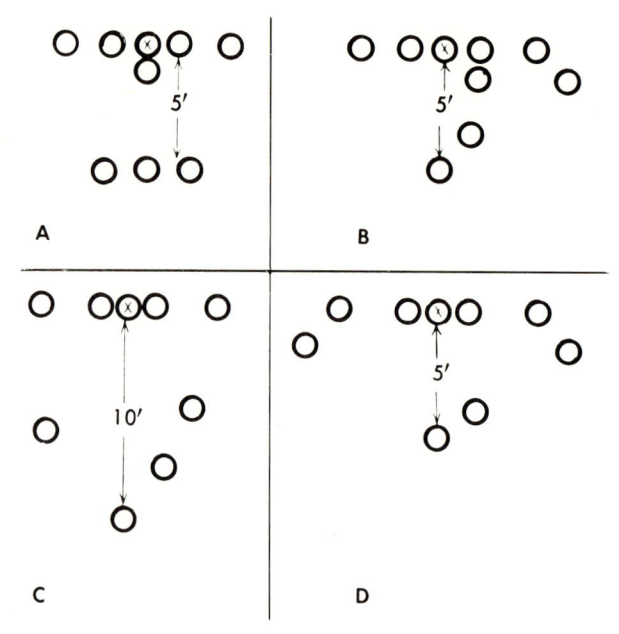

Fig. 24-8. Offense for nine men. **A,** T formation. **B,** Single wing. **C,** Punt. **D,** Double wing.

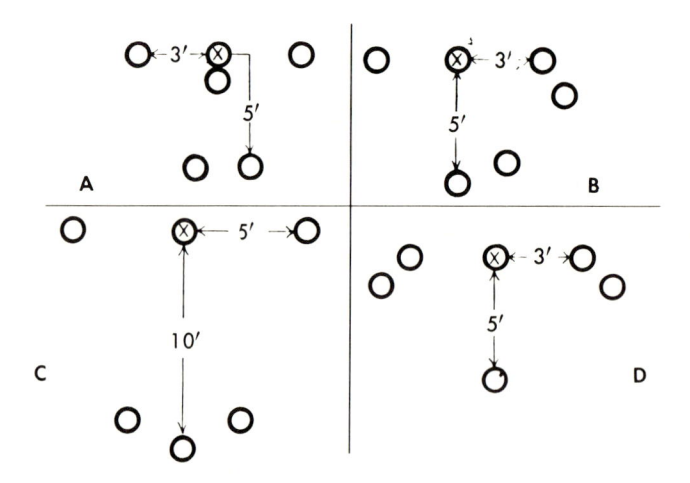

Fig. 24-9. Offense for six men. **A,** T formation. **B,** Single wing. **C,** Punt. **D,** Double wing.

6. Be under the ball as well as possible.
7. Try not to change stride unless the ball will fall short.

FUNDAMENTALS OF OFFENSE AND DEFENSE

In introducing offense, the following steps seem most logical:

1. Explanation of positions, including duties and conventional formation (See Figs. 24-8 and 24-9.)
2. Kick formation and assignments involved
   (a) Protection
   (b) Getting downfield fast
   (c) Kicker acting as safety
3. Forward passes and related plays
   (a) Numbers system. Number each player, and call number in designating approximate assignment; for instance, "No. 3, flat to strong side."

TOUCH FOOTBALL 311

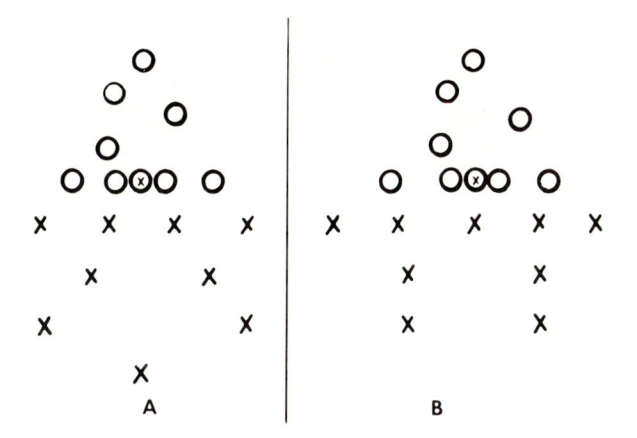

Fig. 24-10. Defense, x, formation for nine-man football. **A,** 4-2-2-1. **B,** 5-2-2.

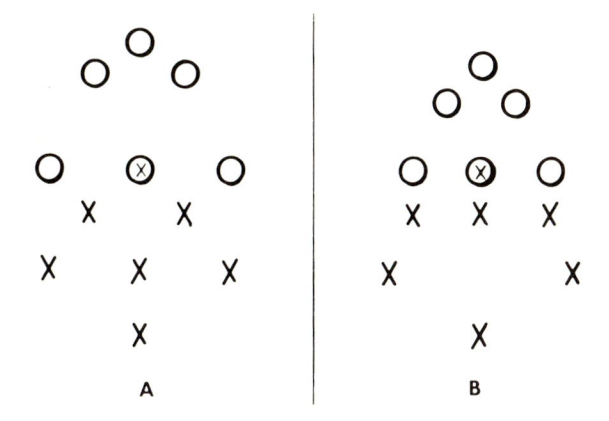

Fig. 24-11. Defense, x, for six-man football. **A,** 2-3-1. **B,** 3-2-1.

    (b) Other members decoy
    (c) Always alert to lateral
4. Running plays
    (a) Buck—for short but essential yardage
    (b) End run
    (c) Simple reverse
    (d) Laterals
5. Running with ball
    (a) Be relaxed.
    (b) Have ball-carrying arm wrapped around the ball securely.
    (c) Have the hand wrapped around the visible end of the ball.
    (d) Be alert at all times and ready to outguess defensive players.
    (e) Be able to sidestep to either the right or left.
    (f) Be able to pivot in either direction.
    (g) Never run backward.
    (h) When you catch a defensive player off-balance, break.
    (i) Follow your interference.
6. Defense
    (a) Regular line defensive positions (See Figs. 24-10 and 24-11.)
    (b) Backing up fast on running plays
    (c) Pass defense
        (1) Rushing the passer
        (2) Covering receivers by zone, man-to-man, or combination
    (d) Punt defense
        (1) Rushing the kicker
        (2) Assuming offensive tactics as soon as the ball is in the air
7. Playing suggestions
    (a) Assignments should not be tipped off by players' leaning or pointing the eyes, head, or body, or by changing facial expression.
    (b) Remember that the passer is a

ball carrier as long as the ball is in his or her hands.
- (c) Vary your style of defense play when flanked by an offensive player. Move out and set, move out and come back in motion, and move and dart through the split if it is wide enough.
- (d) Early in the game discover which defense players are weak in covering passes.
- (e) Set up plays by sacrificing one or two downs in order to make the plays function properly.
- (f) Plays should be set up in a sequence, including both pass and running plays.

FLAG FOOTBALL

In the game of flag football each player has a piece of material attached to the back of the clothing. To catch a player carrying the ball the flag must be removed. All the other rules of touch football are used.

SAFETY PRECAUTIONS

Instructors should inspect all wearing equipment to ensure safety and minimize injuries.

See that competent officials know and enforce such rules as not allowing the feet to leave the ground in blocking and declaring the ball dead on all fumbles.

Officials should inspect the field and clear it of all obstacles that might cause injuries.

Injured players should be given immediate medical attention.

TEACHING AND LEARNING PROCEDURES IN THE SKILL TECHNIQUES

1. History of touch football
2. Brief description of the game
3. Necessary equipment
4. Discussion of rules over several class periods
    - (a) Length of game
    - (b) Scoring
    - (c) Players and substitutions
    - (d) Playing regulations
    - (e) Fouls and penalties
    - (f) Officials
5. Skill fundamentals
    - (a) The stance
        - (1) Offensive line stance
        - (2) Defensive line stance
        - (3) Offensive backfield stance
        - (4) Defensive backfield stance
    - (b) Blocking
        - (1) Shoulder block
        - (2) Body block
    - (c) Tagging
    - (d) Kicking
        - (1) Punting
        - (2) Place-kick
    - (e) Passing
        - (1) Forward pass
        - (2) Lateral pass
        - (3) Center pass
    - (f) Catching the ball
        - (1) From punt
        - (2) From forward pass
    - (g) Tackling
6. Fundamentals of offense and defense
    - (a) Conventional formations and positions of players
    - (b) Kick formation and assignments
    - (c) Forward passes and related plays
    - (d) Numbers system
    - (e) Running plays
    - (f) Defense

GLOSSARY OF TOUCH FOOTBALL TERMS

backfield The men behind the line who usually handle the ball.
balanced line Having the same number of players on each side of the center.
block Using the body, but not the arms, to intercept a defensive player or to stop a defensive player from touching the ball carrier.
bootleg play Faking a pass to another player.
clipping Landing on the back of the leg or legs of a player not carrying the ball.
cut-back To change direction; usually done by the receiver or ball carrier.
double wingback An offensive formation; two backs are placed about one yard outside of their ends, one back is placed either to the right or left behind a guard, and the tailback about five yards behind the center.

fair catch A catch designated by the player catching the ball by raising the hand.

lateral pass Passing the ball backward or sideward behind the line of scrimmage.

line of scrimmage An imaginary line marking the position of the ball at the start of each play.

REFERENCES

Grombach, J. V.: Touch football, New York, 1942, A. S. Barnes & Co.

Menke, Frank G.: Encyclopedia of sports, ed. 3, New York, 1966, A. S. Barnes & Co.

U. S. Naval Institute: Football, Annapolis, 1950, The Institute.

25 Track and field

ORIGIN

The equivalent of track and field events originated almost with the beginning of man. In order to survive, man had to be both a gymnast and a sprinter. Survival depended upon his ability to outperform his challenger, man or beast. When he was not in search of sustenance or being pursued, he kept physically fit by engaging in running, jumping, or throwing activities with his immediate family or group.

Games involving the fundamentals of track and field were first formulated by the Greeks during their Golden or Homeric Age. The most famous of these games were the Olympics which began in 776 B.C. and continued to be held every five and then four years until A.D. 392, at which time they were abolished by the Romans. In 1896 they were reorganized again by Baron Pierre de Coubertin of France, and since that time they have been conducted as an international festival. One of the strong motivations behind our whole national sports program is the meeting together every four years of the many champions of the various countries of the world. With some exception, the United States Olympic teams have done well in most track and field events.

Research is constantly being conducted to improve the technique of performance so that the competitor will realize better time for a sprint, a little better distance in the broad or long jump, or a greater height in the high jump. With the application of scientific principles, records are constantly being broken.

CONSTITUENCY

Track and field consists of four different types of events: running, jumping, vaulting, and weight throwing. The track events are running and hurtling; the field events are long jump, triple jump, high jump, pole vault, shot put, discus, javelin, and hammer throws.

Running events

Sprints: Outdoor sprints include 100- to 220-yard dashes. Indoor sprints are from 40 to 80 yards.

Middle distances: Outdoors or indoors, any distance that falls within 300 to 1000 yards is considered a middle distance. The most common distances are the 440- and the 880-yard races.

Distances: Outdoor and indoor distance events range from 1 to 3 miles.

Hurdles: Outdoors and indoors, high hurdles covering a distance of 120 yards are used. The low hurdles for men consist of ten barriers, 2½ feet high, placed 20 yards apart. The high hurdles consist of ten barriers, 3½ feet high, placed 10 yards apart for men, 3¼ feet high for boys, and 2 or 2½ feet for girls and women. Women run the 80-meter hurdles. There are also intermediate hurdles.

Relays: Outdoors and indoors, relay teams consist of four members, each of whom (except in shuttle relays) carries a baton and passes it to the next runner in succession until the last runner carries it across the finish line. The relays include four times 110 yards, four times 220 yards, four times 440 yards, four times 880 yards, and four times 1 mile. The medley relays are the sprint, the distance, and the high school.

Jumping events

Long jump and triple jump: The runway varies from 130 to 160 feet. The styles of long jump that are used are the float, hitch kick, and hang.

High jump: Various styles of jumps are used, including straddle, eastern, western, and back-flip.

Pole vault: The pole vault is a spectacular event, for the vaulter must be able to bring into action practically every muscle in the body. The pole-vaulter must be able to sprint, jump, and do pull-ups and push-ups. One of the best poles is the new fiber glass vaulting pole. The runway used is from 125 to 140 feet in length.

Weight-throwing events

Shot put: For college, A.A.U., and Olympic competition, 16 pounds are used; for high school, 12 pounds; and 8 pounds for grade school. The shots are made of a cast-iron, bronze, or brass shell with a lead center. The shot is thrown from a circle 7 feet in diameter.

Discus: The collegiate discus is wooden with a metal rim, measures 8.622 inches in diameter, and weighs 4 pounds, 6.548 ounces. It is thrown from a starting circle 8 feet, 2½ inches in diameter. For high schools the discus must be not less than 3 pounds, 9 ounces in weight.

Hammer: The hammer consists of a round weight attached to a triangular handle by a wire. It weighs 16 pounds, and its total length may not exceed 48 inches. It is thrown from a circle 7 feet in diameter.

Javelin: The javelin is a wooden spear with a metal point. The length is approximately 8½ feet, and the weight is 1.765 pounds. It has a cord grip 6.3 inches wide around the center of gravity.

Other track and field events

In the Olympic games there are other track and field events such as 10,000- and 50,000-meter walks and the decathlon.

FACILITY

A satisfactory facility for track and field is the combination football area surrounded by an oval-shaped 440-yard track as shown in Fig. 25-1. At both ends the track has curves with an 80- to 110-foot radius. The straightaway is the side with the extended track. Six to eight running lanes are usually marked off. Around the periphery of the field are located the pits and circles for the

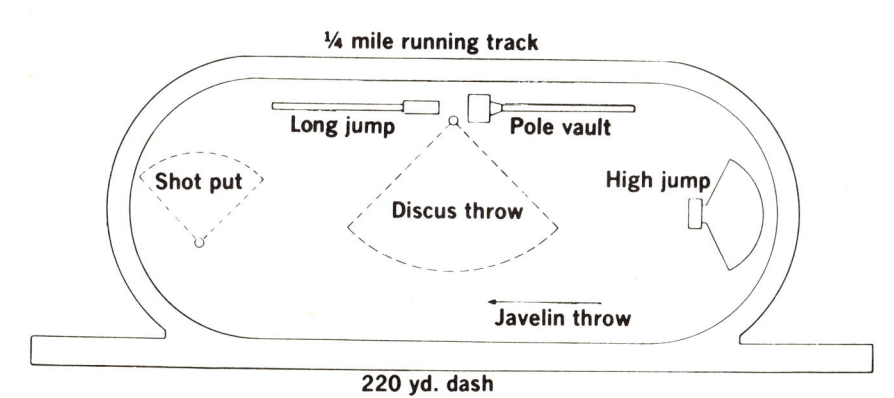

Fig. 25-1. Track and field facility.

316 BASIC SKILLS IN SPORTS FOR MEN AND WOMEN

field events. A good layout is one in which two or more events can be conducted simultaneously.

SHOES

The style or fit of shoes may determine whether a competitor is a winner or a loser. Most coaches are convinced that the best shoe is one that is made of yellow-backed kangaroo leather with an oak sole, stitched by hand. Shoes are now being constructed that permit the interchanging of a variety of spikes. The proper spikes should be worn for each event, except in the shot put and discus.

OBJECTIVES OF TRACK AND FIELD

1. To assist in the development of all physical factors—speed, agility, endurance, coordination, balance, strength, and flexibility
2. To encourage participation in the many and varied running, jumping, and throwing activities
3. To develop self-confidence, self-respect, self-assurance, will power, or just to have fun
4. To encourage participation in team sports
5. To promote spectator interest through instruction in the fundamentals of track and field sports

MECHANICAL ANALYSIS OF TRACK AND FIELD EVENTS

Running events

STARTING BLOCKS

Starting blocks are essential to the sprinter, providing a solid base from which to push off and preventing unnecessary slipping or injury to the runner. Adjustable blocks that can be used either indoors or outdoors are the most satisfactory. A 90-degree angle for the foot-supporting surface of the back block and a 45-degree angle for the front block is the recommended adjustment. (See Fig. 25-2.)

STARTING POSITIONS

Due to a wide difference in anatomical proportions among participants, there is a variance in starting positions. However, three main positions are recognized: the bunched, the medium, and the elongated. The bunched position is used mainly by the small participant. However, since the medium starting position is the most widely used, it is the one that will be analyzed.

"On your mark" (see Fig. 25-2, left): Place the front foot 12 to 15 inches back of the hands with the toe pointing straight ahead. Place the rear foot about 30 to 34 inches to the rear so that the knee bisects the front foot. Place the fingers and thumbs in a tripod position on the starting line about shoulder width apart. Focus the eyes on the ground immediately in front of the starting line.

"Set" (see Fig. 25-2, middle): To get set means to distribute the weight of the body in the best possible position to take off. To assume this position the sprinter raises the hips until they are about 20 degrees above the shoulders and the weight is over the arms. The eyes are focused just ahead of the starting line. Concentration at this point should be on the rear leg and opposite arm.

"Go"—discharge of pistol (see Fig 25-2, right): Push off forcefully with the rear leg and reach forward with the opposite arm.

Fig. 25-2. Starting blocks.

This reaction takes practice. The action is to fall as far forward as possible without leaving the feet. The moment of force should be as far in back of the center of gravity as possible. Concentration should be on the first 20 yards. The runner should not shorten the steps or use strides that are too extended or too short.

END OF THE RACE

Hitting the tape: The beginner should sprint on through the tape.

Lunge: This consists of pushing the chest well forward and the arms down and back.

Shrug: This adds a throw of one arm and shoulder toward the finish line.

SPRINTING

The sprinter should be relaxed while running in order to maintain the greatest speed. Many stand up too straight or hold the head too high. This causes fatigue and tension in the back and neck and causes an unnecessary expenditure of neuromuscular energy.

Rhythm must be mastered by coordinating all bodily parts. The arms should be flexed and swung freely at the sides of the body, with the swing of the arms making an arc from the waist to the shoulders. The hands should be open and relaxed. While the sprinter is running, the weight of the body should fall on the balls of the feet. The heels sink, but not entirely to the ground. As the center of weight moves over the feet, the legs straighten. As a leg is flexed and brought forward, all the extensor muscles should be at rest. The length of the stride is determined by the speed attained. Maintenance of a parallel line of gravitation is most important for achieving smoothness and rhythm.

RUNNING THE QUARTER MILE

As the distance increases, the runner assumes a more erect posture, the strides become shorter, and the heels assist in supporting the weight.

A good rule to follow in preparation for competition is to run more than a quarter mile to develop endurance and to run less than a quarter mile to develop speed. Alternate these workouts. Rest a day before a meet.

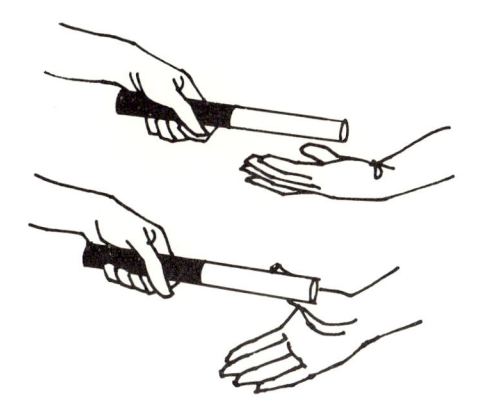

Fig. 25-3. Coordination of the pass.

RELAYS

Method of passing baton: The *visual pass* is a pass that is seen by the receiver. It is used primarily in the long relays where the fatigue of the runner may lessen coordination, decreasing the runner's ability to pass accurately. The baton is passed from the left hand to the right.

The *nonvisual pass* or blind pass is a pass that is not seen by the receiver. This pass is used in sprint relays and must be practiced by the runners. It is a quick, highly coordinated movement—the baton going from the runner to the receiver at top speed. The baton is carried in the extended left hand of the runner and received on the run by the right hand of the receiver. See Fig. 25-3 for the styles of hand positions during the pass.

HURDLING

Good hurdling depends upon the ability to start fast and to generate top sprinting speed. Ten steps are taken to the first low hurdle, and seven in between. Good form for the low hurdles requires that the body not be raised as it passes over the hurdles.

As the front leg is lifted to pass over the barrier (see Fig. 25-4, left), the body leans forward for maintenance of equilibrium. The rear leg is drawn over sideways. (See Fig. 25-4, right.) This position can be practiced on the ground.

For the high hurdles, a 7- or 8- stride start is used with 3 strides between barriers. As described in the low hurdles, the body

Fig. 25-4. Running the high hurdles.

should not rise and fall. The position of the body during the first seven steps is quite similar to that assumed in sprinting. On the eighth stride, the body is inclined forward to allow it to pass over the bar and to present an opportunity to bring the rear leg over without losing balance. Some coaches think it is best to keep both arms forward in hurdling, but it is more common to hurdle with the opposite arm forward. (See Fig. 25-4.)

Jumping events

LONG JUMP

Success or failure in long jumping depends upon the two factors of speed and spring. The distance for the approach to the takeoff board varies from 125 to 140 feet. The jumper should establish the takeoff foot by "running through" the jump a few times and checking for accuracy. In most cases the 2-4-8-stride plan is recommended. This means that the runner marks off three spots which are 2, 4, and 8 strides apart. If the jumper leaves the takeoff board with the right foot, these spots must be hit with the left foot. Other stride plans to which a jumper might adjust better are the 2-4-6 and the 2-4-10 plans.

Two of the most common types of long jumps are the float and the hitch kick. The run should be fast, but a shortening of the stride allows the jumper to hit the board for height and distance or to "foot stamp" the takeoff.

Knee-tuck: This is also called the sit-down style of jumping. After the takeoff, both legs move forward to the landing.

Stride-in-air: In the execution of the stride-in-air the lead leg swings forward,

Fig. 25-5. Straddle.

backward, and then forward and upward while the takeoff leg makes a forceful kick forward and upward.

Hang: The hang-style jump is performed by delaying the leg action. After the body has reached top flight, the legs are swung forward.

The objective of all three types of long jumps is to ensure proper placement of the feet so that the jumper does not fall back. The stride-in-air can add inches to a jump.

HIGH JUMP

Straddle form (see Fig. 25-5): There are a number of high jump styles. One of the best is the straddle. This style is executed by kicking the right foot high into the air if the approach is from the left, jumping forcefully off the left foot, and passing over the bar belly down.

The approach to the bar is made with approximately 12 to 14 strides from a 30-degree angle. Check marks should be placed at 8 strides and 4 strides from the point of takeoff. After a flat-footed stamp on the takeoff, the right foot is kicked up and over the bar with all the force possible. Both the arms are thrown upward with the emphasis on the upward throw of the left

Fig. 25-6. Eastern cut-off.

Fig. 25-7. Western roll.

arm and shoulder. The eyes on the takeoff should be on the crossbar. The landing should be made on the right hand and foot.

Eastern cut-off (see Fig. 25-6): For the eastern cut-off, the right-handed jumper addresses the bar from the right side. The jumper kicks the right foot high above the bar. As the body rises to pass over the bar, the left leg is brought up and under the right. (See Fig. 25-6.) The landing is on the left foot and the hands.

Western roll (see Fig. 25-7): In performing the western roll from the left, kick upward with the right foot, roll to the left, and land on the left foot and the hands. The foot stamp is widely recommended in the western roll as well as in other forms of the high jump. The angle of approach to the bar is approximately 45 degrees. The average jumper ordinarily uses no more than 8 or 9 strides. Check marks should be made at 4 strides and 8 strides from the point of takeoff. The first few steps should be relaxed and somewhat bounding, whereas the remaining ones should be more vigorous. Energy should be utilized for the lift. Therefore, the jumper must be relaxed as the takeoff foot is planted. The last stride should be considered as a part of the uplift because it is through these strides that the kicking leg is swung. The last stride should be fairly short. At the moment of the foot stamp, the left knee should be bent as the center of weight passes over it. As the right leg swings upward, the arms must do likewise. Both arms should, as a matter of fact, assist in the lift.

After the takeoff, the left leg flexes almost completely as the body passes over the bar. The left leg is then dropped for the landing, which is made on the left foot and hands.

The most recent method of high jumping is the backflop. (See Fig. 25-8.)

Fig. 25-8. Backflop.

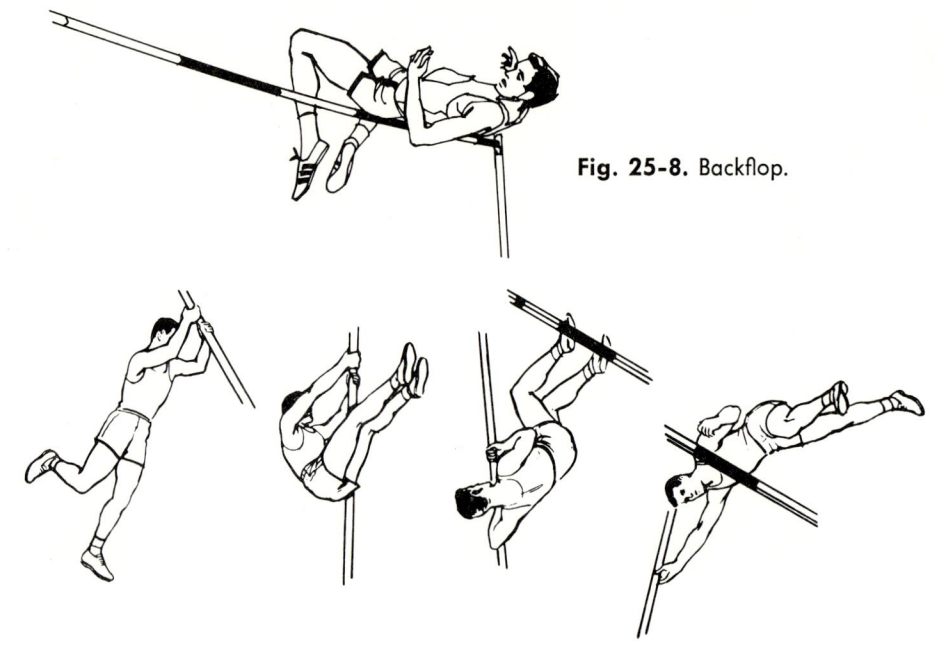

Fig. 25-9. Pole vault, aluminum, alloy, or steel.

Pole Vaulting

Holding the steel pole: The placing of the hands on the pole depends primarily upon the height of the crossbar and secondly on the distance of the hand spread. (See Fig. 25-9.) A vaulter with strong upper arms and a fast approach can use a high hand-hold or high-point carry.

The vaulter grasps the pole in the right hand at a comfortable height and then lowers it to the right side. Next the vaulter grasps the pole with the left hand while keeping the left arm slightly flexed and in contact with the body. The pole should now be held to the right side with the right hand extended well back and the left arm across and in contact with the front of the body. The hand spread should be about 22 inches. This hand position is known as the high-point carry. For the low-point position, extend the left arm. The beginner should practice running while holding the pole in its proper position.

The approach: Three forms of approach are most commonly used: (1) the 2-6-8 plan, (2) the 4-6-8 plan, and (3) the 2-8-10 plan. For these three forms there will be three check marks, which are marked off as explained for the long jump.

The takeoff: As the pole is slipped into the box after the run, the hands should be approximately above the jumper's head, and the arms should be slightly flexed to absorb the reaction of the pole. The right arm should be extended almost completely as the weight of the body shifts to the pole. This offers a maximum swing of the body on the forward-upward motion. The upswing is developed through a pull-up rather than a jump-up.

The swing-up: On the swing-up the arms are partially flexed and the body arched as it leaves the extended leg and the ball of the takeoff foot. As the body swings forward-upward, the vaulter pulls up, flexes the body, and extends it upward and over the bar by dropping the legs and raising the hips. This phase of pole vaulting is called the jackknife. The twist is executed by vigorously kicking upward and outward with the left foot. After the push-up, a flip of the pole with the wrists will send it back and away from the crossbar. This action is the throw away. (See Fig. 25-9.)

Most necessary in the pole vault, of course, is the ability to be relaxed when landing. Strains, sprains, and broken bones can result from improper landing.

Fig. 25-10. Increased flexibility of fiber glass pole.

Fiber glass pole: The fiber glass pole does for the vaulter what the new parallel bars and horizontal bar do for the gymnast. In both cases the resiliency of the apparatus used aids the performer in the quest for greater power. This added power from the flexibility of the pole lifts the performer to greater heights.

The pole-plant for the fiber glass pole is basically the same as that for the aluminum alloy or steel poles. The handhold for the fiber glass pole is different from the one used with the other poles in that the hands are not brought together. They are kept about 16 inches apart. This is done to acquire the maximum bend and body control. (See Fig. 25-10.)

During the foot plant and spring, the ball of the takeoff foot is directly under the midway point between the hands on the pole.

This helps to cause a maximum pole bend. The mechanics of the vault after the liftoff are about the same as those for the steel pole, as was previously described. Because of the bend and whip of the fiber glass pole, the time should be faster and the action of the performer faster.

Weight-throwing events

SHOT PUT

The most common elementary method of holding the shot is at the base of the first three fingers. Elbows should be back and away from the body. A right-hander should stand with the left side toward the direction of the put. The head should be held erect. Observe Fig. 25-11: (1) the left arm is raised for balance as the weight is shifted to the right foot, (2) the putter hops in the putting direction on the right foot, (3) the landing is made on the right foot and the putter crouches for the toss, (4) a sideward step is executed with the left foot for balance and momentum, (5) beginning of the release drive is made from the right leg, abdominal muscles, arms, and chest, (6) the follow-through, and (7) the release. More advantageous mechanical styles have been developed that involve applying force over a longer distance by rotating the body one-half turn at the beginning of the put.

DISCUS

The discus is grasped firmly by the first joints of the fingers. The thumb should remain relaxed. (See Fig. 25-12.)

The feet should be comfortably spread with the left side toward the throwing direction. The discus is held in the right hand, over the left shoulder. It is supported with the left hand. Two or three windup motions are commonly performed with the discus being swung from front to rear as illustrated in (1) and (2) before the first turn of the body. A shift of the center of weight is made to the right foot as the discus is swung backward. From this position (2) the discus is whirled counterclockwise with a shift of weight to the left foot (3) and a one-half twist is made (4). Once again the weight shifts back to the right foot (5) as the discus continues in a circle and another one-half

Fig. 25-11. Progressive steps in the elementary shot put.

Fig. 25-12. Progressive steps in throwing the discus.

Fig. 25-13. Finnish crossover.

twist is executed (6). One step forward is now made with the left foot (7), and the discus whipped out of the hand for the throw. On the release a hop is made from the left to the right foot for stabilization (8). The discus leaves the hand at shoulder height and revolves counterclockwise. Notice that as the body twists, the right arm drags behind until the complete rotation is finished.

Javelin

The Finnish method is the most popular way of handling the javelin. In this method the shaft is held by the thumb and second finger at the edge of the cord.

The average preparatory run is about 115 feet. There are two methods of approach: the crossover and the hop step. The hop-step approach is the most widely used in the United States. Fig. 25-13 shows the crossover style of approach.

During the run in the hop-step method the javelin is carried at the level of the shoulder. On the hop, the hand is brought back for the throw and the left arm is brought forward and upward for balance. On the landing from the hop the right hand and shoulder should be in position for the delivery; that is, the body should be arched and rotated one-fourth twist to the right. The left arm and shoulder should be high. The eyes should be focused in the direction of the throw. On the next left step the javelin is released with an over-the-shoulder throw.

BASIC RULES

Sprinting

1. Tactics to disconcert an opponent cannot be used. Two warnings will cause disqualification.
2. A false start may be called if the runner does not comply with the command "on your mark" or "set."
3. A false start is declared if the runner jumps the gun. Two false starts disqualify a runner.
4. Runners cannot change lanes.

Hurdling

1. The entire body must pass over each hurdle.
2. The hurdler cannot run around a hurdle.
3. The hurdler must stay in the lane.
4. There shall be no disqualifications for knocking over any number of hurdles if all the other rules are obeyed.

Relay races

1. No one runner can be disqualified.
2. The baton must be passed inside the 20-meter passing zone.
3. The baton must be carried in the hand.
4. If the baton is dropped, it must be recovered legally.
5. The last runner of the race must have the baton.
6. After passing the baton, the runner must not interfere with the opponent.

High jump

1. The crossbar must be cleared without displacement.
2. The jump is false if after clearing the bar the jumper is at fault for knocking down the crossbar.

Pole vault

1. The crossbar must be cleared without displacement from either the body or the pole.
2. The pole must not touch beyond the vaulting box.
3. The pole must not fall under the bar.
4. The vaulter, during the vault, must not move the upper hand higher on the pole or the lower hand above the upper hand.

Long jump and triple jump

1. The shoe must not touch the scratch line.
2. The shoe must not extend over the scratch line.
3. The foot must not drag during the jump.

Shot put

1. A legal put must be used.
2. The competitor must put within the proper area.
3. No assisting device can be used.
4. The put must be from within the circle.
5. The competitor must stay within the circle after the put until the distance is marked.

Discus

1. The throw must land within the sector.
2. The competitor must stay within the circle until the distance is marked.
3. The complete throw must be from within the circle.
4. The proper discus must be used.

Javelin

1. The throw must be performed within the sector.
2. The point tip must strike the ground first.
3. The javelin must be held by the cord grip.
4. A regulation javelin must be used.
5. The javelin must not be pointed in the direction of the opponents.

Hammer

1. The throw must be within the sector.
2. The competitor must stay within the

324 BASIC SKILLS IN SPORTS FOR MEN AND WOMEN

throwing area after the throw until the throw is marked.
3. During the throw the competitor must not leave the circle.
4. The implement must be legal.
5. Gloves may be used.

SAFETY PRECAUTIONS FOR TRACK AND FIELD EVENTS

Sprinting
1. Run through a few adaptive conditioning exercises.
2. Do not fall through the tape.
3. Wear the right size shoes.

Hurdling
1. Run through a few adaptive conditioning exercises.
2. Be serious about practice jumps and runs.
3. Constantly strive to improve form.

High jump
1. Warm up with a few adaptive exercises.
2. Always try to land on hands and feet.
3. Do not jump from a wet surface or with wet soles.
4. See that the pit is ready.

Long jump
1. Adaptive exercises should be used for a warm-up.
2. Wear the proper shoe.
3. See that the pit is ready.
4. Be sure that the takeoff board is dry.

Shot put, discus, and javelin
1. Warm up with adaptive exercises.
2. Practice in a secluded area.
3. Do not leave the shot where someone else will carelessly use it.

GLOSSARY OF TRACK AND FIELD TERMS

A.A.U. Amateur Athletic Union.
anchor The last runner of a relay.
approach Method of movement used by the performer just before the throw or jump.
baton An object passed from one runner to another in a relay race.
blind pass Receiving the baton without seeing it.
break Jumping the gun; leaving the block before the gun.
circle Area used for the shot put and discus throw.
clear the watches Setting the watches back to zero.
crossbar A bar over which the high jumper or pole-vaulter must pass.
dead heat A tie of two or more runners.
drive leg The first leg to take off in jumping or vaulting.
exchange zone Area 20 meters long in a lane used for passing the baton in relay races.
false start *see* Break.
flight Preliminary contest for purposes of testing competitors and for elimination; also refers to one lane of hurdles.
follow-through The motion of the body following release of an object.
heat The preliminary round of a race, the winners of which participate in the semifinals and finals.
kick Increased leg speed at the end of a race.
leg of a relay The distance that one runner must run.
medley relay A relay with each runner running different distances.
pace The runner's rate of speed.
shot A cast-iron, bronze, or brass shell with a lead center.
shuttle relay Alternately running from one end of the track to the other or from one line to another.
staggered start Starting a race in which the runners do not start on a straight line.
visual exchange Watching the incoming runner until the pass of the baton is completed.

REFERENCES
Cretzmeyer, F. X., Alley, L. E., and Tipton, C. M.: Track and field athletics, ed. 8, St. Louis, 1974, The C. V. Mosby Co.
Menke, Frank G.: Encyclopedia of sports, ed. 2, New York, 1966, A. S. Barnes & Co.
Official A.A.U. handbook, New York, 1969, The Amateur Athletic Union of the United States.
Official collegiate track and field guide, New York, 1969, The National Collegiate Athletic Association.
Seaton, D. D., Clayton, I. A., Leibee, H. C., and Messersmith, L.: Physical education handbook, ed. 3, Englewood Cliffs, N. J., 1965, Prentice-Hall, Inc.
Track and field guide, Washington, D. C., 1968-1970, D.G.W.S.

26 Trampoline

HISTORY

Rebound tumbling is a relatively new sport in physical education. Two centuries ago it started with a small beginning such as springboards, or a fulcrum placed under both ends of a board. The flexible plank for the leaps grew out of a man's urge to overcome gravity and allowed the performer to leap higher with less effort, thus performing feats otherwise impossible for acrobats and tumblers. The springboard allowed the performer to leap higher and land in nets.

Du Trampoline, a professional circus performer, experimented with crude systems of spring suspensions using aerialist's nets. He reduced the size of the net for practical reasons and developed the earliest form of the apparatus now bearing his name.

Rebound tumbling has gained widespread recognition as a new and exciting gymnastic sport that provides physical benefits for all ages and both sexes. Within recent years this apparatus has been installed in many schools and colleges and has found a place in physical education programs for both sexes.

Rebound tumbling is really a combination of springboard diving and tumbling. The basic skills to be learned are the same.

VALUES

Rebound tumbling is a means of developing muscular control and coordination and a sense of precise balance and timing of bodily movements. It produces poise and confidence in one's own ability. It is appealing to both sexes and is a pleasurable experience.

EQUIPMENT

1. Gym shirt
2. Shorts
3. Supporter
4. Socks
5. Gymnastic shoes or cloth slippers with rubber soles

RULES (A.A.U. COMPETITION)

1. Each contestant shall perform one compulsory and one voluntary routine. The compulsory routine is to have ten skills. The voluntary is to have ten to twelve. The contestant's mark is the added scores of both routines. The count begins as the performer does the first stunt, with a 20-second rest between routines.
2. The performer should stand at attention on the trampoline until the head judge gives the signal to start. At the end of the routine, the performer

should kill the bounce and stop. *Mounts and dismounts are not used.*
3. National collegiate trampoline championship tests consist of the execution of two routines—a compulsory routine set up by the International Trampoline Federation and an optional routine. It is the combined scores of these two routines that determine the individual winners. A trampoline team shall consist of four members. The best three scores on the compulsory routine will be added as part of the team score. These are added to the best three of the optional routines. The optional routine consists of ten movements. Following is a sample of the compulsory routine: 1¾ forward somersault in pike position, baroni ball-out to feet, layout backward somersault, backward somersault with one twist, piked ¾ backward somersault to stomach, tucked cody to feet, forward somersault with 1½ twist, baroni, and tucked double backward somersault.
4. Scoring is based on 10 points per judge. Point distribution should be based on form, execution, control, and difficulty.
5. Officials consist of four judges, one referee, one assistant referee, one counter, and one recorder. High and low scores are discarded and the remaining scores are added together. One judge is the head judge. A scorekeeper is needed to tabulate scores.

SAFETY RULES

1. The trampoline should not be used without official supervision.
2. When not supervised, it should be locked or bolted up against the wall.
3. Inexperienced students should not bounce the trampoline without safety spotters placed strategically around it to prevent injury.
4. The metal frame of the trampoline should be covered with pads.
5. Beginners should be taught how to kill an out-of-control bounce. The technique is the same as that on a springboard.

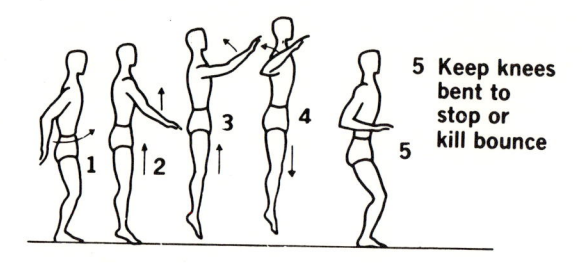

Fig. 26-1. Feet bounce.

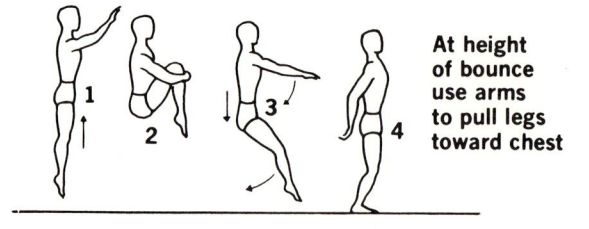

Fig. 26-2. Bounce and tuck.

6. Beginners should not bounce too high at first.
7. Spotters should be on all sides. When extra spotters are available, they should double up on the two ends.

FUNDAMENTAL SKILL TECHNIQUE OBJECTIVES

Nine fundamental bounces

An analysis of the nine fundamental bounces follows. These bounces must be learned in the following progressive sequence—do not take short cuts.

FEET BOUNCE (WORKING THE BED)

The reader should refer to Figs. 26-1 and 26-2.
1. Stand with the body and head erect, eyes spotted on bed, and weight on the balls of the feet. Rise on the toes as the arms are raised; swing the arms down sharply, flexing the hips and knees. This movement presses the bed downward.
2. As the bed recoils, extend the hips and knees as the arms lift up. Extend the toes down against the recoil of the bed as far as possible. Maintain the eye spot on the bed.
3. At the top peak of the bounce, float the arm swing and bring the arms into position for the downswing as the

Fig. 26-3. Hands and knees bounce.

Keep arms straight. Do not bounce too high when first trying stunt!

3 When landing on knees, do not bend at hips!

Fig. 26-4. Knees bounce.

body descends to the bed. Never lose the eye spot on the bed throughout the entire movement. It helps to maintain balance in the air.
4. In landing, swing the arms down sideward and through past the hips. At the same time, extend the hips, knees, and ankles for continuous rebounds. This is called working the bed.

Helpful hints
1. Start with the feet about 10 to 14 inches apart.
2. Look forward and downward at a spot on the bed or end of the frame.
3. Learn at the start to stop or kill the rebound at the end of the exercise by flexing the hips and knees quickly to absorb the recoil of the bed.
4. Swing the arms evenly throughout the exercises; otherwise, balance and rhythm are lost.
5. This exercise is called working the bed, just as the same exercise in springboard diving is called working the board.

HANDS AND KNEES BOUNCE

The reader should refer to Fig. 26-3.
1. As a beginner, start the movement on the hands and knees, back parallel with the bed. From this position, start takeoff by extending hips and knees and swinging arms and head upward. Land again on all fours until the feel of the movement is experienced and improved.
2. Attempt the takeoff now from a standing position and take one or two bounces in the erect position and then drop to the knees and hands, by executing a backward-downward movement. Do not jump forward. On the recoil to regain starting foot position, extend hips and knees, reach upward with the arms. Spot on the bed throughout the movement.

KNEES BOUNCE

The reader should refer to Fig. 26-4.
1. Start the movement with several low foot bounces. Focus the eyes forward and downward. The body must be held erect.
2. To drop on the knees on the descent, flex the knees and hips very slightly and swing the heels up behind so the foreleg is parallel with the bed. The arm swing movement is the same as in the feet bounce, except that at the end of the downswing the elbows are bent sharply to change to a lift motion. Keep the back straight.
3. On recoil, extend the hips, swing the arms up, hold the head erect, spot on the bed, and as the knees leave the bed, extend them and bring the feet down

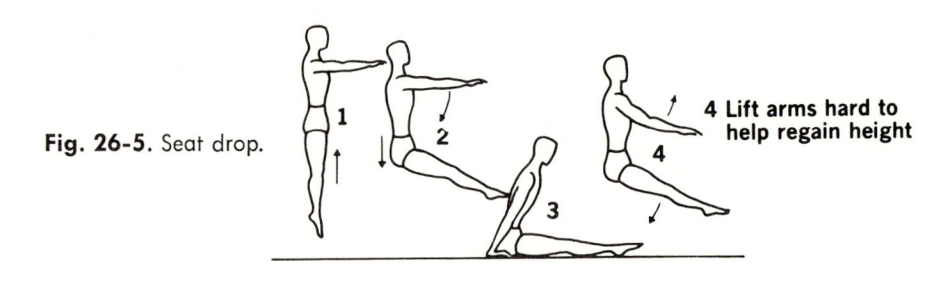

Fig. 26-5. Seat drop.

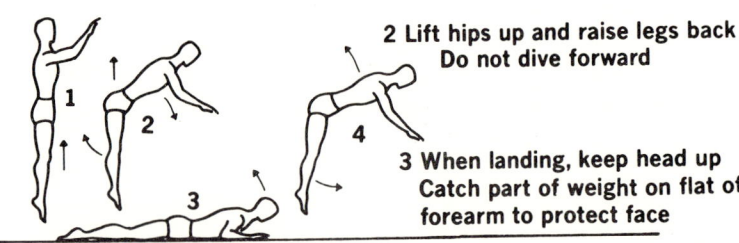

1
2
3
4 Lift arms hard to help regain height

1
2 Lift hips up and raise legs back
Do not dive forward
3 When landing, keep head up
Catch part of weight on flat of forearm to protect face
4

Fig. 26-6. Front drop.

to again land on the bed in an erect feet-bounce position.

Helpful hints
1. Not too much height is needed in this exercise.
2. Land on the knees and on lower legs.
3. When contact is made, drive the bed down by extending the hips.
4. As a beginner, attempt several continuous drops and rebounds to get the feel of the movement and balance.

SEAT DROP

The reader should refer to Fig. 26-5.
1. Execute this exercise from the feet bounce.
2. On the drop, hold the trunk and head erect, focus forward and down on the bed, holding the arms above the head on the reach, swing the legs forward with the knees straight but flex the hips. Lower the hands forward and down to a position behind the hips, palms down. Land on the hands, buttocks, thighs, and heels simultaneously. Do not jump forward.
3. In executing the rebound, push the bed down with the hand and swing the arms up to the lift; extend the hips and press the legs down on clearing the bed.
4. Land again in the feet-bounce position. Maintain the spot throughout for balance.

Helpful hints
1. Use the arms for balance but keep them level throughout the entire exercise.
2. Several continuous repetitions help the performer to gain balance and confidence.
3. During the takeoff, pull the head and shoulders back slightly.
4. At the takeoff, reach high with the arms in order to achieve a high lift and to regain feet.

FRONT DROP

In the front drop the body lands on the bed in an extended prone position (face down) on the hands and forearms, chest, abdomen, thighs, and ankles. From this position, regain the feet-bounce position. (See Fig. 26-6.)
1. Start the exercise from the feet-bounce position.
2. Execute the drop from a reasonably high bounce. Flex the hips and knees slightly and lift the hips simultaneously with this movement; lower the arms, as well as the head and shoulders, forward and down as if to land on all fours. This gives a forward rotation to the body, similar to executing a somersault. Continue the rotation forward until the back is parallel to the bed, the upper arms and thighs flexed sufficiently to be perpendicular to the

Fig. 26-7. Back drop.

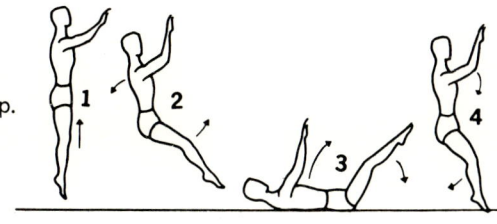

3 Keep head forward so as not to whip back against bed

trunk under the body. The body actually has the appearance of landing on all fours.
3. To stop or check forward rotation, raise the head when the trunk is horizontal, spot down, and prepare for landing on the bed.
4. To land, extend the legs out straight and raise the head. Land flat on the hands, chest, abdomen, hips, thighs, and feet simultaneously. Do not land on the elbows.
5. Rebound by pushing forcefully with the hands. Raise the arms, head, and shoulders, and then bend the hips and swing the legs down.
6. As the body now begins to drop to the feet bounce, extend the hips and straighten the body to the erect position.

Helpful hints
1. The takeoff is the same as for the feet bounce.
2. Not too much height is needed on the bounce.
3. In dropping for the front drop, keep the legs low.
4. Separate the feet about shoulder width throughout the exercise.

BACK DROP

The back drop is executed from the feet-bounce position. The performer lands on the back and recovers again to the starting position. (See Fig. 26-7.)
1. Use a low bounce when first attempting this exercise.
2. First start a backward rotation with the body.
3. This is executed on the upward bounce by lifting the arms overhead and pressing the abdomen and hips forward. Permit the shoulder girdle to bear and give backward at the same time. As the body drops preparatory to landing on the back, draw the knees up toward the chest.
4. Land flat on the back, holding the back firmly rigid, hold the head forward with the chin on the chest, and spot at the far end of the trampoline.
5. To rebound, raise the head forward and straighten the legs forward. As the body lifts strongly, press the hip forward and now swing the legs downward toward the bed. The body should descend to the bed in the feet-bounce position.

Helpful hints
1. This fundamental skill will be very difficult for the beginner to learn and execute while still maintaining balance.
2. At the top of the rebound, the body should be arched. The legs are pressed down under the center of body weight.

HALF-TWIST AND FULL-TWIST BOUNCE

This feet bounce and twist is performed exactly like the front jump* dive in springboard diving. The student should learn the basic techniques of body twister movements as soon as the bounces discussed previously have been mastered.

From the feet bounce the arms are reached upward while the body is held in vertical alignment as it leaves the bed. If the twist is to be made to the right, the right arm remains elevated as the twisting mechanics are executed with the left arm.

Swing the left arm down and across close to the chest and push it upward past the opposite shoulder and slightly beyond head

---
*See jump dives in Armbruster, D. A., Allen, R. H., and Billingsley, H. S.: Swimming and diving, ed. 6, St. Louis, 1973, The C. V. Mosby Co.

330 BASIC SKILLS IN SPORTS FOR MEN AND WOMEN

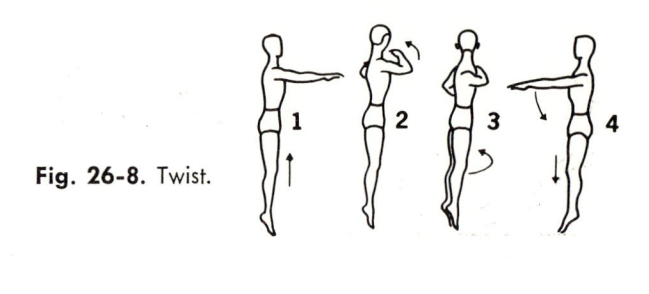

Fig. 26-8. Twist.

Half twist to left
2 Pull left arm back and throw right arm to left as shown in 2 and 3; at same time turn head to left

To stop twist, 4, brake arms out from folded position

3 Bring legs up to touch hands. Do not bend upper body forward

Fig. 26-9. Jackknife.

level. As the left arm passes in front of the right shoulder, simultaneously the head does an about-face, the eyes are focused, and the right arm is lowered with the elbow bent pushing backward to square the shoulders. When landing on the bed, the body faces in the opposite direction from the beginning of the stunt. (See Fig. 26-8.)

The full-twist bounce is just an exaggeration of the half-twist bounce. This sometimes is called the pirouette, as in dancing.

The student should try twisting to both left and right to determine which way is best.

In rebound tumbling parlance this exercise is sometimes called swivel hips.

The twisting should occur just as the body approaches the peak of its upward movement.

Tuck and bounce

From the feet bounce, lift straight up and, while near the full height, draw the legs up to the chest and hook the hands around the shins. This is a tuck position. On the way down, drop the legs and land in a standing position.

Split jackknife bounce

From the feet bounce, lift straight up and, while near full height, spread and lift the legs until they are horizontal with the bed, hold the knees straight, and touch the toes with the hands. On the down drop, lower the legs and land on the feet. (See Fig. 26-9.)

Advanced turns and twists

These preliminary exercises serve as warm-ups or feelers. They form the basic foundation for acquiring confidence and courage in preparation for more advanced turns and twists such as those to be described.

Swivel hips

The swivel hips is a combination seat drop, half twist, to seat drop. From the seat drop, throw the arms straight up over the head, lower the legs, and twist the upper body. The rotation is around the vertical axis. Drop the arms and raise the legs for the landing. If this is done correctly, the arms will describe a full circle. (See Fig. 26-10.)

Half turntable

The half turntable is one of the few movements that rotate around the dorsoventral axis or short axis. First execute the belly drop. On the rebound, push forcibly to the right if the turn is to be to the left and throw the whole upper body to the left. To make a full turn, flex the knees and tuck. (See Fig. 26-11.)

TRAMPOLINE 331

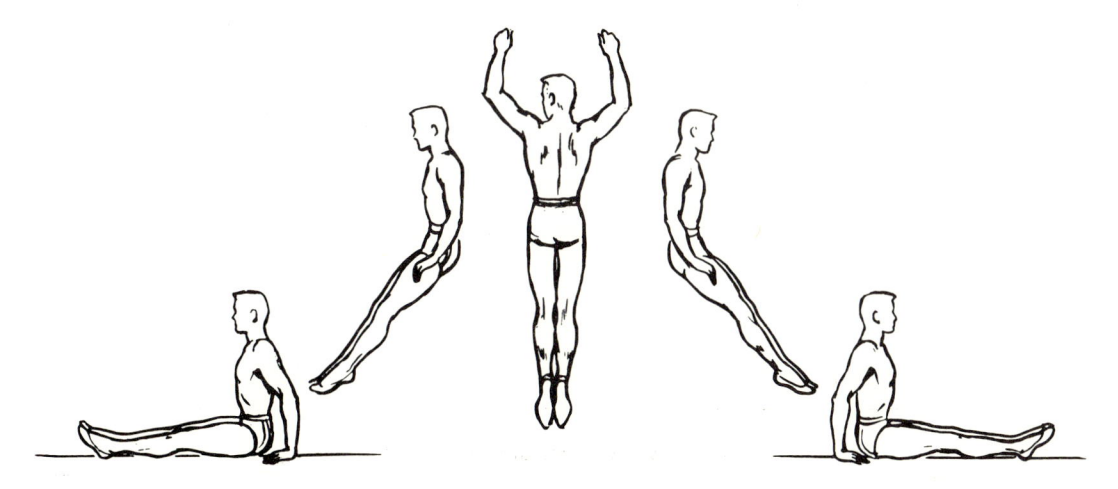

Fig. 26-10. Swivel hips.

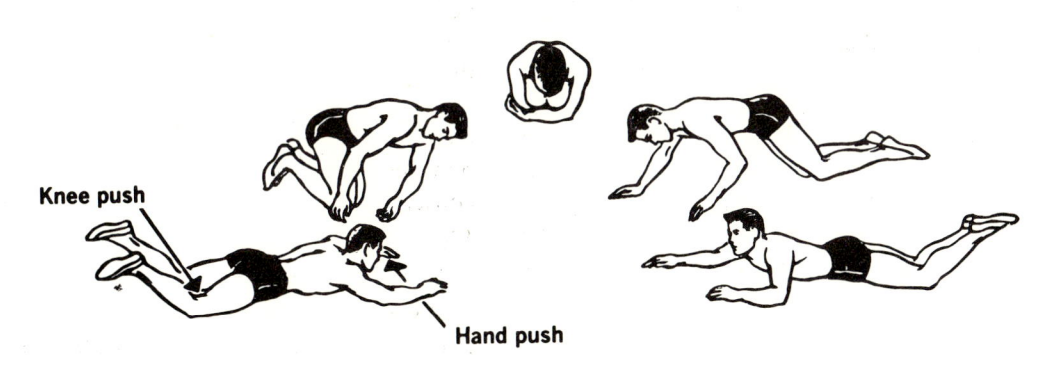

Knee push

Hand push

Fig. 26-11. Half turntable.

Fig. 26-12. Cradle.

Fig. 26-13. Front airo or somersault.

Cradle

The cradle revolves first around the horizontal axis, then the vertical axis, and then the horizontal again. This is a back drop, half twist, and back drop. First learn the back drop half twist to the feet. This is accomplished by pushing hard with the opposite hand from the twist and rotating the hips in the desired direction. To execute the cradle, speed up the forward rotation, bringing the feet up after the twist, and land on the back. (See Fig. 26-12.)

Front Airo or Somersault

Execute the regular forward-upward lift to get sufficient elevation, and then throw down with the hands, flex the head on the chest, and lift the hips. Tuck tightly but untuck immediately. Learn this first in the safety belt. (See Fig. 26-13.)

Back Airo or Somersault

There are a number of different types of back airos: the tuck back, the loose back or consecutive back, the cannonball or vertical shoot, the jackknife, and the layout back. Illustrated here is the loose back—the one best suited for doing a series of backs. These airos should be initiated and completed in the center of the bed. As the body leaves the bed, the head is extended and the chest lifted for rotation. To return to the area of the bed from which the airo was started, the body must make a forward-upward movement from the takeoff. Many rebound tumbling performers prefer to tuck during their consecutive turns. Use the safety belt. (See Fig. 26-14.)

Brandy or Baroni

If performed correctly, the brandy is a half twist around the vertical axis while doing a forward airo. (See Fig. 26-15.)

Take off with the body slightly flexed at the waist. (See example 1.) Drop the upper body down and raise the hips. (See example 2.) Rotate the right shoulder back and lower the left shoulder. (See example 3.) Keep the eyes on the bed at all times and pike the body. (See examples 4 and 5.) Flex at the knees for the landing. (See example 6.)

Develop the brandy by first doing the knee drop, cartwheel, and knee drop. Next try a knee drop and round off to the feet.

Cody (Back Airo from Front Drop)

Push forcibly with the arms and hands off the front drop. As the body ascends and

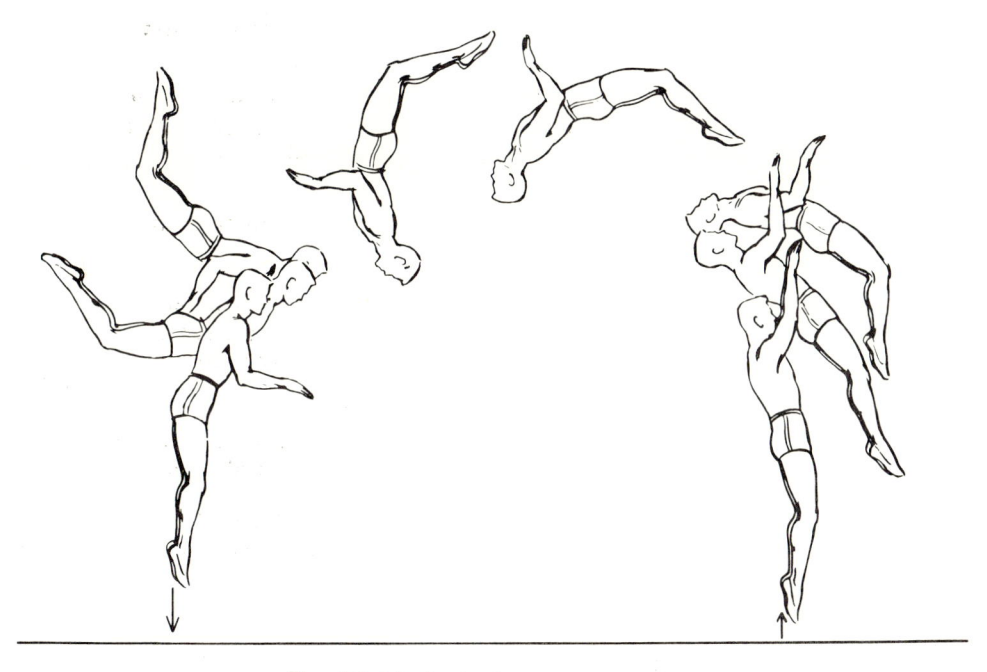

Fig. 26-14. Back airo or somersault.

Fig. 26-15. Brandy or baroni.

passes over the 45-degree angle, tuck tightly for the rotation. This stunt must be initiated from a high preliminary bounce. Use the safety belt. (See Fig. 26-16.)

COMBINATION ROUTINES

Once the preceding routines have been learned and confidence has been gained, combinations can be worked up as a routine. The following suggested sequence of progressions is recommended:

1. Front drop to seat drop
2. Half twist to back drop
3. Half twist to front drop
4. Seat drop to front drop
5. Back drop to front drop
6. Front drop to back drop
7. Front drop to half turntable
8. Front drop to full turntable
9. Seat drop to half twist to seat drop
10. Seat drop to full twist to seat drop
11. Front three-quarter somersault to seat drop
12. Seat drop to back somersault to feet

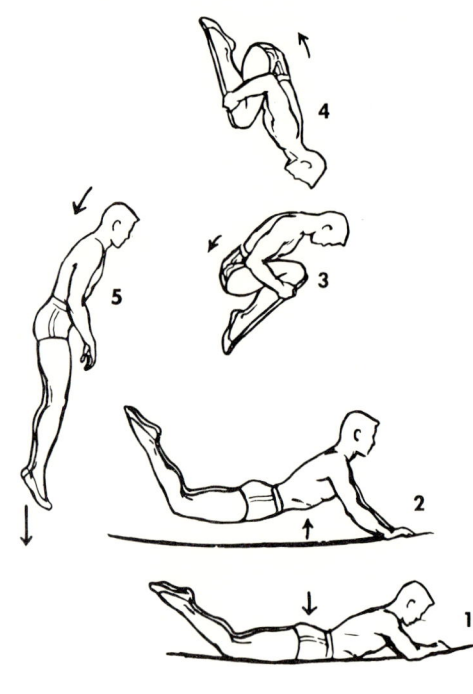

Fig. 26-16. Cody.

13. Cat twist (back drop, full twist, and back drop)
14. Back somersault to seat drop
15. Back airo from knees to seat (tuck)
16. Front turnover to hands and knees, to feet
17. Back airo to hands and knees

REFERENCES

Kenney, Chuck: Trampolining illustrated, New York, 1961, The Ronald Press Co.
LaDue, Frank, and Norman, Jim: This is trampolining, ed. 2, Cedar Rapids, 1965, Nissen Trampoline Co.
Musker, Frank, Irwin, Leslie, and Casady, Don: The gymnastic guide, New York, 1968, The Macmillan Co.
Norman, Randi: Gymnastics for girls and women, Dubuque, Iowa, 1965, William C. Brown Co., Publishers.

FILMS

Elementary tumbling, Audio Visual Aids Department, University of Iowa.
The official A.A.U. gymnastic championships, A.A.U. Motion Picture Library, New York, N. Y.
Up in the air, Nissen Trampoline Co., Cedar Rapids, Iowa.
Whatever goes up, Universal International Films, Inc., New York, N. Y.

27 Tumbling

DESCRIPTION

Tumbling is the art of manipulating the body in feats of skill without the use of apparatus. Tumbling maneuvers include rolls, somersaults, twists, springs, heels overhead, balances on hands, and manipulation of the body in unusual positions.

From primitive times and through all stages of development, mankind has nurtured desires and impulses to learn new ways to move the body. Tumbling offers such an outlet.

BRIEF HISTORY

The earliest historical records, in the form of painting, sculpture, and literature, indicate that tumbling was connected with the dance, the most fundamental art of living of the people. The research findings of N. de Garis Davies show that tumblers had a distinct place in the professional dance groups of Egypt and that they participated in religious ceremonies, celebrations, processions, and funerals.

Tumblers of early times had an important influence upon entertainment and the theater, and in Greece and Rome the tumblers entertained at private dinner parties and social occasions.

The word "tumble" is Teutonic in origin and meant "to dance violently, to dance with posturing, balancing, and contortions." Tumbling was very popular during the middle ages. The terms used by other nationalities showed similar spelling and embodied the same activities of somersaulting, rolling, and contorting the body.

From the fifteenth to the eighteenth century, tumbling was a favorite entertainment of royalty. Queen Elizabeth, an ardent admirer of tumbling, maintained a company of tumblers that was quite famous.

About 1810, Frederick Jahn and Adolph Spiess founded and developed the German system of gymnastics that included marching, tumbling, mat stunts, and heavy apparatus work. Jahn organized his students into clubs called Turnverein.

About 1850, a wave of German immigration brought these clubs to the United States and the name was changed to the Turner Society.

About this time, wandering entertainers, tumblers, jugglers, and rope dancers came to America from other countries and found favor with the people in spite of the hostility of some religious groups.

An act of Congress prohibited tumbling along with all other forms of entertainment during the Revolutionary War. However, following the Revolution the art was no longer banned, and tumblers performed in circuses and on showboats.

The professional tumbler exerted influence in bringing tumbling into the modern program of physical education as a skill activity in the schools, colleges, and Y.M.C.A.s. The popularity of the sport was also responsible for the organization of the American Turners, the Swiss Gymnastic Association, the American Sokol, and other groups.

There is no question that springboard diving in swimming pools and rebound tumbling on the modern trampoline are outgrowths of the tumbling art.

EQUIPMENT

A firm and nonslippery mat or a grassy field is all that is necessary. Gym shoes and a proper gymnasium costume with supporter are adequate.

For competition, the mat should be 5 feet wide and at least 60 feet long.

FUNDAMENTAL SKILL TECHNIQUES

Tumbling provides an excellent means for developing agility, poise, and balance and for building total muscular strength. Success in learning new skills gives the individual self-confidence, courage, and determination.

Lead-up developmental exercises

Figs. 27-1 to 27-9 (animal walks) should be utilized as part of the conditioning program. Fig. 27-9, the snail drag, is especially good for developing the upper body.

Tumbling stunts

Figs. 27-10 to 27-20 are considered progressive ability stunts of the first level of proficiency.

Spinal rock: Keep the head up, grasp the shins, pull tight, and rock. (See Fig. 27-10.)

Forward roll: Reach forward, duck the head well under, round the back, roll, and tuck. (See Fig. 27-11.)

Fig. 27-1. Galloping dog. Run on all fours.

Forward roll to back: Complete the forward roll but do not lift the head after passing over it. (See Fig. 27-12.)

Forward roll—arms folded: Cross the arms, place the head on the mat, and then roll. Keep the arms folded until back on the feet. (See Fig. 27-13.)

Forward roll—arms horizontal: Extend the arms to the side, place the head on the mat, and roll with a tight flexion. Keep the

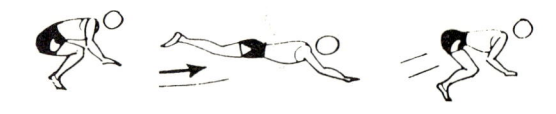

Fig. 27-2. Squirrel hop. Dive to hands and land in squat.

Fig. 27-3. Crab walk. Belly up.

Fig. 27-4. Elephant walk. Keep knees stiff and spread feet.

Fig. 27-5. Wet-cat footwalk. Walk on three limbs and shake one.

Fig. 27-6. Bear walk. Same as elephant walk but feet together.

Fig. 27-7. Duck waddle. Keep knees bent with hands on hips.

TUMBLING 337

Fig. 27-8. Kangaroo hop. Place hands on mat, kick feet in air, and land in squat position with hands still on mat. Reach forward and repeat.

Fig. 27-9. Snail drag. Keep legs inactive and drag body with arms.

Fig. 27-10. Spinal rock.

Fig. 27-11. Forward roll.

Fig. 27-12. Forward roll to back.

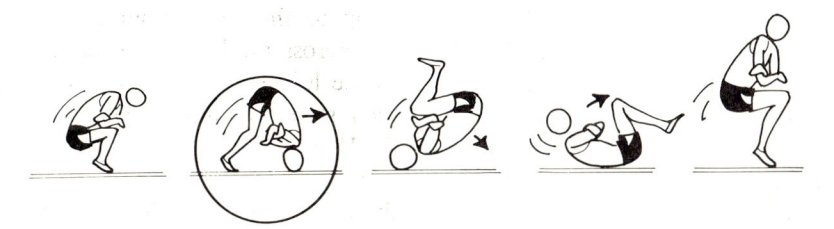

Fig. 27-13. Forward roll—arms folded.

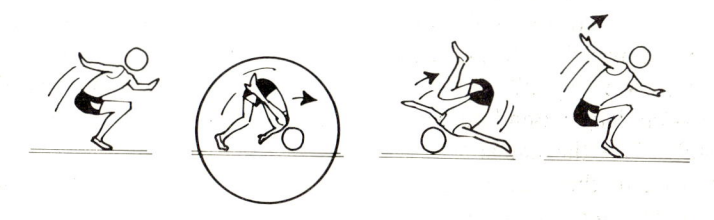

Fig. 27-14. Forward roll—arms horizontal.

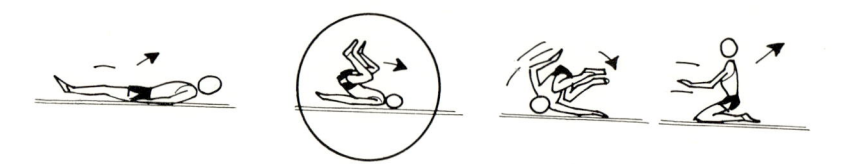

Fig. 27-15. Backward roll over shoulder.

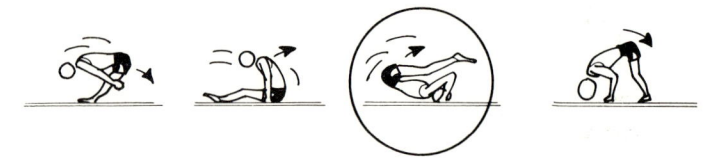

Fig. 27-16. Backward roll—jackknife.

Fig. 27-17. Backward extension roll.

arms horizontal until completion of the roll. (See Fig. 27-14.)

Forward roll—legs crossed: Cross the legs first. Reach well forward, duck the head well under, roll tight, and tuck. Make a half turn on ascending.

Forward roll—holding toes: Spread the knees apart and do a deep knee bend. Reach down between the knees and grasp the toes. Now place the head on the mat and roll. Force the head and shoulders forward.

Forward roll—hands behind head: Lace the fingers behind the head, do a deep knee bend, place the head on the mat, and roll with a tight flexion.

Backward roll over shoulders: Lie down on the mat face up, place the right hand down by the side and the left arm out to the side, turn the head to the right and bring the knees up and over the left shoulder. Land on the knees. (See Fig. 27-15.)

Backward roll—jackknife: Bend forward with the knees stiff, place the hands behind the thighs, drop back to the seat, raise the legs, and roll straight over the head. (See Fig. 27-16.)

Backward extension roll: Start this one the same as the backward roll, jackknife, but when going over the head, shoot the legs to the ceiling and push hard with the hands. (See Fig. 27-17.)

Football roll: Spread the feet apart, bend over, and place the left hand on the mat. Reach under the left arm with the right. Drop to the right shoulder, roll over, and roll across the back from the right shoulder to the left hip. Get up on the left knee and then step up on the right foot. (See Fig. 27-18.)

Squat headstand: Make a triangle with the head and hands. Slowly place the knees on the elbows. (See Fig. 27-19.)

Flying angel: Bottom performer pulls the top performer over the body slowly. Top performer then arches the back and raises the head. (See Fig. 27-20.)

Headstand: Be sure that the head and hands are in a good triangle. Place the forehead, not the top of the head, on the mat. Raise the hips slowly, maintaining balance at all times. Now raise the legs slowly. (See Fig. 27-21.)

Fig. 27-18. Football roll.

Fig. 27-19. Squat headstand.

Fig. 27-20. Flying angel.

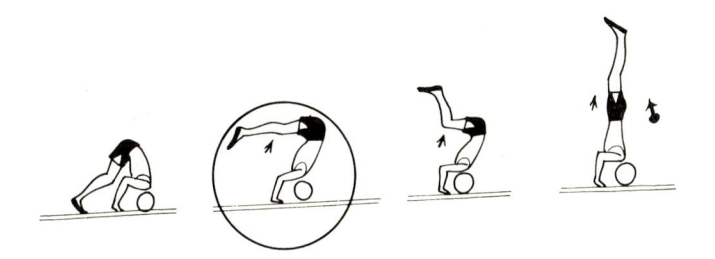

Fig. 27-21. Headstand.

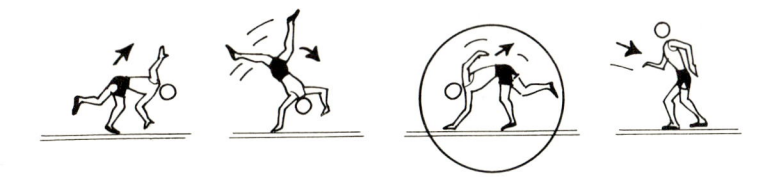

Fig. 27-22. Cartwheel.

Fig. 27-23. Cheststand on partner.

Cartwheel: In doing a cartwheel, step and face into the handstand position. Place the foot in the opposite direction when landing. (See Fig. 27-22.)

Cheststand on partner: Place the chest on the back of the partner, grasp the upper arm and thigh, kick slowly into position, hold tight, and arch the back. (See Fig. 27-23.)

Two high: The important move here is the hand position. Top performer-to-be stands in back of the bottom performer-to-be. Bottom performer reaches over the shoulders with the palms up. Top performer

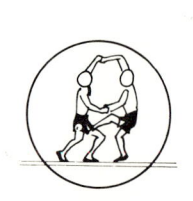

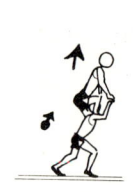

Fig. 27-24. Two high.

Fig. 27-25. Handstand support.

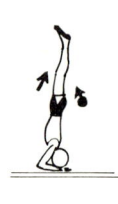

Fig. 27-26. Headstand in hands.

places the palms in the bottom performer's. Holding this hand position, the two face each other. The position now should be like shaking hands with the left hands, right hands over the head. Top performer-to-be places the left foot on the bottom performer's left thigh. This is done from the side with the toe of the top performer pointing in toward the middle of the bottom performer's body. As the bottom performer pulls with the right hand, the top performer steps up on the shoulder. (See Fig. 27-24.)

Handstand support: Keep the head up as you kick up. The catcher should stand to the side to prevent being kicked in the face. (See Fig. 27-25.)

Headstand in hands: Place the forehead in the hands and the forearms on the mat. Kick up slowly. (See Fig. 27-26.)

Snail roll: Lie down on the belly and place the hands on the hips. Turn the head to the left and raise the hips as high as possible. Now turn the head under so that the back of the head is on the floor and the chin is on the chest. The elbows should now be resting on the floor. Transfer the weight of the body from the right shoulder to the left and lower the hips back to the floor by extending the body. (See Fig. 27-27.)

• • •

Figs. 27-28 to 27-46 are exercises for the student who has advanced to a more progressive level of tumbling skill, and they represent the second level of proficiency.

Triple roll: From the three-performer lying position, the middle performer rolls to the left and the performer on the left springs from the hands and knees over the middle performer, landing in the middle. The middle performer executes only one full turn and comes to rest on hands and knees. This is repeated from left to right. (See Fig. 27-28.)

Dive and roll over three performers: First teach a simple dive and roll. Use a two-foot takeoff. Be sure to dive high enough. Land first on the hands, then duck the head, and roll. Flex the body tight and tuck if possible. (See Fig. 27-29.)

Headsnap over mat: The best way to learn this is to do a flexed headstand. Let the body fall off-balance. Just as the balance

Fig. 27-27. Snail roll.

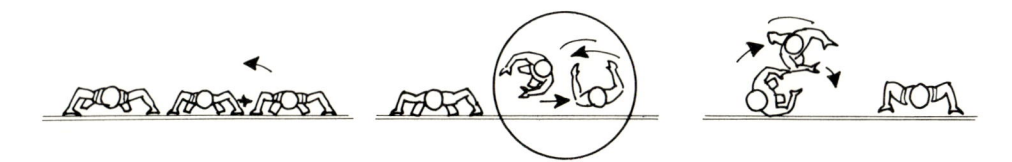

Fig. 27-28. Triple roll.

Fig. 27-29. Dive and roll over three men.

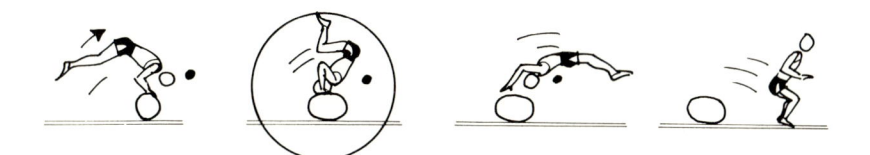

Fig. 27-30. Headsnap over mat.

Fig. 27-31. Double roll with partner.

is lost, kick hard and push with the hands. (See Fig. 27-30.)

Double roll with partner: Hold onto each other's ankles, as shown in Fig. 27-31. Flex the knees and place the feet on the floor close to the thighs. Spread the knees apart so that the performer on top can duck the head and roll. This is important. Work hard to help the other performer.

Fish dive: This is done from the standing position. Kick either foot backward and upward and jump off the other foot. Land on the hands with the feet over the head. At this point the body should be in the handstand position. Now bend the arms and let the body down, rolling from the chest to the knees. Flex at the waist and push hard with the hands until the weight is back over the feet. Lift the body to the squat stand. (See Fig. 27-32.)

Arabian cartwheel: To do this stunt properly, take about a 10-yard run, finish with

Fig. 27-32. Fish dive.

Fig. 27-33. Arabian cartwheel.

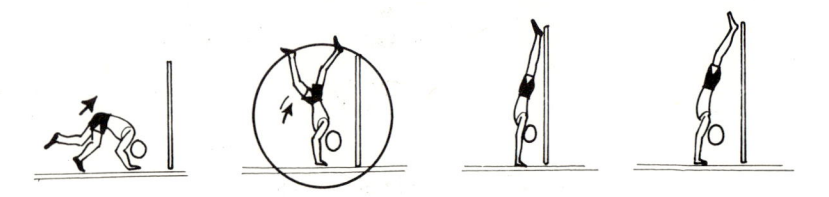

Fig. 27-34. Handstand against wall.

Fig. 27-35. Tiger stand.

a short hop, dive about 5 feet, and do a cartwheel. (See Fig. 27-33.)

Handstand against wall: The main thing to remember in kicking up against the wall is to keep the head up. If the head is not kept up, the body usually falls in a heap. (See Fig. 27-34.)

Tiger stand: Try to keep the upper arm perpendicular to the floor and kick up slowly. (See Fig. 27-35.)

Round-off: Important: do not forget the short hop at the end of the run. Whip the hands down to the mat. Keep the arms fully extended. Put the left hand down with a quarter turn and the right one down with a half turn. Snap to the feet. (See Fig. 27-36.)

Mule kick: The best way to start this is from the handstand. Bend the knees a little and the arms. Snap the legs downward and push hard with the arms. This is the true landing position—body bent forward and arms reaching backward and upward. Immediately use the lift of the arms and jump back up into the handstand position. As the jump is made, keep the head down. (See Fig. 27-37.)

Fifteen-second handstand: Kick into a good balance and lock. Keep the head up and use the fingers. Point the toes and tighten the muscles through the hips.

Pitch-back airo: Top performer stands in the palms of the bottom performer. On the

Fig. 27-36. Round-off.

Fig. 27-37. Mule kick.

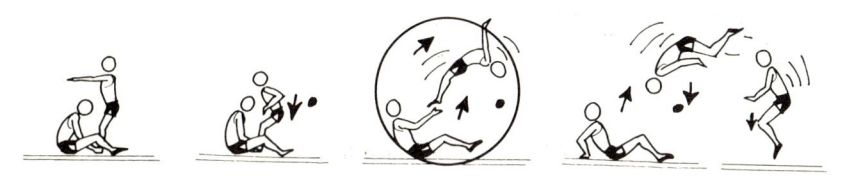

Fig. 27-38. Pitch-back airo.

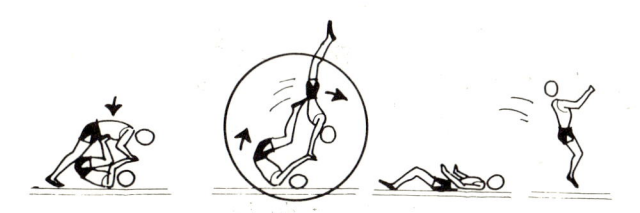

Fig. 27-39. Pitch from belly.

count of three, the top performer throws the arms straight for the ceiling and jumps with all strength. The top performer then throws the head back and forcibly brings the knees up to give rotation. As the top performer jumps, the bottom performer lifts straight up and sits back to prevent being kicked in the face. The thing to watch for in this stunt is the overthrow. Be sure to have a spotter or safety belt. This is very important. Never teach this skill without spotting. (See Fig. 27-38.)

Pitch from belly: This is a handspring with the assistance of the bottom performer. The top performer places the stomach on the bottom performer's feet. The feet are placed in a V position—heels together, toes apart. The bottom performer pulls the top performer forward, and as all the top performer's weight is felt, the bottom performer pulls the top performer's upper body forward and pushes hard with the feet. As the top performer's weight passes over, the bottom performer pushes with the hands. It is important to have at least one spotter assisting so that the top performer will not overthrow. (See Fig. 27-39.)

Kip from mat: While in the lying position, place the hands over the shoulders on the floor and roll back until the weight is on the

344 BASIC SKILLS IN SPORTS FOR MEN AND WOMEN

back of the head and shoulders. As the body is rolled forward slightly, shoot the legs up in the air and push hard with the hands. The legs should go up and forward. (See Fig. 27-40.)

Roll-over kip from mat: Start this as a forward roll. Immediately on contact of the shoulders with the floor or mat, kip as in the preceding exercise. (See Fig. 27-41.)

Headspring: This is executed from the top of the head. Place the head on the mat with the hands slightly forward. Keep the

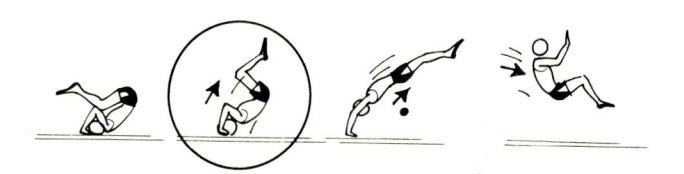

Fig. 27-40. Kip from mat.

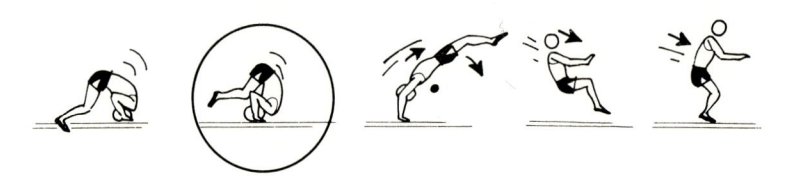

Fig. 27-41. Roll-over kip from mat.

Fig. 27-42. Headspring.

Fig. 27-43. Handspring.

Fig. 27-44. Back airo.

Fig. 27-45. Front airo.

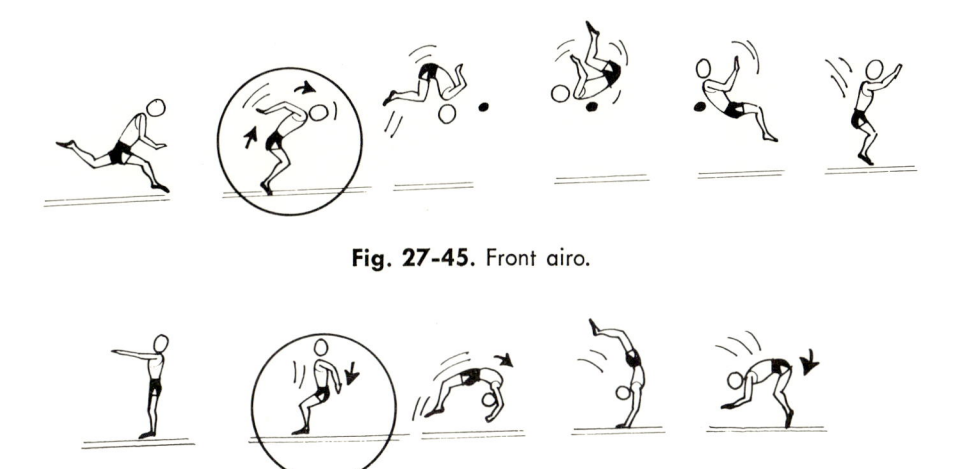

Fig. 27-46. Back flip.

knees flexed as the body falls over off-balance. As the body rolls past center, kick hard as in the kip and push hard with the hands. (See Fig. 27-42.)

Handspring: Take about a 10-yard run, hop, and whip the hands to the mat. Kick one foot hard backward and upward and push hard with the other. Keep the head up and the arms extended. As the legs pass over the head, give a little kick, flex at the wrist, and land on the feet. (See Fig. 27-43.)

Back airo: Follow the examples in Fig. 27-44. Stand with the arms outstretched. Drop the arms down and flex the knees to about a quarter knee bend. Throw the arms over the head as hard and fast as possible so that the body is lifted off the floor. Jump with the arm lifted as high as possible. Throw the head back and bring the knees up to the chest. Tuck and let out. This should never be done without a spotter. The overhead mechanic should be used.

Front airo: There are many different ways to throw this stunt, but the best is the two-arm backward-upward lift. Take about a 10-yard run. Use a two-foot takeoff. From the takeoff, which is executed in a one-quarter forward bend, jump hard and throw the arms with much force backward and upward. Roll over in the air into a tight tuck and let out. (See Fig. 27-45.)

Back flip: This is performed as though sitting on a chair. Sit with the back straight and swing the arms down and back. Keep the feet flat on the floor. Just as the body falls off-balance, whip the arms over the head and throw the head back. As the arms are thrown back, reach for the floor and throw the belly to the ceiling. Snap to the feet. (See Fig. 27-46.)

There is a great number of stunts and tumbling skills that can be used in a physical education program. Those presented are individual, elementary, and fundamental for a student to advance to the more difficult skills. There is also a vast number of companion (or pairs of) exercises that can be introduced into an interesting program. Pyramid building can also be used in tumbling.

Beginning tumblers should never work alone. Use safety belts when necessary. See that mats are always in place.

RULES

For rules governing tumbling competition, see Gymnastics, N.C.A.A. and A.A.U. Rules of Competition.

REFERENCES

Bunn, John: Scientific principles of coaching, Englewood Cliffs, N. J., 1955, Prentice-Hall, Inc.

Cotteral, B., and Cotteral, C.: Tumbling and pyramid building, New York, 1936, A. S. Barnes & Co.

Harby, S. F.: Tumbling for students and teachers, Philadelphia, 1932, W. B. Saunders Co.

LaPorte, W. R., and Renner, A. G.: Tumbler's manual, Englewood Cliffs, N. J., 1944, Prentice-Hall, Inc.

McClow, L. L.: Tumbling illustrated, New York, 1931, A. S. Barnes & Co.

Price, Hartley D., and others: Gymnastics and tumbling, Annapolis, 1959, U. S. Naval Institute.

Ryser, Otto: Teacher's manual for tumbling and apparatus stunts, Dubuque, 1951, Wm. C. Brown Co., Publishers.

FILMS

Tumbling, 35 min., Ideal Pictures, New York, N. Y.

Tumbling advanced, 35 min., Ideal Pictures, New York, N. Y.

28 Volleyball

HISTORY

Volleyball was developed in 1895 by William J. Morgan, who at that time was physical education director of the Y.M.C.A. in Holyoke, Massachusetts. His reason for inventing this game was to provide an indoor game for the winter months in which relatively large groups of men could participate in a small gymnasium. Mr. Morgan employed the principal features of tennis, but the net was raised and the players struck the ball with their hands instead of rackets.

The Y.M.C.A. is chiefly credited with promoting this very fine game to prominence. It soon spread to the Orient and South America. It spread widely in America, and today is played regularly on playgrounds, in recreation centers, camps, school gymnasium classes, and school and college intramural leagues. It is one of the best of the after-school carry-over team sports.

The Y.M.C.A. held its first National Volleyball Championships in 1922. Since that time this has been an annual tournament for Y.M.C.A. teams and has done much to further popularize the game, not only as a pleasurable sport, but also as a fine competitive game.

The A.A.U. has since taken over the game of volleyball as a competitive sport in America, and under its jurisdiction, as an amateur competitive sport, annual national championships are held.

Volleyball is now being competed in by N.C.A.A. colleges.

It has become an excellent recreational game in the armed services, and was used in this capacity in both World War I and World War II.

GENERAL DESCRIPTION AND EQUIPMENT

The game of volleyball for men and women is played on a rectangular court 60 feet long by 30 feet wide, divided by a tightly stretched net 3 feet wide. For men, the top of the net is 8 feet from the floor. (See Fig. 28-1.) For women, it is 7 feet, 4¼ inches from the floor. A backcourt spiking line is drawn across the court 10 feet from and parallel to the center line. Six players comprise a team. The six players are designated as right, center, and left forwards and right, center, and left backs.

An inflated leather or rubber-case ball is used, measuring not less than 25 inches and not more than 27 inches and weighing between 9 and 10 ounces. It is somewhat smaller than a basketball and resembles a soccer ball or water polo ball in size.

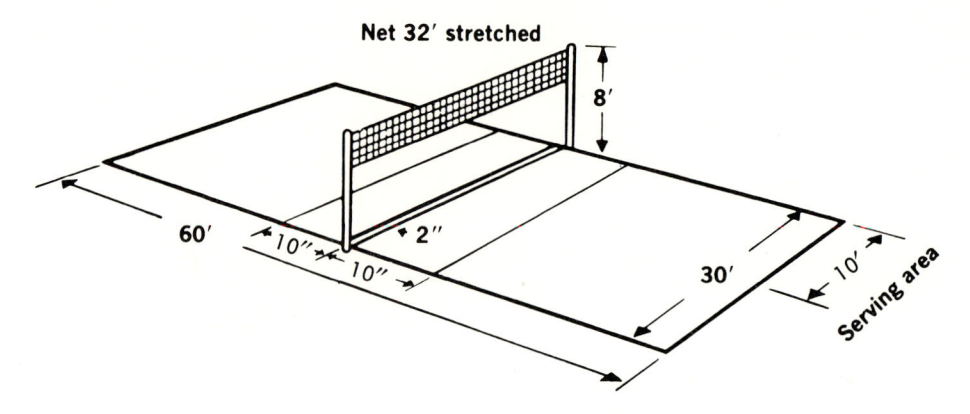

Fig. 28-1. Volleyball court for men.

The play begins with a serve. The server stands with both feet in the service area—an area 6 feet in depth and 10 feet in width to the right and in back of the end line. The right boundary line of this area is an extension of the right side line of the court. The serve consists of hitting the ball with the hand so that it goes clearly over the net. The team on the other side of the net, known as the receiving team, must return the ball over the net before it touches the floor. The ball is batted back and forth until either team makes an error. If the receiving team makes an error and fails to return the ball, a point is scored. If the serving team makes the error, it loses the serve, and the other team serves.

The ball must be batted (in volleyball, called a "pass"). A maximum of two passes is permitted to a team before returning the ball over the net.

Only the serving team may score points. Players in a men's volleyball game may never hit the ball twice in succession.

A server who once starts to serve continues to serve as long as points are scored. However, when the player's side is out and the ball comes back again, the next player in line serves. This is a rotational system used so that every player rotates not only in serving but in position on the floor. This is one of the excellent features of the game. No one player specializes in any one position. All players on a team should learn the skill of playing all positions on the floor and should adroitly play the ball in that position.

ABRIDGED RULES AND REGULATIONS

See any manual for rules governing the positions of the various players.

Playing area and court specifications

The net should be 7 feet 4¼ inches high in the center for women. For the official measurements of the court and playing area for men see Fig. 28-1.

Officials and their duties

1. The referee is the superior official and decides when the ball is in play or dead and when point or side out is made and imposes penalties for rule infractions.
2. The umpire, stationed beneath and at the opposite end of the net from the referee, assists the referee wherever possible but is primarily responsible for net and center line violations and for supervision of substitutions.
3. The scorer, seated on the side of the courts opposite the referee, keeps the record on points scored, substitutions made, and time outs called and supervises rotations of servers.
4. The linesmen are stationed at opposite corners of the court where they can make decisions concerning boundary plays.

Players and substitutes

1. In official matches each team must consist of only six players. Player posi-

tions along the net are designated right forward, center forward, and left forward; those in the backcourt are called right back, center back, and left back.

When the ball is served, players must be in their own positions. After a serve, players may cover any section of their own court in playing the ball, but deliberate interchange of positions is a foul.

2. A substitute may replace any player when the ball is dead, provided the player has reported to the scorer and received permission of the umpire. A player taken out of a game may re-enter it once but must return to the original position.

Service and rotation of positions

1. Choice of which team is to serve first at the start of a match is determined by the toss of a coin. After each game the team that lost the previous one serves first in the succeeding game.
2. The player in the right back position makes the serve and continues as the server until "side out" is called. After side out is called, an opponent becomes the server.
3. Each member of a team, upon receiving the ball for service, rotates clockwise one position, and remains in this new position until side out has been called on an opponent's serve.
4. When a game is completed, teams change courts, and alterations in rotation of players must be made at that time.
5. In serving, the server must stand entirely outside the court in the service area until the ball is struck. The server must bat the ball with one hand clearly over the net, so that if untouched, it would land within the opponent's court. A serve is good if it clears the net and is touched by an opponent regardless of where it might have fallen.

Receiving and returning, playing the ball

1. A return may be batted in any direction. Under DGWS and NCAA rules a player can use any part of the body above the waist. Under the international rules the feet and lower legs cannot be used.
2. A return that passes over that part of the net between the sidelines is in play even if it touches the top of the net while in flight.
3. A return may be recovered from the net, provided the player avoids contact with the net.
4. After once contacting the ball, a player may not touch it again until it has been touched by some other player. (*Note:* In receiving a hard-driven spike, a defense player is allowed to make multiple contacts, even if they are not simultaneous, provided they are on the same play.)

Points and side out

If any member of the receiving team commits any of the infractions listed below, 1 point is credited to the serving side; if the infraction is made by the serving team, side out is called.

1. Serving illegally or serving out of turn.
2. Catching or holding the ball or failing to make a legal return.
3. Dribbling the ball or touching it twice in succession.
4. Contacting the net or reaching over it while the ball is in play. A player is not considered to have contacted the net if a hard-driven ball causes it to touch him or her. (*Note:* Should two opponents contact the net simultaneously, neither player is penalized, and the serve is made over.)
5. Touching the ball when it has already been played three times without passing over the net.
6. Touching the floor on the opposite side of the center line or the center line extended. (*Note:* While playing the ball, a player is allowed to reach under the net, but must not touch the floor over the center line.)
7. Reaching under the net and touching the ball or an opponent while the ball is in the opponent's court.
8. Changing player positions during a

game (until after the serve has been made). Until the serve is made, players on each team must be in their relative playing positions.
9. Violating substitutions or time out regulations.
10. Unnecessarily delaying the game.

Time out

1. Time out can be called only by the referee upon request of a team captain when the ball is dead.
2. Time out for substitutions is not charged against a team, provided play is resumed in 1 minute.
3. Time out for rest is limited to twice in each game, and play must be resumed in 1 minute, with the following exception: if a player has been injured but is to remain in the game, the rest period may last 3 minutes.
4. Time out between games is 3 minutes.

Scoring

1. Failure of the receiving team to return the ball legally over the net into the opponents' court scores 1 point for the team serving.
2. A game is won when either team scores a 2-point lead with 15 or more points or by the team ahead after 8 minutes of play, whichever occurs first. Under DGWS rules, actual playing time is 8 minutes.
3. The score of a forfeited game is 15-0.
4. A match is won by the team that first scores two out of three games. Courts are changed in the middle of the third game.

FUNDAMENTAL SKILLS AND TECHNIQUES

Volleyball is a game that challenges the participant's skill in the use of the hands and agility in jumping, twisting, reaching, and batting. Batting motions that require the use of good body control and muscular coordination are constantly demanded. It is an excellent remedial activity in that it develops good body and shoulder posture.

Passing

The most fundamental skill to be learned is the ability to deflect the ball to a teammate, which is required on almost all plays.

Fig. 28-2. Two-hand pass.

VOLLEYBALL 351

Fig. 28-3. Two-hand wrist pass.

Fig. 28-4. Underhand pass "palms-up" method. Seldom used today. Contact the ball only with the fleshy parts of the fingers.

Two-hand passes

Two-hand passes should always be used because of greater accuracy and control. To execute such a pass, the hands are held close together with the fingers forming a cup the size of the ball, all ten fingers contacting the ball simultaneously. This is commonly known as the ten-point method of passing. (See Fig. 28-2.)

The official rules do not permit carrying the ball, which occurs during any open-handed underhand hit below the chest. If the ball is hit underhand, the player should clasp the hands together and hit the ball on top of the wrists (see Fig. 28-3), lower arms, and tops of the thumbs. If the ball is hit with the open hand, the player should use extended fingers and hit the ball with the heel of the hand. (See Fig. 28-4.) In an emergency the player should hit the ball with a one-handed underhand fist. If the ball is received higher than chest level the hands are held with the thumbs almost touching as the ball is received.

For the most favorable and most accurately controlled pass, the player should receive the ball at a point directly above the upturned face.

One-hand passes

One-hand passes are not used except in a position in which it is impossible to use both hands. Such passes are less accurate and should not be used when two hands can do a better job.

Feeding

Feeding is very definitely a skill to be mastered early in one's learning experience. The player bats the ball or deflects it to a teammate in an arc at least as high as the net and aimed so that the ball would fall on the teammate's head. If playing in the backcourt, the player feeds it up to the forwards who are in a more advantageous position to place the ball in the opponent's court.

Setups

A boost or setup is a pass directed in such a way that the ball is arched 10 to 12 feet and falls close enough for the spiker to effectively spike or play it advantageously.

Serving

A player should learn to serve accurately and carefully, avoiding trick serves, since a team cannot score unless the serve is made good. The success of a serve therefore depends primarily upon accuracy, control, and consistency. Regardless of the type of serve used, the server should attempt to place the ball in the opponents' backcourt so that the opposing forwards cannot spike it. Most serving errors are the result of carelessness. A serve should be placed into the opponents' backcourt, preferably in the corners.

How to hit the ball in serving

The most common methods (see Fig. 28-5) of hitting the ball are as follows:

352 BASIC SKILLS IN SPORTS FOR MEN AND WOMEN

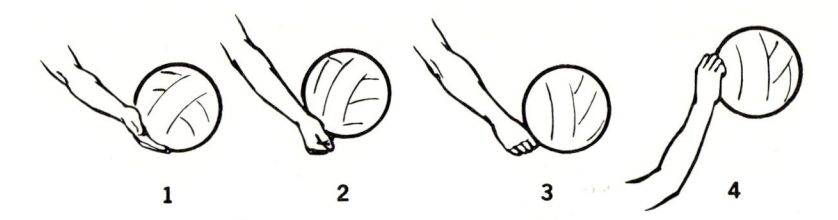

Fig. 28-5. Methods of serving.

Fig. 28-6. Open hand serve.

1. The open hand
2. The heel of the hand
3. The thumb and forefinger with partially closed fist
4. Overhand with fist partially or wholly closed

The open hand is the most accurate method. The use of the fist or heel of the hand is less accurate but, if mastered, will give greater speed to the served ball as well as a twisting line of flight deceptive to the opposing receivers. (See Fig. 28-6.)

TYPES OF SERVICE

There are usually three basic types of service: the underarm, the overarm, and the sidearm.

Underarm serve: The underarm serve is the easiest and simplest for beginners to use to start the play.

In executing this serve, the player faces the net with the left foot in front (if right-handed) of the other, rests the ball in the left hand at about knee height, and hits it off the holding hand. The hitting arm swings as in bowling a ball. The hand follows the ball straight through.

Overarm serve: The chief asset of the overarm serve is its speed and often a weaving line of flight, making it difficult for opponents to return. It often takes a looping and deceptive line of flight. The overhand serve is the one most used by expert players and most often recommended for college players.

This serve is executed by tossing the ball high into the air above and slightly in front of the head. The left side of the body faces the net, feet well apart. Draw the hitting arm back beyond the hips, and as the ball falls to the desired hitting spot, swing the arm in a motion similar to a tennis serve, hitting the ball with the hand. The hips move forward and turn to the left while the arm follows through across the body, which faces the net. The arm may be held perfectly straight or bent while hitting.

Sidearm serve: The sidearm serve is not often used. Its chief assets are its deceptive curves and the twist that the line of flight often creates. It is very unreliable as a consistent serve but can be used as a change of pace.

The ball is held about hip level and is tossed about a foot into the air while the arm swings parallel to the floor. The left side of the body faces the net, left foot forward as in a forehand stance in tennis, and the swing of the arm is similar to the forearm swing.

RECEIVING THE SERVE

The ball should be advanced from the rear court to the forecourt in preparation for either spiking or placement in the opponents' court.

Fig. 28-7. Spiking.

Fig. 28-8. Blocking.

Spiking

In spiking, the ball should go higher than the net, and the player should jump into the air from either a stationary or a running position, striking the ball with great force in a downward direction into the opponents' court. (See Fig. 28-7.)

To accomplish this, the player must learn to coordinate the arm and leg movements in both the standing and running attack. In the standing attack the spiker should stand ready with the left side to the net, both arms relaxed, knees slightly flexed, and weight forward on the feet. As the jump for the contact with the ball is made, the right arm swings backward and upward. At the moment of downward swing the wrist is flexed and the hand or fist makes contact with the ball, sending the ball downward. In the running spike the jump is the same but the momentum must be considered in making contact with the ball. The running spike will allow for greater height and power.

Spiking may be accomplished in both the men's and women's game by the backs from a 10-foot line.

Blocking

Blocking is a method of defense set up by an opponent or opponents against the spike or any other placement play. Essentially, the block consists of a defensive player's or players' jumping into the air directly in front of the spiker, with arms extended in an effort to block the ball and at the same time to rebound it off the arms back into the spiker's court. (See Fig. 28-8.)

To block effectively, one should time the jump with that of the spiker.

Retrieving the ball from net

To play the ball from the net, crouch low, legs spread and bent, with the body facing the sideline. As the ball rebounds from the net, the fists employ an upward-backward striking motion so that a teammate may be able to play the ball. If the ball hits the net near the top, it will drop almost straight down. If it hits low in the net, it may rebound several feet, and the retreiver must be stationed accordingly.

Team play

The idea of the game of volleyball is not just merely to hit the ball back and forth over the net. Essentially, the game offers many opportunities for team play, both offensive and defensive. When these skills are smoothly executed, performed, and developed, a real sense of enjoyment is derived by all players as a unit.

Offense or attack

First of all, the ball should go from service receiver to setup to attack. The ball should be in front of the attack so that all players face the attack.

A player should anticipate the course of the ball and movements of teammates.

The attack is used to develop and establish a playable situation that will deliver to the opponents an unplayable ball. This situation requires team play. The spiker should aim the ball into an unguarded area of the opponents' court. Somtimes as a surprise play the spiker lobs the ball over the blocker's head or directs it to either side of the blocker.

In placing team members in the various court positions, the serving order should be arranged so that rotations will always have a good spiker and feeder in alternate positions.

When the ball is received in the backcourt, the team immediately swings into action for a kill setup. The rear line player feeds an easy lob up to a forward who in turn deflects the ball above the net and within a foot or two of it to the spiker for the kill.

Serve quickly when piling up points. Study the opposing team and play to its weaknesses and holes. The spiker should spike laterally and not straight forward.

Defense

Primarily, good defensive methods are formations set up to most effectively block a hard-hit or well-placed ball. A block is usually set up by grouping two or three blockers together, while the other players place themselves so as best to cover a large court area and crouch low with hands near the floor, ready for a low, fast, spiked ball.

Return quickly to original position when drawn out on a play. The server should assume position immediately following a serve.

OBJECTIVES

1. To teach the proper serve, pass, and setup shots
2. To teach a scientific method of play
3. To teach the rules of the game
4. To teach an intensive type of game rather than a volleying game

TESTS
Achievement test

1. Ability to serve to
    (a) Right back
    (b) Left back
2. Pass from right back, center back, and left back to right forward, center forward, and left forward
3. Setup
    (a) Ability to set up for attack from forward position
    (b) Ability to set up from the back position
4. Demonstration of proper attack
5. Demonstration in play of proper pass, setup, and kill
6. Demonstration of correct blocking of the ball
7. Correct placement of serve
    (a) Ability to serve 4 out of 5 into right backcourt
8. Ability to pass 4 good out of 5 trials
9. Reception of the ball
    (a) Good if handled properly
    (b) Poor if just able to get it away
10. Result of pass
    (a) Good if high and in general forward direction
    (b) Fair if not high but forward
    (c) Poor if setup player has to chase it or if ball is too speedy
11. Setup—4 good out of 5 trials
    (a) Good if the setup is 5 feet above the net and within 1 foot of the net
    (b) Fair if setup is low or too high
    (c) Poor if setup is away from the net and back more than 2 feet
    (d) Very poor if the setup is over or into the net or below the top of the net
12. Attack—3 good out of 5 trials
    (a) Good if the ball is spiked within the front half of the court
    (b) Fair if the ball is spiked within the back half of the court

(c) Poor if there is no control of the ball

Final examination
1. Rules
2. Plays
3. Defense
4. Offense

GLOSSARY OF VOLLEYBALL TERMS

actual playing time Time from the service to dead ball; eight minutes constitutes a game for women's play.

add on Points scored after a tie of 14.

blocking A defensive play; attempting to block or stop the returning ball close to the net.

body foul Ball touches below the waist.

dead ball Ball that is out of play.

defaulted game Game in which one team does not have six players to start; score of a defaulted game is 2-0.

delaying the game Deliberately doing something to slow down the game.

deuce Tie score from 14 points on.

double foul Simultaneous fouls.

foot fault To step on or over the end line before or during the serve, or to step over the center line.

game point The last point in the game.

illegal hit The ball coming to rest momentarily on any part of the body above the waist.

match To win two out of three games.

point Awarded the serving team for any infringement of the rules by the receiving team.

rotation Shifting positions clockwise just before the next person serves.

service Putting the ball into play by the right back.

service area Area 6 feet in depth and 10 feet in width at the right rear of the court from which the ball is served.

side out Ending of a team's right to serve following an infringement of a rule by a member of the team.

term of service Serving the ball until side out is called.

time out Stopping the game for rest, substitutions, or injuries.

violation Committing a foul.

REFERENCES

Bratton, Robert: Power volleyball for players, teacher and coach, Toronto, 1968, CVA Publications.

Egstrom, Glen H., and Schaafsma, Francis: Volleyball, Dubuque, Iowa, 1972, William C. Brown Co.

Emery, Curtis R.: Modern volleyball, New York, 1953, The Macmillan Co.

Hartman, Paul: Volleyball fundamentals, Columbus, Ohio, 1968, Charles E. Merrill.

Laveaga, Robert E.: Volleyball, New York, 1960, The Ronald Press Co.

Menke, Frank: Encyclopedia of sports, ed. 3, New York, 1966, A. S. Barnes & Co.

Neal, Patsy: Coaching methods for women, Reading, Mass., 1969, Addison-Wesley.

Official guide for women, Washington, D. C., 1973-75, American Association for Health, Physical Education, and Recreation, N.S.W.A.

Official volleyball guide, 1973.

Official volleyball rules and guide, Washington, D. C., 1967, AAHPER, Division for Girls' and Women's Sports.

Welch, J. Edmund (ed.): How to play and teach volleyball, New York, 1960, Association Press.

FILMS

Fun playing volleyball, 16 mm., 11 min., Marjorie Fish, Orange Gardens, Kissimmee, Fla.

Fundamentals of volleyball, 16 mm., 10 min., All American Productions, Riverside, Calif.

29 Water polo

HISTORY

Bored with conventional swimming races and stunts, a group of British aquatic athletes set out during the 1860s to create a new type of game. Contested originally in lakes with eleven players per side and rafts used as goals, water polo has since undergone numerous refinements until today it ranks as perhaps the most demanding of all aquatic sports.

Admitted to the Olympic Games in 1900, water polo has always appealed to swimmers throughout the world, especially in Europe, but because there have been relatively few swimmers until recent years, it has remained a rather obscure sport.

Now, however, with the boom in swimming pools and the availability of well-trained professional swimming coaches, resulting in the tremendous increase in the number of competent swimmers around the world, water polo has blossomed into one of the fastest-growing of all sports. In fact, of the thirty-two sports on the Olympic agenda, the United States Olympic Development Committee rated water polo as the third fastest growing sport in this country.

For various reasons the United States has never exactly followed the rules used by most other nations, which are referred to as the FINA (International) rules. Earlier in this century the United States promoted what was called "softball" water polo in which a soft, semi-inflated ball was used; the ball could be taken underwater, and much of the action occurred beneath the surface.

This game attracted very few spectators, since no one could see what was happening underwater. Furthermore, the referee, who was situated at poolside, could not see what was taking place, and therefore an increasing number of underwater injuries occurred. Most swimmers and swimming coaches were disinterested, since there was little relationship between swimming on the surface, as the swimmers did, and wrestling underwater, as the poloists did.

In the late 1940s and throughout the 1950s, a small group of California swimming coaches brought United States water polo back to the surface of the water and created a style of play that appealed to California high school and college swimmers and which, during the 1960s, spread rapidly across the entire country.

It is generally acknowledged by almost all poloists, both here and abroad, that the United States interscholastic and intercollegiate style of play, as embodied in the

NCAA rules, creates the fastest, cleanest, and most attractive brand of water polo. The FINA (International) rules are slowly but surely being changed to conform more closely to the United States NCAA rules, and when this change is fully accomplished, the United States is certain to be in contention for World and Olympic supremacy. Even now, the United States is close to the top, usually ranking between fourth and sixth on the international water polo scene out of the ninety or more polo-playing nations.

NCAA RULES

This style of play is based on two popular sports: swimming and basketball.

Playing is done on the surface of the water by teams of seven players each. The size of the playing area is 25 yards by 15 yards, which is the size of the typical high school or college indoor pool. The deeper the water, the better. If the entire playing area is deep—6 feet or more—this is ideal, although most indoor pools have a shallow end.

The goalpost must be ten feet apart, and the cross bar must be 3 feet above the water surface when the water depth is 5 feet or more; when the water depth is less than 5 feet the cross bar must be 8 feet from the floor of the playing area. Canvas backing and sides must enclose the goal area. The depth of the goal space must be a minimum of 18 inches.

At the start of the game each team shall consist of 6 field players and a goalkeeper, each wearing trunks and a cap. The captain of each team must be a player in the water. Substitutions may be made by the officials during the game.

The goalie is the only player on the team who can stand or jump from the bottom (if it is shallow enough to permit this), or catch and pass the ball with both hands at the same time, or hit the ball with a clenched fist. However, the goalie may not swim across or pass the ball across the middle of the pool.

The guards and forwards on each team may swim freely up and down the pool as they see fit, interchanging positions as often as they wish. They may not stand on or jump from the bottom, nor may they touch the ball with more than one hand at a time when catching, passing, or shooting it, nor may they enter inside the opposing team's 2-yard line unless preceded by the ball.

EQUIPMENT

Each team must have two sets of caps.

The goalie on the visting team must wear a cap with alternating colored and white quarters and with the number 1 clearly marked on it; the teammates must wear white caps numbered 2 through 21.

The goalie on the home team must wear a quartered colored cap with the number 22 clearly marked on it; the teammates must wear colored caps numbered 23 through 42.

The ball is similar to a soccer ball, except that it is yellow and covered with a waterproofing substance that makes it easier to handle, even with one hand.

PLAYING TIME

In intercollegiate competition the game consists of four 7-minute quarters, the teams changing ends after every period of play. In high school competition the game consists of four 5- or 6-minute quarters, depending on the ages of the participants, and the teams change ends after every period. There is a very brief interval between each quarter.

STARTING THE GAME

At the start or restart of a game, the goalkeeper must be in position between the goalposts and the field players must take up their positions at least one yard apart on their respective goal lines. They may grasp the wall of the pool ready to push off.

The game is started by a blast of the whistle by the referee who then throws the ball into the center of the pool. If the ball is not thrown properly, it may be thrown again. If a player on one team jumps the whistle, the ball is given to the opposing team on the halfway line.

OFFICIALS

The head referee walks along one side of the pool watching for infractions, and in this endeavor is aided by the assistant referee, who patrols the opposite side of the pool. The referees are both equipped with shrill whistles and official flags. These flags must be 12 inches square and correspond in color to the color of the caps worn by the opposing teams. The white flag will be fastened onto one end of a 36-inch stick and the colored flag onto the other end.

Whenever one of the referees sees an infraction committed by a player, the referee blows the whistle and signals with the flag. For example, if a player wearing a white cap commits a foul, the referee will blow the whistle and extend the colored flag, pointing it toward the spot where the foul occurred. This means the nearest player on the team wearing the colored caps, against which the foul was committed, may take possession of the ball.

Whenever one of the referees blows the whistle, it is vitally important for all the participating players on both teams to glance hurriedly up and ascertain which flag is being extended. This determines which team will have possession of the ball on offense and which will have to fall back on defense.

In addition to the two referees, other necessary officials include a timer and a scorer, both of whom should be seated at the score's table at poolside. For important competition, there should also be goal judges situated at each end of the pool, whose primary duty is to help the referees in determining whether the shots taken by the players enter the goal for a score or do not enter the goal.

As in all sports, it is important that all the officials be skilled and competent. This is especially true in water polo where the players are somewhat submerged and out of sight, thus inviting underwater holding and kicking unless the referees are adept at interpreting what is happening beneath the surface.

TECHNICAL FOULS

The following are some of the common technical fouls:

1. To start before the referee blows the whistle to open the quarter.
2. To hold onto or push off from the sides of the pool during actual play.
3. To take or hold the ball underwater when "tackled" by an opposing player. Tackled is to have made bodily contact.
4. To swim inside the opposing team's 2-yard line unless preceded by the ball.
5. To touch the ball with both hands at the same time (goalie excepted).
6. To stand on, walk on, or jump from the bottom when taking an active part in the game (goalie excepted).

When a technical foul occurs, the referee will blow the whistle and by proper extension of the flags award possession of the ball to the team against which the infraction was committed. The player on the team awarded possession who was nearest the point of infraction then has 5 seconds to put the ball back into play; this may be done by passing to a teammate or by dropping the ball into the water and swimming with it.

PERSONAL FOULS

The following are some of the common personal fouls:

1. To commit any of the aforementioned technical fouls for the purpose of scoring a goal or preventing an opponent from scoring
2. To hold onto, duck, pull, push off from, swim over, or impede the arm or leg movement of any opponent who is not touching the ball
3. To splash water in the face of an opponent

When a personal foul occurs, the referee will follow the same procedure as with a technical foul, blowing the whistle and properly extending the flags to award possession of the ball to the team against which the infraction was committed. At the same time the referee will also call out loudly and clearly the number of the player who was guilty of the infraction, and a personal foul shall be marked against the player by the official scorer.

After accumulating five personal fouls, a player "fouls out" and must be replaced by a substitute, as in basketball.

PENALTY SHOT

A penalty shot can be awarded by either of the referees or the scorer when (1) an offensive player inside the opponents' 4-yard line but not touching the ball is held, ducked, pulled back, kicked, or struck, and (2) a team has accumulated a total of ten personal fouls against it. When the former occurs, the head or assistant referee should immediately blow the whistle and by holding the two-flagged stick in a vertical position above the head signal that a penalty shot has been awarded. When the latter occurs, the scorer should use a buzzer located at the scorer's table to signal that one team has accumulated ten personal fouls, thereby entitling the other team to a penalty shot.

A penalty shot is taken from the 4-yard line in front of the goal. All players except the defending goalie must leave the 4-yard line until the shot is taken, and no player can be within 1 yard of the shooter.

After ascertaining that the shooting player is on the 4-yard line and the goalie is on the goal line, the referee will ask the shooter to lift the ball up, and, when the player does, the referee will give a sharp, quick blast of the whistle. At the whistle, the shooter must shoot without delay and without any faking at the goal. The goalie may try to block the shot; if the shot is blocked, or is otherwise missed, the ball is immediately in play and action continues.

WHEN A GOAL IS SCORED

When a goal is scored, either from a shot taken by a player out in the field or by virtue of a penalty shot, the defending goalie must then pass the ball to the nearest referee. The referee will then pass the ball back to the goalie, who puts it in play by a pass to a teammate as soon as possible. The opposing team may fall back into its half of the pool to set up a defense, or it may choose to execute a full-pool press. Either way, both teams should be "ready to go" almost immediately after a goal has been scored; there should be no let up in the action. This rule, like the others discussed previously, tends to make the NCAA brand of water polo a fast, clean, exciting contest.

SWIMMING SKILLS

The better one can swim, the better chance that person has at becoming a competent water poloist. In California, over the past decade, it has been discovered that the teams that excel at swimming are the ones that excel at water polo, and vice versa.

It is practically impossible for a swimmer of limited ability to play a respectable game of water polo under the NCAA rules, which place a premium on speed, clean play, and continual action.

The ordinary *freestyle,* or *crawl stroke,* is used most commonly in water polo. However, because each player must remain alert to the positioning of other players and the location of the ball, it is necessary to swim with the head raised. This results in a type of crawl stroke in which the arms are a bit higher and the legs a little lower than normal, but by and large, there is not too much dissimilarity to the regular racing crawl stroke used by competitive swimmers; basically the same muscles are called upon to propel the body through the water.

The second most important stroke for the water poloist is the *breaststroke* in which a whip or frog kick is used. This type of kick, especially when refined into the "eggbeater" kick, does the best job of enabling the player to raise the body high out of the water. The higher a player rides in the water, the more advantageous it is.

To perform the *eggbeater kick* the poloist simply uses the familiar breaststroke whip or frog kick but moves the legs alternately rather than simultaneously; in short, when one leg is bent in the frog position, the other is extended, and vice versa. This kick, when mastered, enables the player to raise the body several inches and sometimes as much as a foot up out of the water.

The *sidestroke kick* is also of importance, since a single sidestroke or scissors kick, done from a prone, stationary position, will quickly provide momentum with which the player may get started, after which the crawl stroke will usually be used.

The *backstroke* is useful since there will be times in every game when the player is sprinting downpool ahead of the ball. By turning over on the back, the player can look and see where the ball is while continuing to swim down the pool on the back.

The *butterfly stroke* is not used much in actual water polo competition, but most coaches use it during their practices to help their players build up their shoulder and arm muscles.

Normally the first 30 or 40 minutes of every water polo practice are devoted to the swimming skills just discussed, since a poloist must be able to perform several different strokes with finesse and speed. Since a game lasts 20 or 24 minutes in high school competition and 28 minutes in college competition, not including the time used for changing ends after each quarter or for time outs, during all of which the player remains in the water either swimming or treading, a high degree of stamina is obviously necessary. A poloist participating in a complete water polo game from start to finish will usually be in the water twice as long as a swimmer competing in a mile-long race! Furthermore, the necessity for making continued stops, pivots, and directional changes in midpool adds to the requirement for possessing stamina.

Many champion swimmers have used water polo for conditioning purposes, and an increasing number of swimmers are finding that they enjoy the tactics provided by water polo more than they enjoy mere swimming up and down the pool.

DEFENSIVE SKILLS AND TACTICS

As in basketball and various other team sports, a water polo team can elect to use any one of a number of defenses in order to prevent its opponents from scoring. The three types of defenses commonly used in water polo are the full-pool press, the half-pool man-to-man, and the zone.

1. In the *full-pool press,* the defensive team members pick up and closely guard their opponents on a man-to-man basis all over the pool. When executed correctly, such a defense can prevent the opposing team from advancing the ball down the pool and will, hopefully, result in the interception of a pass in the middle of the pool. This requires close guarding in all corners of the pool. There are two disadvantages to the full-pool press. Because of the close guarding, a number of personal fouls can be accrued by the defensive players. Also, by guarding all over the pool, the defenders leave themselves open to a swift-swimming, fast-breaking attack by the opposing team, especially if the opponents happen to be faster swimmers.

2. In the *half-pool man-to-man,* the defensive team members fall back into their half of the pool area whenever the opponents capture possession of the ball. As soon as the opponents swim past midpool, the defenders pick them up and guard them man-to-man. The half-pool man-to-man is effective at shutting off the opposing team's fast break, but it allows the opponents to take their time setting up their attack, and it also removes all defensive players from the opposing team's goal area and therefore eliminates a quick counterattack in case the ball is intercepted or stolen.

3. In the *zone defense,* the defensive team members fall back into a cluster around their own goal and defend a particular segment of the goal area rather than a player on the opposing team. By doing this the defensive team shuts off almost all close-in shots that the attacking team might want to take but challenges the attackers to shoot freely from far out; this necessitates good goaltending by the defensive goalie. Slow-swimming teams have used the zone type of defense successfully to stop faster-swimming opponents, but it places an emphasis on defense rather than offense and does not lend itself well to a lot of scoring by the team relying on it.

No matter what kind of tactics are used by a team defensively, each guard and forward must possess individual skills. Guarding an opponent is not easy. Each player when guarding must determine whether the opponent likes to swim around a lot or remain in one position, handles the ball with the right or left hand, is intimidated by close, breathing-down-the-neck guarding, or uses illegal underwater tricks to gain an advantage or not.

A good guard will stay very close to the opponent, being prepared to execute a "tackle" whenever possible. It is permissible to tackle an opponent by impeding the arm or leg movement, by swimming over, or by ducking the opponent, *provided the opponent is touching the ball*. This makes water polo a rough, tough sport at times.

The guard must beware, however; if the guard becomes overanxious in the guarding and executes a tackle just a few seconds before or after the opponent touches the ball, the guard will be guilty of an infraction and will be called for a personal foul by one of the referees. Therefore, a good guard must be constantly alert to tackle the opponent but careful not to do so at the wrong moment. This takes proper defensive positioning, quick reflexes, and experience.

Many beginning water poloists are competent swimmers and have enough ball-handling ability to do a good job offensively at the start, but good guarding is an entirely separate skill that must be practiced endlessly. The poloist who can keep a particular opponent from scoring while causing some bad passes to be thrown and some good passes to be fumbled is a valuable asset to any team.

GOALTENDING

As in soccer, field hockey, and other sports, the goalie in water polo has special privileges and restrictions. The goalie's position in the field of play and duties are unique.

The water polo goalie should play about 2 or 3 feet in front of the goal being defended. Although the goalie cannot score any goals, just being present will keep the opposing team from shooting anything but good shots, and even then, a good goalie will block at least half the good shots taken at the goal. In short, a skilled goalie's value cannot be underestimated; the goalie is the backbone of the team, always being in a position to compensate for errors made by teammates.

It is true that a goalie needs swimming speed and stamina less than the guards and forwards, but there will come times when a loose ball occurs in front of the goal, and the goalie's speed in swimming to it might save a score by the opposition. So speed helps.

Furthermore, the goalie must tread water throughout the entire game, and since this can take as long as 45 minutes, counting between-quarter breaks and time-outs, stamina helps, too.

From the position in front of the goal, the goalie can see all that is taking place in the pool, and should not be hesitant to shout directions to teammates.

The goalie should be able to move quickly from side to side across the goal when opposing players swim in from different angles to shoot, and should also be able to stand up to strong shots without flinching. More than any other player, the goalie's ability to execute the eggbeater kick and raise the body high out of the water is important; a goalie who is up high in the water with outstretched arms and a confident expression on the face can be an imposing sight to a player swimming in and preparing to shoot.

Needless to say, the goalie should be an adept ball-handler. Since the goalie is the only member of the team allowed to catch and pass the ball with both hands at the same time, poor ball-handling is inexcusable.

To summarize, the goalie should have some swimming speed and stamina, a good eggbeater kick, the ability to "talk it up" to teammates, fast reactions, better-than-average ball-handling skill, plenty of courage, and enough strength to withstand a degree of physical contact, since the goalie, like any other player, can be tackled when touching the ball.

Goalie is a demanding position to play, and only the best athletes can succeed at it.

OFFENSIVE SKILLS AND TACTICS

The team in possession of the ball has just one objective: to advance the ball down the pool by dribbling and passing and then to score by shooting the ball into the opposing team's goal.

Dribbling is done by controlling the ball between the arms while swimming with the head-raised crawl stroke. The arms are carried a bit higher than normal on the recovery in order to protect the ball from opponents. Proficient poloists can dribble with amazing speed, but a better way to advance the ball is by passing. This seemingly simple skill is actually very difficult to perform. It must be remembered that the passer can pick up the ball with only one hand, and when doing so, can immediately be tackled by an opponent. Therefore, the passer must first assume a position to make the pass without being grabbed, ducked, or otherwise impeded; this requires some adroit body maneuvering.

Because the players are usually so low in the water, the passer frequently has a tough time finding a teammate to whom to pass midst all the splashing that is taking place, so sharp eyesight can be helpful.

Finally, the passer must lift the body up out of the water with a powerful kick so that the passing arm clears the surface of the water and the ball, when thrown, clears the outstretched arms of the opposing team members.

It is essential that the pass arrive on target; if it is even a foot or two off target, the receiver may have trouble catching it, since just one hand can be used and the catch must be made in such a manner to avoid being tackled.

If the pass receiver is stationary in the water and has secured an advantageous position over an opponent, the pass thrown to the receiver should be a dry pass, one that travels from the passer to the receiver entirely in the air without touching the water.

If the pass receiver is swimming down the pool or is closely guarded by an opponent, the pass thrown to the receiver should be a wet pass, one that lands in the water in front of the receiver if the receiver is swimming or at the side away from the opponent if the receiver is closely guarded.

Whether it is wet or dry, the pass must be thrown with accuracy, and it must then be caught and handled adeptly. The mark of a good water polo team is its ability to advance the ball down the pool with accurate passes and without losing control or possession.

There are three types of offenses commonly being used throughout the United States today, each based on the personnel needed to use it. If all the guards and forwards on a team are fast swimmers and in top physical condition, the team is likely to use a "fast break" form of offense. When the team captures possession of the ball, no matter what type of defense they have been utilizing, all the players break as swiftly as possible toward the opposing team's goal. This takes some practice and coordinated effort so the players do not swim into each other, but when executed properly, one or two of the players are almost assured of breaking into the open, and if they are then given an accurate pass, they will have a good shot at the goal.

A fast-breaking team can often run up as many as fifteen or twenty goals against an inferior opponent, but this type of attack requires a whole team of swift, well-conditioned athletes, plenty of practicing, and accurate passing. Furthermore, if the attack does not result in a score, the team members will have to use their speed to get back on defense hurriedly.

The two other types of offensive attacks revolve around a player stationed on the opposing team's 2- or 3-yard line. Whenever the player's team takes possession of the ball, it is quickly thrown to the player on the 2- or 3-yard line. Needless to say, the player will be closely guarded by one or possibly even two opponents, but if the player is big, combative, and a highly skilled shooter, five or six points might be scored during the game. The player's teammates, meanwhile, are able to concentrate on defense and will try to prevent the opposing team from scoring more than three or four times.

If the player on the 2- or 3-yard line finds that points cannot be scored because the opponents are excellent defenders, the player can then become a decoy. In this type of offense, the ball is thrown to the player on the 2- or 3-yard line, but instead of shooting, the player waits until one or two teammates break into scoring position, and then makes an accurate pass to them so they can take the shot.

Whether a team uses a fast-breaking offense, or depends on a single shooter stationed near the opposing team's goal to do most of the scoring, or utilizes two or three players breaking in and around the player on the 2- or 3-yard line, no scores

WATER POLO

can be recorded without some strong, accurate shooting.

SHOOTING SKILLS

The goal at which the players are shooting is big, being 10 feet across with the crossbar 3 feet above the water surface when the water is 5 feet or more in depth and 8 feet from the floor of the playing area when the water is less than 5 feet in depth. Yet when a goalie is positioned in front of the goal with the body held high and the arms outstretched, the goal looks surprisingly small to the attacking player. Furthermore, whenever the attacker touches the ball or lifts it up in preparation for taking the shot, opponents can tackle the attacker.

Thus it takes much practice to become a good shooter, one who can handle the ball easily with one hand, outmaneuver opponents to avoid being tackled, and shoot past a waiting goalie. A player who, under these conditions, can score on 50 percent or more of shots taken over an entire season of competition is doing well.

FREQUENTLY USED SHOTS

Power shot: When unguarded and unhurried, the shooter can simply assume a vertical position in the water, rear back, and shoot as hard as possible toward the goal.

Bounce shot: From the same unguarded and unhurried vertical position, the shooter can throw the ball in such a manner that it hits the water in front of the goal and bounces up into the goal.

Lob shot: Taken from almost any position facing the goal, the lob shot is designed to be thrown high into the air, so that it sails gently over the goalie's outstretched arms into the corner of the goal in the rear.

Tip shot: An accurate pass thrown to a player positioned on the 2- or 3-yard line can be tipped, or deflected, into the goal without ever being caught or otherwise handled.

Backhand shot: A good shot for a player on the 2- or 3-yard line, this is performed with the shooter's back to the goal.

Slap shot: When swimming in toward the goal and closely pursued, a player often cannot stop and shoot without being caught

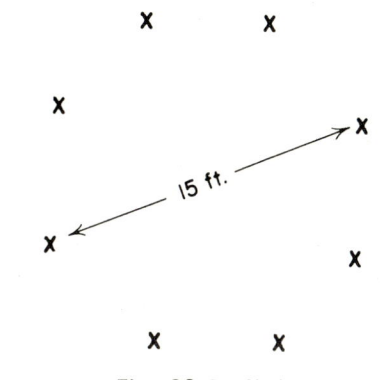

Fig. 29-1. Circle drill.

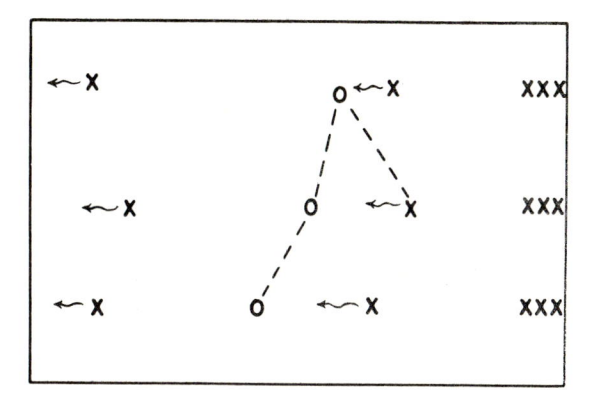

Fig. 29-2. Three-player passing drill.

from behind and tackled; therefore, from the swimming position, the player can bat the ball a few inches into the air with the underwater arm and then slap the ball goalward with the other arm as it swings forward on the recovery.

PASSING DRILLS
Circle drill

This is an excellent drill for practicing the dry pass. Catching the ball softly with the fingers spread wide should be emphasized. Have all of the students practice with both the left and right hands. If the class is large enough for two or more circles, competition can be easily established by having each group count the number of good passes and receptions without the ball touching the water. (See Fig. 29-1.)

A keep-away drill could also be used by having three or four defenders in the center of the circle trying to intercept the ball. Such a drill would emphasize sharp, quick passes to the open player on the part of the offense and quick reaction and hustle on the part of the defense.

Three-player passing drill

This is a very simple drill for practicing the wet pass. (See Fig. 29-2.) Leading the receiver should be emphasized, but not so much that the defense has a chance for the ball. Have all players vary positions and use both hands.

• • •

Water polo players should take at least fifty practice shots daily, and they should learn to master as many different kinds of shots as possible. Every player, whether a guard or forward, should be able to score through hard, accurate shooting when the opportunity presents itself.

FINA RULES

While the NCAA rules governing high school and college competition provide for a fast, clean, exciting game, the FINA (International) rules must be learned by poloists aiming to take part in the Olympic Games, the Pan-American Games, or other international competition. Generally, United States poloists can learn to follow the FINA rules by engaging in local, regional, and national tournaments conducted around the country by the Amateur Athletic Union, which has the responsibility for readying United States water polo players for all forms of international action.

The FINA rules—the ones followed by the Amateur Athletic Union in this country—rely on just one referee, instead of two, and this obviously opens the door to more underwater fouling and rough play.

Until recently, a player could commit as many fouls as desired without ever being banished, and this resulted in some very rough, tough games on the international level. Now, however, the FINA rules are starting to incorporate some of the United States NCAA rules, and whenever a player commits a major foul under the FINA rules that player must leave the game for one minute without being replaced, so the team must play one player short. The threat of having to leave the game for 1 minute keeps many players from committing fouls that used to be commonplace in international competition.

In another attempt to make the game faster and cleaner, the FINA rules committee has just instituted a rule stating that a team in possession of the ball must take a shot within 45 seconds or else lose possession.

REFERENCES

Hines, Charles: How to play and teach water polo, New York, 1967, Association Press.
Lambert, Arthur F., and Gaughran, Robert: The technique of water polo, North Hollywood, Calif., 1969, Swimming World Publications.
NCAA official water polo rules, 1973.
Wilks, Roy: NCAA water polo casebook (issued annually), California Water Polo and Swimming Coaches and Officials Association.
Wilks, Roy: Water polo scoreboard, monthly magazine, La Puente, Calif.

FILMS

Beginning water polo, James Schultz, available from American Swimming Coaches Association.
U. S. water polo, prepared by Olympic Development Committee and narrated by Burt Lancaster, available from U. S. Olympic Water Polo Committee and American Swimming Coaches Association.

30 Weight training, weight lifting, and circuit training

HISTORY

In the ancient days of the Greeks, Egyptians, and Romans, weight training played an important role in preparing and strengthening men for war. Practically all sports were performed with weights upon the hands. During the sixth century B.C., Greece stressed weight training as its chief means of building strength.

About the seventeenth century, modern dumbbells became known in Europe. It is believed that the dumbbell was originated in England. Originally two bells, with clappers removed, were fastened one at each end of a stick or axe handle. Hence, the term "dumb" bells. They were designed so that exercising with them would develop the entire body.

In 1728, John Paugh conceived the idea that the use of apparatus with dumbbells would be of great value in physical training. The idea was accepted in Germany because of the demand for strength and power. Dr. Frederick Jahn, father of German gymnastics and founder of the Turnverein, set up a program that included weight training with dumbbells.

Between 1859 and 1872, Dr. G. B. Winship toured the United States and Canada, giving exhibitions of weight lifting and pioneering the movement in this country. He had been influenced by three German refugees who were protégés of Jahn.

Alan Calvert started a progressive movement in weight lifting in America at the turn of the nineteenth century. In 1905 he also founded the first barbell company.

Weight lifting soon found its way into Y.M.C.A.s, athletic clubs, and exhibitions on the vaudeville stage.

In 1896 weight lifting was included in the modern Olympic Games for the first time.

In America, the A.A.U. took over jurisdiction of the event and included it in its amateur program of competition. In 1929, the A.A.U. held its first National Championships in America. In 1932, the United States entered its first weight-lifting team in the Olympic Games.

In the 1936 Olympic Games, Terlazzo of the United States won the first individual championship in the feather-weight class. In 1946, the United States won its first world championship in Paris, France. In the 1947 World Championship Meet, the United

States made a grand slam victory in every body-weight class. In the 1948 Olympic Games, the United States won the team championship by winning four out of six body-weight classes. In the 1949 World Championship Meet, Egypt always a powerful contender, squeezed out the United States by one point.

The United States' rise in this sport in the very short space of a few years has been phenomenal.

In recent years the Russians have produced some outstanding weight-lifting teams. The Russian and American teams have dominated weight lifting in the past few years, with the competition being very intense. Both nations have developed the individuals who have repeatedly broken the world record. Paul Anderson, of the United States, established a new world record of a total of over 1100 pounds lifted in the three Olympic lifts. He turned professional after having created several new records.

Weight training, as it is called today in the modern physical education program, is constantly increasing in popularity in colleges, clubs, and Y.M.C.A.s. Also, it is not at all uncommon to find a set of barbells in the rumpus rooms of many American homes.

Muscular strength and power can be developed more rapidly through progressive weight training than through almost any other convenient means. Modern weight training is a systematic method of progressive body building.

Weight training has become a great aid to the adaptive and remedial branch of the physical education program. It is valuable in developing and strengthening neck muscles and injured muscles. It is also valuable in rebuilding muscles affected by atrophy following surgery or immobilization.

OBJECTIVES

1. To continue to develop interest in, and appreciation of, weight training as a worthwhile physical skill activity
2. To develop a fair degree of skill in the execution of the various lifts
3. To teach an appreciation of the differentiation of vigorous and modified exercises based on individual differences in age and weight

Fig. 30-1. Two-hand curl.

4. To teach weight training as an enjoyable body builder and as a carry-over activity
5. To increase all-around physical strength and endurance
6. To increase the abilities of all athletes by increasing their muscular power

WARM-UP

Before starting weight exercises, a class or individual should do freehand warm-up exercises, such as:

1. Running in place for 2 minutes
2. Ten push-ups with stiff back
3. Ten thigh dips without weight
4. Fifteen sit-ups on an inclined board

FUNDAMENTAL SKILL TECHNIQUES
Two-hand regular curl (develops biceps muscles of arms)

Stand close to the barbell and grasp it with both hands, palms out; stand erect. Slowly, without moving the elbows, curl the weight to the shoulders and lower the barbell to the first position. (See Fig. 30-1.) Continue the movement, doing from 6 to 10 repetitions. Do three series of exercises, first with 40 pounds, then with 50 pounds, and finally with 60 pounds. Add poundage as strength increases.

Stiff-leg dead lift (develops powerful muscles of lower back)

Stand close to the barbell, feet 12 to 18 inches apart. Grasp the barbell with both

Fig. 30-2. Dead lift.

Fig. 30-3. Military press.

hands at shoulder width and lift it to the chest. Steadily push the barbell to arm's length overhead. (See Fig. 30-3.) Lower it to the chest and repeat the movement, doing 6 to 10 repetitions each with 60 pounds, 70 pounds, and 80 pounds. Add weights as strength increases.

Shoulder shrug (develops shoulder girdle)

Stand close to barbell, feet 12 to 18 inches apart. Grasp the barbell with both hands slightly more than shoulder width apart and stand erect, barbell against thighs. Without bending the elbows, raise the shoulders as high as possible and then lower. Continue the movement doing from 6 to 10 repetitions each with 60 pounds, 70 pounds, and 80 pounds. Add weights as strength increases.

Rowing motion (develops upper back and upper arm muscles)

Stand close to the barbell, feet 12 to 18 inches apart. Grasp the barbell with both hands slightly more than shoulder width apart and lift it a few inches from the floor without bending the legs. With the upper body still bent over, pull the barbell to the chest, lower it to within a few inches of the floor, and continue the movement, doing 6 to 10 repetitions each with 60 pounds, 70 pounds, and 80 pounds. Add weights as strength increases.

Raise on toes (develops calves and strengthens feet and arch)

Stand close to the barbell, feet 12 to 18 inches apart. Grasp the barbell with both hands at extreme width and pull it up to the chest. Lift the barbell overhead and place it on the back of the neck, raise up on toes as far as possible, and lower the heels to the floor. Continue the movement, doing 10 repetitions with feet in each position (30 repetitions in all), first with 80 pounds, then with 90 pounds, and finally with 100 pounds. Add weights as strength increases.

Deep knee bend (develops all muscles and teaches balance)

Stand close the barbell, feet 12 to 18 inches apart. Grasp the barbell with both hands slightly more than shoulder width

hands at shoulder width and stand erect, barbell against the thighs. Without bending the legs, lower the barbell to the floor. (See Fig. 30-2.) Come back to an erect position and continue the movement, doing 15 repetitions each with 80 pounds, 90 pounds, and 100 pounds. Add weights as strength increases.

Two-hand military press (develops shoulder and triceps)

Stand close to the barbell, feet 12 to 18 inches apart. Grasp the barbell with both

Fig. 30-4. Squats or deep knee bend.

apart and lift the barbell to the chest. Then lift the barbell overhead, place it across the back of the neck, and lower the body into a full squat position. (See Fig. 30-4.) Come to an erect position and repeat the movement, doing 10 to 15 repetitions each with 80 pounds, 90 pounds, and 100 pounds. Add weights as strength increases.

Two-hand reverse curl (develops forearm muscles and biceps)

Stand close to the barbell, feet 12 to 18 inches apart. Grasp the barbell with both hands, palms facing in, about shoulder width apart. Stand erect, bringing the barbell to the thighs. Curl the barbell to the shoulders, lower it to the thighs, and repeat the movement, doing 6 to 10 repetitions each with 20 pounds, 30 pounds, and 40 pounds. Add weights as strength increases.

Bench press (develops arm, shoulder, and chest muscles)

Lying on the back on a bench, push the barbell to a full arm's length. (See Fig. 30-5.) Repeat this exercise 6 to 10 times. A spotter should stand above the head, ready to assist.

Pull-overs (develop arm and chest muscles)

Lie on the floor, face up. Reach over the head and grasp the barbell. Raise the arms up over the head and face to the vertical

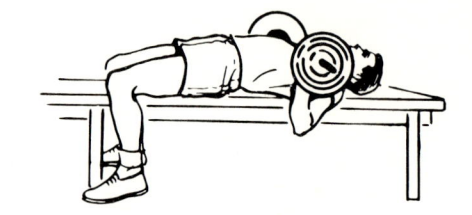

Fig. 30-5. Bench press.

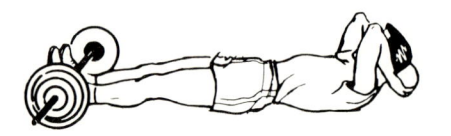

Fig. 30-6. Sit-ups.

position. Return the barbell to the floor. Repeat this exercise 6 to 10 times. Do three sets.

Sit-ups (develop abdominal muscles)

Lie supine on the floor (face up), and support the feet with a barbell or have someone hold them. Place a 10- or 15-pound dumbbell behind the neck and hold it in place while 8 to 15 sit-ups are performed. (See Fig. 30-6.)

Straddle jumps (develop leg, ankle, and feet muscles)

Standing with a weight of about 35 pounds held behind the neck and across the shoulders, jump with the feet apart, then

DAILY WEIGHT-TRAINING EXERCISE CHART*

AREA BENEFITING AND EXERCISE	W†	R‡	W	R	W	R	W	R
1. Arm pressing exercises								
Military press								
Bench press								
Dumbbell								
2. Arm curling exercises								
Two-hand curls								
Reverse curls								
Dumbbell								
3. Leg exercises								
Deep squats								
Heel raising								
Straddle jump								
4. Chest exercises (dumbbells)								
Pull-overs								
Supine laterals								
Inclined press								
5. Shoulder exercises								
Shoulder shrugs								
Upright rowing								
Bent-over rowing								
6. Back exercises								
Ordinary dead lift								
Stiff-leg dead lift								
Forward trunk bend								
7. Abdomen exercises								
Sit-ups with weight								
Inclined sit-ups								
Leg raising (boots)								
8. Neck exercises								
Backward raise								
Wrestler's bridge								
9. Forearm exercises								
Ordinary wrist roll								
Reverse wrist roll								
10. Lifting exercises								
Repetition snatch								
Repetition clean								
Repetition jerk								

*1, The range of repetitions for barbell exercises is 6 to 10. 2, The range of repetitions for dumbbell exercises is 6 to 10. 3, Each time an exercise is performed, insert the poundage in the appropriate square. 4, When the maximum number of repetitions (10) is achieved, encircle the poundage and increase the weight 5 or 10 pounds on the subsequent performance. 5, In all other exercises, insert the number of repetitions.
†Weight.
‡Repetitions.

with the feet together. Repeat the exercise about 40 times in rhythm.

SAFETY SUGGESTIONS

1. Do not start to lift when cold.
2. Warm up thoroughly before lifting.
3. Do not lift a bar without collars; check to see if they are on tight.
4. When doing heavy lifts, use spotters at each end of the barbell.
5. Do not drop heavy weights on the floor.
6. In starting, keep poundages light until you know your capabilities.
7. Do not walk in front of or near or talk to anyone attempting heavy lifts, especially in competition.
8. Be especially careful not to use too much weight with the straight-leg dead lift.

HELPFUL AIDS AND SUGGESTIONS

1. Do not expect magical results overnight; regular workouts, three or four days a week, are necessary.
2. Have regular workouts for good conditioning.
3. As the muscles become adjusted to the routine of exercises, and when they are thoroughly warmed up, strengthen them further by repeated exercises or increased poundages.
4. It takes hard work to get good results.
5. Work a movement to one's extreme range.
6. When lifting, always look straight ahead.
7. One's head is the key to keeping the back straight.
8. Use magnesium chalk on the hands when they are damp.
9. Place a 1- or 2-inch plank under the heels and a pad on the back of the neck under the bar when doing deep knee bends.
10. Follow a definite routine with variations at different times.
11. In weight training do not hold the breath. Inhale on the upward lift and exhale on the downward movement. Breathe through the mouth.
12. Use on ordinary grasp with the palms toward the thighs and the thumb circled around the bar.
13. Before progressing to heavier weights, be able to lift the currently used weight only about 8 to 12 times. Continue with that weight until it can be continuously lifted at least 13 times.
14. Keep a record of repetitions and progression. (See chart, p. 369.)

OFFICIAL A.A.U. WEIGHT LIFTING
Recognized lifts

1. Two-hand clean and press
2. Two-hand snatch
3. Two-hand clean and jerk

Power lifts

1. Two-hand bench press
2. Deep knee bend
3. Two-hand dead lift

Governing body-weight classes in competitive lifting

Bantamweight	123½ pounds and under
Featherweight	132¼ pounds and under
Lightweight	148¾ pounds and under
Middleweight	165¼ pounds and under
Light heavyweight	181¾ pounds and under
Middle heavyweight	198¼ pounds and under
Heavyweight	unlimited

DESCRIPTION OF COMPETITIVE LIFTS
Two-hand clean and press

FIRST MOTION

Place the bar horizontally in front of the legs. Grip the bar with both hands and bring it in a single, distinct motion to the shoulders, either lunging or springing on bent legs. Rest the bar on the chest or on the arms, which are thoroughly bent; bring the feet back on the same line, separated by a distance of 16 inches at maximum.

SECOND MOTION

After completing the first motion, press the bar over the head as rapidly as possible with no added shoulder motion and hold it overhead until the referee gives the signal to lower the weight. During the whole execution of the second motion, that is to say the press proper, the body should be maintained in the same position. The head may move back if needed at the onset of the press.

REMARKS

As a rule, the bar must touch the chest before the execution of the second motion, which must not begin before the referee gives the signal. Athletes who are unable to rest the bar on the chest must inform the officials of this fact before commencing the execution. Any departure of the body or the head from the vertical position, any twisting, any foot motion, any bending—however little—of the legs, and any uneven extending of the arms during the develop (press) are forbidden.

Two-hand snatch

EXECUTION

Place the bar horizontally in front of the legs. Grip the bar with both hands and pull it in one motion from the floor to the end of the arms vertically above the head, either splitting or bending the legs.

REMARKS

The bar will pass with a continuous non-stop movement along the body, of which no part other than the feet must touch or graze the ground during the execution of the movement. The lifted weight must be held in the final motionless position, arms and legs stretched and feet on the same line, until the referee gives the signal to lower the weight. The distance between the hands is not specified, but the hands may not, in any case, move or slide along the bar during the execution. An obvious stop or pause or touching of the ground with a knee when lifting is forbidden.

Two-hand clean and jerk

EXECUTION

Place the bar horizontally in front of the legs. Grip the bar with both hands and pull it up in a single, distinct motion from the ground to the shoulders while splitting or bending the legs. Bring the feet back to the original position, that is, on the same line. Bend the legs and extend them as well as the arms suddenly, thus jerking the bar to arm's length vertically. The weight must be held in the final motionless position to await the referee's signal to replace the bar on the platform.

REMARKS

The jerk may not be repeated. In the clean, the bar must not touch any part of the body before its arrival at the shoulders although the competitor may change the width of the grip.

GENERAL RULES GOVERNING WEIGHT LIFTING COMPETITION
Number of trials

Each competitor has the privilege of three trials for each scheduled event, but not for each weight. The increase of weight between each trial must not be less than 10 pounds, except for the last trial, when it may be 5 pounds. A premature increase by 5 pounds denotes the last try. In no case may a competitor carry out a trial with a weight less than that employed in the preceding trial. The athletes must themselves decide on the weight with which they wish to begin. In no case can a weight once tried be replaced by a lesser weight. When an athlete fails to complete a lift, the judges shall grant a rest period of not more than 3 minutes before the next attempt.

Ties

In case of a tie in a weight division, the lighter of the two competitors will be declared the winner.

BASIC SKILLS PERFORMANCE TEST IN WEIGHT LIFTING

Those students who wish to take the basic skills test in weight training must conform to their corresponding weight classes. Three lifts, with the corresponding poundage listed below, must be satisfactorily performed.

Two-hand clean and press

123-pound class	90 pounds
132-pound class	95 pounds
148-pound class	100 pounds

165-pound class — 110 pounds
181-pound class — 120 pounds
198-pound class — 130 pounds
Heavyweight class — 135 pounds

Two-arm snatch

123-pound class — 90 pounds
132-pound class — 95 pounds
148-pound class — 100 pounds
165-pound class — 110 pounds
181-pound class — 120 pounds
198-pound class — 130 pounds
Heavyweight class — 135 pounds

Two-hand clean and jerk

123-pound class — 115 pounds
132-pound class — 125 pounds
148-pound class — 135 pounds
165-pound class — 145 pounds
181-pound class — 155 pounds
198-pound class — 165 pounds
Heavyweight class — 170 pounds

EQUIPMENT

For class work

1. Barbells—160 pounds (12 sets)
2. Dumbbells—5, 10, 20, 25, 35, and 50 pounds (8 sets)
3. Iron boots (6 sets)
4. Abdominal boards (3)
5. Neck strap (6)
6. Forearm apparatus

For competitive work

1. Weight-lifting platform—14 × 14 feet (made of 2- × 8-inch boards)
2. Olympic type barbell set—360 pounds

CIRCUIT TRAINING

The term circuit training was introduced to the United States in 1958 by a group of gymnasts who were invited here to demonstrate a new method of exercising on the apparatus they had developed in Sweden. In the method various types of exercises were performed at the many stations set up in the gymnasium. Many schools are now using this method of rotation, but the types of exercises have been changed. Many different types are now being used. The important thing to keep in mind in setting up a routine of exercises is to alternate the use of body parts. Below are listed eight stations and a few of the many exercises that can be used. Use one of each exercise per workout and then change.

Station 1—neck

1. Assume the wrestler's bridge position. Now rock forward and back.
2. Stand with the feet apart, hands on the hips. Now twist the head to the right and then to the left.
3. Two students working together—one student on hands and knees and the other standing. The student who is on hands and knees hangs the head. The standing student places one hand on the head of the student on hands and knees and resists as the student on hands and knees tries to raise the head.
4. Partners in the same position as 3. The student on hands and knees raises the head and the standing student places a hand on the forehead and resists as the student on hands and knees attempts to lower the head.

Station 2—shoulders

1. Push-ups. The number may be set at 25.
2. Barbell—over the head press (military press). Start with 35 pounds.
3. Headstands or cartwheels.
4. Isometrics—take a long piece of rope. Hold the two ends and loop the center under the feet. Now try to pull the rope either forward-upward or sideward-upward.

Station 3—upper back

1. Pull-ups on the horizontal bar.
2. Bent over rowing motion with the barbell (can be found in the weight training chapter).
3. Use of wall weights or chest weights.
4. Isometrics—extend the arms sideward. Now flex the arms so that the hands touch the chest. Now take a short piece of rope and once again assume this position. Try to pull the rope apart and at the same time force the elbows back.

Station 4—lower back

1. While holding a light weight, bend down and touch the toes.
2. Lie on your stomach on the floor. Place the hands at the side. Now raise the chest and head off the floor.

3. While standing on the head raise and lower the legs. Make several attempts to kickup to a handstand.
4. Isometrics—hold the ends of the piece of rope in each hand and loop the center of the rope under the feet. Bend over and take up on the rope so that it is tight. The body should be parallel to the floor. Hold tight and try to straighten up.

Station 5—abdomen

1. Do a number of sit-ups. Go for 150.
2. Hang on the horizontal or adjusto bar and flex the legs to the chest.
3. Have someone hold the feet and sit back over the edge of a bench. Sit up and lower over the edge of the bench again. Try to do 15.
4. While lying on the mat have someone hold the feet while attempting to sit up with a light weight behind the neck.

Station 6—legs

1. Do 40 to 50 straddle jumps with a light barbell held behind the neck. Try 35 pounds.
2. Do partial knee bends to sitting on a bench with about 100 pounds to start.
3. Jump rope. Do high repetitions.
4. Jog a couple of blocks or 5 laps around the gym. Try squat jumps.

Station 7—biceps

1. Pull-ups on the horizontal bar.
2. Try two-hand curls with a light barbell or two dumbbells.
3. Climb the rope, first using the legs and then no legs.
4. Isometrics—partially bend your knees. Take a piece of rope and hold an end in each hand while you loop the center in back of your knees. Try to flex the arms.

Station 8—triceps

1. Try kicking up to the handstand against the wall.
2. Execute the two-hand bench press. If there is no bench available, do the exercise while lying on the mat. Try 80 pounds.
3. Two-hand military press or two-hand alternate over-the-head press with dumbbells.
4. Isometrics—take a long piece of rope. Hold the rope about half way up over the head and loop it under the feet. Hold the rope tight and try to push it up.

Time to rotate

Divide the number of minutes that the class has to work out by the number of stations. Set the number of repetitions of each exercise to the number of minutes at each station. Rotate on the blow of the whistle. Be sure that all exercises are posted at each station.

REFERENCES

Eallon, M.: Weight training for sports and fitness, New York, 1957, Soccer Associates.
Hoffman, Robert: Weight training for athletes, New York, 1961, The Ronald Press Co.
Menke, Frank G.: Encyclopedia of sports, ed. 2, New York, 1960, A. S. Barnes & Co.
Murray, J., and Karpovich, P.: Weight training in athletics, Englewood Cliffs, N. J., 1956, Prentice-Hall, Inc.
Official weight lifting rules, New York, 1972, The Amateur Athletic Union of The United States.

31 Wrestling

HISTORY

Wrestling is one of the oldest sports known to man. In the ancient Olympic Games, wrestling was an integral part of the Pentathlon, a form of all-round athletic championship featuring running, jumping, wrestling, and throwing the discus and javelin. The ancient Greeks were not the first to engage in the sport. Earlier peoples, the Babylonians, Egyptians, and Hindus, taught their youth some form of wrestling as a matter of military need.

Although in various countries there have been minor differences in the rules and objectives of wrestling, making about as many systems as nations engaging in this sport, there is no basic fundamental difference in the various systems. About eighty years ago the French compiled a set of rules that are still in use today with very little change.

Today the value of wrestling is universally recognized. There are several distinct styles of wrestling, including the catch-as-catch can, the Graeco-Roman, judo, and sumo. Catch-as-catch-can, the style used in the United States, permits any holds except those believed dangerous, the main objective being to bring the opponent's shoulders to the mat. The Graeco-Roman, a style used in Europe, is restricted to holds only above the waist and employs the flying fall, in which the object is to touch both of the opponent's shoulders to the mat for a fraction of a second. The freestyle, a compromise between catch-as-catch-can and the Graeco-Roman style, permits any holds not dangerous. In judo, a style used in Japan, the objective is to force the opponent to surrender by joint-locking or by strangling the opponent. Sumo, another Japanese style, has become a national sport in Japan. The primary requisite is great strength.

THE MAT

The wrestling area of the mat shall be no less than 24 feet square or, if circular, 28 feet in diameter. All new mats shall have a wrestling area not less than 32 feet square or a circular area 32 feet in diameter. There should be at least a 5 foot width of mat around this area. The mat should have the shock quality of a 2-inch thick hair felt mat. In the center of the mat there should be painted a circle 10 feet in diameter. A 12-inch arc should be painted on each side of the circle, one arc red and the other green. It is from these arcs that the wrestlers start their match. (See Fig. 31-1.)

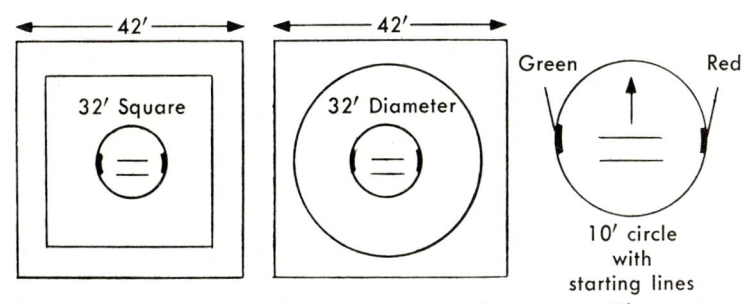

Minimum mat size provides for a circle with a diameter of 28' as a legal wrestling area or a 24' square wrestling area with a mat area of at least 5' in width extending round wrestling area proper.

Fig. 31-1. Recommended mat sizes.

ABRIDGED RULES
Weight classification
INTERCOLLEGIATE

The classes for intercollegiate wrestling are as follows:

> 118 pounds and under
> 126 pounds and under
> 134 pounds and under
> 142 pounds and under
> 150 pounds and under
> 158 pounds and under
> 167 pounds and under
> 177 pounds and under
> 190 pounds and under
> unlimited

In all dual college meets there is no weight allowance at weigh-in.

HIGH SCHOOL MODIFICATION

> 98 pounds and under
> 105 pounds and other
> 112 pounds and under
> 119 pounds and under
> 126 pounds and under
> 132 pounds and under
> 138 pounds and under
> 145 pounds and under
> 155 pounds and under
> 167 pounds and under
> 185 pounds and under
> unlimited

All high school competition will be governed by the NCAA Wrestling Guide—high school modification.

Major differences between scholastic and collegiate rules
WEIGH-IN FOR DUAL MEETS

Schools: 1 hour maximum and 30 minutes minimum before scheduled starting time of match.
College: 5 hours maximum and 30 minutes minimum before scheduled starting time of match.

WEIGH-IN FOR TOURNAMENTS

Schools: 3 hour maximum and 30 minutes minimum.
College: 5 hour maximum and 4 hour minimum.

WEIGHT ALLOWANCE

Schools: 2 pounds additional in January and 1 pound in February (3 pound total).
College: No weight allowance (in tournaments 1 additional pound allowance each day of tournament; 1 pound allowance when traveling and wrestling on successive days).

LENGTH OF BOUT

Schools: Three 2-minute periods (tournaments—overtime two 1 minute periods; consolidation—three periods—first period, 1 minute; second and third periods, 2 minutes each).
College: Three periods—first period, 2 minutes; second and third periods, 3 minutes (tournaments—overtime, three 1-minute periods; consolidation—three 2-minute periods).

SWEATBOX

Schools: Prohibited.
College: Permissible.

WEIGHT CLASS RESTRICTION

Schools: May wrestle one weight class above actual weight at time of weigh-in; unlimited above 175 pounds.
College: No restriction.

Conduct of match

The first period starts with the men opposite each other on their feet, one standing on the green area and the other on the red. The wrestlers will first come forward and shake hands and then go back to their area. When the referee blows his whistle they will commence wrestling. A fall during this period or during one of the others terminates the match. If no fall is secured in the first period, a coin is tossed and the winner of the toss chooses his position, either on the bottom or top. The third period starts with the alternate man on the bottom. The referee starts all wrestling with the whistle. If during the match no falls occur, the winner is decided by the point system. Wrestlers must return to and remain on their respective areas until the winner is declared, or a penalty will be imposed. In case of a tie there will be three overtime periods of 1 minute each. Wrestlers' positions will be the same as when beginning a match and are decided in the same way, by the toss of a coin. If there is still a tie at the end of overtime, the winner shall be selected by a ballot of the jury. The jury is made up of two judges and a referee.

In college and high school wrestling if the men wrestle off the mat, they are brought back to the center of the mat with the man that had advantage on top. If neither one had control, they start again on their feet.

Scoring for high school and college

POINT-SCORING SYSTEM FOR MATCHES IN WHICH NO FALL OCCURS

1. For "takedown," or bringing the opponent to the mat from standing, 2 points
2. For escaping from a defensive position on the mat, 1 point
3. For reversal of position from a defensive position on the mat, 2 points
4. For a near fall, or a situation in which the offensive wrestler has control of his opponent and a fall is imminent, 3 points
5. For one minute or more of superior, accumulated time advantage behind an opponent, 1 point, 1 point being the maximum awarded for the match

TOURNAMENT SCORING

1. First place in each weight, 10 points
2. Second place in each weight, 7 points
3. Third place in each weight, 4 points
4. Fourth place in each weight, 2 points
5. For each fall secured throughout the meet, 1 additional point
6. Default scores, 1 point
7. Forfeit scores, 1 point
8. Advancement scores, 1 point; consolation, ½ point
9. Disqualification, 1 point
10. Decision, ½ point

DUAL MEETS SCORING

1. Fall, 6 points (Fall: any part of both shoulders held in contact with the mat for 2 seconds; high school, 1 second)
2. Decision, 4 points
3. Draw, 2 points for each team
4. Forfeit, 6 points
5. Default, 6 points
6. Disqualification, 6 points

Illegal holds*

The following holds are illegal: hammerlock, above the right angle, the twisting hammerlock, front headlock, headlock without the arm, the straight head scissors, over scissors, flying mare with the palm up, full nelson, strangle holds, all body slams, toe holds, twisting knee lock, key lock, overhead double arm bar, the bending, twisting, or forcing of the head or any limb beyond its normal limits of movement; locking the hands behind the back in a double arm bar from a neutral position; full back suplay from a rear standing position; and any hold used for punishment alone.

EQUIPMENT

For practice, the necessary equipment includes an athletic supporter, sweat suit, and trunks. Only rubber-soled shoes without heels should be used on the mat.

For competition, a pair of long tights and a sleeveless overshirt are needed.

---

*See N.C.A.A. rule book for technical and dangerous holds.

Fig. 31-2. Open stance.

Fig. 31-3. Closed stance.

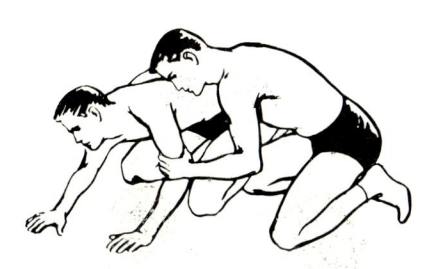

Fig. 31-4. Starting position on the knees.

Contestants shall be clean shaven and free of mustaches and sideburns and hair shall be trimmed and well groomed.

Protective head gear must be worn.

FUNDAMENTAL TECHNIQUES

Descriptions are given from one side only. However, they may be applied from the other side by changing right to left and left to right.

Wrestling positions

OPEN STANCE

If possible, stand as tall as the opponent but not too straight. Feet should be apart about width of shoulders, knees slightly bent, and weight distributed evenly on both feet so that movement is free and easy. Arms should be extended forward, with elbows bent and close to the body. (See Fig. 31-2.)

CLOSED STANCE

Grasp the back of the opponent's head with the right hand, with right elbow down and in toward his chest. The left hand is on the opponent's right elbow. (See Fig. 31-3.) The object is to secure a well-balanced stance in order to be ready for offense and defense.

STARTING POSITION ON THE MAT

The reader should refer to Fig. 31-4.

Defensive wrestler: The rule states that the defensive wrestler must be on his knees with his hands in the center of the mat. He must keep both knees on the mat and must not spread them more than the width of the shoulders. The legs must be parallel with the toes turned neither out nor under in an exaggerated position. The heels of the hands must be on the mat and not less than 12 inches in front of knees.

Offensive wrestler: The offensive wrestler must be on his knees at the side of his opponent with his head along the midline of his opponent's back (Fig. 31-4). The palm of his right (or left) hand must be placed loosely against the defensive man's navel at the waistline and his left (or right) hand must be placed loosely on the opponent's left (or right) elbow. Both of his knees must be on the mat outside of the defensive wrestler's near leg. His knee must not touch the near leg of his opponent and must be even with or ahead of the defensive man's foot.

Wrestling objectives

OFFENSIVE

1. Takedown—To take the oppent to the mat
2. Controlling—To keep the opponent under control on the mat
3. Breaking—To force an opponent off-balance when down on the mat
4. Pinning—To bring the opponent's shoulder blades in contact with the mat for 2 seconds

Fig. 31-5. Double-leg takedown.

Fig. 31-6. Arm drag and go behind.

Defensive

1. Reverse positions—To change from a defensive position on the mat to an offensive position
2. Escaping—To free one's self from the grasp of an opponent while in a defensive position on the mat

Takedown skills

Double- or single-leg takedown: From the referee's standing position, grasp the opponent's right elbow with the left hand and force the arm up. Grasp one or both of the opponent's legs and force him off-balance. (See Fig. 31-5.)

Counter: Defensive man resists by moving the feet back, dropping to the knees, and forcing the opponent's head to the mat.

Arm drag: Start from standing position, opponents facing each other. The objective is to go behind standing. Grasp the opponent's left wrist with the right hand and then with the left hand grasp his left arm above the elbow and pull with both hands to his left until he is partly turned. Then slip the right arm around the opponent's waist and with the right foot step behind. Lock the hands around the opponent's waist. (See Fig. 31-6.)

Counter: Resist and keep facing the offensive man when he attempts to pull your arm.

Drop with leg trip: The objective is to take the opponent down when standing behind. Your hands are locked with the arms around the opponent's waist and your head is resting on his left hip. Then drop to the left knee and grasp his left ankle with the left hand. Place your right leg in front of the opponent's right leg. Then force your

Fig. 31-7. Bar-arm waist lock.

Fig. 31-8. Far arm and far ankle.

right shoulder to the opponent's buttock and force him forward while at the same time pulling his ankle.

Counter: Open the body lock by tearing the opponent's hands apart.

BREAKDOWNS AND RIDES

To break a man down means to put him on his hands and knees on the mat from the starting position. Because of the low center of gravity and the four points of support this is a difficult thing to do. The technique to be used here is to disengage one of the points of support.

Bar arm and waist lock: From the starting position pull the near arm out from under and force him to the mat by pulling him down with the arm that is around his waist. (See Fig. 31-7.)

Counter: After the tie-up, bottom man rolls toward top man. Then he takes his left arm, which is free, wraps it over and around top man's arm and grasps top man's wrist and prys it loose.

Far ankle and far arm: The object is to quickly reach under the bottom man and to grasp his far arm above the elbow. Now pull this arm to you and at the same time grasp his far ankle with the other hand. Turn him over by applying leverage with your body to his. (See Fig. 31-8.)

Counter: The best way to counter this

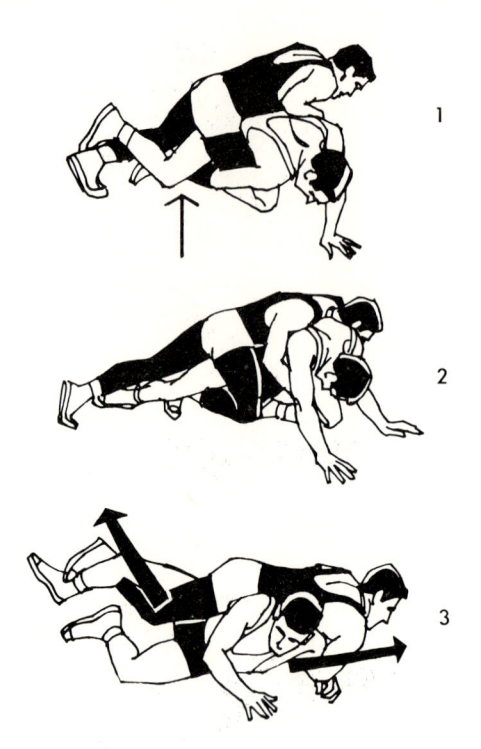

Fig. 31-9. Grapevine and arm bar.

move is for the bottom man to pull the right arm away or the left arm away if it happens to be from the other side.

Grapevine and bar arm: This can be accomplished only if the top man is extremely fast. He must quickly move upon the bottom man's back and wrap his right leg in between the bottom man's arm and leg. He then places his body across the bottom man's. While in this position he grasps, from above, the bottom man's arm.

Counter: Bottom man should expect this and not allow the top man to place his foot between his arm and leg. However, if the leg of the top man does go through, the bottom man should push it through further than he wanted it to go. (See Fig. 31-9.)

Head pry and near arm: To execute this breakdown the top man moves his right knee to a position in between bottom man's legs. He then slides his left hand down to the wrist of the bottom man. As he lifts the bottom man's arm up and slightly to the side, he places his head in back of the bottom man's arm and applies pressure. This pressure and the pressure forward of his right thigh forces the bottom man to the mat. (See Fig. 31-10.)

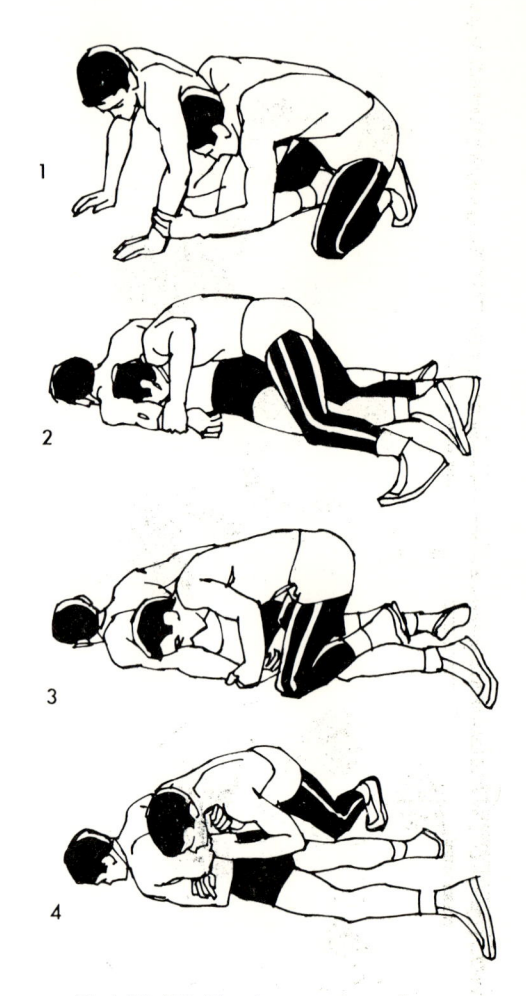

Fig. 31-10. Head pry and arm bar.

Counter: Bottom man should try to pull his arm forward as the top man moves his hand from the elbow to wrist.

Grapevine and bar nelson: Execute a grapevine as previously described, placing the right forearm behind the opponent's neck, pushing the left arm under the opponent's left arm, and locking hands (bar nelson).

Grapevine and half nelson: Execute a grapevine as described previously, placing the left arm under the opponent's left arm with the forearm behind the opponent's neck (half nelson).

Body scissors and half nelson: Place the right foot between the opponent's right arm and right thigh with the left foot in a similar position, locking the feet (body scissors). Execute a half nelson as before.

Fig. 31-11. The set out.

Escapes and reversals

Side roll: The man in the defensive position locks the opponent's right wrist by pressing his own arm close to his own body, then rolling to his right, bringing his opponent over and under (side roll) or shoving the right arm between the opponent's legs (crotch hold).

Set out: Step the right foot forward first. Then shoot the left foot out and forward and land on the left side with the left arm

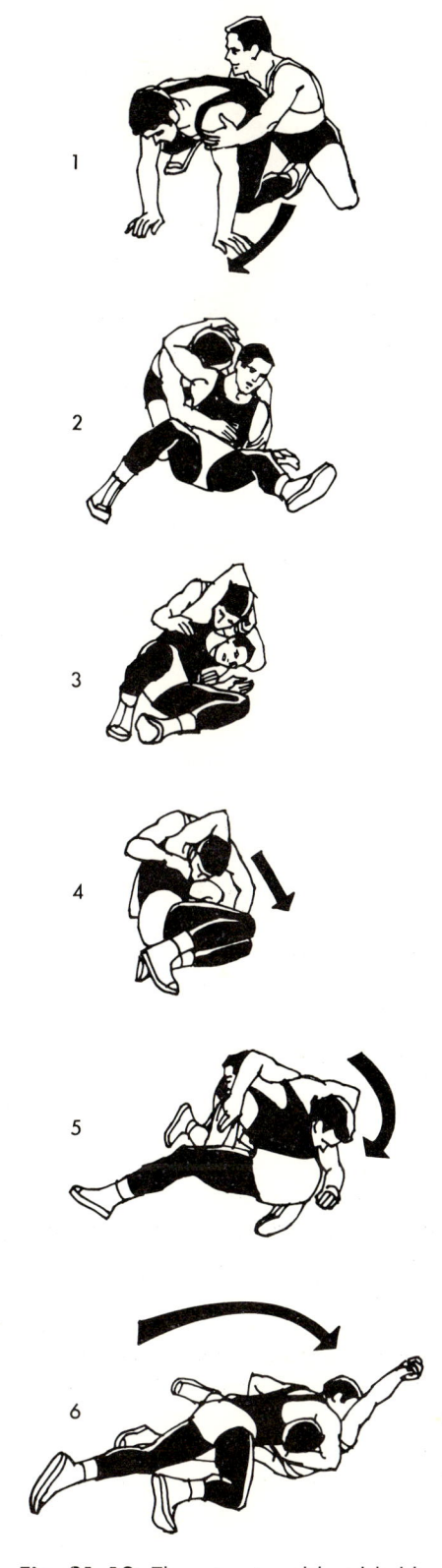

Fig. 31-12. The set out and head hold.

382 BASIC SKILLS IN SPORTS FOR MEN AND WOMEN

at the side. From this landing, roll to the left on the left shoulder. (See Fig. 31-11.)

Counter: Top man should break the left arm down as the bottom man attempts to execute the kick out with the left leg.

Set out and head hold: The bottom man shoots both feet out as he did in the set out. Now, while in this position, he grasps the top man's head with the right arm, drops the left shoulder to the floor, and turns to the left still holding the head. The top man should end up with a half nelson ready to try for a pinning hold.

Counter: Top man should break down bottom man's left arm or try for a chin hold with the left hand. Top man should then bring his right hand under the bottom man's right arm pit and grasp the bottom man's chin. Top man now tries to pull bottom man back for a fall. (See Fig. 31-12.)

The switch: Begin the switch by crossing the right hand over the left (if the referee's position is on the right side). Now place the weight on the left foot. Kick the right foot forward and to the left. Keep the hips off the mat. With the left arm reach over the top man's left arm and grasp his left thigh from the inside. Lean back and apply force to his left shoulder. Now pivot on the right foot and grasp the top man around the waist. (See Fig. 31-13.)

Counter: Break down bottom man's right arm as he attempts to pivot just after he kicks out.

PINNING HOLDS

Chicken wing and half nelson: This is done from the starting position on the mat. The top man is on the right side. He releases his grip on the bottom man's elbow and moves his hand around the left arm and up on the back of the bottom man. This is called the chicken wing. With the hand flat on the left scapula of the bottom man, he now moves to bottom man's right side over his back. As top man continues to circle to the right, he applies a half nelson with the right hand. The pressure of the half nelson turns the bottom man's head under. The top man continues to move counterclockwise, turning the bottom man over on his shoulders in position for the fall.

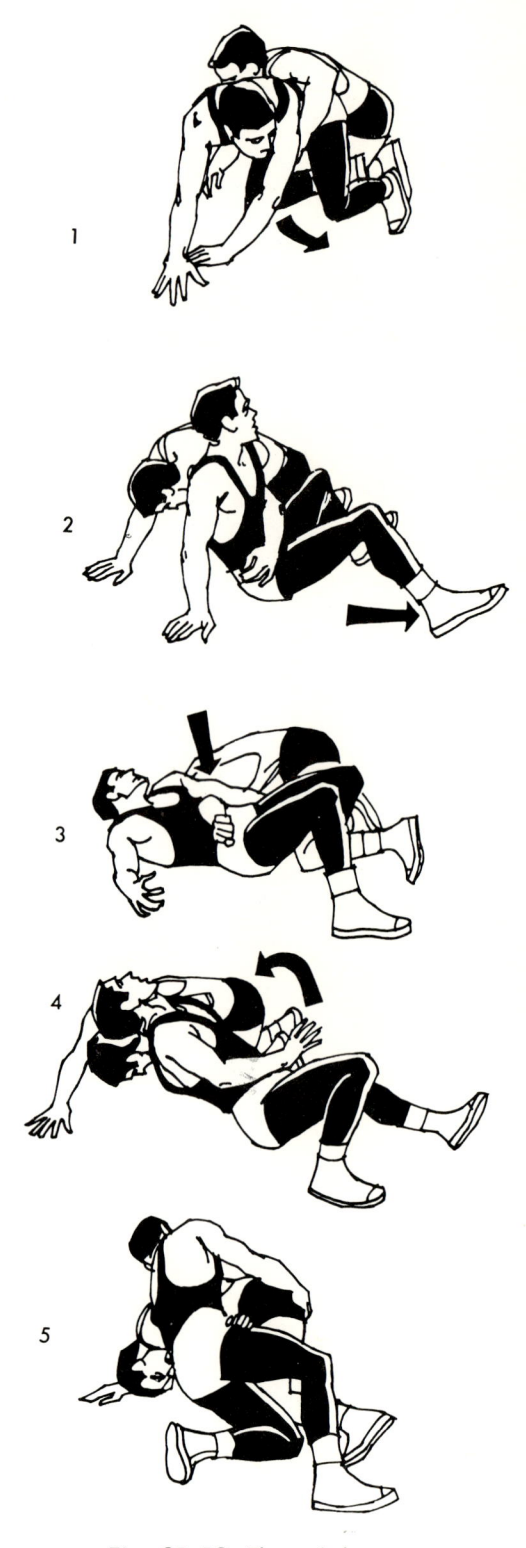

Fig. 31-13. The switch.

Fig. 31-14. Side roll.

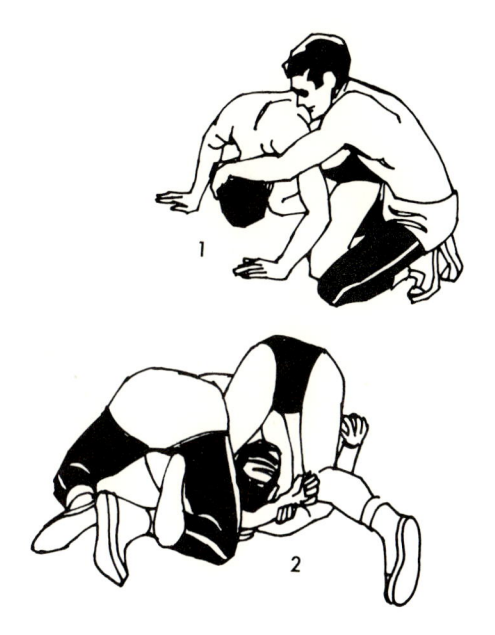

Fig. 31-15. Three-quarter nelson.

Side roll to cradle: This move is executed from the kneeling position. (See Fig. 31-14.) The bottom man straightens his left leg and at the same time grasps top man by the wrist (right). Bottom man then brings his right leg to his left, drops on his right shoulder and rolls top man over him. As top man hits his right side, bottom man turns to face him. Bottom man now places his left arm over top man's right shoulder and around his head to a half nelson. The last move is for the bottom man to insert his right arm between his opponent's legs, raise his left leg, and then lock his hands. Locking the hands or arms around opponent's leg and head is called the cradle.

Three-quarter nelson: This also is executed from the kneeling position. Top man places his right knee behind bottom man. He then moves his right arm from bottom man's waist, reaches under bottom man with the right hand, and locks hands over the back of bottom man's head. Next he pulls bottom man's head under and moves to the left. To keep the bottom man from rolling out, top man retains control of bottom man's leg with his own right leg. (See Fig. 31-15.)

The guillotine: This is done from either the kneeling or the referee's position. (See Fig. 31-16.) Starting from the cross-body ride the top man reaches over the body of bottom man and places his right hand on the mat for support. Then he grasps bottom man's left wrist with his left hand. Top man then lifts bottom man's left arm up over his head and then falls back pinning bottom man's shoulders.

Counter: Bottom man should not allow top man to lift his left arm.

Penalty chart: See the penalty chart (Fig. 31-17) for the awarding of points.

384 BASIC SKILLS IN SPORTS FOR MEN AND WOMEN

Fig. 31-16. Guillotine.

Infractions	Warning	First penalty	Second penalty	Third penalty	Fourth penalty	Rule 10 sections
Illegal holds*	No	1 pt.	1 pt.	2 pts.	Disqualify	
Technical violations*	No	1 pt.	1 pt.	2 pts.	Disqualify	
Stalling	Yes	1 pt.	1 pt.	2 pts.	Disqualify	
Unnecessary roughness†	No	1 pt.	1 pt.	2 pts.	Disqualify	
Abusive and/or unsportsmanlike conduct	Yes	Deduct 1 team point	Remove from premises	(Removal is for duration of dual meet or tournament session only)		
Flagrant misconduct	No	Disqualify on first offense and deduct 1 team point				
Greasy substance on skin, objectionable pads and braces, illegal equipment, or illegal costume		Disqualify if not removed or corrected in allotted time				

Summary of technical violations (Rule 10, Sec. 8 and 9, N.C.A.A. Handbook)
    Interlocking hands (Sec. 8, a)
    Holding legs (Sec. 9, b)
    Leaving mat without permission (Sec. 8, b)
    Delaying match (Sec. 8, c)
    Intentional forcing opponent off mat (Sec. 8, d)
    Intentional going off mat (Sec. 8, e)
    Stalling (Sec. 9, a-b-c)
    Grasping clothing, etc. (Sec. 8, g)
Reminder:
    Penalties for any infractions are accumulative throughout the match including overtime.

*Note 1—Disqualification due to technical violation, illegal holds, or less flagrant unnecessary roughness does not eliminate a contestant from further competition in tournaments. Disqualification for any other reason eliminates a contestant from further competition in tournaments.

†Note 2—Points for unnecessary roughness may be awarded in addition to points earned.

‡Also Rule 7, Sec. 6.

Fig. 31-17. Penalty chart.

OBJECTIVES

1. To teach knowledge and rules of wrestling
2. To teach fundamental wrestling positions and holds easily understood by the beginner
3. To increase proficiency in executing holds in the proper order of sequence
4. To develop interest in a sport that is a great physical developer

ACHIEVEMENT TESTS

Achievement tests should cover the following basic skills:
1. Proper stance
2. Timing of offensive and defensive moves
3. Recovery after offensive and defensive moves
4. Ability to rest in periods between efforts
5. Aggressive ability (follow-through)
6. Defensive ability

FINAL GRADE

The final grade is based upon tests given in regular short bouts and a written examination on salient points in National Collegiate Wrestling Rules and combination of holds and counters.

GLOSSARY OF WRESTLING TERMS

default Winning a match through the inability of an opponent to continue the match; 1 point in tournament scoring.

escape Gaining a neutral position by the defensive wrestler while the supporting points of either wrestler are within the wrestling area.

fall Any part of both shoulders or area of both scapulas held in contact with the mat for a designated time: NCAA, 1 second; high school, 2 seconds.

forfeit Winning a match through the failure of an opponent to appear; one point in tournament scoring.

near-fall Position in which the offensive wrestler holds the opponent's shoulders or the scapula area in contact with the mat for a designated time (NCAA: less than one second; high school: one second) or when one shoulder of the defensive wrestler is touching the mat and the other shoulder is held within one inch or less of the mat for two full seconds; three points are awarded.

neutral position Position in which neither wrestler has control.

out-of-bounds Having the supporting parts of either wrestler outside the boundary lines.

position of advantage Having control of an opponent.

predicament Position in which the offensive wrestler has control of his opponent in a pinning situation; two points are awarded.

reversal Act of moving from a defensive position to an offensive position.

stalemate Neither wrestler is able to improve his situation; the referee stops and restarts the match.

starting position on the mat Position in which the defensive wrestler is on his knees with his hands in the center of the mat. The offensive contestant is on his knees at the side of his opponent with his nearest arm around the opponent's waist and the other hand just above the opponent's nearest elbow.

takedown Bringing an opponent from a standing position to the mat and under control.

time advantage Accumulated time during which a wrestler is in a position of advantage over his opponent; no more than two points may be awarded in any one match meaning that two or more minutes have been accumulated in a position of advantage.

REFERENCES

Brown, Robert L., and Ober, Kenneth D.: Complete book of high school wrestling, Englewood Cliffs, N. J., 1962, Prentice-Hall, Inc.

Donnelly, R., Helms, W., and Mitchell, E.: Active games and contests, ed. 2, New York, 1958, The Ronald Press Co.

Kapral, Frank S.: Coach's illustrated guide to championship wrestling, Englewood Cliffs, N. J., 1964, Prentice-Hall, Inc.

Menke, Frank G.: Encyclopedia of sports, ed. 2, New York, 1966, A. S. Barnes & Co.

Official wrestling guide, New York, 1974, The Amateur Athletic Union of the United States.

Official wrestling guide, New York, 1974, The National Collegiate Athletic Association.

Keen, C. P., and others: Championship wrestling, Annapolis, 1964, U. S. Naval Institute.

U. S. Naval Institution: Championship wrestling, Annapolis, Md., 1973, U. S. Naval Institution.

APPENDIX # Miscellaneous field and court dimensions

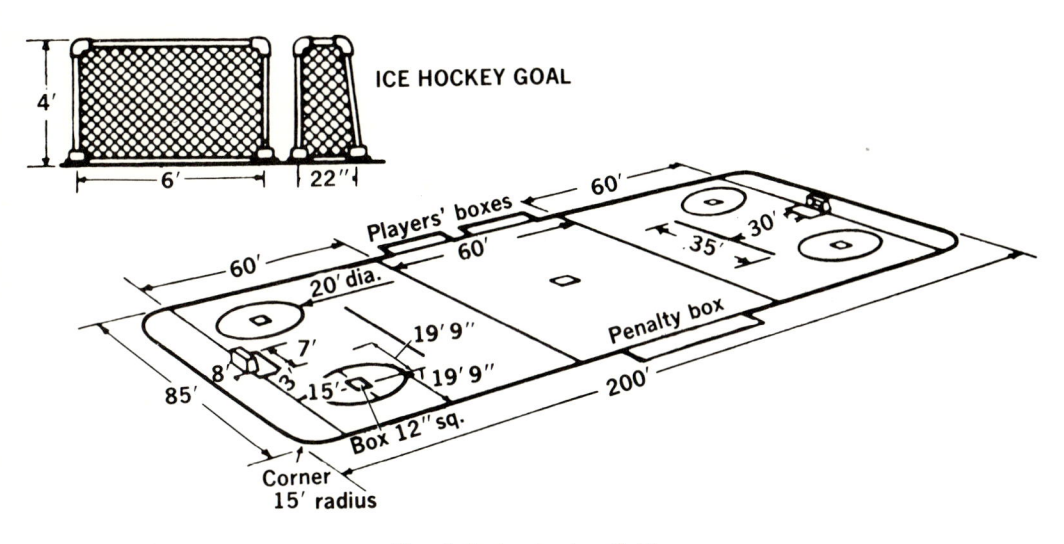

Fig. A-1. Ice hockey field.

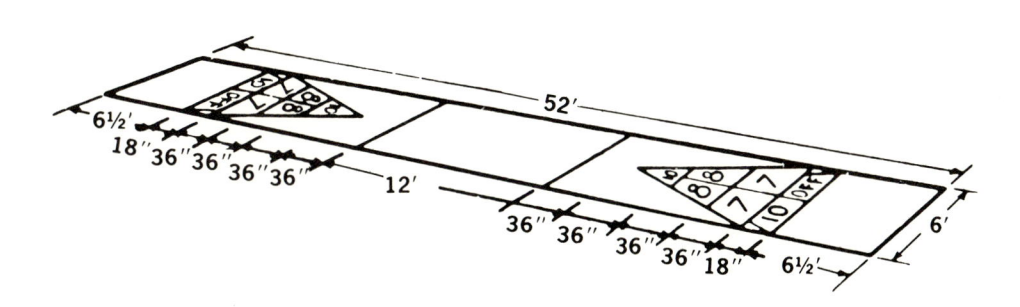

Fig. A-2. Shuffleboard court.

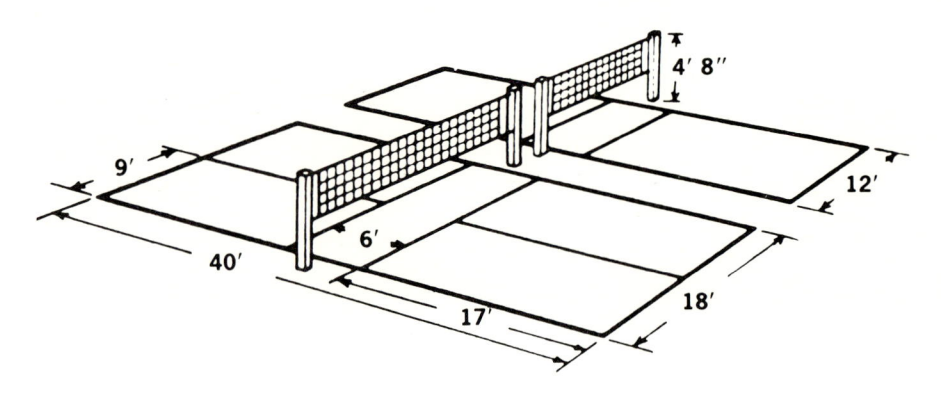

Fig. A-3. Deck tennis (double and single) courts.

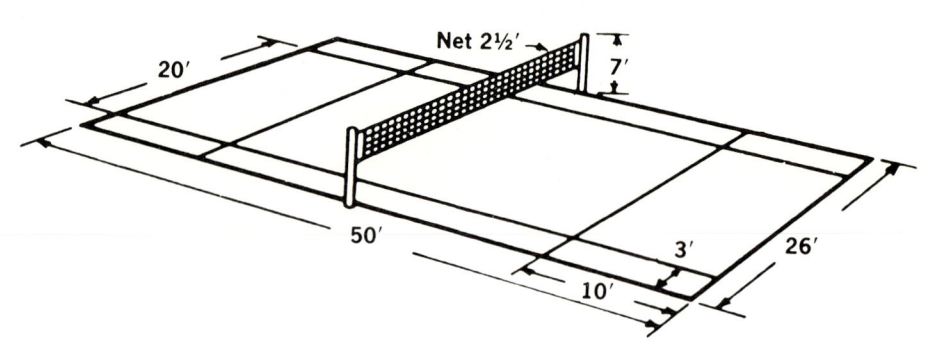

Fig. A-4. Aerial tennis court.

APPENDIX 389

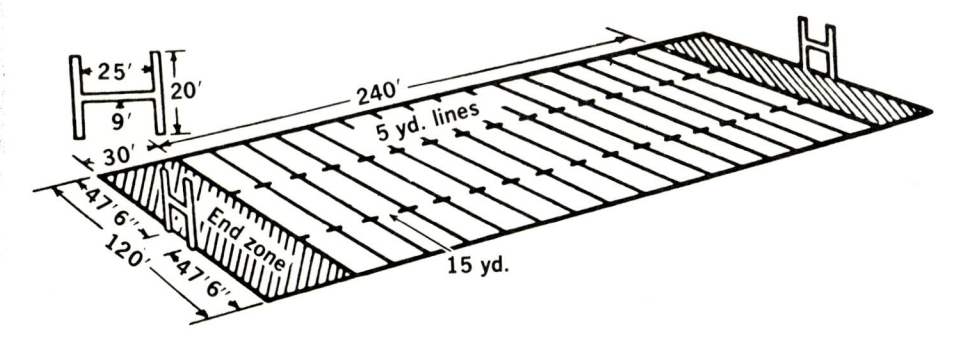

Fig. A-5. Six-man football field.

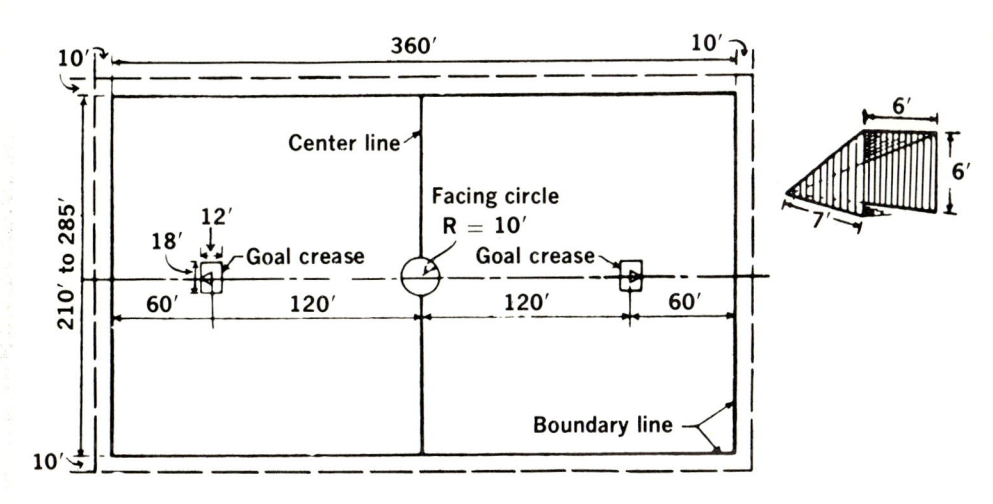

Fig. A-6. Lacrosse field.

1
2
3
4
5
6
7
8
9
10
11
12
13
14

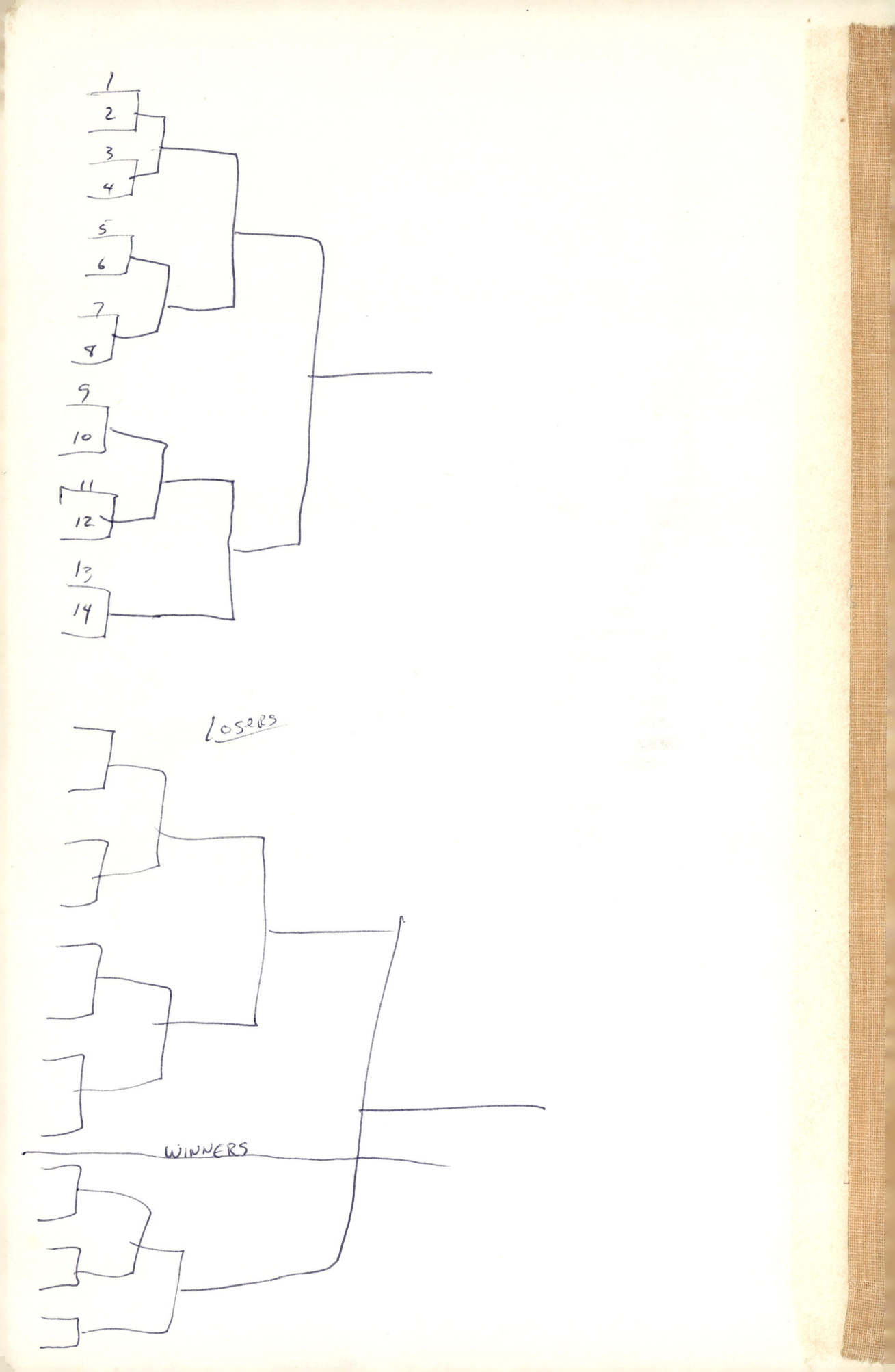

LOSERS

WINNERS